Writing That Works

Communicating Effectively on the Job

NINTH EDITION

Writing That Works
Communicating Effectively on the Job

Walter E. Oliu
Communications Consultant

Charles T. Brusaw
Communications Consultant

Gerald J. Alred
University of Wisconsin–Milwaukee

Bedford/St. Martin's
Boston ♦ New York

For Bedford/St. Martin's

Developmental Editor: Ellen Kuhl
Assistant Editor: Amy Hurd Gershman
Production Supervisor: Andrew Ensor
Marketing Manager: Karita dos Santos
Text Design: Books By Design, Inc.
Project Management: Books By Design, Inc.
Cover Design: Donna Lee Dennison
Cover Photo: Messy Office Desk © Matt Gray/Photonica/Getty
Composition: Pine Tree Composition, Inc.
Printing and Binding: RR Donnelley & Sons, Inc.

President: Joan E. Feinberg
Editorial Director: Denise B. Wydra
Editor in Chief: Karen S. Henry
Director of Marketing: Karen Melton Soeltz
Director of Editing, Design, and Production: Marcia Cohen
Manager, Publishing Services: Emily Berleth

Library of Congress Control Number: 2006929092

Manufactured in the United States of America.

2   1   0   9   8

f

For information, write: Bedford/St. Martin's, 75 Arlington Street, Boston, MA 02116 (617-399-4000)

ISBN-10: 0-312-44844-9
ISBN-13: 978-0-312-44844-8

Acknowledgments

Figure 2–21: Copyright © 2006 by the American Academy of Audiology. Reprinted with permission. Courtesy the American Academy of Audiology.

Figure 3–6: Society for Technical Communication, excerpt from "Overcoming Writer's Block" from *Capital Letter* 31, no. 3 (December 1999). Copyright © 1999. Reprinted with permission.

Figures 3–7 and 3–8: Steve Coffel and Karen Feiden, excerpt and illustration from *Indoor Pollution*. Copyright © 1990 by Steve Coffel and Karen Feiden. Reprinted with the permission of Ballantine Books, a division of Random House, Inc.

Acknowledgments and copyrights are continued at the back of the book on pages 642–643, which constitute an extension of the copyright page.

Preface

Writing That Works has been successful through eight editions because it effectively prepares students to apply the writing process to the documents and situations they will encounter in the workplace—regardless of their academic background or occupational interest. Informed by the decades of professional and academic experience we have between us, the book integrates practical coverage of the writing process with clear guidelines for specific types of workplace writing—correspondence, reports, proposals, instructions, presentations, and more—supported by a wealth of sample documents, hundreds of exercises and projects, and the most current advice for using technology in today's workplace.

The ninth edition continues to offer the structure and features that instructors have told us are effective. Workplace communications, however, is not a static field. Tools, sources of information, and practices continue to evolve, in both the classroom and the workplace. In preparing this edition, we looked critically at every facet of the book and added and updated material to keep it current. Our focus has been on helping students prepare for an increasingly global and technical environment as well as on helping them become aware of the ethical concerns of workplace writing. We have also streamlined the book significantly, reorganized several chapters to make them easier to use, added new material throughout, and created a thoroughly integrated set of additional resources that are, for the first time, available in course management systems for courses taught either completely or partially online. (For a detailed description of what's new to this edition, see pages vii–ix.)

■ About This Book

Informed Guidance on the Writing Process at Work

The advice, assignments, and features in Writing That Works all draw on our real-world and classroom experiences and have been honed by the suggestions and contributions of more than a hundred teachers and writers over the years. Divided into four parts, the book is structured so that it begins with an overview of the writing process and then applies that process to the specific tasks and types of business writing, all of them illustrated by an impressive number of samples that are annotated to clarify what they demonstrate.

- **Part One: The Writing Process**   Chapters 1 through 4 guide students through the steps of planning, organizing, drafting, and revising, with a focus on the contexts and practices distinctive to workplace writing.
- **Part Two: Essential Skills**   Chapters 5 through 7 help students develop additional communication skills essential to workplace writing. The chapter on collaborating includes advice on how to peer-review and edit shared documents; the research chapter covers primary, print, and online research, with guidelines for documenting sources; and the design chapter offers concrete advice and examples for creating effective visuals and integrating them into documents and presentations.
- **Part Three: Writing at Work**   Chapters 8 through 16 help students apply the skills learned in Parts One and Two, guiding them through the many types of writing and communications they will face in any workplace, with detailed advice on routine correspondence — e-mail messages, letters, and memos — informal and formal reports, instructions, and proposals. These chapters also cover creating and delivering presentations, conducting meetings, writing for the Web, and finding a job.
- **Part Four: Revision Guide**   This self-contained handbook provides help with sentence errors, punctuation, and mechanics, and it features a section tailored to students who speak English as a second language (ESL).

Easy to Use, with an Emphasis on Practical Skills

Long appreciated for its straightforward approach, *Writing That Works* is flexible enough to accommodate different courses and teaching styles. It is also thorough enough for students to use on their own.

Boxed features integrated throughout the text summarize important information and include checklists for considering audience and purpose, drafting and revising, designing effective documents, and using the latest communications technologies, as well as tips for ESL students. Marginal notes point students to supporting content in the text and on the companion Web site. Indeed, *Writing That Works* presents visually-oriented information throughout: Screened edges highlight the most-referenced material (documentation models and the "Meeting the Deadline" features) and colored boxes highlight all tips and checklists with icons that identify their topics.

More than 300 assignments in the book and on the companion Web site give students unparalleled opportunities to practice their skills, either on their own or in class. Most of them class-tested, the assignments at the end of each chapter include exercises, collaborative writing projects, research projects, and Web-based projects.

Focused on Success

To connect the book's advice with the real world, each chapter opens with brief commentaries called Voices from the Workplace. These popular profiles — featuring the photos and words of both experienced professionals and those who are new to the workplace—provide firsthand experience and advice for writing, communicating, facing challenges, and succeeding on the job. This edition has 32 commentaries, half of which are new.

To prepare students for the real demands of professional life, *Writing That Works* offers advice for writing successfully, even under the pressure of a tight deadline. The book's popular Meeting the Deadline sections offer practical help for approaching time-sensitive memos, proposals, and presentations.

New to This Edition

As with each edition of *Writing That Works*, this revision has been guided by the thoughtful reviews and suggestions of business and technical writing instructors across the country. In response to their feedback and to better meet the needs of the variety of courses in which *Writing That Works* is taught, we have made several improvements.

Streamlined and Easier to Navigate

While retaining the comprehensiveness applauded in previous editions, we have thoroughly reworked every chapter for clarity and conciseness. The chapters on developing instructions (12) and proposals (13) in particular were extensively reorganized. Heeding the advice of adopters, we condensed the eighth edition's two revision chapters into one (now Chapter 4) and replaced the handbook section with a brief Revision Guide that focuses on the stylistic and editing concerns with which business writers are most likely to need help. New reference features—including chapter previews and marginal cross-references—help students locate answers to specific writing questions.

Greater Attention to Global Communication

Because of the growing importance of global communication in today's workplace, we have expanded our coverage of this important topic throughout the book and added new sections on considering international audiences to the chapters on writing the draft (3), designing documents and visuals (7), and writing instructions (12). Several of the sample documents, exercises and writing projects, and Voices from the Workplace now reflect the book's increased emphasis on global communication.

Greater Attention to Ethics

Two dozen new ethics notes throughout the book alert students to the need for personal as well as corporate integrity and highlight advice for handling ethical issues frequently encountered in workplace writing, such as the use of misleading visuals, biased language, and dishonesty. We have also greatly expanded the discussion of plagiarism and copyright violation in Chapter 6.

Fresh Sample Documents and Visuals

Approximately 75 new or revised figures—including letters, memos, informal reports, résumés, charts, graphs, drawings, tables, internationally recognized symbols, illustrated descriptions, and visual instructions—reflect a broader range of careers, the increasingly global workplace, and the prominence of electronic communication.

Ample New Assignments

Nearly 100 new exercises, collaborative writing projects, research projects, and Web projects—many of which thread through multiple chapters—focus on ethics, intercultural communication, and a wide variety of real-world scenarios. For every chapter, we now offer additional activities on the Web site, giving instructors more options than ever.

New Material Throughout

To better reflect the choices and resources available to workplace writers, we have added, updated, and expanded several sections, including the following:

- **A new discussion of context** (Chapter 1) to help writers convey enough background information so that readers understand the purpose and value of a document.
- **Updated guidance on research** (Chapter 6) that includes the latest information on finding, evaluating, and documenting primary and secondary source material.
- **A new section on the politics of memo protocol** (Chapter 8) that highlights the importance of context to writing in corporations and other complex organizations.
- **New advice on instant messaging** (Chapter 8) that explains how to make the most of this emerging workplace tool.
- **Expanded treatment of visual communication,** including a new chart for selecting the right visual for the right purpose (Chapter 7), a discussion of international symbols (Chapter 7), clearer guidelines on formatting correspondence (Chapter 8), and new advice on preparing visual-only instructions for a global audience (Chapter 12).
- **A new explanation of usability testing** (Chapter 12) that emphasizes the need to systematically integrate input from the target audience in developing complex instructions.
- **Coverage of grant and research proposals** (Chapter 13) that points students to resources for tackling these challenging documents.
- **Updated advice on finding a job** (Chapter 16) that offers new tips for using résumé summary statements, combining chronological and functional

formats, and writing and formatting print and electronic résumés. New sample résumés designed by Kim Isaacs, the Résumé Expert at Monster.com, and new sample cover letters provide up-to-date models.

- **New Digital Tips** give advice on proofreading (Chapter 4), reviewing collaborative documents (5), using Wikis (5), interviewing by e-mail (6), storing research results (6), designing documents with a word processor (7), instant messaging (8), creating styles and templates (10), and using PDF files (15). All of the tips throughout the book are up to date, and several are now enhanced by step-by-step instructions at the companion Web site.

Ancillaries

Book Companion Web Site: <bedfordstmartins.com/writingthatworks>

The companion Web site for *Writing That Works* (illustrated on the back cover of this book) augments the material in the book with a gallery of sample documents, more than 100 additional exercises and writing projects, tutorials, expanded Digital Tips with step-by-step guides, additional advice and resources for finding a job or an internship, and links to helpful Web sites related to every topic in the book. Integrated On the Web marginal notes throughout the book point to specific resources and activities available online.

Online Instructor's Manual: <bedfordstmartins.com/writingthatworks>

The comprehensive online Instructor's Manual provides chapter overviews and teaching tips, quizzes, suggested responses to the exercises and writing projects, PowerPoint slides, transparency masters, classroom handouts, course-planning help, and sample syllabi.

Content for Online Courses

A variety of student and instructor resources developed for this textbook is ready for use in course management systems such as WebCT and Blackboard.

Additional Resources for Business and Technical Writing: <bedfordstmartins.com/bustech>

This site provides helpful resources for students — access to a *Web Design Tutorial* by Mike Markel and to *Research and Documentation Online*, a reference guide by Diana Hacker for finding and documenting sources in multiple disciplines.

In addition, all the resources within Re:Writing (<bedfordstmartins.com/rewriting>) are available to users of *Writing That Works*. Resources include tutorials, exercises, diagnostics, technology help, and model documents — all written by our most widely adopted authors.

ix visual exercises for techcomm

This CD-ROM, which can be packaged for free with copies of *Writing That Works*, introduces the fundamentals of visual composition in an interactive medium, using brochures, instructions, reports, and other examples of technical communication. To see a sample tutorial, visit <bedfordstmartins.com/ixtechcomm>. For ordering information, contact your local sales representative or e-mail us at <sales_support@bfwpub.com>.

Document-Based Cases for Technical Communication

This brief supplement by Roger Munger (Boise State University), which can be packaged for free with *Writing That Works*, introduces students to seven context-rich cases by providing a range of common workplace documents, including business graphics, definitions and extended descriptions, letters, memos, e-mail messages, proposals, technical reports, instructions, and presentation graphics. Four realistic workplace tasks in each case ask students to analyze sample documents, to use information to solve a problem, and to produce their own thoughtful documents. Electronic copies of case documents are available for students to download and work with at <bedfordstmartins.com/techdocs>, and suggested responses for instructors offer possible approaches to case tasks in an instructor-only area of <bedfordstmartins.com/techdocs>.

■ Acknowledgments

We would like to thank Lisa-Anne Culp of the University of South Florida for her thoughtful work on the Ninth Edition's writing assignments and projects, the companion Web site, and the Instructor's Manual. We thank Sandy Petrulionis of Pennsylvania State University and her students Susan Litzinger, Shana L. Richardson, and Eric Shoop for the formal report and sales proposal included in this book. Thanks also to Johan De Beer of Mitsubishi Engines North America for permission to include an adaptation of one of his trip reports, to Chris Helms of the *Cambridge Chronicle* for providing a model of a functional résumé, and to Peggy Edwards for letting us include the student résumé that helped her land her current job as an inspector for the Salem County Department of Health in New Jersey.

We are grateful to Sandy Fuhr, University Librarian at Southwest Minnesota State University, for her contributions to the research chapter; to Matthias Jonas, Niceware International, LLC, for developing the new advice and samples for instant messaging in the workplace; and to Stuart Selber and Tony Ceraso of Pennsylvania State University, Altoona, for preparing the Digital Tips (in the book and on the Web site) on wikis. For their contributions to previous editions of this book, we would like to thank Candy Henry of Pennsylvania State University for her ESL advice and work on the book's writing assignments and companion Web site,

Suzanne Karberg of Purdue University both for her contributions to the Meeting the Deadline coverage in the presentations chapter and for her work on the writing assignments and projects, and Kate Williams of Oglethorpe University for developing the advice for finding a job or an internship provided on the book's Web site.

We wish to thank the following instructors who have substantially strengthened the Ninth Edition by generously sharing their helpful comments and recommendations: Luann Okel Adams, Mid-State Technical College; D. Michelle Adkerson, Nashville State Community College; David Beach, George Mason University; Maureen S. Bogdanowicz, Kapi'olani Community College; Stephanie J. Brown, Saginaw Valley State University; Kerry J. Burner, Tallahassee Community College; Dave Clark, University of Wisconsin–Milwaukee; Helyn Elisabeth Evatt, Clemson University; Sonia Feder-Lewis, Saint Mary's University of Minnesota; Julie Freeman, Indiana University–Purdue University Indianapolis; Brenda Glascott, University of Pittsburgh; Paul Graham, West Virginia University; Richard Hay, University of Wisconsin–Milwaukee; Jacqueline Justice, Kent State University; Susan M. Katz, North Carolina State University; Jeff Kerssen-Griep, University of Portland; Anne M. Kuhta, George Mason University; Kirk Lockwood, Illinois Valley Community College; Jennifer M. Love, Lane Community College; Joan McNamara, Boston College; Ron McNeel, New Mexico State University at Alamogordo; Neil Pagano, Columbia College Chicago; Lori A. Paige, Westfield State College/American International College; Susan Marie Plachta, Saginaw Valley State University; Laurie Brown Pressly, Clemson University; Charles Riley, City University of New York Bernard M. Baruch College; Debra Lattanzi Shutika, George Mason University; Eric Smith, Kent State University; Jeanne Smith, Kent State University; Kim Thomas-Pollei, Westminster College; Jane Jones Turnbull, Community College of Baltimore County; Yong-Kang Wei, University of Texas at Brownsville; Linda Woodson, University of Texas at San Antonio. We also gratefully acknowledge the ongoing contributions and help of the students and faculty at the University of Wisconsin–Milwaukee, as well as our colleagues in the United States and abroad.

For kindly sharing their experiences of writing and communicating at work and for contributing to our Voices from the Workplace feature, we would like to thank Anne Basanese, Toxics Use Reduction Institute; James Bates, U.S. Department of Housing and Urban Development; Beth Blazon, St. Joseph's Hospital; Steve Bramlage, Vectren Energy Delivery of Ohio; Debra Canale, Roadway Express; Paul Clark, John Deere; Johan De Beer, Mitsubishi Engines North America; Robert Demers, Philips Medical Systems; Howard Ellis, Compuware Corporation; Deborah Gilpin, Children's Museum of Phoenix; Liz Goodwin, Melrose Public Library; Paul B. Greenspan, EMC Corporation; Claire Harrison, Claire Harrison Communication Services; Steven K. Hurd, U.S. Department of Veterans Affairs; Ted Kalo, Office of Representative John Conyers Jr.; Susan U. Ladwig, Reinhart Boerner Van Deuren; Stephen Lin, Smarter Living, Inc.; Brian Manning, Molecular, Inc.; Maureen March, Lincoln Elementary School; Patrick Martinack, Council on International Educational Exchange; Ulrike Mueller, SAP AG; David Noyes, HLM Design—Heery International; Sherri Pfennig, University of

Wisconsin–Milwaukee; Judy Prono, Los Alamos National Laboratory; Joseph G. Rappaport, Taxis for All Campaign; Victoria Ravin, Translations.com; Robert Repetto, Novia Associates, Inc.; Rebecca Schlei, Harry W. Schwartz Bookshops; Sarah Schwerdel, Bay State Community Services; Kelli Strieby, Condé Nast (New York); Annika Tamura, Boston.com; and Adam Thompson, *Denver Post*.

We are also greatly indebted to the leadership of Bedford/St. Martin's, beginning with Joan Feinberg, president; Charles Christensen, retired president; Denise Wydra, editorial director; Karen Henry, editor in chief; and Leasa Burton, executive editor, for helping us to re-imagine our approach to this edition and for their unstinting support throughout the revision process. Amy Hurd Gershman deserves praise for keeping everything moving, locating and coordinating the new Voices from the Workplace, and developing an impressive companion Web site. We thank Emily Berleth, who, with the help of Herb Nolan at Books By Design, oversaw the difficult task of producing this book. We are grateful to Janis Owens at Books By Design for the creative design, and to Kathleen Benn McQueen and Faith Hanson for their careful copyediting and proofreading.

Finally, this edition benefited significantly from our collaboration with Ellen Kuhl, our developmental editor at Bedford/St. Martin's. Her contributions were invaluable in helping us re-imagine key features throughout the text. She was especially helpful in the reorganization of several chapters and in streamlining the Revision Guide. Beyond these efforts, she was instrumental in updating samples throughout the book, locating good "voices" for the Voices in the Workplace feature, and keeping us all focused on the ethics and global communications content. This edition is stronger throughout because of her superb editing skills and attention to conciseness.

Walter E. Oliu
Charles T. Brusaw
Gerald J. Alred

About the Authors

Walter E. Oliu until recently served as Chief of the Publishing Services Branch at the U.S. Nuclear Regulatory Commission. He is a communications consultant in the Washington, D.C., area and has taught at Miami University of Ohio, Slippery Rock State University, and Montgomery College.

Charles T. Brusaw worked for twenty years as a technical writer for the NCR Corporation and has also worked in advertising, public relations, and curriculum development. He has served as a business-writing consultant for corporations worldwide and taught at both NCR Corporation's Management College and Sinclair Community College.

Gerald J. Alred is professor of English at the University of Wisconsin–Milwaukee, where he teaches courses in professional writing and directs the Graduate Certificate Program in International Technical Communication. He is a recipient of the 2004 Jay R. Gould Award for Excellence in Teaching Technical Communication from the Society for Technical Communication. He is also the associate editor of *Journal of Business Communication*.

All three are coauthors of *The Business Writer's Handbook,* Eighth Edition; *Handbook of Technical Writing*, Eighth Edition; *The Business Writer's Companion*, Fourth Edition; and *The Technical Writer's Companion,* Third Edition.

Brief Contents

Contents

Chapter 3   Writing the Draft   64

Chapter 4   Revising the Draft   94

Chapter 7

Designing Effective Documents and Visuals   205

Voices from the Workplace: Howard Ellis; Paul Clark   206

PART THREE Writing at Work: From Principle to Practice   259

Chapter 9   **Writing Business Correspondence**   313

Voices from the Workplace: Robert Repetto; Victoria Ravin   314

Writing That Works

Communicating Effectively on the Job

PART ONE

The Writing Process

In Part One, you will learn techniques for developing, drafting, and revising letters, memos, and a wide array of other on-the-job writing tasks. Using these strategies will help you produce clearly written, well-organized documents, because effective on-the-job writing always reflects the writer's attention to the work that goes on before the finished memo or letter emerges from the printer.

◆ **Determining Audience and Purpose.** Chapters 1 through 3 provide discussion and exercises to help you clearly define your reader's needs and the message you intend your document to convey.

◆ **Brainstorming and Gathering Information.** Chapter 1 includes detailed examples and discussion of methods you can use to generate ideas and collect and begin to organize information.

◆ **Outlining.** Chapter 2 describes how you can organize your information into an outline that is appropriate to your purpose and audience. It also offers examples in a wide range of outline styles.

◆ **Writing the Draft.** Chapter 3 discusses and offers examples of the process through which writers turn an outline into a successful rough draft.

◆ **Revising.** Chapter 4 describes the kinds of problems you need to evaluate when you revise your draft. You will learn to review your draft to see how well it communicates to its intended audience, to be sure it is complete and coherent, to look for ways to emphasize key ideas, to check information for accuracy, to consider the ethical implications of your writing, and to proofread for correctness.

1 Assessing Audience and Purpose: A Case Study

AT A GLANCE: The Writing Process

This chapter describes how one employee successfully completed an important on-the-job writing task from first thought to final product. The process occurs in a systematic series of steps applicable to all workplace writing:

Christine Thomas was aware of a potential opportunity at HVS Accounting Services, where she worked as the company's systems administrator. The company was prospering. In just the past year, Harriet Sullivan, the president and founder of the small company, hired five new employees to handle the increasing workload of tax preparation, financial planning, and investment services. HVS now had 12 full-time employees, about half of whom commuted over an hour each way. Christine was also aware that the company recently lost several promising job applicants because they did not wish to spend two or more hours a day driving to and from work.

With this information in mind, Christine had carefully reviewed several management magazines and Web sites about the benefits of telecommuting for companies and their employees. Companies that offered this option to their employees had a more satisfied workforce, less absenteeism, and greater productivity per employee.

So, with all the information in hand and confident of the value of her suggestion, Christine wrote an e-mail message to Harriet Sullivan (Figure 1–1). Two days later, Christine received the

> **To:**   Harriet V. Sullivan, President
> **From:**   Christine Thomas, Systems Administrator
> **Date:**   May 5, 2006
> **Subject:** Telecommuting and HVS Accounting Services
>
> I believe that HVS Accounting would benefit greatly if we permitted our employees to telecommute one or more days a week. A growing number of companies, large and small, permit employees to perform company work at home on a schedule they jointly agree to. The companies can communicate with these employees during the workday in a variety of ways — by phone, e-mail, and fax.
>
> Such a policy has many advantages that would help HVS and our employees. Employees would save the time and expense necessary to commute every day. They would also suffer less stress and be in a better frame of mind to tackle their work. This would result in greater worker productivity. Please consider my suggestion that we offer our employees the opportunity to perform their HVS work at home one or more days a week.
>
> Christine

Figure 1–1   First Proposal (E-mail)

following terse return e-mail from Harriet: "Not right for HVS." Christine was not only disappointed but also puzzled. She knew that her suggestion was timely and reasonable because she had checked all the facts before writing the e-mail. Yet she had failed to convince Harriet Sullivan.

■ Writing Systematically

In writing her e-mail message, Christine Thomas committed the most common mistake made by people who write on the job: She lost sight of the purpose of her message and overlooked the needs of her audience. Christine was so convinced of the value of her suggestion that she did not realize that Harriet was not familiar with the information her research had produced and could not see the situation from her perspective. Had she kept her primary purpose and her reader clearly in mind, Christine would have been able to generate ideas, establish her scope, and organize her thoughts in a way that ultimately might have achieved her objective.

The last three steps are important: Even with her reader and her purpose clearly in mind, Christine would not have been ready to write her e-mail to Harriet. She would simply have established a framework in which to develop her message. Once they have identified their purpose and their audience, some writers don't know what to do next and stare at a blank page or computer screen waiting for inspiration.

A systematic approach helps writers over this hurdle. Before beginning to write, careful writers not only identify their purpose and audience but think seri-

Voices from the Workplace

Deborah Gilpin, Children's Museum of Phoenix

Writing is a critical tool for museum president and CEO Deborah Gilpin. In her work, Deborah is often required to help others understand and visualize the learning, creative, and social development that happens at her museum — experiences that are highly objective and difficult to put into words. Deborah also faces the challenge of writing for a number of different audiences and purposes. "Thank-you notes for contributions express gratitude and strengthen the personal connection the donor has to the museum's purpose," Deborah explains. "Proposals, on the other hand, serve as an invitation to contributions, participation, and collaborative work. Writing helps to bring my work into focus — it requires me to refine the details, to identify where accountability lies, and to imagine the greatest possible outcome."

Patrick Martinack, Council on International Education Exchange

Writing is an important part of customer-service manager Patrick Martinack's daily routine at Council on International Educational Exchange (CIEE), a company that specializes in placing students and professionals in international-study and work-abroad programs. From business correspondence to the development of customer-service training materials, Patrick faces the challenge of writing for a multilingual audience. "When writing to customers participating in one of our work-exchange programs," Patrick explains, "I have to sense the English ability of the person. . . . He or she may have limited English skills and is likely in the United States for the first time. With that in mind, my purpose is like that of an ambassador. To accomplish my goal, I have to consider why the correspondence is happening and anticipate what useful information I need to include in addition to the conversation at hand."

ously about the context of their writing and strive to organize and present information for ease of understanding. This process involves first listing all the ideas and facts the writer might wish to include, refining that list by examining each item from the perspectives of audience and purpose, and organizing what's left in a way that satisfies both the writer's purpose and the audience's needs.

WRITER'S CHECKLIST
Planning Your Document

- ☑ Determine your purpose.
- ☑ Assess your audience's needs.
- ☑ Consider the context of your writing.
- ☑ Generate, gather, and record ideas and facts.
- ☑ Organize your ideas in a list.
- ☑ Establish the scope of coverage for your topic.
- ☑ Organize the list based on the needs of your purpose and audience.

Determining Your Purpose

Everything you write has a purpose. You want your readers to know, to believe, or to be able to do something when they have finished reading what you have written. Determining your purpose is the first step in preparing to write; unless you know what you hope to accomplish, you cannot know what information you should present.

Purpose gives direction to your writing. The more precisely you can state your primary purpose at the outset, the more successful your writing is likely to be. (You may also have a secondary purpose, such as to motivate or reassure.) Christine Thomas might have said that her purpose was "to allow HVS employees to telecommute" — but permitting employees to telecommute was the *result* she wanted; it was not the precise purpose of her memo. Further thought would have led Christine to recognize the specific goals of the e-mail itself. To make sure that your purpose is precise, put it in writing. In most cases, you can use the following pattern to guide you:

▶   My primary purpose is to _____ so that my audience _____ .

By filling in the blanks, Christine Thomas might have developed the following statement of purpose:

▶   My primary purpose is to explain the advantages of telecommuting so that my reader,
    Harriet Sullivan, will be persuaded that the idea has enough merit for the company
    and its employees that she will permit it at least for a trial period.

With this statement of purpose, Christine would have recognized that her purpose was more complicated than it had at first appeared and that she would have to present persuasive evidence to be effective.

Assessing Your Audience's Needs

Your job as a writer is to express your ideas so clearly that your audience cannot misinterpret them. An important element of the purpose statement is the phrase "so that my audience . . .". Simply identifying the response you would like is very different from actually achieving it. Although a purpose statement addresses a problem from the writer's point of view, the audience's needs must also be taken into account if you are to be persuasive. Yet many writers often forget that they have an audience, and they focus solely on their own purposes.

After you have stated your purpose, ask yourself, "Who is my audience?" Often you will know the answer. For example, if you are writing a memo attempting to persuade your manager to fund a project, you know who your reader is. In another situation, however, you might be writing a letter to someone you do not know in another company. In this case, you would try to imagine your reader, taking into consideration what you know about that company, your reader's position in the company or department, and his or her responsibilities regarding the topic you are writing about. You could not know what your reader's needs are until you know at least that much about him or her.

 CONSIDERING AUDIENCE AND PURPOSE
Writing for Your Reader

Try to answer each of the following questions in as much detail as possible to help focus on your reader's needs in relation to your subject. This process is helpful for all types of writing, but it will be especially important for longer, more complex tasks.

- Who is your audience?
- Do you have more than one audience?
- What do you want your audience to know, to believe, or to be able to do after reading your writing?
- Have you narrowed your topic to best focus on what you want your audience to know?
- What are your audience's needs in relation to the subject?
- What does your audience know about the subject?
- If you have multiple audiences, do they have different levels of knowledge about your subject?
- What are your audience's feelings about your subject — sympathetic? hostile? neutral?
- Does your writing acknowledge other or contrary points of view about the subject?
- Have you selected the right medium — e-mail, memo, letter, booklet, and so on — for your subject and audience?
- Is your tone respectful?
- Does your format enhance audience understanding?

When you know enough about your reader that you can actually picture him or her responding to what you have written, you have an advantage. However, even if you know your audience very well, a little reflection is necessary. Without careful thought, Christine Thomas might have answered the question "Who is my reader?" from only one point of view:

▶ My reader is Harriet Sullivan, and she's been my manager for ten years. We've worked together since she founded the company, so she'll no doubt understand that I have her best interests in mind.

Had Christine carefully analyzed Harriet as the reader of her e-mail, she would have considered Harriet's role in the company, her lack of familiarity with the topic, and her anxiety about taking such a step. Bearing these concerns in mind, Christine might have answered the question differently.

▶ My reader is Harriet Sullivan, president of HVS Accounting Services. Harriet founded HVS ten years ago with modest savings and a substantial loan. Cautious, industrious, and a stickler for detail, Harriet has built HVS into a sound business and is now be-ginning to see some return on her investment. Harriet is also a hands-on executive. She puts in long hours at the office and is in frequent contact with the staff by e-mail, telephone, and face-to-face conversations. In addition to a regularly scheduled staff meeting every Wednesday, she holds informal meetings several times a week. She may strongly resist the loss of hands-on access to her staff when they work at home. She values computer technology and purchased laptop computers for the account-ants and financial analysts to help them as they visit clients around the metropolitan area. However, although she uses e-mail regularly, she does so reluctantly and prefers memos.

ON THE WEB

For online resources for determining audi-ence and purpose, see Chapter 1, bedfordstmartins.com/ writingthatworks

Based on this analysis, Christine would have been better prepared to provide the information that Harriet needed to understand, agree with, and act on Christine's proposal.

Considering the Context

In the workplace, everything is written in a context. The environment or situation in which you write a document (such as a proposal, letter, or report) will affect how your audience interprets its meaning. Even a good idea will fail to get support if the writer does not take into account the circumstances—both inside and out-side the organization—that could influence its acceptance. Christine Thomas, for example, had to consider her manager's style and the company's infrastructure. Aware of Harriet's hands-on approach to management, Christine needed to ad-dress her potential anxiety about the staff being away from the office one or more days a week. Christine also had to consider the larger context of how telecom-muting might affect the company as a whole. For example, she needed to think about each staff member's personal situation and commuting habits, equipment requirements, communications technologies, customer confidentiality and con-venience, jobs most and least suitable for telecommuting, and any expenses her suggestions might incur. Without addressing these issues, she could not ade-quately develop a proposal that would merit Harriet's serious consideration.

WRITER'S CHECKLIST
Assessing Context

Use the following questions as a starting point as you assess the context for your topic:

- ☑ What is your professional relationship with your readers and how might that af-fect the tone, style, and scope of your writing?
- ☑ What is "the story" behind the immediate reason you are writing; that is, what series of events or previous documents led to your need to write?
- ☑ What medium do your readers prefer — memo, letter, report, or e-mail?
- ☑ What specific factors or values, such as competition, finance, and regulation, are important to your readers' organization or department?
- ☑ What is the corporate culture in which your readers work?

☑ What are the professional relationships among your readers?

☑ What recent or current events within or outside an organization or a department may influence how readers interpret your writing?

☑ What national cultural differences might affect your readers' expectations for or interpretations of a document?

Generating, Gathering, and Recording Ideas and Facts

When you have determined your purpose, assessed your reader's needs, and considered the context for your writing, you must decide what information will satisfy these demands. Several techniques are available for gathering and recording information.

Brainstorming

A good way to start generating ideas is to tap into your own knowledge and experience. You may find that you already have enough information to get started. The technique of interviewing yourself, commonly known as *brainstorming*, may also suggest ways to obtain additional information.

To begin, list as many ideas as you can think of about the general subject of your document as they occur to you. (This type of research also works well with a group of writers or project team members.) Jot down what you already know and, if possible, where you learned of it, using a computer, a dry-erase board, a pad of paper, or note cards.

Reporters and other writers have long used the following questions as a guide to ensure that they have answered the questions their audience is likely to have about a particular story: *What* happened? *Why* did it happen? *When* did it happen? *How* did it happen? *Where* did it happen? *Who* was involved? Rarely will you be able to apply all these questions to any single on-the-job writing situation, but the range of information they cover can help to start your thinking.

Once you have assembled a list of ideas, examine each item and decide whether it contributes to your purpose or satisfies your audience's needs. Then mark the item with a *P* for purpose or an *A* for audience. Some items will satisfy both your purpose and your audience, others will appear to satisfy only one, and still others will appear to have nothing to do with either. When you have finished marking your list, cross out any item that is not marked. Be sure to reconsider an unmarked item from the perspectives of both your purpose and your audience, making certain that the item fits neither before eliminating it. Ideally, you will have a comprehensive list of items beside which you have placed both a *P* and an *A*. The more common ground your purpose and your audience's needs share, the more effective your writing will be.

As you review your list, you will find that items relating clearly to both your purpose and the needs of your audience are easiest to work with. Items that your audience might need but that would get in the way of your purpose are trickier. Harriet Sullivan, for example, needs to know that after the program begins, she will have less direct access to employees working from home. Because she's a "hands-on" manager, this break with her customary practice will be difficult for Harriet to accept. Christine, however, might be reluctant to mention this fact because it appears to undermine her purpose, which is to persuade Harriet to support telecommuting. However, to reconcile Harriet's interests and her own, Christine would have to point out this aspect of the program. To have credibility, you need to acknowledge opposing points of view when they are relevant; doing so allows you to respond to your audience's objections rather than leaving them unanswered.

ETHICS NOTE

Acknowledge any real or potential conflicting opinions; doing so is honest, allows you to anticipate and overcome objections, and builds your credibility.

Turning a writer's list of ideas into a reader's list of information should be neither difficult nor mysterious; thoroughness is the key. Christine Thomas, for example, might have generated the well-balanced list shown in Figure 1–2, using one or more of the methods described here. Such a list will give you an idea of the content of the project. The list will probably be sketchy or missing information, but that's actually helpful in showing where additional research is needed. It will also give you a framework for where to integrate the details of the additional research.

Using Other Sources of Information

Brainstorming may not produce all the information you need. Christine, for example, read about telecommuting by reviewing trade journals and Web sites in the field. To get enough information to meet the needs of your audience, you may have to conduct formal, systematic research. In such cases, you should have some idea of how thoroughly you will cover your subject. To consult the appropriate sources, you will have to know how much detail is required. If you know what you are looking for and where to find it, research presents few problems.

◆ These different sources of information are discussed in detail in Chapter 6, Researching Your Subject.

The library provides books, articles, reference works, and other material for your research. The Internet, used carefully, provides access to vast amounts of information from commercial, educational, governmental, and other sources. A personal interview with an expert can provide you with up-to-date information not readily available in printed material. A questionnaire permits you to obtain the views of a group of people and requires less time and money than numerous personal interviews.

Establishing Your Scope

Having refined your list of ideas and facts, you must review it once again to establish the scope of coverage for your topic. Your *scope* is the degree of detail you decide is necessary to cover each item in your list, and you must determine it based on your purpose and the needs of your audience. As you contemplate each item, ask yourself, "How much information should I include to support my purpose and satisfy my audience's needs?" Often you will find that you have omitted important

ITEMS FOR TELECOMMUTING PROPOSAL

A   Harriet needs to see benefits of new practice

P   Current commutes too long

AP   Employee morale down because of long commutes

A   Good feature for recruiting and keeping skilled staff

A   Productivity gains

P   Saves employees time and money

A   Done elsewhere?

~~P   Eliminate the need for current office space?~~

P   Need for additional equipment — computers? phones? faxes?

A   Cost of additional technology

A   Do on trial basis

A   Is home work space OK?

A   Need to establish home working hours

~~P   Advantages to community~~

P   Benefits to employees of avoiding long commutes

A   Advantages to customers?

PA   Benefits to employees with special needs

~~P   Employee isolation~~

P   Is this a program for everyone?

A   Management can't look in on workers — not physically in office

P   Not all jobs lend themselves to telecommuting

A   What about staff meetings?

A   What about meetings with clients?

A   What about taking confidential information home?

A   How can Harriet assess employee productivity?

A   Danger of losing employee loyalty?

A   What are the benefits for HVS?

A   Will employees be distracted at home?

AP   Does program apply to all HVS employees?

~~A   Will those not in program resent those who are?~~

A   How will work be coordinated among employees?

Figure 1–2   Brainstorming List for a Proposal

points or need to research your subject further to obtain necessary facts or figures. At other times, you will find that your list is cluttered with unnecessary detail.

Had Christine Thomas drawn up the list shown in Figure 1–2 and then reviewed it to establish her scope, she would have discovered that some of the items on her list needed detailed information to satisfy Harriet Sullivan's concerns. Entries such as "Cost of additional technology" would tell her that she had to either provide detailed figures for the cost of this equipment or explain why no additional expense is necessary. However, other items requiring more detail might be more difficult to identify: "How can Harriet assess employee productivity?" indicates Christine's sense that evaluating productivity would present a cost-conscious person like Harriet with a challenge. She would want to know how this could be done effectively. Figure 1–3 shows the list in Figure 1–2 after the scope has been established.

Be careful when establishing your scope. Writers who know a lot about a subject tend to unload information on audiences who have no time or need to wade through a catalog of topics or details to get to the point. Understand, too, that establishing your scope in the classroom may be different from doing so on the job. The scope of topics for classroom assignments must often be limited because of accessibility of information, the goals of the course, or other learning objectives. Consider these limitations as part of the purpose of an assignment. In whatever context you establish the scope of your writing, always be guided by your purpose and your audience's needs.

Organizing Your Ideas

Once you have established your scope, you should have a list of the ideas and facts to be included in your writing. Examine this list and look for relationships among the items in it. Group the related ideas and arrange them under headings — short

---

POINTS TO COVER

- *Good feature for recruiting and keeping skilled staff*
- *Productivity gains — note industry data*
- *Saves employees time and money*
- *Our competitors permit telecommuting*
- *Costs of additional technology and types needed — although HVS is set up well right now*
- *Do on trial basis — recommend three months, two days/week*
- *Need to establish home working hours*
- *Advantages to community — less congestion and pollution*
- *Advantages to customers — maybe?*
- *Benefits to employees with special needs — two HVS employees can use now!*
- *Employee morale down because of long commutes*
- *Management can't look in on workers — not physically in office*
- *Not all jobs lend themselves to telecommuting — such as receptionist*
- *Scheduling staff and client meetings*
- *Need to protect confidential information when home*
- *Show how Harriet can assess employee productivity*
- *Possible danger of losing employee loyalty*
- *Address possibility that employees will be distracted at home*

Figure 1–3   Notes for Proposal

phrases that identify the kind of items in each group. As you group the related ideas, consider the following questions: Is the time sequence among items important? If so, organize them chronologically. Do you need to compare the features of one item with those of one or more other items? Organize accordingly. Should you present the most important information first or, instead, build a case that ends with the most important information? Organize items by decreasing order of importance or by increasing order of importance, respectively.

As you assemble and arrange the groups of ideas, add, delete, and move ideas around until you feel that you have the best possible organization. For example, Christine turned her brainstorming list of thoughts, shown in Figure 1–2, into the Points to Cover list in Figure 1–3 after narrowing the topic. She then organized these points into the three major subtopics covered in Figure 1–4.

◆ *For a detailed discussion of organizing techniques, see Chapter 2, Organizing Your Information.*

◆ *For large or complex subjects, a more formal outline is often helpful. See Chapter 2, Organizing Your Information.*

---

1. **COMPANY BENEFITS**
   - Productivity gains
   - Done elsewhere—by competitors
   - Advantages to customers?
   - Special-needs employees
   - Do on trial basis only—low risk
   - Worker recruitment and retention

2. **COMPANY CONCERNS**
   - Need for additional equipment
   - Need to establish home working space and hours
   - Not for all jobs/employees
   - Can't observe workers firsthand
   - Staff meetings
   - Client meetings
   - Confidential information
   - Assessing productivity
   - Employee loyalty
   - Distractions at home
   - Coordinating work

3. **EMPLOYEE BENEFITS**
   - Help special-needs employees
   - Improve morale—less time on the road
   - Save time and expenses

Figure 1–4 Revised Notes for Proposal

■ Writing for Results

Soon after she received the disappointing response to her e-mail, Christine found the courage to step into Harriet's office. Christine explained, "I've really investigated the situation, and I'm sure my suggestion would be in our best interest. Perhaps if I gave you more information, you'd reconsider my suggestion." Harriet thought for a moment and then said, "All right. Give me the major benefits and any associated disadvantages and costs by next Monday. If they are convincing, I'll meet with you and Fred Sadowski as soon as I get the chance. And, by the way, give me the information in a memo. An e-mail is too informal for what you're suggesting." Christine Thomas left Harriet Sullivan's office both relieved and determined that this time she would convince Harriet.

Christine wrote a statement of purpose; determined the general needs of her reader; generated, gathered, and recorded the key ideas and facts; and established her scope of coverage. As she prepared to organize her information, Christine thought again about Harriet as her reader. Knowing that Harriet is a practical businessperson concerned about money and wary of change, Christine realized that she must organize her ideas to first convince Harriet of the advantages of telecommuting before going on to address what Harriet would see as the potential disadvantages. After organizing her notes (see Figure 1–3), Christine was ready to write a rough draft. Note that a first draft is less concerned with creating a coherent, correct, and persuasive memo than it is with getting all the needed information down in a reasonably organized manner.

◆ *For a discussion of specific revision techniques and strategies, see Chapter 4, Revising the Draft.*

Christine wrote a draft and put it aside, planning to reread her work the next morning to discover any problems with clarity, coherence, and correctness. She also e-mailed the draft to a trusted colleague and asked for suggestions. The coworker said that Christine had obviously researched her subject with care and that she presented the appropriate information about starting the new program, but that she needed to do a better job of anticipating some of Harriet's questions. The coworker suggested also that Christine might rephrase and reorganize the memo with a sharper eye for Harriet's needs. She noted, for example, that the memo would benefit from headings to introduce subtopics and commented that Harriet would appreciate being told that the new program would benefit both the company and its employees. Finally, she told Christine that the writing was too choppy and needed to be smoothed out. She handed Christine a copy of the draft that included her handwritten suggestions (Figure 1–5).

◆ *For detailed guidance on memo format, see page 288 in Chapter 8, Understanding the Principles of Business Communication.*

◆ *For help in locating and correcting sentence-level errors, see Part Four: Revision Guide.*

Christine considered her coworker's suggestions and reviewed the brainstorming lists she'd written earlier. She then added to her introduction and conclusion and reworked the body of the memo. The extra attention she gave to Harriet's needs provided a helpful point of focus she could use to restructure and polish her writing. She also heeded the format advice to add topic headings to guide Harriet through the proposal. When she finished her revisions, Christine proofread her work for grammatical and mechanical errors and sent the final version of the memo to Harriet Sullivan (Figure 1–6). Note that the content and style of the finished memo reflect the suggestions made by Christine's coworker. Christine's story had a happy ending: Harriet was persuaded by Christine's final memo and started the work-at-home program on a trial basis that September.

Memo   DRAFT

Date: May 9, 2006
To: Harriet V. Sullivan, President
From: Christine Thomas
Subject: Telecommuting and HVS Accounting Services

Make subject line more descriptive

I believe that HVS Accounting Services and its employees would benefit if we permit our professional staff to telecommute two days a week. Telecommuting is becoming increasingly common through-out the United States. I suggest that we try the program for three months. That would give us a trial basis. I suggest that we begin on September 1. That would be before our busy end-of-year and winter tax-preparation period.

Sentences too choppy — smooth out

Such a program offers a lot of advantages to HVS. The biggest ad-vantage is that employee productivity could increase. I looked at a dozen trade-journal articles and they show average gains of from 15–30%. I spoke with other financial services companies at monthly Accounting Society meetings. They mention gains in the 20–30% range. We need to pull even with the competition.

Add topic headings for readability

Include list of articles and publications they appear in?

Reasons?

This would also benefit our employees. They save time and money on the days they work at home. They also wind up being less frazzled. Employees say that the time savings and better frame of mind are two reasons why they can better focus on their jobs. Also, the com-petition is doing it. They say they have an easier time recruiting and keeping employees. This is an important option that we can offer to our employees. The current job market is very competitive.

Name one or two specific competitors doing this?

The program would also be good for Bill Mayhue and Mabel Chong. Bill is having a hip replacement next month. He will be away from work for up to 6 weeks. Part of this time away could be used pro-ductively if he's allowed to work at home. Mabel's baby is due in September. She plans to spend 3 months at home after the birth and wants to keep up with her projects. Instead of losing their services,

Figure 1–5   **Draft Proposal (with Notes from Coworker)** (continued)

page 2

Note that staff has well-defined tasks

we would all mutually benefit. This would be a great boost for employee morale, too.

Will the program work in practice? One key issue is keeping track of employees working away from the office. HVS currently has details on staff productivity by billable hours. This system would apply to work-at-home employees. I will work with Fred Sadowski to set up and maintain measurable goals for those in the program. We would then review these goals in the middle and at the end of the 3-month trial period with you.

I wouldn't approach Fred w/o Harriet's permission

OK for all jobs at HVS?

I believe that Mondays and Fridays would be ideal work-at-home days. That would leave Tuesday through Thursday as core business days. Keeping in touch with employees at home will not be difficult. Everybody has a telephone. Our staff also has home desktop computers with Internet access. They also have fax machines and printers. Several also have small copiers. HVS has secure electronic information exchange. That's how we send and receive confidential client information electronically. Those in the program can be given password access to this information with their current remote-access software. In other words, they can log into and work on their office computer from their home computer. Finally, we can put home e-mail addresses and phone and fax numbers on our internal Web site. We can give that information to clients, also.

Long-distance calls?

Who pays for paper? Other supplies?

Any costs to HVS?

Will employees mind sharing their info?

Everyone I have spoken with already maintains a home office. So, they have access to private work space at home already. They also believe that they would not lose touch with everyone else at HVS if they're only gone for a day or two a week. Our staff has a proven record of getting the job done. This makes them well suited to a work-at-home program.

Any evidence?

Maybe auditors?

Figure 1–5   Draft Proposal (with Notes from Coworker) (continued)

HVS Memo

DATE: May 12, 2006
TO: Harriet V. Sullivan, President
FROM: Christine Thomas, Systems Administrator *CT*
SUBJECT: The Advantages of Telecommuting

I believe that HVS Accounting Services and its employees would benefit if we permit our professional staff to telecommute one or more days a week. Telecommuting is becoming increasingly common throughout the United States for several important reasons. I have researched the topic and talked with colleagues here and among our competitors. This memorandum presents the results of my findings and proposes that HVS set up a work-at-home program on a three-month trial basis beginning September 1. The trial period would occur well before our busy end-of-year and winter tax-preparation period.

What Are the Advantages?

The program would offer HVS several important advantages:

- Improved employee productivity
- Enhanced ability to recruit and retain good employees
- Mutually beneficial arrangements for employees with special needs

The foremost advantage to HVS is that employee productivity for those in a work-at-home program would very likely increase. I have reviewed a dozen trade-journal articles in our field and several Web sites that show average productivity gains of from 15 to 30 percent. In conversations with other financial-services companies at monthly Accounting Society meetings, they mention gains in the 20 to 30 percent range. This is an area where I believe we need to pull even with the competition.

Preprinted memo stationery

Memo heading

Author initials paper copy

Introduction to proposal for a new program

Heading signals an upcoming topic

List of key points focuses attention on advantages to company

Development of key points

Figure 1–6   Final Proposal (continued)

Harriet V. Sullivan   2   May 12, 2006

Advantages to employees

Telecommuting would provide important advantages to the staff that would help us to recruit and retain qualified employees. Several of our employees commute over an hour each way daily. Telecommuting would permit them to save time and money on the days they work at home. They would also be less frazzled on those days. Employees who telecommute report that the time savings and better frame of mind are two reasons they can better focus on their jobs. As you are aware, we have lost qualified job candidates because of their objections to long commutes. Our competitors note that they have an easier time recruiting and retaining valuable employees when they offer telecommuting as an option. This is an important benefit that we can offer to our employees, especially in the current competitive job market.

The program would also be strongly beneficial to HVS and two employees in particular: Bill Mayhue and Mabel Chong. Bill is scheduled for a hip replacement in two months and will be away from work for up to six weeks. Part of this time away could be used productively if he's allowed to work at home. Mabel's baby is due in September. She plans to spend three months at home after the birth and would also be a good candidate for this program. Instead of losing their services for extended periods—and their ongoing contacts with their clients—we would all benefit. This would be a great boost for employee morale, too.

How Would Telecommuting Work at HVS?

Any new program of this kind raises questions about how well it will work in practice. I believe that the key questions are the following:

List focuses attention on company concerns

- How can we track the work of those in the program?
- Should everyone participate?
- Which days of the week would work best?
- Are there startup or ongoing costs to HVS?

Figure 1–6   Final Proposal (continued)

Harriet V. Sullivan   3   May 12, 2006

HVS Accounting Services is in an ideal position to be able to keep track of employees working away from the office. Each member of the professional staff has well-defined tasks in financial and estate planning for families, in tax preparation and auditing for financial and estate planning for families, and in tax preparation and auditing for both families and small businesses. As you know from our monthly reports, HVS currently maintains detailed information that quantifies staff productivity by billable hours. This system would apply equally well to work-at-home employees. Also, with your approval, I will work with Fred Sadowski to set up and maintain measurable goals for those in the program. We would then review these goals in the middle and at the end of the three-month trial period with you. Not all jobs at HVS would be suitable for the program. The receptionist, mail staff, several of our temporary employees, and I need to be at the office during business hours, so we would not participate.

Development of key points

I believe that Mondays and Fridays would be ideal work-at-home days. That would leave Tuesday through Thursday as core business days for staff meetings, client conferences, and other activities better done at the office. Even on Mondays and Fridays, keeping in touch with employees at home will not be difficult in this electronic era. In addition to telephones, everyone eligible for the program already has home desktop computers with Internet access, fax machines, and printers. Several also have small copiers. Essentially, no startup expenses for HVS are associated with the program. The staff can keep a log of long-distance business calls and bring in their telephone bill monthly for reimbursement.

Can We Protect Customer Confidentiality?

Heading signals shift in topic

Customer confidentiality would also be protected. HVS has secure electronic information-exchange software that allows us to send and receive client confidential information electronically. Those in the program can be given password access to confidential and other client information at home using pcEverywhere, our current remote-access software. The software allows employees to connect to and work on their office computers from their home computers.

Figure 1–6   Final Proposal (continued)

Harriet V. Sullivan   4   May 12, 2006

Finally, I can post the home e-mail addresses and phone and fax numbers for everyone in the program on our internal Web site and provide that information to the appropriate clients. I will also program everyone's phone speed-dial feature with the home numbers of participants.

Because everyone I have spoken with already maintains a home office, having access to private work space at home is not a hindrance. Having this space also minimizes the possibility of interruptions or other disturbances during the day while still permitting employees to schedule home-repair visits rather than having to leave work to meet a repair person, as happens now. The staff also believes that they would not lose touch with everyone else at HVS if they're gone for only a day or two a week. As you know, the auditing staff is periodically away from the office for a week or two at a time at client sites until an audit is completed. Working away from the office is customary to them and causes few disruptions. Finally, everyone in the program would keep the same business hours, minus the commute, of course. Another indirect benefit of telecommuting is that it allows us to help do our part to reduce air pollution and traffic congestion in the area.

Can We Make It Happen?

Closing

Our staff has a proven record of getting the job done regardless of where they are working, which I believe makes them well suited to a work-at-home program. I look forward to discussing this option with you at your convenience.

Figure 1–6   Final Proposal (continued)

DIGITAL TIPS: Using Word Processors

- Avoid the temptation of writing first drafts without any planning. After brainstorming a list of ideas, use the outline feature to organize them. As you create the draft, you can use the cut-and-paste feature to try alternative organizations.

- Set your word processor to automatically save your draft at regular intervals. Routinely create backup copies of all of your files.

- Use the Find-and-Replace command to locate and delete wordy phrases (such as "that is," "there are," "the fact that," and "to be"); to find technical terms that may need further explanation or inclusion in a glossary; or to find words you have a tendency to overuse.

- Use a spell-check or grammar-check feature to identify and correct typographical errors, misspellings, and grammar problems. Remember, however, that a spell checker cannot determine that you meant "here" if you incorrectly typed "hear." Also, consider grammar-check recommendations as suggestions only because the software cannot interpret the context of your writing.

- Practice effective document design by defining styles for headings and other repeated text elements, by using the Copy and Paste commands to create and duplicate parallel headings throughout your text, and by allowing extra white space to set off examples and illustrations (refer to pages 206–216 in Chapter 7, Designing Effective Documents and Visuals, for more information). Style sheets from your instructor or employer will help you create uniform document designs.

CHAPTER 1 SUMMARY: GETTING READY

Successful writing on the job is the result of careful preparation. Review the following checklist to ensure that your writing assignments—in the classroom and on the job—are adequately planned.

- Have I determined the purpose of my writing?
- Have I considered my audience's needs and perspectives?
- Have I considered the context in which my audience will evaluate the document?
- Have I gathered and recorded all the ideas and facts necessary to fulfill my purpose and address my audience's needs?
- Have I established the appropriate scope of coverage?
- Have I organized my ideas into related groups and determined the best sequence to link these groups for my audience?
- Have I revised the draft to emphasize the points most important to my audience?
- Have I reviewed my draft for problems with clarity, coherence, and correctness?
- Have I formatted the final draft to highlight key ideas?

ON THE WEB

For an online quiz on audience and purpose, go to Chapter 1, bedfordstmartins.com/ writingthatworks

■ Exercises

1. Select a problem at your place of employment (past or present) or on your campus. Using the pattern in this chapter, create a statement of purpose for a memo you could write about a suggested solution for this problem. Your reader should be able to make a decision regarding your suggestion. Give the reader's name and position in your statement of the purpose. As your instructor directs, prepare the following:

    a. Brainstorm a list of items for the subject selected. Try to list 15 to 20 items; even if they seem inappropriate, just keep listing. Mark the items with a *P* for purpose or an *A* for audience.

    b. Eliminate the items in your list from 1a that clearly do not meet the audience's needs or contribute to your purpose. Then establish your scope and rewrite the list, grouping the items into three or more categories. Next, arrange the items in each category in sequence.

    c. Using the groups of items created in 1b, write a memo suggesting a solution to the problem.

2. For three of the following topics, or topics of your own choosing, list the topic, the audience, one possible purpose for a document, and the information needed to achieve that purpose. (List kinds of information, not sources of information.) Because the following topics are broad, you will need to select some particular aspect of each topic that you choose.

Banking	Office procedures
Computer programming	Personal computers
E-commerce	Photography
Electronics	Printing
Health care	Real estate
Highway construction	Small businesses
The Internet	Sports
Marketing	Television
Music	Welding
Occupations	

The following is a sample list:

Topic	Internet faxing
Audience	The average computer user
Purpose	To instruct the average computer user on how to set up and send a fax message to a friend, a fellow student, a coworker, or an instructor.
Kinds of information	Required hardware, Internet access, e-mail address, fax number, location (Web address) of one or more Internet faxing services, detailed instructions on how to send and receive faxes over the Internet

3. Using the techniques described in this chapter, write a memo explaining how to perform your job (or a job you've had) for an employee who will be replacing you while you are on vacation. Write two versions of this memo: Write one to a temporary employee hired through a temporary job agency and write a second to an

employee who works in your department but not in the same job. (See Chapter 8, Understanding the Principles of Business Communication, for memo-format examples.)

4. Write a memo to your manager asking for tuition reimbursement to attend this or another course. Assume that you work for a large organization that does not have a regular procedure for such a request and thus requires approval beyond your department. Therefore, you will need adequate background information and detail for someone who may not be familiar with your job duties or this request. Use the course, text descriptions, and the syllabus to prepare your memo. This memo will be most successful if you help your audience see the value of this course. You may wish to attach supporting material (such as the course syllabus). (See Chapter 8, Understanding the Principles of Business Communication, for memo-format examples.)

5. Your company is experiencing financial difficulties, which has resulted in a hiring freeze. Because of limited support-staff positions and internships, upper-management personnel will now have to do more of their own office tasks, such as photocopying and faxing. First, consider the possible reactions and feelings regarding the change in responsibilities. Then write a memo from the human resources department to upper management, describing the situation and explaining the new policy.

6. Your company's human resources manager has asked you to create an employee manual that details how to use the following office machines: the fax, the photocopier, and the phone system. Brainstorm about the amount of detail (the scope) that you would have to provide in this manual for the following groups of employees: interns with no office work experience; administrative assistants with one to two years of office experience; and senior management personnel who have over 10 years of office experience but who have relied on staff to complete faxing, copying, and telephone tasks. Write a brief e-mail to the human resources manager, suggesting the number of manuals needed and for whom. Support your claims.

7. Using the list of topics in Exercise 2, select a product or service and write a complaint letter about a problem you, the consumer, have had with this product. Before writing, consider the purpose of your letter, the exact nature of your complaint, the audience you are addressing, and what you want the company to do about the problem or what you think the resolution to the problem should be. Bring your letter to class. (For advice on writing complaint letters, see pages 324–326 and 329, Chapter 9, Writing Business Correspondence.)

8. Your manager has asked you to report on the in-house food-service vendors that your company uses. Because you do not have enough information to begin your assignment, create a list of questions to ask your manager to clarify your assignment. Include details about purpose and priorities.

Collaborative Classroom Projects

1. Discuss similarities and differences between writing for the audience in Exercise 3 and writing for the audience in Exercise 4.

ON THE WEB

For more collaborative classroom projects, go to Chapter 1, bedfordstmartins.com/writingthatworks

2. The manager of your company's publications department believes that sharing a printer among four employees is slowing down their productivity on company manuals, brochures, and other communications pieces. In the long run, this slowdown might cause his department to miss publication deadlines. The manager of the information technology (IT) department, however, doesn't want to purchase a new printer because it is near the end of the fiscal year and an equipment purchase could push her department over budget, making IT look bad to upper management.

   a. Divide the class into two groups, one that represents the publications department and the other the IT department. Instruct each group to brainstorm separately a list of reasons that support your manager's concerns and needs.

   b. Debate your position with the other group. Acknowledge each other's concerns and address them. At the end of the debate, discuss what you have learned and research possibilities that would be beneficial to both sides (for example, would a used or refurbished printer be a possible solution?).

   c. The publications department group should now draft a memo to send to the IT department manager. The IT department group should draft a memo to send to the publications department manager. For either memo, state your group's needs, acknowledge the other side's concerns, and suggest possible compromises or solutions that could resolve this issue amicably.

3. Divide into groups of four to six students. For 20 to 25 minutes, brainstorm and develop a list of problems that make studying on campus difficult. Then take 15 minutes to revise the list into two versions: (1) a list for the dean's office committee whose assignment it is to make studying on campus easier and (2) a list for the residence-hall planning committee in charge of designing a new dormitory on campus. Discuss how the different purposes and audiences affected your lists.

■ Research Projects

ON THE WEB

For extra research projects, go to Chapter 1, bedfordstmartins.com/ writingthatworks

1. Find an article on a subject of interest to you in two different types of publications—for example, a newspaper or a general-interest magazine (such as *Discover*) and a technical journal (such as the *Journal of the American Medical Association*). After you have read the two articles, do the following:

   a. Identify the target audience of each publication. Compare the approaches taken in each article toward the intended audience. Look specifically for indicators of the audience's knowledge of the subject, such as the presence or absence of technical terms and the kind and number of illustrations used.

   b. Create statements of purpose for each article, as if you had been the writer.

   c. Discuss how well the writers met the needs of their audiences. (Respond only after you have completed a and b.)

2. Interview at least three current or former instructors about how they prepare their class lectures for their different groups of students. For example, you might ask them how their style of teaching first-year students differs from teaching juniors or seniors (or graduate students). Or, you might ask how the style of their exams or essay questions varies, depending on the class for which they are written. Write

your findings and present them to the class. (*Note:* Before you begin, read pages 150–152 about interviewing for information in Chapter 6, Researching Your Subject.)

■ Web Projects

ON THE WEB

For more Web projects, go to Chapter 1, bedfordstmartins.com/ writingthatworks

1. Suppose that the company you work for provides a week's paid vacation package as a reward to the Employee of the Year and his or her immediate family. Your manager has asked you to select this year's vacation package at a location that has educational value. You have a budget of $4,000. Using the Web, compare and contrast different vacation packages and then outline your reasons for your recommendation. Keep the checklists Planning Your Document on page 5 and Writing for Your Reader on page 8 in mind as you write a concise memo to your manager.

2. Imagine that you volunteer several hours a week at an adult community learning center where you teach basic computer skills to people over the age of 65. They usually are interested in learning how to use e-mail or research information on wills or planning trips. However, their lack of experience with the Internet leaves them vulnerable to scams, particularly ones that require them to send e-mails to receive free things or that ask them to verify bank account or credit-card information. Go to sites that debunk online scams and sites that offer advice on how to spot scams. Write a memo to your students warning them about these scams and how to avoid them. Be sure to give examples.

2 Organizing Your Information

AT A GLANCE: Organization

How do business and technical writers arrange facts and ideas to serve their purposes and meet the needs of different audiences? This chapter reviews proven organizing techniques and describes a wide range of organizing strategies that you can apply to your own writing.

When a motion picture is being filmed, the scenes are usually shot out of sequence. Different locations, actors' schedules, weather conditions, and many other circumstances make working out of sequence necessary. If it were not for a skilled film editor, the completed film would be a jumble of random scenes. The editor, following the script, carefully splices the film together so that the story moves smoothly and logically from one event to the next, as the screenwriter and the director planned. Without a plan, no such order would be possible because the editor would have no guide for organizing the thousands of feet of film.

Organizing a movie and organizing a written document are obviously different tasks, but they have one element in common—both must be planned ahead of time. For a film, planning means creating a script. For a written document, it means organizing information into a sequence appropriate to the subject, the purpose, and the audience.

Voices from the Workplace

Steve Bramlage, Vectren Energy Delivery of Ohio

Steve Bramlage is the president of Vectren Energy Delivery of Ohio and East Operations, a gas and electric utility serving approximately 1.2 million customers in Indiana and Ohio. The scope of Steve's responsibilities and the many demands on his time require him to be extremely organized, especially when he approaches writing. Because he does not have time to work through several drafts, he decides what he wants to say *before* he sits down to write. "If you don't organize your thoughts before you hit the keyboard," he says, "you're sure to end up writing several drafts instead of getting it right the first time. In today's business world, you can't afford inefficiency in communication. There just isn't time."

Adam Thompson, *Denver Post*

As a sportswriter for the *Denver Post*, Adam Thompson must think about how to organize the information in his news stories to attract and hold his readers' attention. He offers the following suggestions for keeping readers interested. "As you go from highlight to highlight, try to use transition sentences that connect one to the next. It creates a much smoother flow. Save a zinger for the end — to reward your readers or listeners who stayed with you. You want to guide your readers, taking them down the path of your choice — it takes conscious effort to keep your readers interested. Some careful thought about how you place your points takes little time and can make all the difference in the world."

Outlining

Organizing your information before you write has two important advantages. First, it forces you to reexamine the information you plan to include to be sure that you have sufficient facts and details to satisfy your audience's needs and achieve the purpose of your writing. Second, it forces you to order the information logically so that your audience understands it as clearly as you do.

The importance of these advantages emerged from a study of the writing habits that separated good from poor writers in a corporate setting. According to the researcher, more than three times the number of good writers as compared with poor writers use a written outline. In fact, 36 percent of the poor writers said they never use an outline or plan, either written or mental.[1]

Not every piece of writing benefits from a full-scale outline, of course. For relatively short items, such as memos and letters, you may need only to jot down a few notes to make sure that you haven't left out any important information and that you have arranged the information in a logical order. These notes then guide you as you write the draft.

◆ *For an example of informal organizational notes, see Figure 1–4.*

---

[1] Christine Barabas, *Technical Writing in a Corporate Culture: A Study of the Nature of Information* (Norwood, N.J.: Ablex Publishing Corp., 1990), p. 188. "Good" and "poor" writers were so classified by their readers within the corporation.

ON THE WEB

For online resources
for outlining, go to
Chapter 2,
bedfordstmartins.com/
writingthatworks

Longer documents generally require more elaborate planning, such as a formal outline. In addition to guiding your first draft, an outline can be circulated for review by your colleagues and superiors. They can easily see in the outline the scope of information you plan to include and the sequence in which it is organized. Their reviews can help you find and fix major problems before you've committed a great deal of time to writing your draft. Any outline, including one you circulate, is tentative and represents your best thinking at that point. It need not be labored over so that it becomes virtually an end in itself. This chapter introduces conventions for creating simple and complex outlines and provides techniques for verifying that your outline is sound.

Traditional Roman Numeral Outline

The most common type of outline emphasizes topics and subtopics by means of Roman numerals, letters, and Arabic numbers in the following sequence of subdivisions:

I. Major section
   A. First-level subsection
      1. Second-level subsection
         a. Third-level subsection
            1) Fourth-level subsection

Creating a Roman numeral outline enables you to recognize at a glance the relative importance of topics and subtopics within your subject. Your subject will seldom require four subdivisions, but dividing it this way allows for a highly detailed outline if one is necessary. Stop at the level at which you can no longer subdivide into two items. For every Roman numeral *I*, you should have at least a Roman numeral *II*. For every *A*, you should have at least a *B*, and so on.

When you are ready to write, you should know your topic well enough to be able to identify its major sections. Begin your outline by writing them down. Then consider them carefully to make sure that they represent the logical divisions of the subject. For example, assume that you are writing an article about the development of the Internet for a company magazine. You might start with the following major sections.

   I. History of the Internet
  II. Growth of Internet technology and future societal issues for the Internet

After a moment's reflection, you decide that the first-level heading is actually the overall topic of the article. After reviewing your research notes, you realize that the topic of the first section should be the background and developments that led to Internet technology, so you revise the outline accordingly.

   I. Background of Internet technology
  II. Growth of Internet technology and future societal issues for the Internet

You quickly decide, however, that you have put too many topics in your second major section, so you make another effort.

    I.   Background of Internet technology
    II. Growth of Internet technology
    III. Future societal issues for the Internet

Now you are satisfied that you have appropriately identified the major sections for your topic.

Once you have established your major sections, look for minor divisions within each section. For example, you might first arrive at the following minor divisions within your major sections.

    I.   Background of Internet technology
        A. Pioneers
        B. Later developments
    II. Growth of Internet technology
        A. Network technology
        B. Improvements in network technology
    III. Future societal issues for the Internet
        A. E-commerce and intellectual stakeholders
        B. Domain space
        C. "Digital divide"
        D. Privacy issues

This outline is a start, but it is weak. The second-level divisions are too vague to be useful. After considering Growth of Internet Technology, for example, you might produce the following revision:

    II. Growth of Internet technology
        A. Competing network techniques and protocols throughout the mid-1970s and early 1980s
        B. Improvements and standardization of techniques and protocols with increased users in the mid-1980s
        C. Transition from a community of scholars, scientists, and defense contractors to widespread infrastructure in the late 1980s and early 1990s
        D. Expansion of Internet in business, academic, and government institutions from the late 1990s and beyond

After evaluating the whole outline, you are now ready to insert any information that you compiled during your research under the appropriate major and minor divisions, as shown in Figure 2–1. When you have finished, you have a complete outline. However, although the outline looks final at this point, you still may need to revise it. Make sure that corresponding divisions present material of equal importance (that is, that major divisions are equal to one another and minor divisions are equal to one another in importance). Likewise, ensure that every head is divided into at least two parts if it is to be divided at all. Subtopics are typically

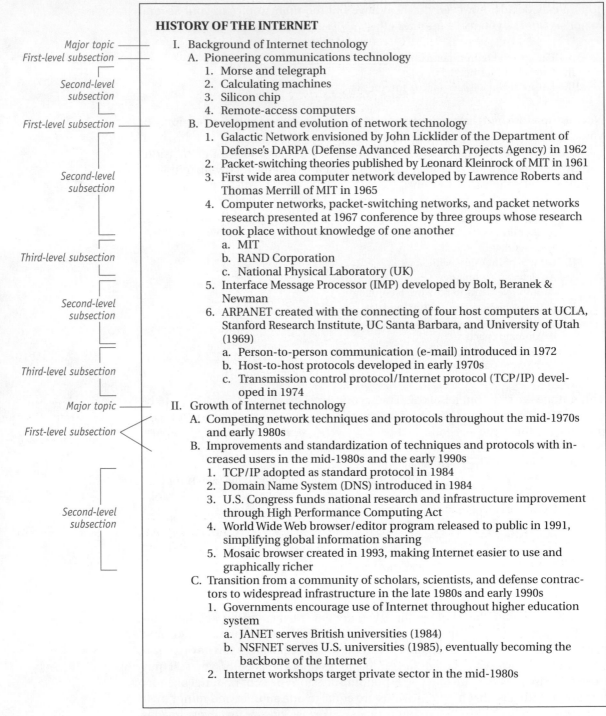

HISTORY OF THE INTERNET

Major topic —
I. Background of Internet technology

First-level subsection —
  A. Pioneering communications technology

Second-level subsection
    1. Morse and telegraph
    2. Calculating machines
    3. Silicon chip
    4. Remote-access computers

First-level subsection —
  B. Development and evolution of network technology

Second-level subsection
    1. Galactic Network envisioned by John Licklider of the Department of Defense's DARPA (Defense Advanced Research Projects Agency) in 1962
    2. Packet-switching theories published by Leonard Kleinrock of MIT in 1961
    3. First wide area computer network developed by Lawrence Roberts and Thomas Merrill of MIT in 1965
    4. Computer networks, packet-switching networks, and packet networks research presented at 1967 conference by three groups whose research took place without knowledge of one another

Third-level subsection
      a. MIT
      b. RAND Corporation
      c. National Physical Laboratory (UK)

Second-level subsection
    5. Interface Message Processor (IMP) developed by Bolt, Beranek & Newman
    6. ARPANET created with the connecting of four host computers at UCLA, Stanford Research Institute, UC Santa Barbara, and University of Utah (1969)

Third-level subsection
      a. Person-to-person communication (e-mail) introduced in 1972
      b. Host-to-host protocols developed in early 1970s
      c. Transmission control protocol/Internet protocol (TCP/IP) developed in 1974

Major topic —
II. Growth of Internet technology

First-level subsection
  A. Competing network techniques and protocols throughout the mid-1970s and early 1980s
  B. Improvements and standardization of techniques and protocols with increased users in the mid-1980s and the early 1990s

Second-level subsection
    1. TCP/IP adopted as standard protocol in 1984
    2. Domain Name System (DNS) introduced in 1984
    3. U.S. Congress funds national research and infrastructure improvement through High Performance Computing Act
    4. World Wide Web browser/editor program released to public in 1991, simplifying global information sharing
    5. Mosaic browser created in 1993, making Internet easier to use and graphically richer
  C. Transition from a community of scholars, scientists, and defense contractors to widespread infrastructure in the late 1980s and early 1990s
    1. Governments encourage use of Internet throughout higher education system
      a. JANET serves British universities (1984)
      b. NSFNET serves U.S. universities (1985), eventually becoming the backbone of the Internet
    2. Internet workshops target private sector in the mid-1980s

Figure 2–1   Sample Outline (continued)

> 3. Commercialization of networking products influences vendors of technology to be competitive as well as interoperative
> 4. E-commerce era begins in 1990s, transforming Internet to a "commodity" service
> III. Future societal issues for the Internet — Major topic
>   A. E-commerce and intellectual stakeholders to drive evolution and innovation
>   B. Contending stakeholders to vie for control of domain space
>   C. Protection of privacy to continue to be a challenge
>   D. "Digital divide" between developed and developing countries to narrow

Figure 2–1   Sample Outline (continued)

divided into at least two parts (for every 1 there should be a 2), although doing so may not always be possible.

NOT

A. Pioneering communications technology
  1. Morse and telegraph, calculating machines, silicon chip, and remote-access computers

BUT

A. Pioneering communications technology
  1. Morse and telegraph
  2. Calculating machines
  3. Silicon chip
  4. Remote-access computers

Finally, review your outline for completeness, determining whether you need additional information. If you find that your research is not really complete, return to your sources and locate the missing material.

◆ *For detailed information on researching information, go to Chapter 6, Researching Your Subject.*

Decimal Numbering System Outline

The sample outlines shown to this point use a combination of numbers and letters to differentiate the various levels of information. Many science and technology authors use a decimal numbering system instead, such as the following, to develop their outlines.

1. MAJOR IDEA
  1.1 Supporting idea for 1
  1.2 Supporting idea for 1
    1.2.1 Example or illustration of 1.2
    1.2.2 Example or illustration of 1.2
      1.2.2.1 Detail for 1.2.2
      1.2.2.2 Detail for 1.2.2
  1.3 Supporting idea for 1
2. MAJOR IDEA

◆ *For a discussion of how this system applies to formal reports, see pages 394–395 in Chapter 11, Writing Formal Reports.*

This system should not go beyond the fourth level because the numbers get too cumbersome past that point. In many technical articles and reports, the decimal numbering system is carried over from the outline to the final version of the document for ease of cross-referencing sections. Typical uses for the decimal outline include procedural manuals, mathematical texts, and scientific and technical material of many kinds.

Remember that the outline is only a means to an end, not an end in itself. Don't view it as being cast in concrete. Outlines are preliminary by their nature. If you suddenly see a better way to organize your material while you are writing the draft, depart from your outline and follow the better approach. The main purpose of the outline is to bring order and shape to your information before you begin to write.

WRITER'S CHECKLIST
Creating an Outline

☑ Complete your research and know your topic well enough to be able to write about it. Break a large topic into its major divisions and write them down. Does the sequence fit the organizing pattern you have decided to use? (See pages 35–37 for organizing patterns.) If not, resequence and label the topics with Roman numerals (I, II, III, and so on).

☑ Repeat the process for each major topic. Break each into its logical subtopics and list them under each major topic. Then sequence the subtopics to fit your pattern of development and label them with capital letters (A, B, C, and so on).

☑ If necessary, repeat the process for each subtopic, breaking each into its logical sub-subtopics and list them under each subtopic. Sequence them to fit your pattern of development, and label them with Arabic numbers (1, 2, 3, and so on).

☑ Now go to your notes and key each one to the appropriate place in your outline (for example, placing II-C beside any note that fits the portion of your outline labeled II-C).

☑ Merge your notes and your outline, placing every note under the appropriate head, subhead, or sub-subhead in your outline. Then organize the notes under each head in the most logical sequence.

☑ To convert your detailed outline into your first draft, put the first head on your computer screen and expand the notes listed under it into sentences and paragraphs.

▉ How Audience and Purpose Shape Organization: A Case Study

The kinds of information and organization that shape your outline will vary according to your purposes for writing and your audience's specific needs. Let us say, for example, that a writer needs to prepare two documents about the Lifemaker System, a home gym that combines the features of ten separate resistance machines into a compact weight-and-cable exercise system. The first document will be a sales brochure directed at potential purchasers of the Lifemaker; the second document will be a maintenance manual written for customers who have already purchased the system.

Both documents share several aspects of audience and purpose. The sales brochure and the maintenance manual both need to describe the design and structure of the Lifemaker System, although they will do so in different ways and for different reasons. The audience for each document is composed of nonspecialists, so each document should contain a minimum of technical language and avoid terms that would be familiar only to technicians, engineers, and sales representatives. The writer of either document might assume that the readers, whether they are potential or current customers of Lifemaker, will know some things about the design features common to exercise systems, so descriptions of the exercise equipment for either document need not be too detailed. Much of the information gathered and used for brainstorming and outlining will be useful for both the sales brochure and the maintenance manual.

However, these documents reflect different purposes in two important ways. Consider how a written statement of purpose might look for each.

◆ See page 6 in Chapter 1 for an explanation of written statements of purpose.

SALES BROCHURE	My primary purpose for writing is to describe the benefits and features of the Lifemaker System so that my readers will want to purchase it.
MAINTENANCE MANUAL	My primary purpose for writing is to explain the assembly and maintenance requirements of the Lifemaker System so that the customer knows exactly how to put it together and take care of it.

The writer of a brochure will need to select and organize the information so that it persuades the reader to purchase the system. The brochure's outline, then, should offer more general comments about the design and structural features of the system and specific comments about the benefits of buying it.

ETHICS NOTE

Readers are persuaded in part if they believe the source is credible. Therefore, be careful not to overstate the claims you make. Although comparing your product or service with that of a competitor is an effective persuasive strategy, speaking negatively or disparagingly about a competitor is not.

The maintenance manual will be directed at readers who have already purchased the system, so the writer will not be concerned with organizing information to form a persuasive argument. Instead, the writer will want to create an outline that will lead to clearly written, step-by-step instructions on how to assemble and maintain the Lifemaker. References to structural features will be very specific and more technical than they would be for the sales brochure. (The audience is still made up of nonspecialists, so the writer needs to keep the use of technical terms to a minimum and might leave places in the outline for diagrams that will eventually appear in the manual to clarify the instructions.)

The outline for the sales brochure (Figure 2–2) notes specific design details (cast-iron plates, adjustable cables, 1 ft by 7-ft size), but this information is organized to support the brochure's persuasive purpose. The purpose of the maintenance manual is to instruct rather than to persuade the audience, so the manual's organization would differ from that used for the sales brochure. Figure 2–3 is

Organized to compare benefits with other systems

Organized by division of features, according to function in system

Organized to compare benefits with other systems

LIFEMAKER:
The Compact, Affordable Home Gym

I. General benefits of owning Lifemaker
   A. More compact than other systems
   B. Provides better training programs than other systems
   C. Lower-priced and easier to assemble and maintain than other systems

II. Design benefits/features
   A. Multiple stations, so two people can work out at the same time
   B. Takes up minimal space (measures only 4′ by 7′)
   C. Designed to work all muscle groups (40 different combinations of exercises)

III. Structural benefits/features: Weights
   A. Dual weight stacks that total 200 pounds of cast-iron plates
   B. Adjustable weight stacks with resistance range of 10 to 150 pounds
   C. Varied individual weights with resistance adjustable in 5-, 10-, and 15-pound increments

IV. Structural benefits/features: Cables
   A. Adjustable cables that increase tension at stations working strongest muscle groups
   B. Reconfigurable weight stacks (cables permit reconfiguring of weights without dismantling entire system)
   C. Reversible tension (cables can increase/decrease tension in mid-set)

V. Financial and maintenance benefits
   A. More reasonably priced than leading system: $999.99
   B. Two-year guarantee for all parts
   C. Easy maintenance (no oiling or solvents necessary)

Figure 2–2 Outline for a Sales Brochure

Maintenance steps organized sequentially

MAINTAINING YOUR LIFEMAKER

I. Maintenance and troubleshooting
   A. Inspect and safeguard all parts each time you:
      1. Inspect parts for wear
         a. Check cables for fraying
         b. Check weights for cracks
         c. Replace worn parts immediately
      2. Tighten tension on cable #1
         a. Find end of 125″ cable (#43 on diagram)
         b. Turn end of cable clockwise
         c. Thread cable farther into weight tube (#35 on diagram)
      3. Tighten tension on cable #2
         a. Find end of 265″ cable (#46 on diagram)
         b. Turn end of cable clockwise
         c. Thread cable farther into weight tube (#35 on diagram)
      4. Clean parts
         a. Clean with damp cloth
         b. Use nonabrasive detergent
         c. Use no solvents or oils

Figure 2–3 Outline for Instructions in a Maintenance Manual (Excerpt)

an excerpt from the outline for the maintenance manual. This outline follows a *sequential (step-by-step)* organization of information (see pages 36–38), which is an ideal pattern to use when instruction, rather than persuasion, is the major purpose for writing. In contrast, the outline for the sales brochure uses a *general-to-specific* sequencing of information (see pages 48–50), which is more appropriate when the purpose for writing is to persuade the audience with a general argument supported with special details. Within the major topic divisions, the sales brochure also uses two other types of organization: *comparison* to emphasize its features against those of its competitors and *division* to illustrate how its features (weights and cables) function in the system. These differences are summarized as follows:

Lifemaker Brochure
- *Purpose:* Describe benefits and features to attract purchasers
- *Audience:* Nonspecialists who are potential Lifemaker customers
- *Organizing Patterns:* General to specific; comparison; division

Lifemaker Maintenance Manual
- *Purpose:* Explain maintenance requirements for system customers
- *Audience:* Nonspecialists who have purchased the Lifemaker system
- *Organizing Pattern:* Sequential (step by step)

Thus, although both documents are drawn from the same source and speak to nontechnical audiences, their different purposes call for different patterns of organization.

◆ *For drafts and revisions of this sales brochure, see Chapters 3, Writing the Draft, and 4, Revising the Draft.*

 DIGITAL TIPS: Formatting Your Outline

Using the outline feature of your word-processing software enables you to do the following:

- Format your outline automatically.
- Fill in, rearrange, and update your outline.
- Experiment with the organization and scope of information while retaining the outline format.
- Rearrange sections and subsections easily on-screen.
- Create Roman numeral or decimal numbering outline styles.

Experiment with the default settings of the outline feature to make the best use of this software. For step-by-step instructions, see <bedfordstmartins.com/writingthatworks> and select *Digital Tips*, "Creating an Outline."

Essential Organizing Patterns

The choice of a pattern of organization comes naturally for some types of writing. Instructions for how to process an invoice or operate a piece of machinery are arranged step by step. A trip report usually follows a chronological sequence. When a subject does not lend itself to one particular pattern, you can choose the best sequence or combination of sequences by considering your purpose and your audience's needs. Suppose, for example, that you report on a trip to several offset-printing companies to gather information on the most efficient way to arrange equipment to improve workflow through the printing shop where you work. You would probably organize the details of the trip chronologically, but your description of the various shop layouts, emphasizing the physical locations of the equipment, would be organized spatially. If you went on to make recommendations about the most workable arrangement for your shop, you might organize them according to decreasing order of importance by presenting the most efficient arrangement first, the second most efficient arrangement next, and so on.

Table 2–1 lists and describes the most common ways to organize, or sequence, information in on-the-job writing.

Table 2–1   Patterns of Organization

Patterns	*Description*
Sequential	Consecutive order of steps, not connected to a specific time
Chronological	Sequence of steps or events related to time
Spatial	Description from top to bottom, front to back, and so on
Division and classification	Division into parts and grouping of parts by class
Decreasing order of importance	Order beginning with the most important item and leading to the least important item
Increasing order of importance	Order beginning with the least important item and leading to the most important item
General to specific	Order leading from an overview to a detailed explanation
Specific to general	Order leading from the details of a topic to a broad overview or conclusion
Comparison	Assessment of traits or characteristics of two or more items to determine their relative value

Sequential

In the sequential pattern, you divide your subject into steps and then present the steps in the order in which they occur. This arrangement is the most effective way to describe the operation of a mechanism, such as a digital photocopier, or to explain a process, such as cardiopulmonary resuscitation (CPR). Sequencing is the logical pattern for writing instructions. For example, the instructions for installing printer software on a desktop computer follow a step-by-step sequence.

▶   To install printer software:
1. Make sure that your printer is plugged in and connected to your computer.
2. Turn your computer on.
3. When you see the "New Hardware Found" screen, insert the Printing Software CD-ROM in the CD-ROM drive.
4. The printer's installation software loads automatically, so follow the instructions on the screen.

The greatest advantage of presenting your information in sequential order is that it is easy for a reader to understand and follow the process because the sequence of steps in your writing corresponds to the order of the process being described. If you were to write instructions for the proper way to download files from a digital camera for e-mailing, for example, you would present the information in a step-by-step sequence (Figures 2–4 and 2–5). When you present your information in steps, you must carefully consider the needs of your audience. Do not assume that your readers are as familiar with your subject as you are; if they were, they wouldn't need your instructions. Even for a simple process, be sure that you list all steps and that you explain in adequate detail how each step is performed. Sometimes you must also indicate the purpose or function of each step.

In some instructions or process descriptions, the steps can be presented in one sequence only. For example, the steps for installing printer software must be carried out in the sequence in which they are listed. In many other instructions or process descriptions, however, the steps can be presented in the sequence that the writer thinks is most effective. The steps in the process by which a company solicits proposals for new equipment from vendors, for example, may vary in sequence from the steps a company uses to solicit proposals for services.

OUTLINE:
How to E-mail a Picture from a Digital Camera

1. Transferring photos from camera to computer
   a. Connect camera to computer by plugging the camera cable into the computer port.
   b. Click on Camera icon on desktop to view images stored in the camera.
   c. Decide which photos you want to transfer.
2. Saving photos on computer
   a. Create and name a folder on your hard drive or on your desktop.
   b. Open and view images (as described in step 1).
   c. Select images you wish to save; drag them to the designated folder or save them by using imaging software.
   d. Delete images from camera.
   e. Back up images on a zip disk.
3. Modifying photos
   a. Crop, change resolution, or add effects, using imaging software.
   b. Save the edited image by using the Save As or Export command, renaming the image to reflect changes.
4. Attaching photos to an e-mail
   a. Open e-mail box and click on Attachment icon.
   b. Locate designated folder and click on file to be sent.
   c. Before sending, check with recipient about file size restrictions.

Figure 2–4   Outline for Sequential Instructions

HOW TO E-MAIL A PICTURE FROM A DIGITAL CAMERA

The following step-by-step instructions describe how to transfer images from your camera to your computer, save them, and then e-mail the images to your friends, relatives, or business colleagues.

1. Transferring Your Photos from Camera to Computer

Connect the cable from the camera to your computer at the USB, or serial port, to enable the camera to serve as its own disk drive. If your digital camera includes a docking station, place the camera in the docking station cradle to automatically connect it to the computer. In most cases, an icon of your camera or a folder for it will appear on your screen after you hook it to your computer. Double-click on the icon to open and view the image files stored on your camera.

2. Saving Photos on the Computer

To save images to your computer, create and name a folder on your hard drive. If you're working on an ongoing project that will have many images, include the dates of the images or other useful identifying information. After you create the folder, open and view the images stored on your camera as described in step 1, select the files you wish to save, highlight them, and drag them into the folder you've created on your hard drive. You can also save the images in software, such as Adobe's PhotoShop, using the software's File/Open command to select a file directly from your digital camera.

Most digital cameras will default to save images in either GIF or JPEG format. However, if yours does not, then the imaging software that came with the camera should provide a way to save the image in either of these formats.

3. Modifying Photos

Use imaging software, such as Adobe's PhotoShop, to crop your image, to change the resolution, and to add other effects. Once you're done making changes to your image, use the File/Save As command or, in some imaging programs, the File/Export command, to make a copy of the image. At this point, you can give the image a more useful name than your camera will have given the file because digital cameras typically assign images a number.

4. Attaching Photos to E-mail Messages

To attach the file to an e-mail message, open your outgoing e-mail box and click on the Attachment icon or box. When your file directory opens, select the folder where your photo images are stored, highlight the file you wish to send, and click Open. Your photo file is now attached to your e-mail box.

5. Checking on File Size Restrictions

Before e-mailing an image, check with your recipients to ensure that their e-mail program can accept a file of the size you're sending. Some recipients have mailbox quotas that may not accommodate your image. E-mail attachments are sometimes used to transmit computer viruses, so letting recipients know in advance that you intend to send an image makes them feel more comfortable opening the attachment.

Figure 2–5 Sequential Instructions

Chronological

Sequential and chronological patterns overlap because each describes steps in a process. In a chronological sequence, however, you focus on the order in which the steps or events occur in time, beginning with the first event, going on to the next event, and so on, until you have reached the last event. Trip reports, work schedules, minutes of meetings, recipes, laboratory test procedures, and certain accident reports are among the types of writing in which information may be organized chronologically. In the outline and memo shown in Figures 2–6 and 2–7, a plant superintendent reports the course of an accidental fire at a chemical plant.

ON THE WEB

For another example of chronological order, go to Model Documents Gallery, bedfordstmartins.com/writingthatworks

OUTLINE

I. Conditions Before Fire
  A. Building A
    1. Three piles of scrap paper 100 ft. outside building
    2. Six pallets of Class I flammable liquids along west wall
  B. Building B approximately 150 ft. from scrap paper outside Building A

II. Chronology of Fire
  A. 6:00 a.m
    1. Spark initiated fire in electric shop of Building A
    2. Night watchman called Ardville Volunteer Fire Department
    3. Fire spread to drums of flammable liquid, engulfing Building A
    4. Fire spread to scrap paper
  B. 6:15 a.m.
    1. Watchman hosed down scrap paper
    2. Watchman set up lawn sprinklers between Buildings A and B
    3. Watchman noticed smoke coming from Building B
  C. 6:57 a.m. (approx.)
    1. Volunteer fire department arrived
    2. Firefighters began pumping water

III. Results of Fire
  A. Building A destroyed
  B. Building B suffered $250K damage to roof . . .

Figure 2–6   Outline for a Chronological Description (Excerpt)

Spatial

In a spatial sequence, you describe an object according to the physical arrangement of its features. Depending on the subject, you may describe the features from top to bottom, from side to side, from east to west (or west to east), from inside to outside, and so on. Descriptions of this kind rely mainly on dimension (*height, width, length*), direction (*up, down, north, south*), shape (*rectangular, square, semicircular*), and proportion (*one half, two-thirds*). Features are described in relation to one another:

▶ One end is raised six to eight inches higher than the other end to permit the rain to run off.

Memorandum

To: Charles Artmier, Chairman, Safety Committee
From: Willard Ricke, Plant Superintendent, Sequoia Chemical Plant   WR
Date: November 17, 2006
Subject: Fire at the Sequoia Chemical Plant in Ardville on November 12, 2006

The following description provides an account of the conditions and development of the fire at our Sequoia Chemical Plant in Ardville on November 12, 2006. Because this description will be incorporated in the report that the Safety Committee will prepare, please let me know if I should add or clarify any details.

Clear headings allow readers to see major steps at a glance

Conditions Before Fire

Three piles of scrap paper were located about 100 feet south of Building A and 150 feet west of Building B at our Sequoia Chemical Plant in Ardville. Building A, which consisted of one story and a partial attic, was used in part as an electric shop and in part for equipment storage. Six pallets of Class I flammable liquids in 55-gallon drums were temporarily stored just outside of Building A, along its west wall.

Cause of and Response to Fire

All steps are timed to inform the audience of the sequence of events

A spark created in the electric shop in Building A started a fire. The night watchman first noticed the fire in the electric shop at about 6:00 a.m. and immediately called the Ardville Volunteer Fire Department and the plant superintendent. Before the fire department arrived, the fire spread to the drums of flammable liquid just outside the west wall and quickly engulfed Building A in flames. The fire then spread to the scrap paper outside, with a 40 mph wind blowing it in the direction of Building B.

During this time, the watchman began to hose down the piles of scrap paper between the buildings to try to keep the fire from reaching Building B. He also set up lawn sprinklers between the fire and Building B to protect Building B from the fire. However, he saw smoke coming from Building B at 6:15 a.m., in spite of his best efforts to protect it.

The volunteer fire department, which was 20 miles away, reached the scene at 6:57 a.m., nearly an hour after the fire was discovered. It is estimated that the fire department's pumps were started after the fire had been burning in Building B for at least 20 minutes.

Results of the Fire

Building A was destroyed, along with its contents, and the fire burned into the hollow joisted roof of Building B, which sustained a $250,000 loss. . . .

Figure 2–7   A Chronological Description (Excerpt)

Features are also described in relation to their surroundings:

▶ The lot is located on the east bank of the Kingman River.

The spatial pattern of organization is commonly used in descriptions of building layouts; emergency evacuation plans; proposals for landscape work; construction-site progress reports; and, in combination with a step-by-step sequence, many types of instructions.

Figure 2–8 presents an outline and Figure 2–9 a description for a house inspection using a bottom-to-top, clockwise (*south to west to north to east*) sequence, beginning with the front door.

OUTLINE

    I. Ground floor
       A. Front hall and stairwell
       B. Dining room
       C. Kitchen
       D. Bathroom
       E. Living room
   II. Second floor
       A. Hallway
       B. Southwest bedroom
       C. Northwest bedroom

Figure 2–8 Outline for a Spatial Description

Division and Classification

An effective way to organize information about a complex subject is to divide it into manageable parts and then discuss each part separately. You might use this approach, called *division*, to describe a physical object, such as the parts of a fax machine; to examine an organization, such as a company; or to explain the components that make up the Internet. The emphasis in division is on breaking down a complex whole into a number of like units—because it is easier for an audience to consider smaller units and to examine the relationship of each to the other.

If you were a financial planner describing the types of mutual funds available to your investors, you could divide the variety available into three broad categories: money-market funds, bond funds, and stock funds. Although this division is accurate, it is only a first-level grouping of a complex whole. These three can, in turn, be subdivided into additional groups based on investment strategy. The second-level grouping could lead to the following categories:

Money-Market Funds
- taxable money-market funds
- tax-exempt money-market funds

Interior of Two-Story, Six-Room House

Ground Floor

Front hall and stairwell. The front door faces south and opens into a hallway seven feet long and ten feet wide. At the end of the hallway is a stairwell that begins on the right-hand (*east*) side of the hallway, rises five steps to a landing, and reverses direction at the left-hand (*west*) side of the hallway.

Dining room. To the left (*west*) of the hallway is the dining room, which measures 15 feet along its southern exposure and ten feet along its western exposure.

Kitchen. North of the dining room is the kitchen, which measures ten feet along its western exposure and 15 feet along its northern exposure.

Bathroom. East of the kitchen, along the northern side of the house, is a bathroom that measures ten feet (*west to east*) by five feet.

Living room. Parallel to the bathroom is a passageway the same size as the bathroom and leading from the kitchen to the living room. The living room (*15 feet west to east by 20 feet north to south*) occupies the entire eastern end of the floor.

Second Floor

Hallway. On the second floor, at the top of the stairs, is an L-shaped hallway, five feet wide. The base of the L is 15 feet long. The vertical arm of the L is 13 feet long.

Southwest bedroom. To the west of the hall is the southwest bedroom, which measures ten feet along its southern exposure and eight feet along its western exposure.

Northwest bedroom. Directly to the north, over the kitchen, is the northwest bedroom, which measures 12 feet along its western exposure and ten feet along its northern exposure.

Figure 2–9   A Spatial Description

Bond Funds
- taxable bond funds
- tax-exempt bond funds
- balanced funds — mix of stocks and bonds

Stock Funds
- balanced funds — mix of stocks and bonds
- equity-income funds
- growth and income funds
- domestic growth funds
- small capitalization funds
- specialized funds

Specialized funds can be further subdivided as follows:

Specialized Funds
- communications
- real estate
- energy
- financial services
- technology
- environmental services
- gold
- worldwide capital goods
- health services
- utilities

After you have divided the variety of mutual funds into accurate categories, or parts, you could classify them by their degree of relative risk to investors. To do so, you would reorganize your original categories based on the criterion of risk. Depending on how risk is defined, this classification might look as follows:

Low-Risk Funds
- taxable money-market funds
- tax-exempt money-market funds

Low- to Moderate-Risk Funds
- taxable bond funds
- tax-exempt bond funds
- balanced funds
- equity-income funds
- growth and income funds

High-Risk Funds
- domestic growth stock funds
- international growth stock funds
- aggressive growth funds
- small capitalization funds

High- to Very High-Risk Funds
- specialized stock funds

The process by which a subject is classified is similar to the process by which a subject is divided. While *division* is the separation of a whole into its parts (such as a piece of equipment, a company's organization, the U.S. budget), *classification* is the grouping of a number of units into related categories (such as herbicides for weed control, allergens affecting people in Hawaii, or types of virus-checking software for desktop computers).

When dividing or classifying a subject, you must observe some basic rules of logic. First, divide the subject into its largest number of equal units. The basis for division depends, of course, on your subject and your purpose. If you are describing the *structure* of a four-cycle combustion engine, for example, you might begin by dividing the subject into its major parts—the pistons, the crankshaft, and the housing that contains them. If a more-detailed explanation were needed, each of these parts, in turn, might be subdivided into its components. A discussion of the *function* of the same engine, however, would require a different logical basis for the division; such a breakdown would focus on the way combustion engines operate: (1) intake, (2) compression, (3) combustion and expansion, and (4) exhaust.

Once you have established the basis for the division, you must apply and express it consistently. Put each item in only one category so that items do not overlap categories. An examination of the structure of the combustion engine that listed the battery as a major part would be illogical. Although it is part of a vehicle's ignition system (which starts the engine), the battery is not a part of the engine itself. A discussion of the parts of the ignition system in which the battery is not mentioned would be just as illogical.

An outline provides a clear expression of classification and is especially useful in preparing a breakdown of any subject at several levels. In the following example, two Canadian park rangers classify typical park users according to four categories; the rangers then discuss how to deal with potential rule-breaking by members of each group. The rangers could have classified the visitors in a variety of other ways, of course: as city and country residents, backpackers and drivers of recreational vehicles, U.S. and Canadian citizens, and so on. However, for law-enforcement agents in public parklands, the size of a group and the relationships among its members were the most significant factors (Figures 2–10 and 2–11).

OUTLINE

    I. Types of campers
       A. Family groups
       B. Small groups
       C. Large groups
       D. Hostile groups
   II. Dealing with groups of campers
       A. Groups A and B
          1. One on one
          2. Courses of action
       B. Groups C and D
          1. Large groups
             a. Make the leader responsible
             b. Course of action
          2. Hostile groups
             a. Make the leader responsible (once determined)
             b. Course of action

Figure 2–10   Outline for a Memo Organized by Division and Classification

Memo

To: All Employees
From: Canadian National Park Service, Office of Rangers
Date: June 15, 2006
Subject: Dealing with Campers in Violation of National Park Rules

To respond to campers breaking National Park Rules and Codes for Safety and Conduct, first, recognize the various types of campers. They can be categorized as follows:

A. Family groups
B. Small groups (up to six well-acquainted members)
C. Large groups or conventions (organized, but not always well-acquainted)
D. Hostile groups (may not have an evident leader)

Groups divided into major categories

Groups A & B

Persons in groups A and B can often be dealt with on a one-on-one basis. For example, suppose a member of the group is picking wildflowers, which is an offense in most of our park areas. Two courses of action are open. You could either issue a warning or charge the person with the offense. In this situation, a warning is preferable to a charge. First, advise the person that this action is an offense, but, more important, explain why. Point out that the flowers are for all to enjoy and that most wildflowers are delicate and die quickly when picked.

Group C

For large groups, other approaches may be necessary. Every group has a leader. For a large group or convention, find out who the event organizer is (this is likely to be the person who reserved the campsite). Hold the group's leader responsible for the group's behavior and take action — issue a warning or charge the leader with the offense — according to the guidelines of the National Park Rules and Codes for Safety and Conduct.

Each group is then classified according to specific criteria

Group D

For hostile groups without an obvious leader, observe the group's behavior to learn which person(s) assumes control of the group's actions, and try to deal with that person. Ultimately, it is best to regain control over a group through one or two individuals within the group. In a potentially hostile environment, always request backup of at least one other ranger on duty. Issue a warning or charge the leader of the group with the offense according to the guidelines of the National Park Rules and Codes for Safety and Conduct. If necessary, eject the group from the premises, as outlined in the Codes.

Figure 2–11   Memo Organized by Division and Classification

Decreasing Order of Importance

When you organize your information in decreasing order of importance, you begin with the most important fact or point, then go on to the next-most-important, and so on, ending with the least important. Newspaper audiences are familiar with this sequence of information. The most significant information usually appears first in a news story, with related but secondary information completing the narrative. Minor details go last, where they may be cut to accommodate a last-minute need for column space.

Decreasing order of importance is an especially appropriate pattern of organization for a report addressed to a busy decision-maker, who may be able to reach a decision after considering only the most important points—and who may not have time to read the entire report. This sequence of information is useful, too, for a report written for a variety of audiences, some of whom may be interested in only the major points and others in all the points. The outline and memo shown in Figures 2–12 and 2–13, respectively, present an example of such an approach.

OUTLINE

    I. Most-qualified candidate: April Jackson, Acting Chief
       A. Positive factors
          1. Twelve years' experience in claims processing
          2. Thoroughly familiar with section's operations
          3. Strong production record
          4. Continually ranked "outstanding" on job appraisals
       B. Negative factors
          1. Supervisory experience limited to present tenure as Acting Chief
          2. Lacks college degree required by job description
   II. Second-most-qualified candidate: Michael Bastick, Claims Coordinator
       A. Positive factors
          1. Able administrator
          2. Seven years' experience in section's operations
          3. Currently enrolled in management-training course
       B. Negative factors
          1. Lacks supervisory experience
          2. Most recent work indirectly related to claims processing
  III. Third-most-qualified candidate: Jane Fine, Administrative Assistant
       A. Positive factors
          1. Skilled administrator
          2. Three years' experience in claims processing
       B. Negative factors
          1. Lacks broad knowledge of claims procedures
          2. Lacks supervisory experience

Figure 2–12 Outline for a Memo Organized by Decreasing Order of Importance

Memo

To: Tawana Shaw, Director, Human Resources Department
From: Frank W. Russo, Chief, Claims Department
Date: November 13, 2006
Subject: Selection of Chief of the Claims Processing Section

The most-qualified candidate for chief of the Claims Processing Section is April Jackson, who is at present acting chief of the Claims Processing Section. In her 12 years in the Claims Department, Ms. Jackson has gained wide experience in all facets of the department's operations. She has maintained a consistently high production record and has demonstrated the skills and knowledge that are required for the supervisory duties she is now handling in an acting capacity. Another consideration is that she has continually been rated "outstanding" in all categories of her job-performance appraisals. However, her supervisory experience is limited to her present three-month tenure as Acting Chief of the section, and she lacks the college degree required by the job description.

Memo begins with most important information (strongest candidate) and includes reasons why

Michael Bastick, claims coordinator, my second choice, also has strong potential for the position. An able administrator, he has been with the company for seven years. Further, he is currently enrolled in a management-training course at the university. He is ranked second because he lacks supervisory experience and because his most recent work has been with the department's maintenance and supply components. He would be the best person to take over many of April Jackson's responsibilities if she should be made full-time chief of the Claims Processing Section.

Second and third paragraphs rank and evaluate other candidates

Jane Fine, my third-ranking candidate, has shown herself to be a skilled administrator in her three years with the Claims Processing Section. Despite her obvious potential, she doesn't yet have the breadth of experience in claims processing that would be required of someone responsible for managing the Claims Processing Section. Jane Fine also lacks on-the-job supervisory experience.

Figure 2–13   Memo Organized by Decreasing Order of Importance

Increasing Order of Importance

When you want the most important of several ideas to be freshest in your readers' minds, organize your information by increasing order of importance. This sequence is useful in argumentative or persuasive writing when you wish to save your strongest points until the end. The sequence begins with the least important point or fact, then moves to the next-least-important, and builds, finally to the most important point at the end.

Writing organized by increasing order of importance has the disadvantage of beginning weakly, with the least important information. Your readers may become impatient or distracted before reaching your main point. However, for writing in which the ideas lead, point by point, to an important conclusion, increasing order of importance is an effective pattern of organization. Reports on production or personnel goals are often arranged by this pattern, as are oral presentations. Figures 2–14 and 2–15 present an outline and a memo, respectively, that show the use of increasing order of importance as a pattern of organization.

OUTLINE

    I. Staffing problem
       A. Too few qualified electronics technicians
       B. New recruiting program necessary
    II. Apprentice program
       A. Providing insufficient numbers
       B. Enlistment bonuses tempting the high school graduates into the military
    III. Technical school
       A. Enrollment at area and regional technical schools up, but fewer students studying electronics
       B. Keen competition from the military for technical school graduates
    IV. Military veterans
       A. Relied heavily on veterans in the past
       B. Military reenlistment incentives have all but removed this source
    V. Strategy to compete with the military

Figure 2–14 Outline for Information Organized by Increasing Order of Importance

General to Specific

In a general-to-specific sequence, you begin your writing with a general statement and then provide facts or examples to develop and support that statement. For example, if you begin a report with the general statement "Companies that diversify their products or services are more successful than those that do not," the remainder of the report would offer examples and statistics that prove to your reader that companies that diversify are, in fact, more successful than companies that do not.

To: Phillip Ting, Vice President, Operations
From: Harry Mathews, Human Resources Department
Date: May 19, 2006
Subject: Recruiting Qualified Electronics Technicians

As our company continues to expand, and with the planned opening of the Lakeland Facility late next year, we need to increase and refocus our recruiting program to keep our company staffed with qualified electronics technicians. In the past five years, we have relied on our in-house apprentice program and on local and regional technical schools to fill our needs.

Although our in-house apprentice program provided a qualified pool of employees in the past, military enlistment bonuses are tempting graduating high school seniors to join a branch of the military services rather than join our apprentice program or attend the technical schools. This is particularly tempting to graduating high school students because the military often sends them to a technical school free of charge while they are in the service. Even our most vigorous Career Day recruiting at the technical schools has yielded disappointing results.

We have also in the past relied on recruiting skilled veterans from all branches of the military. With the military now offering very attractive reenlistment incentives, however, this source of technicians has all but disappeared.

I would like to meet with you soon to devise a strategy for competing with the military's enlistment and reenlistment incentives.

The point-by-point description of the dilemma leads the reader to the urgency of the conclusion

Final paragraph states the e-mail's most important message

Figure 2–15   E-mail Organized by Increasing Order of Importance

A memo or report organized in a general-to-specific sequence discusses only one point. All other information in the memo or report supports the general statement (Figures 2–16 and 2–17). Examples and data that support the general statements are frequently accompanied by charts and graphs, providing data to support your general point.

◆ *For guidelines for creating and presenting charts, tables, and other visuals, see pages 217–252 in Chapter 7, Designing Effective Documents and Visuals.*

OUTLINE

The company needs to locate additional suppliers of computer chips because of several related events.

    I. The current supplier is reducing output.
   II. Domestic demand for our laptop computers continues to increase.
  III. We are expanding into the international market.

Figure 2–16   Outline for Information Organized from General to Specific (Excerpt)

General statement

LOCATING COMPUTER-CHIP SUPPLIERS

On the basis of information presented at the supply meeting on April 14, we recommend that the company locate additional suppliers of computer chips. Several related events make such action necessary.

Supporting infor-
mation includes
specific details

Our current supplier, ABC Electronics, is reducing its output. Specifically, we can expect a reduction of between 800 and 1,000 units per month for the remainder of this fiscal year. The number of units should stabilize at 15,000 units per month thereafter.

Domestic demand for our computers continues to grow. Demand during the current fiscal year is up 25,000 units over the last fiscal year. Sales Department projections for the next five years show that demand should peak next year at 50,000 units and then remain at that figure for at least the following four years.

Finally, our expansion into Eastern Europe will require additional shipments of 5,000 units per quarter to each country for the remainder of this fiscal year. Sales Department projections put computer sales for each country at double this rate, or 40,000 units in a fiscal year, for the next five years.

Figure 2–17   Document Organized from General to Specific (Excerpt)

Specific to General

When you organize information in a specific-to-general pattern, you begin with specific information and build to a general conclusion. The examples, facts, and statistics that you present in your writing support the conclusion that comes at the end. For example, if your subject were highway safety, you might begin with details of a specific highway accident, go on to generalize about how that accident was similar to many others, and then present recommendations for reducing the probability of such accidents. If your purpose is to persuade a skeptical audience by providing specific details, this pattern is useful because it suspends the general point until your case has been made. This pattern of organization is somewhat like increasing order of importance in that you carefully build your case and reach your conclusion at the end, as shown in Figures 2–18 and 2–19.

OUTLINE

    I. Study of 4,500 accidents involving nearly 7,200 adult front-seat passengers showed only 20 percent of the vehicles equipped with passenger-side air bags

   II. Study shows adult front-seat passengers in vehicles without air bags twice as likely to be killed as those in vehicles with air bags

       A. Children riding as front-seat passengers can be killed by deployment of air bags

       B. Children should ride in the backseat

 III. Estimated 40 percent of adult front-seat passenger vehicle deaths could be prevented if passenger-side air bags were installed

Figure 2–18   Outline for Information Organized from Specific to General

FACTS ABOUT AIR BAGS

Recently, a government agency studied the use of passenger-side air bags in 4,500 accidents involving nearly 7,200 front-seat passengers. Nearly all these accidents occurred on routes that had a speed limit of at least 40 mph. Only 20 percent of the adult front-seat passengers were riding in vehicles equipped with passenger-side air bags. Those not riding in vehicles equipped with passenger-side air bags were more than twice as likely to be killed as passengers riding in vehicles that were so equipped.

Statistical details build the case for the final paragraph

A conservative estimate is that 40 percent of the adult front-seat passenger vehicle deaths could be prevented if all vehicles came equipped with passenger-side air bags. Children, however, should always ride in the backseat because other studies have indicated that a child can be killed by the deployment of an air bag. If you are an adult front-seat passenger in an accident, your chances of survival are far greater if the vehicle in which you are riding is equipped with a passenger-side air bag.

General conclusion

Figure 2–19   Document Organized from Specific to General (Excerpt)

Comparison

When you use comparison as a pattern of development, you evaluate the relative merits of the items you are considering. Comparison works well in determining which of two or more items is most suitable for some specific purpose, such as selecting the best color printer for digital photographs, determining the most cost-effective messenger service for your company, or choosing the most-qualified applicant for your job opening. Showing such information in tables often facilitates item-to-item comparisons when you have more than a few options to consider, as in Table 2–2. The advantage of a table is that it provides a quick reference, allowing readers to see and compare all the information at once. The disadvantage is that a table cannot convey as much related detailed information as a narrative description.

ON THE WEB

For more examples of comparison, go to Model Documents Gallery, bedfordstmartins.com/ writingthatworks

TABLE 2–2   Table Layout for a Comparison

Comparison of Woodworking Glues				
	White Glue	*Aliphatic Resin Glue*	*Plastic Resin Glue*	*Contact Cement*
Bonding strength	Low	Moderate	High	High
Moisture resistance	Low	Moderate	High	High
Setting time	30 minutes	30 minutes	4 to 6 hours	Bonds on contact
Common uses	Light construction	General purpose	General purpose	Laminate and veneer to wood

——— *Types of glue*

Characteristics

◆ *For a discussion of tables see pages 220–224 in Chapter 7, Designing Effective Documents and Visuals.*

To be sure that your choice will be the best one, you must determine the basis (or bases) for making your comparison. For example, if you were comparing the features commonly used to evaluate woodworking glues, you could organize them as shown in Table 2–2.

Once you decide on the bases important to your comparison, you can determine the most effective way to structure your comparison: whole by whole or part by part.

- In the *whole-by-whole* pattern, all the relevant characteristics of one item are discussed before those of the next item are considered.

- In the *part-by-part* pattern, the relevant features of each item are compared one by one.

Hearing aids, for example, may be compared in a variety of ways: style, size, correction range, control features, and more. To help consumers comparing hearing-aid options, the whole-by-whole pattern would allow them to consider each type in turn. The outline shown in Figure 2–20 and the discussion in Figure 2–21 comparing types of hearing aids are organized according to the whole-by-whole pattern. The writer describes each type according to its size and placement, features, and drawbacks before going on to the next type.

OUTLINE: COMMON TYPES OF HEARING AIDS

  I. Completely in the Canal
     A. Size and placement
     B. Special considerations
        1. Correction range
        2. Volume control
        3. Amplification range
     C. Potential problems
        1. Acoustic feedback
        2. Ear-wax maintenance
        3. Wind noise
 II. In the Canal (Partial)
     A. Size and placement
     B. Special considerations
        1. Correction range
        2. Volume control
        3. Amplification range
     C. Potential problems
        1. Acoustic feedback
        2. Ear-wax maintenance
        3. Wind noise

Figure 2–20   Outline for a Whole-by-Whole Comparison (continued)

III. In the Ear
    A. Size and placement
    B. Special considerations
        1. Correction range
        2. Volume control
        3. Amplification range
    C. Potential problems
        1. Acoustic feedback
        2. Ear-wax maintenance
        3. Wind noise
IV. Behind the Ear
    A. Size and placement
    B. Special considerations
        1. Correction range
        2. Volume control
        3. Amplification range
    C. Potential problems
        1. Missing outer ear
        2. Cosmetic appeal
        3. Acoustic feedback

Figure 2–20   Outline for a Whole-by-Whole Comparison (continued)

COMMON TYPES OF HEARING AIDS

Hearing aids are tiny instruments worn in or behind the ear that amplify sounds for people with hearing loss. The following comparison describes the most common types of hearing aids and their advantages and disadvantages. Figure 1 illustrates their placements.

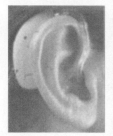 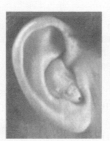 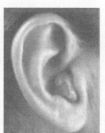 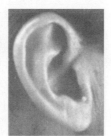

Types of hearing aids being compared

Behind the Ear (BTE)   In the Ear (ITE)   In the Canal (ITC)   Completely in the Canal (CIC)

Figure 1.   Common Hearing Aids and Their Placement
Source: American Academy of Audiology (<www.audiology.org>)

Figure 2–21   Whole-by-Whole Comparison (Excerpt) (continued)

Completely in the Canal

Completely in-the-canal (CIC) hearing aids are the smallest type of hearing aid manufactured. They are custom fitted for insertion in the ear canal next to the ear drum and are virtually invisible when worn, which makes them cosmetically appealing. They require no outside wires or tubes and are removed by the wearer with a transparent wire. CIC hearing aids are especially effective for mild to severe hearing loss; they are not designed for profound hearing loss.

Despite their size, CIC hearing aids offer a variety of special features that allow users to control for certain types of hearing-loss conditions. . . .

The CIC's advantage in size does result in certain kinds of problems that can impede their effectiveness. Their small size often limits their power and the range of frequencies they pick up. It can make manipulating their controls and changing their tiny batteries challenging, too. Acoustic feedback (whistling) can occur because the microphone is close to the speaker in this model.

In the Canal (Partial)

This style is larger than the CIC model, but it is still small and discreet. Although partially visible when worn, it too affords the wearer cosmetic appeal. Like the CIC model, it is effective for mild to severe hearing loss; it is not effective for profound hearing loss.

This model offers additional control functions compared with the CIC model, like the capability to hold a telecoil for telephone conversations and a directional microphone. . . .

Problems impeding effectiveness include its size, which requires manual dexterity to manipulate its controls and change the battery. Without frequent cleaning, it can be damaged by ear wax. As with the CIC model, a small ear canal may not afford adequate space for this style of aid.

In the Ear

This style is larger than the full or partial in-the-canal models and is fully visible when worn. It is custom made to fit the contours of the outer ear and fits just outside the opening to the ear canal. In-the-ear (ITE) devices are effective for mild to severe hearing loss but not for profound hearing loss.

Because of their size, in-the-ear devices afford a wide array of user-controlled features, such as directional microphones, tone control, and a telecoil to enhance hearing during telephone conversations. . . .

Certain models can be damaged by ear wax, so they require frequent cleaning. . . .

Detailed descriptions of advantages and disadvantages provide basis for comparison

Figure 2–21   Whole-by-Whole Comparison (Excerpt) (continued)

Behind the Ear

The behind-the-ear (BTE) style is the largest of the common models. It fits snugly behind one or both ears and can be fully or partially hidden, depending on the wearer's hairstyle. The BTE device is connected to a plastic ear mold inside the outer ear. It can also be attached to eyeglasses. It is designed for severe to profound hearing loss. Its size and placement minimize the likelihood of acoustic feedback and make manipulating the controls and changing the battery easier than in the smaller models.

The BTE devices can be connected to a variety of external sound sources, such as television sets and infrared listening devices that make targeted sounds, such as speakers in a classroom or an auditorium, easier to hear. . . .

This type of device cannot be worn by those with deformed or missing outer ears. Eyeglass wearers also require a special adaptation to wear this style. The BTE devices are prone to acoustic feedback (whistling) if poorly fitted. Finally, their size and location reduce their cosmetic appeal.

Figure 2–21 Whole-by-Whole Comparison (Excerpt) (continued)

As is often the case when the whole-by-whole pattern is used, the purpose of this comparison is to weigh the advantages and disadvantages of each type of device against the others. However, if your purpose were to compare, one at a time, the major *functions* of hearing aids, the information might be arranged according to the part-by-part pattern (Figures 2–22 and 2–23). Note that this pattern emphasizes the specific characteristics of the hearing aids rather than the different types of hearing aids. The features being compared can be further highlighted by word order and by mechanical highlighting (*italic*, **boldface**, or <u>underlining</u>), as in the narratives comparing hearing aids in Figures 2–21 and 2–23.

OUTLINE: EVALUATING HEARING-AID CHARACTERISTICS

  I. Size and Placement
      A. Completely in the canal
      B. In the canal
      C. In the ear
      D. Behind the ear
  II. Special Considerations
      A. Hearing-correction range
         1. Mild to moderate
         2. Moderate to severe
         3. Severe to profound
      B. Special features
         1. Volume control
         2. Telecoil for phone use
         3. Connection to external sound source
         4. Amplification range
         5. Vents to facilitate high-frequency sounds
         6. Circuitry that limits maximum volume of sound to tolerable level
         7. Cell-phone compatibility
         8. On/off capability
         9. Preprogrammed memory
        10. Directional microphone
 III. Potential Problems
      A. Acoustic feedback
      B. Ear-wax maintenance
      C. Wind noise
      D. Cosmetic appeal

Figure 2–22   Outline for a Part-by-Part Comparison

EVALUATING HEARING-AID OPTIONS

Hearing aids are tiny instruments worn in or behind the ear that amplify sounds for people with hearing loss. The following comparison describes the features that consumers in need of hearing aids should evaluate in selecting the model most appropriate to their hearing loss and ease of use.

Size and Placement

Characteristics that distinguish different kinds of hearing aids

Comparison of features organized by topics important to consumers

The most common types of hearing aids are classified according to their size and location in or behind the ear. *Completely in the canal* (CIC) hearing aids, the smallest type manufactured, are worn deep inside the ear canal next to the ear drum. *In the canal* (*partial*) (ITC) hearing aids, although larger than the CIC devices, are small and discreet. *In the ear* (ITE) hearing aids are worn in the contour of the outer ear, just outside the opening to the ear canal. *Behind the ear* (BTE) models fit snugly behind the ear and are the largest of the common models.

Figure 2–23   Part-by-Part Comparison (Excerpt) (continued)

Correction Range and Special Features

Hearing loss is categorized from mild to profound. *Mild to severe* loss can be helped with CIC, ITC, and ITE hearing aids. *Severe to profound* hearing loss can be helped with the BTE style.

Hearing aids provide a variety of features to improve the user's quality of hearing. All models offer on/off capability, volume control, and circuitry to limit maximum volume of sound to tolerable levels. The ITC and ITE models can hold a telecoil. The BTE model can be connected to external sound sources, such as TV sets, radios, and infrared listening devices. . . .

Potential Problems

Acoustic feedback (whistling) is most often a problem for the smallest models because of the close proximity of the microphone to the speaker. Except for the BTE model, the others can be damaged by ear wax. The BTE hearing aid is the least cosmetically appealing because of its size. . . .

Figure 2–23   Part-by-Part Comparison (Excerpt) (continued)

CONSIDERING AUDIENCE AND PURPOSE
Organizing Information

Organize your writing from the perspective of your audience and purpose. Keep in mind that some types of writing lend themselves logically to only one kind of organization and will best convey information to your reader by that pattern.

- **Sequential** organization takes your reader step by step through the stages of a process in the order in which the process occurs. (Example: instructions in a user's manual)

- **Chronological** organization takes your reader step by step through the stages of an activity or event as it occurs *in time* from beginning to end. (Example: a trip report)

- **Spatial** organization describes physical objects, areas, and phenomena at the level of detail necessary for your reader to envision their appearance or how they occurred. (Example: an accident report)

- **Division** is a way of organizing information about a complex whole by breaking it down into smaller units for your reader, making it easier to understand. (Example: a description of the parts of a computer)

- **Classification** is a way of organizing information that groups disparate units into categories recognizable to your audience. (Example: a description of different types of vacation packages)

- **Decreasing order of importance** introduces your reader to your main, or most important, points at the beginning of your writing, followed by background information that supports your main points. (Example: a news story or formal report for busy readers)

- ■ **Increasing order of importance** leads your reader through the thought process and details that support conclusions you reach at the end of your writing. (Example: a persuasive presentation)
- ■ **General-to-specific** organization of information introduces your reader to the main or general point you wish to make at the beginning of your writing and leads your reader through the facts and other supporting information that describes how you reached your general point. (Example: memo or proposal that begins with a recommendation)
- ■ **Specific-to-general** sequence leads your reader through the facts and other supporting information you use to build your case for reaching the conclusion you state at the end of your writing. (Example: a report that begins by giving the details of an event)
- ■ **Comparison** allows your reader to evaluate the relative strengths of the items that are under evaluation after you establish the basis for the comparison. (Example: a memo that considers a variety of options)

CHAPTER 2 SUMMARY: ORGANIZING YOUR INFORMATION

Before you begin to write, consider the following questions as you organize your information into a logical sequence.

- ■ Will I need a brief list or a full-scale outline to organize my information?
- ■ Will I need to circulate the outline to colleagues or superiors?
- ■ Is the outline divided into parts and subparts that reflect the logical divisions of the topic?
- ■ Will my word-processing software structure the outline automatically?
- ■ Does the topic lend itself naturally to one of the following patterns of development?
  - • Sequential
  - • Chronological
  - • Spatial
  - • Division and Classification
  - • Decreasing Order of Importance
  - • Increasing Order of Importance
  - • General to Specific
  - • Specific to General
  - • Comparison
- ■ Does the topic need to be organized by more than one pattern of development?

ON THE WEB

For additional exercises, go to Chapter 2, bedfordstmartins.com/ writingthatworks

■ Exercises

1. Determine the best method of organizing each of the following topics — sequential, chronological, spatial, division and classification, decreasing order of importance, increasing order of importance, general to specific, specific to general, or

comparison. You will use some of the methods more than once and at least one method not at all. It is possible for a topic to fit more than one method. Be prepared to defend your choice.

ON THE WEB

For an online quiz on organization, go to Chapter 2, bedfordstmartins.com/ writingthatworks

- Explaining how to register for classes at your school
- Supporting an argument against smoking
- Describing different types of dogs at a dog show
- Determining the job that is right for you
- Explaining how to get the job you want
- Describing the most important room in your house
- Announcing the winners of a contest
- Describing the fire-escape route for a building
- Determining the best computer to buy
- Describing the planets in our solar system
- Explaining the changing educational system in your state
- Supporting an argument for or against specific environmental-protection laws

2. Identify the method of organization that would be most effective for each of the following topics and explain how consideration of audience and purpose might affect your decision.

- Instructions for performing CPR
- A report of the results of a police stakeout or other police activity
- A report on the different kinds of news, drama, and comedy programs on prime-time television
- A report on the differences among the major personal computer manufacturers
- Instructions for preparing a five-course meal, including recipes
- A report on the different types of media coverage of a world event
- A report on the results of a governmental election and its importance
- Instructions for buying or selling a house

3. Pretend that you are the author of this textbook and a textbook from another course. Complete the following written statement of purpose for both textbooks: "My primary purpose for writing [textbook's title] is to _____ so that my readers will be able to _____."

a. Based on the table of contents from both textbooks, practice outlining by breaking down the chapters and the material in the chapters, using either a Roman numeral or decimal numbering system outline.

b. Now compare both outlines. Do you see any organizational strategies on the part of these textbook authors in presenting their material to students? Do you agree with the authors' organization of the material in the textbooks? Assuming that your statements of purpose are correct, do you believe that the organization of these textbooks helped the authors achieve their goals in writing? Present your findings to the class.

c. Now imagine that you are an author of either a textbook for academic readers or a how-to book for general readers. Pick a subject of interest to you and create a statement of purpose for a book on that topic. Then outline the chapters and materials using the Roman numeral or decimal numbering system. Have another student peer-review your work. Will your organization help you achieve your goal as a writer? What works well? What would need to be changed? Rework your statements or outline and present them to the class.

4. Make a list of topics and create an outline for one of the following writing projects, organizing each *sequentially.* As your instructor directs, use the outline to write a document of assigned length.

- Preparing a household budget for clients of a financial planner
- Tuning a guitar for customers with little musical training
- Setting up a personal computer for use in a home office: parts, peripherals, and desktop configuration
- Applying for a personal loan for customers of a local bank
- Finding an apartment to rent: a guide for foreign students
- Repairing a broken window for customers of a hardware store
- Maturing of a monarch butterfly egg to an adult for a display at a nature center
- Hosting a social event for members of a networking group
- Purchasing a product on the Internet (text to be included at a Web site)
- Buying a car for business travelers

5. Make a list of topics and create an outline for one of the following descriptions, organizing each *spatially.* As your instructor directs, use the outline to write a description of assigned length. Without relying on illustrations, describe the topic clearly enough so that a classmate, if asked, could create an accurate drawing or diagram based on your description.

- The layout of your apartment or of a floor in your home (as it is, or as you would like it to be)
- The layout of the reference room or other area of the school or community library
- The dimensions and most significant features of a public park or building
- The layout of a garden for a home-improvement Web site
- The layout of the shop, office, or laboratory where you work for new employees
- The physical process for disinfecting a hospital room or for painting or wallpapering a room

6. Make a list of topics and create an outline for one of the following writing projects, organizing each by a *decreasing-order-of-importance* sequence. As your instructor directs, use the outline to write a document of assigned length.

- Your job qualifications and career goal to be used in a letter of application and résumé
- The advantages of living in a particular city or area of the country for an employee relocation guide
- The importance of preventive maintenance of a specific machine or piece of equipment for a manual
- The importance of preventive care in one health-related area (diet, exercise, dental care, and so on)
- The advantages of having paychecks directly deposited into checking accounts, of having savings automatically deducted from paychecks, or of using online banking for credit union members
- The advantages of recycling for a city council booklet
- The advantages of owning life insurance for an agent training manual
- The advantages of carpooling for an employee intranet Web site

7. Make a list of topics and create an outline for one of the following writing projects, organizing each by an *increasing-order-of-importance* sequence. As your instructor directs, use the outline to write a document of assigned length.

    - Why smoking should or should not be permitted in restaurants for legislators who must debate the issue
    - The advantages of learning to pilot a small airplane for prospective students of a flying school
    - The reasons you deserve a pay raise for a possible meeting with or a memo to your manager
    - The advantages of alternatively fueled vehicles for an environmental-resource organization
    - A proposal to change a procedure where you work for your management

8. For this exercise, use a *general-to-specific* sequence. Choose one of the following statements, then support it with pertinent facts, examples, anecdotes, and so on. As your instructor directs, outline the information to write a document of assigned length.

    - Volunteer jobs and internships provide valuable experience in the working world.
    - For families living within limited means, budgeting is essential.
    - Capable managers are willing to delegate authority.
    - Post–high school education or technical training is essential in today's job market.
    - Ongoing computer education and training is fundamental in today's workplace.
    - A sound human resources training program pays off for companies.

9. Create a topic outline for one of the following subjects, organizing it by *division and classification*. Using the outline, write a document of assigned length as instructed.

    - Personal digital assistants (including pocket PCs)
    - Conventional and alternative medical therapies
    - Weight-loss strategies and programs
    - Home exercise equipment
    - Bicycles (for example, racing, mountain)
    - Cameras (for example, quality, convenience, price ranges)
    - Cable TV channels (select a single category: for example, news, information, public access, shopping, special interest)

10. Create a topic outline for one of the following subjects, organizing it by the *comparison* method of development. Using the outline, write a document of assigned length appropriate to the topic or as your instructor directs.

    - The features of two or more word-processing or spreadsheet software programs
    - U.S. intellectual property laws (for example, copyright law, trademark law, and patent law)
    - Features of at least five specialized library databases (for example, InfoTrac, Clearinghouse, Health AtoZ, Thomas Legislative Information, Zip Code Lookup)

ON THE WEB

For more collaborative classroom projects, go to Chapter 2, bedfordstmartins.com/ writingthatworks

■ Collaborative Classroom Projects

1. Following is an example of a poorly developed outline. In small groups and within the allotted time frame, revise this outline, using the guidelines provided in this chapter. Select a spokesperson from your group to present your outline to the class.

   Company Sports
   I. Intercompany sports
      A. Advantages to the company
         1. Publicity
         2. Intercompany relations
      B. Disadvantages
         1. Misplaced emphasis
         2. Athletic participation not available to all employees
   II. Intracompany sports
      A. Wide participation
      B. Physical fitness
      C. Detracts from work
      D. Risks injuries

2. Bring five common tools to class (a can opener, a pencil sharpener, and so on). In small groups, outline a narrative description of one or more of the tools, keeping in mind the particular function of the tool(s). When finished, exchange papers and critique one another's outlines based on whether the outline effectively describes the tool.

3. In small groups, create an outline for a guide for new students who need to learn how to sign up for classes. First, consider the obvious things students have to do, like learn their student identification numbers, meet with their advisors, and go over the course catalog and class schedules. Then, evaluate the scope of signing up for classes. (Review pages 10–12 in Chapter 1, Getting Ready, for advice on considering scope in your writing.) Would it help to start at the very beginning—with enrollment at the university, required immunizations, and learning the locations of classroom buildings, for example? Determine the amount of information necessary before creating the outline; be prepared to defend your choices.

ON THE WEB

For extra research projects, go to Chapter 2, bedfordstmartins.com/ writingthatworks

■ Research Projects

1. Locate a government, a business, or an industry report or an article in a professional journal. Analyze the organization of information in the report or article, and write an outline that mirrors the organization. Develop the outline to the level of detail of the outline shown in Figure 2–1, or to the level of detail specified by your instructor. Then assess the report or article for its use of the methods of organization described in this chapter, citing specific sections or paragraphs in which each method is demonstrated. Finally, describe how the organization of the report or article made it easier or more difficult to understand its content.

2. Material that will be read quickly is often organized by decreasing order of importance. Newspaper articles and news releases (announcements of upcoming events

or company news created by public relations writers) are two such types of material. At a university or college, the university relations or advancement office often sends news releases about campus events to local newspapers and news stations, hoping to persuade reporters or camera crews to attend an event and write an article or present a film segment about it. Newspaper editors and television producers get many news releases a day, so they don't spend much time reading each one.

a. Go to your university public relations office (or its link on your school's Web site) and ask for several examples of news releases about major events on your campus. You can also go to PR Newswire at <www.prnewswire.com> and look for news releases about your school. Then in groups, analyze the order of the information in these releases. Create an outline of a news release based on your analysis.

b. Next, ask someone in your university public relations office for copies of articles that were published by local newspapers based on the news releases they received. (You can also find articles in the Lexis/Nexis database at your school's library.) In the same groups, analyze how these newspaper articles were written. Then create an outline of a newspaper article based on your analysis. Present your findings to the class.

c. Finally, members of your group should imagine that they work in your school's university public relations office. Using your outline, write a news release about an upcoming event at your school (for example, a writing contest, a guest lecturer, or a sports event).

■ Web Projects

ON THE WEB

For more Web Project options, go to Chapter 2, **bedfordstmartins.com/ writingthatworks**

1. Visit five or more government Web sites and analyze the variety of ways that information is organized at each site; use specific examples to support your analysis. Write one to three paragraphs that detail the effectiveness or ineffectiveness of how information is presented at each site. Compare the sites. Write another one to three paragraphs explaining how other methods of organization and the use of outlining (as discussed in this chapter) could improve each of these sites.

2. As noted in this chapter, writers should not overstate claims they make about a product or service, nor should they speak negatively or disparagingly about a competitor. Search the Web for products that are usually marketed with a large degree of hype, like diet products, sports drinks, or home electronics.

a. Print out several examples of online advertisements or Web pages for a particular type of product. First look at the visual persuasive strategies that the graphics and Web designers have chosen to use. (*Note:* Before you begin, read about graphics and design in Chapter 7, Designing Effective Documents and Visuals.) Describe the pictures on the pages, the colors used, and the fonts used. What do the visuals say about these products?

b. Next, examine the sites' persuasive writing strategies. For example, do they include action words? Repetitious use of certain words? Lots of exclamation points?

c. Write your findings in a memo to the class. How have the visual and rhetorical strategies added to or subtracted from the designers' and writers' persuasiveness?

3   Writing the Draft

AT A GLANCE: Drafting

Once you have gathered and organized your information, you are ready to write. But how do you turn an outline into a workable document? This chapter describes and illustrates several well-established strategies for preparing a first draft.

This chapter describes proven techniques for successfully writing your draft as well as staying connected to your audience and developing your topic as you do so. It also guides you through the process of writing effective openings and closings and continues the development of the Lifemaker brochure introduced in Chapter 2, Organizing Your Information.

The most effective way to start and to keep going is to use a good outline as a springboard and a map for your writing. The outline also serves to group related facts and details. Once these facts are grouped, you are ready to construct unified and coherent paragraphs—the major building blocks of any piece of writing. Keep in mind, however, that first drafts are necessarily rough and unpolished. Writing and revising are two very different tasks. Trying to write something perfectly the first time puts undue pressure on you that can become self-defeating. In fact, any attempt to correct or polish your writing only stimulates your internal critic and

Voices from the Workplace

Maureen March, Lincoln Elementary School

In her job as a first-grade teacher in Coquille, Oregon, Maureen March writes lesson plans, formal student observations, e-mail correspondence with staff and parents, and report cards. Strong writing skills are crucial to Maureen as an educator because she serves as a model to her students, their parents, and the community. To make her message clear and concise, Maureen often goes through multiple drafts as part of her writing process. She explains, "I jot down the message I want to communicate and then revise it to meet the formality required for that specific type of correspondence and for the intended audience — whether it's a parent, principal, or colleague. Report cards take the longest. I begin writing my comments early, so I can revise and redraft before sending them out."

Debra Canale, Roadway Express

As a competitive intelligence manager, Debra Canale writes for a diverse audience of logistics professionals. From researching and preparing presentations for officers to disseminating competitive analyses on strategic direction, she finds that drafting is the most challenging part of the writing process. "Organizing your thoughts and your work space is essential in writing for business," she says. "I find it helps to keep to-do and date-due lists and to re-prioritize my writing responsibilities on a daily basis in order to accommodate interruptions, emergencies, and ever-changing business priorities." Once Debra knows the objective and audience for a piece, she must set aside time to think creatively about the topic, conduct research, and determine her audience's knowledge level. For those working in a fast-paced business environment, she suggests: "Pay close attention to the first draft of a writing project. In the corporate world, the less you need to rewrite the better."

undermines your ability to complete your draft. When you write the draft, your goal is to transcribe and expand the notes from your outline into paragraphs without worrying about grammar, refinements of language, or spelling. Experienced writers use the tactics described in this chapter to start, keep moving, and get the job done; you will discover which ones are the most helpful to you.

◆ For detailed advice on outlining ideas before drafting, review Chapter 2, Organizing Your Information.

◆ The revision process is explained in detail in Chapter 4, Revising the Draft.

◆ For editing guidelines, see Part Four, Revision Guide.

■ Time-Management Tactics

Because on-the-job writers must work not only under constant deadlines but also with several assignments at once, managing time is an essential part of the writing process.

You may not feel inspired to begin, but you will gain confidence as you continue writing. Use positive motivation: Remember that your goal at this point is to write a draft, not a polished final product.

ON THE WEB

For online resources for drafting, go to Chapter 3, bedfordstmartins.com/writingthatworks

◆ *For tips on practicing freewriting to get your ideas down quickly, see Drafting on Your Computer on page 67.*

WRITER'S CHECKLIST
Developing Confidence

☑ Nothing builds a writer's confidence more than adequate preparation.

☑ Remember past writing projects—you have completed something before, and you will this time.

☑ Don't wait for inspiration to write the rough draft—treat writing the draft as you would any on-the-job task.

☑ Think of writing a rough draft as simply transcribing and expanding the notes from your outline into paragraphs.

☑ Don't worry about a good opening—that can wait until you've constructed your paragraphs.

☑ Concentrate on ideas without attempting to polish or revise. Don't worry about precise word choices, usage, syntax, grammar, or spelling.

☑ Keep writing quickly to achieve unity, coherence, and proportion.

☑ Don't criticize yourself for not being able to write a smooth, readable sentence the first time; it is natural for first drafts to be clumsy and long-winded.

☑ Remind yourself that you are beginning a *draft* that no one else will read.

Allocating Your Time

Keep a calendar on your desk or computer that indicates various deadlines for projects, appointments for interviews, and time periods for gathering information. Your daily calendar should also include "writing appointments," times set aside for writing that you must keep (without interruptions) as if you had an appointment with another person.

Begin small. Within the deadlines set by teachers, managers, and others, set your own short-term, manageable deadlines for completing sections of a draft and other tasks. Concentrating on such small goals can help you meet the overall deadline, and it can also relieve some of the pressure of writing the draft. Some professional writers think of the completion of small goals as building a draft one brick at a time.

List these goals, together with your other job tasks; then schedule each task for a specific time. As you set your schedule, remember that time-management experts advise working on the most difficult or unpleasant tasks during the time of day when your mind is keenest.

◆ *For guidelines on writing three types of time-sensitive documents, see*
• *Meeting the Deadline: The Time-Sensitive Memo on pages 289–291*
• *Meeting the Deadline: The Time-Sensitive Proposal on pages 468–469*
• *Meeting the Deadline: The Time-Sensitive Presentation on pages 495–498.*

Preparing Your Work Environment

Another useful time-management strategy is to prepare your writing environment and assemble your materials before you begin. Find an isolated place or a method of isolating yourself for writing the draft; then hang out the "Do Not Disturb" sign. Especially when a deadline is in jeopardy, finding a quiet area away from phones and meetings can be effective.

Put order into your writing environment by arranging your materials and supplies. Use whatever writing technology (pen and pad, computer, or tape recorder) is most comfortable for you. You may even discover that certain props will help you

DIGITAL TIPS: Drafting on Your Computer

■ Try freewriting to overcome writer's block: Turn off the monitor and write your thoughts as quickly as possible without stopping to correct mistakes, to complete sentences, or to polish your writing. After you finish, you can turn the monitor back on and review, revise, and reorganize as appropriate.

■ If a difficult section hinders your progress, use the highlighting or comment feature to make note of it and move on.

■ Save each draft separately so that you can return to earlier versions if necessary, but do not create separate drafts for minor corrections.

■ Use a consistent naming pattern for multiple drafts, such as course abbreviation, assignment number, and draft number or date.

get started. Sitting in a favorite chair, opening computer files, or placing a reference book on your desk may symbolize your commitment to yourself and your work.

Remaining Flexible

Start with your outline as a guide, but remember that it is not cast in concrete. Feel free to improve your organization as you work. Consider starting with the easiest or most interesting part to get moving and build some momentum. You may find that just writing a statement of your purpose will help you get started.

◆ *For more on statements of purpose, see Determining Your Purpose on page 6.*

Once you are rolling, keep going. You may wish to write comments to yourself while you are writing the rough draft if that tactic keeps you moving. When you reach landmarks (such as the subgoals described earlier) or feel powerfully tempted to start revising, you may need to take a break. When you do, leave a signpost, such as a printout of an unfinished section or a note in the outline recording the date and time you stopped, so you will not waste time searching for your place when you resume work. When you finish a section, reward yourself with a cup of coffee, a short walk, or another small diversion. Physical activity serves as an excellent break for writers. If possible, avoid immersing yourself in another mental activity while you are on your break. If you are not under mental pressure, you may discover a solution to a nagging writing problem.

When you resume, reread what you have written so that you can recall your frame of mind. Some writers also like to change their writing tools or environment when they resume writing the draft.

WRITER'S CHECKLIST
Writing a Rough Draft

☑ Set up a quiet writing area with the necessary equipment and materials, then hang out the "Do Not Disturb" sign.

☑ Start with the section that seems easiest or most interesting to you.

☑ The first rule of good writing is to help your audience by clearly communicating to them. Write in a plain and direct style that is comfortable and natural for both you and your audience.

(continued)

WRITER'S CHECKLIST (continued)

☑ To make your writing more direct and conversational, imagine a typical reader sitting across the desk from you as you explain your topic.

☑ If you are writing instructions or procedures, visualize your readers actually performing the actions you are describing. This will help you envision the necessary steps and ensure that you provide adequate information in the right sequence and level of detail.

☑ If you are writing a sales letter, think of your arguments from the reader's point of view. Imagine how the features you describe can best be translated into benefits for a prospective customer.

☑ Give yourself a 10- or 15-minute time limit in which you write continually, regardless of how good or bad your writing seems to you. The point is to keep moving.

☑ Stop writing when you've finished a section (or before you're completely exhausted) and give yourself a small reward.

☑ Reread what you have written when you return to your writing. Often, seeing what you have written will trigger the frame of mind that was productive.

■ Keeping Your Audience in Mind

When writing the draft, focus on communicating with your readers. Think of your subject from your readers' perspective. Ask: "What does my reader probably know?" and "What are my reader's feelings about the subject—sympathetic? Hostile? Neutral?" These questions will always help improve the effort required to think about them. For international readers, keep language and cultural differences in mind and consult someone from the target audience for guidance if possible. For persuasive writing, support your ideas convincingly, acknowledge opposing points of view, and use the appropriate medium for your message. In all your writing, adopt the tone of voice—formal, authoritative, conversational—appropriate to your audience and purpose.

◆ *For detailed advice on analyzing an audience, see pages 6–7 in Chapter 1, Assessing Audience and Purpose.*

Writing from the Audience's Point of View

Whether your reader is a coworker, customer, or company president, he or she is interested in the problem you are addressing more from his or her point of view than from yours. Imagine yourself in your reader's position, perhaps by visualizing your reader performing a set of activities or taking certain actions based on your writing. Taken together with what you know about your reader's background, this picture will help you predict your reader's needs and reactions and ensure that you clearly provide all the information your reader needs.

For instance, suppose you work for a bicycle manufacturer and you need to write assembly instructions so that people who buy the new model 1050J can get from opening the carton to riding the bicycle with a minimum of frustration. You would break down the assembly process into a sensible series of easy-to-follow steps. You would avoid technical language and anticipate questions that your audience would be likely to have, making it unnecessary for them to consult other sources to follow your directions. You would also include assembly diagrams, a list of parts, and a list of the tools necessary for assembly. You would not explain the engineering theory that is responsible for the bicycle's unique design.

You would approach the situation differently if you were preparing assembly instructions for a bicycle dealer. You could use standard technical terms without defining them, and you would probably combine related steps because the dealer would be familiar with bicycle assembly and able to follow a more-sophisticated set of instructions. Your audience would not need a list of tools required for assembly; the shop would no doubt have all the necessary tools, and the dealer would know which ones to use. You might well, in a separate section, include some theoretical detail, too. The dealer could possibly use this information to explain to customers the advantages of your bicycle over a competitor's.

Accommodating Multiple Audiences

When you write for readers similar in background and knowledge—all sales associates, for example, or all security officers—picture a typical representative of that group and write directly to that person. Occasionally, however, you may need to write for readers with widely different work environments, technical backgrounds, or professional positions. For example, if you were to write a technical report that would be used by company executives, field-service engineers, and sales associates, you might address each audience separately in clearly identified sections of your document: an executive summary for the executives, the body of the document for the sales associates, and an appendix for the service engineers. When you cannot segment your writing this way, determine who your primary audience is, and make certain that you meet all of that audience's needs. Then try to meet the needs of other readers—only if you can do so without placing a burden on your primary audience.

Figures 3–1 and 3–2 are from a technical-assessment report that describes to an organization the advantages of acquiring media-streaming technology. The first part of the report (Figure 3–1) provides an overview of the topic for policymakers who may be unfamiliar with this technology and its uses. The second part (Figure 3–2) is targeted at technical experts who must understand the hardware and software requirements for the system.

◆ *For an explanation of how the different parts of a formal report address the needs of different audiences, see Chapter 11, Writing Formal Reports.*

Writing for an International Audience

The prevalence of global communication technology, international trade agreements, and the emergence of Europe as a single market have made communicating with audiences from varied cultural backgrounds an essential skill. Language differences, of course, create the biggest obstacle to writing for readers whose primary language is not English.

The communications habits and expectations of audiences whose primary language is not English often will differ from those common in North America. Organizational patterns, forms of courtesy, and ideas about efficiency can vary significantly from culture to culture. What might seem direct and efficient in the

Overview and purpose of report

INTRODUCTION

This report demonstrates how the Office of the Chief Information Officer can improve the distribution of agency information and enhance communications with the staff, the nuclear industry, other federal agencies, the media, and the public by using media-streaming technology (MST). This report explains this technology and its advantages to our organization, details the resources necessary to deploy it, and recommends a course of action to achieve these goals.

Definition of a key term

Media-streaming is the receipt of audio and video broadcast media over the Internet at one's desktop computer. The advantages of providing this capability to the agency are threefold:

List of high-level advantages to organization

- To enhance the agency's ability to collaborate with the nuclear industries, the states, other federal agencies, the public, and other agency stakeholders
- To provide desktop delivery of training, commission meetings, public meetings at remote locations, staff safety programs, nuclear industry standards, and much else
- To build partnerships with government and private-sector organizations

This report provides no single solution to deploying MST. Agency requirements are not static and will require alternative configurations over time at headquarters and the regional offices.

Statement defines intended audience (decision-makers)

Accordingly, the coverage includes necessary background information for decision-makers in the following areas:

- Business requirements for and cost of supporting MST

Statement of scope of report

- Technology cost alternatives based on a variety of agency program requirements
- A new internal Web site focusing on MST to assist management and staff in determining how the technology can be used to improve agency programs and customer relations

Figure 3–1   Introduction to a Report (for a General Audience)

ARCHITECTURE OF THE REAL SYSTEM

Real System G2 is a client-server application that delivers live and on-demand MST content across TCP/IP networks. The Real System architecture has three main components: Real Server, Real Player, and content publishing tools. Real Server streams live and on-demand Real Audio, Real Video, Real Flash animation, Real Pix (GIF and JPEG images), and Real Text content across the Internet and NGN. Real System G2 supports most other existing media file formats, such as ASF, AVI, JPEG, MPEG, VIV, and WAV. The Real Player is used on client workstations to play the MST content. Real System publishing tools, such as the Real Producer and Real System G2 Authoring Tool, are used to create MST content. . . .

Technical vocabulary and abbreviations for expert audience

Figure 3–2   Subsection of a Report (for a Technical Audience)

United States, for example, could be seen as blunt and even impolite in other cultures.

Cultural differences and the reasons behind them are often so subtle that only someone who is very familiar with a culture can explain the effect those differences may have on others from the culture. For that reason, consult with someone from your intended reader's culture before writing a draft or preparing a presentation for an international audience. The reasons behind these differing attitudes are complex and have given rise to important studies because of their significance to international business. The following books are useful starting points for communicating with international audiences:

◆ For a fuller discussion of cultural differences, see Writing International Correspondence on pages 300–305 and, for presentations, see Reaching Global Audiences on pages 495–496.

- Andrews, Deborah C. *Technical Communication in the Global Community.* 2nd ed. Upper Saddle River, N.J.: Prentice-Hall, 2000.
- Scollon, Ron, and Suzanne Wong Scollon. *Intercultural Communications: A Discourse Approach.* 2nd ed. Cambridge, Mass.: Basil Blackwell, 2001.
- Varner, Iris, and Linda Beamer. *Intercultural Communication in the Global Workplace.* 3rd ed. New York: McGraw-Hill/Irwin, 2004.
- Victor, David A. *International Business Communication.* New York: HarperCollins, 1992.

ON THE WEB

Intercultural Press provides publications aimed at specific cultures and that cover a wide variety of subjects from cross-cultural theory to international business. For links to this and other resources for global communication, go to Chapter 3, **bedfordstmartins.com/writingthatworks**

Persuading Your Audience

Suppose you and a friend are arguing over whether the capital of Maine is Portland or Augusta. The issue is a simple question of fact that easily can be checked in an almanac or an atlas. (It's Augusta.) Now suppose you are trying to convince management at your company that it ought to adopt flexible working hours for its employees or to upgrade software to improve communications with its customers. A quick look in a reference book will not settle the issue. You will have to persuade management that your idea is a good one.

In all on-the-job writing, strive to keep your reader's needs, as well as your own, clearly in mind. Doing so is especially important in persuasive writing, in which your purpose may often be to ask your reader to change working procedures or habits. You may think that most people would automatically accept a recommendation for an improvement in the workplace, but people tend to resist change. Your proposed idea may be a threat to a staff member's pet project, or it may make the accumulated knowledge and experience of a veteran employee seem out of date. To overcome resistance, you'll have to establish the need for your recommendation and support it with convincing, objective evidence.

The memo in Figure 3–3 was written by an MIS (management information systems) administrator to persuade her staff to accept and participate in a change to a new computer system. Notice that not everything in this memo is presented in a positive light. Change brings disruption, and the writer acknowledges that fact.

For persuasive communications outside the company, you must take equal if not greater care in the way you present information. In the letter in Figure 3–4, the

ON THE WEB

To see a draft of a persuasive letter with a peer editor's suggestions, go to *Model Documents Gallery,* **bedfordstmartins.com/writingthatworks**

Memo

TO: Engineering Sales Staff
FROM: Bernadine Kovak, MIS Administrator   *BK*
DATE: April 7, 2006
SUBJECT: Plans for Changeover to NRT/R4 System

Writer's initials for printed memo

Background of problem

As you all know, our workload has jumped by 30 percent in the past month. It has increased because our customer base and resulting technical support services have grown dramatically. This growth is a result, in part, of our recent merger with Datacom.

Statement of problem

This growth has meant that we have all experienced the difficulty of providing our customers with up-to-date technical information when they need it. In the next few months, we anticipate that the workload will increase another 20 percent. Even a staff as experienced as ours cannot handle such a workload without help.

Statement of solution

To cope with that expansion, in the next month we will be installing the NRT/R4 mainframe and QCS enterprise software with Web-based applications and global sales and service network. The system will speed processing dramatically as well as give us access to all relevant companywide databases. It should enable us to access the information both we and our customers need.

Candid acknowledgment of disruption

The new system, unfortunately, will cause some disruption at first. We will need to transfer many of our existing programs and software applications to the new format. And all of us need to learn to navigate in the R4 and QCS environments. However, once we have made those adjustments, I believe we will welcome the changes.

Call for cooperation

I would like to put your knowledge and experience to work in getting the new system into operation. Let's meet in my office to discuss the improvements on Friday, April 14, at 1:00 p.m. I will have details of the plan to discuss with you. I'm also eager to get your comments, suggestions, and—most of all—your cooperation.

Figure 3–3   Persuasive Memo (sent on paper)

Commuter Aircraft Corporation
7328 Wellington Drive
Partridge, Ohio 45424

March 7, 2006

Adele Chu, Permissions Editor
Poet's Press, Inc.
One Plaza Way, Suite 3
Boston, MA 02116

Dear Ms. Chu:

Thank you for responding so quickly to my request for permission to reprint the poem "Flight" in the pilot's manual for our new Aerosoar 100 Commuter.

Complimentary and courteous opening

I am writing to express concern about the fee you have requested for the use of this selection. It is much higher than we expected. Because the manual is an instructional booklet distributed to pilots free of charge, the budget for this project is strictly limited, particularly for nontechnical, ancillary materials such as poetry. We continue to feel that the poem would interest and even inspire our readers, however, and we would like to ask you to consider lowering your fee to make this possible. To meet the demands of our budget, we are able to pay no more than $300 for each selection in the manual—considerably less than the $900 you have requested.

Statement of problem, its basis, and counteroffer

I hope you understand our position and that you will consider reducing your fee for the use of this material. Thank you for considering my request. I look forward to hearing from you.

Restatement of request and respectful closing

Sincerely,

J. T. Walters

J. T. Walters
Publications Manager

cc: Legal Department

(890) 321-1231
Fax (890) 321-5116
jtw@commair.com

commair.com

Figure 3–4   Persuasive Letter

writer is disappointed with the response to a request, but she attempts to persuade her audience to reconsider. Instead of responding with anger or sarcasm
("Your fee is highway robbery!"), the writer thanks the publisher and gets quickly
to the point: her concern for the high fee and her wish to have it reduced.
Throughout, her tone and language are courteous and respectful.

When writing to persuade your audience, do not overlook opposing points of
view. Most issues have more than one side, and you should acknowledge them, as
does the writer proposing a disruptive change in Figure 3–3. By including differing points of view, you gain several advantages. First, you can show that you are
honest enough to recognize opposite views when they exist. Second, you can
demonstrate the advantage of your viewpoint over those of others. Third, by anticipating and bringing up opposing views *before* your readers do, you may be able
to anticipate some or all of their objections.

Finally, use the appropriate medium for communicating with your audience.
As the writer of the memo in Figure 3–3 recognized, a brief e-mail message was
not the appropriate means to present her proposal. Her staff needed the formality and readability that a memo permits. As you plan your writing and prepare the
draft, consider how you want to package your finished communication.

Establishing Your Role and Voice as the Writer

Writers must also assume roles. As an on-the-job writer, for example, you may
need to assume the role of a teacher who guides the audience through the process
of learning a new task. In this case, you must do more than explain or persuade—
you must also anticipate your audience's reactions and growing understanding of
the subject. You must be alert to questions that readers might ask, such as "Why do
I need to read this document?" "How much time must I spend to learn this subject?" and "Where can I find a quick answer to my problem?" By anticipating that
the audience will ask such questions, you will be more likely to answer them in
your draft.

You may discover that an audience's interests do not always coincide with its
needs. Some audiences, for example, would prefer not to read your document at
all; however, they are interested in completing a task or solving a problem as
quickly as possible. You must demonstrate how your document links the audiences' interests with their need to read the document.

As you write the draft, consider which voice your audience should hear.
Should it be authoritative or friendly, formal or accessible, provocative or reassuring—or somewhere in between? Determine the voice you adopt by considering
what is appropriate to your specific purpose. The guidelines shown in Figure 3–5
are intended for respiratory-care therapists who assess patients to develop a plan
of care. The writer's voice is slightly formal (the guidance is in the imperative
mood) yet caring in tone, as befits the subject.

By contrast, newsletter readers may expect a voice that is fast-paced and re-
portorial. Consider the attention-getting approach used in the opening of an article in a professional association newsletter (Figure 3–6).

◆ *For more on persua-
sive writing, see pages
437–438 in Chapter 13,
Writing Proposals.*

◆ *For a description of
options available to
help you make this
decision, see Selecting
the Appropriate
Medium and Form
on pages 263–267
in Chapter 8, Under-
standing the Principles
of Business Communi-
cation.*

◆ *For guidance on
writing for users averse
to reading instructions,
see Chapter 12, Writing
Instructions.*

◆ *For guidance on
whether to use the first
or third person in your
writing, see pages
107–108 in Chapter 4,
Revising the Draft.*

RESPIRATORY-CARE PLAN

1. Let the patient know exactly what is being done.
2. Maintain a good rapport; answer questions the patient may ask to allay fear.
3. Maintain the privacy and dignity of the patient at all times.
4. Be prepared. A stethoscope, a watch with a sweep second hand or a stopwatch, and a pen are basic items essential to this process.
5. Document your findings as soon as time permits; otherwise, you may forget important points.

Authoritative voice instructs yet reassures

Figure 3–5   Formal Voice (in Medical Instructions)

OVERCOMING WRITER'S BLOCK

Um, er, I would have delivered this article earlier, perhaps even on time, but, er, you see, I had writer's block!

Has this ever happened to you? Hah! Of course it has. It happens when you're writing to your Aunt Hattie to thank her for the butterfly book she gave you for your birthday as easily as when you're writing a crucial report to your boss or looking for a different way of presenting a procedure. Nobody is immune; it happens to us all at various times. November's meeting . . . dealt with how three successful writers cope with this near universal problem. . . .

Source: *Capital Letter,* Society for Technical Communications (December 1999).

Conversational voice directly engages audience

Figure 3–6   Conversational Voice (in a Professional Association Newsletter)

 CONSIDERING AUDIENCE AND PURPOSE
Preparing to Write a Draft

When preparing to write a draft, ask yourself the following questions:

- What is my purpose in writing this document? What action do I want my readers to take after reading it?

- Who are my readers? Is there a secondary audience? What do my readers know and how do they feel about the subject I'm addressing or the idea I'm proposing?

- Does my audience include international clients or colleagues?

- Why do my readers need to read this document or e-mail message? (To perform a task? To obtain basic information? To investigate a problem? To make a decision?)

- How much information will my readers need to understand the subject or to be persuaded by my idea? What is the best way to clearly present this material?

- What objections might my readers have to the subject or proposed idea?

- What medium would be most appropriate? (E-mail? Memo?)

- What voice would best convey my message? (Authoritative? Friendly? Provocative? Reassuring?)

ETHICS NOTE

Keep in mind that the way you present your ideas is as important as the ideas themselves. Respect your audience's needs and feelings by applying some basic manners in your writing. Avoid sarcasm or any other hostile tone that will offend your audience. Also avoid exaggerating or being overly enthusiastic. Your audience may interpret such an attitude as insincere or presumptuous. Of course, you should not conceal genuine enthusiasm; just be careful not to overdo it.

■ Development Strategies

The following strategies for developing your ideas will help you to convey information and to present evidence persuasively:

- **Explaining a process:** tells how something works or how something happened
- **Describing information:** describes how something looks or is planned to look
- **Defining terms and concepts:** clarifies the meanings of ideas crucial to your topic
- **Explaining cause and effect:** explains why something happened

Although this section focuses on each method separately, the methods are often used in combination. For investigative and accident reports, for example, the writer must state exactly what happened (explaining a process), which may also require the writer to physically describe people, places, or equipment (describing information), and to explain language or ideas that the audience may not understand (defining terms and concepts). Finally, the writer must try to explain why the event or accident happened (explaining cause and effect). A skillful integration of these methods to present evidence will do much to convince your audience that your findings and recommendations are accurate and appropriate.

Explaining a Process

When you explain a process, you tell your audience how something works, happened, or is done. The process you explain might be an event that occurs in nature (the tidal pull of the moon), a function that requires human effort (conducting a marketing survey), or an activity in which people operate machinery to produce goods or services (automobile assembly-line production).

The explanation of a process is composed of steps and may also include illustrations that show the process from beginning to end. As in all on-the-job writing, you must aim your writing at a level appropriate to your audience's background and be as clear, accurate, and complete as possible. Beginners require more basic information and less technical vocabulary than do experienced workers.

In your opening paragraph, tell your audience why it is important for them to become familiar with the process you are explaining. Before you explain the steps necessary to form a corporation, for example, you could cite the tax savings that incorporation would permit. To give your audience a framework for the details that will follow, you might present a brief overview of the process. Finally, you might describe how the process works in relation to a larger whole of which it is a part. In explaining the air-brake system of a large dump truck, for example, you might note that the braking system is one part of the vehicle's air system, which also controls the throttle and transmission-shifting mechanisms.

A process explanation can be long or short, depending on how much detail is necessary. The passage in Figure 3–7 explains the process by which drinking water is purified. It provides essential background information in the context of a discussion of how drinking water may be contaminated as it is treated before distribution to homes. The information is intended for the average homeowner, but the vocabulary does assume an elementary familiarity with biological and chemical terms. The explanation is enhanced by a step-by-step illustration that complements the pattern of the writing by providing an overview image (first panel in Figure 3–8) and then three more-detailed drawings of the water-treatment process (remaining three panels of Figure 3–8).

DRINKING WATER TREATMENT PROCESS

After it has been transported from its source to a local water system, most surface water must be processed in a treatment plant before it can be used. Some groundwater, on the other hand, is considered chemically and biologically pure enough to pass directly from a well into the distribution system that carries it to the home. *Background to process*

Although there are innumerable variations, surface water is usually treated as follows: First, it enters a storage lagoon where a chemical, usually copper sulfate, is added to control algae growth. From there, water passes through one or more screens that remove large debris. Next, a coagulant, such as alum, is mixed into the water to encourage the settling of suspended particles. The water flows slowly through one or more sedimentation basins so that larger particles settle to the bottom and can be removed. Water then passes through a filtration basin partially filled with sand and gravel where yet more suspended particles are removed. (See "Drinking Water Treatment Process" illustration [Figure 3–8].) *Overview of steps in the process*

At that point in the process, the Safe Drinking Water Act has mandated an additional step for communities using surface water. . . . [W]ater is to be filtered through activated carbon to remove any microscopic organic material and chemicals that have escaped the other processes. Activated carbon is extremely porous—one pound of the material can have a surface area of one acre. This honeycomb of minute pores attracts and traps pollutants through a process called adsorption. . . . *Definition of key term*

The final stage of water treatment is disinfection, where an agent capable of killing most biological pathogens is added to the water. Until the chlorination process was developed, devastating epidemics—such as the outbreak of typhoid and cholera that took 90,000 lives in Chicago in 1885. . . . *Basis for importance of the process*

Figure 3–7   Explanation of a Process   *Source:* S. Coffel and K. Feiden, *Indoor Pollution* (1990). Reprinted by permission of Ballantine Books, a division of Random House, Inc.

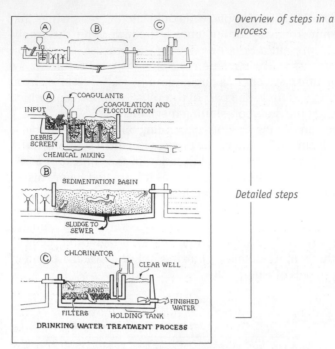

Overview of steps in a process

Detailed steps

Figure 3–8   Illustration for Explanation of a Process   *Source:* S. Coffel and K. Feiden, *Indoor Pollution* (1990). Reprinted by permission of Ballantine Books, a division of Random House, Inc.

Describing Information

When you give your audience information about an object's size, shape, construction, or other features of its appearance, you are describing it. The kinds of description you write will vary—engineers must describe products they design according to corporate specifications, marketing professionals must describe the products they are marketing to potential customers, software developers face the daunting task of describing something the audience cannot see, police must describe accident scenes, and so on. Your description may be of something concrete, such as a machine, or of something abstract, such as computer software. The key to writing an effective description is to accurately present details. To select appropriate details, determine what your audience will use the description for—to identify something? To assemble or repair the object being described?

When describing a physical object or system, give an overview before describing its parts in detail. Descriptions can be brief and simple, or they can be highly complex; they should always be clear and specific. Simple descriptions usually require only a listing of key features. A purchase order, shown in Figure 3–9, is a typical example of simple descriptive writing. Notice that even an order for something as ordinary as trash-compactor bags needs (in addition to the part number) four specific descriptive details to ensure accuracy.

Complex descriptions, of course, require more detail than simple ones. The details you select should accurately and vividly convey what you are describing. If

PURCHASE ORDER		
Part No.	Description	Quantity
GL/020	Trash-compactor bags, 31″ × 50″ tubular, nontransparent, 5-mil thickness, including 100 tie wraps per carton	5 cartons@ 100 per carton

Specifications for trash-compactor bags

Figure 3–9   Simple Description

it is useful for your audience to visualize an object, for instance, include details—such as color and shape—that appeal to the sense of sight. Sometimes, you may want to describe the physical characteristics of an object and at the same time itemize the parts that go into its makeup. To describe a piece of machinery, for example, you would probably find this approach, called the whole-to-parts method, the most useful for your purpose. You would first present a general description of the device as a frame of reference for the more specific details that follow—physical description of the various parts and the location and function of each in relation to the whole. The description would conclude with an explanation of how the parts work together.

Illustrations can be powerful aids in descriptive writing, especially when they show details too intricate to explain completely in words. Do not hesitate to use an illustration with a complex description if doing so creates a clearer image. Figure 3–10 describes a body harness and includes an illustration for occupational safety officials who must assess such devices as they seek ways to protect worker health and safety on the job. Figure 3–11 illustrates a storm-shutter installation that small businesses can use to protect windows from windborne debris damage. The illustration, with callouts highlighting important features, largely eliminates the need for extensive written details to describe their relationship to one another and their function.

◆ *For detailed instructions on the use of illustrations, see Chapter 7, Designing Effective Documents and Visuals.*

Defining Terms and Concepts

Accurate definitions are crucial to many kinds of writing, especially for an audience unfamiliar with your subject. Depending on your audience's needs, your definition can be formal, informal, or extended.

A *formal definition* places a term in a class of related objects or ideas and shows how it differs from other members of the same class. (An auction is a public sale in which property passes to the highest bidder through successive increased offers.) An *informal definition* uses a familiar word or phrase as a synonym for an unfamiliar word or phrase. (Plants live in a symbiotic, or mutually beneficial, relationship with certain kinds of bacteria.) Informal definitions permit you to explain the meaning of a term with a minimum of interruption in the flow of your writing.

Background safety information

Approximately 50 ironworkers fall to their deaths each year in the United States. The latest fall-protection system may change all this. The following illustration shows a system that protects ironworkers from falls without interfering with their work. This system complies with the Occupational Safety and Health Administration's strict fall-protection requirements.

Specific details of system components and operation

Known as the Beamwalker, the system consists of two stanchions that clamp to a standard I-beam. A 40-foot line, to which workers can attach their lifelines, runs between the stanchions. The Beamwalker is installed while the beam is on the ground.

The Beamwalker

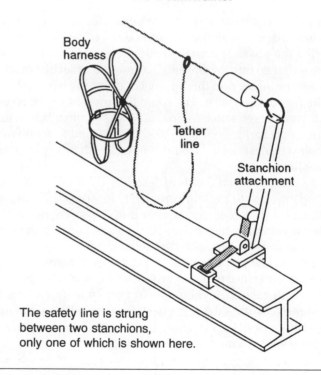

Subsystem detail

The safety line is strung between two stanchions, only one of which is shown here.

Figure 3–10   Illustration to Aid Description

When more than a phrase or a sentence is needed to explain an idea, use an *extended definition*, which explores a number of qualities of the item being defined. How an extended definition is developed depends on your readers' needs and on the complexity of the subject. Readers familiar with a topic might be able to handle a long, fairly complex definition, whereas readers less familiar with a topic might require simpler language and more basic information.

Perhaps the easiest way to define a term is to give specific examples of it. Listing examples gives readers easy-to-picture details that help them see and thus

Protect Windows and Doors

Protecting windows and doors is one of the most effective actions you can take to reduce your risk of wind damage. High winds and windborne debris can easily break unprotected windows and cause doors to fail. Once wind enters a building, the likelihood of severe structural damage increases, and the contents of the building will be exposed to the elements. The most reliable method of protecting windows and doors is installing permanent storm shutters. Alternatives include using temporary plywood covers, replacing existing glass with impact-resistant glass, and covering existing glass with a protective film.

Permanent storm shutters are usually made of aluminum or steel and are attached to a building in such a way that they can be closed quickly before a storm arrives. One type is the "rolldown" shutter (as shown here), which is contained in a housing mounted above the window and lowered when necessary. Manually operated and motor-operated models are available.

ROLLDOWN SHUTTER PERMANENTLY ATTACHED TO BUILDING

SHUTTER IS HELD BY GUIDE TRACKS ALONG SIDES OF WINDOW

SHUTTER IS SECURED BY LATCH AT BASE OF GUIDE TRACK

Description concentrates on the types of shutters available and their function

Illustration appears next to or immediately after the text that discusses it

Figure 3–11   Detailed Description (with Illustration)   *Source:* Federal Emergency Management Agency (<www.fema.gov>).

understand the term being defined. To clarify the abstract term *metadata,* the definition in Figure 3–12 provides specific examples of how metadata is used to identify subject matter at Web sites.

Another way to define a difficult concept, especially when you are writing for nonspecialists, is to use an analogy to link the unfamiliar concept with a simpler or more-familiar one. An analogy can help the reader understand an unfamiliar

Metadata. Literally, "data about data." Examples of metadata include the author's name, creation date, content category, content type, intended audience, and access control properties. Metadata can be used to generate automated content directories, drive dynamic behavior, and support site measurement

Figure 3–12   Extended Definition, Using Examples   *Source:* Gartner, Inc., *Dealing in Web Currency* (2001).

Management by objective has been quite popular, but it is important to remember that carefully selecting objectives is the key to successfully applying this principle. Think, for example, of a golfer who wishes to improve by hitting the ball farther. The golfer sets a goal of hitting every drive as far as possible. Every decision the golfer makes is governed by that goal—hitting the ball as far as possible. The golfer would then be managing his or her game by objective. However, the golfer is shortsighted because golf is as much a game of accuracy as it is of hitting balls for distance. Some of the decisions the golfer makes to hit the ball farther, therefore, might well be counterproductive to achieving the larger goal of obtaining the lowest possible score. In the same way, when a company decides to use a management-by-objective strategy, it must be certain that the objective is appropriate for achieving the desired results.

Figure 3–13   Extended Definition, Using Analogy

term by showing its similarities to a more familiar term. In Figure 3–13, the writer uses analogy to define *management by objective.*

Sometimes it is useful to point out what something is *not* to clarify what it *is.* A what-it-is-not definition is effective only when the reader is familiar with the item with which the defined item is contrasted. If you say *x* is not *y,* your audience must understand the meaning of *y* for the explanation to make sense. In a crane operator's manual, for instance, a "negative definition" is used to show that, for safety reasons, a hydraulic crane cannot be operated in the same manner as a lattice boom crane (Figure 3–14).

A hydraulic crane is not like a lattice boom crane [a friction machine] in one very important way. In most cases, the safe lifting capacity of a lattice boom crane is based on the weight needed to tip the machine. Therefore, operators of friction machines sometimes depend on signs that the machine might tip to warn them of impending danger. This practice is very dangerous with a hydraulic crane. . . .

Figure 3–14   Negative Definition   *Source: Operator's Manual* (Model W-180), Harnishfeger Corporation.

Explaining Cause and Effect

When your purpose is to explain why something happened, or why you think something will happen, cause-and-effect analysis is a useful writing strategy. For instance, if you were asked to report on why the accident rate for the company truck fleet rose by 30 percent, you would use cause-and-effect analysis to work from an effect (higher accident rate) to its cause (bad driving weather, inexperienced drivers, poor truck maintenance, and so on). If you were to report on the possible effects that switching to a four-day workweek (ten hours per day) would have on the office staff, you would also use cause-and-effect analysis—but this time you would start with cause (the new work schedule) and look for possible effects (changes in morale, in productivity, in absenteeism, and the like).

The goal of cause-and-effect analysis is to make as plausible as possible the relationship between a situation and either its cause or its effect. The conclusions you draw about the relationship should be based on the evidence you have gathered. Because not all facts and arguments will be of equal value to you as you draw conclusions, it's a good idea to keep the following guidelines in mind.

- *Evidence should be relevant to your topic.* Be careful not to draw a conclusion that your evidence does not lead to or support. You may have researched some statistics, for example, that show that an increasing number of Americans are licensed to fly small airplanes. You cannot use that information as evidence for a decrease in new car sales in the United States— the evidence does not lead to that conclusion.

- *Evidence should be adequate.* Incomplete evidence can lead to false conclusions. If, for example, you know two people who completed driver training classes but later crashed their cars, you do not have sufficient evidence to conclude that driver training classes do not help prevent automobile accidents. A thorough investigation of the usefulness of driver training classes in keeping down the accident rate would require more than one or two examples: It would also require a comparison of the driving records of those who had completed training with the driving records of those who had not.

- *Evidence should be representative.* If you conduct a survey to obtain your evidence, do not solicit responses only from individuals or groups whose views are identical to yours; be sure you obtain a representative sampling. A survey of backpackers in a national park on whether the park ought to be open to off-road vehicles would more than likely show them overwhelmingly against the idea. Such a survey should include opinions from more than one interested group.

- *Evidence should be demonstrable.* Two events that occur close to each other in time or place may or may not be causally related. For example, that new traffic signs were placed at an intersection and the next day an accident occurred does not necessarily prove that the signs caused the accident. You must demonstrate the relationship with pertinent facts and arguments.

To show a true relationship between a cause and an effect, you must demonstrate that the existence of the one *requires* the existence of the other. It is often difficult to establish beyond any doubt that one event was the cause of another event. More often, a result will have more than one cause. As you research your subject, your task is to determine which cause or causes are most plausible.

When several probable causes are equally valid, report your findings accordingly, as in Figure 3–15. The paragraph is an excerpt from an article on the use of a furnace-vent damper, an energy-saving device that can be dangerous if it fails to

> One damper was sold without proper installation instructions, and another was wired incorrectly. Two of the units had slow-opening dampers (15 seconds) that prevented the [furnace] burner from firing. And one damper jammed when exposed to a simulated fuel temperature of more than 700 degrees.

Figure 3–15   Paragraph Linking Cause and Effect   *Source:* Don DeBat, "Save Energy But Save Your Life, Too." *Family Safety.*

work properly. The investigator located more than one cause of damper malfunctions and reported on them. Without such a thorough account, recommendations to prevent similar malfunctions would be based on incomplete evidence.

■ Writing an Opening

As discussed earlier in this chapter, you do not need to begin your draft by writing the opening; however, understanding the purposes of an opening and the strategies for writing one can help you start the draft. The opening statement of your writing should (1) identify your subject, (2) provide any necessary context for the subject, and (3) catch the interest of your audience.

The title of your report or the subject line of the memo or e-mail message will announce the subject. The first paragraph of the opening should describe the context for why you are writing—the "story" behind the document. That is, what series of events led to your need to write: to answer a request for information, to recommend a new process to accomplish a goal, to propose that a new employee be hired, or to pass on information to someone.

◆ *For a discussion of assessing an audience's needs, see pages 6–8 in Chapter 1, Assessing Audience and Purpose.*

Most audiences of on-the-job writing are preoccupied with other business when they begin to read a memo, a letter, a report, or even an e-mail message. To catch your audience's interest, you first must know your audience's needs. An awareness of those needs will help you determine which details your audience will find important and thus interesting.

Consider the opening from a memo written by a human resources manager to her supervisor (Figure 3–16). This opening not only states the subject of the report (its context) but also promises that the writer will offer solutions to a specific problem. Solutions to problems are always of interest to audiences.

◆ *For examples of openings for special types of writing, such as application letters, complaint letters, and formal reports, refer to specific entries in the Index.*

For most types of writing done in offices, shops, and laboratories, openings that simply get to the point are more effective than those that provide detailed background information. Furthermore, the subject line of a memo or the title of a report is often, by itself, enough to catch the audience's interest. The openings in Figures 3–17 and 3–18 are typical; however, do not feel that you must slavishly follow these patterns. Rather, always first consider the purpose of your writing and the needs of your audience and then tailor your opening accordingly. Notice that these openings do not introduce irrelevant subjects or include unnecessary details. They give the audience exactly what they need to focus their attention on

Memo

To: Paul Route, Corporate Relations Director
From: Sondra L. Rivera, Human Resources Manager   *SLR*
Date: November 1, 2006
Subject: Decreasing Applications from Local College Graduates

This year, only 12 local college graduates have applied for jobs at Benson Tubular Steel. Last year, over 30 graduates applied, and the year before 50 applied. This decline in applications is occurring despite increasing enrollments at each school. After talking with several college counselors, I am confident that we can solve the problem of decreasing applications from local colleges.

First, we could resume our advertisements in local student newspapers. . . .

Concise statement of a problem sets the stage for a proposed solution

Figure 3–16   Opening of a Memo

PENROSE FIRST INVESTOR'S BANK
12 Powell Square
Penrose, Maine 04291
penrosefib.com

March 3, 2006
Mr. George Whittier
12 Nautical Dr.
Penrose, ME 04291

Dear Mr. Whittier:

You will be happy to know that we have corrected the error in your bank balance. The new balance shows . . .

Figure 3–17   Opening of a Letter

MEMO

To: David Diehl, Director of Athletics
From: Marylynn Scott, Project Engineer   *M.S.*
Subject: Progress Report on Rewiring the Sports Arena
Date: August 22, 2006

The rewiring program at the Sports Arena is continuing ahead of schedule. Although the cost of certain equipment is higher than our original bid had indicated, we expect to complete the project without exceeding our budget because the speed with which the project is being completed will save labor costs.

Work Completed

As of August 15, we have . . .

Opens with a prediction

Figure 3–18   Opening of a Progress Report

what is to follow. As direct as they are, they establish context by noting the background for the communication (an error was made, specimens were submitted for analysis, a rewiring program is underway).

■ Writing a Closing

A good closing is concise and ends your writing emphatically. It not only ties your points together but also may recommend a course of action, offer a value judgment, speculate on the implications of your ideas, make a prediction, or summarize your main points. Even if your closing only states, "If I can be of further help, please call me" or "I would appreciate your comments," you are showing consideration for your audience and thereby gaining goodwill.

The way you close depends on the purpose of your writing and the needs of your audience. For example, a committee report about possible locations for a new production facility might end with a recommendation that is realistic given the circumstances, a lengthy sales proposal might conclude persuasively with a summary of the proposal's salient points and the company's main strong points, or the closing of a company's annual report might offer a judgment about why sales are up or down. A report for a retail department store about consumer buying trends could end by speculating on the implications of these trends, perhaps even suggesting new product lines that the store might carry in the future. Figures 3–19 and 3–20 illustrate typical closings.

Although my original estimate on equipment ($20,000) has been ex-ceeded by $2,300, my original labor estimate ($60,000) has been re-duced by $3,500. Therefore, I will easily stay within the limits of my original bid. In addition, I see no difficulty in having the arena finished in time for the December 23 Christmas program.

Ends with a summary of costs and a final prediction

Figure 3–19   Closing of a Progress Report

However you close, be careful not to resort to a cliché or a platitude, such as "While profits have increased with the introduction of this new product, the proof of the pudding is in the eating" or "Please feel free to contact us at your earliest convenience," when the contents don't call for a response of any kind. Also be careful not to introduce a new topic in your closing. A closing should always relate to and reinforce the ideas presented in the opening and body of your writing.

I recommend that ABO, Inc., participate in the corporate membership program at Aero Fitness Clubs, Inc., by subsidizing employee memberships. Implementing this program will help ABO, Inc., reduce its health-care costs while building stronger employee relations by offering employees a desirable benefit. If this proposal is adopted, I have some additional thoughts about publicizing the program to encour-age employee participation. I look forward to discussing the details of this proposal with you and answering any questions you may have.

Ends with a recom-mendation and an offer to discuss the proposal in more detail

Figure 3–20   Closing of a Company Internal Proposal

■ Case Study: Drafting the Lifemaker Brochure

The techniques for drafting discussed in this chapter can be applied to any kind of workplace document. Figure 3–21 shows the rough draft of a sales brochure meant to persuade consumers to purchase the Lifemaker home gym. It follows the gist of the writer's initial outline and uses many of the drafting skills and develop-ment strategies discussed in this chapter.

◆ *For an outline of this brochure, see Figure 2–2, page 34.*

The draft is quite rough—loosely organized, lacking in transitions and punc-tuation, ungrammatical, inconsistent in upper- and lowercase letters and point of view, and cluttered with jargon and unnecessary phrases. Still, as drafts go, this one reflects a strong start for the writer. Not only has she followed the basic or-ganization of her outline, but she has managed also to work through so-called writer's blocks and to jot down the new idea of emphasizing financial incentives.

◆ *For a marked-up ver-sion of a later draft of this memo, along with the final version, see Figures 4–2 and 4–3, pages 119–120.*

LIFEMAKER: The Compact Exercise System You Can Afford

DRAFT

Tentative cause-and-effect linkage

For opening—say something about how owning a Lifemaker will give you healthy bones and teeth, straighten your hair, improve your love life . . . no . . . Whether you are young or young at heart, male or female, developing well-conditioned muscles will help your body perform better, look better, and help you maintain an ideal level of fitness (Needs work!! Keep going, go back to it later. Get to the muscle of the matter.)

Tentative description of system compared with competitors' systems

(*Description*) The Lifemaker design more compact than leading competitor's, eliminates hassle and expense of going to health club to work out. The Lifemaker fits easily into small space—4 × 7 ft living room can accommodate the Lifemaker with more ease than many home gym systems, offers more stations and more exercises because of its multiple stations. What's the point I'm making? More compact than many fancy systems, offers 40+ exercises, more than most systems priced at a comparable level—comparably priced and sized systems. OK OK, don't compromise your exercise needs with an overpriced or ineffective system. The integration of an exercise program to suit your lifestyle and budget is possible with Lifemaker.

(I'm writing all over the place and I sound like I'm making a coronation speech—don't pick, THINK. Headings, use headings you used in outline.)

Cast-Iron Weight Stack

Physical description

Dual weight stacks total 200 pounds of cast-iron plates. You can arrange stacks to offer a resistance range of 10 to 150 pounds and they are adjustable in 10-pound increments.

Adjustable Cables

Combined process and physical description

Resistance can be increased—no—The unique cable system is engineered to increase resistance at the stations that work the strongest muscle groups. The cables can quickly be redesigned—restructured—reconfigured without taking apart the entire system. Just pulling the center rod permits adding or removing as many plates as needed.

Process description

The cable tension is also adjustable within sets to make sure that your muscles get the most resistance from each exercise for maximum efficiency and results.

(*Closing*) Heading? Low Maintenance—Easily Affordable

Best of all, no it's not best of all, think later about transition. . . . The Lifemaker is easy to assemble and requires little maintenance. And at $999.99, it is priced lower than the leading competitor.

Need to emphasize financial perks—mention low-interest monthly payment plan. Lifemaker will fit your back and your budget.

Figure 3–21   Draft of a Sales Brochure (with Writer's Notes)

She can now go on to write a second draft, develop an opening and closing that will help her tighten her focus, and then revise the entire document by using the techniques covered in Chapter 4, Revising the Draft.

CHAPTER 3 SUMMARY: WRITING THE DRAFT

Gathering the details you need (see Chapter 1) and grouping them in an outline (see Chapter 2) will enable you to write a good rough draft. When writing the draft, remember that your task is to produce only a working document, not a polished piece of writing. Polish will come with revision (see Chapter 4). Use the following guidelines as you write the draft:

- Concentrate solely on getting your draft written.
- Do not confuse writing with revising; they are different tasks, and each requires a different frame of mind.
- Avoid revising as you write—do not worry about perfection at this point in the writing process. Focus on *what* you are writing, not on *how* you are writing.
- Allocate your time efficiently.
- Prepare a comfortable work environment.
- Sustain momentum once you begin writing.
- Take brief breaks after reaching milestones.
- Keep your intended readers actively in mind, visualizing them if possible, and address your topic from their point of view.
- Consider the voice your readers should hear—concerned, neutral, and authoritative.
- Be persuasive:
  - Take your readers' feelings into account.
  - Appeal to your readers' good sense.
  - Acknowledge other points of view where an issue is controversial.

Consider the following kinds of writing:

- Explain a process:
  - Introduce the process with information about its purpose and significance.
  - Divide the process into steps.
  - Present each step in its proper sequence.
  - Illustrate steps and procedures when this aids clarity.
  - Present the information at a level appropriate to your readers' background.
  - Write concisely.
- Describe information:
  - Select details carefully, based on what use your readers will make of the description.
  - Provide a brief explanation of the function of any physical objects you describe, such as equipment.
  - Do not overwhelm your readers with unnecessary details.
  - Include illustrations where they add clarity.
- Define terms and concepts.
- Explain cause and effect:
  - Establish a plausible relationship between an event and its cause.

- Evaluate evidence for the relationship carefully:
  - Is it pertinent?
  - Is it sufficient?
  - Is it representative?
  - Is it plausible?
- Do not overstate conclusions.

■ Write an opening that identifies your subject to focus your readers' attention.

■ Get to the point first, even when providing essential background information in the opening.

■ Create closings that reinforce, summarize, or tie together the ideas in the body of your writing.

■ Do not introduce ideas in the closing that have not been discussed elsewhere in your writing.

ON THE WEB

For an online quiz on drafting, go to Chapter 3, bedfordstmartins.com/writingthatworks

ON THE WEB

For a detailed freewriting assignment, go to Chapter 3, bedfordstmartins.com/writingthatworks

■ Exercises

1. Write an opening paragraph for two of the following purposes and the audiences specified.

   - The instructor from whom I learned the most (for a letter nominating him or her for a teaching award)
   - Ways to improve employee participation in a blood donation (or similar) program (to the president or head of the organization that employs you)
   - Ways to improve student use of the career counseling office at your school (to the dean of students or someone in an equivalent position)
   - What to look for in housing in your area (for a guide for transferred employees)
   - Important features to consider when purchasing a new automobile, cellular phone, or personal computer (for a consumer guide)
   - The advantages of setting up a budget or checking account on a personal computer (for an informational handout at a senior center or for students seeking help at your college mentoring center)

2. Building on Exercise 1, write a closing for the same topics and audiences.

3. Using the Lifemaker compact exercise system as your topic (see Figure 3–21), write three different opening paragraphs for a Lifemaker System 40 sales brochure geared toward each of the following audiences (one paragraph for each):

   - college students
   - retired persons
   - industry executives

4. Building on Exercise 3, write three different closing paragraphs for a Lifemaker System 40 sales brochure geared toward each of the following audiences (one paragraph for each):

   - college students
   - retired persons
   - industry executives

5. Summarize in a list all of the differences you had to be aware of when writing for different audiences and for different purposes in Exercises 3 and 4 (for example, time constraints, mobility constraints, and so forth).

6. Write a letter to a high school guidance counselor who wants to inform students about your chosen course of study. With your audience and purpose in mind, draft a letter that includes an effective opening, specifies important elements of the program and other relevant details in the body, and uses an appropriate closing. Use correct business-letter format when preparing your letter. For guidelines on format, see Chapter 8, Understanding the Principles of Business Communication.

7. Assume that the administration of your college or university is contemplating creating a learning center that will offer math and English tutoring. To implement this program, offices will need to be created from classroom space, tutors will need to be paid from the Student Services program, and a director will need to be hired. Reaction to this center is mixed. As the president of a student organization, you have been asked to write a letter to the administration about your organization's position on the creation of the center.

   a. Make a list of several possible points of view on this center. (Consider, for example, the perspectives of the admissions office, computing services, maintenance, faculty, and students.) Realize that different audiences may share both supportive and unsupportive views on the same topic for different reasons.

   b. Based on the points of view you have listed, draft an outline of a letter that supports creating the center, supports it with conditions, or opposes it.

   c. Write a letter to the administration, explaining your organization's point of view on the creation of the learning center. Be sure you have addressed the potential multiple points of view in your letter. If you are for the center, offer strategies to address the concerns of those who are unsupportive; if you are against the center, address the concerns of those who believe such a center is needed.

■ Collaborative Classroom Projects

ON THE WEB

For more collaborative classroom projects, go to Chapter 3, bedfordstmartins.com/ writingthatworks

1. Building on Exercise 7, form a small group and read each other's letters. Choose a spokesperson from your group to contact the director of your school's real learning center (if your school has one) for an interview. Select two or three people from your group to interview this person about the creation of the center. Ask questions about the many points of view and concerns that had to be addressed regarding funding, staffing, location, and so on. You can also interview faculty and staff about their experiences related to the creation of the center. (You should read the section on interviewing in Chapter 6, Researching Your Subject, first.) Are there similarities between your letters in Exercise 7 and what happened in the creation of a real center? If your school does not have a learning center, interview someone in administration about creating one. What concerns does the administration have about such a project? In either case, write a memo to the class about your group's findings.

2. Bring to class an advertisement from a magazine for a personal computer, a cellular phone, a fax machine, or a similar item. Create an outline and then draft a brief

narrative describing the product and its technology to a person who knows nothing about this product. Or, draft a letter or memo aimed at a particular type of consumer whom you would like to persuade to purchase this product. Begin by assessing your audience and creating a brief outline.

3. In small groups, design a draft of a brochure that helps volunteer relief workers put together a personal supplies kit. (You might refer to Chapter 7, Designing Effective Documents and Visuals.) This brochure should detail items they should bring with them when they travel to the site of an earthquake, hurricane, or similar natural disaster—for example, alcohol-based hand sanitizer, toilet paper, sunblock, insect repellent, soap, shampoo, lightweight clothing, boots, rain gear, rubber gloves, flashlights, and a cell phone. What kinds of clip art or photos would you use to represent different categories of supplies? Be ready to share your ideas with the class.

ON THE WEB

For extra research projects, go to Chapter 3, bedfordstmartins.com/ writingthatworks

■ Research Projects

1. Assume that the brochure that you prepared for Collaborative Classroom Project 3 created a surge of interest in the fields of relief work, outdoor rescue, and survival skills. Research businesses that offer courses and products related to wilderness medicine. Based on your findings, write a rough draft of an informal report for a local volunteer group. (For guidance, see Chapter 10, Writing Informal Reports.) Be sure to define what wilderness medicine is, what kinds of courses are offered, and whether there are certifications or degrees in the field. Also, describe what kind of products these companies sell for rescue work. Support your findings with examples. Be sure to locate and discuss information that is supportive as well as critical of the field, schools, and products.

2. Research a business or technological advancement that you are curious about. Narrow your topic to one particular aspect of that field and write an informal report entitled "Recent Breakthroughs in _____ [a particular field]: _____ [specific breakthrough]." (Again, for guidance, see Chapter 10, Writing Informal Reports.) Analyze the topic and support your analysis with information that you've researched. For example, if you decided to write about a new medical procedure, your analysis might be that the risks do or do not outweigh the benefits; you would then support your opinion with the findings that persuaded you.

   a. Submit a four- to five-page draft with an outline to your instructor.
   b. Meet with your instructor to discuss his or her suggestions for revision.
   c. Conduct further research if necessary.
   d. Write a second draft.

ON THE WEB

For more Web projects, go to Chapter 3, bedfordstmartins.com/ writingthatworks

■ Web Projects

1. Locate at least three companies on the Web that hire business or technical writers. For example, what companies in the area of medicine, technology, or environmental engineering hire writers? What kinds of documents or other materials do writers for these companies produce? (Search the companies' Web sites for docu-

ments produced by their professional writers.) How would the information covered in Chapter 3 apply to the writing required by these companies? Prepare a brief draft of your reply.

2. Many companies have offices overseas and need to prepare their employees for traveling and living abroad. Imagine that you are in charge of an orientation program for several employees who will be going on tours of major cities in Africa, the Near East, East Asia and the Pacific, or South Asia. Outline and draft a memo that will begin with general information on traveling overseas, followed by specific advice on traveling to one of these regions. After you conduct your research, you will need to decide how to organize the information for each major category.

a. Begin by researching general information on traveling overseas, such as visa and passport requirements, immunizations, and security issues. (Two good sources of information for Americans traveling overseas are the U.S. State Department and the Centers for Disease Control and Prevention (CDC); see <www.state.gov/travel/> and <www.cdc.gov/travel/>.) Make a list of topics you'll want to address in the general travel information section of your memo. Put these in your outline.

b. Pick three to five countries that you imagine employees will visit, and research the major cities in each. (The U.S. State Department has links to information about these four regions at <www.state.gov/r/pa/ei/bgn/>; another good source is the Library of Congress's Country Studies page at <http://lcweb2.loc.gov/frd/cs/cshome.html>.) Make a list of topics to address and put them in your outline.

c. Following your outline, draft a memo to the employees who will be traveling to one of the regions. Refer to the Writing a Rough Draft checklist on page 67–68 as needed.

d. Have your classmates peer-review your draft. Make necessary changes and present your outline, drafting strategies, and travel information to the class.

4 Revising the Draft

AT A GLANCE: Revision

Have you ever found after writing a first draft that you knew you could do better, but you did not know how to improve it? If your answer is yes, you are not alone. All writers—including professional writers—have the same problem at some time or another. This chapter introduces the elements essential to effective revision, such as:

- Ensuring that the scope of coverage is adequate / 96
- Improving organization / 96
- Unifying, linking, and highlighting ideas / 98
- Ensuring that the language throughout is precise, concise, unbiased, and free of affectation / 108
- Editing and proofreading your draft / 115
- Checking your draft for appropriate physical appearance / 116

One of the enduring legends of American history is that President Abraham Lincoln wrote the Gettysburg Address as he made the train trip from Washington, D.C., to Gettysburg, Pennsylvania. The address is a remarkable accomplishment, even for a writer as gifted as Lincoln. It is the eloquent testimony of a leader with a powerful intellect and a compassionate heart.

The facts of how the Gettysburg Address was composed do not support the legend, however. Lincoln actually worked on the address for weeks and revised the draft many times.[1] What Lincoln was doing on the train to Gettysburg was nothing more than what any of us must do before our writing is finally acceptable: He was revising. What is remarkable about the address is that Lincoln made so many revisions of a speech of well under 300 words. Obviously, he wanted it to fit the occasion for which it was intended, and he knew that something written hastily and without reflection would not satisfy his purpose and audience.

This principle is as true for anyone who writes on the job (which, of course, is what the president was doing) as it was for Lincoln. Unlike the Gettysburg Address, however, most on-the-job writing should not strive for oratorical elegance; the more natural a piece of writing sounds to the audience, the more effort the writer has probably put into revising it.

---

[1]Tom Burnam, *The Dictionary of Misinformation* (New York: Perennial Library, 1986), pp. 93–94.

Voices from the Workplace

Claire Harrison, Claire Harrison Communication Services

Claire Harrison provides corporate communication services to clients in government and business. Her expertise lies in writing reports, speeches, public-relations pieces, and more. "Most projects require three drafts," Claire says. "The first draft should never be 'rough.' It is the best I can do with the material the client gives me. This draft organizes the information in a coherent, logical way and sets a style suitable for the audience." She revises after the client makes changes. "I address style issues in the second draft. I aim for conciseness, smooth flow, and ways to make the text more interesting to readers. I like to create snappy headers and vary text rhythm by mixing paragraphs with bulleted lists." Claire uses the third draft to polish the piece, making only minor word and style changes and doing "a careful proofreading to ensure consistency in formatting, spelling, and punctuation."

Steven K. Hurd, U.S. Department of Veterans Affairs

Steven Hurd is the chief of voluntary services at the U.S. Department of Veterans Affairs in Togus, Maine. As a liaison between hospital administrators, volunteers, donors, and sometimes the veterans themselves, he says that written communication is a vital part of his job. Policy circulars, letters, speeches, and proposals are just a few of the documents Steven creates on a regular basis. "It's challenging to meet the needs of such a diverse audience, "he says. "I often have to write multiple drafts, depending on the intended reader. Sometimes we have drafts reviewed by people in the field who will give us smart, honest feedback. When writing to a potential donor in particular, I have to choose my tone and words carefully. It has to be just right because the hospital depends on volunteers and donations."

Revising requires a different frame of mind than does writing the draft. Immediately after you write a rough draft, ideas are so fresh in your mind that you cannot read the words, sentences, and paragraphs objectively. You must detach yourself from them to be able to look at the writing critically. Do not allow yourself to think, "Because my ideas are good, the way I've expressed them must also be good." The first step of revision is to develop a critical frame of mind—to become objective.

During revision, be eager to find and correct faults and be honest. Be hard on yourself for the benefit of your readers. Read and evaluate the draft as if you were a reader seeing it for the first time. Experiment to discover your own methods of becoming objective. One writer, for example, finds that she can be more critical if she writes her first draft on yellow paper. Another creates his first draft on a computer because he cannot be critical when looking at his own handwriting. Some people like to revise with a felt-tip pen; others prefer using colored pencils. The particular methods that work for you are not important. What is important is that you develop an effective technique for evaluating your writing—and then use it as the basis of your revision.

ON THE WEB
For online resources for revising, go to Chapter 4, bedfordstmartins.com/ writingthatworks

WRITER'S CHECKLIST
Revision Strategies

☑ Allow for a cooling period. Wait a day or two (or even a few hours) between writing a rough draft and revising it—you will be able to look at the writing itself more objectively.

☑ Pretend that a stranger has written your draft. This will help you to see the faults of the draft. If you can look at your writing and ask, "How could I have written that?" you are in the right frame of mind to revise.

☑ Revise your draft in multiple passes. Don't try to improve everything all at once. Concentrate first on larger issues, such as content and coherence; then turn to improving emphasis and polishing your language. Save mechanical corrections, like spelling and punctuation, for later proofreading.

☑ Be alert for your most frequent problems. Be sure that you are aware of the errors you typically make, and watch for them as you revise.

☑ Read your draft aloud. Listening to sentences aloud often enables you to detect flawed word order or other problems.

☑ Ask someone else to read and critique your draft. Someone unfamiliar with your draft can see it objectively and identify problems that you need to address as you revise.

■ Content and Organization

Once you have put yourself in a frame of mind to view your work objectively, what should you look for? Begin with the whole-text tasks that involve your purpose and organization. Then in separate passes look for the accuracy of your content. Do you need to add content to bolster meaning or delete redundant information? Are your recommendations adequately supported by your conclusions? Ensure, too, that topics mentioned in the introduction are not left out of the summary or conclusion.

The easiest way to test the soundness of your organization is to write an outline of your rough draft—a technique most useful for longer drafts but helpful with smaller ones, too. The advantage of outlining is that it breaks down blocks of text to essential ideas and makes the sequence of points easy to evaluate; it enables you to experiment with sequences and to lay out the most direct route to achieving your purpose. Does the outline of your draft conform to your planning outline? It may not because you probably rethought some ideas or added or deleted information as you wrote. If you find a problem with the logic of the sequence or with the amount or type of information included or omitted, revise the outline—and then your draft—to reflect the solution.

In revising your draft for completeness, you may also think of new information that you failed to include when you were preparing and writing your outline. This is the time to insert any missing facts or ideas. Always carefully consider such new information in the context of your audience and purpose. If the information will help satisfy your audience's need and accomplish the purpose of your writing, by all means add it now. However, if the information—no matter how interesting—does not serve these ends, it has no place in your writing.

WRITER'S CHECKLIST
Revising for Ethical Considerations

On the job, ethical dilemmas do not always present themselves as clear-cut choices. To help avoid ethical problems in your writing, ask the following questions as you complete your revision:

☑ Is the communication honest and truthful?

☑ Am I ethically consistent in my communication?

☑ Am I acting in the best interest of my employer? The public? Myself?

☑ What would happen if everybody acted or communicated in this way?

☑ Does the action or communication violate anyone's rights?

☑ Am I willing to take responsibility for the communication, publicly and privately?

Above all, keep in mind that your language choices and their ethical implications are important—they influence how the audience perceives your ethical stance *and* your employer's integrity.

A review of the relevant information in Chapters 1, 2, and 3 will be especially helpful as you reassess the effectiveness of your draft when it comes to these larger issues. Review in Chapter 1, Assessing Audience and Purpose, the sections titled Establishing Your Scope (page 10) and Organizing Your Ideas (page 12). Further evaluate the logic of your organization by reviewing the material in Chapter 2, Organizing Your Information, on outlining (pages 27–35). See Chapter 3, Writing the Draft, for guidance on ensuring that you address the right audience in the right voice (pages 68, 74). Once you complete this review, you are ready to tackle the smaller, more-detailed steps of the process described in the remainder of this chapter.

ESL TIPS   Supporting an Argument

- Remember that your goal is to persuade your audience—and that most American readers expect arguments to be backed up with concrete evidence, not general analogies or traditional wisdom.

- Support arguments, opinions, recommendations, and conclusions with specific facts and examples.

- Be direct and straightforward, rather than subtle or circuitous.

WRITER'S CHECKLIST
Evaluating Your Draft

☑ Is the purpose of the document clear?

☑ Is the information organized in the most effective sequence?

☑ Does each section follow logically from the one that precedes it?

☑ Is the scope of coverage adequate? Is there too little or too much information?

(continued)

WRITER'S CHECKLIST (continued)

☑   Are all the facts, details, and examples relevant to the stated purpose?

☑   Is the draft written at the appropriate level for the reader?

☑   Are the main points obvious? Are subordinate points related to main points?

☑   Are contradictory statements resolved or eliminated?

☑   Do the descriptions and illustrations aid clarity? Are there enough of them?

☑   Are any recommendations adequately supported by the conclusions?

☑   Are any topics mentioned in the introduction and text also addressed in the conclusions?

■ Coherence

Writing is coherent when the relationship between ideas is clear to your audience. Each idea should relate clearly to the others, with one idea flowing smoothly to the next. Coherence must be tested after writing. As you revise, ask "Can my reader move from this sentence or from this paragraph to the next without feeling a break in meaning?"

The basic building blocks of a coherent draft are paragraphs. Effective paragraphs must be unified around a central idea so that every sentence is related to the idea stated in the topic sentence. Paragraphs must also be coherent, with all ideas arranged in a logical order, and with transitional devices linking sentences and paragraphs throughout the draft so that the audience can follow your reasoning from sentence to sentence and from paragraph to paragraph.

Paragraph Unity

When every sentence in a paragraph contributes to developing one central idea, the paragraph has unity. If a paragraph contains sentences that do not develop the central idea, it lacks unity.

The most effective way to make sure that your paragraph has unity is to provide a topic sentence that clearly states the central idea of that paragraph and double-check that every sentence directly relates to the topic sentence.

Consider the following example, from a report evaluating possible locations for a company's new distribution center:

▶   Probably the greatest advantage of Chicago as the location for our new distribution center is its excellent transportation facilities. The city is served by three major railroads. In fact, Chicago was at one time the hub of cross-country rail transportation. Chicago is also a major center of the trucking industry, and most of the nation's large freight carriers have terminals there. We are concerned, however, about the delivery problems that we've had with several truck carriers. We've had far fewer problems with air freight. Both domestic and international air cargo services are available at O'Hare International Airport. Finally, except in the winter months when the Great Lakes are frozen, Chicago is a seaport, accessible through the St. Lawrence Seaway.

Although the paragraph opens with a clearly stated topic sentence, every sentence should have been about the advantages of Chicago's transportation facilities. Three sentences do not develop that central idea: The sentence about Chicago as the former hub of railroad transportation, although historically accurate, is not relevant to the company's assessment; the two sentences about the relative merits of truck and air carrier delivery are not relevant here. Stripped of these sentences, the paragraph becomes unified:

▶   Probably the greatest advantage of Chicago as the location for our new distribution
    center is its excellent transportation facilities. The city is served by three major rail-
    roads. Chicago is also a major center of the trucking industry, and most of the nation's
    large freight carriers have terminals there. Both domestic and international air cargo
    services are available at O'Hare International Airport. Finally, except in the winter
    months when the Great Lakes are frozen, Chicago is a seaport, accessible through the
    St. Lawrence Seaway.

For workplace writing, it's best to place a topic sentence at the beginning of a paragraph. With this placement, the writer can more easily construct a unified paragraph because every sentence supports the topic sentence and the central idea it expresses. The reader knows immediately what the paragraph is about because the opening sentence states the central idea.

A paragraph should be just long enough to deal adequately with the central idea stated in its topic sentence. Begin a new paragraph whenever you change the subject significantly. Keep in mind that long paragraphs can intimidate your reader by failing to provide manageable subdivisions of thought. Overly short paragraphs have a disadvantage, too: They may make it difficult to adequately develop the point stated in the topic sentence. A series of short paragraphs can also sacrifice unity by breaking a single idea into several pieces.

Transitions

Effective paragraphs take the reader logically from one idea to the next. Providing transitions will help you achieve a smooth flow of ideas from sentence to sentence, paragraph to paragraph, and subject to subject. Transition is a two-way indicator of what you have said and what you are about to say; it provides readers with guideposts for linking ideas and clarifying the relationship between them.

Transitions between Sentences

Within a paragraph, transitional expressions clarify and smooth the movement from idea to idea. The words and phrases in Table 4–1 commonly function as transitional devices. Some transitional words and phrases in this table are nearly synonymous but imply somewhat different logical connections. Be sure that the transitional words and phrases you choose convey the precise meaning you intend.

You can achieve effective transitions between sentences by repeating key-words or key ideas from preceding sentences and by using pronouns that refer to

Table 4–1   Common Transitions

To add information

also	besides	moreover	furthermore
in addition	finally	next	additionally
first, second, etc.	last		

To give an example or to illustrate a point

for example	for instance	to illustrate	specifically
in particular	in this case	to demonstrate	notably

To compare or contrast

on the other hand	on the contrary	likewise	however
although	similarly	nevertheless	meanwhile
whereas			

To prove

because	moreover	furthermore	besides

To show time

initially	eventually	during	thereafter
finally	then	later	previously
formerly	first, second, etc.	next	afterward
at last	before	at the same time	currently

To show sequence

next	now	finally	simultaneously
first, second, etc.	after	consequently	concurrently
thus	therefore		

To conclude

in conclusion	therefore	thus	as a result
finally	all in all		

Conjunctions

and	or	nor	so
yet	for	but	

antecedents in previous sentences. Consider the following short paragraph, which uses both of those means:

▶   Over the past several months, I have heard complaints about the Merit Award *Program*. Specifically, many employees feel that this *program* should be linked to annual *salary increases*. They believe that *salary increases* would provide a much better incentive than the current $1,000 and $1,500 *cash awards* for exceptional service. In addition, these *employees* believe that their supervisors consider the *cash awards* a satisfactory alternative to *salary increases*. Although I don't think this practice is widespread, the fact that the *employees* believe that it is justifies a reevaluation of the Merit Award *Program*.

Transitions between Paragraphs

Transitional devices between paragraphs serve the same function as they do between sentences: They signal the relationship of one to the other. For paragraphs, however, longer transitional elements are often necessary. One technique is to begin a new paragraph with a sentence that summarizes the preceding paragraph, as in the following excerpt from an environmental report:

▶   Each year, forest fires in our region cause untold destruction. For example, wood ashes washed into streams after a fire often kill large numbers of fish. In addition, the destruction of the vegetation along stream banks causes water temperatures to rise, making the streams unfit for several varieties of cold-water fish. Forest fires, more-over, hurt the tourist and recreation business because vacationers are not likely to visit flame-blackened areas.

      These losses, and many other indirect losses caused by forest fires, damage not only the quality of life but also the economy of our region. They also represent a huge drain on the resources and personnel of the Department of Natural Resources. For ex-ample, our financial investment last year in fighting forest fires . . .

If used sparingly, another effective transitional device between paragraphs is to ask a question at the end of one paragraph and answer it at the beginning of the next.

▶   New technology has always been feared because it has at times displaced some jobs. However, it invariably creates many more jobs than it eliminates. Almost always, the jobs eliminated by technological advances have been menial, unskilled jobs, and workers who have been displaced have been forced to increase their skills, which resulted in better and higher-paying jobs for them. *In view of these facts, is new technology really bad?*

      Certainly technology has given us unparalled access to information and created many new roles for employees. . . .

When you use this transitional device, make sure that the second paragraph does, in fact, answer the question posed in the first.

WRITER'S CHECKLIST
Creating Effective Paragraphs

☑   Unify the paragraph around a central idea.

☑   Ensure that every sentence relates to the topic sentence.

☑   Arrange ideas (and sentences) in a logical order.

☑   Use transitions to help readers follow the sequence of your ideas.

◾ Emphasis

Effective writing is emphatic writing—it highlights the facts and ideas that the writer considers most important and subordinates those of less importance. By fo-cusing the reader's attention on key elements, emphatic writing enables the reader to determine how one fact or idea in a sentence is related to another. You can achieve emphasis by using any number of the techniques described in this section.

Active and Passive Voice

A sentence is in the active voice if the subject of the sentence acts; it is in the passive voice if the subject is acted on.

ACTIVE   Rajesh Patel prepared the design for the new pump.
                           [The subject— *Rajesh Patel*—acts on *the design*—the direct object.]

PASSIVE   The design for the new pump was prepared by Rajesh Patel.
                           [The subject— *the design*—receives the action.]

In business writing, it is often important to emphasize who or what performs an action. Because the active voice is generally more direct, more concise, and easier for readers to understand, use the active voice unless the passive voice is more appropriate. Using the active voice allows your audience to move quickly and easily from the actor (the subject) to the action performed (the verb) to the receiver of the action (the direct object).

The passive voice can be useful, too. For example, when the doer of the action is less important than the receiver of the action, the writer can emphasize the receiver by making it the subject of the sentence.

EFFECTIVE PASSIVE   Sharon Gleason was appointed chief pathologist of Pine Cone
                      County Hospital by the hospital's board of directors.

The important person in this sentence is Sharon Gleason, not the board of directors who made the appointment. To give her—the receiver of the action—the needed emphasis, the sentence makes sense in the passive voice. The same principle holds true in the sciences for situations where the data are more important than the scientist collecting that data. Laboratory or test reports are good examples of the proper use of the passive voice.

EFFECTIVE PASSIVE   The test was conducted to identify the soil pH levels at the site.

Finally, the passive voice is also useful when the performer of the action either is not known or is not important.

EFFECTIVE PASSIVE   The wheel was invented thousands of years ago.
                      [Who invented it is not known.]

As you revise, select the voice, active (usually) or passive (occasionally), appropriate to your purpose and topic.

Subordination

First drafts are often plagued by an overabundance of short, staccato sentences. Read the following passage, for example:

▶   The landscape designer's proposal was extensively illustrated. It covered ten pages.

ETHICS NOTE

Do not use the passive voice to avoid responsibility for an action or to obscure an issue, as in the following examples: "Several mistakes were made in the processing of your claim" (Who made them?) and "It has been decided that annual bonuses will be discontinued this year" (Who has decided?). Although writers sometimes use the passive voice and vague language unintentionally, attempts to evade responsibility for a problem or future commitment clearly involve an ethical choice.

ESL TIPS   **Choosing Voice**

Different languages place different values on active-voice and passive-voice constructions. In some languages, the passive is used frequently; in others, hardly at all. As a nonnative speaker of English, you may have a tendency to follow the pattern of your native language. But remember, even though business writing may sometimes require the passive voice, active verbs are highly valued in English.

The writing in this passage is monotonous because both sentences have the same subject-verb structure; it is unemphatic because each idea is given equal weight. The key to transforming a series of repetitive, unemphatic sentences is *subordination*, a technique in which a fact or an idea is shown to be secondary to another fact or idea in the same sentence. You can subordinate an element in a sentence by making it a dependent clause, a phrase, or a single modifier.

DEPENDENT CLAUSE	The landscape designer's proposal, *which covered ten pages*, was extensively illustrated.
PHRASE	The landscape designer's proposal, *covering ten pages*, was extensively illustrated.
SINGLE MODIFIER	The landscape designer's *ten-page* proposal was extensively illustrated.

You can also shift the focus from one idea to another by its placement in a sentence. If you wish to highlight an item, place it either at the beginning or at the end of the sentence; if you wish to subordinate an item, place it in the middle of the sentence.

WITHOUT SUBORDINATION	Blast furnaces are used mainly in the smelting of iron. They are used all over the world.
EMPHASIZES PURPOSE	Blast furnaces, *in use all over the world*, arc used mainly in the smelting of iron.
EMPHASIZES EXTENT	Blast furnaces, *used mainly in the smelting of iron*, are used all over the world.

Although subordination can help you to write clear and readable sentences, it can be overdone. Be careful not to pile one subordinating clause on top of another — doing so will force your reader to work harder than necessary to understand what you are saying. The following sentence is hard to read because the bottleneck of subordinate clauses prevents the reader from moving easily from one idea to the next.

TOO MUCH SUBORDINATION	When the two technicians, who had been trained to repair Maurita printers, explained to Erin that the new Maurita 5090 printer, which she had told them was not working properly, needed a new part, she decided that until the part arrived the department would have its sales letters reproduced by an independent printing supplier.
EFFECTIVE SUBORDINATION	Erin told the two Maurita technicians that the new Maurita 5090 printer was not working properly. The technicians examined the printer and explained to her that it needed a new part. She decided that until the part arrived, the department would have its sales letters reproduced by an independent printing supplier.

ETHICS NOTE

Highlighting advantages in a document is appropriate, but subordinating or failing to mention related disadvantages could easily mislead the audience. Even making a bulleted list of advantages, where they stand out, and then burying a disadvantage in the middle of a paragraph could unfairly mislead the target audience. At the same time, you might be tempted to dramatically highlight a feature or service that your audience would find attractive but that may be available only with some models of a product or at extra cost. In that case, the audience could justifiably object that you have given them a false impression in order to sell a product or service, especially if the extra cost was also deemphasized.

Parallel Structure

Parallelism can produce an economy of language, clarify meaning, indicate the equality of related ideas, and frequently achieve emphasis. Parallel structure allows your audience to anticipate a series of units within a sentence. A reader who has sensed the pattern of a sentence can go from one idea to another more quickly and confidently.

Parallel structure requires that sentence elements—words, phrases, and clauses—that are alike in function be alike in structure as well. The strategy you choose to make a sentence parallel depends on the degree of emphasis you wish to create: Words produce some emphasis, phrases produce more emphasis, and clauses produce the most emphasis.

PARALLEL WORDS	If you want to pass the customer-service training program, you must be *punctual, courteous,* and *conscientious.*
PARALLEL PHRASES	If you want to pass the customer-service training program, you must recognize the importance *of punctuality, of courtesy,* and *of conscientiousness.*
PARALLEL CLAUSES	If you want to pass the customer-service training program, *you must arrive punctually, you must behave courteously,* and *you must study conscientiously.*

To make the relationship among parallel units clear, repeat the word (or words) that introduces the first unit.

> *in*
> The advantage is not in the pay but the greater opportunity.

> *a*
> The study of electronics is a necessity and challenge to the trainees.

Lists

Lists can save readers time by allowing them to see at a glance specific items, questions, or directions. Lists also help readers by breaking up complex statements and by allowing key ideas to stand out. When you use a list of phrases or short sentences, be sure to keep all elements parallel, as in the following example.

> Please note the following policy changes:
> - Do not use company phones for personal long-distance calls.
> - Use low-grade yellow paper rather than bond for any written copy that is not to go out of the office.
> - Make double-sided copies rather than one-sided photocopies of all internal correspondence.

Although lists help focus readers' attention, avoid overusing the technique. When a document consists almost entirely of lists, the audience is unable to distinguish the relative importance of ideas. To make sure a list fits with the surrounding sentences, provide adequate transition before and after it.

WRITER'S CHECKLIST
Using Lists

- ☑ List only comparable items.
- ☑ Use parallel structure throughout.
- ☑ Use only words, phrases, or short sentences.
- ☑ Provide context by introducing lists with complete sentences, followed by a colon.
- ☑ Provide adequate transitions before and after lists.
- ☑ Use numbers when rank or sequence is important.
- ☑ Use bullets when rank or sequence is not important.
- ☑ Do not overuse lists.

Other Ways to Achieve Emphasis

You can create a feeling of anticipation in your audience by arranging a series of facts or ideas in climactic order. Begin such a series with the least-important or lowest-impact idea and end it with the most-important or highest-impact one.

> The hostile takeover of the company will result in some employees being relocated to different cities, some being downgraded, and some being let go.

The writer leads the audience step by step from the lowest potential impact on employees to the highest: (1) employee relocation, (2) downgraded jobs, and (3) the loss of jobs.

An abrupt change in sentence length can also highlight an important point.

▶ We have already reviewed the problems that the accounting department identified during the past year. We could continue to examine the causes of our problems and point an accusing finger at all the culprits beyond our control, but in the end it all leads to one simple conclusion: *We must cut costs.*

Sometimes, simply labeling ideas as important creates emphasis.

▶ *But most important*, we can do everything in our power to make sure that we are producing the best communication equipment on the market.

♦ *For additional highlighting devices, see pages 209–212 in Chapter 7, Designing Effective Documents and Visuals.*

If you don't overuse them, direct statements such as *most important* should make your audience take particular notice of what follows.

Important information may also be brought to the audience's attention by a special format — the material may be boxed, for instance — or by attention-getting devices such as dashes, ALL-CAPITAL letters, <u>underlined words</u>, or a distinctive typeface, such as **boldface** or *italic* type. These features can be used to emphasize important words and phrases in warnings.

WARNING

DO NOT proceed to the next instruction until you have unplugged the equipment. The electrical power generated by this equipment can kill!

Overuse of typographical devices may cancel their effectiveness, however. Readers quickly learn to gloss over these devices if they are used for subordinate as well as truly important material.

WRITER'S CHECKLIST
Achieving Emphasis

☑ Use the active voice.

☑ Subordinate secondary ideas.

☑ Use parallel structure to focus attention on how ideas are related.

☑ Use lists to highlight ideas by setting them apart from surrounding text.

☑ Arrange ideas in least-important to most-important order.

☑ Label key ideas as important.

☑ Selectively use typographical devices such as ALL-CAPITAL LETTERS or *italic*, **boldface**, or <u>underlined text</u>.

Point of View

Point of view shows the writer's relation to the information presented. First-person point of view indicates that the writer is a participant or an observer. Second- and third-person points of view indicate that the writer is giving directions, instructions, or advice or writing about other people or something impersonal.

FIRST PERSON	*I* scrolled down to find the Settings option.
SECOND PERSON	Scroll down to find the Settings option and double-click. [*You* is understood.]
THIRD PERSON	*He* scrolled down to find the Settings option.

Many people think they should avoid the pronoun *I* in their business writing. Such practice, however, often leads to inappropriate passive constructions or to awkward sentences with writers referring to themselves as *one* or as *the writer* instead of as *I*.

▶ ~~It is regrettable~~ that the equipment shipped on the 12th ~~is unaceptable.~~
   I regret   *we cannot accept*

▶ ~~One~~ can only conclude that the bond rate is too low.
   I

Do not use the personal point of view, however, when you need to emphasize the subject matter over the writer or the reader. In the following example, it does not help to personalize the situation; in fact, the impersonal version may be more tactful.

PERSONAL	I received objections to my proposal from several of your managers.
IMPERSONAL	Several managers have raised objections to the proposal.

Whether you adopt a personal or an impersonal point of view depends on your purpose and readers. For example, in an informal e-mail to an associate, you would most likely adopt a personal point of view. However, in a report to a large group, you would probably emphasize the subject by using an impersonal point of view.

ETHICS NOTE

In correspondence on company stationery, use of the pronoun *we* may be interpreted as reflecting company policy, whereas *I* clearly reflects personal opinion. Use the appropriate pronoun according to whether the matter discussed in the letter is a corporate or an individual concern.

▶ *I* understand your frustration with the price increase, but *we* must now include the cost of the import tax in our pricing.

> **ESL TIPS**   **Stating an Opinion**
>
> In some cultures, stating an opinion in writing is considered impolite or unnecessary, but in the United States, readers expect to see a writer's opinion stated clearly and explicitly. The opinion should be followed by specific examples to help the reader understand the writer's point of view.

■ Language

The words you use matter. Focus on them carefully as you revise. Ensure that you use the right word in the right context throughout and that your writing is economical by eliminating redundant or otherwise needless language. Now is also the time to evaluate your draft for any stated or implied bias toward people or groups. Finally, consider the necessity for technical, legal, or other specialized vocabulary that may be inappropriate for members of your audience. The plainer your language, the more time and effort you will usually save your readers.

Context and Word Choice

As Mark Twain once said, "The difference between the right word and almost the right word is the difference between 'lightning' and 'lightning bug.'" Precision requires that you choose the right word.

When you write, be alert to the effect that a word may have on your audience—and try to avoid words that might, by the implications they carry, confuse, distract, or offend your audience. For example, in describing a piece of machinery that your company recently bought, you might refer to the item as cheap—meaning inexpensive. However, because "cheap" often suggests "of poor quality" or "shoddily made," your audience may picture the new piece of equipment as already in need of repairs.

In selecting the appropriate word, you will want to keep in mind the *context*—the setting in which the word appears. Suppose instead of "cheap" you call the new machine "inexpensive." The exact meaning of the word would depend on the context. While a $1,000 desktop laser printer might be overpriced, an audience unfamiliar with the cost of printing machinery might be surprised to learn that an $80,000 printing press is a good buy. It is up to you, the writer, to provide your audience with a context—to let them know, in this case, the relative costs of printing equipment.

The context will also determine whether a word you choose is specific enough. When you use the word *machine*, for instance, you might be thinking of an automobile, a lathe, a cash register, or a sewing machine. *Machine* is an imprecise word that must be qualified, or explained, unless you want to refer in a general way to every item included in the category *machine*. If you have a particular kind of machine in mind, then you must use more precise language. Figure 4–1 illustrates just how specific a particular context might require you to be. To include

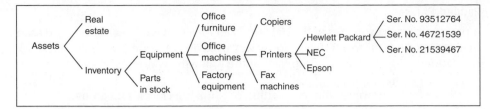

Figure 4–1   Abstract-to-Concrete Words

printer model numbers in a company's annual report, a detailed parts list in a sales brochure, or highly technical language in a memo to the accounting department would, of course, be inappropriate. In all the writing you do, you must decide what your purpose is and who your audience will be, and then select terms that are neither too general nor too specific for the context.

ETHICS NOTE

Use words correctly and appropriately. Consider the company document that stated, "A *nominal* charge will be assessed for using our facilities." When clients objected that the charge was very large, the writer pointed out that the word *nominal* means "the named amount" as well as "very small." In this situation, the audience had a strong case in charging that the company was attempting to deceive. In other circumstances, various abstract words, technical or legal jargon, and euphemisms—when used to mislead an audience or to hide a serious or dangerous situation—are unethical, even though technical or legal experts could interpret them as accurate.

Conciseness

As you revise, focus on removing unnecessary words, phrases, clauses, and sentences from your writing. Wordiness, as well as stilted or pretentious language, can place a barrier between you and your audience by making your ideas difficult to understand. As you revise your writing, be particularly alert for two types of wordiness: redundancy and padded phrases.

Redundancy

When selected carefully, modifiers—whether adjectives, adverbs, prepositional phrases, or subordinate clauses—can make the words they describe vivid and specific (for example, a *frosty* night). However, avoid modifiers that simply repeat the idea contained in the word they modify, such as the expressions in the following list:

blue in color	plan ahead
resume again	basic essentials
square in shape	attach together
brief in duration	visible to the eye
completely finished	present status
final outcome	round circle

Padded Phrases

A padded phrase expresses in several words an idea that could easily be expressed in a word. *Due to the fact that* is a wordy way of saying *because*. Examine your work for padded language, often composed of the following words: *case, fact, field, factor, manner,* and *nature.*

Sometimes, however, longer wording or phrasing clarifies meaning.

▶   *In terms of* gross sales, the year has been successful; *in terms of* net income, however, it has been discouraging.

Instead of being redundant, the phrase *in terms of* balances the sentence and highlights the contrast in meaning. Expressions such as these must be evaluated individually. If the expression does not contribute to the meaning of the sentence, use its simpler substitute.

Bias

Biased words and expressions offend because they make inappropriate assumptions or stereotypes about gender, ethnicity, physical or mental disability, age, or sexual orientation.

ETHICS NOTE

The easiest way to avoid bias is simply not to mention differences among people unless the differences are relevant to the discussion. Keep current with accepted usage, and, if you are unsure of the appropriateness of an expression or the tone of a passage, have several classmates or colleagues review the material and give you their honest assessment.

Sexist Language

Sexist language can be an outgrowth of sexism, the arbitrary stereotyping of men and women—it can breed and reinforce inequality. To avoid sexism in your writing, treat men and women equally, and do not make assumptions about traditional or occupational roles. Accordingly, use nonsexist occupational descriptions in your writing.

Instead of	Consider
chairman, chairwoman	chair, chairperson
foreman	supervisor
manpower	staff, personnel, workers
policeman, policewoman	police officer
salesman, saleswoman	salesperson
male nurse	nurse
female chemist	chemist

Use parallel terms to describe men and women.

Instead of	**Consider**
man and wife	husband and wife
Ms. Jones and Bernard Weiss	Ms. Jones and Mr. Weiss; Mary Jones and Bernard Weiss
ladies and men	ladies and gentlemen; women and men

Sexism can creep into your writing by the unthinking use of male pronouns where a reference could apply equally to a man and a woman. One way to avoid such usage is to rewrite the sentence in the plural.

> *All employees* *their managers* *their travel vouchers.*
> ▸ ~~Every employee~~ will have ~~his manager~~ sign ~~his travel voucher.~~

Other possible solutions are to use *his or her* instead of *his* alone or to omit the pronoun completely if it is not essential to the meaning of the sentence.

> *an*
> ▸ Everyone must submit ~~his~~ expense report by Monday.

He or she can become monotonous when repeated constantly, and a pronoun cannot always be omitted without changing the meaning of a sentence. Another solution is to omit troublesome pronouns by using the imperative mood whenever possible.

> *Submit all*
> ▸ ~~Everyone must submit his or her~~ expense reports by Monday.

Other Types of Biased Language

Identifying people by racial, ethnic, or religious categories is simply not relevant in most workplace writing. Telling readers that an engineer is Native American or that a professor is African American almost never conveys useful information. Similarly, linking a profession or a characteristic to race or ethnicity reinforces stereotypes, implying that it is rare or expected for a person of a particular background to have achieved a certain position.

Consider how you refer to people with disabilities. If you refer to "a disabled employee," you imply that the part (*disabled*) is as significant as the whole (*employee*). Use "an employee with a disability" instead. Similarly, the preferred usage is "a person who uses a wheelchair" rather than "a wheelchair-bound person"; the latter expression inappropriately equates the wheelchair with the person. Likewise, references to a person's age can also be inappropriate, as in expressions like "middle-aged manager" or "young Web designer."

In most workplace writing, such issues are simply not relevant. Of course, in some contexts race, ethnicity, religion, disability, or age should be identified. For example, if you are writing an Equal Employment Opportunity Commission report about your firm's hiring practices, the racial composition of the workforce is relevant. In such cases, you need to present the issues in ways that respect and do not demean the individuals or groups to which you refer.

Plain Language

Strive to communicate with your audience in language that is both uncomplicated and accurate. Even with the best of intentions, however, you cannot always avoid using specialized terms and concepts. This section will help you sort out the difference between writing that is plain and accurate and writing that is either too complicated or too simplistic.

ETHICS NOTE

Many states have created "plain-language" laws, which require that documents be written in clear, understandable language. The federal government also now requires that all its new regulations be written in plain language.

Affectation

Do not use language that is more formal, technical, or showy than it needs to be to communicate information to your reader. Such inflated language creates a smoke screen that the audience must penetrate to discover your meaning. Consider the following example, in which a company needs to tell employees about its policy for personal phone calls.

INFLATED   It is the policy of the company to provide the proper telephonic apparatus to enable each employee to conduct the interoffice and intra-business communication necessary to discharge his or her responsibilities; however, it is contrary to company policy to permit telephones to be utilized for personal employee communications.

PLAIN   Your telephone is provided for company business; do not use it for personal calls.

Most people would have to read the first version of the policy several times before deciphering its message. The meaning of the revised version, which uses direct, simple, and precise language, is evident at a glance.

Another common type of affectation is adding prefixes and suffixes to simple words. For example, *analyzation*, *summarization*, and *notation* are simply fancy-sounding versions of *analysis*, *summary*, and *note*. The extra syllables tacked on such words do not make them mean anything more precise; they make them incorrect and long-winded.

Understanding the possible reasons for affectation is the first step toward avoiding it. Review and revise your writing if you recognize any of the following tendencies:

- *Impression.* Some writers use pretentious language in an attempt to impress others. Evidence and logic will create a much more positive impression, whether you are a student trying to impress a teacher or an employee trying to impress a superior or customer.

- *Insecurity.* If you are unsure of your facts, conclusions, or arguments, don't try to cover these gaps with a smoke screen of pretentious language. Continue to research the topic until you are certain of what to say.

- *Imprecision.* Try to be as precise as possible rather than filling in for missing information with vague language. Don't say "the policy will have a positive impact on the department" unless you can describe precisely how the policy will in fact positively affect the department.

- *Imitation.* Avoid the tendency to imitate the poor writing you see around you. For example, maybe everyone in your company refers to themselves as *the writer* rather than *I* in letters and memos. These practices are frequently simply bad habits thoughtlessly repeated rather than formal company policy. At least find out before falling into the habit with everyone else.

- *Initiation.* If you just completed your education or training for an occupation, it's natural to feel that one way to prove your professional standing is to use technical terminology and jargon as much as possible. Although this impulse usually passes with time, be especially careful to avoid it in your writing for senior officials and customers. These readers are much less likely to be as technically knowledgeable as you.

- *Intimidation.* A few writers, consciously or unconsciously, try to overwhelm their readers with pretentious language, often to protect themselves from criticism.

WRITER'S CHECKLIST
Avoiding Affectation

☑ Write in the first person (*I*); avoid *the writer* and *one*.

☑ Choose simple words that say exactly what you mean—do not substitute big, imprecise, or unusual words for well-thought-out, precise language.

☑ Avoid trying to impress your reader with pretentious language—such as *discharge responsibilities, aforesaid, hereto*—or with vague or trendy language—such as *factoid, infomercial, right-sizing, solution* (used to mean a product or service).

☑ Be certain of your facts, conclusions, and arguments. Insecurity in these areas can lead to inflated language.

☑ Revise your writing, identifying wording that should be replaced with clearer, shorter, common words and phrases.

Technical Terminology

Technical terms are standard, universally recognized words used in a particular field to refer to specific principles, processes, or devices. Unlike inflated language, technical terms are useful and often essential in communicating accurately and concisely. For example, the term *divestiture* has a specific meaning for audiences familiar with management strategies. Similarly, the term *logic gate* would be understood by an audience who studied computer science or electrical engineering.

◆ *For guidance on how to define terms accurately and incorporate them smoothly into your writing, see Defining Terms and Concepts on pages 79–82 in Chapter 3, Writing the Draft.*

If you are certain that your audience (and potential audience) will understand a technical term, use it to ensure precision. If you are at all uncertain, however, define the term in plain language when you first use it. If your audience is likely to be confused by a concept, explain it, perhaps including an easy-to-understand example. Digressing into an explanation, though less efficient than using a technical term, is sometimes required to make your writing easily understandable—your ultimate goal.

WRITER'S CHECKLIST
Revising for Clarity

- ☑ Organize your writing logically.
- ☑ Use effective transitions between sentences, paragraphs, and sections.
- ☑ Be consistent in your point of view toward your topic.
- ☑ Emphasize key ideas and subordinate ancillary ideas.
- ☑ Choose precise language to ensure accuracy and to eliminate vagueness and ambiguity.
- ☑ Strive for conciseness by eliminating words, phrases, and sentences that are not necessary to your subject, purpose, and audience.

Jargon

Jargon is highly specialized technical slang that is unique to an occupational group. If you are addressing a particular occupational group, jargon (like technical terminology) may provide a time-saving and efficient means of communicating with them. For example, human resource professionals adopted the term *headhunters* to describe the recruitment of professional and executive personnel. Such terms should be used only in the appropriate context. Technical shorthand is not a satisfactory substitute for everyday language outside the field in which it is standard.

Another type of jargon is used to define occupations euphemistically. Tactfulness dictates that if you are writing to an undertaker and must refer to his or her occupation, you should use the term *funeral director*. For similar reasons, a trash collector is frequently called a *sanitation worker*.

When jargon becomes so specialized that it applies only to one company or subgroup of an occupation, it is referred to as "shop talk." For example, an automobile manufacturer might produce a "pollution-control valve—Model LV-20." In the department where the device is built, it may be referred to as an "LV-20." Obviously, shop talk is appropriate only for those familiar with its special vocabulary and should be reserved for speech, informal memos, and e-mail messages within a company.

■ Proofreading

Proofreading is your final opportunity to review your content for accuracy and for sentence-level corrections in grammar, punctuation, mechanics, and the like. Even though you are familiar with your content at this point, inadvertent errors can remain unless you methodically examine the draft for them.

 For an easy-access reference to grammar, punctuation, mechanics, and spelling while revising, see Part Four: Revision Guide.

DIGITAL TIPS: Grammar and Spell Checkers

Do not rely entirely on computer grammar checkers and spell checkers. They will help with proofreading, but they can make writers overconfident. If a typographical error results in a legitimate English word (for example, *coarse* instead of *course*), the spell checker will not flag the misspelling. Because grammar checkers cannot anticipate the meaning of your sentences, they have a tendency to flag proper usage as incorrect and to suggest inappropriate revisions. Therefore, you still must proofread your work carefully—both on your monitor and on paper.

Above all, your information must be accurate. Although accuracy is important in all types of writing, it takes on special significance when you write on the job. One misplaced decimal point, for example, can create a staggering budgetary error. Incorrect or imprecise instructions can cause injury to a worker. At the very least, if your writing is not accurate you will quickly lose the confidence of your readers. They will be confused, for example, if a figure or fact in your writing differs from one in a chart or graph. These kinds of inaccuracies are easily overlooked as you write a first draft, so you must correct them during revision.

Whether the material you examine is your own writing or that of someone else, consider editing and proofreading in several stages. Although you need to tailor the stages to the specific document and to your own problem areas, the Proofreading in Stages checklist that follows provides a useful starting point for proofreading.

WRITER'S CHECKLIST
Proofreading in Stages

First-Stage Review

- ☑ Appropriate format, as for reports or correspondence
- ☑ Typographical consistency (headings, spacing, fonts)

Second-Stage Review

- ☑ Specific grammar and usage problems
- ☑ Appropriate punctuation
- ☑ Correct abbreviations and capitalization
- ☑ Correct spelling (especially names and places)
- ☑ Complete Web or e-mail addresses and the like

(continued)

WRITER'S CHECKLIST (continued)

☑ Accurate figures and consistent units of measurement in tables and lists

☑ Cut-and-paste errors; for example, a result of moved or deleted text and numbers

Final-Stage Review

☑ Final check of your goals: readers' needs and purpose

☑ Appearance of the document (see Layout and Design in Chapter 7, Designing Effective Documents and Visuals)

☑ Review by colleague for crucial documents

Use the standard proofreaders' marks shown on page 588, especially for proofreading someone else's document.

■ Physical Appearance

The most thoughtfully prepared, carefully written, and conscientiously revised writing will quickly lose its effect if it has a poor physical appearance. In the classroom or on the job, a sloppy document will invariably lead your reader to assume that the work that went into preparing it was also sloppy. In the classroom, that carelessness will reflect on you; on the job, it can reflect on your employer as well. Unless your instructor provides other specific instructions, use the following guidelines for preparing your document:

◆ *For format guidelines for letters and memos, see Chapter 8, Understanding the Principles of Business Communication.*

◆ *For guidance for formal reports, see Chapter 11, Writing Formal Reports.*

◆ *For guidance on page design, see Chapter 7, Designing Effective Documents and Visuals.*

- Use good-quality, white paper.
- Check that your printer produces a clear, dark image.
- Use at least one-inch margins on all sides of the page.
- Number all pages.
- Leave ample white space to separate sections.

🖱 DIGITAL TIPS: Proofreading for Format Consistency

An effective way to check formatting, spacing, and typographical consistency as well as general appearance of documents is to view the whole page on-screen in your word-processing program. You may also wish to view multiple pages or "tile" separate documents side by side for comparison. For more on this topic, see <bedfordstmartins .com/writingthatworks> and select *Digital Tips*.

■ Case Study: Revising the Lifemaker Brochure

A variety of the revision techniques discussed in this chapter apply to the Lifemaker sales brochure that was outlined and drafted in Chapters 2 and 3. In Figure 4–2, the writer has taken her second draft and, after allowing for a cooling-

DIGITAL TIPS: Revising Your Draft

- Print a double-spaced copy of your draft. Write notes and revisions on paper before returning to the computer to enter changes and corrections.

- Move blocks of text as needed.

- Use the Find command to locate inappropriate diction such as *a lot;* padded phrases such as *that is*, *there are*, *the fact that*, and *to be*; jargon that needs to be eliminated or technical terms that may need further explanation; and your most commonly misused words.

- Use spell and grammar checkers carefully, and reread the text for accuracy. Spell checkers can identify a misspelled word, but they cannot determine whether you mean *course* or *coarse.* Likewise, grammar checkers cannot interpret your intent or the context of your writing.

off period, critiqued her work, using the main points covered in this chapter as her guide. Figure 4–3 shows a revised version of the draft. Notice that the writer has not simply made mechanical, sentence-level corrections to her work. She used her marginal comments to revise the structure and organization as well as its sentences.

ON THE WEB

For samples of an original and revised draft of a persuasive letter, go to *Model Documents Gallery*, **bedfordstmartins.com/ writingthatworks**

The Lifemaker System 40
The Compact, Affordable Home Gym
Designed for Maximum Fitness Conditioning

DRAFT

Home gyms were designed to eliminate the hassle and expense of going to a health club to work out, but most of them are too bulky and awkward to fit either your budget or your wallet. The Lifemaker System 40 is designed for (limped) living space, a modest budget, and maximum fitness needs.
sp

Compact Design

too much jargon

The Lifemaker's multiple stations provide a technologically sophisticated strength training program, (and is) architecturally configured for minimal space and maximal efficiency. (At 4 (fett) wide and 7 feet long,) your living room can (easily) accommodate the Lifemaker with more (ease) than other home systems. At the same time, the Lifemaker offers more stations and more exercises. —— *faulty comparison*
Point of view

missing pronoun

sp

misplaced modifier

redundant

Move this ¶ to introduction

(One) need not compromise (your) exercise needs with an (overside) or ineffective system. Our home gym lets you integrate a complete home exercise system into your available space and your budget.
sp

Cast-Iron Weight Stack

need direct object "of plates"

agreement

The dual cast-iron weight <u>stacks totals</u> 200 lbs. Which can be arranged to offer a resistance range of 10 to 150 pounds. In addition, Lifemaker offers the <u>only weight system</u> on the market that can be adjusted in (multiplied) increments.
sp

not true!!

too vague "can be adjusted in 5, 10, 15 pound increments"

Adjustable Cables

missing subject-verb agreement

The Lifemaker's unique cable system (allows) quick (reconfiguring) of the weight stacks without taking apart the entire system. <u>Just pulling</u> the center rod and <u>one can</u> add or remove as many plates as you need.

verb agreement; point of view

Figure 4–2 Draft Sales Brochure Copy (Marked for Revision) (continued)

page 2

too much jargon; too vague

The cable tension can also be adjusted to make sure your muscles are working against all the possible resistance in each exercise to increase reflexor capacity and resistance ability.

Easy Assembly and Maintenance

sounds awkward

You <u>can</u> assemble the Lifemaker yourself in under an hour; we even in-clude all the tools needed for assembly. The system requires little <u>main-tenance and upkeep</u>; simply check all parts each time you exercise and

redundant

tighten cable tensions. You can clean the system by wiping all parts with a damp cloth; <u>unlike most other systems,</u> no special cleaning flu-ids or oiling is necessary.   *not true!! most systems don't require special treatment*

make more personal "is pleased to offer you . . ."

Affordable

Lifemaker, Inc. is offering this state-of-the-art, compact home gym at only $999.99. All parts carry a two-year guarantee, and replacement parts can be shipped to you in under 24 hours by calling our 800 number.

For a limited time, you can also purchase the Lifemaker System 40 on a no-interest monthly payment plan, because at Lifemaker, Inc., we be-lieve that an exercise system should strengthen your back, not flatten your wallet.

add bit about talking to service rep

dangling modifier and sounds wrong — "within 24 hours of placing an order"

Figure 4–2   Draft Sales Brochure Copy (Marked for Revision) (continued)

The Lifemaker System 40
The Compact, Affordable Home Gym
Designed for Maximum Fitness Conditioning

Introduces major benefits from Figure 2–2

Home gym systems are designed to eliminate the hassle and expense of working out at a health club, but most systems take up too much space and can injure both your budget and your back. The Lifemaker System 40 offers a solution to the problem of oversized, overpriced, and ineffective home gyms, because Lifemaker is designed to fit a limited living space, a modest budget, and maximum fitness requirements. Purchasing a Lifemaker System 40 will let you integrate a complete weight and cable exercise system into your living space and your budget.

Headings make brochure inviting to readers

Compact Design

The Lifemaker's comprehensive strength-training program is designed to occupy minimal space. The system offers more than 40 exercise combinations, but because it measures only 4 feet wide and 7 feet long, Lifemaker will fit easily into almost any room.

Multiple Stations

Three workout stations let you move through your conditioning program as efficiently as if you owned a roomful of weight and cable machines. In addition, the multiple stations are designed so that two people can work out at the same time.

Cast-Iron Weights

The Lifemaker features dual weight stacks totaling more than 200 pounds of cast-iron plates. The dual stacks offer a resistance range of 10 to 150 pounds; resistance can be adjusted in 5-, 10-, or 15-pound increments.

Expands equipment fitness, maintenance, and affordability benefits from introductory paragraph

Adjustable Cables

A unique cable system allows you to reconfigure the dual weight stacks without taking apart the entire system. Simply pull the rod located between the stacks and you can add or remove as many plates as you need for a particular exercise. The cable tension can also be adjusted to increase or decrease the amount of resistance within exercise sets.

Easy Assembly, Easy Maintenance

The Lifemaker System 40 can be assembled in less than an hour; no special tools are needed for assembly. You can maintain the Lifemaker in good condition simply by wiping down the system with a damp cloth; no oiling or scrubbing of parts is ever necessary. All parts carry a two-year guarantee and can be shipped to you within 24 hours of your placing an order.

Affordable

Lifemaker, Inc., is pleased to offer you this state-of-the-art, compact home gym for only $999.99. You can also purchase the Lifemaker on a low-interest monthly payment plan. Call (800) 554-1234 and we will be happy to arrange a plan that works with your financial needs. At Lifemaker, Inc., we believe that owning a home gym system should strengthen your back, not flatten your wallet.

Figure 4–3   Final Sales Brochure Copy

CHAPTER 4 SUMMARY: REVISING THE DRAFT

Use the following checklist to help you remember the various aspects of revision that this chapter has covered. Refer to this list both before and after you write the final draft of any document; fix any problems before your reader sees them.

- Have I allowed a cooling period?
- Have I included all the information my readers need?
- Is the writing organized logically?
- Do any potential ethical problems need to be resolved?
- Does each paragraph have a topic sentence?
- Are the sentences in each paragraph related to the paragraph's central idea?
- Have I included enough transitions, so readers can follow the logical relationships among ideas?
- Are active and passive voices used appropriately?
- Are secondary ideas subordinated to primary ideas?
- Are ideas of equal importance written in parallel structure?
- Are other highlighting devices used appropriately?
- Is the point of view appropriate and consistent?
- Does the language accurately and precisely suit the topic and the audience?
- Is the writing concise?
- Is the writing free of actual or implied bias?
- Does the vocabulary avoid unnecessary technical terminology and jargon?
- Have all errors—grammatical and factual—been corrected during proofreading?
- Is the document's appearance crisp and clean?
- Is the document appropriately formatted?

ON THE WEB

For an online quiz on revision, go to Chapter 4, bedfordstmartins.com/ writingthatworks

■ Exercises

ON THE WEB

For additional exercises, go to Chapter 4, bedfordstmartins.com/ writingthatworks

1. Well-constructed paragraphs enable readers to quickly understand their content and writers to achieve their purpose. Read the following paragraph and then (a) underline its topic sentence and (b) cross out any sentences that do not contribute to paragraph unity.

  ▶ Frequently, department managers and supervisors recruit applicants without working through our corporate human resources office. Our human resources departments at all of our locations across the country have experienced this problem. Recently, the manager of our tool-design department met with a graduate of MIT to discuss an opening for a tool designer. The graduate was sent to the human resources department, where she was told that no such position existed. When the tool-design manager asked the director of human resources about the matter, the manager learned that the company president had ordered a hiring freeze for two months. I'm sure that our general employment situation will get better. As a result of the manager's failure to work through proper channels, the applicant was not only disappointed but bitter.

2. The sentences in the following paragraph have been purposely placed in the wrong order. Examine key terms and transitional devices, and then rearrange the sentences so that the paragraph moves smoothly and logically from one sentence to the next. Indicate the correct order of the sentences by placing the sentence numbers in the order in which the sentences should appear.

(1) If such improvements could be achieved, the consequences would be significant for many different applications. (2) However, the most challenging technical problem is to achieve substantial increases in the quantities of electrical energy that can be stored per unit weight of the battery. (3) The overall process yields about 70 percent of the electricity originally put into the battery. (4) A storage battery is a relatively efficient way of storing energy.

3. Each of the following pairs of sentences lacks a transition from the first sentence to the second. From the list of transitional devices in Table 4–1, select the most appropriate one for each sentence pair. Then rewrite the sentences as necessary.

a. The Doctors Clinic was able to attain its fund-raising goal on time this year. Mercer Street Hospital was forced to extend its fund-raising deadline for three months.

b. When instructing the new tellers, the branch manager explained how to deal with impatient customers. The personal-banking assistant told the new employees that they should consult her if they had difficulty handling those customers.

c. A car may skid on ice for several reasons. The driver may be going faster than road conditions warrant.

d. Unit sales dropped 12 percent between the first and second quarters. Revenue increased by 6 percent.

4. Bring to class a document that you have written either in this (or another) class or at your job. Under the direction of your instructor, take the following steps:

a. Create a rough outline of your document by writing a one-sentence summary of each paragraph in the order that the paragraphs appear.

b. Determine whether your sequence of points is logical and effective.

c. Make a note of any information that you could have added or deleted to make the document more effective.

d. If you find a problem with the logic of the sequence or with the amount or type of information included or omitted in your paper, revise the outline and then your draft.

5. Bring to class a document that you have written either in this (or another) class or at your job. (You may use the same document you examined for Exercise 4 if you wish.) Under the direction of your instructor, take the following steps:

a. Circle all the words or phrases that provide transition between sentences.

b. If you find two sentences that do not have adequate transition, place an X in the space between them.

c. For sentences that seem not to have adequate transition, insert a word, phrase, or clause that will improve the transition.

6. To persuade readers to take a specific course of action, successful workplace writers support their suggestions with evidence. When such details are missing in a first draft, they must be added at the revision stage. Referring to the opening and closing paragraphs you wrote for Exercises 1 and 2 in Chapter 3, outline and draft a letter that takes into account the following questions:

    a. What concrete details can you include in your letter to persuade your audience?

    b. What specific examples, facts, and statistics will you include as evidence?

    c. What point of view (first person, second person, or third person) would be most effective for your purpose?

7. Rewrite the following sentences to eliminate excessive subordination.

    a. The duty officer who was on duty at 3:30 a.m. was the one who took the call that there was a malfunction in the Number 3 generator that had been repaired at approximately 9:00 a.m. the previous morning.

    b. I have referred your letter that you wrote to us on June 20 to our staff attorney who reviewed it in the light of corporate policy that is pertinent to the issue that you raise.

    c. Will your presentation that is scheduled for the 12th of next May and that will answer questions submitted in advance be circulated before the 12th to those who will be attending the workshop?

8. Each of the following sentences contains a redundant word, phrase, or clause. Rewrite the sentences to eliminate the redundant elements.

    a. We began the project in the month of April.

    b. He opened the conversation with a reference to the subject of inflation.

    c. The field of engineering is a profession that offers great opportunities.

    d. The human resources manager spoke to the printing-plant supervisor with regard to the scheduling of employee vacations.

    e. Our experienced salespeople, who have many years of work behind them, will plan an aggressive advertising campaign to sell the new product.

    f. Any two raceway assemblies can be connected together with the plate as shown.

    g. Dissatisfied employees should give their complaints to the manager who is in charge as supervisor.

9. The following passages contain unnecessary jargon, padded phrases, and affectation. Revise the passages.

    a. I hereby designate Mr. Samson, who has been holding the position and serving in the capacity of assistant technical supervisor, to be named and appointed to the position and function of deputy director of customer relations. In his newly elevated position Mr. Samson will report, in the first instance, directly to the department director—that is, to me.

    b. Purchasers of the enclosed substance should carefully and thoroughly follow the instructions provided herein for the use of the substance, and should in no case whatsoever consume, or otherwise partake of, said substance without proceeding in the manner set forth on the accompanying circular of instructions.

10. Some of the following sentences violate the principles of parallel structure. Identify the incorrect sentences and revise to make them parallel. The sentences may be correctly changed in more than one way.

    a. We expected to be disappointed and that we would reject the proposal.

    b. Etiquette is important in social life, and you need it in business too.

    c. To type fast is one thing, but typing accurately is another.

    d. Do you prefer filing, typing, or balancing the budget?

e. Is your home well heated and with adequate ventilation?

f. The mailing notation should not only appear on the original but also on the copies.

g. The office has not only been cleaned but also newly decorated.

h. Our friends enjoy winter sports like hockey, skiing, and to skate.

i. Ms. Jory either wants Anna or me to proofread the galleys for our annual report.

j. The desk was neither the correct size nor the right model.

k. You may either send a check or a money order.

l. We are afraid that either the package is lost or stolen.

m. Next week, we plan to rent a cabin, hire a guide, and hiking through the countryside.

n. Mr. Levesque is a well-read and an interesting person.

ON THE WEB

For more collaborative classroom projects, go to Chapter 4, bedfordstmartins.com/ writingthatworks

Collaborative Classroom Projects

1. Affected language can confuse both native and nonnative speakers. During the next 15 minutes, in groups try to figure out common proverbs buried in these overwritten substitutes. Then, translate these proverbs and put them into regular sentences that might appear in a business-oriented document. When finished, the groups may be asked to exchange papers to evaluate the results.

   EXAMPLE   Everything that coruscates with effulgence is not ipso facto aureous.

   TRANSLATION   Everything that glitters is not gold.

   REWRITE   Sometimes things that appear valuable are not as valuable as they seem: "Despite the large amount of advertising and public relations that went into the shoe company's new product line, the design of its new athletic shoes is really not appealing to consumers."

   a. Never calculate the possible number of juvenile poultry until the usual period of incubation has been accomplished.

   b. People who reside in transparent domiciles should not cast geological specimens.

   c. The warm-blooded, feathered, egg-laying vertebrate animal that is among the first invariably comes in the possession of a small, legless crawling invertebrate animal.

   d. Where there is gaseous evidence of flammable matter, there is an indicated insinuation of incendiary pyrotechnic.

   e. Ornithological specimens of identical plumage tend to congregate in close proximity.

   f. Do not utter loud or passionate vocal expressions because of the accidental overturning of a receptacle containing a whitish nutritive liquid.

   g. Do not traverse a structure erected to afford passage over a waterway prior to the time of drawing nigh to the same.

   h. Hemoglobin is incapable of being extracted from the edible root of brassica rapa.

   i. Deviation from the ordinary or common routine is that which gives zest to the cycle of existence.

   j. A donee would be wise to abolish the habitual casting of glances into the oral cavity of equestrian specimens.

2. Rewrite each of the following sentences so that the verb is in the active voice. Whenever a potential subject is not given in a sentence, supply one as you write. When you have finished your sentences, divide into groups to share and discuss them. Is there much variation in the wording of your sentences? Is the meaning of the sentence affected by the differences in wording? Is a different tone implied?

   a. The entire building was spray-painted by Charles and his brother.
   b. It was assumed by the superintendent that the trip was postponed until next Tuesday.
   c. The completed form should be submitted to Tim Hagen by the 15th of every month.
   d. The fluid should be applied sparingly and should be allowed to dry for eight to ten seconds.
   e. The metropolitan area was defined as groups of counties related by commuting patterns by the researchers.

3. Imagine that members of your group are heading up a technical writing division of a university publishing company. You have learned that jargon and acronyms often impede the work of your native and nonnative student writers, editors, and proofreaders. For example, your company often hires U.S. and international engineering students to write the content in computer manuals. Some of the international students are often confused by the e-mail acronyms and jargon that are sent to them by the U.S. student editors and proofreaders. Meanwhile, many of your proofreaders are U.S. students from nontechnical fields who get confused by the Internet computer jargon that the engineering students use.

   a. As a group, research and then draft a document that lists and defines the following e-mail acronyms and jargon: BTW, FYI, IMHO, RTFM, LOL, RSN, ROTFL, and <g>. (You can add more if you wish.)
   b. As a group, research and then draft a document that lists and defines the following Internet and Web jargon: Boolean logic, browsers, cache, cgi, cookie, domain name, field searching, FTP, host, IP address or IP number, and ISP. (You can add more if you wish.)
   c. Now review your drafts using the Evaluating Your Draft checklist on pages 97–98. Present your final documents to the class.

■ Research Projects

ON THE WEB

For extra research projects, go to Chapter 4, bedfordstmartins.com/ writingthatworks

1. As discussed in this chapter, affected language is very hard to read. In small groups, visit the U.S. government's Plain Language Web site at <www .plainlanguage.gov>, which has as its purpose "to promote the use of plain language for all government communications." Divide up the work so that each person researches the history of Plain Language, describes what it is, examines samples of government documents written before and in Plain Language style, or makes a list of ways to use Plain Language. Write a draft of your findings and be ready to submit them to the class for peer review.

2. Find a document (instructions, direct-mail advertising, or other sample) that you believe demonstrates one or more of the ethical problems discussed in this chapter: using language that attempts to evade responsibility, to mislead the audience,

to deemphasize or suppress important information, or to emphasize misleading or incorrect information. As your instructor directs, (1) report what ethical problems you see and describe how the document might be revised to eliminate those problems, and (2) rewrite the samples to eliminate the ethical problems.

ON THE WEB

For more Web projects, go to Chapter 4, bedfordstmartins.com/ writingthatworks

■ Web Projects

1. Following up on Research Project 1, in your groups go to at least two government agency Web sites and review their Plain Language guidelines. You can find them by typing "Plain Language Initiative" into a search engine. What are these government agencies and what is the purpose of their communication with U.S. citizens? What guidelines are these agencies implementing? What are the agencies' goals in implementing these guidelines as they relate to U.S. citizens reading their material? Take your findings and add them to the draft of the document you wrote earlier about Plain Language. Have another group proofread your work, using the Proofreading in Stages checklist on pages 115–116. (Your instructor can determine if your work should be peer reviewed in stages by different groups.) Distribute your final document or present your findings to the class, as your instructor directs. (You may want to visit Chapter 14, Giving Presentations and Conducting Meetings.)

2. Imagine that you work for an employment agency that specializes in recruiting nursing staff for major hospitals. Your company needs to hire a variety of different types of nurses (prenatal, triage, and so on) in the coming months, and you are part of a committee that is working to find the best candidates. The lead recruiter is concerned because this is a competitive market and your company's online ads have not been attracting the most-qualified candidates. For example, one of the ads reads: "Desperately need hospital nurses for multiple locations and shifts. We offer lots of benefits like daily pay, 401K, and uniform programs!"

   a. You have been asked to review the ads of local hospitals and competing employment agencies to see why they are more successful. Go to the Web sites of several local hospitals and nursing employment agencies and make notes about their nursing ads (be careful to note what kind of nurse each ad refers to) and compare them to one another.

   b. Then, in a memo to the lead recruiter, discuss the lack of content in your company's ad. Based on your research, revise this ad for a particular type of nurse so that it attracts the right candidates and persuades them to contact your employment agency. As you prepare your recommendation, refer to the section on Content and Organization on pages 96–97.

Essential Skills: Collaboration, Research, and Design

While Part One discussed the principles of effective writing that apply to all on-the-job writing, Part Two focuses on skills that you will need to approach more complex projects requiring collaboration, research, and design. The following chapters will help you prepare for the specific writing and communicating presented in Part Three — such as writing correspondence, reports, and proposals, and developing presentations.

◆ **Collaboration.** Chapter 5 discusses the importance of writing strategies learned in Chapters 1 through 4 to collaborative writing projects on the job, whether you are a member of a collaborative writing team or the team leader.

◆ **Research.** Chapter 6 provides extensive treatment of researching your subject, including using the library and Internet, interviewing, using questionnaires, and making firsthand observations. You will also find advice for using the APA (American Psychological Association) and MLA (Modern Language Association) styles of documenting your research.

◆ **Design.** Chapter 7 gives detailed advice on formatting effective documents; developing illustrations, charts, and graphs; and successfully integrating them with your text. Attention to format and design is key to your success in creating instructions, reports, proposals, presentations, and other communications that will appeal to your audience.

5 Collaborative Writing

AT A GLANCE: Collaboration

Workplace writing is often collaborative writing—working with other people on a team to produce a single document. Like any team project, it requires the cooperation of people with different personalities and backgrounds working toward a common goal. Achieving the goal can be stressful but rewarding. To help achieve the goal successfully, this chapter describes the following classroom- and workplace-tested process for successful collaboration:

On the job or in the classroom, no one works in a vacuum. To some degree, everyone must rely on the help of others to do their jobs. No matter what you write or how often you write, you will likely have to collaborate with other people. Collaborative writing occurs when two or more people work together as a team to produce a single document, with each team member contributing to the planning, designing, and writing. It also involves sharing equal responsibility for the end product.

Collaborative writing is generally done for one of three reasons:

1. The project requires expertise or specialization in more than one subject area.
2. The project will benefit from merging different perspectives into a unified perspective.
3. The size of the project, time constraints, or the importance of the project to your organization requires a team effort.

The larger and more important the document, the more likely it is to be produced collaboratively. Sales proposals, for example, often require contributions from many different types of experts (engineers, systems analysts, scientists, financial specialists, sales managers, and so on). Formal reports and technical specifications are among other documents that are commonly

ON THE WEB

For online resources for writing collaboratively, go to Chapter 5, bedfordstmartins.com/writingthatworks

written by teams. For collaborative writing projects, the writing process varies only by the addition of a team-review step; otherwise, the process itself is no different, consisting of planning, researching, writing, reviewing, and revising. Typically, one person edits the final draft to unify the writing style and manages the reproduction and distribution of the finished document.

■ Advantages and Disadvantages of Collaborative Writing

Collaborative writing offers many benefits.

- *Many minds are better than one.* Collaborative teams usually produce work that is considerably better than the work produced by any one member. Team members stimulate each other to consider ideas and perspectives different from those they would have explored individually.

- *Team members provide immediate feedback.* Even if it is sometimes contested and debated, feedback is one of the great advantages of collaborative writing. Fellow team members may detect problems with organization, clarity, logic, and substance—and point them out during review. Receiving multiple responses also makes criticism easier to take; if three out of three team members make the same point, you can more readily accept its validity. Collaborating is like having your own set of critics who have a personal stake in helping you do a good job.

- *Team members play devil's advocate for each other.* That is, they take contrary points of view in an attempt to make certain that all important points are covered and that all potential problems have been exposed and resolved.

- *Team members help each other past the frustrations and stress of writing.* When one team member needs to make a decision, someone is always available to talk it over with.

- *Team members write more confidently.* Knowing that peers are depending on your contribution and will offer constructive criticism—not to find fault but to make the end product better—reduces anxiety.

- *Team members develop a greater tolerance of and respect for the opinions of others.* Team members become more aware of and involved in the planning of a document than if they were working alone. The same is true of reviews and revisions.

The primary disadvantages of collaborative writing include the demand it can place on your time, energy, and ego as a writer. Collaborative writing takes more time and energy than writing alone and exposes your writing to criticism. In fact, conflicts sometimes arise when not all team members participate or share equally in the team's work. Unless the final document is edited for the clarity and consistency of its content and style, it will be difficult to read and possibly incorrect.

Voices from the Workplace

Ulrike Mueller, SAP AG

Senior information developer Ulrike Mueller works at a software-development company in Germany, where she manages the efforts of a group of technical writers based in Ireland. Collaborative writing allows Ulrike and her colleagues to share the workload and make each document and its concept more diverse. It also requires a lot of extra planning. Ulrike comments, "In our case, working for a global player, you might have to deal with different time zones, different cultures, and different mentalities and work ethics. All this creates a need for more coordination, which you normally do not have to such a large extent." Another challenge is streamlining the final document. "Toward the end of the project," Ulrike explains, "more time needs to be spent on aligning the different parts and making it coherent in style."

Joseph G. Rappaport, Taxis for All Campaign

As an advisor with Taxis for All Campaign, a coalition dedicated to making all New York City taxicabs wheelchair accessible, Joseph Rappaport produces fact sheets, leaflets, press releases, and legislative testimony. Many of the documents that Joseph and his colleagues create are written collaboratively. "One person usually takes the lead in getting a letter or leaflet out the door. I try hard to respond quickly to drafts composed by that person. I always make a concrete suggestion if I don't think a word, a phrase, or a sentence works. There is nothing less helpful than getting a letter marked up with notes that say 'This doesn't work' and no ideas on what might work better. Quick turnaround and detailed suggestions for revision help the collaborative writing process work smoothly."

■ Functions of a Collaborative Writing Team

◆ *Read the section Conducting Productive Meetings on pages 499–509 in Chapter 14, Giving Presentations and Conducting Meetings, before calling your first meeting.*

Writing teams collaborate on every facet of the writing process:

- Planning the document
- Researching the subject and writing the draft
- Reviewing the drafts of other team members
- Revising the draft on the basis of comments from all team members

Planning

The team collectively identifies the readers, purpose, and scope of the project. Collaborators work together to conceptualize the document to be produced, create a broad outline of it, divide the work into segments, and assign each segment to individual team members, usually on the basis of their expertise.

In the preliminary planning stage, the team plans, as a group, as much of the document as is practical and produces a schedule for each stage of the project. The agreed-on schedule should include due dates for drafts, for team reviews of drafts, and for revisions. (Individual team members must plan how they will meet their assigned responsibilities.) For the project to succeed, team deadlines must be met, even if it means submitting a draft that is sketchy or not quite as good as desired. The other team members will have the opportunity to comment on drafts and suggest improvements. A deadline missed by one person may hold up the work of the entire team, so all members must be familiar with the schedule and submit their drafts and revisions on time.

As part of the planning process, the team should also agree on a standard reference guide for style and format. The guidelines should provide for uniformity and consistency in each team member's writing, which is especially important because different team members are preparing separate sections of the same document.

Lacking a standard guide, the team should establish project style guidelines that address the following issues:

- Levels of headings and their style: all-capital letters, all underlined, first letter capitalized, boldfaced, italicized, or some combination of these
- Spacing and margin guidelines
- Distinction between research sources that must be cited and those that need not be cited
- Use of the active voice, the present tense, and the imperative mood
- Format for References or Works Cited (if they are used)
- Capitalization of words in the text
- Abbreviations, acronyms, and symbols
- Standards for terms that should be written as one word, two words, or hyphenated (*on site/onsite*, *e-mail/email*, *on-line/online*)
- Format and wording of disclaimers (to satisfy legal or policy requirements)

ON THE WEB

For a list of standard reference guides, go to Chapter 5, bedfordstmartins.com/writingthatworks

 DIGITAL TIPS: Using Wikis for Collaborative Work

Wikis are Web sites whose content and organization can be quickly and easily edited by site visitors. Although most Web sites operate like printed documents, presenting text and other content to users who are trying to solve problems or accomplish tasks, wikis allow users to become authors by providing them with basic editing functions and the ability to post comments or questions. These features are especially useful in certain types of writing situations, such as collaboratively developing a report or paper. A writer posts a draft to a wiki, and then collaborators can edit the draft; the edits are tracked so that users can see who revised what.

In the workplace, wikis can be used for a variety of purposes, including coauthoring and coediting documents, sharing and distributing information, managing projects, and providing communication spaces for clients and customers. They are especially helpful for geographically separated collaborators and for reducing problems with tracking multiple versions because the system displays all changes by author and date.

For more-detailed advice on creating and editing documents in a wiki, see <bedfordstmartins.com/writingthatworks> and select *Digital Tips*, "Using Wikis for Collaborative Work."

In addition, the team must agree on the format and handling of project software files. The most efficient means of sharing drafts electronically is for everyone to use the same operating system and word-processing, graphics, and spreadsheet software. If that's not possible, the team must decide on an effective alternative. (To set up and share a document for electronic review, refer to the Digital Tips boxes on pages 132 and 136.)

◆ *The revision strategies outlined in Chapter 4, Revising the Draft, work well for most collaborative work.*

WRITER'S CHECKLIST
Planning a Collaborative Writing Project

☑ Establish guidelines to ensure that all team members are working toward the same goal and moving in the same direction.

☑ Agree on a standard reference guide for matters of style and format.

☑ Make sure that work assignments are appropriate to each person's particular talents.

☑ Establish a schedule that includes due dates for drafts, for team reviews of drafts, and for revisions.

☑ Agree on how to exchange project software files and whether to use collaborative software.

Research and Writing

The planning stage is followed by the research and writing stages. These are periods of intense independent activity by the individual team members. At this point, you gather and research information for your assigned segment of the document, create a master outline of the segment, flesh out the outline by providing the necessary details, and produce a first draft.

◆ *For guidelines on planning and writing a rough draft, see Chapters 2, Organizing Your Information, and 3, Writing the Draft.*

Collaboration requires flexibility. The team should not insist that individual members rigidly follow an agreed-on outline if it proves to be inadequate or faulty in one or more areas. When a writer pursues a specific assignment in detail, he or she may find that the general outline for that segment was based on insufficient knowledge and is not appropriate, or even possible, as written. During the research process, in particular, a writer may discover highly relevant information that is not covered in the team's working outline. In such cases, the writer must have the freedom to alter the outline. If the deviation is great enough, the writer should consult with the other team members before proceeding.

◆ *For a detailed explanation of the research process, see Chapter 6, Researching Your Subject.*

Revise your draft until it is as good as you can make it. Then, by the deadline established for submitting drafts, send copies of the draft to all other team members for their review. You may circulate the draft by distributing hard copy, by sending an attachment through e-mail, or by sharing files online.

Review and Revision

During the review stage, team members attempt to prevent in advance any problems that might arise for a given reader—a customer, a senior official in the organization, or the board of directors, for example. Each team member reviews the

◆ For a discussion of writing for international audiences, see pages 69–71 of Chapter 3, Writing the Draft, pages 300–305 of Chapter 8, Understanding the Principles of Business Communication, and pages 491–492 of Chapter 14, Giving Presentations and Conducting Meetings.

work of the other team members carefully and critically (but also with sensitivity to the person whose work is being reviewed), checking for problems in content, organization, and style. A good reviewer evaluates a document in terms of audience and purpose, coherence, emphasis, and accuracy. For a document intended for an international audience, this is the stage to have it reviewed by someone familiar with the country or culture of that audience.

The review stage may lead to additional planning. If, for example, a review of the first draft reveals that the original organization for a section was not adequate or correct, or if new information becomes available, the team must return to the planning stage for that segment of the document to incorporate the newer knowledge and understanding.

Figures 5–1 and 5–2 represent one section of a proposal that was written by Brady Associates to persuade a prospective client to merge a company's profit-sharing plans. The proposal describes the merger process and shows its associated costs. Two people collaborated to prepare the document; Figure 5–1 shows one team member's initial draft with the other's review comments. Because the final report will be submitted to a company president, whose time is limited and who has only a general knowledge of profit-sharing plans and mergers, the reviewer carefully noted any parts of the proposal that were not appropriate for a nonexpert reader.

Revising collaborative writing is much like revising any other type of writing: The writer considers suggested changes, checks questionable facts, and reworks the draft as appropriate. At this point, you, as a writer, must be careful not to let your ego get in the way of good judgment. You must consider each suggestion objectively on the basis of its merit, rather than reacting negatively to criticism of your writing. Writers who are able to accept criticism and use it to produce a better product participate in the most productive kind of collaboration.

ON THE WEB

For a sample of a reviewer's handwritten comments on a draft, go to *Model Documents Gallery,* bedfordstmartins.com/ writingthatworks

WRITER'S CHECKLIST
Reviewing Drafts by Other Writers

- ☑ Does the draft meet the established purpose of the document?
- ☑ Does the draft meet the needs of the target audience?
- ☑ Does the material fall within the predetermined scope of coverage?
- ☑ Does the draft generally follow the agreed-on outline?
- ☑ Is the content complete?
- ☑ Are there technical errors? Does anything seem technically questionable?
- ☑ Do details and examples support the main points?

Part II. Merger of Plans/Amending and Restating Plans/Applications for Determination Letters

Comment [EMK1]: Title is too technical—"Costs/Benefits of Merging"?

[DRAFT]

We can no longer test the Oakite product services 401(k) Profit Sharing

Plan separately for coverage and nondiscrimination because combined,

Oakite products and Oakley services have fewer than 50 employees.

Attempts to state problem and offer a solution

The merger of the 401(k) Profit Sharing Plans takes care of this problem

while reducing the implementation and audit costs. We will need to amend

and restate the new plan to bring it into compliance with tax law 409921-65.

Comment [WO2]: This is covered in Part I (make this into transition)

Comment [WO3]: sp

Comment [WO4]: #

Provides costs but no incentives

The cost of merging, amending, restating, and redesigning the surviving

401(k) Profit Sharing Plan and for filing of notices 54-90 and 36-98 and

applications 56-98 and 45-98 would be between $18,000 to $25,000.

Comment [EMK5]: Too technical and you need to emphasize benefits

Comment [WO6]: Cost reduction over 2 years

Additional Comments: Team Member #2 (B. Reisner, Sales Development)

Information sounds correct, but the prospective client will need definitions and explanations for many terms and names (notices 54-90 and 36-98). Also note in your opening that Part I explains the problems associated with maintaining separate plans. Doing so will give you a better lead into your section than you've got at this point.

Further, break down specific financial costs and benefits that will result from the merger. Don't go into detail here; remember, Part III describes the details of the merger process. Simply note specific costs for specific services in a table, and give an estimate of the client's projected financial gain. NOTE: The range for costs is $19,000 to $26,000, not $18,000 to $25,000. CHECK: Can client deduct merger costs from gross profit?

Finally, promote our services with more vigor. You're not simply reporting information so that Mr. B. can phone up another company to do the merger—you're talking him into working with Brady Associates.

Figure 5–1   Draft Section of a Proposal, with Comments of a Team Member

Statement of problem and offer of solution

Incentives for selecting proposed solution

PART II. BENEFITS AND COSTS OF MERGING CURRENT PROFIT-SHARING PLANS

As Part I of this report explains, the separate profit-sharing plans for your two companies, Oakite Products and Oakley Services, can no longer ensure that each employee is assigned the correct number of shares and the correct employer contribution. In addition, administrative costs for maintaining separate plans are high. If you commissioned Brady Associates to merge the plans, however, adequate tests could be performed to ensure accuracy, and administrative costs would be greatly reduced.

Further, although a merger would require you to make certain changes to your current profit-sharing procedures, Brady Associates would help you amend and restate the new plan so that it complies with the most recent tax legislation. Brady Associates will also prepare and file necessary merger documents with the Departments of Taxation and Labor.

The estimated cost for merging, amending, and refiling the profit-sharing plans would be between $19,000 and $26,000. Please see Table 1 for a breakdown of specific costs.

In reality, you would incur no cost if Brady Associates merged your profit-sharing plans because of reduced administrative costs. According to our estimates, the merger would give you a yearly net reduction of $36,000 in administrative costs. Thus, you would save approximately $11,000 during the first year of administering the plan and at least $36,000 annually after the first year. See Table 2 for a breakdown of net reductions in administrative costs.

Figure 5–2   Revised Section of Draft Proposal in Figure 5–1

 DIGITAL TIPS: Reviewing Collaborative Documents

Adobe Acrobat and many word-processing packages have options for providing feedback on the drafts of collaborators' documents. You can add text or voice annotations to the text, allowing your readers to read or hear your comments; you can also add track changes in your text and allow readers to accept or reject each change. In Acrobat, you can use a drawing tool to input traditional proofreaders' marks.

For more on this topic, see <bedfordstmartins.com/writingthatworks> and select *Digital Tips*, "Reviewing Collaborative Documents."

 DIGITAL TIPS: Using E-mail for Collaborative Writing

■ E-mail encourages members of a collaborative team to communicate with each other often, share information, ask questions, and solve problems.

■ Although e-mail can reduce the frequency of face-to-face communication, it does not eliminate the need for a group to meet in person when possible, especially during project planning periods.

■ A draft sent as an attachment enables collaborative team members to solicit feedback electronically and revise the original draft based on comments received.

■ Individual team members can solicit feedback and revise accordingly until all sections are in final form and ready for consolidation into the master copy maintained by the team leader.

◼ The Role of Conflict in Collaborative Writing

It is critically important to the quality of any team-written document that all contributors' viewpoints be considered. However, when writers collaborate, conflicts occur. These may range from a relatively minor difference over a grammatical point (such as whether to split an infinitive) to a major conflict over the basic approach to a document (such as how much detail is necessary). Regardless of the severity of a conflict, it must be worked through to a conclusion or compromise that all team members can accept, even though all might not entirely agree. When a group can tolerate some disharmony and work through conflicting opinions to reach a consensus, its work is enhanced.

Although mutual respect among team members is necessary, too much deference can inhibit challenges—and that reduces the team's creativity. You have to be willing to challenge another team member's work while still being sensitive to that person's ego. The same rule applies to collaborative writing that applies whenever critical give-and-take occurs: Focus on the problem and how to solve it rather than on the person.

Conflicts over valid issues almost always generate more innovative and creative work than does passive acceptance. However, even though the result of conflict in a peer-writing team is usually positive, it can sometimes produce doubt about yourself or your team members. Remember that conflict is a natural part of group work. Learn to harness it and turn it into a positive force.

To maximize the benefits and minimize the negative effects of conflict, the team members should emphasize areas of agreement. They then should identify differences of opinion and ask why they exist. If differences occur over facts, simply determine which are or are not correct. If there is a problem of differing goals, review the project's purpose statement to ensure common understanding. When conflict arises for other reasons, define the problem, describe or brainstorm possible solutions, and select the one solution—or compromise—that best satisfies the views of each team member and of the overall team.

The following suggestions can help you manage conflict:

- Avoid taking a win-or-lose stand, which gains one person's victory at another person's expense. This approach is not constructive because, by definition, there must be a loser. Most conflicts don't start out this way, but when a team member faces personal defeat, reaching a productive compromise is almost impossible.

- Avoid accusations, threats, or disparaging comments. Instead, emphasize common interests and mutual goals, bearing in mind that conciliation fosters cooperation. Expressing a desire for harmonious relations can have a very disarming effect on an aggressive personality in the group.

- Support your position with facts. Show how your position is consistent with precedent, prevailing norms, or accepted standards (if true, of course). Point out the ways that your position could benefit the team's ultimate goal and tactfully point out any disadvantages or logic errors in the other person's point of view. Again, focus on the problem and its so-lution, not the person.

- Use bargaining strategies to arrive at an exchange of concessions until a compromise is reached. Both parties win through a compromise. Even if you settle for less than you initially wanted, you don't risk losing out alto-gether as in a win-or-lose struggle. A successful compromise satisfies each participant's minimum needs.

Used well, collaboration resolves conflicts. Each team member must accept the group's goals and all must work to achieve the best outcome for the team. A flexible, exploratory attitude is a prerequisite for collaboration; always strive to understand each others' points of view and meet the group's needs.

WRITER'S CHECKLIST
Working in a Collaborative Group

- ☑ Know the people on your team and establish a good working rapport with them.
- ☑ Put the interests of your team ahead of your own.
- ☑ Think collectively, as a group, but respect the views of members with subject-area expertise.
- ☑ Participate constructively in group meetings.
- ☑ Be an effective listener (see Listening on pages 492–494 in Chapter 14, Giving Presentations and Conducting Meetings).
- ☑ Be receptive to constructive criticism.
- ☑ Provide constructive feedback to your team members.
- ☑ Meet your established deadlines.

■ Leading a Collaborative Writing Team

Although the team may designate one person as its leader, that person shares decision-making authority with the others while assuming the responsibility of co-ordinating the team's activities, organizing the project, and producing the final product. Leadership can be granted by mutual agreement to one team member or it can be rotated if the team produces many documents over time. The teams that collaborate best are composed of people who are professionally competent, who have mutual respect for the abilities of the other members, and who are compatible enough to work together harmoniously toward a common goal.

On a practical level, the team leader's responsibilities include scheduling and leading meetings, writing and distributing minutes of meetings, and main-taining the master copy of the document during all stages of its development. To make these activities as efficient as possible, the leader should prepare and dis-tribute forms to track the project's status. These forms should include style guidelines mutually agreed to in the project planning meeting (covering the issues listed on page 130), a project schedule, and transmittal sheets to record the status of reviews.

Schedule

All team members must know not only what is expected of them but when it is expected. The schedule provides this information. Schedules come in different formats. Figure 5–3, for example, shows a schedule used for a team project for a business writing class. Figure 5–4 shows a bar-chart schedule for the production of a software user's manual that required coordination among the writing, review, and production staffs over a five-month period. Regardless of the format, the schedule must state explicitly who is responsible for what and when the draft of each section is due.

Review Transmittal Sheet

The team leader should provide review transmittal sheets if drafts will be circulated on paper. Writers attach the sheets to their drafts or to a file folder or an envelope that holds it. Each reviewer signs off after reviewing the draft, then distributes it to the next reviewer on the list. The review transmittal sheet shows at a glance where the project is in its progression through the review cycle. It also lists in order those who must review the draft, as shown in Figure 5–5.

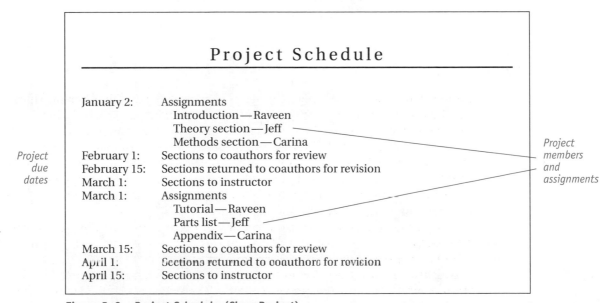

Project due dates

Project Schedule

January 2:	Assignments
	Introduction — Raveen
	Theory section — Jeff
	Methods section — Carina
February 1:	Sections to coauthors for review
February 15:	Sections returned to coauthors for revision
March 1:	Sections to instructor
March 1:	Assignments
	Tutorial — Raveen
	Parts list — Jeff
	Appendix — Carina
March 15:	Sections to coauthors for review
April 1:	Sections returned to coauthors for revision
April 15:	Sections to instructor

Project members and assignments

Figure 5–3   Project Schedule (Class Project)

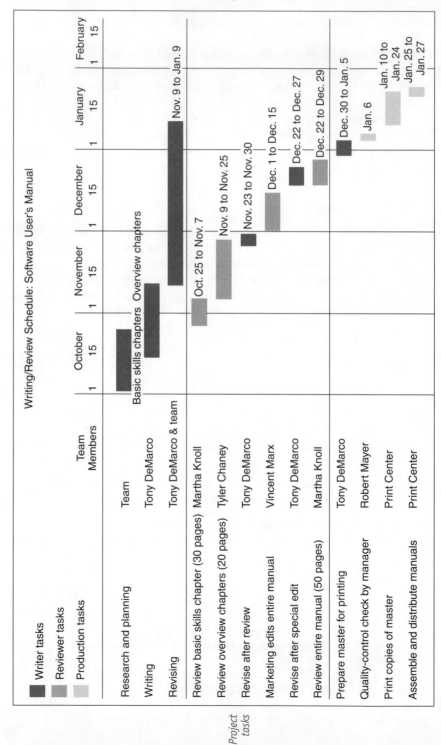

Figure 5–4   Project Schedule Presented as a Bar Chart (Workplace Project)

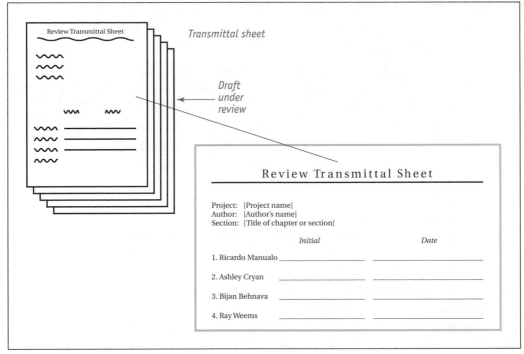

Figure 5–5   Review Transmittal Sheet Attached to a Draft

Collaborating with Other Departments

In some work settings, writing-team leaders also arrange for the cooperation of different departments within the organization in the creation or publication of final documents. For example, the team leader may need to meet with art, media, or Web production staff to

- Plan for the creation of graphs, charts, drawings, maps, and so on.
- Plan for the document's cover.
- Arrange for photographs to be taken or scanned.
- Determine the date for posting the document to the organization's Web site.

◆ *For guidance on posting documents to Web sites, see pages 530–531 in Chapter 15, Writing for the Web.*

The team leader may also meet with print production staff or the off-site printer to

- Inform them when to expect the manuscript.
- Discuss any special printing requirements, such as color, special bindings, document size, foldout pages, and so on.
- Ensure that the publication date meets the project deadline.

In addition, the team leader may need to obtain reviews and approval from other departments, such as the sales and legal departments.*

---

*In the classroom, your instructor or group team leader may take these roles.

CHAPTER 5 SUMMARY: COLLABORATIVE WRITING

Form a collaborative writing team when

- Your project requires specialists in more than one subject area.
- Your project would benefit from the merging of different perspectives.
- Your project's size, importance, or deadline requires a team effort.

As a member of a collaborative writing team, you are expected to

- Work with others as a team of peers to plan, design, and write a single document.
- Ensure that all important points are discussed and that all problems are addressed.
- Research the topics of your assigned section.
- Write your draft.
- Review the work of other team members.
- Revise your draft based on comments from other team members.
- Maintain the project schedule.
- Share equal responsibility for the end product.
- Respect the opinions of others.

As a team leader, you are expected to

- Share decision-making authority with other team members.
- Coordinate the activity of team members.
- Maintain the project schedule.
- Coordinate the production of the final product.

ON THE WEB

For an online quiz on collaborative writing, go to Chapter 5, bedfordstmartins.com/ writingthatworks

ON THE WEB

For additional exercises, go to Chapter 5, bedfordstmartins.com/ writingthatworks

■ Exercises

1. a. Draft a 300-word summary of a news article related to a professional or technical development, then exchange it with a study partner by e-mail. Review each other's work, make suggestions for revision, and return the file by e-mail. Refer to Digital Tips on pages 132 and 136. Together decide which method you will use to mark the files. Also review the Reviewing Drafts by Other Writers checklist on page 134.
   b. Bring a hard-copy draft of your writing assignment to class and exchange it with another student. Each student makes comments and suggestions for revision and returns the draft for rewriting.

2. Schedule a telephone, an e-mail, or a personal interview with a health-care, a business, a technology, or an industry representative who is part of a collaborative writing team. Before the interview, review this chapter to help you prepare a list of questions to ask about details of the collaborative writing style used by his or her group or company. Keep your interview to no more than 20 to 30 minutes. Consider asking about planning meetings and how they are conducted, collaboration with other specialists or peer reviews, preparing drafts of documents and how they are circulated and commented on for revision, and any positive or negative experi-

ences your interviewee found most helpful during the collaborative writing process. After the interview, prepare an outline, a draft, and a final report on your findings. Be ready to share your interview report with your classmates, and send the person you interviewed a thank-you letter.

3. Assume that your collaborative writing team of three or four students has been hired by a restaurant's national headquarters to conduct an evaluation of a local restaurant. Appoint a team leader who will assign specific items for each group member to observe while in the restaurant—for example, the cleanliness of the silverware and restrooms, the attentiveness of the wait staff, the quality of the food, and so on. As a group, summarize your findings in an outline and then create a draft letter addressed to the person who hired your team.

4. Assume that a group of you work as staff in your school's career-development center and you are concerned about some students not getting interviews. You call various recruiters and find out that they are turned off by the students' use of emoticons and silly addresses in their e-mail messages. Collaborate with classmates to develop a memo that could be sent to all students, advising them of proper e-mail etiquette. (You may want to review Writing and Formatting Memos on pages 282–288 and Sending E-mail and Instant Messages on pages 291–300 in Chapter 8, Understanding the Principles of Business Communication.)

5. Form a collaborative writing team with two or three classmates and choose a product or service, then create a company name. Decide on the nature of your business (service, manufacturing, and so on), the scope and size of your business (international, many branches), and the audience (client, consumer group) for your company's product or service. Develop and design a logo, letterhead, and business card appropriate to your company and clients. Submit your finished products to your instructor.

6. Form a collaborative writing team with your classmates based on common occupational interests, such as agriculture, communications, early childhood education, or engineering. Assume that you have been asked by your university's recruiting staff to create a document based on your experience as a student, explaining why your campus is a great place to prepare for the occupational interest you and your team have chosen. In your group, appoint a team leader and a team recorder, and decide how to organize and write this assignment so that recruiters can use your material to persuade students to attend your university.

7. Form a collaborative writing group that will meet weekly for the rest of the semester to discuss and write about the new material you learned in class and the assigned reading that you did that week. Your group will submit a brief, informal memo to your instructor each week that summarizes your group's discussion. Individually, you will also keep a weekly journal that records the group's interactions, activities, conflicts, and progress throughout the semester. In your final journal entry, comment on whether you think your writing group functioned as a productive writing team and analyze why or why not.

8. Write a brief narrative explaining why collaborative writing experiences are (or are not) a productive part of learning business writing skills. Review this chapter before you begin your draft, then use your own academic and on-the-job collaborative writing experiences as a basis for your conclusions.

9. Collaborate with a classmate to develop a process that your class can follow to review and comment on each other's written work. Before you begin, review this

chapter. Then create an outline and a rough draft for a plan that facilitates peer feedback. Highlight the specific benefits of your plan and be ready to share your plan with the rest of the class.

10. Form a collaborative group of no more than six members in which both genders are represented equally. Appoint a group leader and a group recorder. Based on your personal experiences, brainstorm as a group to create a list of gender-related issues that you have encountered as college students, such as the stereotyping of women and men with regard to verbal or mathematical abilities or technological skills. Use your collaborative lists to generate a brief report about these campus gender issues for your college's Office of Diversity (or comparable unit) that includes the ideas of each group member. Be ready to share your report with the rest of the class or write an individual report, summarizing the personal interactions of your group during your meetings.

ON THE WEB

For more collaborative classroom projects, go to Chapter 5, bedfordstmartins.com/ writingthatworks

◼ Collaborative Classroom Projects

1. An important stage of the collaborative writing process is the planning stage, during which time all members of the team need to work toward the same goal, select a reference guide, set up a schedule, and agree on how to enforce the standards that have been established. Assume that your manager has given you a collaborative writing assignment on a topic specific to the company's main product. In groups of five or fewer, take the next 30 minutes to

   a. Become acquainted with one another's expertise by asking each person to talk about his or her background for two minutes or less.
   b. Select a team leader.
   c. Decide the schedule for making initial assignments and submitting drafts, coauthor reviews, and revisions.
   d. Decide what method you will use to enforce the timeline.
   e. Decide what other guidelines are necessary to ensure the group's success.

   Keep in mind that unstated policies can lead to confusion about responsibilities. Therefore, when your group has discussed project guidelines, the team leader will summarize these policies in a list.

2. Using the same group you selected for Collaborative Classroom Project 1, experiment with positive conflict, which almost always generates more innovative and creative work than does passive acceptance. Assuming that half of the members of your team have young children and half do not, as a team write a recommendation on whether your company should provide space for on-site day care. The parents on the team claim that an unused storage room in the building is large enough to accommodate a day-care center, while those without young children feel it would be more productive to convert the space into an employee lounge. As a team, spend 45 minutes developing an outline of the pros and cons for both sides of the issue.

   a. Quickly establish who is a parent of young children and who is not.
   b. Appoint a team leader.
   c. Brainstorm your list of pros and cons for first one side of the issue and then the other.

    d. During the next 15 minutes, quickly draft your collaborative outline and be ready to share it with the class.

3. Imagine that several of you have been hired as a collaborative writing team for a national home décor and architecture magazine. This magazine has won awards for its high-end presentation of celebrity homes and parties, but its senior editor and upper management have recently been lured away by a competing publication. The last two issues have suffered as new hires and interns struggle to come up with successful story ideas, coordinate celebrity interviews and photo shoots, get error-free copy from advertisers and freelance writers on time, coordinate with the graphics department so that the issues are laid out properly, and meet the printer's deadlines. The magazine publisher is very worried about the upcoming holiday issue, which is usually popular with readers and advertisers.

    Magazines typically have a six-month lead time. For example, December magazine articles are assigned to writers in July. Choose someone to be team leader, then using Figures 5–3, 5–4, and 5–5, create a schedule for the holiday issue and transmittal sheets. Decide on the final production deadline (when everything is ready to go to the printer) and then individual production deadlines for the following:

    a. Help the editorial staff determine all of the copy (written material) that will be included in the issue, the dates freelance and staff writers need to start writing the copy, and the copy deadlines (make them due at least six weeks before the production due date). Don't forget the time the editorial staff will need to edit the copy and fact-check it. Create a Review Transmittal Sheet (see Figure 5–5) to ensure all of the editors, proofreaders, and fact-checkers have reviewed the drafts.

    b. Help advertising staff determine the number of ads for this issue and make them due at least seven weeks before the production due date. Then help the graphics staff determine when they need to have the artwork for the ads (display artwork) completed (no more than a week or two after the ads come in). Remember to have the artwork and ads proofread by members of the editorial staff.

    c. Help the graphics staff schedule the time needed to lay out the entire magazine and then have it proofread by members of the editorial staff to make sure everything was included in the issue and copy or ads weren't accidentally forgotten.

■ Research Projects

ON THE WEB

For extra research projects, go to Chapter 5, bedfordstmartins.com/writingthatworks

1. Form a collaborative writing team to research and write a major report for a department manager, recommending the purchase of laptop computers for traveling staff. In your proposal, identify the type and brand of computer you will be evaluating, as well as how and where you will gather information on the product (in person at a retail location, on the Internet, and so on).

    a. Decide on a team leader and an evaluation board, then
- Write a memo requesting your instructor's approval for your team to undertake the project and to evaluate specific computer brands and models.
- Create biweekly progress reports, to start as soon as your team has received project approval and to continue for the duration of the project.

b. Have the team leader delegate research responsibilities so that members are able to collect information that answers why the computers are needed and how many are needed; describe the specific features the portable computers should have (such as memory size, operating speed, and compatibility with personal computers already installed at the company); describe the types of software that should be installed; define what the total cost will be and whether an educational discount or a quantity discount is available; and explain how the computers should be kept secure and how borrowing them would be controlled.

c. Decide collaboratively on dates for submission of the proposal, progress reports (every two weeks from project approval), the final report, and the final presentation.

d. Present an oral description of your research to the other team members, as well as a report on the results of your preliminary evaluation. Each team member should do the same.

e. Have the team leader present the final results of the project and the recommendations to an evaluation board.

f. Finally, (1) prepare and submit a joint (single) copy of the proposal, progress reports, and formal report, and (2) make group oral presentations. Provide handouts of any printed information you have obtained or of any important text from your proposal (see Using Handouts on page 488 in Chapter 14, Giving Presentations and Conducting Meetings). As a team, consider how much the visual appearance of your report will influence whether your recommendations receive approval. If the department manager likes what he or she reads, your report may be attached to his or her budget request to demonstrate why the computers are needed (this is commonly known as "the justification"). Consequently, the quality of your report, both in appearance and in content, can help convince those readers who will approve the expenditure for your request. Your instructor will award a group mark for each assignment, which all team members will receive.[1]

2. Teamwork is used in corporations around the globe. Form a collaborative writing team to research at least two different countries' perspectives on the need for teamwork in the workplace. Compare your findings to the American perspective on teamwork in the workplace. Present your findings to the class. As your instructor directs, use some of the strategies from earlier collaborative assignments.

ON THE WEB

For additional Web projects, go to Chapter 5, bedfordstmartins.com/ writingthatworks

■ Web Projects

1. One of the major experts in teamwork and corporate success is W. E. Deming, who created Total Quality Management (TQM). Form a collaborative group and research and write a report on Deming and TQM. The presentation should consist of an introduction and a conclusion and the following three parts that form the middle of the report:

---

[1] This project is adapted, with permission, from "An Integrated Collaborative Writing Project" by Ron S. Blicq, in *Collaborative Technical Writing: Theory and Practice*, ed. Richard Louth and Martin Scott (Hammond, LA: Association of Teachers of Technical Writing, n.d.), pp. 57–60.

    a. A definition and an explanation of TQM, with background on the history of TQM and its creator.

    b. An explanation of TQM's 14 principles and how TQM supports teamwork. Give examples of why companies like General Motors have used or continue to use TQM.

    c. An explanation of the both positive and negative issues that need to be addressed regarding TQM or other teamwork programs. One might be that people from different cultures may have different problems adapting to teamwork. For example, many Americans value individualism, which may at times conflict with teamwork principles.

2. Several of today's successful companies encourage collaborative writing on the job. Search the Web to learn how such companies advertise their team approach when hiring. You might explore the job listings on Web sites for companies such as Saturn and the Kimberly-Clark Corporation, as well as the job descriptions on career sites such as Monster.com and HotJobs.com. Outline the kinds of collaborative writing assignments that a writer at a particular company might encounter. Your outline should cover areas such as product information, warranty information, employment training, management styles, and so on.

6 Researching Your Subject

Tom Cabines, Production Manager of Nebel Desktop Publishers, received a memo from Alice Enklend, Purchasing Director, asking him how many copies of an employee manual a corporate customer had commissioned the firm to print. Tom probably had the answer at his fingertips or was able to find it after a quick look at his computer's production-scheduling

Voices from the Workplace

Susan U. Ladwig, Reinhart Boerner Van Deuren

Susan Ladwig is an associate attorney in the Employee Benefits Department at Reinhart Boerner Van Deuren in Milwaukee, Wisconsin. Among her responsibilities are researching legal issues and developing legal memoranda and legal documents reflecting her research. Susan describes the Internet as a powerful tool and resource in her business: "The Internet has become a basic research tool for attorneys who must quickly access the most up-to-date information on law changes, corporations, court decisions, and various legal subjects. Learning how to critically evaluate and efficiently gather key data from the Internet is an important skill."

Liz Goodwin, Melrose Public Library

As a librarian's assistant, Liz Goodwin works at the ciruclation desk, where she helps patrons find books and conduct research on specific subjects. In addition to helping other people locate information, Liz often conducts her own research as part of her job. Once, for example, she "was given the task of finding out what were the most-popular books of [the year]. We wanted to know how often these books were checked out of the library so we could petition for more funding to buy more books. I consulted a few Internet resources, like the *New York Times* best-seller list and <www.amazon.com>. Because I knew these sites were reputable, I could base my research on their findings."

spreadsheet. Tom's *research*—or tracking down of information on the topic—would be minimal.

Suppose, instead, that Tom were asked to write a market-research report for the president of Nebel Desktop Publishers about developing a Web publishing division. How would he go about obtaining the necessary information? For this task, he would have to do some extensive work, which could involve primary research—conducting interviews or collecting questionnaire responses on the topic—or secondary research—gathering information from the library, the Internet, or both.

ON THE WEB

For online resources for conducting research, go to Chapter 6, bedfordstmartins.com/ writingthatworks

■ Conducting Primary Research: Experience, Interviews, Observations, and Questionnaires

Primary research is the gathering of raw data from such sources as firsthand experience, interviews, direct observations, and questionnaires. In fact, direct observation and interaction are the only ways to obtain certain kinds of information about human and animal behavior, natural phenomena, and the operation of systems and equipment. For example, you might use primary research to test the usability of instructions you have created.

◆ *For more on usability testing, see page 428 in Chapter 12, Writing Instructions.*

In an academic setting, you may talk about resources with your peers, your instructors, and especially a research librarian. On the job, you may rely on your own knowledge and experience and that of your colleagues. In business, the most-important sources of information may include market research, questionnaires and surveys, focus groups, public meetings, shareholder meetings, and the like. In this setting, begin by brainstorming with colleagues about what sources will be most useful for your project and how you can track them down.

Beginning with Experience

◆ *For detailed advice on using outlines, see pages 27–35 in Chapter 2, Organizing Your Information.*

If your research topic deals with something familiar (a hobby or an area of interest, for example) or relates to an occupation you are in or hope to be in, you may already know enough to get started. In addition, you can check your home or office files for any materials you have acquired on the subject. Based on this background, make a rough outline—it will tell you how much you know about the topic. Your own experience is a starting point from which you can expand your knowledge by finding and using other sources discussed in this chapter.

Interviewing for Information

To learn from the experience of others, you may be able to do some of your research by interviewing someone who is an expert on the subject. This process includes determining the proper person to interview, preparing for the interview, conducting the interview, and expanding your notes immediately after the interview.

Determining Whom to Interview

Many times, your subject or purpose logically points to the proper person to interview for information. If, for instance, you were writing about how to use the Web to market a software-development business, the logical experts to interview would include someone with extensive experience in Web marketing and someone who has built a successful business developing software. The following sources can help you identify an appropriate person to interview: (1) workplace colleagues or faculty in relevant academic departments, (2) a local firm or organization whose staff includes experts on your subject, (3) information from Internet research, (4) local chapters or Web pages of professional societies, and (5) yellow or business pages of the local telephone directory.

Preparing for the Interview

Once you have selected the person or persons you would like to interview, learn as much as possible about each person and the organization for which he or she works. When you contact the prospective interviewee, explain who you are, why you would like to interview him or her, the subject and purpose of the interview, and how much time it will take. Also let your interviewee know that you will allow him or her to review your draft.

After you have made the appointment, prepare a list of questions to ask your interviewee. Avoid vague, general questions such as "What do you think of the Internet?" Instead, ask specific but open-ended questions such as "How do you use the Internet to help clients?" and "How has use of the Internet helped your organization?" Such questions prompt interviewees to provide specific information. Organize your questions so that you begin with the least-complex aspects of the topic, then move to the more-complex aspects.

Conducting the Interview

Arrive for your interview on time and be prepared to guide the discussion. Once you've introduced yourself, take a few minutes to chat informally—this will help both you and your interviewee to relax. During the interview, follow the guidelines listed in the Interviewing Successfully checklist.

◆ *See also Listening on pages 492–494 in Chapter 14, Giving Presentations and Conducting Meetings.*

WRITER'S CHECKLIST
Interviewing Successfully

- [ ] Be pleasant but purposeful. You are there to get information, so don't be timid about asking leading questions on the subject.

- [ ] Use the list of questions you have prepared, starting with the less-complex aspects of the topic to get the conversation started and then going on to the more-complex aspects.

- [ ] Let your interviewee do most of the talking. Remember that he or she is the expert.

- [ ] Be objective. Don't offer your opinions on the subject. You are there to get information, not to debate.

- [ ] Some answers prompt additional questions; ask them as they arise.

- [ ] Stay on track. If the interviewee strays too far from the subject, ask a specific question to redirect the conversation.

- [ ] Be flexible. If a prepared question is no longer suitable, move to the next question.

- [ ] If you plan to use a tape recorder, first obtain the interviewee's permission to do so. If permission is granted, do not let the recorder lull you into relaxing so that you neglect to ask crucial questions.

- [ ] As the interview comes to a close, take a few minutes to skim your notes. If time allows, ask the interviewee to clarify anything that is ambiguous. After thanking the interviewee, ask permission to telephone to clarify a point or two as you complete your interview notes.

Expanding Your Notes after the Interview

Immediately after leaving the interview, use your memory-jogging notes to help you mentally go over the interview and record your detailed notes. Review your notes, fill in any material that is obviously missing, and summarize the speaker's remarks. Do not postpone this step. No matter how good your memory is, you will forget some important points if you do not do this at once. As soon as possible, convert the notes to complete sentences. Select the important information you need and transfer it to your outline or working draft.

A day or two after the interview, thank the interviewee in a brief letter or e-mail.

 DIGITAL TIP: Using E-mail to Ask Questions

Even if geography or scheduling prevents you from interviewing an expert in person, you may be able to ask some questions through e-mail. To locate an expert's e-mail address, check the author notes at the end of articles and bibliographies; academic and company Web sites are also good resources for electronic contact information.

When sending questions by e-mail, be as concise and informative as possible in the Subject line. Send the request from your school or work e-mail account to avoid the impression that your request is spam, and do not include any attachments. In the body of your message, briefly describe your quest, write out a few questions, and ask your expert for a referral if he or she is unable to respond. (See also Inquiries on pages 314–318 in Chapter 9, Writing Business Correspondence.) Above all, remember that the person you are writing to is not obligated to answer your e-mail. To improve your chances of a reply, be brief, clear, and respectful.

Observing Firsthand

Visiting a location and conducting firsthand observations may provide valuable information about how a process or procedure works or how a group interacts. If you are planning research that involves observation, choose your sites and times carefully, and be sure to obtain permission in advance. During your observations, remain as unobtrusive as possible and keep accurate, complete records that indicate date, time of day, duration of the observation, and so on. Save interpretations of your observations for future analysis.

Using a Questionnaire

Consider expanding the number of people you gather information from beyond those you've interviewed by using a questionnaire. A questionnaire—a series of questions on a particular topic, sent out to a number of people—is an interview on paper. It has several advantages over the personal interview, and several disadvantages.

Advantages

- A questionnaire allows you to gather information from more people more quickly than you could through personal interviews.
- It enables you to obtain responses from people who are hard to reach or who are in scattered geographical locations.
- Respondents have more time to think through their answers than they would under the pressure of composing thoughtful and complete answers to an interviewer.

- The questionnaire may yield more-objective data because it reduces the possibility that the interviewer's tone of voice or facial expressions might influence an answer.
- The cost of distributing and tabulating a questionnaire is lower than the cost of conducting numerous personal interviews.

Disadvantages

- The results of a questionnaire may be slanted in favor of those people who have strong opinions on a subject because they are more likely to respond than those who have only moderate views.
- Even if a questionnaire is designed to let one question lead logically to another, the questionnaire does not allow specific follow-up to answers.
- Distributing questionnaires and waiting for replies may take considerably longer than conducting a personal interview.

Selecting Questionnaire Recipients

Selecting the proper recipients for your questionnaire is crucial if you are to gather representative and usable data. If you wanted to survey the opinions of large groups in the general population—for example, all medical technologists working in private laboratories or all independent garage owners—your task would not be easy. Because you cannot include everybody in your survey, you need to choose a representative cross section—for example, include enough people from around the country, of both genders, and with varied educational training. Only then could you make a generalized statement based on your findings from the sample. (The best sources of information on sampling techniques are marketing-research and statistics texts.)

ON THE WEB

For online resources related to marketing, marketing research, and more, go to Chapter 6, bedfordstmartins.com/ writingthatworks, and select *Web Links*.

Preparing and Designing Your Questionnaire

A key goal in designing a questionnaire is to keep it as brief as possible. The longer it is, the less likely the recipient will be to complete and return it. Next, the questions should be easy to understand. A confusing question will yield confusing results, whereas a carefully worded question will be easy to answer. Ideally, recipients should be able to answer most questions with a "yes" or "no" or by checking or circling a choice among several options. Such answers are simple to tabulate and require minimum effort on the part of the respondent, thus increasing your chances of obtaining a response.

▶ Do you recommend that the flextime program be made permanent?

❏ Yes   ❏ No   ❏ No opinion

If you need more information than such questions produce, provide an appropriate range of answers, as in the following example.

▶ How many hours of overtime would you be willing to work each week?

❏ 4 hours   ❏ 8 hours   ❏ Over 10 hours
❏ 6 hours   ❏ 10 hours   ❏ No overtime

Questions should be neutral; their wording should not lead respondents to give a particular answer, which can result in inaccurate or skewed data.

SLANTED   Would you prefer the freedom of a four-day workweek?

NEUTRAL   Would you choose to work a four-day workweek, ten hours a day, with
                 every Friday off?

ETHICS NOTE

Follow your company's policy or applicable laws when requesting information about the respondent's age, gender, occupation, or other private information. Include such information only if it will be of value in interpreting the answers to the questionnaire. Also be clear about whether the respondent's identity and any information he or she provides will be kept confidential.

The sample cover memo and questionnaire in Figures 6–1 and 6–2 were sent to employees who had participated in a large organization's six-month program of flexible working hours.

Luxwear Products Corporation
MEMO

To: All Company Employees
From: Nelson Barrett, Human Resources Director
Date: October 17, 2006
Subject: Review of Flexible Working Hours Program

Please complete and return the questionnaire enclosed regarding Luxwear's trial program of flexible working hours. Your answers will help us decide whether we should make the program permanent.

Return the completed questionnaire to Ken Rose, Mail Code 12B (Fax 212-936-8358), by October 27. Your signature on the questionnaire is not necessary. All responses will be confidential and given serious consideration. Feel free to raise additional issues pertaining to the program.

If you want to discuss any item in the questionnaire, call Pam Peters in the Human Resources Department at extension 8812, or send her an e-mail at pp1@lpc.com.

Enclosure: Questionnaire

Figure 6–1   Questionnaire Cover Memo

Flexible Working Hours Program
Questionnaire

1. What kind of position do you occupy?

   ☐ Supervisory
   ☐ Nonsupervisory

2. Indicate to the nearest quarter of an hour when you begin work under flextime.

   ☐ 7:00 a.m.   ☐ 8:15 a.m.
   ☐ 7:15 a.m.   ☐ 8:30 a.m.
   ☐ 7:30 a.m.   ☐ 8:45 a.m.
   ☐ 7:45 a.m.   ☐ 9:00 a.m.
   ☐ 8:00 a.m.   ☐ Other (specify)

3. Where do you live?

   ☐ Talbot County   ☐ Greene County
   ☐ Montgomery County   ☐ Other (specify)

4. How do you usually travel to work?

   ☐ Drive alone   ☐ Walk
   ☐ Bus   ☐ Carpool
   ☐ Train   ☐ Motorcycle
   ☐ Bicycle   ☐ Other (specify)

5. How has flextime affected your commuting time?

   ☐ Increase: Approximate number of minutes
   ☐ Decrease: Approximate number of minutes
   ☐ No change

6. If you drive alone or in a carpool, has flextime increased or decreased the amount of time it takes you to find a parking space?

   ☐ Increased   ☐ Decreased   ☐ No change

7. How has flextime affected your productivity?

   a. Quality of work
      ☐ Increased   ☐ Decreased   ☐ No change

   b. Accuracy of work
      ☐ Increased   ☐ Decreased   ☐ No change

   c. Quiet time for uninterrupted work
      ☐ Increased   ☐ Decreased   ☐ No change

8. Have you had difficulty getting in touch with coworkers who are on different work schedules from yours?

   ☐ Yes   ☐ No

Figure 6–2   Questionnaire (continued)

9. Have you had trouble scheduling meetings within flexible starting and quitting times?

   ☐ Yes   ☐ No

10. Has flextime affected the way you feel about your job?

    ☐ Yes   ☐ No

    If yes, please answer (a) or (b):

    a. Feel better about job
       ☐ Slightly   ☐ Considerably

    b. Feel worse about job
       ☐ Slightly   ☐ Considerably

11. How important is it for you to have flexibility in your working hours?

    ☐ Very   ☐ Not very   ☐ Somewhat   ☐ Not at all

12. Has flextime allowed you more time to be with your family?

    ☐ Yes   ☐ No

13. If you are responsible for the care of a young child or children, has flextime made it easier or more difficult for you to arrange babysitting or day-care services?

    ☐ Easier   ☐ More difficult   ☐ No change

14. Do you recommend that the flextime program be made permanent?

    ☐ Yes   ☐ No

15. Please describe below or on a separate page any major changes you recommend for the program.

Thank you for your assistance.

Figure 6–2   Questionnaire (continued)

WRITER'S CHECKLIST
Creating a Questionnaire

☑ Prepare a cover letter, a memo (if the questionnaire is to be circulated within an organization), or an e-mail explaining who you are, the questionnaire's purpose, the date by which you need a response, and how and where to send the completed questionnaire. Include your contact information (mailing address, phone number, and e-mail address).

☑ Include a stamped, self-addressed envelope if you are using regular mail.

☑ Construct as many questions as possible that can be quickly answered with "yes," "no," or a checkmark.

☑ Include a section for additional comments, where respondents may clarify their overall attitude toward the subject.

☑ Consider offering some tangible appreciation to those who answer the questionnaire by a specific date, such as a copy of the results or, for a marketing questionnaire, a gift certificate.

Conducting Secondary Research: The Library and the Internet

Secondary research is the gathering of information that has been previously analyzed, assessed, evaluated, compiled, or otherwise organized into accessible form. Sources include books and articles, as well as reports, Web documents, online discussion forums, audio and video recordings, podcasts, business letters, minutes of meetings, operating manuals, brochures, and so forth. To find these materials, you will need to conduct research using your library and the Internet.

Developing an effective search strategy entails considering what you already know and ferreting out further questions about the topic. Early stages may have dead ends and enticing side trips as you begin to focus your topic. Review the Developing a Search Strategy checklist to analyze your assignment and consider the type, quantity, and format of information you need.

WRITER'S CHECKLIST
Developing a Search Strategy

Your answers to the following questions will help to limit the kind of information you are seeking and determine where you should look.

☑ What is the scope of your project? Is it a 5-minute oral presentation? A 20-page research paper? A combined group presentation?

☑ How much information is needed? Is currency a factor?

☑ What kinds of sources (newspapers, signed encyclopedia articles, scholarly journal articles, books, Web sites) are appropriate?

☑ What formats (visual images, audio, print, or electronic) are needed?

☑ Do you need others' opinions or points of view?

☑ What are your deadlines?

As you look for sources, keep in mind that in many cases the more recent the information, the better. Articles in periodicals and newspapers provide current sources. Academic (.edu), organizational (.org), and government (.gov) Web sites may include recent research, works in progress, interviews, articles, papers, and conference proceedings.

When a resource seems useful, consider its authorship and other aspects of a text or document as outlined in the Evaluating Print Resources (page 170) and Evaluating Online Resources (page 171) checklists. Then read the material carefully and take notes that include any additional questions about your topic. Some of your questions may eventually be clarified in other sources; questions that remain unanswered may point to future research projects.

Library Research

Libraries provide organized paths into scholarship, information, and the ever-expanding Internet. Library resources include online catalogs useful for locating books, videos, and government documents; licensed online databases and indexes necessary for locating and retrieving articles; specialized tools; and subject directories for using the Web.

Go to the best library in your area and take advantage of it. The mission for most librarians is to help patrons answer questions. Librarians can tell you where to begin, how to refine your search strategy, and how to find research materials related to your topic. They can also interpret your questions and guide your search toward the best print or online resources for your topic, often saving you time. A brief conversation may help to focus your research and alert you to the most-productive information sources. Keep in mind that in addition to providing help in person and on the phone, an increasing number of libraries now offer e-mail or live chat access for answering reference questions and giving research support. Use your library's homepage (Figure 6–3) to access this feature, as well as the library catalog, article databases, Web directories, and more.

Your search strategy depends on the kind of information you are seeking. For example, if you need the latest data on obesity-prevention programs, you might start by checking your library's subject directory to the Web. For additional information, you could then search a database subscribed to by your library—such as Academic Search Premier—for journal articles on the subject. Do you want to include opinions about the impact of obesity in the workplace? Search the newspaper databases. For an overview of a subject, check your library's reference materials. For in-depth discussions, the best resources are books and periodicals.

Using Online Catalogs to Locate Books

A library's online catalog—accessed through a library computer or the Internet, as shown in Figure 6–3—allows you to search a library's holdings, tells you an item's location and availability, and may even permit you to search the holdings of other libraries in the region or around the world. (Check with the library staff or the library homepage for interlibrary loan policies and requirements.)

ON THE WEB

For resources for finding libraries in your area or online, go to Chapter 6, bedfordstmartins.com/ writingthatworks, and select *Web Links*.

ON THE WEB

For glossaries of common library and Internet research terms, go to Chapter 6, bedfordstmartins.com/ writingthatworks

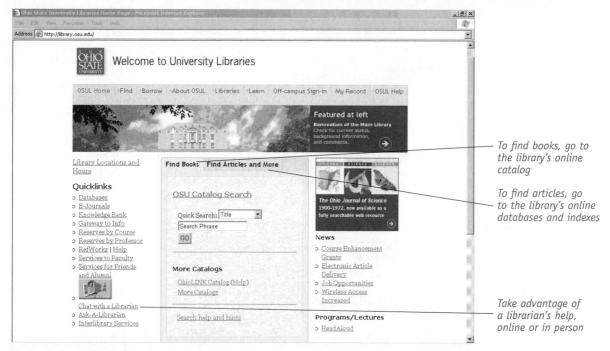

To find books, go to
the library's online
catalog

To find articles, go
to the library's online
databases and indexes

Take advantage of
a librarian's help,
online or in person

Figure 6–3   College Library Homepage

Methods for searching online catalogs vary. Typically, you can search by author, title, subject, or keyword. Become familiar with the way your library's catalog works. If you are at the library, ask a reference librarian to give you a brief tour of the catalog; otherwise, check the library's homepage or catalog page for guidelines or FAQs (Frequently Asked Questions). Help screens (Figure 6–4) can be particularly useful in learning the best strategies for locating appropriate materials. Getting information on a few basic tools and reviewing the directions for locating materials will prepare you to start your research and will often help you streamline the search process.

Follow these basic steps to search an online catalog:

1. *Start with a question or a thesis statement.* If your topic is unfamiliar, try to find a background article on it. Is there a specialized encyclopedia, reference book, or summary that brings some of the research and history of the topic together in one location? Talk to a reference librarian to identify good starting points.

2. *Limit the scope of your search.* Do you need to describe why the topic is important? Will the chronology of changes in the topic strengthen your argument? The catalog may provide a shortcut to the library's online reference section. Hyperlinks can be helpful but also very distracting—keep your focus.

ON THE WEB

For access to online library catalogs, go to Chapter 6, **bedfordstmartins.com/ writingthatworks,** and select *Web Links.*

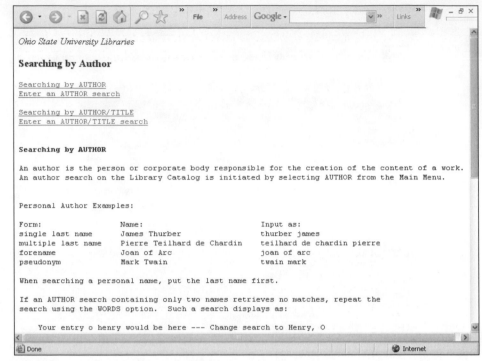

Defines meaning of search term with examples

Describes advance search options

Figure 6–4　Online Catalog Help Screen

ON THE WEB

For online tours of the Library of Congress and Dewey decimal organizing systems, go to Chapter 6, **bedfordstmartins.com/ writingthatworks**, and select *Web Links*.

3. *Sum up your thesis in two or three key terms.* What words might you use to conduct keyword or key subject searches? If you are using an American academic library, consider checking the subject headings issued by the Library of Congress at <www.loc.gov> for categories relevant to your topic. Public libraries most often use the older Dewey decimal system for classifying information in their collections.

If your search turns up too many results, narrow your search by using the Limit Search or Advanced Search option offered by many catalogs. An example of an advanced search by keyword is shown in Figure 6–5.

Using Databases and Indexes to Locate Articles

Libraries subscribe to databases, also known as periodical indexes, that provide citations for print resources and electronic collections of full-text articles; they can be searched within the library building or through remote access available to registered students, faculty, and staff. Figure 6–6 is an example of a library page that provides access to articles in journals organized by subject area. A library's database and index subscriptions might include any or all of the following:

- *EBSCOhost's Academic Search Premier:* the world's largest academic multidisciplinary database, which provides full text for nearly 4,600 scholarly publications, including full text for more than 3,500 peer-reviewed journals

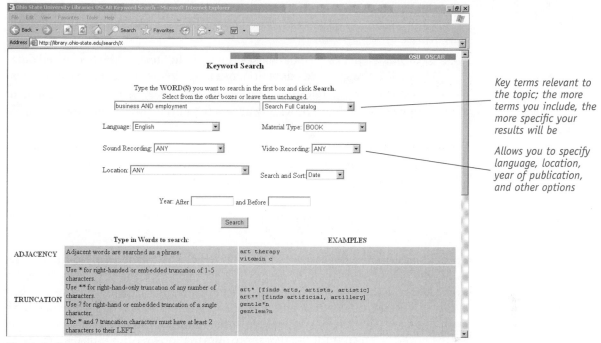

Figure 6–5   Advanced Catalog Search by Keyword

Key terms relevant to the topic; the more terms you include, the more specific your results will be

Allows you to specify language, location, year of publication, and other options

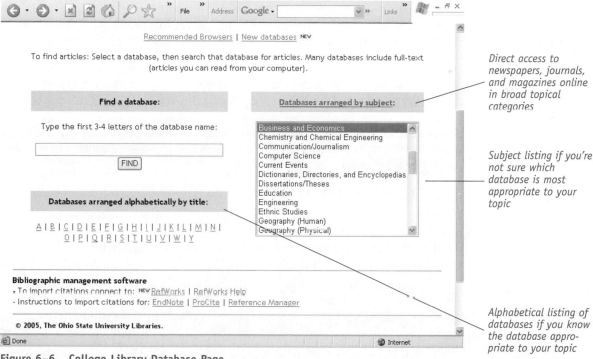

Figure 6–6   College Library Database Page

Direct access to newspapers, journals, and magazines online in broad topical categories

Subject listing if you're not sure which database is most appropriate to your topic

Alphabetical listing of databases if you know the database appropriate to your topic

- *InfoTrac:* another enormous database, covering general-interest and scholarly journals, plus business, law, and health-care publications (many in full text)
- *ProQuest:* a package of databases (many in full text) with specialized databases for newspapers, education, nursing, biology, psychology, and others
- *ERIC* (Education Resources Information Center): a U.S. Department of Education database, providing access to journal and nonjournal resources in education
- *JSTOR:* a full-text, archival collection of journals in humanities, social sciences, and sciences
- *Lexis/Nexis Academic:* a collection of databases that is particularly strong for news, business, legal, and corporate and financial information (most articles in full text), as well as congressional, statistical, and governmental resources

These databases are excellent resources for articles published within the last ten to twenty years. Some include descriptive abstracts and full texts of articles. To find older articles, you may need to consult a print index, such as the *Readers' Guide to Periodical Literature* and the *New York Times Index,* both of which have been digitized and may be available in some libraries. Check the subject listings for the coverage on your topics. (For more information on print indexes, see Using Reference Works to Locate Facts, Overviews, and Statistics, on pages 162–164.)

To locate articles within a particular database, conduct a keyword search. If your search turns up too many results, narrow your search by connecting two search terms with *AND*—"business writing AND employment"—or use other options offered by the database, such as a limited, modified, or advanced search, as shown in Figure 6–7.

 DIGITAL TIP: Storing Search Results

Most databases allow users to customize and save their searches; some, such as ProQuest, will even create a bibliography for you. Several databases also offer the option of sending a citation or the full text of a journal article to an e-mail account. To manage this information, create electronic folders for each of your projects and make a habit of organizing your search results within them. Copying the folders onto a CD-ROM or a flash drive can make your research portable and available as you move among the classroom, the library, and home.

Using Reference Works to Locate Facts, Overviews, and Statistics

In addition to articles and books, you may want to consult reference works such as encyclopedias, dictionaries, and atlases for a brief overview of your subject. *Bibliographies,* which are lists of works written about a topic, can direct you to more-specialized sources. Ask your reference librarian to recommend reference works and bibliographies that are most relevant to your topic. Many are located online and can be accessed through your library's homepage.

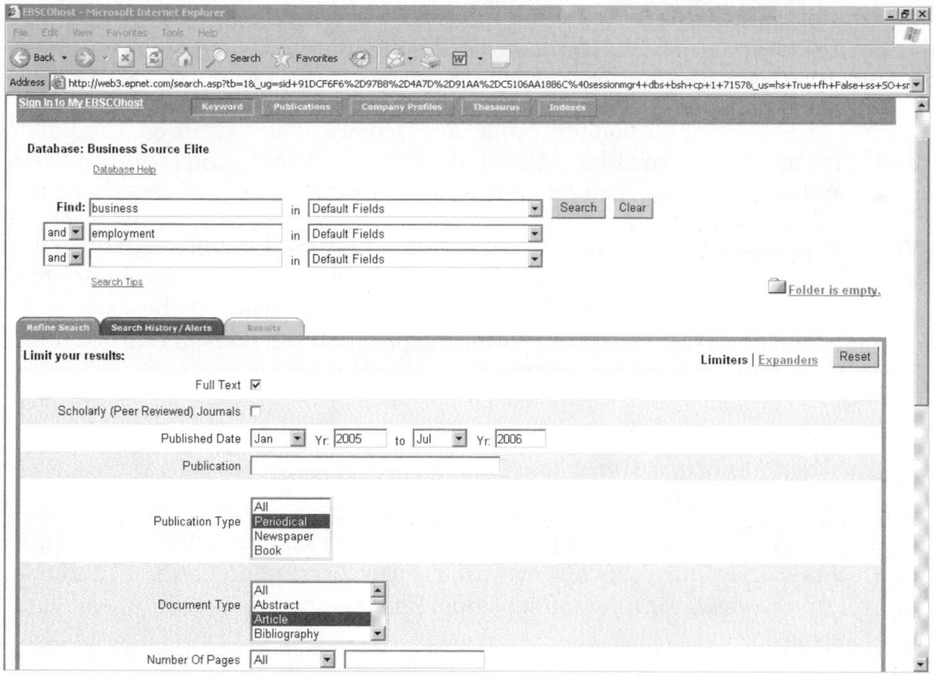

Area to specify keyword search

Separate screen to help refine search

More options for focusing your search; results will include only 2005–2006 articles available in full text

Search results provide access to the articles in periodicals

Figure 6–7 EBSCOhost Search for Articles

Encyclopedias. Encyclopedias are comprehensive, multivolume collections of articles arranged alphabetically. Some, such as the *Encarta Encyclopedia* at <http://encarta@msn.com>, cover a wide range of subjects, while others, such as *The Encyclopedia of Careers and Vocational Guidance,* 13th ed., edited by William Hopke (Chicago: Ferguson, 2005), and the *McGraw-Hill Encyclopedia of Science and Technology,* 9th ed. (New York: McGraw-Hill, 2002), are targeted to specific subjects. One lively development is *Wikipedia* at <www.wikipedia.org>, a free online encyclopedia that users are encouraged to update (because it has no editorial filter, use it only with extreme caution).

Dictionaries. General and specialized dictionaries are available in print and online. General dictionaries can be compact or comprehensive, unabridged publications. Specialized dictionaries define terms used in a particular field, such as engineering, computers, architecture, or consumer affairs, and offer detailed definitions of field-specific terms, usually written in straightforward language.

Handbooks and manuals. Handbooks and manuals are typically one-volume compilations of frequently used information in a particular field. They offer brief definitions of terms or concepts, standards for presenting information, procedures for documenting sources, and visuals such as graphs and tables.

Bibliographies. Bibliographies provide annotated lists of books, periodicals, and other research materials published in areas such as engineering, medicine, the humanities, and the social sciences. They can be invaluable time savers. As with other research materials, the format for many bibliographies is moving from print to online. Check with your research librarian.

General guides.   The annotated *Guide to Reference Books,* 12th ed., by Robert Kieft (Chicago: American Library Association, 2000), can help you locate reference books, indexes, Web sites, and other research materials.

Atlases and statistical sources.   Atlases provide representations of the physical and political boundaries of countries, climate, population, or natural resources. Statistical sources are collections of numerical data. They are the best source for such information as the U.S. gross domestic product, the consumer price index, or the demographic breakdown of the general population.

Atlases

> *Microsoft® Encarta® World Atlas 2001.* CD-ROM for Windows®. Microsoft Corporation, 2001.
>
> *Google Earth,* <http://earth.google.com/>. Using satellite images and maps, this site permits users to view virtually any location on earth, tilt and rotate site views for three-dimensional images, and save or share search results.
>
> *MapQuest,* <http://www.mapquest.com/>. Allows users to conduct searches for specific locations (area or neighborhood) and view maps of the site with detailed directions to it.

Statistical Sources

> *American Statistics Index.* Washington, D.C.: Congressional Information Service, 1978–. Monthly, quarterly, and annual supplements.
>
> *FedSTATS,* <www.fedstats.gov/index.html>. The gateway to statistics from over 100 federal agencies.
>
> *OFFSTATS: official statistics on the Web,* <www.library.auckland.as.nz/subjects/stats/offstats>. Hosted by the University of Auckland Library, this site compiles other sites and provides free social and economic statistics with a concentration on current data and time series.
>
> U.S. Bureau of the Census. *Statistical Abstract of the United States.* Washington, D.C.: Government Printing Office, 1879–. Annual. <http://www.census.gov/prod/www/statistical-abstract-1995_2000.html>.

WRITER'S GLOSSARY
Common Library Terms

■ *Abstract:* a brief version of a long document that gives the reader its main points

■ *Bibliographic information:* the author, title, and publication information needed to locate an item in a journal article or book

■ *Bibliography:* (1) a listing of sources used in the writing of a document; (2) in the MLA format, it is called a Works Cited page; in the APA format, it is called the References page

■ *Bound periodical:* several issues of a journal or magazine that are secured together in book form

■ *Call number:* the number assigned to every item in the library to help locate the item

■ *Circulation desk:* the desk where a patron can check out, return, and renew library materials

■ *Interlibrary loan:* material requested from another library and sent to the patron's library for use

■ *Journal:* a periodical containing scholarly articles written by experts in a particular subject area

■ *Peer review:* the journal-publishing practice in which experts review articles for accuracy, completion, and adherence to the highest research standards prior to publication

■ *Magazine:* a popular periodical meant for the general public; articles are written by paid journalists

■ *Microform:* books or articles in film or fiche format that must be viewed on a particular machine

■ *Periodical:* a publication issued regularly, such as a newspaper, magazine, or journal

Internet Research

Anyone with Internet access can search through the staggering amount of information that it offers (including access to many public university library catalogs and databases). The Internet contains a wealth of information; unlike a library, however, it has no one indexing scheme—no single catalog that brings the information together for browsing or easy access. Search engines and Web directories can streamline your search process.

Using Search Engines and Web Subject Directories

To locate specific subjects, you can use two types of search tools: a subject directory and a search engine. A subject directory (also known as an index) organizes information by broad subject categories (business, entertainment, health, sports) and related subtopics (marketing, finance, investing). Many college and university libraries produce their own Web directories like the one shown in Figure 6–8; check your library's homepage. A subject-directory search eventually produces a list of specific sites that contain information about the topics you request. Once you locate a site of interest that you want to revisit, you can bookmark it.

A search engine locates information based on words or combinations of words that you specify. The software engine then lists for you the documents or files that contain one or more of these words in their titles, descriptions, or text. Also available are metasearch engines—tools that do not maintain an internal database but

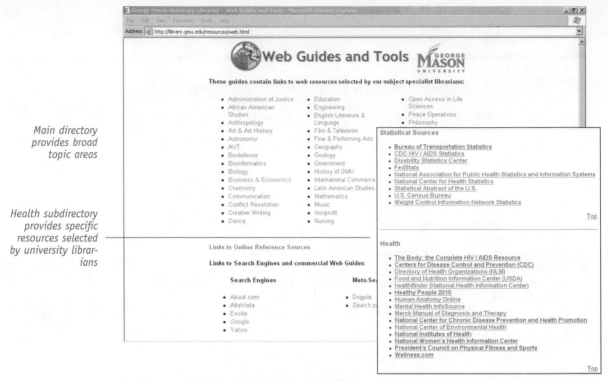

Main directory provides broad topic areas

Health subdirectory provides specific resources selected by university librarians

Figure 6–8   College Library Subject Directory to the Web

instead launch your query to multiple databases of various Web-based resources (other search engines or subject directories). Most major search engines, such as Google and Yahoo!, also offer directories. The following subject directories, search engines, and metasearch engines are among the most widely used on the Web.

Web Subject Directories

Ask Jeeves, <www.ask.com/>. Ask Jeeves, Inc., delivers world-class information retrieval products through a diverse blend of Web sites, portals, and downloadable applications. Sites are categorized as sponsored or nonsponsored Web sites and include suggestions for narrowing topics.

Infomine, <http://infomine.ucr.edu/>. Infomine is a Web directory specializing in scholarly Internet resources of interest to academics and scholars.

Internet Public Library (IPL), <www.ipl.org>. Developed by the University of Michigan School of Information, the IPL's collection of over 45,000 links are hand picked, organized, and described by librarians and library students.

Librarians' Internet Index, <www.lii.org>. A publicly funded weekly newsletter, the Librarians' Internet Index is a searchable, annotated directory of

continuously updated Internet resources that are evaluated and annotated by research librarians. It is a great example of how a portal can save
time.

Internet Scout Project, <http://scout.wisc.edu/>. Published continuously
since 1994, Internet Scout presents the efforts of librarians and educators
at the University of Wisconsin–Madison, who have selected and annotated more than 10,000 academically useful Web sites.

WWW Virtual Library, <http://vlib.org>. The Virtual Library is a noncommercial
catalog of the Web started by the creator of HTML and the World Wide Web.

SEARCH ENGINES

Google, <www.google.com>. Probably the most-popular search engine, with
new versions offered continuously. In addition to a basic Web search, you
can look for U.S. government sites at <www.google.com/unclesam>, try
the book search at <http://books.google.com/>, or find scholarly articles
at <http://scholar.google.com/>.

Yahoo! <www.yahoo.com>. The best-known and popular Yahoo! is a search
engine, directory, and portal.

METASEARCH ENGINES

Dogpile, <www.dogpile.com>. Dogpile searches other search engines for
responses to your query and sifts the findings.

Metacrawler, <www.metacrawler.com>. Metacrawler searches Yahoo!,
Google, and other search engines for responses to your query, lists the
search engines where relevant sites were found, and allows you to e-mail
the results. Try <www.metafind.com> if searching for a business.

As comprehensive as search engines and directories may seem, none is complete. Many, for example, do not index Adobe portable document format (PDF)
files or Usenet Newsgroups, and most cannot index databases and other non-
HTML–based content. Further, a search engine's ranking of the sites recommended
as relevant to your topic is based on a number of different strategies. Some sites
base relevance on how high on the given page your search term appears, on the
number of appearances of your term, or on the number of other sites that link to
the page. Almost all major search sites now sell high rankings to the highest bid-
ders, so your results may not highlight the pages most relevant to your search.

Your best strategy is to investigate how your favorite search engines work;
nearly all provide detailed instructions on their help pages. Many search engines
also give you the option of conducting an advanced search, which provides you
with a number of ways to obtain more-selective results. Figure 6–9 shows an advanced search conducted on Google for information about remote sensing, forest
management, and pesticides.

Although search engines vary in what and how they search, you can use some
of the basic strategies in Digital Tips: Using Search Engines.

ON THE WEB

For information on
evaluating search en-
gines, go to Chapter 6,
bedfordstmartins.com/
writingthatworks

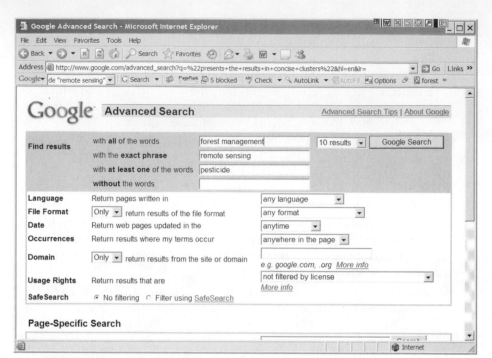

*Specify key terms
and number of
results desired*

*Limit your search to
a specific domain
(.org, .edu, .com,
and so on)*

Figure 6–9   Advanced Google Search

DIGITAL TIPS: Using Search Engines

■ Enter words and phrases that are as specific to your topic as possible. For example, if you are looking for information about *nuclear power* and enter only the term *nuclear,* the search will also yield listings for *nuclear family, nuclear medicine,* and *nuclear winter.*

■ Use Boolean operators (AND, OR, NOT) to narrow your search. For example, if you're searching for information on breast cancer and are finding references to nothing but prostate cancer, try "breast AND cancer NOT prostate." Consider conducting an advanced search (see Figure 6–9) to further narrow your search.

■ Check any search tips available at the engine you use. For example, some engines allow you to narrow your search by combining phrases with double quotation marks: "usability testing" will return only pages that have the full compound phrase.

■ Try a variety of search engines and consider how well they provide information relevant to your search. You may want to stick to using your favorite engine, but you will get more varied results if you use more than one.

■ If you are interested in obtaining as many hits as possible, consider using a metasearch engine such as Dogpile at <www.dogpile.com> and Metacrawler at <www.metacrawler.com>.

Locating Business and Government Sites

The Web includes numerous sites devoted to specific subject areas. Following are some suggested resources for researching a business topic.

BUSINESS RESOURCES

Business Internet Resources, <www.pace.edu/library/links/links.html>.

Business Reference Services: Science, Technology, and Business Division, <www.loc.gov/rr/business/>. This site is developed and maintained by the Library of Congress. See the Subject Guide to Internet Resources.

globalEDGE™, <http://globaledge.msu.edu/>. Created by the Center for International Business Education, this site is a rich resource for international business information.

Google Directory: Business, <www.google.com/Top/Business/>.

Yahoo! Directory: Business and Economy, <http://dir.yahoo.com/Business_and_Economy/>.

GOVERNMENT RESOURCES

American FactFinder, <http://factfinder.census.gov>. Population, housing, economic, and geographic data.

Federal Government Agencies Directory, <www.lib.lsu.edu/gov/fedgov.html>.

FIRSTGOV, <www.firstgov.gov/>. The U.S. government's official Web portal.

Library of Congress: Thomas, <http://thomas.loc.gov/>. Legislative information.

■ Evaluating, Recording, and Acknowledging Research Sources

As you research your topic, use your sources carefully. Once you've decided which materials to use, you will need to record information from each source so that you can accurately quote, paraphrase, and summarize it in your paper or report. Recording your sources is especially important so that you can acknowledge where your information came from, thereby avoiding plagiarism.

Evaluating Sources

After you have located a number of promising books, articles, and Web resources, you need to decide which ones to continue to use in your research. As you interview for information or work with print or online material, evaluate each source by asking yourself the following questions:

- Is the information accurate and up to date?
- Is the speaker or author reputable and qualified?

- Is the publisher or sponsoring organization well established and respected in the field?

Also consider the points in the Evaluating Print Resources checklist.

> ## WRITER'S CHECKLIST
> ## Evaluating Print Resources
>
> *For a Book*
>
> ☑ Is the text up to date and relevant to your topic?
>
> ☑ Who is the author? Does the preface or introduction indicate the author's purpose?
>
> ☑ Does the author present information in an objective way? Are the language, tone, and style unbiased?
>
> ☑ Does the table of contents relate to your topic? Does the index contain terms related to your topic? Does the text contain a bibliography, reference list, or footnotes?
>
> ☑ Are the chapters useful? (Skim through one that seems related to your topic — notice especially the introduction, headings, and closing.)
>
> ☑ Does the book contain informative diagrams or other visuals?
>
> *For an Article*
>
> ☑ Is the article up to date and relevant to your topic?
>
> ☑ Is the publisher of the magazine or other periodical well known? Who is the publication's main audience? (Is it the mainstream public? A small group of specialists?)
>
> ☑ Does the publication target or show bias toward a particular audience?
>
> ☑ What is the article's purpose? (For a journal article, read the abstract; for a newspaper article, read the headline and the lead sentences.)
>
> ☑ Does the article contain informative diagrams or other visuals that indicate its scope?

Evaluate the usefulness of information on the Internet with the same standards that you use to evaluate information from other sources. Is it accurate? Is it up to date? Is the author qualified and reputable? Is the sponsor of the site or journal reputable? These standards apply for printed material, for people you interview, and for any other source.

The easiest way to ensure that information is valid is to obtain it from a reputable source. For example, data from the Bureau of Labor Statistics, the Securities and Exchange Commission, and the Bureau of the Census are widely used by U.S. businesses. Likewise, online versions of established, reputable journals in medicine, engineering, computer software, and other fields merit the same level of trust as the printed versions. However, as you move away from established, reputable sites, exercise more caution. Be especially wary of blogs, unmoderated discussion groups on Usenet, and other public bulletin-board systems. Remember that anyone with access can place information on the Internet, so for many sources no editorial checks and balances are in place. Treat information obtained from these sources cautiously.

WRITER'S CHECKLIST
Evaluating Online Resources

☑ *Who* is the author? Why should that author be trusted?

☑ *What* is the main focus of the page? Does it make sense?

☑ *Where* does the site originate? Is it put out by an organization, an individual, or an institution?

☑ *When* was the site put online? Is it updated regularly?

☑ *Why* does that page exist? Can you find a purpose statement or an "about us" page? Is there a particular bias?

☑ *How* does the information available compare with at least two other reputable online sources?

Keep in mind the following four criteria when evaluating any source, whether print or online: authority, accuracy, bias, and currency.[1]

Authority

Consider the author's reputation: Is the writer an authority in the field? Has he or she written other, highly regarded books or articles? If you don't know, ask a librarian, an instructor, or an expert who is familiar with the subject area, whether the author of a book or an article has an established reputation.

Because anyone can publish on the Web, it is sometimes difficult to determine authorship of a document, and frequently a person's qualifications for speaking on a topic are absent or questionable. If you do not recognize the author or the organization sponsoring the site as well known and respected in the field, check the site's "about us" page or mission statement if available. This information should give you a sense of the site's purpose and perspective. Ask the following questions to help you determine the authority of a site or document.

- Is the author's document listed in or linked from a reliable source or document?

- Is the author referenced or mentioned positively by another author or organization whose authority you trust?

- Does the document give ample biographical information about the author so that you can evaluate his or her credentials, or can you get this information by linking to another document?

If the publisher or sponsor is an organization, you can usually assume that the document meets the standards and aims of the group. Consider also the following:

- The suitability of the organization to address this topic

- Whether this organization or agency is recognized and respected in the field

ON THE WEB

For more resources for evaluating Web content, go to Chapter 6, **bedfordstmartins.com/ writingthatworks**

---

[1] Adapted from Leigh Ryan, *The Bedford Guide for Writing Tutors*, 3rd ed. (Boston: Bedford/St. Martin's, 2002).

- The relationship of the author to the publisher or sponsor (Does the document tell you something about the author's expertise or qualifications?)

Accuracy

Criteria for evaluating accuracy would include the following:

- Other sources that the document relies on are linked or are included in a bibliography.
- Background information can be verified.
- Methodology is appropriate for the topic.
- With a research project, data that were gathered include explanations of research methods and interpretations.
- The graphs and visuals are free of distortion.
- The site is modified or updated regularly.

Bias

To determine bias, consider how the context reveals the author's knowledge of the subject and his or her stance on the topic. Check for the following:

- The publication or site identifies in some form the audience it targets.
- The book, article, or site was published or developed by a recognized academic institution; government agency; or national, international, or commercial organization with an established reputation in the subject area.
- The author shows knowledge of theories, techniques, or schools of thought usually related to the topic.
- The author shows knowledge of related sources and attributes them properly.
- The author discusses the value and limitations of the approach, if it is new.
- The author acknowledges that the subject itself or his or her treatment of it is controversial, if you know that to be the case.

Currency

If currency is important, consider whether the document has a publication or "last updated" date or includes date of copyright, gives dates showing when information was gathered, or gives information about new material when appropriate.

Taking Notes

The purpose of taking notes is to condense and record information from the books, articles, Web sites, and other sources used for your research. The notes you take will furnish much of the material for your outline and final written work.

Document the following information about any book that you decide to include in your research:

Call number

Author (if the author is an organization, indicate that fact)

Title

City of publication

Publisher's name

Year of publication

For an article, record the following information:

Author

Title of the article

Name of the journal in which the article appears

Journal volume and issue numbers

Date of publication

Page numbers of the article

When you are ready to prepare a bibliography for your research report, you can do so easily using this information. To document sources, you can use the Print Screen key to print out the search screen containing the full bibliographic citation. You can also download the bibliographic citation from an online database to your hard drive, or you can e-mail the citation to yourself. You can do the same for the texts of articles you retrieve.

If you make a habit of sending your search results and articles to your e-mail address, you will have a record of your research—and the sources themselves— ready for your use when you begin to draft your paper or presentation.

When working with paper sources (books and journals), you can photocopy material and highlight important passages with a highlighter, jot notes on index cards, or key them into your laptop or desktop computer. If you are using Internet sources, you can highlight passages and cut and paste them into a word-processing file, in addition to taking notes. When you cut and paste information from the Internet, be very careful: Consider changing the font or color of the text so that you can easily distinguish borrowed material from your own notes; at the very least, put quotation marks around the material. Always include the source to provide proper credit in your final work. Otherwise, you will be plagiarizing from the source. If the source is copyrighted, you may also be guilty of copyright infringement. (A full discussion of avoiding plagiarism and copyright infringement begins on page 178.)

Whichever method you use, identify the source of the information and include the author's last name (also include first name or initials if you have two authors with the same last name) and the page number or numbers on which the material appears in the original source. If you have consulted more than one book or article by an author, include the title as well; for long titles, you may use a shortened form.

As you take notes, make a list of the topics you will cover in your research. Identify your notes as appropriate with these topics (sometimes called *slugs*). When you arrange the cards or word-processing notes by topic in preparation for creating an outline, you can use the slugs as a guide in organizing your material.

◆ *For a sample list of research topics, see Christine Thomas's notes on page 13 of Chapter 1, Assessing Audience and Purpose.*

For the sake of accuracy and correctness, be careful to distinguish whether you are quoting directly from your source, paraphrasing (restating the text you're using in your own words), or summarizing (writing down a highly condensed version of the text). If you are a beginning researcher, you should probably stick to writing down direct quotations. Then, when you turn to actually writing your research paper, you can decide whether you want to quote directly, paraphrase, or summarize.

Quoting from Your Sources

When you quote directly from another source, use only the information you need to make your point. This section describes long-standing techniques to help you do so and to credit your information sources.

Direct Quotations

A direct quotation is a word-for-word copy of the text of an original source. Choose direct quotations (which can be of a word, a phrase, a sentence, or, occasionally, a paragraph) carefully and use them sparingly. Enclose direct quotations in quotation marks and separate them from the rest of the sentence by a comma or colon. The initial capital letter of a quotation is retained if the quoted material originally began with a capital letter.

▶ The economist stated, "Regulation cannot supply the dynamic stimulus that in other industries is supplied by competition."

When a quotation is divided, the material that interrupts the quotation is set off, before and after, by commas, and quotation marks are used around each part of the quotation.

▶ "Regulation," he said in a recent interview, "cannot supply the dynamic stimulus that in other industries is supplied by competition."

Indirect Quotations

An indirect quotation is a paraphrased version of an original text. It is usually introduced by the word *that* and is not set off from the rest of the sentence by punctuation marks.

▶ In a recent interview, he said that regulation does not stimulate the industry as well as competition does.

Deletions or Omissions

Deletions or omissions from quoted material are indicated by three ellipsis points (. . .) within a sentence and a period plus three ellipsis points (. . . .) at the end of a sentence.

▶ "If monopolies could be made to respond . . . we would be able to enjoy the benefits of . . . large-scale efficiency. . . ."

When a quoted passage begins in the middle of a sentence rather than at the beginning, ellipsis points are not necessary; the fact that the first letter of the quoted material is not capitalized tells the reader that the quotation begins in mid-sentence.

▶ Rivero goes on to conclude that "coordination may lessen competition within a region."

Regardless of where the ellipsis appears, be careful to retain the accuracy and grammatical consistency of the original passage.

Inserting Material into Quotations

When it is necessary to insert a clarifying comment within quoted material, use brackets.

▶ "The industry is an integrated system that serves an extensive [geographic] area, with divisions existing as islands within the larger system's sphere of influence."

When quoted material contains an obvious error or might be questioned in some other way, the expression *sic* (Latin for "thus"), in italic type and enclosed in brackets, follows the questionable material to indicate that the writer has quoted the material exactly as it appeared in the original.

▶ The company considers the Baker Foundation to be a "guilt-edged [*sic*] investment."

ETHICS NOTE

When you use quotation marks to indicate that you are quoting, do not make any changes or omissions in the quoted material unless you clearly indicate what you have done. For further information on incorporating quoted material and inserting comments, see Avoiding Plagiarism and Copyright Violations on pages 178–179 and Incorporating Quotations into Text on pages 175–176.

Incorporating Quotations into Text

Quote word for word only when your source concisely sums up a great deal of information or reinforces a point you are making. Quotations must also relate logically, grammatically, and syntactically to the rest of the sentence and surrounding text.

Depending on the length, two methods of handling quotations in your text are available. For Modern Language Association (MLA) style, a quotation of three or fewer lines is incorporated into the text and enclosed in quotation marks. For American Psychological Association style, a quotation of fewer than 40 words is incorporated into the text and enclosed in quotation marks.

Material that runs four lines or longer (MLA style) or at least 40 words (APA style) is usually set off from the body of the text by being indented from the left margin ten spaces (MLA style) or five to seven spaces (APA style). The quoted passage is spaced the same as the surrounding text and is not enclosed in quotation marks, as shown in the following example, which uses MLA style. If you are not following a specific style manual, you may block indent ten spaces from both the left and right margins for reports and other documents.

▶   After reviewing a large number of works in business and technical communication, Alred sees an inevitable connection between theory, practice, and pedagogy:

> Therefore, theory is necessary to prevent us from being overwhelmed by what is local, particular, and temporal. In turn, pedagogy both mediates practice and transforms our theory. Indeed, one reason I find this work rewarding is that I sense it puts me at the intersection of theory, practice, and pedagogy as they are involved with writing in the workplace. (ix–x)

> The use of the Web today has reinforced this connection because it calls on the Web-page designer to engage in a teaching function as well as reflect on the practice of Web design. For example, the widespread use of . . .

Notice that the quotation blends with the content of the surrounding text, which uses transitions to introduce and comment on the quotation. At the end of the document, the following entry appears in the MLA-style list of works cited as the source of the quotation in the example.

▶   Alred, Gerald J., Charles T. Brusaw, and Walter E. Oliu. The Business Writer's Handbook. 8th ed. Boston: Bedford, 2006.

Do not rely too heavily on the use of quotations in the final version of your document. Generally, avoid quoting anything that is more than one paragraph.

Paraphrasing

Paraphrasing is restating or rewriting in your own words the essential ideas of another writer. Because the paraphrase does not quote the source word for word, quotation marks are not necessary. However, paraphrased material should be credited because the *ideas* are taken from someone else. The following example is an original passage explaining the concept of object blur. The paraphrased version restates the essential information of the passage in a form appropriate for a report.

ORIGINAL   One of the major visual cues used by pilots in maintaining precision ground reference during low-level flight is that of object blur. We are acquainted with the object-blur phenomenon experienced when driving an automobile. Objects in the foreground appear to be rushing toward us, while objects in the background appear to recede slightly.

—Wesley E. Woodson and Donald W. Conover,
Human Engineering Guide for Equipment Designers

PARAPHRASED   Object blur is an optical illusion that affects people in fast-moving vehicles: nearby objects seem to rush toward the observer, while distant objects seem to move away slightly (Woodson and Conover).

Strive to put the original ideas into your words without distorting them.

Summarizing

A summary is a highly condensed version, in the researcher's own words, of an original passage. Summary notes present only the essential ideas or conclusions of the original and are considerably shorter than paraphrases of the same passage. As with directly quoted and paraphrased material, the source of summarized information must be credited in a footnote.

Following this passage is a brief summary of its content.

ORIGINAL   Now that we have learned something about the nature of elements and molecules, what are fuels? Fuels are those substances that will burn when heat is applied to them. Some elements, in themselves, are fuels. Carbon, hydrogen, sulfur, magnesium, titanium and some other metals are examples of elements that can burn. Coal, charcoal and coke, for example, are almost pure carbon; hydrogen, another element, is a highly flammable gas. But the most familiar combustible materials are not pure elements; they are compounds and mixtures. Wood, paper and grass are principally composed of molecules of cellulose, a flammable substance. If we examine the chemical makeup of this compound, we will discover what elements form the basic fuels in most solid materials. The cellulose molecule contains twenty-one atoms: six carbons, ten hydrogens and five oxygen atoms: $C_6H_{10}O_5$. Since oxygen is not flammable . . . , it follows that the carbon and hydrogen found in most common combustible solids are the elements that burn. This conclusion becomes even stronger when we look at common flammable liquids. Gasoline, kerosene, fuel oils, and other petroleum compounds are composed of only carbon and hydrogen atoms, in varying amounts. These compounds, called hydrocarbons (hydrogen + carbon), will all burn.

—James H. Meidl, *Flammable Hazardous Materials*

SUMMARIZED   The chemical makeup of a substance determines whether it is flammable. Carbon and hydrogen are highly flammable elements, so material made up largely of these elements, called hydrocarbons, are good fuels (Meidl 8–9).

Take summary notes to remind yourself of the substance of a research source. Summarized information can also be useful to your reader because it condenses passages that give more details than the reader needs.

ON THE WEB

For a tutorial on using sources correctly, go to bedfordstmartins.com/ writingthatworks and select *Tutorials,* The St. Martin's Tutorial on Avoiding Plagiarism. For links to other helpful resources, select *Web Links.*

Avoiding Plagiarism and Copyright Violations

Plagiarism is the use of someone else's ideas without acknowledgment, or the use of someone else's exact words without quotation marks and appropriate credit. Plagiarism is considered to be the theft of someone else's creative and intellectual property and is unacceptable in any field. If you intend to publish, reproduce, or distribute material that includes quotations from published works, including Web sites, you may need to obtain written permission from the copyright holders of those works.

Acknowledging Your Sources

The gold standard for avoiding problems is to carefully document your sources of information. This standard applies both in the classroom and on the job, regardless of whether your primary audience is your instructor, your company management, or the readers of a publication or Web site. (Details regarding commonly used systems for documenting sources begin on page 179.)

Quoting a passage—including cutting and pasting a passage from the Internet into your work—is permissible only if you enclose the passage in quotation marks and properly cite the source. Likewise, you may paraphrase the words and ideas of another *if you document your source.* Although you do not enclose paraphrased ideas or materials in quotation marks, you must document their sources. Paraphrasing a passage without citing the source is permissible only when the information paraphrased is common knowledge.

Common Knowledge

Common knowledge generally refers to information that is widely known and readily available in handbooks, manuals, atlases, and other references. For example, the distances between two cities, the names of routes, and the geographic features of an area found on virtually every travel map qualify as common knowledge. You need not document the source of such information. Common knowledge also refers to information within a specific field that is generally known and understood by most others in that field—even though it may not be widely known by those outside the field. For example, the fact that the 1918 Spanish Flu pandemic killed millions of Americans is common knowledge among public health officials, epidemiologists, and influenza researchers. The source for this information need not be documented. However, the number of deaths caused by the 1918 flu among members of the U.S. military or among the population of a North American city would not be common knowledge and would require a citation. An indication that something is common knowledge is whether it is repeated in multiple sources without citation. If you are in any doubt about whether information meets this standard, document its source.

Copyright

Most published material—written or visual—is copyrighted. In workplace writing, you must obtain prior approval to reproduce virtually all copyrighted information and cite the source of that information in your final work. However, small amounts of material from a copyrighted source may be used, especially for educational purposes, without permission or payment as long as you indicate that it is someone else's material and the use satisfies the "fair use" criteria of the U.S. Copyright Office.

To seek permission to reproduce copyrighted material, write to the copyright holder. In some cases, it is the author; in other cases, it is the editor or publisher of the work. For Web sites, read the site's "terms-of-use" information (if available) and e-mail your request to the appropriate party. State specifically which portion of the work you wish to reproduce and how you plan to use it. The copyright holder has the right to charge a fee and specify conditions and limits of use.

ON THE WEB

The "fair use" criteria are described on the Web site of the U.S. Copyright Office at <www.copyright.gov/>.

Public Domain Materials

Works created by or for U.S. government agencies are in the public domain — that is, they are not copyrighted. Some older written works may also be in the public domain because their copyright has lapsed; the rules governing copyright can be complex, however, so it's generally wise to assume that any work not created by the U.S. government is protected. Public-domain works, including text and visuals from publications and Web sites, can be reproduced without permission unless the information is classified or otherwise protected. As with other material you use in your own work, however, you must give appropriate credit to the source from which the material is taken (see the next section, Documenting Sources).

In-House Materials

In the workplace, employees often borrow from in-house manuals, reports, and other company documents and Web sites. Because the company is considered the author of works prepared by its employees on the job, using such information (called "boilerplate") is neither plagiarism nor a violation of copyright. Hence, there is no need to acknowledge such sources because the information is simply being used in a different setting by the organization to which it already belongs.

ETHICS NOTE

In the classroom, borrowing published and Web-based information is necessary and acceptable, whether quoted or paraphrased, but you must document the source.

Documenting Sources

As a writer, by documenting your sources, you identify where you obtained the facts, ideas, quotations, and paraphrases you used in preparing a written report. This information can come from books; newspaper, magazine, or trade journal articles; manuals; proposals; investigative reports; interviews; e-mail; the Internet; and other sources. Documenting sources achieves three important purposes:

- It allows readers to locate and consult the sources used and to find further information on the subject.

- It enables writers to support and lend credibility to their assertions and arguments in such documents as proposals, reports, and trade journal articles.
- It helps writers to give proper credit to others and thus avoid plagiarism by identifying the sources of facts, ideas, quotations, and paraphrases.

This section shows citation models and sample pages for two principal documentation systems: APA and MLA.

> American Psychological Association. *Publication Manual of the American Psychological Association.* 5th ed. Washington, D.C.: American Psychological Association, 2001. See also <www.apastyle.org>.

The APA system of citation is often used in the social sciences. It is referred to as an author/date method of documentation because parenthetical in-text citations and a references list (at the end of the paper) emphasize the author(s) and date of publication so that the currency of the research is clear.

> Gibaldi, Joseph. *MLA Handbook for Writers of Research Papers.* 6th ed. New York: Modern Language Association of America, 2003. See also <www.mla.org>.

The MLA system is used in the humanities. MLA style uses parenthetical citations and a list of works cited (at the end of the paper), and places greater importance on the pages on which cited information can be found than on the publication date.

APA Style

APA In-Text Citations

To document direct quotations in text, give the author's last name, the year of publication, and the page number in parentheses.

▶ The "first electronic war" (Butrica, 2000, p. 2) was fought as much in the research laboratory as on the battlefield.

The page number is optional for paraphrased information and ideas.

▶ World War II was the occasion of radar's first application in warfare, and Great Britain led the way in radar research (Butrica, 2000).

If the author's name is mentioned in the text, give only the year of publication and the page number in parentheses.

▶ According to Butrica (2000), the use of radar as an offensive and defensive warfare agent made World War II "the first electronic war" (p. 2).

Include no more information than is necessary to enable readers to find the corresponding entry in the reference list. If the author's name and the year of publication are mentioned in the text, give only the page number for direct quotations.

▶ As Butrica pointed out in his 2000 research, "technology forever changed the way we make war" (p. 196).

Omit parenthetical information for paraphrased material.

▶ In his 2000 research, Butrica pointed out the impact of technology on warfare.

If the citation follows a block quotation, place the citation after the final punctuation mark, as shown in Figure 6–10 on page 188. Use the spacing shown in the examples. Within the citation itself, separate the name, date, and page number with commas. Allow one space after each comma. Use the abbreviation *p.* or *pp.* before page numbers.

If your reference list includes more than one work by the same author published in the same year, add the lowercase letters *a*, *b*, *c*, and so forth, to the year in both the reference-list entries and the text citations: (Ostro, 1993b, p. 347). When a work has two authors, cite both names joined by an ampersand: (Maddie & Khoshaba, 2005). For the first citation of a work with three, four, or five authors, include all names.

▶ As Burns, Brooks, and MacNeil (2006) argued . . .

For subsequent citations, include only the name of the first author followed by et al. (not italicized).

▶ Burns et al. (2006) put forth the alternate theory . . .

For a work with six or more authors, use the name of the first author followed by et al. in all citations.

▶ Their findings led to a radical change in the way the metals were processed (Hargrove et al., 2003, p. 21).

When two or more works by different authors are cited in the same parentheses, list the citations alphabetically and use semicolons to separate the citations: (Loftus, 2004; Testerman, Kuegler, & Dowling, 2000; Van Gremergen, 2001).

If you are citing a source created by a corporation or an organization, use its name as the author.

▶ However, high employment rates in the Midwest affected this trend considerably (U.S. Department of Labor, 1999).

If you are quoting a source by an unknown author, use a brief version of the title in your citation.

▶   Textile manufacture had replaced the local maritime trade well before the mid-nineteenth century ("A Short History," p. 19).

If two or more sources have authors with the same last name, use first initials in your citation (J. Kellogg, p. 414). When citing e-mail messages, phone calls, or personal interviews, use the words *personal communication* in your parenthetical citation.

▶   Linda Waters (personal communication, November 28, 2000), an executive at CorTex, stated the case succinctly. . . .

To refer to an entire Web site (not just to a particular article or document at that site), include the URL in your parenthetical citation.

▶   The U.S. Department of Commerce provides current statistics on international trade at the Bureau of Economic Analysis Web site (http://www.bea.doc.gov/bea/rels.htm).

However, you should not include the Web site in your reference list if you are citing the entire site. If you are citing a specific document from a Web site, you should follow the format that you would for a print document (citing the author, year, and page or paragraph number). If the online document has no page or paragraph numbers, include just the author and the year in your parenthetical citation (you will provide further details in the reference list).

▶   In his previous address to the group, he expressed his belief in the value of using technology in the classroom (Maxwell, 2002).

APA Citation Format for a References List

The references list should begin on the first new page following the end of the text. Begin each new entry at the left margin, and indent the second and subsequent lines five spaces or one-half inch from the left margin. (Your instructor may require you to use a paragraph indent instead. If so, begin at a paragraph indent, with subsequent lines continuing at the left margin.) Double-space within and between entries.

Include full page numbers when citing a range of pages for articles (119–124, not 119–24) and indicate with a comma if the page flow of an article is interrupted (119–124, 128–132). Use the abbreviation *p.* or *pp.* only with articles in newspapers (not in magazines or other sources), chapters in edited books, or proceedings.

Include only sources that were essential to the preparation of your document; do not include background reading. Do not include forms of personal communication, such as letters, e-mail messages, messages from electronic bulletin boards, and telephone conversations. Cite these sources only in the text.

The following listing specifies the APA format and order of elements in a reference list.

Author

- Alphabetize the list by author's last name and initials.
- List multiple works by the same author in publication date order, from earliest to latest.
- For works by corporations or government agencies, alphabetize by organizational name.
- When no author is given, alphabetize by the first significant word in the title.

Publication Date

- Enclose in parentheses.
- For journals and books, give only the year.
- For periodicals other than journals, give the year, comma, and month or day.

Title

- Capitalize the first word of the title and subtitle of books, articles, or chapters.
- Lowercase all other words except proper nouns.
- Italicize the titles of books and periodicals.
- Do not use quotation marks or italics for titles of articles or chapters from books.
- End book and article titles with a period.

Multiple Volume or Series Publications

- List the series number following the title.
- List the volume number following the title.
- List the edition number following the title, if it is not the first.

Publishing Information

- List the publishing information last for citations to books, pamphlets, and conference proceedings.
- Show a shortened form of the publisher's name.
- Include the publisher's city and state. (If the publisher's city is well known—e.g., New York—omit the state name.)
- Abbreviate the state name using the postal code.
- Omit terms like *Publisher*, *Co.*, and *Inc.*
- Do not abbreviate the words *Books* and *Press*.

Periodicals

- Show the title of a journal, magazine, or newspaper in upper- and lower-case letters.
- Capitalize only the first word of the title and subtitle and any proper nouns; do not italicize or enclose the title in quotation marks.
- List the volume and page numbers after the title.
- Italicize the title and volume numbers.
- Separate elements with commas and end with a period.

Online Sources

- Review the guidelines for citing electronic sources beginning on page 185.

Figure 6–11 on page 189 shows a sample APA-style References page.

APA Documentation Models

BOOKS

Single Author

Van Grembergen, W. (2001). *Information technology evaluation methods and management*. New York: Idea.

Multiple Authors

Testerman, J. O., Kuegler, T. J., Jr., & Dowling, P. J., Jr. (2000). *Web advertising and marketing* (3rd ed.). Rocklin, CA: Prima.

Corporate Author

Ernst and Young. (2001). *Ernst and Young's retirement planning guide* (3rd ed.). New York: Wiley.

Edition Other Than First

Van Horne, J. C. (2000). *Financial market rates and flows* (6th ed.). New York: Prentice Hall.

Multivolume Work

Standard and Poor. (2004). *Standard and Poor's register of corporations, directors and executives* (Vols. 1–3). New York: McGraw-Hill.

Work in an Edited Collection

Griswold, C. L. (2002). Happiness and Cypher's choice: Is ignorance bliss? In W. Erwin (Ed.), *The Matrix and philosophy* (pp. 126–137). Chicago: Open Court.

Encyclopedia or Dictionary Entry

Gibbard, B. G. (2003). Particle detector. In *World Book Encyclopedia* (Vol. 15, pp. 186–187).
  Chicago: World Book.

ARTICLES IN PERIODICALS (See also ELECTRONIC SOURCES)

Magazine Article

Limp, F. (2001, June). Enterprise deployment. *Business Geographics, 26,* 18–27.

Journal Article

Loza, J. (2004). Business-community partnerships: The case for community organization capacity
  building. *Journal of Business Ethics, 53,* 297–311.

Newspaper Article

Loftus, P. (2004, August 31). Small business: Enterprise. *Wall Street Journal,* p. B4.

Article with Unknown Author

CFOs remain optimistic on economy. (2004, September 27). *The Business Journal,* p. 33.

ELECTRONIC SOURCES

An Entire Web Site

The APA recommends that, at minimum, a reference to a Web source should provide a document title or description, a date (of the publication or retrieval of the
document), an address (URL) that links directly to the document or section, and
an individual or corporate author, whenever possible. On the rare occasion that
you need to cite multiple pages of a Web site (or the entire site), provide a URL that
links to the site's homepage.

Association for Business Communication. (2006). Retrieved September 20, 2006, from
  http://www.businesscommunication.org [no period after URLs]

A Document on a Web Site, with an Author

Locker, K. O. (2002). *The history of the ABC.* Retrieved September 20, 2004, from
  http://www.businesscommunication.org/about/history/history.html

Document on a Web Site, with a Corporate or an Organizational Author

General Motors. (2003). *Company profile.* Retrieved September 20, 2004, from
  http://www.gm.com/company/corp_info/profiles/

Document on a Web Site, with an Unknown Author

Forgotten inventors. (2001). Retrieved September 20, 2004, from
    http://www.pbs.org/wgbh/amex/telephone/sfeature/index.html

Article or Other Work from a Database

Goldbort, R. C. (2001, March). Scientific writing as an art and as a science. *Journal of
    Environmental Health, 63*(7), 22–25. Retrieved September 20, 2004, from Expanded Academic
    ASAP database.

Article in an Online Periodical

Tiernen, R. (2001, April 18). Waiting for wireless. *SmartMoney.com.* Retrieved September 20, 2004,
    from http://www.smartmoney.com/techmarket/index.cfm?story=20010418

E-mail

Personal communications (including e-mail and messages from discussion groups
and electronic bulletin boards) are not cited in an APA reference list. They can be
cited in the text as follows: "According to J. D. Kahl (personal communication,
October 2, 2006), Web pages need to reflect . . .".

Publication on CD-ROM

Money 2004. (2004). [CD-ROM]. Redmond, WA: Microsoft.

MULTIMEDIA SOURCES

Map or Chart

Asia. (2001). [Map]. Retrieved April 20, 2001, from
    http://www.maps.com/explore/atlas/political/asia.html

Wisconsin. (2000). [Map]. Chicago: Rand.

Film or Video

Lawrence, D. (Director), & Christopher, J. (Editor). (2001). *Emergency film group video* [Video].
    Retrieved April 20, 2006, from http://www.efilmgroup.com/video1.rm

Massingham, G. (Director), & Christopher, J. (Editor). (2003). *Introduction to hazardous chemicals*
    [Motion picture]. Edgartown, MA: Emergency Film Group.

Radio or Television Program

Norris, R. (Host). (2001, April 3). Energy supplies. *All things considered* [Radio broadcast]. Boston:
    WGBH. Retrieved April 20, 2001, from http://www.npr.org/programs/atc

Duran, D. (Host). (2006, July 17). Danger robots. *The Science Channel: Discoveries this week* [Television broadcast]. Washington, DC. The Discovery Channel.

OTHER SOURCES

Published Interview

Gates, B. (2000, April 17). The view from the very top [Interview]. *Newsweek, 135,* 36–39.

Personal Interview and Letters

Personal communications (including telephone conversations) are not cited in a reference list. They can be cited in the text as follows: "According to J. D. Kahl (personal communication, October 2, 2001), Web pages need to reflect. . .".

Brochure or Pamphlet

Library of Congress. U.S. Copyright Office. (2004). *Copyright registration for online works* [Brochure]. Washington, DC: U.S. Government Printing Office.

Government Document

U.S. Department of Energy. (2004). *The August 14, 2003, blackout one year later* (Technical Publication No. 137-2004-12176). Washington, DC: U.S. Government Printing Office.

Report Published in a Collection

Rude, C. D. (2002). Legal and ethical issues in editing. In K. J. Harty (Ed.), *Strategies for business and technical writing,* 5th ed. (pp. 367–378). New York: Pearson.

Report Published Separately

Bertot, J. C., & McClure, C. R. (2000). *Public libraries and the Internet 2000: Summary findings and data tables.* Washington, DC: U.S. Government Printing Office.

Unpublished Data

Wisniewski, K., & Hussar, D. (2002). [Oregon small business statistics by county]. Unpublished raw data.

APA Sample Pages

Shortened title and page number

One-inch margins; text double-spaced

14   Ethics Cases

This report examines the nature and disposition of the 3,458 ethics cases handled companywide by CGF's ethics officers and managers during 2004. The purpose of such reports is to provide the Ethics and Business Conduct Committee with the information necessary for assessing the effectiveness of the first year of CGF's Ethics Program (Davis, Marks, & Tegge, 2001). According to Matthias Jonas (2004), recommendations are given for consideration "in planning for the second year of the Ethics Program" (p. 152).

The CGF Aircraft Corporation takes its commitment to an ethical work environment seriously. Throughout its 64-year history, CGF has fostered high ethical standards in its relations with its customers, suppliers, and employees. The size, diversity, and decentralized locations of our workforce make it imperative that CGF's ethical committment—both in principle and in practice—be formalized.

The Office of Ethics and Business Conduct was created to administer the Ethics Program. The director of the Office of Ethics and Business Conduct, along with seven ethics officers throughout CGF, was given the responsibility for the following objectives, as described by Rossouw (1997):

Long quote indented five to seven spaces, double-spaced, without quotation marks

> Communicate the values, standards, and goals of CGF's Program to employees. Provide companywide channels for employee education and guidance in resolving ethics concerns. Implement companywide programs in ethics awareness and recognition. Employee accessibility to ethics information and guidance is the immediate goal of the Office of Business Conduct in its first year. (p. 1543)

In-text citation gives name, date, and page number

The purpose of the Ethics Program, established by the Committee, is to "promote ethical business conduct through open communication and compliance with company ethics standards" (Jonas, 2001, p. 89). To accomplish this purpose, any ethics policy must ensure confidentiality and anonymity for employees who raise genuine ethics concerns. The procedure developed at CGF guarantees appropriate

Figure 6–10   APA Sample Page

Ethics Cases   21

References

Davis, W. C., Marks, R., & Tegge, D. (2001). *Working in the system: Five new manage-ment principles.* New York: St. Martin's Press.

Hassab, J. C. (1997). *Systems management: People, computers, machines, materials.* New York: CRC.

Jonas, M. (2001). Ethics in organizational communication: A review of the litera-ture. *Journal of Ethics and Communication, 29,* 79–99.

Jonas, M. (2004). The Internet and ethical communication: Toward a new para-digm. *Journal of Ethics and Communication, 27,* 147–177.

Library of Congress. U.S. Copyright Office. (2004). *Copyright registration for online works* [Brochure]. Washington, DC: U.S. Government Printing Office.

The one-minute manager. (1998). [CD-ROM]. Boston: Bedford/St. Martin's.

Rossouw, G. J. (1997). Business ethics in South Africa. *Journal of Business Ethics, 16,* 1539–1547.

Heading centered

List alphabetized by authors' last names and double-spaced

Hanging-indent style used for entries

Figure 6–11   APA Sample List of References

ON THE WEB

For additional sample documents in APA style, go to **bedfordstmartins.com/ writingthatworks** and select *Model Documents Gallery.*

MLA

MLA Style

MLA In-Text Citations

When you cite a source in text, give only the author's last name and the page number or numbers in parentheses.

▶ Preparing a videotape of measurement methods is cost-effective and can expedite training (Peterson 151).

If the author's name is mentioned in the text, give only the page number of the source in parentheses.

▶ Peterson summarized the results of these measurements in a series of tables (183–91).

If two or more sources have authors with the same last name, include their initials (or first names if their names begin with the same letter) to avoid confusion.

▶ These results were summarized 40 years ago (R. Peterson 183–91). S. Peterson has recently suggested the reevaluation of these findings (29).

Include no more information than is necessary to enable readers to find the corresponding entry in the list of works cited. To cite an entire work rather than a particular page in a work, mention the author's name in the text and omit the parenthetical citation.

Place a parenthetical citation in text between the closing quotation mark or the last word of the sentence (or clause) and the end punctuation mark (usually a period). Use the spacing shown in the examples.

▶ The results of these studies have led even the most conservative managers to adopt technologies that will "catapult the industry forward" (Peterson 183–84).

If the parenthetical citation refers to an indented quotation, however, place it outside the last sentence of the quotation, as shown in Figure 6–12 on page 197.

If you are citing a page or pages of a multivolume work, give the volume number, followed by a colon, a space, and the page number(s): (Jones 2: 53–56). If the entire volume is being cited, identify the author and the volume: (Smith, vol. 3).

For more than one work by the same author, give the title of the work (or a shortened version if the title is long) in the parenthetical citation, unless you mention it in the text. If, for example, your works-cited list includes more than one work by Thomas J. Peters, the citation for his book *The Pursuit of Wow: Every Person's Guide to Topsy-Turvy Times* would appear as (Peters, *Pursuit* 93). Use only one space between the title and the page number.

To cite a source written by two or three authors, include all of the names in your parenthetical citation: (Rotherson and Peters 467–75); for a source written by four or more authors, include the first author's name followed by "et al." (and others; not italicized) or give all the authors' last names (depending on the style used in the works-cited list). To cite a source in which a separate work is quoted, provide the name of the person being quoted.

▶ According to Billings, there is "a greater potential for a small business to succeed in an urban area" (qtd. in Kooper et al. 421).

To quote a source written by a corporation or an organization, use that name as the author.

▶ However, many declining industries that fueled the economy of the 1950s are now being faced with a government mandate to clean up and preserve the environment (Environmental Protection Agency 16–17).

To quote a source by an unknown author, use a brief version of the title in your citation.

▶ The benefits of this treatment have been known since the early 1980s ("Audio Therapy" 56).

For a sentence that refers to two separate sources, include both in your parenthetical citation, separating them with a semicolon.

▶ Some analysts believe that the impact of electronic commerce caused the extreme market fluctuations of the late 1990s (Jones 174; Dragonetti 267).

To cite electronic sources, follow the same rules that you would for print sources, including as much identifying information as available (names and page numbers).

▶ As pointed out in a recent Slate.com article, America's poor are more numerous, but less visible than ever (Connors).

If no names are indicated in the electronic source, use the title (full or shortened) in your citation; if no page numbers are indicated, do not cite any numbers, unless there are paragraph or section numbers. In this case, use the abbreviation *par.* or *sec.* in your citation. Do not include URLs in your parenthetical citations, but do include them in your works-cited list.

▶ According to one online article, the organization's stated mission is to connect North American exporters with appropriate markets in Eastern Europe ("Business to Go" par. 18).

MLA Citation Format for a List of Works Cited

Begin the list of works cited on the first new page following the end of the text. Each new entry should begin at the left margin, with the second and subsequent lines within an entry indented five spaces or one-half inch. Double-space within and between entries. Use the following format for dates: day, month, year, with no commas (19 Jan. 2003). Abbreviate all months except May, June, and July.

The following listing specifies the format and order of elements in a list of works cited.

Author

- Alphabetize the list by the author's last name for a single author and by the last name of the first author for works with more than one author.
- List multiple works by the same author in alphabetical order by first significant word in the title. Put three hyphens and a period in place of the author's name for the second and subsequent titles.
- When a corporation or government agency is the author, alphabetize by organizational name, followed by a period.
- When no author is given, alphabetize by the first significant word in the title.
- For edited works, follow the editor's name with a comma, space, and *ed.* or *eds.* (for more than one editor).

Title

- Capitalize the first word in the title and subtitle and all significant words thereafter.
- Underline the title of a book, pamphlet, journal, or newspaper.
- Put quotation marks around the titles of articles in periodicals, essays in collections, or papers in proceedings.
- End titles of books and articles with a period.

Multiple Volume or Series Publications

- Give the name of the series and series number followed by a period after the title.
- Specify the edition if not the first.

Publication Information

- List the place of publication, publisher's name, and date of publication.
- Use a shortened form of the publisher's name.
- When publication information cannot be found, use *n.p.* (no publication place), *n.p.* (no publisher), and *n.d.* (no date).
- For familiar reference works, list only the edition and year of publication.

Periodicals

- For journal articles, list the volume number, date, and page numbers after the title of the periodical.
- For an article in a magazine or newspaper, omit the volume and issue numbers.
- For a newspaper, give the edition and page number(s).

Online Sources

Standards continue to evolve for citations of online and electronic sources. When citing online information, the two primary goals are to give credit to the author and to enable readers to retrieve the source.

- Include the author, title, and, if the information is included in a printed version, publication information.
- Indicate the date the document was created or updated and the date the information was retrieved and include in angle brackets the Web address (the URL) or enough address information to allow the reader to retrieve the source. Underline titles of entire Web sites.
- Treat any articles or graphics included at the site as you would those from print sources.
- For personal communications, such as e-mail messages and bulletin-board postings, follow the format for letters and interviews.

See Figure 6–13 on page 198 for a sample list of works cited in MLA style.

MLA Documentation Models

BOOKS

Single Author

Van Grembergen, Wim. Information Technology Evaluation Methods and Management. New York: Idea, 2001.

Multiple Authors

Testerman, Joshua O., Thomas J. Kuegler, Jr., and Paul J. Dowling, Jr. Web Advertising and Marketing. 3rd ed. Rocklin, CA: Prima, 2000.

Corporate Author

Ernst and Young. Ernst and Young's Retirement Planning Guide. 3rd ed. New York: Wiley, 2001.

Edition Other Than First

Van Horne, James C. Financial Market Rates and Flows. 6th ed. New York: Prentice Hall, 2000.

Multivolume Work

Standard and Poor. Standard and Poor's Register of Corporations, Directors and Executives. 3 vols. New York: McGraw, 2004.

Work in an Edited Collection

Griswold, Charles L. "Happiness and Cypher's Choice: Is Ignorance Bliss?" The Matrix and Philosophy. Ed. William Irwin. Chicago: Open Court, 2002. 126–37.

Encyclopedia or Dictionary Entry

Gibbard, Bruce G. "Particle Detector." World Book Encyclopedia. 2003 ed.

ARTICLES IN PERIODICALS (See also ELECTRONIC SOURCES)

Magazine Article

Limp, Fred. "Enterprise Development." Business Geographics June 2001: 19.

Journal Article

Loza, Jehan. "Business-Community Partnerships: The Case for Community Organization Capacity Building." Journal of Business Ethics 53 (2004): 287–311.

Newspaper Article

Loftus, Anna Patrick. "Small Business: Enterprise." Wall Street Journal 31 Aug. 2004: B4.

Article with Unknown Author

"CFOs Remain Optimistic on Economy." Business Journal 27 Sept. 2004: 33.

ELECTRONIC SOURCES

Entire Web Site

Association for Business Communication. Aug. 2004. Assn. for Business Communication. 20 Sept. 2005 <http://www.businesscommunication.org/>.

Short Work from a Web Site, with an Author

Locker, Kitty O. "The History of the Association for Business Communication." Association for Business Communication. Oct. 2002. Assn. for Business Communication. 20 Sept. 2004 <http://www.businesscommunication.org/about/history/history.html>.

Short Work from a Web Site, with a Corporate Author

General Motors. "Company Profile." General Motors. 2003. 20 Sept. 2004 <http://www.gm.com/company/corp_info/profiles/>.

Short Work from a Web Site, with an Unknown Author

"Forgotten Inventors." Forgotten Inventors. PBS Online. 2001. 19 Apr. 2001 <http://www.pbs.org/
    wgbh/amex/telephone/sfeature/index.htm>.

Article from a Database (Subscription)

Goldbort, Robert C. "Scientific Writing as an Art and as a Science." Journal of Environmental Health
    63.7 (2001): 22. Expanded Academic ASAP. InfoTrac. Salem State Coll. Lib., Salem, MA. 19
    Apr. 2001 <http://infotrac.galegroup.com>.

Article in an Online Periodical

Eberstadt, Nicholas, "Doon and Demography." The Wilson Quarterly XXX.1 (2006): 5 pp. April 2006
    <http://www.wilsoncenter.org/index.cfm?fuseaction=wq.essay&essay_id=162417>.

Publication on CD-ROM

Money 94. CD-ROM. Redmond, WA: Microsoft, 2004.

E-mail Message

Kahl, Jonathan D. "Re: Web page." E-mail to the author. 2 Oct. 2001.

MULTIMEDIA SOURCES

Map or Chart

Wisconsin. Map. Chicago: Rand, 2000.

"Asia." Map. Maps.com. 2000. 20 Apr. 2006 <http://www.maps.com/explore/atlas/political/
    asia.html>.

Film or Video

Massingham, Gordon, dir., and Jane Christopher, ed. Introduction to Hazardous Chemicals.
    Videocassette. Edgartown, MA: Emergency Film Group, 2003.

Lawerence, Detrick, prod. Accident Investigation--DVD. 2001. 10 Jan. 2006 <http://www
    .efilmgroup.com/>.

Radio or Television Program

"Cheering China's Baby Stops." Lou Dobbs Tonight. Host Lou Dobbs. CNN. 22 July 2005.

"Tailor-Made Cartography with Google Maps." Host Robert Siegel. All Things Considered. Natl. Public
    Radio. WGBH, Boston. 8 Jan. 2006. 17 Jan. 2006 <http://www.npr.org/programs/atc/>.

Television Interview

Aziz, Shaukat. Interview. The Charlie Rose Show. By Charlie Rose. Public Broadcasting System. 18 Jan. 2006.

OTHER SOURCES
Published Interview

Gates, Bill. "The View from the Very Top." Interview. Newsweek 17 Apr. 2000: 36–39.

Personal Interview

Sariolgholam, Mahmood. Personal interview. 29 Nov. 2004.

Personal Letter

Pascatore, Monica. Letter to the author. 10 Apr. 2004.

Brochure or Pamphlet

Library of Congress. US Copyright Office. Copyright Registration for Online Works. Washington: GPO, 2004.

Government Document

United States. Dept. of Energy. The August 14, 2003, Blackout One Year Later. Technical Pub. 137-2004-12176. Washington: GPO, 2004.

Report Published in a Collection

Rude, Carolyn D. "Legal and Ethical Issues in Editing." Strategies for Business and Technical Writing, 5th ed. Ed. Kevin J. Harty. New York: Pearson Education, 2005. 367–378

Report Published Separately

Bertot, John Carlo, and Charles R. McClure. Public Libraries and the Internet 2000: Summary Findings and Data Tables. Washington: GPO, 2000.

Lecture or Speech

McKinney, Scott. Lecture. Demarest Hall, Hobart and William Smith Colls., Geneva, NY. 3 May 2002.

Krug, Steve. "Don't Make Me Think: The Art of Designing User-Friendly Websites." New England School of Art & Design at Suffolk U. Boston Public Lib. 3 Apr. 2001.

MLA

MLA Sample Pages

This report examines the nature and disposition of the 3,458 ethics cases handled companywide by CGF's ethics officers and managers during 2004. The purpose of such reports is to provide the Ethics and Business Conduct Committee with the information necessary for assessing the effectiveness of the first year of CGF's Ethics Program (Davis, Marks, and Tegge 142). According to Matthias Jonas, recommendations are given for consideration "in planning for the second year of the Ethics Program" ("Internet" 152).

The CGF Aircraft Corporation takes its commitment to an ethical work environment seriously. Throughout its 64-year history, CGF has fostered high ethical standards in its relations with its customers, suppliers, and employees. The size, diversity, and decentralized locations of our workforce make it imperative that CGF's ethical committment — both in principle and in practice — be formalized.

The Office of Ethics and Business Conduct was created to administer the Ethics Program. The director of the Office of Ethics and Business Conduct, along with seven ethics officers throughout CGF, was given the responsibility for the following objectives, as described by Rossouw:

> Communicate the values, standards, and goals of CGF's Program to employees. Provide companywide channels for employee education and guidance in resolving ethics concerns. Implement companywide programs in ethics awareness and recognition. Employee accessibility to ethics information and guidance is the immediate goal of the Office of Business Conduct in its first year. (1543)

The purpose of the Ethics Program, according to Jonas, is to "promote ethical business conduct through open communication and compliance with company ethics standards" ("Ethics" 89). To accomplish this purpose, any ethics policy must ensure confidentiality and anonymity for employees who raise genuine ethics concerns. The procedure developed at CGF guarantees appropriate discipline, up to and

Author's last name and page number

One-inch margins; text double-spaced

Long quote indented one inch (or 10 spaces), double-spaced, without quotation marks

In-text citations give author name and page number; title used when multiple works by same author cited

Figure 6–12   MLA Sample Page

MLA

Litzinger 21

Works Cited

Association for Business Communication. Aug. 2004. Assn. for Business
 Communication. 16 Mar. 2005 <http://www.businesscommunication.org/>.

Davis, W. C., Roland Marks, and Diane Tegge. Working in the System: Five New
 Management Principles. New York: St. Martin's, 2001.

Hassab, Joseph C. Systems Management: People, Computers, Machines,
 Materials. New York: CRC, 1997.

Jonas, Matthias. "Ethics in Organizational Communication: A Review of the
 Literature." Journal of Ethics and Communication 29 (2001): 79–99.

---. "The Internet and Ethical Communication: Toward a New Paradigm." Journal
 of Ethics and Communication 32 (2004): 147–77.

Library of Congress. US Copyright Office. Copyright Registration for Online
 Works. Washington: GPO, 2004.

The One-Minute Manager. CD-ROM. Boston: Bedford, 1998.

Rossouw, George J. "Business Ethics in South Africa." Journal of Business Ethics
 16 (1997): 1539–47.

Sariolgholam, Mahmood. Personal interview. 29 Nov. 2004.

*Heading
centered*

*List alphabetized
by authors' last
names or title and
double-spaced*

*Hanging-indent style
used for entries*

ON THE WEB

For additional sample
documents in MLA
style, go to
**bedfordstmartins.com/
writingthatworks**
and select *Model
Documents Gallery.*

Figure 6–13   MLA Sample List of Works Cited

Other Style Manuals

Many professional societies, publishing companies, and other organizations publish manuals that prescribe bibliographic reference formats for their publications or for publications in their fields. In addition, several general style manuals are well known and widely used.

Biology

Council of Science Editors. *Scientific Style and Format: The CBE Manual for Authors, Editors, and Publishers.* 6th ed. New York: Cambridge University Press, 1994. See also <www.councilscienceeditors.org>.

Chemistry

American Chemical Society. *ACS Style Guide: A Manual for Authors and Editors.* 2nd ed. Washington, D.C.: American Chemical Society, 1998. See also <www.acs.org>.

Government Documents

United States Government Printing Office. *Style Manual.* Washington, D.C.: U.S. Government Printing Office, 2000. See also <www.gpoaccess.gov/stylemanual/>.

Journalism

Goldstein, Norm, ed. *Associated Press Stylebook and Briefing on Media Law.* Rev. ed. New York: Associated Press, 2005. See also <www.ap.org>.

Law

Harvard Law Review et al. *The Bluebook: A Uniform System of Citation.* 17th ed. Cambridge, Mass: Harvard Law Review Association, 2000. See also <www.legalbluebook.com>.

Medicine

American Medical Association. *American Medical Association Manual of Style.* 9th ed. Baltimore: Williams, 1998. See also <www.ama-assn.org>.

Political Science

American Political Science Association. *Style Manual for Political Science.* Rev. ed. Washington, D.C.: APSA, 2001. See also <www.apsanet.org>.

Social Work

National Association of Social Workers. *Writing for the NASW Press: Information for Authors.* See also <http://www.naswpress.org/resources/tools/01-write/guidelines_toc.htm>.

CHAPTER 6 SUMMARY: RESEARCHING YOUR SUBJECT

Information sources available to you as you research job-related topics include the record of firsthand observations that you gather directly and the results of research published by others that is available in print or online.

■ Firsthand observations and experiments are essential to gather information about behavior, natural phenomena, and the functions of processes or equipment. To gather observational information:

- Choose sites and times carefully and, as necessary, request permission in advance.

- Keep complete, accurate records and note dates, times, durations, and other details.

- Remain as unobtrusive as possible to not interfere with the process under observation.

■ Your own knowledge, training, and experience may provide essential information.

■ Personal interviews with subject-matter experts can provide up-to-date information not readily available elsewhere, but interviews require thoughtful preparation.

- Select the subject-matter expert most likely to be helpful.

- Prepare specific questions before the interview.

- Take careful notes during the interview.

- Review and summarize your notes immediately after the interview.

■ Questionnaires permit you to obtain the views of groups of people without the time and expense necessary for conducting numerous personal interviews.

- Design the questionnaire to gather as much information as you need with as little effort as possible on those answering the questions.

- Formulate questions so that the answers can be readily tabulated.

- Select respondents carefully to ensure that their responses represent a cross section of the population to which you wish to generalize your results.

■ Libraries provide organized access to a wealth of information in their print, audiovisual, and digitized collections. Researchers can access the information through online catalogs, databases and indexes, and reference works.

■ The Internet provides online access to immense amounts of information, although its lack of a coherent organization makes locating salient information a challenge. To increase the odds of locating what you need, use subject directories of sites, search engines, and metasearch engines.

- Evaluate print and online sources of information for their relevance, timeliness, and accuracy.

- Review the information source for its depth and breadth of coverage of your topic.

- Ensure that the source is reputable.

- Evaluate the information for any evidence of bias.

- Keep detailed records of these sources for your bibliography.

■ Take notes that accurately summarize the information relevant to your topic.

■ Avoid plagiarism by giving complete and accurate credit to all your information sources, which will:

- Allow readers to locate the source of the information given.

- Establish your credibility by supporting your work with information from existing sources.
- Give proper credit to your sources.

■ Document the information that you quote, paraphrase, or summarize in your text

- In brief *parenthetical citations* in text, with full information in an alphabetical list of works cited.
- In *numbered references* in text that refer to full information in a reference section, where citations are listed numerically in the order of their first citation in text.
- In *notes* that appear either at the bottoms of text pages (footnotes) or in a separate section at the end of a chapter or section (endnotes).

ON THE WEB

For an online quiz on research, go to Chapter 6, bedfordstmartins.com/writingthatworks

■ Exercises

1. Review the online catalog search in this chapter (illustrated in Figures 6–4 through 6–6). Choose a topic related to your area of study and conduct a step-by-step online catalog search by keyword. What three to five books would you consider using, and why?

2. For each sentence in the following passage, decide whether it is necessary to add quotations or cite a source. Explain your reasoning.

> Many people have made money investing in real estate in the past couple of years. However, what goes up, comes back down (1). EZHomeBuilders, a corporation that builds luxury homes, just announced that they believe the market for new homes is slowing and home prices are flattening out (2). After they announced this, shares of EZHomeBuilders fell 10% on the New York Stock Exchange, closing at $27.14 per share (3). Shares of other major builders fell as well (4).
>
> My aunt, Shelly Maughn, who is a residential real estate broker, says she thinks the market will return to the way it was about a decade ago, with prices increasing more slowly (5). She also used to work in retail sales and sold furnishings and appliances for homes where she watched sales go up and down with the housing market (6). When business for home builders slowed, business slowed for us, she says (7).
>
> I worked as an intern in Aunt Shelly's real estate office last summer and I really enjoyed it (8). One day, I hope to become a residential real estate broker and investor even though real estate can be a challenging career (9).

3. Prepare an MLA-style works-cited page, using the following list of sources:

- Allen, R.C. Guiding Change Journeys. New York: John Wiley & Sons, Inc., 2002
- Eula Bingham, Barbara Cohrssen, Charles H. Powell, Editors. Patty's Toxicology: Hydrocarbons/Organic Nitrogen Compounds, Volume four. Fifth edition, John Wiley & Sons, New York, 2001
- Kuhn, Thomas S. 1996. The Structure of Scientific Revolutions. 3rd edition, University of Chicago Press, Chicago, Illinois, 1996
- Richard Saul Wurman, Information Anxiety 2, Que, Indianapolis, Indiana, 2001
- Highsmith's Complete School & Library Catalog. Highsmith Inc., Fort Atkinson, WI, 1998

ON THE WEB

For additional exercises, go to Chapter 6, bedfordstmartins.com/writingthatworks

- Lee Hopkins, Do You Know What Day Tomorrow Is? Scholastic Inc., New York, 1989
- Bob Boiko, Content Management Bible, Hungry Minds, New York, NY, 2002
- Edward R. Tufte, Visual Explanations: Images and Quantities, Evidence and Narrative. Graphics Press, Cheshire, Connecticut, 1997.
- Karen A. Schriver, Dynamics in Document Design. John Wiley & Sons, New York, NY, 1997.
- Wayne Applehans, Alden Globe, and Greg Laugero. Managing Knowledge: A Practical Web-based Approach, Addison-Wesley Information Technology Series. Reading, Mass., Addison-Wesley Longman. 1999.

4. Using the list of sources provided in Exercise 3, prepare an APA-style references page.

5. Use one of your library's online periodical databases (such as Academic Search Premier) to find articles related to a recent discovery or an important trend in your field. Write a three-page report of your findings, using the APA or MLA style of documentation. Cite your sources within your text and include an APA-style reference list or an MLA-style list of works cited.

6. Paraphrase the following passage. Then summarize the information. Identify the topic of the passage for each version.

> To keep pipes from freezing, wrap the pipes in insulation made especially for water pipes or in layers of old newspaper, lapping the ends and tying them around the pipes. Cover the newspaper with plastic to keep out moisture. When it is extremely cold and there is real danger of freezing, let the faucets drip a little. Although this wastes water, it may prevent freezing damage. Know where the valve for shutting off the water coming into the house or apartment is located. You may as a last resort have to shut off this main valve and drain all the pipes to keep them from freezing and bursting.

7. For Research Project 2 in Chapter 1, you interviewed instructors about how they prepare their class lectures for their different groups of students. Go back to your interview transcripts and incorporate at least two direct quotes and two paraphrases of your interviewees' comments into your written findings.

8. The use of cell phones, laptop computers, and digital cameras has created a growing need for the recycling of portable rechargeable batteries. Many retail stores are promoting goodwill with their customers and helping to preserve the environment by shipping spent battery packs to recycling centers. Create a questionnaire designed to determine if people are aware of the need to recycle portable rechargeable batteries and how people feel about companies that provide recycling programs. Give the questionnaire to at least 20 people, tally your results, and present your findings to the class.

9. Select a topic from your career field or another area of interest. Using the online catalog in your library, locate five books on your topic. Document your sources according to the MLA or APA guidelines in this chapter.

10. Using a periodical database that your college library has access to, locate five articles—from magazines, newspapers, or journals—on the topic you chose for Research Project 9. Document your sources according to the MLA or APA guidelines in this chapter.

■ Collaborative Classroom Projects

1. This project involves doing some research and bringing that research into class before you can begin working with your classmates. Assume that you work in the public relations department of General Motors (GM) and that the company has been frustrated by a popular story that claims to show the consequences of failing to do proper research before introducing new products to international markets. According to the story, the Chevrolet Nova sold poorly when it was introduced to Latin America in the 1970s because GM failed to recognize that the translation of "no va" is "it doesn't go." Despite this example's inclusion in many marketing and business textbooks, however, many sources say the story is untrue.

   a. Research the history of this urban legend on the Web and bring the information to class.
   b. Create a questionnaire (see pages 152–157) that you can use to survey students and professors about this story—where they heard it, if they believe it, and so on. (You may want to survey respondents from all majors, or business and marketing students and professors in particular.)
   c. Tabulate the responses to your survey. What were your findings? Based on your research and your questionnaire, write a memo to your supervisor at General Motors explaining how the legend got started and addressing how your department might prevent the spread of such stories in the future.

2. Bring to class information related to your area of study from three Web sites. Print out relevant pages from each site and draft a brief synopsis of the resources provided there. Form groups with three to five students who share your major. Review the guidelines in this chapter for evaluating a Web site and draft a list of questions to consider when evaluating a Web site as a research resource specific to your field. Evaluate and compare each of the sites that your group members have found and decide which sites would be the most valuable for your research. Write a brief group summary of your findings to share with the class.

3. Using the online sources that you brought to class for Collaborative Classroom Project 2, work in a group of three to five students to create an MLA-style list of works cited and an APA-style list of references from your collective online sources. (Refer to the Documenting Sources section of this chapter as needed.)

■ Research Projects

ON THE WEB

For extra research projects, go to Chapter 6, bedfordstmartins.com/writingthatworks

1. Choose a topic related to your area of study and interview someone knowledgeable about your subject. Incorporate the information that you gathered at your interview into a research paper and document the interview according to MLA or APA style. Submit to your instructor your organized notes of the interview and the letter or e-mail message that you sent to request the interview.

2. Imagine that you have decided to expand the story in Exercise 2 for publication in a local newspaper. Your goal is to explore trends in your local real estate market over the last three years, using primary sources (interviews and questionnaires, for example) and research published by others.

a. Begin researching your state's real estate data by going to industry-specific Web sites (such as the Media Center of the Florida Association of Realtors at <http://media.living.net/releases/archive.htm>) and national government sites (like FedStats at <www.fedstats.gov/>).

b. Use newspaper databases such as LexisNexis (available through your school's library) to locate relevant newspaper articles. NewsLink at (<http://newslink.org/news.html>) lists newspapers and their respective Web sites in all states.

c. After you have reviewed your notes and have a good idea of local real estate market trends, conduct primary or firsthand research by interviewing a real estate agent or broker from your market, or someone who researches real estate for his or her job—an economics or statistics professor, for example. Your goal is to include quotes from qualified sources in your story.

Write a story incorporating all of your research. Be sure you paraphrase, quote, and cite your sources correctly.

ON THE WEB

For more Web projects, go to Chapter 6, bedfordstmartins.com/ writingthatworks

■ Web Projects

1. Assume you are a manager at a small manufacturing firm (you may choose the product that your company produces). Because of a rising national concern about the environment and land use, the board of directors has asked your department to develop a policy statement outlining your corporation's views on the conservation of natural resources. Use your library's Web subject directory to locate information about how government environmental policy affects your business. Submit your list of at least five sites with your notes, describing the information contained at each site and giving reasons why you chose these sites. Include with your notes an APA-style reference list or an MLA-style list of works cited.

2. Imagine that you work in public relations at an engineering college and your department is hosting a "brain teaser" competition for local high school students as a strategy to get more of them interested in the sciences and especially in your university. Many engineering professors and consultants will be in the audience. You decide to create a list of questions about space shuttles and go to several sites to research their history, height, wingspan, which three are still in service, and the missions they have flown. You also decide to include quotes from former and current crew members. It is very important that you not only have accurate answers for your questions but also that you have credible sources in case someone doubts your answers.

Designing Effective Documents and Visuals

At a Glance: Design

Workplace—and classroom—communications require more than words. They often require tables, drawings, photos, maps, graphs, and charts, elements that must be integrated with text into a unified whole. The integration of text and images takes careful thought if these components are to blend effectively to advance your purpose and meet your audience's needs. This chapter describes effective ways to plan, create, and integrate these nontext elements, by doing the following:

- Designing special-purpose documents to make them easy for readers to understand / 206
- Creating or locating the most appropriate visuals to accurately depict images and ideas / 217
- Creating or selecting accurate and culturally sensitive images for international audiences / 246

This chapter is divided into two main parts: The first, Designing Documents, offers detailed information for document layout and design; the second, Creating Visuals, provides guidelines and models for designing illustrations, for integrating them with text, and for using graphics to communicate with an international audience.

Clarity and consistency are important not only for good writing but also for the design and layout of any document—especially one that includes visuals—and to the creation and use of the visuals themselves. Effectively designed documents help readers locate the information they need and grasp how the parts fit together. The Designing Documents section describes how to achieve these goals, by providing your readers with carefully selected visual cues. Whether you are creating a memo, a report, or a newsletter, everything from your choice of type size and style to the arrangement of text and visuals on each page contributes to your reader's comprehension.

The Creating Visuals section of this chapter focuses on how to use visual aids to increase your reader's understanding of your topic. Tables, graphs, drawings, charts, maps, and photographs—often collectively called *visuals*—can express ideas or convey information that words alone cannot. Clear, concise visuals support your text and help your readers focus on key points. By allowing readers to understand and interpret data at a glance, visuals can encourage faster decision-making and be used to persuade your audience.

Voices from the Workplace

Howard Ellis, Compuware Corporation

As an information analyst at Compuware Corporation in Milwaukee, Wisconsin, Howard Ellis centers the majority of his writing on the creation, modification, and delivery of technology. His audience varies significantly — from executives to developers to end users — and so does their ability to understand technical ideas and concepts. To satisfy their diverse needs, Ellis relies heavily on the use of visuals. He says, "Visuals play a significant role in the work I do; it would be impossible for me to write effectively about technology without them." Tailoring his visuals to his intended audience is also important: "For a highly technical audience, I may present detailed visuals from some aspect of a project, including tables, screen shots, and possibly graphs. For another audience, such as a group of executives, I'll pare back the details."

Paul Clark, John Deere

Paul Clark is a former employee and current contractor at John Deere, where he helps to develop a Web-based system to plan and track the process required for producing products. Because the system is complex, Paul gives a lot of thought to how it looks. He explains, "I find that using diagrams and visuals is extremely important to the transfer and understanding of ideas. I spend a lot of time creating documents showing exactly what the screens will look like and how they will work. . . . This is time well spent because it allows both engineers and programmers to visualize the desired results. These diagrams greatly increase the probability that the final product will meet the expectations because most of the questions are covered."

■ Designing Documents

Most memos, letters, meeting minutes, progress reports, and other routine communications are formatted according to a predetermined set of standards. Business-correspondence formats, for example, are discussed in Chapter 8, Understanding the Principles of Business Communication; formal-report formats are discussed in Chapter 11, Writing Formal Reports. However, certain high-visibility, complex, or special-purpose documents, such as those aimed at customers, stockholders, or clients, require special layout-and-design consideration.

This section introduces you to the document layout-and-design principles for such nonroutine materials. Thoughtfully applied, these principles will make even the most complex information look accessible and give readers a favorable impression of the writer and the organization that produced it. To accomplish these goals, any document's design should

1. Offer a simple and uncluttered presentation of the topic.
2. Highlight structure, hierarchy, and order.

3. Help readers find information easily.

4. Reinforce an organization's image.

The same content can read differently with and without a well-designed page layout. Figure 7–1, for example, is a sample page from a software instruction manual without any conscious design devices. Note the effort necessary to follow the logic of the instructions—the words and sentences run together without any breaks or pointers to the content's organization and logic. Figure 7–2 shows the same information with a layout that both highlights the content's sequence and cues the reader to the location of this material within the manual.

Reference numbers have three parts: the basic reference number, a transposition check digit (TCD) that helps verify correct entry of the number and a suffix that lets the system link related reference numbers such as an incoming message and the reply to that message. The system adds hyphens to longer reference numbers to make them easier to read. Parts of a reference number: in the sequence 123-456789–B123, 123-456789 is the basic reference umber, B is the TCD, and 123 is the suffix.

System messages are informational, advisory, or error messages that appear on screens. Simple messages appear on the last line of any screen. Multiple messages appear on the Message Screen, which is accessed by pressing MESSAGE. The start of the message indicates the message type. Information Message is a confirmation that the system accepts your transaction. ⊵ Important: The most important informational message is TRANSACTION ACCEPTED AND POSTED TO FILES, which indicates the transaction has been successfully completed and is now part of the record for that account, instrument, or instruction. Look for this message as you post each message.

Figure 7–1   Page without Layout or Design

Effective design is based on visual simplicity and harmony, such as using compatible fonts and the same highlighting device for similar items. Design should reveal hierarchy by signaling the difference between topics and subtopics, between primary and secondary information, and between general points and examples. Writers can achieve effective layout and design through their selection of fonts, their choice of devices to highlight information, and their arrangement of text and visual components on a page. Such visual cues make information easy to find. Finally, the design of a document should project the appropriate image of an organization. For example, if clients are paying a high price for consulting services, they may expect a sophisticated, polished design; if employees inside an organization expect management to be frugal, they may accept—even expect—economical and standard company design.

ON THE WEB

For more information on designing effective documents and visuals, go to Chapter 7, bedfordstmartins.com/writingthatworks

Header with rule

Two-column design

Boxed figure with caption

Headings

White space
Icon and boldface

Rule and footer

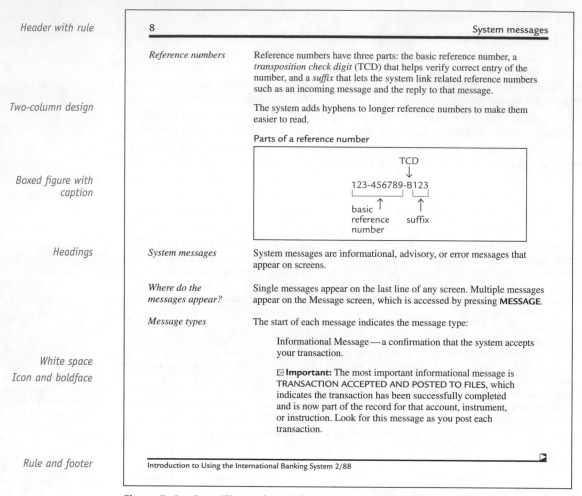

Figure 7–2   Page Illustrating Design and Layout Choices

Typography

Typography refers to the style and arrangement of type on a printed page. A complete set of all the letters, numbers, and symbols available in one typeface (or style) is called a *font*.

Typeface

For most on-the-job writing, select a typeface primarily for its simplicity and legibility. Focus on legibility by avoiding typefaces that may distract readers with contrasts in thickness or with odd-looking features, as is often the case with script and cursive typefaces. Choose popular typefaces with which readers are familiar, such as Times New Roman, or any of the following:

Baskerville	Century	Gill Sans	Palatino
Bodoni	Garamond	Helvetica	Univers

Do not use more than two or three typefaces in a single document—using too many typefaces will create visual disharmony in your document. To create a dramatic contrast between headings and text, as in a newsletter, use a typeface for the heading that is distinctively different from that of the text. You can also use a noticeably different typeface within a graphic element. In any case, experiment before making your final decision. (Keep in mind that not all fonts have the same assortment of symbols and other characters that you may need for your graphics.)

One major distinction among typefaces is the presence or absence of serifs. Serifs are the small projections at the end of each stroke in a letter. The text of this book is set in Utopia, a serif typeface, while all headings are in Officina Sans, a sans serif typeface. Serif type is easier to read, especially in the smaller sizes, and it works best for main text. Sans serif (without serifs) type, however, works well for headings (like the ones in this book). The simpler design of sans serif letters also makes them ideal for use with text on Web sites and for use in other documents read on-screen.

Type Size

Ensure that your text is easily readable. Small print can cause eyestrain and make the text look crammed and intimidating. Six-point type, for example, is too small for almost anything other than dating a source and classified ads. Likewise, type that is too large makes reading difficult for a general audience and is inefficient. Ideal point sizes for text in paper documents range from 10 to 12 points. For documents that will be read from a distance or that are geared toward visually impaired readers, use large type sizes. Figure 7–3 on page 211 illustrates a range of type sizes.

◆ *Ideal type sizes for presentation slides and Web sites are discussed in Chapters 14, Giving Presentations and Conducting Meetings, and 15, Writing for the Web.*

Highlighting Devices

Highlighting devices can give a document a visual logic and organization. For example, rules and boxes can set off steps and illustrations from surrounding explanations. Consistency is important: Use the same technique to highlight a particular feature throughout your document. However, be selective about how you use typographical devices and special graphics; too many design devices clutter a page and interfere with comprehension. Writers use a number of methods to emphasize important words, passages, and sections within documents:

- Typographical devices
- Headings and captions
- Headers and footers
- Rules, icons, and color

◆ *For additional guidance on highlighting facts and ideas, see Emphasis on pages 101–106 in Chapter 4, Revising the Draft.*

Figure 7–2 illustrates a variety of highlighting devices.

DIGITAL TIP: Designing Documents with a Word Processor

A variety of word-processing features can help you adhere to the requirements of your instructor or employer or to customize the text layout and other elements affecting the appearance of your document.

- *Page margins.* Page margins, usually preset at one or one-and-a-quarter inches on all sides of a page, can be changed for an entire document, for a given page, or for blocks of text within a page.

- *Columns.* Lines of text can be arranged to run across the page from left to right or to run in two or more columns. The columns feature can also be used for data in tables, membership lists, financial statements, rosters, and the like.

- *Margin alignment.* Headings, columns, blocks of text, and visuals can be centered, aligned solely on the left margin, or aligned on both left and right margins.

- *Centering.* Words, lines of text, and blocks of text can be centered between the right and left margins, a feature useful for creating titles, letterheads on stationery, and captions for tables and figures.

- *Line, word, and letter spacing.* The space between lines of text can be adjusted (single-, double-, triple-spaced, and so on), and unnecessary space between words and letters on a line can be eliminated.

- *Headers and footers.* Headers (titles at the top of a page) and footers (titles at the bottom of a page) can be inserted automatically on each page.

- *Type fonts.* The text for letters, reports, manuals, and other types of documents can be printed with a variety of type fonts that you deem appropriate to your purpose and readers. (A *font* is a complete set of letters, numbers, and other type characters with a distinctive and uniform design.)

- *Type style.* The text may also be printed using a variety of type styles within the basic font chosen. Type-style options include **boldface,** *italic,* and underlining to highlight or otherwise create distinctive text.

- *Preview mode.* Preview mode allows you to view a full page of your document on-screen exactly as it will look when it is printed. Save time and paper by evaluating the overall look of a page and adjusting it if necessary before you print.

- *File type.* When it is important to preserve the format of a document you send by e-mail, you can create it as a word-processing file and send that as an attachment, scan and save the document as a graphic file, or convert it to PDF format using Adobe Acrobat software. Whichever format you use, confirm in advance that your recipient can open a program you use.

- *Style sheets and templates.* For multiple documents that need a uniform look, create and save format specifications as a separate file. The file can be called up and automatically applied to subsequent versions of the same kind of document.

For a tutorial on these options, see <bedfordstmartins.com/writingthatworks> and select *Tutorials,* "Designing Documents with a Word Processor." For step-by-step instructions for setting margins, alignment, columns, and other design elements, select *Digital Tips,* "Laying Out a Page."

6 pt.	This size might be used for dating a source.
8 pt.	This size might be used for footnotes.
10 pt.	This size might be used for figure captions.
12 pt.	This size might be used for main text.
14 pt.	This size might be used for headings.

Figure 7–3   Samples of 6- to 14-Point Type

Typographical Devices

When used sparingly, **boldface,** *italics,* and ALL-CAPITAL LETTERS can help you achieve emphasis.

- Use **boldface** type for headings or short passages of text that you wish to draw attention to.
- Use *italics* to highlight a key term or phrase, or if you wish to slow readers, as in cautions or warnings.
- Use ALL-CAPITAL LETTERS for headings (if you don't use boldface) or to alert readers to crucial steps in a process, as in instructions, or to indicate danger, such as in a caution or warning message.

Headings and Captions

Headings—titles and subtitles within the body of a document—divide material into comprehensible segments by highlighting the main topics and signaling topic changes. They indicate the hierarchy within a document and help readers decide which sections they need to read. Captions—titles that highlight or describe illustrations or blocks of text—often appear below figures, above tables, and in the left or right margins next to blocks of text.

Headings appear in many typeface variations (**boldface** being most common) and often use sans serif typefaces. The most common positions for headings and subheadings are centered, flush left, indented, or by themselves in a wide left margin. Insert an additional line of space above a heading to emphasize the division on the page. Major section or chapter headings normally appear at the top of a new page. Never leave a heading as the final line on a page—the heading will be disconnected from its text and thus ineffective. Instead, move the heading to the start of the next page.

◆ *For detailed advice on using and formatting headings in formal reports, see pages 389–395 in Chapter 11, Writing Formal Reports.*

Headers and Footers

A header is identifying information carried at the top of each page; a footer contains similar information at the bottom of each page. (The header at the top of the next page reads "Chapter 7 Designing Effective Documents and Visuals," and includes the page number.) Document pages may have headers or footers or both. They carry such information as the topic or subtopic of a section, the section numbers, the date the document was written, page numbers, the document name, or the section title. Although headers and footers are important reference devices, limit the amount of information in them to avoid visual clutter. Headers and footers are usually in a smaller type size than the main text.

Rules, Icons, and Color

Rules are vertical or horizontal lines used to divide one area of the page from another or to create boxes; used in moderation, rules isolate and highlight important information for ease of reading. Figure 7–2 illustrates the effective use of rules to separate the header and footer from the main text.

An icon is a pictorial representation of an idea; it can be used to identify specific actions, objects, or sections of a document. Commonly used icons include the small envelopes on Web pages to symbolize e-mail links and national flags to symbolize different language versions of a document. Their advantage is that they convey ideas without words, so they are especially useful in communications with international audiences. To be effective, however, icons must be simple and easily recognizable to your reader. Figures 7–36 and 7–37, for example, illustrate internationally recognized icons (also called symbols).

Color and screening (or shading) can distinguish one part of a document from another or unify a series of documents. Color and screening can set off sections within a document, highlight examples, or emphasize warnings. They are especially useful in graphs, maps, and drawings to differentiate boundaries and to depict the actual colors of geological and biological samples. In tables, you can use screening to highlight column titles or sets of data to which you want to draw the reader's attention. Figure 7–13, for example, uses screening to differentiate the data for 2000 and 2001.

Page Design

◆ *For information about using graphics and typography at Web sites, see pages 527–529 in Chapter 15, Writing for the Web.*

Page design is the process of combining the various elements on a page to make a coherent whole. The flexibility of your design is based on the capabilities of your software, how the document will be reproduced, and your budget. (High-quality offset color printing, for example, is far more expensive and time consuming to reproduce than black-and-white printing.)

Thumbnail Sketches

ON THE WEB

For examples of well-designed newsletters and brochures, go to bedfordstmartins.com/writingthatworks, and select *Model Documents Gallery*.

Before you spend time positioning text and visuals on a page, you may want to create a thumbnail sketch, in which blocks indicate the placement of elements. The thumbnails are usually sketched by hand on lined tablet or graph paper, although some software programs make sample layout and design easy to experiment with on-screen. Your sketches need not be formal or even neat. They are simply a way to brainstorm design options before you begin the actual layout of a report, newsletter, brochure, or other document. Figure 7–4 shows thumbnail sketches of designs for an 8 1/2-by-11-inch report with two columns per page and for an 8 1/2-by-11-inch newsletter with three columns per page. You can go further by roughly assembling all the thumbnail pages, showing size, shape,

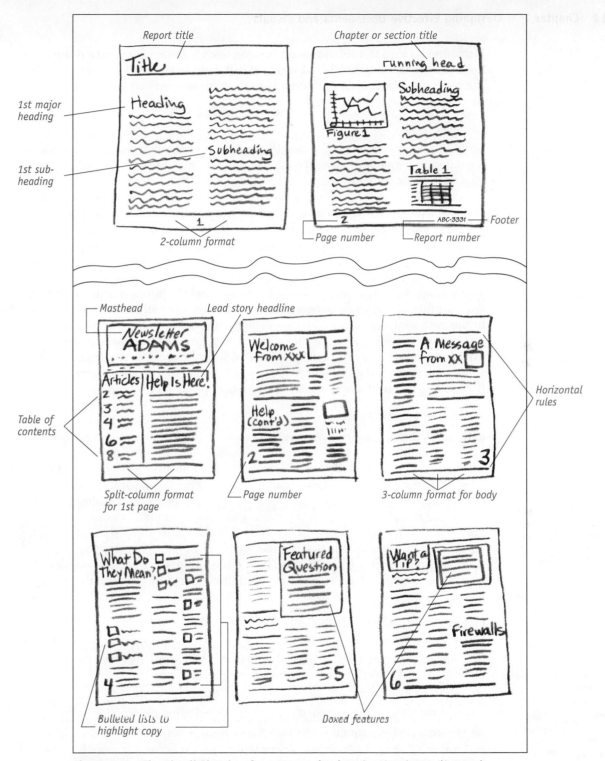

Figure 7–4 Thumbnail Sketches for a Report (*top*) and a Newsletter (*bottom*)

form, and general style of a large document. Such a mock-up, called a *dummy*, allows you to see how a finished document will look. As you work with elements on the page, experiment with different layouts to make sure that your ideas work in practice.

Columns

As you design pages, consider the size and number of columns. A single-column format works well with larger typefaces, double-spacing, and left-justified margins. For smaller typefaces and single-spaced lines, the two-column structure enhances legibility by keeping text columns narrow enough so that readers need not scan back and forth across the width of the entire page for every line. Check your document for single words or parts of words that appear alone as first or last lines of your columns. Figure 7–5 shows a report formatted in two columns.

White Space

White space visually frames information and breaks it into manageable chunks. For example, white space between paragraphs helps readers see the information in the paragraphs as units. White space between sections is also a visual cue that one section is ending and another is beginning. You need not have access to sophisticated equipment to make good use of white space. Use the default margin setting on your word processor (usually 1 or 1 1/4 inch), but allow extra space for the binding if your document will be three-hole punched for binders.

Left- or Full-Justified Margins

Left-justified margins are generally easier to read than full-justified margins because the uneven contour of the right margin (or "ragged" right) allows the spacing within and between words to be more uniform. Full justification causes word-processing software to insert irregular-sized spaces between words, producing unwanted gaps or unevenness in blocks of text, often making your document more difficult to read. Full-justified text is more appropriate for publications such as corporate annual reports, consumer booklets, sales brochures, and other documents aimed at a broad readership that expects a more-formal, polished appearance. Full justification is often useful with multiple-column formats because the spaces between the columns (alleys) need the definition that full justification provides. Figure 7–5 shows the same document with left-justified and full-justified columns.

Lists

Lists are an effective way to highlight words, phrases, and short sentences. Further, they are easy to read. Lists are particularly useful for certain types of information:

- Steps in sequence
- Materials or parts needed
- Items to remember
- Criteria for evaluation
- Concluding points
- Recommendations

Avoid both too many lists and too many items in lists.

ON THE WEB

For advice on using word-processing software to lay out your document, go to Chapter 7, **bedfordstmartins.com/ writingthatworks**

◆ *For more information about using lists effectively, see page 105 in Chapter 4, Revising the Draft.*

Optical and Handwritten Character Recognition Software: Recent Developments

Since the inception of computers, programmers have been teaching them to mimic humans. One such task that humans often take for granted is literacy. The process of reading printed text with a computer is called Optical Character Recognition (OCR). This method is optical because it uses a scanner to measure the reflected light off a piece of paper much like a copy machine does (Srihari and Lam 1–4). Along with OCR technology came handwriting recognition. Handwriting recognition occurs when the computer identifies each character the user writes with an electronic pen. Both OCR and handwriting recognition currently allow the computer almost 100 percent accuracy in understanding the writing of its human counterpart ("Looking Forward" 213).

What Are the Practical Applications?
OCR and handwriting recognition are used daily for such tasks as reading your tax forms and checking your passport at customs. The IRS, for example, receives about 200 million tax forms every year. So OCR is an important technology in processing tax forms because of OCR's speed and accuracy co... with ma... terpreta-

to 45,000 pieces of mail an hour (Srihari and Lam 12). . . .

How Does Scanning Work?
When the computer scans a page of text it does so graphically. All the computer sees at first is a grid of many small dots where each dot is either black or white. A typical scanner reads 300 of these dots per square inch.

The Letter R as printed (*left*) and as scanned into a matrix of dots (*right*).

In the first step of processing a page of text, the computer looks at the whole document and decides which regions contain text, and within regions ... rches f... dividual

Left-justified columns

Optical and Handwritten Character Recognition Software: Recent Developments

Since the inception of computers, programmers have been teaching them to mimic humans. One such task that humans often take for granted is literacy. The process of reading printed text with a computer is called Optical Character Recognition (OCR). This method is optical because it uses a scanner to measure the reflected light off a piece of paper much like a copy machine does (Srihari and Lam 1–4). Along with OCR technology came handwriting recognition. Handwriting recognition occurs when the computer identifies each character the user writes with an electronic pen. Both OCR and handwriting recognition currently allow the computer almost 100 percent accuracy in understanding the writing of its human counterpart ("Looking Forward" 213).

What Are the Practical Applications?
OCR and handwriting recognition are used daily for such tasks as reading your tax forms and checking your passport at customs. The IRS, for example, receives about 200 million tax forms every year. So OCR is an important technology in processing tax forms because of OCR's speed and accuracy compared with manual interpretation

to 45,000 pieces of mail an hour (Srihari and Lam 12). . . .

How Does Scanning Work?
When the computer scans a page of text it does so graphically. All the computer sees at first is a grid of many small dots where each dot is either black or white. A typical scanner reads 300 of these dots per square inch.

The Letter R as printed (*left*) and as scanned into a matrix of dots (*right*).

In the first step of processing a page of text, the computer looks at the whole document and decides which regions contain text, and within those regions it searches for individual letters

Full-justified columns

Figure 7–5 Left-Justified (*top*) and Full-Justified (*bottom*) Text Columns

Illustrations

Readers notice illustrations, especially large ones, before they notice text. Therefore, choose the size of an illustration according to its relative importance within your document. For newsletter articles and publications aimed at wide audiences, consider especially the proportion of the illustration to the text. In magazine design, for example, page layout is more dramatic and appealing when the major illustration (photograph, drawing, and so on) occupies three-fifths rather than half the available space. The same principle can be used to enhance the visual appeal of a report. While aesthetic considerations are important, it's most important that your document is clear and useful. For example, placing illustrations at the end of a report usually makes the writer's task easier, but placing them in the text closer to their accompanying explanations gives readers more-convenient access to them and provides visual breaks from blocks of text. (Creating visuals and integrating them with text are discussed in the next section.)

DESIGNING YOUR DOCUMENT
Laying Out the Page

- Select typefaces for legibility in style and size, not simply for variety.
- Emphasize important information with consistent typographical and design devices, using the following:
  - All-capital, italic, and boldface type styles selectively
  - Headings (in boldface or italic type) to denote major sections and topic changes
  - Captions to identify figures and tables, and to emphasize boxed information
  - Headers and footers to orient readers at the page level
  - Rules, icons, and color to highlight crucial information
- Integrate the typographical and page-level design elements into a consistent, coherent whole.
  - Experiment with the positions of text and visuals on a variety of thumbnail sketches to evaluate how the elements look together.
  - Create a mock-up copy, or dummy, of the whole document by assembling the thumbnail sketches for review.
  - Experiment with one- and two-column text layouts.
  - Allow adequate white space between paragraphs and around visuals and text boxes.
  - Use lists to highlight comparable types of information by setting them off from the surrounding text.
  - Position visuals in proportion to their importance and set them off with adequate white space.

Creating Visuals

Visuals can express ideas or convey information in ways that words alone cannot. For example, tables allow readers to easily compare large numbers of statistics that would be difficult to understand in sentence form. Graphs make trends and mathematical relationships immediately evident. Drawings, photographs, charts, and maps render shapes and spatial relationships more concisely and efficiently than text can. By allowing the reader to interpret data at a glance, visuals not only encourage faster decision-making but may add to the persuasiveness of your document or Web site. The guidelines in Table 7–1 can help you select the most-appropriate visuals based on their purpose and special features.

Designing and Integrating Visuals with Text

◆ *For guidance on preparing presentation graphics, see pages 484–488 of Chapter 14, Giving Presentations and Conducting Meetings.*

When using tables, graphs, or illustrations, consider your purpose and your reader carefully. For example, a drawing of the major regions of the brain for a high school science class would be different from an illustration provided for research scientists studying brain abnormalities. Be aware, though, that even the best visual only enhances, or supports, the text. It is your writing that must carry the burden of providing context for the visual and pointing out its significance.

To make the most-effective use of visuals and to integrate them smoothly with the text of your document, consider your graphics requirements even before you begin to write. Plan your visuals—tables, graphs, drawings, charts, maps, or photographs—when you're planning the scope and organization of your final work, whether it's a report, newsletter, brochure, presentation, or Web site. Make graphics an integral part of your outline, noting approximately where each should appear throughout the text. At each place where you plan to include a visual, either make a rough sketch of the visual or write "illustration of . . ." and enclose each suggestion in a box in your outline. If you are working on your computer, you can copy and paste graphics directly into your outline at the appropriate places, using your computer's clipboard feature. Like other information in a working outline, these boxes and sketches can be moved, revised, or deleted as required.

The following guidelines, which apply to most visual materials you might use to supplement or clarify the information in your text, will help you create and incorporate your visual materials within your documents effectively. (If you have an international audience, be sure to read Using Graphics to Communicate Internationally, beginning on page 246.)

- **Why include your visual?** Explain in the text why you've included the illustration. The description for each visual will vary with its complexity and its importance. Consider your audience: nonexperts require lengthier explanations than experts do, as a rule.
- **Is the information in your visual accurate?** Gather the information from reliable sources.

TO SHOW OBJECTS AND SPATIAL RELATIONSHIPS

DRAWINGS CAN . . .

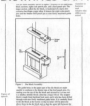

- Depict real objects difficult to photograph
- Depict imaginary objects
- Highlight only parts viewers need to see
- Show internal parts of equipment in cutaway views
- Show how equipment parts fit together in exploded views
- Communicate to international audiences more effectively than text alone

PHOTOGRAPHS CAN . . .

- Show actual physical images of subjects
- Record an event in process
- Record the development of phenomena over time
- Record the as-found condition of a situation for an investigation
- Show the colors essential to the accuracy of information in medical, chemical, botanical, and other fields

TO DISPLAY GEOGRAPHIC INFORMATION

MAPS CAN . . .

- Show specific geographic features of an area
- Show distance, routes, or locations of sites
- Show the geographic distribution of information (e.g., populations by region)

TO SHOW NUMERICAL AND OTHER RELATIONSHIPS

TABLES CAN . . .

- Organize numerical and non-numerical information systematically in rows and columns
- Present large numerical quantities concisely
- Facilitate item-to-item comparisons more easily than if embedded in text
- Clarify trends and other graphical information with precise data

BAR AND COLUMN GRAPHS CAN . . .

- Depict data in vertical bars and horizontal columns for comparison
- Show quantities that make up a whole
- Visually represent data shown in tables

LINE GRAPHS CAN . . .

- Show trends over time in amounts, sizes, rates, and other measurements
- Give an at-a-glance impression of trends, forecasts, and extrapolations of data

Table 7–1   Choosing Appropriate Visuals (continued)

- Compare more than one kind of data over the same time period
- Visually represent data shown in tables

PICTURE GRAPHS CAN . . .

- Use recognizable images to represent specific quantities
- Add visual appeal to help nonexpert readers grasp the information
- Visually represent data shown in tables

PIE GRAPHS CAN . . .

- Show quantities that make up a whole
- Give an immediate visual impression of the parts in proportion to one another
- Visually represent data shown in tables or lists

TO SHOW STEPS IN A PROCESS OR RELATIONSHIPS IN A SYSTEM

FLOWCHARTS CAN . . .

- Show how the parts or steps in a process or system interact from beginning to end
- Show the stages of an actual or a hypothetical process in the correct direction, including recursive steps

SCHEMATIC DIAGRAMS CAN . . .

- Show how the components in electronic, chemical, electrical, and mechanical systems interact and are interrelated
- Use standardized symbolic representations rather than realistic depictions of system components

TO SHOW RELATIONSHIPS IN A HIERARCHY

ORGANIZATION CHARTS CAN . . .

- Give an overview of an organization's departmental components
- Show how the components relate to one another
- Depict lines of authority within an organization: who reports to whom

TO SUPPLEMENT OR REPLACE WORDS

SYMBOLS OR ICONS CAN . . .

- Convey ideas without words
- Save space and add visual appeal
- Transcend individual languages to communicate ideas effectively for international readers
- Communicate culturally neutral images

Table 7–1 Choosing Appropriate Visuals (continued)

- **Is your visual focused?** Include only information necessary to the discussion in the text and eliminate unnecessary labels, arrows, boxes, and lines.

- **Are terms and symbols in your visual defined and consistent?** Define all acronyms in the text, figure, or table. If any symbols are not self-explanatory, include a listing (known as a *key*) that defines them. Keep terminology consistent. Do not refer to something as a "proportion" in the text and as a "percentage" in the illustration.

✦ *For more on evaluating sources, see pages 169–179 in Chapter 6, Researching Your Subject.*

- **Does your visual specify measurements and distances?** Specify the units of measurement used or include a scale of relative distances, when appropriate. Ensure that relative sizes are clear or indicate distance by a scale, as on a map.

- **Is the lettering readable?** Position any explanatory text or labels horizontally for ease of reading, if possible.

- **Is the caption clear?** Give each illustration a concise caption that clearly describes its contents.

- **Is there a figure or table number?** Assign a figure or table number for documents containing five or more illustrations. The figure or table number precedes the title:

  ▶ Figure 1. Projected sales for 2007–2010

  Note that graphics (photographs, drawings, maps, and so on) are generically labeled "figures," while tables (data organized in rows and columns) are labeled "tables."

- **Is a list of figures or tables needed?** In documents with more than five illustrations, list the illustrations by title, together with figure and page numbers, or table and page numbers, following the table of contents. Title figures "List of Figures" and tables "List of Tables."

- **Are figure or table numbers referred to in your text?** Refer to each illustration by its figure or table number in the text of your document.

- **Are visuals appropriately placed?** Place illustrations as close as possible and following the text where they are discussed. Place lengthy and detailed illustrations in an appendix and refer to them in the text of your document.

- **Do visuals stand out from surrounding text?** Allow adequate white space on the page around and within each illustration.

A discussion of specific types of visuals commonly used in on-the-job writing follows. Your topic will ordinarily determine the best type of visual to use.

Tables

A table is useful for showing large numbers of specific, related data in a brief space. The data may be numerical, as in Figure 7–6, or verbal, as in Table 7–2. Because a table displays information in rows and columns, your readers can easily compare data and see their significance more clearly than if they were presented in the text.

Table number

Boxhead

Stub

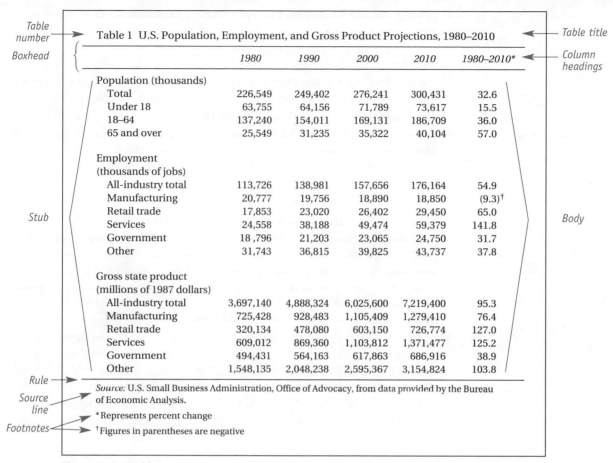

Table title

Column headings

Body

Rule

Source line

Footnotes

Table 1 U.S. Population, Employment, and Gross Product Projections, 1980–2010

	1980	1990	2000	2010	1980–2010*
Population (thousands)					
Total	226,549	249,402	276,241	300,431	32.6
Under 18	63,755	64,156	71,789	73,617	15.5
18–64	137,240	154,011	169,131	186,709	36.0
65 and over	25,549	31,235	35,322	40,104	57.0
Employment (thousands of jobs)					
All-industry total	113,726	138,981	157,656	176,164	54.9
Manufacturing	20,777	19,756	18,890	18,850	(9.3)[†]
Retail trade	17,853	23,020	26,402	29,450	65.0
Services	24,558	38,188	49,474	59,379	141.8
Government	18,796	21,203	23,065	24,750	31.7
Other	31,743	36,815	39,825	43,737	37.8
Gross state product (millions of 1987 dollars)					
All-industry total	3,697,140	4,888,324	6,025,600	7,219,400	95.3
Manufacturing	725,428	928,483	1,105,409	1,279,410	76.4
Retail trade	320,134	478,080	603,150	726,774	127.0
Services	609,012	869,360	1,103,812	1,371,477	125.2
Government	494,431	564,163	617,863	686,916	38.9
Other	1,548,135	2,048,238	2,595,367	3,154,824	103.8

Source: U.S. Small Business Administration, Office of Advocacy, from data provided by the Bureau of Economic Analysis.

*Represents percent change

[†]Figures in parentheses are negative

Figure 7–6   Table

ETHICS NOTE

Whether you reprint a preexisting image or use published information to create your own graph or table, you must acknowledge your borrowings in a source or credit line. Place source information below the caption for a figure and below any footnotes at the bottom of a table. (See Figure 7–0 for an example.) If you wish to use illustrations found on the Web or in printed sources, obtain written permission from the copyright holder. Material that is not copyrighted (generally limited to publications of the U.S. federal government) can be reproduced without permission, but you must still acknowledge the source in a credit line.

Following are the elements of a typical table, as shown in Figure 7–6, with guidelines:

- *Table number.* Number each table sequentially throughout the text.
- *Table title.* Create a title that describes concisely what the table represents; place it above the table.
- *Boxhead.* In the boxhead (beneath the title) provide column headings that are brief but descriptive. Include units of measurement either as part of the heading or enclosed in parentheses beneath it. Standard abbreviations and symbols are acceptable. Avoid vertical or diagonal lettering.
- *Stub.* In the left-hand vertical column of a table, called the stub, list all the items to be shown in the body of the table.
- *Body.* Provide data in the body of your table below the column headings and to the right of the stub. (Each datum element is located in a *cell.*) Within the body, arrange columns so that the terms to be compared appear in adjacent rows and columns. Where no information exists for a specific cell, substitute a row of dots or a dash to acknowledge the gap. If you substitute the abbreviation "N/A" for missing data in a cell, add a footnote to clarify whether it means "not available" or "not applicable."
- *Rules.* Use rules (lines) to separate your table into its various parts. Include horizontal rules below the title, below the body of the table, and between the column headings and the body of the table. You may include vertical rules to separate the columns, but do not use rules to enclose the sides of the table.
- *Source line.* Below the table, include a source line to identify where you obtained the data (when appropriate). Many organizations place the source line below the footnotes.
- *Footnotes.* Include a footnote when you need to explain an item in the table. Use symbols (*, †) or lowercase letters (sometimes in parentheses) rather than numbers to make it clear that the notes are not part of the data or the main text.
- *Continuing tables.* When you must divide your table to continue it on another page, repeat the column headings and give the table number at the head of each new page with a "continued" label ("Table 3, continued"), as shown in Figure 7–7.

To list relatively few items that would be easier for the reader to grasp in tabular form, use an informal table.

▶ The sound-intensity levels (decibels) for the three frequency bands (in hertz) were determined to be the following:

Frequency Band (Hz)	Decibels
600–1,200	68
1,200–2,400	62
2,400–4,800	53

Table 4

Assessment of Electronic Media and Format Standards in Federal Agencies: Number, Percentage, and Basis for Use by Agency

Format	Standard for each format used							
	Agency mandated		Common agency practice		Other		None	
	Number	Percent	Number	Percent	Number	Percent	Number	Percent
Database								
Oracle	7	38.9	8	44.4	1	5.6	1	5.6
WAIS	1	4.3	21	91.3	0	0.0	0	0.0
MARC	1	33.3	1	33.3	0	0.0	0	0.0
Sybase	0	0.0	4	80.0	0	0.0	0	0.0
dBase	0	0.0	8	80.0	0	0.0	0	0.0
Other	2	4.4	21	46.7	12	26.7	9	20.0
Spreadsheet								
Lotus 1-2-3	6	25.0	9	37.5	3	12.5	5	20.8
Excel	4	11.8	24	70.6	0	0.0	4	11.8
Other	0	0.0	0	0.0	0	0.0	2	50.0
Tagged markup								
HTML	21	13.3	114	72.2	6	3.8	15	9.5
SGML	2	13.3	9	60.0	2	13.3	1	6.7
XML	0	0.0	1	33.3	0	0.0	1	33.3
Other	0	0.0	7	53.8	1	7.7	4	30.8
Image								

Table 4, continued

Assessment of Electronic Media and Format Standards in Federal Agencies: Number, Percentage, and Basis for Use by Agency

Format	Standard for each format used							
	Agency mandated		Common agency practice		Other		None	
	Number	Percent	Number	Percent	Number	Percent	Number	Percent
Audio								
WAV	2	15.4	8	61.5	0	0.0	2	15.4
AU	4	66.7	0	0.0	0	0.0	1	16.7
AIFF	1	50.0	0	0.0	0	0.0	0	0.0
Other	0	0.0	1	20.0	2	40.0	1	20.0
Video								
MOV	0	0.0	5	62.5	0	0.0	2	25.0
MPEG	1	10.0	5	50.0	1	10.0	2	20.0
AVI	1	20.0	3	60.0	0	0.0	0	0.0
Other	0	0.0	0	0.0	1	50.0	0	0.0
Text								
ASCII	21	13.3	87	70.7	6	4.9	15	9.5

Figure 7–7 Divided Table (Continued on a Second Page)

Although you need not include titles or table numbers to identify informal tables, you do need to include headings that describe the information provided and columns and rows that are properly aligned. You may also need to acknowledge the source of the information, as discussed in the Ethics Note on page 219.

DESIGNING YOUR DOCUMENT
Creating Tables

■ Use tables to present data that you want readers to quickly evaluate and compare, and that would be difficult or tedious to present in your main text.

■ Identify each table with a concise, descriptive title and a unique table number.

■ Use horizontal lettering, if possible.

■ Do not enclose the left and right sides with vertical rules.

■ Include a source line when necessary to identify where you obtained your data.

■ For tables continued on another page, repeat the table number (followed by "continued"), title, and column headings.

■ Use informal tables—those without a title or number—when there are only a few items to categorize.

Graphs

Graphs, also called charts, present numerical data in visual form, showing trends, movements, distributions, and cycles more readily than tables do. Although graphs present statistics in a format that is easy to understand, they are less accurate than tables. For this reason, they are often accompanied by tables that give exact numbers. (Note the difference between the graph and the table showing the same data in Figure 7–8.) To solve the problem of showing only approximate data in graphs, you can include the exact data for each column—if this will not clutter your graph—giving the reader both a quick overview of the data and accurate numbers. (See Figures 7–9 and 7–13.) The most commonly used graphs are line graphs, bar graphs, pie graphs, and picture graphs, all of which you can easily render on your computer once you have entered your data into a spreadsheet or database application.

Line Graphs

The line graph shows the relationship between two or more sets of figures. The graph is composed of a vertical axis and a horizontal axis that intersect at right angles, each representing one set of data. The relationship between the two sets is readily indicated by points plotted along appropriate intersections of the two axes that are then connected to form a continuous line. The line graph's vertical axis usually represents amounts, and its horizontal axis usually represents increments of time (Figure 7–9). Line graphs with more than one plotted line allow for comparisons between two sets of data. In creating such graphs, label each plotted line, as shown in Figure 7–10. You can emphasize the difference between the two lines

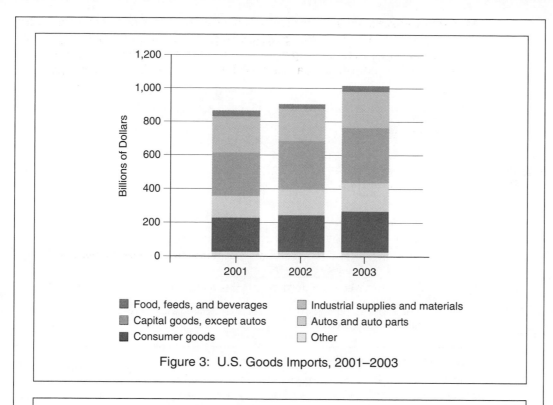

Figure 3: U.S. Goods Imports, 2001–2003

Table 3: U.S. Goods Imports, 2001–2003						
	2001	2002	2003	02–03	98–03	96–03
Imports	Billions of Dollars			Percentage Change		
Total (BOP Basis)*	876.4	917.2	1,030.2	12.3	54.1	92.0
Food, feeds, and beverages	39.7	41.2	43.6	5.7	40.6	57.9
Industrial supplies and materials	213.8	200.1	222.6	10.7	36.7	59.9
Capital goods, except autos	253.3	269.6	296.9	10.1	61.0	121.0
Autos and auto parts	139.8	149.1	179.5	20.4	51.7	95.6
Consumer goods	193.8	216.5	239.6	10.7	63.8	95.3
Other	29.3	35.4	43.9	24.1	106.1	148.0

Source: U.S. Department of Commerce.
*Balance of Payment Basis for Total. Census Basis for Sectors.

Figure 7–8   Graph and Table Showing the Same Data

Vertical axis shows quantity, and horizontal axis shows time increments

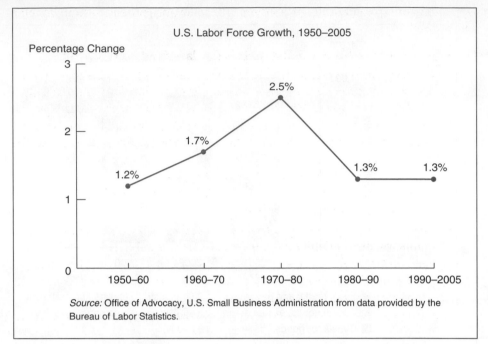

Figure 7–9 Single-Line Graph

Actual data plotted with normal range shaded to highlight difference

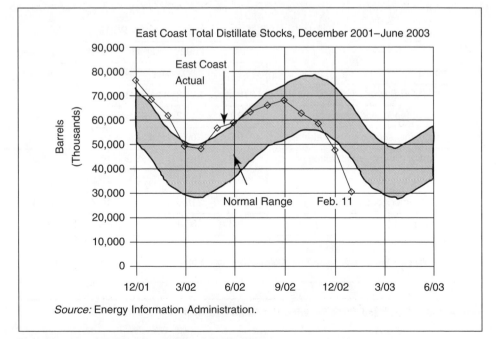

Figure 7–10 Double-Line Graph with Shading

by shading the space that separates them. The following guidelines apply to most line graphs:

- Give your graph a title that describes the data clearly and concisely.

- Indicate the zero point (where the two axes meet). If the range of data makes it inconvenient to begin at zero, insert a break in the scale (Figure 7–11); otherwise, the graph would show a large area with no data.

- Divide the vertical axis into equal portions, from the least amount at the bottom to the greatest amount at the top. The caption for this scale may be placed at the upper left (as in Figure 7–10), or, as is more often the case, vertically along the vertical axis (as in Figure 7–11).

- Divide the horizontal axis into equal units from left to right, and label them to show what values each represents.

- Include enough points to plot—accurately depict—the data; too few data points will distort depiction of the trends (Figure 7–12).

- Keep grid lines to a minimum so that the curved lines stand out. Detailed grid lines are unnecessary because precise values are usually shown either on the graph or in an accompanying table.

- Include a label or a key when necessary to define symbols or visual cues to the data, such as in the box below the data in Figure 7–13.

- Include a source line under the graph at the lower left, indicating where you obtained the data (see Figures 7–9, 7–10, and 7–13).

- Present all type horizontally if possible, although the type for the vertical-axis caption is usually presented vertically (see Figure 7–11).

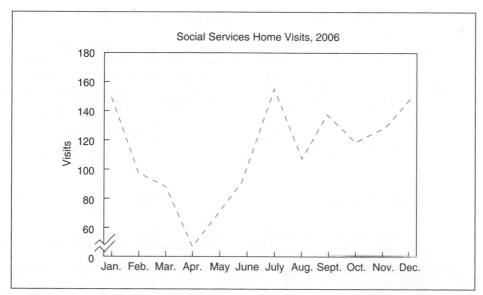

Break in vertical scale to emphasize the zero point

Figure 7–11   Line Graph with Vertical Axis Broken

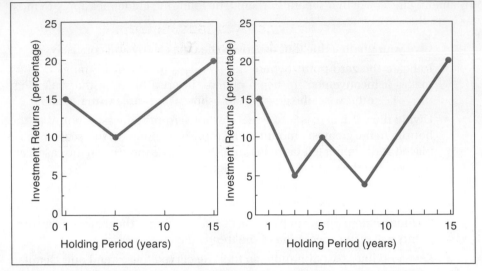

*Time increments
(right) expanded
to render data
free of distortion*

Figure 7–12   Distorted (*left*) and Distortion-Free (*right*) Expressions of Data

Be sure to proportion the vertical and horizontal scales so that they present data precisely and without visual distortion—to do otherwise is inaccurate and potentially misleading. In Figure 7–12, the graph on the left gives the appearance of a slight decline followed by a steady increase in investment returns because the scale is compressed, with some of the years selectively omitted. The graph on the right represents the trend more accurately because the years are evenly distributed without omissions.

ETHICS NOTE

Be careful not to omit or distort the data in your visuals. At the least, misleading visuals call into question the credibility of you and your organization—and they are unethical. Using misleading visuals can also subject you and your organization to lawsuits.

Bar Graphs

Bar graphs consist of horizontal or vertical bars of equal width but scaled in length or height to represent some quantity. They are commonly used to show the following proportional relations:

- Different types of information during different periods of time (Figure 7–13)
- Quantities of the same kind of information at different periods of time (Figure 7–14)
- Quantities of different information during a fixed period of time (Figure 7–15)
- Quantities of the different parts that make up a whole (Figure 7–16)

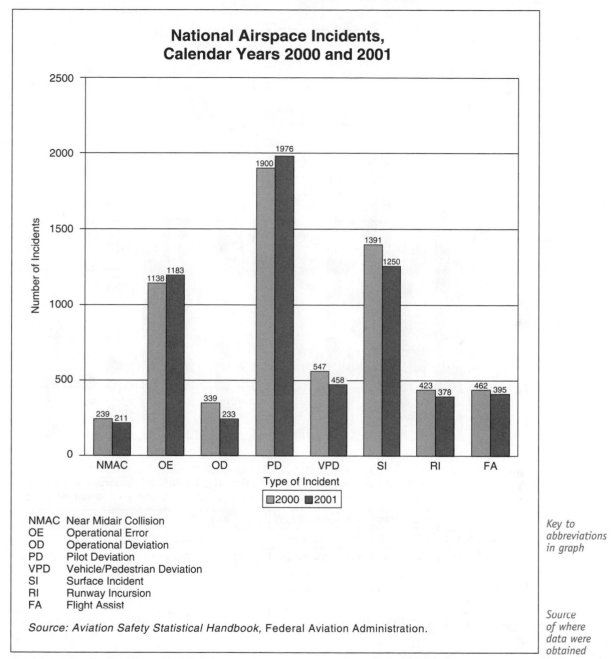

NMAC   Near Midair Collision
OE   Operational Error
OD   Operational Deviation
PD   Pilot Deviation
VPD   Vehicle/Pedestrian Deviation
SI   Surface Incident
RI   Runway Incursion
FA   Flight Assist

Source: Aviation Safety Statistical Handbook, Federal Aviation Administration.

Key to abbreviations in graph

Source of where data were obtained

Figure 7–13   Bar Graph of Different Types of Information during Different Time Periods

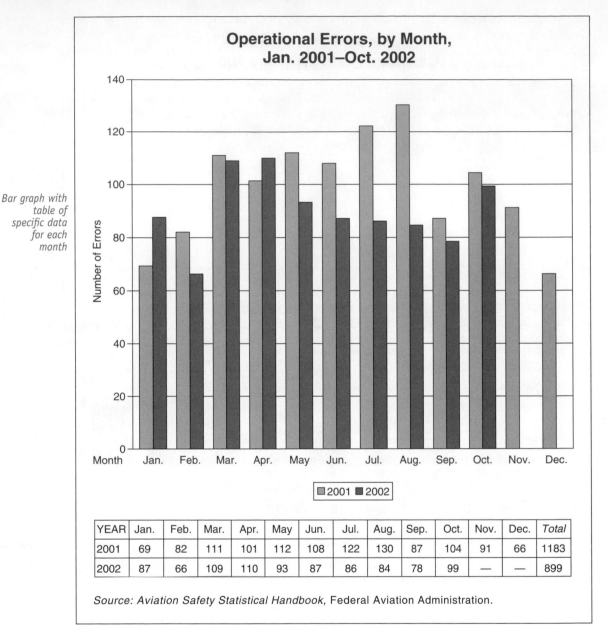

Bar graph with table of specific data for each month

Operational Errors, by Month, Jan. 2001–Oct. 2002

YEAR	Jan.	Feb.	Mar.	Apr.	May	Jun.	Jul.	Aug.	Sep.	Oct.	Nov.	Dec.	*Total*
2001	69	82	111	101	112	108	122	130	87	104	91	66	1183
2002	87	66	109	110	93	87	86	84	78	99	—	—	899

Source: Aviation Safety Statistical Handbook, Federal Aviation Administration.

Figure 7–14   Bar Graph Showing Quantities of the Same Kind of Information at Different Periods of Time

Bar graphs can also indicate what proportion of a whole the various component parts represent. In such a graph, the bar, which is theoretically equivalent to 100 percent, is divided according to the proportion of the whole that each item sampled represents. (Compare the displays of the same data in Figures 7–16 and 7–18.) In some bar graphs, the completed bar does not represent 100 percent because not all parts of the whole have been included or not all are pertinent in the sample (Figure 7–17). Bar graphs are also used to track project schedules, where each bar represents the time allotted for each task of a project. A project-tracking bar graph, also called a *timeline graph,* is shown in Figure 5–4 on page 140.

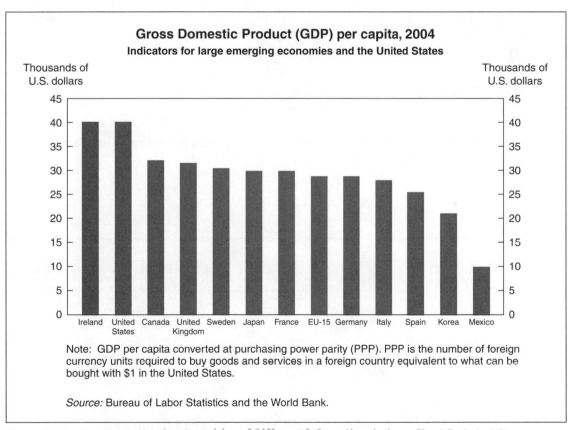

Figure 7–15   Bar Graph Showing Quantities of Different Information during a Fixed Period of Time

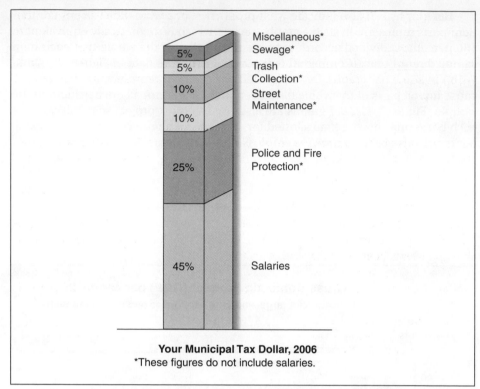

Explanatory note clarifies data

Figure 7–16   Bar Graph Showing Different Quantities of Different Parts of a Whole

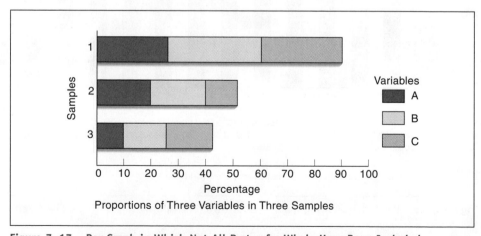

Figure 7–17   Bar Graph in Which Not All Parts of a Whole Have Been Included

Note that in Figure 7–19, a type of bar graph showing travel frequency, the exact quantities appear at the end of each picture column, eliminating the need to have an accompanying table giving the percentages. If the bars are not labeled, as in Figures 7–14 and 7–17, the different portions must be clearly indicated by shading, cross-hatching, or other devices. Include a key that represents the various subdivisions.

Pie Graphs

A pie graph presents data as wedge-shaped sections of a circle. The circle equals 100 percent, or the whole, of some quantity (a tax dollar, a bus fare, the hours of a working day), with the wedges representing the various parts into which the whole is divided. In Figure 7–18, for example, the circle stands for a city tax dollar and is divided into units equivalent to the percentages of the tax dollar spent on various city services. Note that the slice representing salaries is slightly offset (exploded) from the others to emphasize that data. This feature is commonly available on spreadsheet and database software.

The relationships among the various statistics presented in a pie graph are easy to grasp, but the information is often general. For this reason, a pie graph is

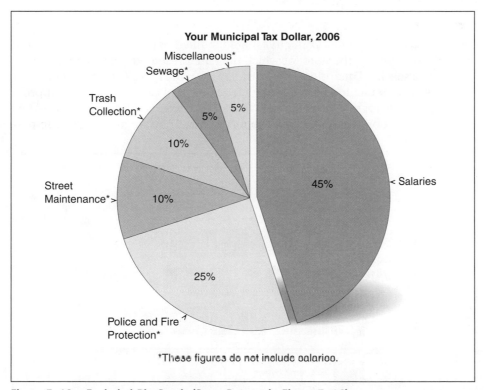

Figure 7–18 Exploded Pie Graph (Same Data as in Figure 7–16)

often accompanied by a table that presents the actual figures on which the percentages in the graph are based.

Following are guidelines for constructing pie graphs:

- Keep in mind that the complete 360° circle is equivalent to 100 percent.
- When possible, begin at the 12 o'clock position and sequence the wedges clockwise, from largest to smallest. (This is not always possible because the default setting for some charting software sequences the data counterclockwise.)
- Apply a distinctive pattern or various shades of gray for each wedge.
- Keep all labels horizontal and, most important, provide the percentage value of each wedge.
- Check to see that all wedges and their respective percentages add up to 100 percent.

Although pie graphs have a strong visual impact, they also have drawbacks. If more than five or six items of information are presented, the graph looks cluttered and, unless percentages are labeled on each section, the reader cannot compare the values of the sections as accurately as on a bar graph.

Picture Graphs

Picture graphs (also called *pictograms*) are modified bar graphs that use picture symbols to represent the item for which data are presented. Each symbol corresponds to a specified quantity of the item, as shown in Figure 7–19. Note that exact numbers are also included because the picture symbol can indicate only approximate figures. Pictograms usually work well for nonexpert audiences because they make the data more vivid and easier to remember. They are also popular in pre-

Quantity increases represented by increased number of symbols

Quantity for each symbol specified

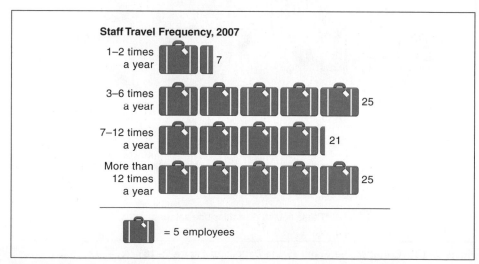

Figure 7–19 Picture Graph

sentations because they add an element of entertainment to the data. Here are some tips on preparing picture graphs:

- Use symbols that are self-explanatory.
- Have each symbol represent a specific number of units and be sure to include accurate numerical quantities for each row of data.
- Show larger quantities by increasing the number of symbols rather than by creating a larger symbol.

Dimensional-Column Graphs

Consider a common on-the-job reporting requirement—tracking a series of expenses over a given period of time. Assume that you wish to show your company's expenses over a three-month period for security, courier, mail, and custodial services. Once you enter the data for these services into a spreadsheet program, you can display them in a variety of graph styles. As you select from among the options available, keep in mind your reader's need to interpret the data accurately and quickly, so keep the graph style as simple as possible for the information shown.

Graphs that depict columns as three-dimensional pillars are popular—they give the data a solid, three-dimensional, building-block appearance. They can, however, obscure rather than clarify the information, depending on how they are displayed. Consider the graph in Figure 7–20. Although the data are accurate, they

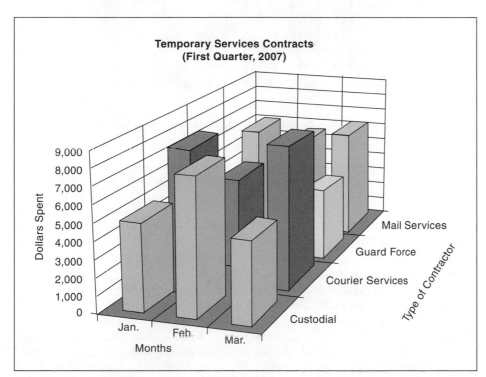

Three-dimensional columns obscure data for February and March

Figure 7–20   Three-Dimensional Column Graph

cannot be interpreted as shown. The axis showing expenditures cannot be correlated with most columns representing the various services. The graph also obscures the columns for courier and guard-force services. Finally, this graph style does not allow readers to spot trends for expenditures over the three-month period, which is key information to decision-makers.

The graph in Figure 7–21 presents more clearly the same data as that shown in Figure 7–20. The trends of expenditures are easy to spot, and all the data are at least visible. Yet this graph is not ideal. To interpret the information, the reader would need to put a ruler on the page and align the tops of the columns with the axis showing expenditures.

Tops of three-dimensional columns cannot be interpreted without a ruler

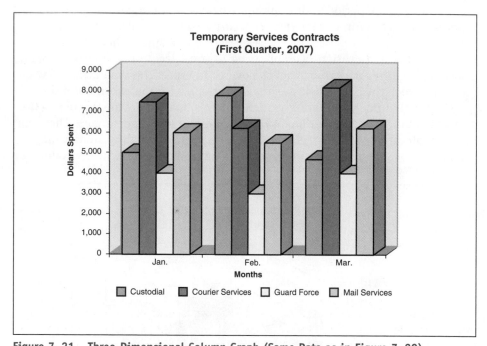

Figure 7–21   Three-Dimensional Column Graph (Same Data as in Figure 7–20)

The three-dimensional appearance can also cause confusion: Is the front or back of each column the correct data point? Also somewhat confusing is that, at first glance, the reader is tricked into interpreting the spaces between the column clusters as columns because they are of equal width.

The graphs in Figures 7–22 and 7–23 would best represent the data, depending on your intent. Figure 7–22 avoids the ambiguity of the graph in Figure 7–21 by showing the data in two dimensions. It also displays the horizontal lines for expenditures on the vertical axis, thus making the data for each column easier to interpret. If you wished to show relative expenses among the four variables for a given quarter, this graph would be ideal. However, if you wished to show trends for

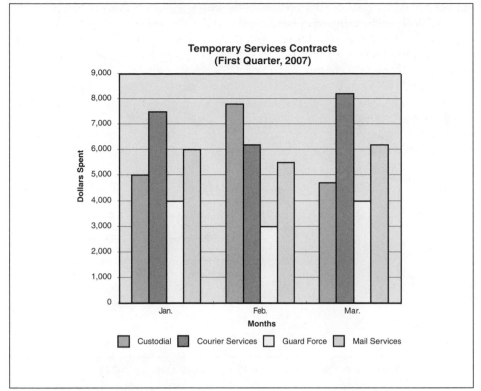

Two-dimensional columns make data easy to interpret at a glance

Figure 7–22   Two-Dimensional Column Graph (Same Data as in Figures 7–20 and 7–21)

the entire three-month period in contract expenditures at a glance, the graph in Figure 7–23 on page 238 is preferable.

When precise dollar amounts for each service are equally important, you can provide a table showing that information. As Figures 7–20 through 7–23 show, the more complicated a graph looks, the harder it is to interpret. On balance, simpler is better for the reader. Use this principle when you review your computer graphics on-screen in several styles and consider your reader's needs before deciding which style to use.

Drawings

A drawing is useful when your reader needs an impression of an object's general appearance or an overview of a series of steps or directions. Note, for example, the sequence of drawings in Chapter 12 that show the steps used to install a waste disposer (Figure 12–9). Drawings are the best choice when you need to focus on details or relationships that a photograph cannot capture. A drawing can emphasize the significant piece of a mechanism, or its function, and omit what is not significant—

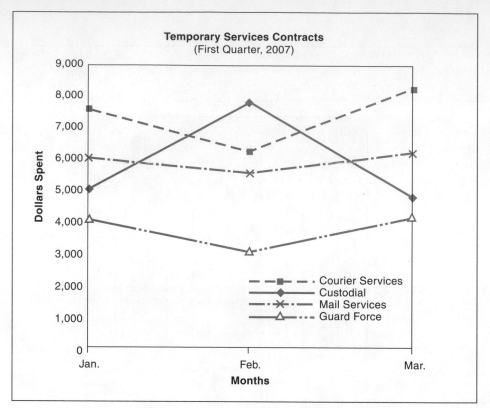

Figure 7–23   Line Graph (Same Data as in Figures 7–20 through 7–22)

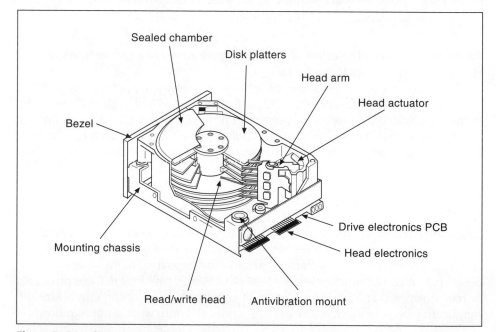

Figure 7–24   Cutaway Drawing

for example, a cutaway drawing can show the internal parts of a piece of equipment in such a way that their relationship to the overall equipment is clear (Figure 7–24). An exploded-view drawing can show the proper sequence in which parts fit together or the details of each individual part (Figure 7–25).

Drawings are also the best option for illustrating simple objects or tasks that do not require photography (Figure 7–26). However, if the actual appearance of an object (a dented fender) or a phenomenon (an aircraft wind-tunnel experiment) is necessary to your document, a photograph is essential. For drawings that require a high degree of accuracy and precision, seek the help of a graphics specialist.

ON THE WEB

For another example of an exploded-view drawing, go to **bedfordstmartins.com/ writingthatworks** and select *Model Documents Gallery*.

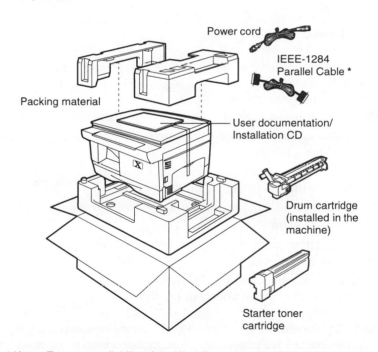

Installation

As you unpack the WorkCentre, familiarize yourself with its contents. After the WorkCentre is installed, and the Ready Indicator is lit, the WorkCentre is ready to make copies.

IMPORTANT: Save the carton and packing materials. They should be used to repack the WorkCentre if it has to be shipped for servicing or in case you move.

Power cord

IEEE-1284 Parallel Cable *

Packing material

User documentation/ Installation CD

Drum cartridge (installed in the machine)

Starter toner cartridge

* Note: To ensure reliability of the WorkCentre use the IEEE-1284 compliant parallel cable that is supplied with the machine. Only cables labeled "IEEE-1284" can be used with your WorkCentre.

Exploded view shows parts of a mechanism, packing container, and part names

Figure 7–25   Exploded-View Drawing

Prevent Repetitive-Motion Injuries

Before beginning keying and during breaks throughout the day, take time to do the stretches as shown.

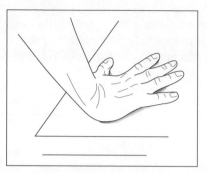

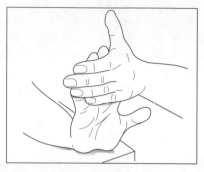

Gently press the hand against a firm flat surface, stretching the fingers and wrist. Hold for five seconds.

Rest the forearm on the edge of a table. Grasp the fingers of one hand and gently bend back the wrist, stretching the hands and wrist. Hold for five seconds.

Figure 7–26   Drawing

Many organizations have their own format specifications for drawings. In the absence of such specifications, the following guidelines should be helpful:

- Show the equipment from the point of view of the person who will use it.
- When illustrating part of a system, show its relationship to the larger system of which it is a part.
- Draw the different parts of an object in proportion to one another, unless you indicate that certain parts are enlarged.
- For drawings used to illustrate a process, arrange them from left to right and from top to bottom.
- Label important parts of each drawing so that text references to them are clear and consistent.
- Depending on the complexity of what is shown, label the parts themselves — see Figure 7–25 — or use a letter or number key.

For general-interest images needed to illustrate newsletters, brochures, or presentation slides, use the clip-art libraries provided with word-processing programs, graphics programs, and the numerous image libraries available on the Web. These sources contain thousands of noncopyrighted symbols, shapes, and images of people, equipment, furniture, buildings, and the like. An added advantage is that you can adjust their size according to your document's layout and

ON THE WEB

For access to image libraries on the Web, go to Chapter 7, bedfordstmartins.com/ writingthatworks

space requirements to fit your space requirements. Figure 7–27 shows examples of clip-art images.

Figure 7–27   Clip-Art Images

Flowcharts

A flowchart is a diagram that shows the stages of a process from beginning to end; it presents an overview that allows readers to grasp essential steps quickly and easily. Flowcharts can illustrate a variety of processes ranging from the stages required to refine bauxite ore into aluminum to the steps required to prepare a manuscript for publication.

Flowcharts can take several forms to represent the steps in a process: labeled blocks (Figure 7–28), pictorial representations (Figure 7–29), or standardized symbols (Figure 7–30). The items in any flowchart are always connected according to

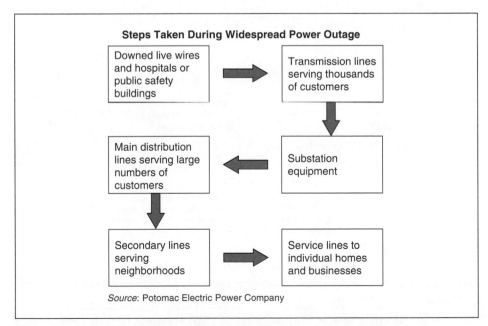

Figure 7–28   Flowchart Using Labeled Blocks (Depicting Electric Utility Power Restoration Process)

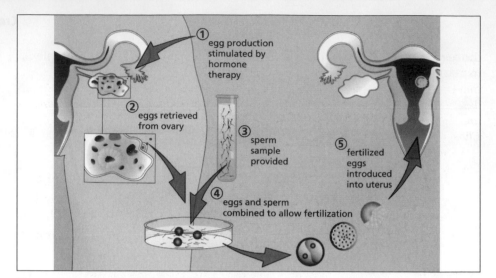

Figure 7–29   Flowchart Using Pictorial Symbols

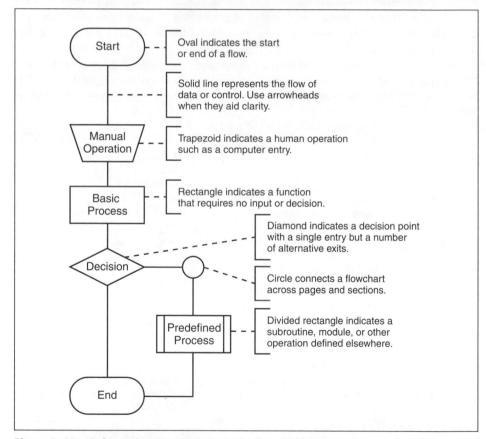

Figure 7–30   Information Standards Organization (ISO) Flowchart Symbols (with Annotations)

the sequence in which the steps occur and typically flow left to right or top to bottom. When the flow is otherwise, indicate it with arrows. Flowcharts that document computer programs and other information-processing procedures use standardized symbols set forth in *Information Processing: Documentation Symbols and Conventions for Data, Program, and System Flowcharts, Program Network Charts, and System Resources Charts,* ISO publication 1985 (E).

Follow these guidelines when creating a flowchart:

ON THE WEB

For additional examples of flowcharts, go to **bedfordstmartins. com/writingthatworks** and select *Model Documents Gallery.*

- With labeled blocks and standardized symbols, use arrows to show the direction of flow, especially if the flow is opposite to the normal direction. With pictorial representations, use arrows to show the direction of all flow.

- Label each step in the process, or identify it with a conventional symbol. Steps can also be represented pictorially or by captioned blocks.

- Include a key if the flowchart contains symbols that your audience may not understand.

- Leave adequate white space on the page. Do not crowd the steps and directional arrows too closely together.

Organizational Charts

An organizational chart shows how the various parts of an organization are related to one another. Such illustrations give readers an overview of an organization or indicate the lines of authority within an organization (Figure 7–31).

The title of each organizational part (office, section, division) is placed in a separate box. These boxes are then linked to a central authority. If useful to your readers, include the name of the person occupying the position identified in each

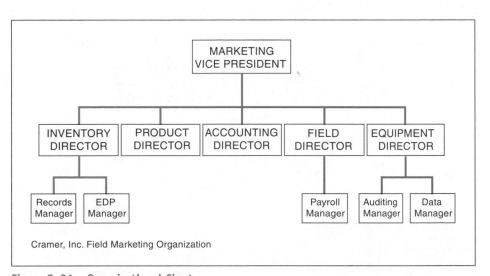

Boxes are linked to show hierarchy of and relationships among units in an organization

Figure 7–31 Organizational Chart

box. As with all illustrations, place the organizational chart as close as possible following the text that refers to it.

Maps

Maps can be used to show the specific geographic features of an area (roads, mountains, rivers) or to show information according to geographic distribution (population, housing, manufacturing centers, and so forth) (Figure 7–32).

Keep in mind the following points as you create maps for use with your text:

- Clearly identify all boundaries within your map. Eliminate those that are unnecessary to the area you want to show.

- Eliminate unnecessary information. For example, if population is the focal point, do not include mountains, roads, rivers, and so on.

- Include a scale of miles or feet, or kilometers or meters, to give your reader an indication of the map's proportions.

- Indicate which direction is north.

- Emphasize key features by using shading, dots, crosshatching, or appropriate symbols, and include a key telling what the different colors, shadings, or symbols represent (Figure 7–33).

Focus of map is location of three sites (highlighted with callouts and arrows)

Note state, reservation and county boundaries; highways; and scales of distance

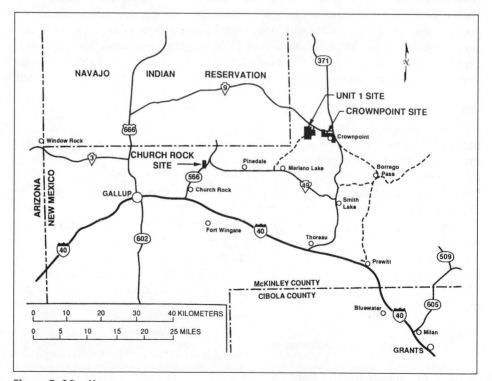

Figure 7–32   Map

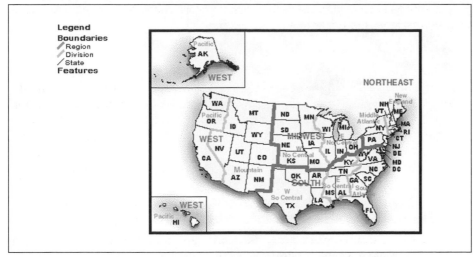

Figure 7–33   Map Showing Legend and Shading to Depict Data
Source: U.S. Census Bureau.

Photographs

Photographs are vital to show the surface appearance of an object or to record an event or the development of a phenomenon over a period of time. Not all representations, however, call for photographs. They cannot depict the internal workings of a mechanism or below-the-surface details of objects or structures. Such details are better shown in drawings or diagrams.

Highlighting Photographic Objects

If you are taking the photo, stand close enough to the object so that it fills your picture frame. A camera will photograph only what it is aimed at; accordingly, select important details and the camera angles that will record these details. To show the relative size of an unfamiliar object, place a familiar object—such as a ruler, a book, a tool, or a person—near the object that is to be photographed, as shown in Figure 7–34.

Ask the printer reproducing your publication for special handling requirements if you use glossy photographs. If you use digital photos, ask about the preferred resolution of the images before you shoot. The higher the resolution, the better the quality. You can digitize film photos using scanners and digital cameras, so ensure that the equipment has the necessary memory for the resolution required by the printer.

Using Color

Color is in many cases the only way to communicate crucial information. In medical, chemical, geological, and botanical publications, for example, readers often need to know exactly what an object or a phenomenon looks like to accurately

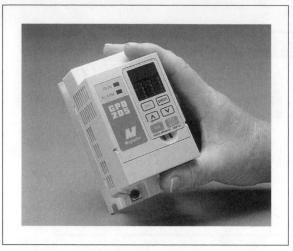

Device being held by a human hand to illustrate its relative size

Figure 7–34   Photo of Control Device
Source: Photo courtesy of Ken Cook Company.

interpret it. In these circumstances, color reproduction is the only legitimate option available.

Posting color images at a Web site is no more complicated or expensive than posting black-and-white images. For publications, however, preparing and printing color photographs are complex technical tasks performed by graphics and printing professionals. If you are planning to use color photographs in your publication, discuss with these professionals the type, quality, and number of photographs required.

Be mindful that color reproduction is significantly more expensive than black-and-white reproduction. Color can also be tricky to reproduce accurately without losing contrast and vividness. For this reason, the original photographs must be sharply focused and rich in contrast.

ON THE WEB

For information on locating photographs and other images for your documents, go to Chapter 7, bedfordstmartins.com/ writingthatworks

Using Graphics to Communicate Internationally

More than ever, business and technical communicators use graphics to communicate with international audiences. As companies expand their markets in Saudi Arabia, China, South America, the countries of the former Soviet Union, and dozens of other places, the marketplace becomes more global—a trend marked by the prevalence of multinational corporations, the international subsidiaries of many companies, multinational trade agreements, the increasing diversity of the U.S. workforce, and even increases in immigration. The audiences for these communications include clients, business partners, colleagues, and current and potential employees and customers. Even though English is rapidly becoming the global language of business and science, many people speak it as a second or third language. For this reason, graphics offer distinct advantages for communicating in a global business climate.

DIGITAL TIPS: Using Graphics Software[1]

■ *Vector graphics* packages allow you to manipulate predefined shapes (boxes, circles, arcs, lines, letters) that you then combine to produce images. Vector packages render crisp, high-resolution images that are ideal for producing complex technical graphics (isometric drawings, exploded views, and detailed line drawings), as well as basic images (flowcharts and organizational charts). These images—lines, shapes, letters—retain high-quality resolution regardless of the size at which they are produced.

■ *Bitmapped* (or *raster*) programs allow you to manipulate individual pixels (picture elements or dots) to produce lines, shapes, and patterns. These programs—also called *paint programs*—work best with images that have broad variations in colors, shapes, or hues, such as photos and detailed drawings. Use these programs to edit photos, create Web graphics, or modify screen shots for use in print and online publications. You can alter these images by manipulating the color and intensity of the dots. The resolution quality of the images is affected by the number of dots they contain—more dots equal higher quality. At lower resolution, the images have a fuzzy or jagged appearance.

Which program should you use? Typical vector programs include Visio, SmartDraw, MSProject, PaintShop, and Adobe Creative Suite. Among the many bitmapped programs, many students use the freeware program InfanView, which is useful for manipulating images. Select the program based on the type of image you will produce.

Use a vector program for

■ Line drawings

■ Blueprints

■ Flow and organizational charts

■ Isometric drawings

■ Network and process diagrams

Use a bitmapped program for

■ Photographs

■ Computer screen shots

■ Web graphics

■ Special effects

Note that most vector programs can convert vector images to dots to create bitmap images for editing with a bitmap image editor. However, bitmap programs cannot convert bitmap images to vector images.

[1] Based on "An Introduction to Illustration Software" by Bryan J. Follas, *Intercom*, September/October 2001: 6–8.

- Graphics can communicate a message more effectively than text, particularly in the context of safety warnings or cautions.
- Graphics can sometimes replace technical terms that are difficult to translate.

Despite their unquestionable value in communicating with international readers, symbols, images, and even colors are not free from cultural associations: How they are perceived depends on many factors—including the values and norms of a given culture. Thus, with the exception of the symbols used in mathematics and certain scientific and engineering disciplines (for example, the voltage symbol used in electrical engineering), no universally accepted graphics standards exist. Writers who create documents for an international audience can avoid confusing and possibly offending their readers by understanding the following cultural differences in connotation.

 DIGITAL TIPS: Computer Graphics

Creating computer graphics allows you to

- ■ Save images for future use and update them as necessary.
- ■ Use images in reports, other documents, and Web sites.
- ■ Send images to presentation software programs such as Microsoft PowerPoint or Apple iWork Keynote to create printed transparencies or digital presentations for meetings.
- ■ Communicate image files to others electronically via e-mail.
- ■ Automate sharing and updating data in images created and maintained in different applications—spreadsheet, database, graphics, word-processing, and presentation programs.

Colors

The use of a particular color can distort or even change the meaning of graphics symbols. Red commonly indicates warning or danger in North America, Europe, and Japan. In China, however, red symbolizes joy. In Europe and North America, blue generally has a positive connotation; in Japan, the color represents villainy. In Europe and North America, yellow represents caution or cowardice; in Arab countries, yellow generally means fertility or strength.

People, Parts of the Body, and Gestures

Depicting people and parts of the body in graphics can be problematic (Table 7–2). If your graphics will reach an international audience, it is better to avoid depictions of people eating or representations of bare arms and feet. Nudity in advertising, for example, generally is acceptable in Europe but not in North America or in predominantly Muslim countries. Even showing isolated body parts could lead to communication difficulties. For example, some Middle Eastern cultures regard the display of the soles of one's shoes to be disrespectful and offensive. Therefore, a technical manual that attempts to demonstrate the ease of running a

Table 7–2   International Implications of Gestures and Body Language

Body Part	Gesture	Country	Interpretation
Head	Nodding up and down	Bulgaria	No
Left hand	Showing palm	Muslim countries	Dirty, unclean
Index finger	Pointing to others	Venezuela, Sri Lanka	Rude
Fingers and thumb	Circular OK	Germany, Netherlands	Rude
Ankle and leg	Crossing over knee	Indonesia, Syria	Rude
Eye	Touching finger below eye	Honduras	Caution

software program by showing a user with his or her feet up on a desk could be considered offensive to that audience.

Consider the graphic warning weightlifters against the use of steroids in Figure 7–35. The image is appropriate for U.S. audiences (and others) but is highly inappropriate in cultures where the image of a partially clothed man and woman in close proximity would be contrary to deeply held cultural beliefs and even laws

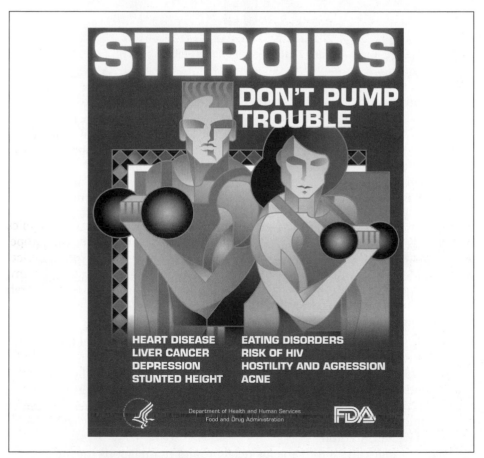

Figure 7–35   Graphic for a U.S. Audience

about the public depiction of men and women. The image in Figure 7–36, however, depicts a weightlifter by using a neutral icon that avoids the connotations associated with more realistic images of people.

Figure 7–36   Graphic for a Global Audience

Communicators producing instructions often use hand gestures such as the victory sign ( ) or the "OK" sign ( ) as positive motivators. However, the meaning of each of these gestures varies by culture. In Australia, for example, the victory sign conveys the same meaning as holding up the middle finger in North America. Similarly, the gesture that means "OK" in North America can mean "worthless" in France, can mean "money" in Japan, and is a sexual insult in many other parts of the world. Even a smile may have different connotations. In Japan, smiling can be a sign of joy or can be used to hide displeasure; in some Asian cultures, smiling may be considered a sign of weakness.

Further, a manual that contains a pointed finger to indicate "turn the page" might offend someone in Venezuela. A writer preparing a manual for export to Honduras could indicate "caution" by using a picture of a person touching a finger below the eye.

Cultural Symbols

Signs and symbols are so culturally rooted that we often lose sight of the fact that they may be understood only in our culture.

A Michigan manufacturer of window fans, for example, wanted to use easily understood symbols to represent the two speeds of its product: fast and slow. The technical communicators selected a rabbit and a turtle. However, recognition of these animals as symbols of speed and slowness requires familiarity with Aesop's fables—a Western tradition.

Symbols that carry simultaneous religious and nonreligious meanings have long been used in North America, where it is common to use the cross as a symbol for first aid or a hospital. In Muslim countries, however, a cross solely represents Christianity; a crescent (usually green) is a symbol for first aid.

The symbols or icons we create to represent technology are also laden with cultural assumptions. If users do not have regular contact with fax machines, photocopiers, computers, or cellular phones, technical and business communicators cannot predict how users will interpret representations of these devices.

Even punctuation marks are affected by cultural expectations. For example, in North America the question mark generally represents the need for information or the Help function in a computer manual or program. In many countries, this symbol is not understood at all. To avoid confusion, when possible include a key that associates the English-language question mark with the local language's equivalent mark.

These and similar examples suggest why international groups, such as the International Organization for Standardization (ISO), have established agreed-on symbols, such as those shown in Figure 7–37, designed for public signs, guidebooks, and manuals.[2]

ON THE WEB

For links to intercultural resources for business writers, go to Chapter 7, **bedfordstmartins.com/ writingthatworks**

Figure 7–37   International Organization for Standardization (ISO) Symbols

Reading Practices

Whether text is read right to left or left to right influences how graphics are sequenced. In the Middle East and in many parts of Asia, for example, text is read from right to left. For these audiences, you will need to alter the design and sequencing of text and graphics.

Directional Signs

The signs we use to represent direction or time are open to misinterpretation. For example, the arrow sign on shipping cartons can be interpreted to mean either that the carton should be placed with the arrow pointing up to the top of the carton, or pointing down to the carton's most stable position. Western cultures tend to indicate the future (or something positive) by pointing to the right ($\rightarrow$) and the past (or something negative) by pointing to the left (←); in the Chinese culture, left represents honor and right self-destruction.

[2]See *Symbol Sourcebook: An Authoritative Guide to International Graphic Symbols,* Henry Dreyfuss (Hoboken, N.J.: John Wiley and Sons, 1984).

Careful attention to the different connotations visual elements may have for an international audience makes translations easier, saves a company from potential embarrassment, and, over time, earns respect for the company and its products and services.

 CONSIDERING AUDIENCE AND PURPOSE

Using International Graphics

- Consult with someone from your intended audience's country who will be able to recognize and explain the effects of subtle visual elements on your intended readers.

- Acknowledge diversity within your company and recognize that not everyone interprets visual information in the same way.

- Learn about the use of gestures in other cultures as a first step to learning about cultural context because the interpretation of gestures differs widely.

- Invite international and intercultural communication experts to speak to your colleagues, and contact companies in your area that may have employees who could be resources for cultural discussions.

- Be sure that the graphics you use have no unintended religious or symbolic implications.

- Use few colors in your graphics. Generally, black-and-white or gray-and-white illustrations are less problematic than color graphics.

- Create simple visuals. Simple shapes with few elements are easier to read in most cultures.

- Use outlines or neutral abstractions to represent human beings. For example, use stick figures for bodies or a circle for a head.

- Be consistent in labeling elements. Use simple, consistent signs for all visual items.

- Explain the meaning of icons or symbols. Include a glossary to explain technical symbols that cannot be changed (for example, company logos).

- Test icons and symbols in context with members of your target audience. Usability testing with cultural experts is critical.

- Organize visual information for intended audiences. North American readers read visuals from left to right in clockwise rotation. Middle Eastern cultures read visuals from right to left in counterclockwise rotation.

CHAPTER 7 SUMMARY: DESIGNING EFFECTIVE DOCUMENTS AND VISUALS

Integrating Visuals and Text

■ Have you noted in your document planning outline the approximate location of your graphics?

■ Does the text preceding a table or figure make clear why the visual is there and what it shows?

■ Do all graphics have clear, concise captions?

■ Is the graphic located as close as possible to—but following—the text describing it? Is the language in the text consistent with the language in the graphic?

■ Have you allowed adequate white space around and within the text and graphics in your documents?

■ Have you obtained permission to reproduce copyrighted graphics in your document?

■ Do the layout and design of your finished document highlight the organization and hierarchy of your information?

Creating Visuals

■ Do your tables organize numerical or verbal information for ease of understanding?

■ Are the trends depicted in your graphs free of distortions?

■ Are graphs supported by accurate data in tables or by exact figures on the graph?

■ Are shading or crosshatching patterns on graphs easy to interpret?

■ Are graphs free of unnecessary details that obscure at-a-glance interpretations?

■ Are drawings shown from the correct perspective and focused on the significant piece of a device or mechanism?

■ Do flowcharts indicate the direction of flow?

■ Are the steps in a pictorial flowchart labeled?

■ Are unfamiliar symbols in a flowchart explained to your audience?

■ Are maps free of details that obscure the features you wish to highlight?

■ Do photographs show key objects and details from the best perspective and degree of visual clarity?

Using Visuals to Communicate Internationally

■ Has someone from your audience's culture or country reviewed your visuals for appropriateness?

■ Do visuals feature culturally neutral shapes and designs?

■ Are important features, including icons and symbols, labeled on the visual or explained in a glossary or key?

ON THE WEB

For an online quiz on designing documents and visuals, go to Chapter 7, bedfordstmartins.com/writingthatworks

ON THE WEB

For additional exercises, go to Chapter 7, bedfordstmartins.com/writingthatworks

Exercises

1. Assume that you work for PLANET (the Professional Landcare Network), a professional association for landscape designers and contractors. You have been asked to create a table for the organization's Web site (<www.landcarenetwork.org/>) that shows the seasonal lawn-maintenance tasks landscape services or homeowners might perform over the period of one year. Use the following information to create your table:

   Mow: April to June (every two weeks), July and August (weekly), and September to October (every two weeks)
   De-thatch: April or September
   Aerate: April or September
   Fertilize: March, May, July, September, November
   Water: Twice a week June through September, or as needed
   Apply weed killer: February, April, June, August, October

2. Assume that a survey of 100 companies resulted in the following distribution percentages by type of industry: computer-related, 32 percent; industrial equipment, 7 percent; business services, 8 percent; telecommunications, 10 percent; media and publications, 10 percent; consumer goods, 10 percent; medical and pharmaceutical, 14 percent; other, 9 percent. Prepare a pie graph showing the distribution.

3. Create a line or bar graph that compares sales in thousands of dollars among the various truck-parts divisions of the ABC Corporation for 2004, 2005, and 2006. Sales for each division are as follows:

   • Axles: 2004 ($225K), 2005 ($200K), 2006 ($75K)
   • Universal joints: 2004 ($125K), 2005 ($100K), 2006 ($35K)
   • Frames: 2004 ($125K), 2005 ($100K), 2006 ($50K)
   • Transmissions: 2004 ($75K), 2005 ($65K), 2006 ($50K)
   • Clutches: 2004 ($35K), 2005 ($30K), 2006 ($15K)
   • Gaskets and seals: 2004 ($28K), 2005 ($25K), 2006 ($20K)

4. Briefly explain whether a photograph or a line drawing would better illustrate features of the following subjects: a dry-cell battery (for an article in a general encyclopedia), a flower arrangement (in a florist's brochure), an electrical-outlet box (in a wiring instructions booklet), or the procedure for wrapping a sprained ankle (for a first-aid handbook).

5. Create a flowchart for a process or procedure important to your field of study or to the topic of your current writing project, as directed by your instructor. Introduce and explain the flowchart, relating it to your topic and explaining discrete actions, decisions, or repetitions of specific procedures that occur in the process that the flowchart depicts.

6. Beginning at the main entrance and ending at the checkout desk, draw a flowchart that traces the path you follow in the process of locating and obtaining books from your library (as outlined in Chapter 6, Researching Your Subject).

7. Create an organizational chart for a club or group to which you belong or for the department in your area of study.

8. Misleading visuals are unethical and can result in a loss of credibility for you and your organization. Sometimes deceptive visuals are based on incorrect statistics;

sometimes statistics are manipulated to help a person or an organization improperly achieve goals. In either case, visuals and the statistics that inform them can help or hurt specific groups. (For example, a graph that accurately shows the number of college binge drinkers could help garner support for the creation of a campus substance abuse counseling center; visuals that inaccurately suggest a lower number of binge drinkers could be used to argue against stricter alcohol regulations on campus.) For each of five subjects from the following list, suggest a potential visual based on statistics and list ways in which that visual might be used to help or hurt the people involved:

- Immigrants seeking asylum in the United States
- Abused children
- Elderly who need financial assistance
- Children with learning disabilities
- Women who give birth in prison
- Disabled veterans
- Battered wives or husbands
- Infants affected by illegal drugs
- Underpaid health-care workers
- Homeless teens
- Adults on Social Security

9. Following up on Exercise 8, imagine that you are planning to create a report for local government leaders on the use and ethics of visuals and statistics as they relate to promoting social programs and public policy. Using the Designing Your Document checklist on page 216, think strategically about the layout of your pages as a means of persuading this audience. For example, how many columns will you use? What kind of font type and size would promote quick and efficient reading? How will you highlight statistics and other crucial information? (You may want to revisit Chapter 1, Getting Ready, for information on audience and their needs.) Use your answers to create a thumbnail sketch of your report.

10. Create a pie chart that breaks down the expense percentages in your monthly budget, including housing, food, utilities, transportation (car, bus, subway), insurance (car, life, property, medical), school, clothing, entertainment, and the like. Support your pie chart with a detailed table that specifies the exact amount you budgeted for each item.

■ Collaborative Classroom Projects

1. Bring to class an explanation of how something works (such as a cell phone or computer chip) that *does not* contain visuals (one good source is <http://howthingswork.virginia.edu/>). Now divide into teams of five or fewer students and choose the explanations for two different objects. Brainstorm with your team about how you would add visuals to these explanations to make them easier to understand. Be sure you have a specific audience in mind before you begin (such as prospective customers overseas, new users, or repair technicians).

   a. Search through this chapter for the types of visuals that would be best suited for this project. List them and give a brief rationale for your choice.

ON THE WEB

For more collaborative classroom projects, go to Chapter 7, bedfordstmartins.com/ writingthatworks

    b. Create thumbnail sketches of the visuals and where they would be placed in relation to the text. Give a brief explanation of your strategy.

    c. Present your work to the class and explain your strategies and why you think they would successfully help your audience to better understand the explanations. Ask for feedback on your work.

ON THE WEB

For extra research projects, go to Chapter 7, bedfordstmartins.com/writingthatworks

    d. As your instructor directs, use your peers' feedback to combine your thumbnail sketches with the text into handouts for the class. (If you want to use clip art or photos from the Web, be sure to review the ethics note on page 221 of this chapter and page 179 of Chapter 6, Researching Your Subject.)

2. Bring to class a set of illustrated instructions (such as assembly instructions for a bookcase or a quick-start guide for a digital video recorder) that you believe could be designed more effectively. As your instructor directs,

    a. Critique the design and create a list of what could be improved.

    b. Recommend specific steps for improving the instructions' clarity.

    c. Create a new set of instructions either yourself or in a group.

3. Bring to class an example of a newsletter from a source on campus, such as a campus group or department, or from a source outside campus, such as a community-service group or business. Divide into groups of five or fewer. For the next forty-five minutes, rank your samples by order of their effectiveness. Which samples best accomplish their purpose? Why? Refer to this chapter for guidelines on page design. Be prepared to defend your choices to your classmates.

◼ Research Projects

ON THE WEB

For more Web projects, go to Chapter 7, bedfordstmartins.com/writingthatworks.

1. Interview someone from another country or culture about a specific aspect of business (or an aspect of another field). Write a report of 500 to 700 words on two cultural differences between ideas held in that country or culture and ideas broadly held in the United States. Consider punctuation marks, religious symbols, colors, body parts, gestures, directional signals, or technology symbols. Do not use any specific examples already discussed in this chapter.

2. Imagine that you just got hired as a graphic artist for a marketing company. Your job is to design visuals for a new promotional campaign your company is creating for a famous sneaker company. You come up with the idea for a graphic, featuring a mound of sneakers piled high to the sky. You decide to copyright your idea. You then create the sneaker graphic and register it in your name instead of the marketing company's. You later run into a friend who shows you an interesting graphic, featuring people running. The artist gave him permission to use that graphic for a project. You ask to use it, too, and your friend gives you permission. Your new boss gets wind of your activities and threatens to fire you unless you learn about copyright laws. Research the basic copyright and fair-use laws regarding graphics to find out what you did wrong. Present your findings to the class in an oral presentation.

Web Projects

1. Create a bar graph showing the median sales price of new single-family homes in the United States for 1975 and at five-year intervals through the most current data available at the Web site of the U.S. Census Bureau at <www.census.gov>.

2. On the Web, you can find sites that use both text and visuals to explain how things work. One excellent source is <www.howstuffworks.com>. After reviewing the guidelines in this chapter for creating documents and integrating visuals:
   a. Choose a hand-held electronic object (such as a video game or digital camera) and search the Web for an explanation of how it works. Print the explanation and evaluate it according to the criteria listed under Designing and Integrating Visuals with Text, beginning on page 217.
   b. Mark the pages of the explanation, indicating any changes you would make to improve its design. Feel free to sketch out your ideas.
   c. Draft a memo to your instructor in which you explain what does and does not work in the explanation's original design, supporting your ideas with information from this chapter. Specify how your changes would improve the document's design. Attach to your memo the marked-up printout of the explanation and any sketches you've created.

PART THREE

Writing at Work: From Principle to Practice

Parts One and Two discuss the principles of effective writing that apply to all on-the-job writing tasks; Part Three focuses on the practical applications of these principles. Chapters 8 through 15 provide explicit guidelines for writing — with plenty of examples — the most-common types of work-related communications: memos, business letters, e-mail messages, instructions, proposals, a variety of formal and informal reports, and content for Web sites. Part Three ends with a chapter that puts everything you learned in the text to its first practical test: finding a job appropriate to your education and abilities.

Understanding the Principles of Business Communication

AT A GLANCE: Communication Principles

Virtually all jobs involve at least some written communication—with cowork-ers, supervisors, staff, clients, vendors, and customers. You can achieve your goals and convey a professional image by using appropriate tone and style in your writing and adhering to expected formats. This chapter covers the fol-lowing skills essential to successful business communication:

- Selecting the appropriate medium and form for your message / 263
- Writing and formatting letters / 267
- Writing and formatting memos / 282
- Working under the pressure of deadlines / 289
- Sending e-mail and instant messages / 291
- Writing international correspondence / 300

Business communication, especially the correspondence among people within organizations or between those people and their clients or customers, is essential to the success of indi-viduals and businesses. Because of their importance, such communications should be well writ-ten; those that are not waste time and money. For example, the poorly written letter shown in Figure 8–1 was actually sent to a law firm (the names have been changed). The staff at the law firm could not understand it, even though a number of attorneys, paralegals, and assistants were fa-miliar with the case. Staff members exchanged e-mail messages and phone calls with Ralph Madison and others at his company without success. Finally, the law firm had to send someone to the company to identify the specific services the company wanted its legal counsel to perform.

This letter wasted the time of a high-paid staff—and caused a delay in legal services to Ralph Madison's company. Further, carelessly written letters or e-mail messages project a poor image of the writer that can result in other kinds of losses. A reader's negative reaction to an un-clear or unprofessional message, for example, can cost a firm its reputation and future business—and can even cost an employee his or her job.

This chapter focuses on the most-common forms of written correspondence—business letters, memos, e-mail messages, and instant messages—and explains how to anticipate the

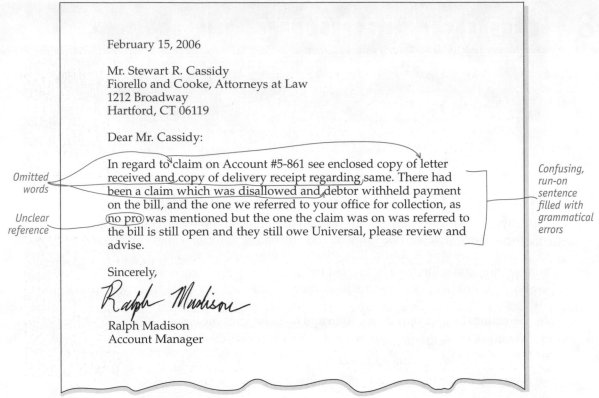

February 15, 2006

Mr. Stewart R. Cassidy
Fiorello and Cooke, Attorneys at Law
1212 Broadway
Hartford, CT 06119

Dear Mr. Cassidy:

Omitted words

Unclear reference

In regard to claim on Account #5-861 see enclosed copy of letter received and copy of delivery receipt regarding same. There had been a claim which was disallowed and debtor withheld payment on the bill, and the one we referred to your office for collection, as no pro was mentioned but the one the claim was on was referred to the bill is still open and they still owe Universal, please review and advise.

Confusing, run-on sentence filled with grammatical errors

Sincerely,

Ralph Madison

Ralph Madison
Account Manager

Figure 8–1   Poorly Written Letter

challenges of communicating with international readers. Writing business correspondence involves many of the steps that go into most other on-the-job writing, as well as some special considerations.

1. Establish your purpose, your reader's needs, and your scope.

2. Outline key points. For a short letter, a memo, or an e-mail, jot down the points you wish to make and the order in which you wish to make them (see Chapter 2, Organizing Your Information).

3. Write a rough draft from the outline (see Chapter 3, Writing the Draft).

4. Allow for a cooling period (see Chapter 4, Revising the Draft), especially when a letter or an e-mail responds to a problem. Don't vent emotions, as illustrated in the cartoon on page 293. Even a lunch-hour break can give you a chance to remove any hasty and inappropriate statements made in the heat of the situation.

5. Revise the rough draft, checking for sense as well as for grammar, spelling, and punctuation (see Chapter 4, Revising the Draft, and Part IV, Revision Guide).

◆ *For an overview of the writing process at work, see Chapter 1, Assessing Audience and Purpose.*

Voices from the Workplace

Robert Demers, Philips Medical Systems

Software engineer Robert Demers helps develop and test equipment that monitors the vital signs of hospital patients. "Almost all of my everyday communication is now electronic," Robert says. "We use e-mail, instant messaging, online meetings, company Web sites, and the telephone — almost all accessible from anywhere, anytime. This provides tremendous flexibility, but sometimes it leads to poorly implemented communications." Robert suggests: "Review your message. Try to get spelling, capitalization, and sentence structure correct and make sure your message is clear. Your recipients will appreciate it and it will reflect well on you. Also, if you must send mass e-mails, send the message only to people who need to read it. Don't just blast out a message to the world and make recipients figure out whether it applies to them."

Kelli Strieby, Condé Nast

Kelli Strieby is an executive assistant to the president of the online division of Condé Nast Publications. Writing interoffice memos, e-mails, and letters is an integral part of her job; she communicates with top executives — both inside and outside her company — daily. "These are very busy people," Kelli explains, "and they need to receive important information quickly, clearly, and efficiently. A well-designed document that includes the date, a clear and concise header — including all of the sender's contact information — and what action needs to be taken by the person receiving the document is extremely important. Also, I cannot stress enough the importance of always running a spelling and grammar check before sending out any and all documents — including e-mails! Sloppiness never looks good."

6. Adjust the format, especially the arrangement and spacing of letter parts (see pages 274–280), and print a copy for review and proofing before signing it.

7. Assume final responsibility: As the author of a letter or a memo, you are responsible for its appearance and accuracy.

ON THE WEB

For more advice on writing and formatting business correspondence, go to Chapter 8, bedfordstmartins.com/writingthatworks

■ Selecting the Appropriate Medium and Form

Important as they are, letters and e-mail messages are not the only means of communication available to businesspeople. The law firm, for example, eventually had to meet with Ralph Madison to interpret his request to "review and advise." You can choose from a wide array of possibilities, including e-mail, instant messaging, fax, voice mail, and videoconferencing in addition to more-traditional means of communication, such as letters and memos, telephone calls, and face-to-face meetings. With so many means of communication available, how do organizations and individuals decide which is preferable in a given situation?

In selecting the appropriate medium, first consider the context, audience, and objective of the communication. For example, when you need to solve an urgent problem, a written message (even one sent electronically) can take too long or create confusion. A telephone call is the more-efficient choice in those circumstances. When you need precise wording and you and your reader need a permanent record of the information exchanged, a written message (letter, memo, or e-mail) will be the best option. When you wish to establish close rapport with someone in the interest of a long-term working relationship, a face-to-face meeting is indispensable. Following is a description of the primary methods of communicating and some of their salient characteristics. All are currently in use because each communicates certain kinds of information better than the others, even though the advantages overlap in some cases.

Letters on Organizational Stationery

Letters are most appropriate for first contacts with new business associates or customers as well as for other official business communications outside a company or an organization. Stationery with an organization's printed letterhead and the writer's handwritten signature communicates formality, respect, and authority. A written promise, conveyed above the signature of an employee who has the authority to act on behalf of an organization, ensures that the information is accurate and that the sender will honor it. For example, a formal letter is often used to summarize the terms and conditions of a proposed business relationship. If you use express or overnight deliveries for letters and other documents, phone or send an e-mail message ahead to alert the recipient that the material has been sent. If speed is essential and the situation requires a signed document, you can fax it and follow up by mailing the original.

Memos

Memos on printed company stationery or attached to an e-mail message are appropriate for internal communications among members of an organization, even when offices are geographically separated. These in-house communications have many of the same characteristics of letters, but memos are convenient for a wider variety of functions—from announcements of organizational policy to short reports.

Memo formats in most organizations are standardized. These formats eliminate the features common to business letters, such as letterhead, an inside address, a salutation, goodwill paragraphs, and formal closing elements. Memo writers must follow their organization's format standards, including whether to use a "MEMO" header; what order to use for "To:," "From:," "cc:," "Date:," and "Subject:"; and where to place your initials or signature, if required.

E-mail Messages

Electronic mail is used to send information, maintain professional relationships, elicit discussions, collect opinions, and transmit many other kinds of messages. E-mail can be a less-formal means of communication than either letters or memos; however, e-mail provides the advantage that the same information can be sent simultaneously at great speed to many recipients. For groups that exchange frequent or recurrent messages, creating a discussion group (or listserv) is convenient. Because e-mail recipients can print copies of the messages they receive and can easily forward them to others, business messages should always be written with care and reviewed for accuracy before being sent.

Instant Messages

Instant messaging (IM) is a communications service that allows the exchange of text messages in real time between two or more people on computers, cell phones, or personal digital assistants (PDAs). Unlike e-mail, IM takes place in real time, like a phone call, and requires that all parties be logged in at the same time.

Instant messaging can be a fast, convenient method for exchanging messages and sharing files with colleagues, suppliers, and partners. It can help people collaborate from scattered work sites, functioning like an abbreviated Internet chat-room discussion. Instant messaging might be useful when a product Web site is down, for example, and staff located in Europe or Asia must communicate to repair it immediately. Of course, you should make sure not only that your readers are comfortable with IM but also that the recipient's IM system is compatible with yours.

Faxes

A fax (facsimile transmission) is most useful when speed is essential and when the information—a drawing or contract, for example—must be viewed in its original form. Faxes are also useful when the recipient does not have access to e-mail or the programs to view e-mail attachments or when graphic material has not yet been converted into electronic form. Note that faxed correspondence may seem less official than a traditional letter, in part because the recipient does not receive the original stationery. However, faxes are acceptable even in legal correspondence (some courts allow filing of official documents by fax). Of course, if an original is also important, the paper copy can be sent separately by overnight or regular mail. Faxed letters should be sent with a cover sheet (available as a word-processing template) or a commercially prepared fax stick-on label.

Telephone and Conference Calls

One of the advantages of phone calls is that they enable participants to interpret tone of voice, so they are often helpful in resolving misunderstandings or clarifying information. Of course, a phone call does not provide the visual cues possible during face-to-face meetings.

Conference calls take place among three or more participants. They are a less-expensive alternative to a face-to-face meeting that would require the participants to travel to a central meeting place. They also provide a setting for the immediate resolution of issues.

Such calls are more efficient if the person setting up the call works from an agenda shared by all the participants. That person must be prepared to direct the

◆ *For further information on preparing agendas and leading meetings, see the discussion of meetings on pages 500–506 in Chapter 14, Giving Presentations and Conducting Meetings.*

discussion as though he or she were leading a meeting. The participants should also take notes on any key points or decisions made during the call. Of course, the call must be planned to ensure that everyone is available at the same time. Timing is especially important when participants are located in different time zones—especially for international calls.

Voice-Mail Messages

Voice-mail systems allow callers to record messages when the person called is not available. Anticipate what you will say if you reach a voice-mail recording instead of the person you've called. Speak clearly and leave your name, phone number, and the date and time of the call. Leave a succinct message ("Call me about the deadline for the new project" or "I got the package from RTL, so you don't need to call the distributor"). If the message is complicated or contains numerous details, use another medium, such as an e-mail message or a letter, to ensure that the information is communicated accurately. If you want to discuss a specific subject, let the recipient know so that he or she can prepare a response when returning your call.

Face-to-Face Meetings

◆ *For a more-detailed discussion of how to conduct effective meetings and record the meeting discussions and decisions, see Conducting a Productive Meeting on pages 499–509 in Chapter 14, Giving Presentations and Conducting Meetings.*

Face-to-face meetings are most appropriate for initial or early contacts with business associates and customers with whom you intend to develop an important long-term relationship. Meetings are also the best medium for exchanges in which you need to solve a serious problem. The most productive meetings occur when all participants come prepared to contribute to a collective effort toward a well-defined objective.

Videoconferencing

Videoconferences are particularly useful for meetings where travel is impractical or too expensive. Unlike telephone conference calls, videoconferences have the advantage of allowing participants to see as well as to hear one another. Videoconferences work best with participants who are at ease in front of a camera.

WRITER'S CHECKLIST
Selecting the Medium

- ☑ Consider your audience, purpose, and what is typical or expected in your organization. Generally, use written forms and messages for precise wording; use telephone, videoconference, and in-person communication when you need, for example, to resolve a misunderstanding.
- ☑ Use letters on organizational stationery for outside business communications; printed letterhead on quality paper communicates formality, respect, and authority.

☑ Use memos (printed and electronic) for in-house business communications — from policy announcements to short reports.

☑ Use e-mail to send messages and electronic documents, maintain professional relationships, elicit discussions, and collect opinions from distant as well as wide audiences.

☑ Use instant messaging when you need to communicate and share files in real time with one or more people in scattered locations who do not have e-mail access at their current locations.

☑ Use faxes when the exact image of nondigital documents must be viewed and when speed matters.

☑ Use telephone and conference calls when give-and-take or tone of voice is important; conference calls, when carefully planned, are a less-expensive alternative to a face-to-face meeting for participants in distant locations.

☑ Use voice mail for short, uncomplicated messages.

☑ Use face-to-face meetings for early contacts with business associates and customers or when solving problems.

☑ Use videoconferencing as a substitute for face-to-face meetings when travel is impractical.

Writing and Formatting Letters

One important consideration in business correspondence is the impression you convey to readers. To convey a professional image — of yourself and your company or organization — take particular care with the tone and style of your writing.

Goodwill and the "You" Viewpoint

When you write a business letter, you are addressing the reader directly. Therefore, you are in a very good position to take that person's needs into account and build goodwill for yourself and for your company. If you ask yourself, "How might I feel if I were the recipient of such a letter?" you can gain insight into the needs and feelings of your reader — and then tailor your message to fit those needs and feelings. Many companies spend millions of dollars to create a favorable public image. A letter to a client that sounds impersonal and unfriendly can quickly tarnish that image; a thoughtful letter that communicates sincerity can greatly enhance it.

Suppose, for example, you are a store manager who receives a request for a refund from a customer who forgot to enclose the receipt with the request. In a letter to the customer, you might write:

▶ The sales receipt must be enclosed with the merchandise before we can process the refund.

However, if you consider how you might keep the goodwill of the customer, you might word that request this way:

▶ Please enclose the sales receipt with the merchandise so that we can send your refund promptly.

◆ *For a discussion of the active and passive voices, see page 104 in Chapter 4, Revising the Draft.*

Notice that this version uses the word *please* and the active voice, while the first version uses only the passive voice. In general, the active voice creates a friendlier, more courteous tone than the passive, which can sound impersonal and unfriendly. Polite wording, such as the use of *please*, also helps to create goodwill. However, you can go one step further. You can put the reader's needs and interests first by writing from the reader's point of view. Often, but not always, doing so means using the words *you* and *your* rather than the words *we, our, I,* and *mine*. That is why the technique has been referred to as using the "you" viewpoint or "you" attitude. For example, consider the point of view of the original sentence in the example just given:

▶ The sales receipt must be enclosed with the merchandise before *we can process* the refund.

The italicized words focus on the writer's need to process the refund. Even the second version, although its tone is more polite and friendly, emphasizes the writer's need to get the receipt "so that we can send your refund promptly." (The writer, of course, may want to get rid of the problem quickly.)

What is the reader's interest? The reader is not interested in helping the business process its accounts. He or she simply wants the refund—and by emphasizing that need, the writer encourages the reader to act quickly. Consider the following revision written from the "you" viewpoint:

▶ So you can receive your refund promptly, please enclose the sales receipt with the merchandise.

This sentence stresses that it is to the reader's benefit to act on this matter.

Be aware, however, that both goodwill and the "you" viewpoint can be overdone. Used thoughtlessly, both techniques can produce a fawning, insincere tone—what might be called *plastic goodwill*. Avoid language full of false praise and sickeningly sweet phrases. Any attempt at goodwill that is insincere will be recognized by your reader and thus will be counterproductive. Consider the opening of the letter that follows from a writer who has corresponded only once with the recipient:

PLASTIC   You are just the kind of customer that deserves the finest service that anyone can offer—and you deserve our best deal. Knowing how careful you are at making decisions, I know you'll think about the advantages of using our consulting service.

In this example, the writer barely knows the customer yet makes an assumption about what "kind of customer" the recipient may be. Further, the writer characterizes the customer as careful "at making decisions." The sentence sounds phony. A far better approach is to make goodwill reasonable for the circumstances and provide specifics that are appropriate to your knowledge of the reader.

APPROPRIATE   From our earlier correspondence, I can understand your need for reliable service—we strive to give all our priority clients our full attention. After you have reviewed our proposal, I am confident you will appreciate our "Five-Star" consulting option.

Organize reader-focused correspondence to achieve goodwill by presenting the main point or good news early—at the outset, if at all possible. The pattern for neutral or good news should be as follows:

1. Main point or good news
2. Explanation of details or facts
3. Goodwill closing

By presenting the main point or good news first, you increase the likelihood that the reader will pay careful attention to details, and you achieve goodwill from the start. Figure 8–2 shows an example of a reader-focused letter.

ON THE WEB

For another example of a reader-focused good-news letter, go to bedfordstmartins.com/writingthatworks and select *Model Documents Gallery*.

WRITER'S CHECKLIST
Using Tone to Build Goodwill

☑ *Be respectful*, not demanding.

DEMANDING   Submit your answer in one week.

RESPECTFUL   I would appreciate your answer within one week.

☑ *Be modest*, not arrogant.

ARROGANT   My report is thorough, and I'm sure that you won't be able to continue without it.

MODEST   This report contains a detailed description of the refinancing options, and I hope you find it useful.

☑ *Be polite*, not sarcastic.

SARCASTIC   I just received the shipment we ordered six months ago. I'm sending it back — we can't use it now. Thanks!

POLITE   I am returning the shipment we ordered on March 13, 2006. Unfortunately, it arrived too late for us to be able to use it.

☑ *Be positive and tactful*, not negative and condescending.

NEGATIVE   Your complaint about our prices is way off target. Our prices are definitely not any higher than those of our competitors.

TACTFUL   Thank you for your suggestion concerning our prices. We have found, however, that our prices are competitive with those of our competitors.

July 28, 2006
Mr. James Longo
Longo's Café and Deli
157 Adams Drive
Trumbull, TN 37802

Dear Mr. Longo:

Main Point

Would you be willing to share your personal history with the Trumbull Historical Society? Mary Tran recommended you as somebody we should talk to because of your long commitment to neighborhood improvement.

Explanation

As you may have heard, Historical Society volunteers are interviewing people whose experiences illustrate Trumbull's rich and varied cultural fabric. The oral history project aims both to document local traditions and to demonstrate that Trumbull is a vibrant neighborhood with strong community ties. At the same time, by sharing oral histories at public forums, the Historical Society hopes to replace negative stereotypes with a truer picture of what the community means to its residents.

We would like to add your voice to the official history of Trumbull. If you choose to participate, you will be asked to recall events, experiences, personal or family memories, and cultural traditions that are important to you. You won't be pressed to discuss anything you're not comfortable with, and you will determine the focus of the conversation. Interviews take about an hour and are scheduled at your convenience.

Closing

I hope I've piqued your interest. I'll call you in the next couple of weeks to discuss the project, but do feel free to contact me before then if I can answer any questions.

Thank you,

Margaret Schweinhurt

Margaret Schweinhurt
Project Coordinator
Trumbull Oral History Project
611.999.9999
oralhistory@mas.com

Figure 8–2   Reader-Focused Request Letter

Negative Messages and the Indirect Pattern

Communicating bad news is sometimes necessary in the workplace. Doing so effectively can benefit the writer and the professional image of any organization. As with any type of writing, consider how your audience will react to your message. Research has shown that people form their impressions and attitudes very early when reading letters. At the same time, bad news is easier to accept when the reasons behind it are explained first. For this reason, presenting bad news or refusals indirectly is often more effective than presenting them directly, especially if the stakes are high.[1] Further, in international correspondence, far more cultures are generally indirect in their business communication than they are direct. Consider the thoughtlessness in the job rejection that follows.

> Dear Ms. Mauer:
>
> Your application for the position of dental hygienist at Southtown Dental Center has been rejected. We have found someone more qualified than you.
>
> Sincerely,

Although the letter is concise and uses the pronouns *you* and *your*, the writer has not considered how the recipient will feel as she reads the letter. The letter is, in short, rude. The pattern of this letter is (1) bad news, (2) curt explanation, (3) close.

A better general pattern for bad-news correspondence is the following:

1. Context (or "buffer")
2. Explanation
3. Bad news
4. Goodwill

The opening (often called a "buffer") should provide a context for the subject and establish a professional tone. Then the body should provide an explanation by reviewing the details or facts that lead, for example, to a negative decision or refusal. Give the negative message simply, based on the facts, but do not belabor the bad news or provide an inappropriate apology. Neither the details nor an overdone apology can turn bad news into something positive. Your goal should be to establish for the reader that the writer or organization has been *reasonable* given the circumstances. To accomplish this goal, you need to organize the explanation carefully and logically.

The closing should establish or reestablish a positive relationship through goodwill or helpful information. Consider, for example, the revised rejection letter shown in Figure 8–3. This letter carries the same disappointing news as the first

◆ For more guidance on organizing information, see Chapter 2, Organizing Your Information.

◆ For more examples, see Sensitive and Negative Messages on pages 323–337 in Chapter 9, Writing Business Correspondence, and Persuading Your Audience on pages 71–74 in Chapter 3, Writing the Draft.

---

[1] Gerald J. Alred, "'We Regret to Inform You': Toward a New Theory of Negative Messages," in *Studies in Technical Communication*, ed. Brenda R. Sims (Denton: University of North Texas and NCTE, 1993), pp. 17–36.

Context (or "buffer") opening

Explanation leading to bad news

Goodwill closing

November 9, 2006

Ms. Barbara L. Mauer
157 Beach Drive
San Diego, CA 92113

Dear Ms. Mauer:

Thank you for your time and effort in applying for the position of records administrator at Southtown Dental Center.

Because we need someone who can assume the duties here with a minimum of training, we have selected an applicant with over ten years of experience.

I am sure that with your excellent college record you will find a position in another office.

Sincerely,

Mary Hernandez

Mary Hernandez
Office Manager

Figure 8–3   Courteous Bad-News Letter

ON THE WEB

For more examples of well-written bad-news letters, go to bedfordstmartins.com/ writingthatworks and select *Model Documents Gallery*.

one, but the writer begins by not only introducing the subject but also thanking the reader for her time and effort. Then the writer explains why Ms. Mauer was not accepted for the job and offers her encouragement in finding a position in another office. Bad news is never pleasant; however, information that either puts the bad news in perspective or makes the bad news seem reasonable maintains respect between the writer and the reader. The goodwill closing is intended to reestablish an amicable business relationship.

Openings and Closings

Most business messages should follow predictable patterns for openings and closings. Openings, for example, must identify the subject and its interest or relevance to your readers.

▶   Yesterday, I received your letter and the pager, number AJ 50172. I sent the pager to our quality-control department for tests.

Carol Moore, our lead technician, reports that preliminary tests indicate . . .

Because business letters are often more personal than reports and other forms, an opening must also establish a tone that is appropriate and achieves your purpose.

▶ I'm seeking advice about organizational communication, and several people have suggested that you are an authority on the subject.

The tone of respect in this opening is not only appropriate but also persuasive, because it appeals to the reader's pride. Other openings might appeal to the reader's curiosity or personal interests, as in the following:

◆ *For a discussion of the principles of writing openings and closings, see pages 84–87 of Chapter 3, Writing the Draft.*

▶ I have a problem you may be willing to help solve.

▶ Mr. Walter Jenkens has given us your name as a reference for his company's services. I hope you'll be willing to help us by answering some specific questions about his company.

Closings for correspondence can also provide an incentive for the reader to act, as in the following:

◆ *For more examples of openings and closings in various types of correspondence, review the figures in Chapter 9, Writing Business Correspondence.*

▶ Please sign the forms today, mark the changes you want made, and return the material to me in the preaddressed envelope. If you can approve everything for me within two days, I should have the amended contract in your hands by the end of the week.

Writing Style and Accuracy

Business messages may legitimately vary from informal, in an e-mail to a close business associate, to formal (or restrained), in a letter to someone you do not know. (Even if you are writing to a close associate, you should always follow the rules of standard grammar, spelling, and punctuation.)

INFORMAL	It worked! The new process is better than we had dreamed.
RESTRAINED	You will be pleased to know that the new process is more effective than we had expected.

You will normally use the restrained style more frequently than the informal one. An overdone attempt to sound casual or friendly, like overdone goodwill, can sound insincere. However, do not adopt a style so formal that your letters or memos read like legal contracts; that type of writing appears wordy, pompous, and affected—and may well irritate your reader.

AFFECTED	Please be advised that we no longer possess an original copy of the brochure requested. Herewith enclosed is a photographic copy for your use. Address any further query to this office for assistance as required.
IMPROVED	We are currently out of original copies of our brochure, so I am sending you a photocopy. If I can help further, please let me know.

◆ *For detailed advice about adopting an appropriate style in your writing, see Language on pages 108–114 in Chapter 4, Revising the Draft.*

The excessively formal writing style of the affected version is full of out-of-date business jargon; expressions such as *query* (for request or question), *be advised that*, and *herewith* are old-fashioned and pretentious. Good business letters have a more conversational style, as the improved version illustrates. The improved version is not only less stuffy but also more concise.

Being concise in writing is important, but don't be so concise that you become blunt. Responding to a written request that is vague with "Your request was unclear" or "I don't understand" could easily offend your reader. Instead, ask for more information and establish goodwill to encourage your reader to provide the information.

▷   I will need more information before I can answer your request. Specifically, can you give me the title and the date of the report you are looking for?

Although this version is longer, it promotes goodwill and will elicit a faster, more helpful response.

A letter, a memo, or an e-mail (as described later) is a written record, so it must be accurate. Facts, figures, and dates that are incorrect or misleading can cost time, money, and goodwill. Remember that when you write a letter, e-mail, or memo, you are responsible for it. Therefore, allow yourself time to review any correspondence carefully before sending it. Whenever possible, ask someone who is familiar with the situation to review an important letter or other message. Listen with an open mind to any criticisms of what you have written. Make whatever changes you believe are necessary.

◆ *Review Proofreading on pages 115–116 in Chapter 4, Revising the Draft.*

Also review your message for punctuation, grammar, and spelling. In business as elsewhere, accuracy and attention to detail are equated with carefulness and reliability. The kindest conclusion a reader can come to about a letter containing mechanical errors is that the writer was careless. Do not give your reader cause to form such a conclusion.

Formatting Business Letters

Letters communicate formality, respect, and authority. Just as the clothes you wear to job interviews play a part in the first impression you make on potential employers, the appearance of a business letter may be crucial in influencing a recipient who has never seen you. A neat appearance alone will not improve a poorly written letter, but a sloppy appearance will detract from a well-written one.

Although word-processing software provides templates for correspondence, it may not always provide appropriate dimensions and spacing. To achieve a professional appearance, use the following guidelines:

- Center the letter on the page vertically and horizontally.
- Use 1- or 1¼-inch margins, the default standard in many word-processing programs.

- When you use organizational stationery, treat the bottom of the letterhead as the top edge of the paper and make the right margin approximately as wide as the left margin.

- For very short letters, increase both side margins to about an inch and a half.

- Use your computer's full-page or print-preview feature to check for proportion.

If your employer requires a particular format, use it. Otherwise, follow the guidelines provided here, and review the formatting shown in Figures 8–4 and 8–5.

The two most-common styles for business letters are the full-block style shown in Figure 8–4 and the modified-block style shown in Figure 8–5. In the full-block style, which should be used with letterhead, the entire letter is aligned at the left margin. In the modified-block style, the return address, date, and complimentary close begin at the center of the page and the other elements are aligned at the left margin. All other letter styles are variations of the full-block and modified-block styles.

ON THE WEB

For models of additional letter styles, go to Chapter 8, **bedfordstmartins.com/ writingthatworks**

Heading

The heading is the writer's full return address—street or post-office box, city and state, postal code—or printed letterhead and the date. Do not include the writer's name in the heading (unless it is part of a printed letterhead) because it appears at the end of the letter. In giving your address, do not use abbreviations for words such as Street, Avenue, First, or West (as part of a street or city name). You may either spell out the name of the state in full or use the standard Postal Service abbreviations. The date usually goes three lines below the letterhead or directly beneath the last line of the address when there is no letterhead. Do not abbreviate the name of the month.

▶ 1638 Parkhill Drive East
Great Falls, MT 59407
April 9, 2007

Begin the heading about two inches from the top of the page. If you are using company letterhead that gives the address, enter only the date three lines below the last line of printed copy.

Inside Address

The inside address is the recipient's full name, title, and address.

▶ Ms. Gail Smith
Production Manager
Docuform Printing Company
14 President Street
Sarasota, FL 33546

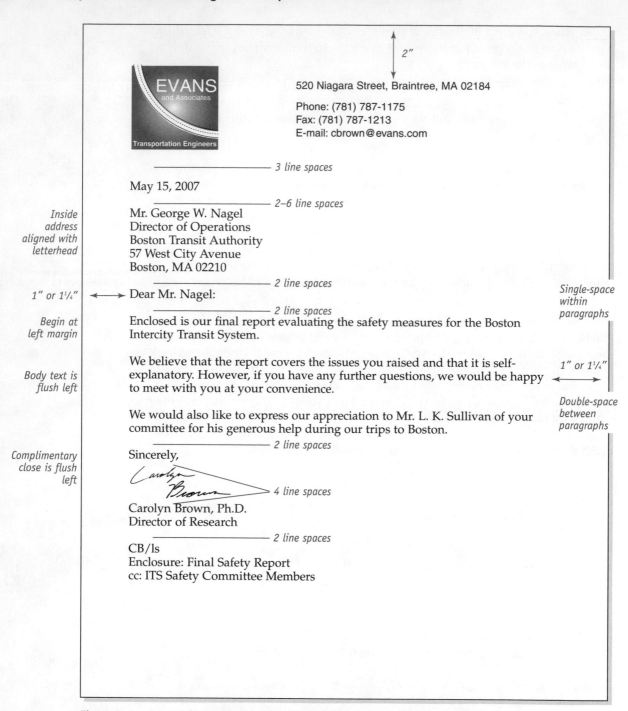

Figure 8–4 Format for a Letter with Letterhead (Full-Block Style)

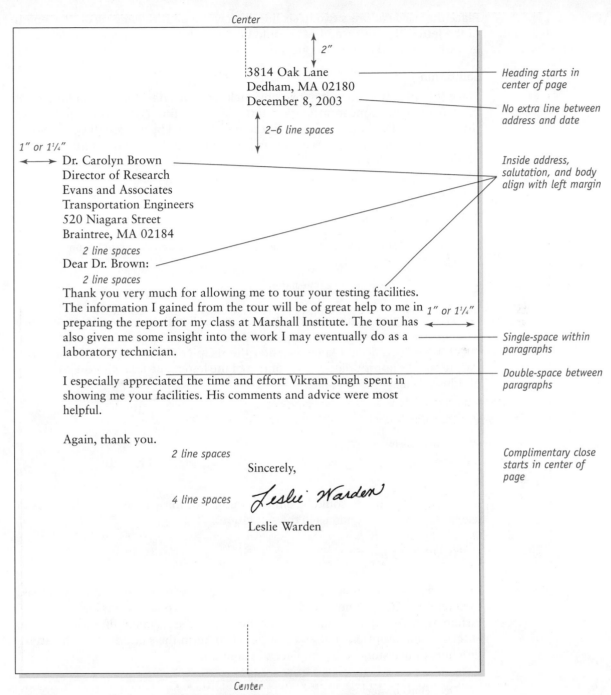

Center

2"

3814 Oak Lane
Dedham, MA 02180
December 8, 2003

Heading starts in center of page

No extra line between address and date

2–6 line spaces

1" or 1¼"

Dr. Carolyn Brown
Director of Research
Evans and Associates
Transportation Engineers
520 Niagara Street
Braintree, MA 02184

Inside address, salutation, and body align with left margin

2 line spaces

Dear Dr. Brown:

2 line spaces

Thank you very much for allowing me to tour your testing facilities. The information I gained from the tour will be of great help to me in 1" or 1¼" preparing the report for my class at Marshall Institute. The tour has also given me some insight into the work I may eventually do as a laboratory technician.

Single-space within paragraphs

Double-space between paragraphs

I especially appreciated the time and effort Vikram Singh spent in showing me your facilities. His comments and advice were most helpful.

Again, thank you.

2 line spaces

Sincerely,

Complimentary close starts in center of page

4 line spaces

Leslie Warden

Leslie Warden

Center

Figure 8–5   Format for a Letter without Letterhead (Modified-Block Style)

Place the inside address two to six lines below the date, depending on the length of the letter. The inside address should be flush with (aligned with) the left margin, which should be at least one inch wide.

Salutation

Place the salutation (greeting) two lines below the inside address, also flush with the left margin. In most business letters, the salutation contains the recipient's title (Mr., Ms., Dr., and so on) and last name, followed by a colon. If you are on a first-name basis with the recipient, you would include his or her title and full name in the inside address but use only the first name in the salutation.

▶ Dear Dr. Smith:

▶ Dear Captain Smith:

▶ Dear Professor Smith: [Note that titles such as Captain and Professor are not abbreviated.]

▶ Dear Gail: [if you are on a first-name basis]

For a recipient who does not have a professional title, use *Mr.* or *Ms.* (if a woman has expressed a preference for *Miss* or *Mrs.* instead, honor her preference). When you do not know whether the recipient is a man or a woman, you may use a title appropriate to the context of the letter. The following are examples of titles you may find suitable:

▶ Dear Customer:

▶ Dear Homeowner:

▶ Dear Service Manager:

When a person's name could be either feminine or masculine, one solution is to use both first and last names in the salutation.

▶ Dear Pat Smith:

In the past, writers to large companies or organizations customarily addressed their letters to "Gentlemen." Today, however, this form of address is inappropriate. Writers who do not know the name or the title of the recipient often address the letter to an appropriate addressee or department in the salutation, in the attention line, or in a subject line in place of a salutation.

▶ Dear Homeowner:

   Take this one-time opportunity to . . .

▶   National Business Systems
    501 West National Avenue
    Minneapolis, MN 55107-5011

    Attention: Customer Relations Department

    I am returning three pagers that failed to operate. . . .

▶   National Business Systems
    501 West National Avenue
    Minneapolis, MN 55107-5011

    Subject: Defective Parts for SL-100 Pagers

    I am returning three pagers that failed to operate. . . .

Body

The body of the letter should begin two lines below the salutation (or below the inside address if no salutation appears). Single-space within paragraphs and double-space between paragraphs with the first line of each new paragraph at the left margin or indented five spaces from the left margin. The right margin should be approximately as wide as the left margin. (In very short letters, you may increase both margins to about an inch and a half.)

Complimentary Close

Start the complimentary close or conventional "good-bye" two lines below the body. Use a standard expression such as *Sincerely yours, Yours truly,* or *Respectfully yours.* (If the recipient is a friend as well as a business associate, you can use a friendly, less-formal close: *Best wishes, Cordially, Sincerely, Best regards.*) Only the first word of the complimentary close is capitalized, and the expression is followed by a comma. Four lines below the complimentary close, and aligned at the left with the close, type your full name. On the next line, place your business title if it is appropriate to do so. Then sign your name in the space between the complimentary close and your typed name. If you are writing to someone with whom you are on a first-name basis, it is acceptable to sign only your given name; otherwise, sign your full name, as shown in Figures 8–4 and 8–5.

Second Page

If a letter requires a second page, always carry at least two lines of the body over to page two. The second page also should have a heading containing the recipient's name, the page number, and the date. (Never use letterhead for a second page.) The heading starts one inch from the top edge of the page and may go in the upper-left-hand corner or across the page, as shown in Figure 8–6.

End Notations

Business letters sometimes require additional information—the initials of the typist (if other than the writer), an enclosure notation, or a notation that a copy of

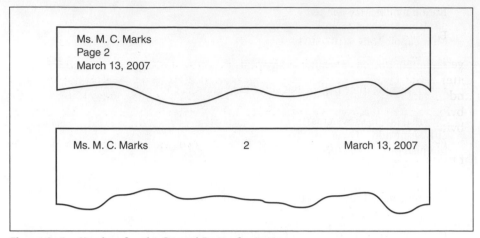

Figure 8–6   Headers for the Second Page of a Letter

the letter is being sent to the named recipients. Place any such information flush left with the margin, two lines below the last line of the complimentary close in a long letter, four lines below in a short letter.

Initials are not used when the writer is also the person typing the letter, as is common. If an assistant has typed the letter, however, that person's initials should appear (all lowercase) two lines below the last line of the complimentary-close block either by themselves or following the author's initials (all uppercase and followed by a slash), as shown in Figure 8–7.

Enclosure notations, which indicate that the letter writer is sending material along with the letter (an invoice, an article, and so on), may take several forms.

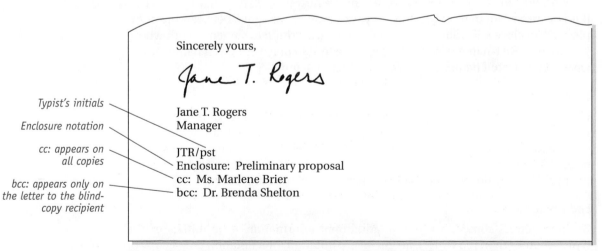

Figure 8–7   Closing with Initials, Enclosure Notation, and Copy Notations

▶ Enclosure [for a single item]

▶ Enclosures (2)

Even though you use an enclosure notation, make a reference in the body of the letter to the enclosed material. Enclosures are described briefly if the letter is long and formal, as shown in Figure 8–4, or if the nature of the enclosed items is not obvious. Enclosures are not described if the letter is short and the enclosures are obvious to the reader.

Copy notations (cc:) tell the reader that a copy of the letter is being sent to one or more named individuals.

▶ cc: Ms. Marlene Brier

 Mr. David Williams

[Brier and Williams receive only the letter.]

▶ cc/enc: Mr. Tom Lee

[Lee receives both the letter and the enclosure.]

A *blind-copy notation (bcc:)* is used when the sender does not want the addressee to know that a copy is being sent to one or more other recipients. That means the blind-copy notation must not appear on the original letter, only on the letter to the blind-copy recipient, as shown in Figure 8–7.

DESIGNING YOUR DOCUMENT
Formatting Letters

- Use good-quality white paper and envelopes of standard size.
- Center the letter on the page, framing it with white space.
- Place the date three lines below the letterhead or directly below the address line when there is no letterhead.
- Place the inside address two to six lines below the date, aligned with the left margin, which should be at least one inch wide.
- Use full-block style with letterhead stationery; use modified-block style on blank paper.
- Place the salutation two lines below the inside address, also aligned with the left margin.
- Begin the body of the letter two lines below the salutation.
- Single-space within paragraphs and double-space between paragraphs.
- Start the complimentary close two lines below the body of your letter.
- If a letter requires a second page, always carry at least two lines of the body over to page two.
- After you have finished writing a letter, check the arrangement and spacing of its parts.

A business letter may, of course, contain all the end notations described in this section (see Figure 8–7).[2]

Writing and Formatting Memos

Much of the general advice on business communication given earlier in this chapter applies to memos. However, the memo—printed or electronic—is routinely used for a wide range of internal correspondence—from short notes to one-page reports and internal proposals. Among their other uses, memos

- Announce policies
- Confirm conversations
- Exchange information
- Delegate responsibilities

- Request information
- Transmit documents
- Instruct employees
- Report results

As this partial list illustrates, memos provide a record of the decisions made and many actions taken in an organization. For this reason, clear and effective memos are essential to the success of any organization. A poorly written memo sends a garbled message that could baffle readers, cause a loss of time, produce costly errors, or even offend.

Memo Protocol

The decision to send memos on paper, attached to an e-mail message, or delivered as an e-mail depends on the organizational practice and the purpose of the communication. Some organizations may prefer the printed memo for announcements and other official messages while reserving e-mail for informal communications. Others may use e-mail almost exclusively not only because of its speed but also because it fosters the easy exchange of information. Even when e-mail substitutes for printed memos, some recipients print copies of important e-mails to highlight sections or to save a hard copy for their records.

Observing Organizational Rank

Although practices vary, be alert to expectations in your organization for who writes and receives certain types of communications. As with all workplace writing, know your audience by learning your organization's procedures for internal communications. Small businesses and organizations, for example, may not need formal guidelines for internal communications, so their expectations and practices will differ from large organizations. In corporations and governmental agencies, however, protocol for internal communications is usually based on lines of authority. For example, staff members at large companies seldom send recommendations directly

---

[2] For more-detailed guidance on business-letter format, see William A. Sabin, *The Gregg Reference Manual,* 10th ed. (New York: Glencoe, 2005).

to senior executives beyond their immediate manager. Doing so could put the sender's immediate supervisor in an awkward position.

Consider also the order in which addressees should be named on the "To" line—senior managers, for example, usually take precedence over junior managers. A company's or agency's organizational chart determines the lines of authority and channels in which internal communications travel.

Organizational policy specifies whether internal paper communications are signed or initialed by the sender. In many organizations, the sender's typed name in the "From" line indicates approval of and responsibility for a document's content; in other organizations, the sender's signature or initials next to the typed name does so. Signatures or initials are unnecessary for memos sent as or attached to e-mail messages.

Distributing Copies

The person listed on the memo or e-mail's "To" line is the primary recipient. To share the same message with others, the sender provides each of them a separate or courtesy copy (*cc:*) of the message. This notation (*cc: Jane Doe*) appears in the memo or e-mail heading and informs all the recipients of who else has received the message.

Courtesy copies are usually sent on a for-your-information basis. While the primary recipient may have to act on a request in the memo (for example, approve hiring a new employee), the courtesy-copy recipients are included because they need to know that the request was made.

Send courtesy copies only to those who need the information, especially when the message contains confidential personnel, medical, or financial information. Unnecessary copies also clog up in-boxes with unwanted information.

Also be aware of lines of authority when you copy recipients. If you send a memo or an e-mail to your immediate supervisor about a pet project, for example, do not copy your supervisor's manager unless you are instructed to do so.

Use blind-copy notation (*bcc:*) when you do not want the addressee to know that a copy is being sent to someone else. A blind-copy notation appears only on the copy, not on the original (*bcc: Dr. Brenda Shelton*).

Writing Style and Tone

To produce a memo that is both effective and efficiently written, outline your memo, even if you simply jot down points to be covered and then order them logically. With careful preparation, your memos will be both concise and adequately developed. Adequate development of your thoughts is crucial to the memo's clarity, as in the following example.

◆ *To review the outlining process, see Chapter 2, Organizing Your Information.*

INCOMPLETE	Be more careful on the loading dock.

DEVELOPED	To prevent accidents on the loading dock, follow these procedures:
	1. Check to make sure . . .
	2. Load only items that are rated . . .
	3. Replace any defective parts . . .

Although the original version is concise, it is not as clear and specific as the revision. Don't assume your reader will know what you mean. State what you mean explicitly. Readers may be pressed for time and misinterpret your memo if it is vague.

Each memo should address only one subject, as the memo in Figure 8–8 illustrates. If you need to cover two subjects, write two memos. Multisubject memos are not only difficult to file (thus easily lost) but also confusing to a hurried reader.

Whether your memo is formal or informal depends entirely on your reader and your objective. Is your reader a coworker, superior, or subordinate? A memo to a coworker who is also a friend is likely to be informal, while an internal proposal to several readers or to someone two or three levels higher in your organization is likely to be more formal. Consider the following versions of a statement:

TO AN EQUAL	I can't go along with the plan because I think it poses serious logistical problems. First, . . . [informal, casual, and forceful response written to an equal]
TO A SUPERIOR	The logistics of moving the department may pose serious problems. First, . . . [formal, impersonal, and cautious response to a superior]

A memo giving instructions to a subordinate should also be relatively formal and impersonal but more direct—unless you are trying to reassure or praise. Using an overly chatty, casual style in memos to your subordinates may confuse them about the relationship and make you seem either insincere or ineffectual. However, if you become too formal, sprinkling your writing with fancy words, you may seem stuffy and pompous. You may also be regarded as rigid and incapable of moving the organization ahead.

Managers who write clear and accurate memos gain respect and credibility. Consider the unintended secondary messages the following notice conveys:

POOR	It has been decided that the office will be open the day after Thanksgiving.

The first part of the sentence ("It has been decided") not only sounds impersonal but also communicates an authoritarian, management-versus-employee tone: Somebody "decides" you work. The passive voice also suggests that the decision-maker does not want to say "I have decided" and thus be identified (in any case, the office staff would undoubtedly know). One solution, of course, is to remove the first part of the sentence.

BETTER	The office will be open the day after Thanksgiving.

Even this statement sounds impersonal. The best solution would be to suggest both that the decision is good for the company and that employees should be privy to (if not a part of) the decision-making process.

BEST	Because we must meet the December 15 deadline for submitting the Bradley proposal, the office will be open the day after Thanksgiving.

PROFESSIONAL PUBLISHING SERVICES MEMO

Standard memo title
Memo heading

TO:	Barbara Smith, Publications Manager
FROM:	Hannah Kaufman, Vice President *HK*
DATE:	April 14, 2006
SUBJECT:	Schedule for ACM Electronics Brochure

Initial or sign if sent
in printed form

ACM Electronics has asked us to prepare a comprehensive brochure for its Milwaukee office by August 9, 2006. We have worked with electronics firms in the past, so this brochure should be relatively easy to prepare. My guess is that the job will take nearly two months. Ted Harris has requested time and cost estimates for the project. Fred Moore in production will prepare the cost estimates, and I would like you to prepare a tentative schedule for the project.

Introduction

Additional Personnel

In preparing the schedule, check the availability of the following:

Headings signal shifts
in topics

1. Production schedule for all staff writers
2. Available freelance writers
3. Dependable graphic designers

Ordinarily, we would not need to depend on outside personnel; however, because our bid for the *Wall Street Journal* special project is still under consideration, we could be short of staff in June and July. Further, we have to consider vacations that have already been approved.

Time Estimates

Please give me the time estimates by April 19. A successful job done on time will give us a good chance to obtain the contract to do ACM Electronics' annual report for its stockholders' meeting this fall.

I know your staff can do the job.

Closing

cc: Ted Harris, President
     Fred Moore, Production Editor

Additional recipients

Figure 8–8   Typical Memo Format (printed form)

By describing the bad news first (the need to meet the deadline), the writer focuses the reader's attention on the reasoning behind the decision to work. Employees may not necessarily like the message, but they at least understand that the decision is not arbitrary because it is tied to an important deadline. As this example illustrates, much of the strategy for business letters discussed earlier in this chapter, such as in Negative Messages and the Indirect Pattern (page 271), applies to memos as well.

Openings

Memo openings are crucial because readers in the workplace are busy meeting deadlines and coping with dozens of messages every day. Although methods of development vary, a memo should begin with a statement of the main idea that the subject line announces.

MAIN IDEA Because the e-mail addresses of individuals make the site vulnerable to hacker attacks, I recommend that we no longer post the e-mail addresses of our laboratory employees on our Web site.

Even if your opening gives the essential background of a problem, state the main point early in the first paragraph.

BACKGROUND Last year we did not hire new staff because of the freeze on hiring. As a result of the increased workload described in this memo, we need to hire two additional application support specialists this year.

When the reader is not familiar with the subject or with the background of a problem, provide an introductory background paragraph before stating the main point (shown in *italics* in the following example) of the memo. Doing so is especially important in memos that serve as records for crucial information months or years later.

MAIN IDEA ACM Electronics has asked us to prepare a comprehensive brochure for its Milwaukee office by August 9, 2006. We have worked with electronics firms in the past, so this job should not cause significant problems. I estimate that it will take two months to complete. Ted Harris has requested time and cost estimates for the project, Fred Moore in production will prepare the cost estimates, and *I would like you to prepare a tentative schedule for the project.*

Generally, longer memos or those dealing with complex subjects benefit most from more-thorough introductions. However, even when writing a short memo about a familiar subject, remind readers of the context. In the following examples, words that provide context are shown in *italics*.

▶ *As we discussed after yesterday's meeting,* we need to set new guidelines for . . .

▶ *As Maria recommended*, I reviewed the office reorganization plan. I like most of the features; however, the location of the receptionist and administrative assistant . . .

Do not state the main point first when (1) the reader is likely to be highly skeptical or (2) you are disagreeing with a person in a position of higher authority. In such cases, a more-persuasive tactic is to state the problem first, then present the specific points supporting your final recommendation.

◆ *For more information on openings and closings, see pages 84–87 in Chapter 3, Writing the Draft.*

Lists and Headings

Using lists is an effective strategy to give your points impact in a memo. Lists can be read and their meaning grasped more quickly than a paragraph that says the same thing. Be careful, however, not to overuse lists. A memo that consists almost entirely of lists is difficult for the reader to understand because he or she must mentally connect the separate and disjointed terms on the page. Further, lists lose their impact when they are overused. A particularly useful type of list is one for messages sent to numerous readers whose responses you need to tabulate.

▶ I can meet at   1 p.m. _____
                2 p.m. _____
                3 p.m. _____

Another attention-getting device, particularly in long memos, is the use of headings. Headings have a number of advantages:

- They divide material into manageable segments.
- They call attention to main topics.
- They signal a shift in topic.

Especially for memos to several readers, headings allow each reader to scan them and read only the section or sections appropriate to his or her needs. Notice the use of both a list and headings in Figure 8–8.

◆ *For additional guidance on using lists, see the Using Lists checklist on page 105 of Chapter 4, Revising the Draft.*

Closings

A memo closing can accomplish many important tasks, such as building positive relationships with readers, encouraging colleagues and employees, and letting recipients know what you will do or what you expect of them.

▶ I will discuss the problem with the marketing consultant and let you know by Monday what we are able to change.

Although routine statements are sometimes unavoidable ("Thanks again for your help"), make your closing work for you by providing specific prompts to which the reader can respond.

▷   If you would like further information, such as a copy of the questionnaire we used, please e-mail me at delgado@prn.com.

Memo Formats and Parts

Memo formats vary from organization to organization. Although no single, standard form exists, Figure 8–8 shows a typical 8 1/2-by-11-inch format with a company name.

Regardless of the parts of the memo included, an element requiring careful preparation is the subject-line title (such as "Schedule for ACM Electronics Brochure" in Figure 8–8). Subject-line titles in both memos and e-mail messages function much like the titles of reports: They announce the topic. They are also an important aid to filing and later retrieval. Therefore, they must be accurate. The memo should deal only with the single subject announced in the subject line, and the title should be complete. However, the title should not substitute for an opening that provides a context for the message.

VAGUE	Subject: Tuition Reimbursement
VAGUE	Subject: Time-Management Seminar
SPECIFIC	Subject: Tuition Reimbursement for Time-Management Seminar

Capitalize the first letter of all major words in a title. Do not capitalize articles, prepositions, or conjunctions of fewer than four letters unless they are the first or last words of the title.

If you are sending a printed memo, the final step is signing or initialing it, a practice that lets readers know that you have approved the memo's contents. (Be aware that not all organizations require initials or signatures.) Where you sign or initial the memo depends on the practice of your organization: Some writers sign their name at the end of a memo, while others sign their initials next to their typed name. Follow the practice of your employer. Figure 8–8 shows a typical placement of initials.

▷ DESIGNING YOUR DOCUMENT
Formatting Memos

- Use your organization's preferred standard in formatting a memo, such as deciding whether to use "MEMO" as a header and what order to use for "To:", "From:", "cc:", "Date:", and "Subject:".

- Use headings and lists to highlight important information.

- Check your memo's general professional look before you initial or sign it, depending on your organization's practice.

■ MEETING THE DEADLINE: The Time-Sensitive Memo _____

More than once in your career you will be asked to do a seemingly impos-sible task—write an important one-page memo that requires some research in less than an hour. Such assignments usually come from a supervisor, often at the last minute, to meet a time-sensitive deadline. These memos are often written for the signature of someone else who is higher up in the organization. When you get such an assignment, do not panic. Instead, use the following straightforward prin-ciples drawn from this book to focus your energies on the task at hand.

Understand the Assignment

Nothing could be worse than to waste time under a short deadline by misunder-standing the purpose or intended reader of the memo. Ask the person giving you the assignment to be as explicit as possible about

- The topic
- The reader and the reader's background
- The purpose and intended outcome
- The key points that must be covered
- The person who will sign the memo

Gather Information

The essential background information for your memo can almost always be lo-cated within your company or organization. Sources include previous letters and memos, press releases, contracts, budget data, handbooks, speeches by senior offi-cials, legal opinions, and the like. Be careful to gather *only* the information pertinent to the memo. The person asking for the memo will usually provide essential back-ground information or tell you where to find it. If the information is not readily available, be sure to ask for it.

As long as the information originated in your organization, fits your context, and is accurate and well written, use as much of it as you need. If necessary, revise such material for consistency of content, style, and format as you draft the memo. When using information from other sources, make sure you avoid plagiarism and any violation of copyright (see Avoiding Plagiarism and Copyright Violations on page 178).

On the job, you will have another source of information that you may not al-ways have in the classroom—your experience. In fact, one reason you may re-ceive such an assignment is your knowledge of the subject, reader, organization, or professional area. Brainstorming, discussed on pages 9–10, will prepare you to draw the most benefit from your experience when you are under pressure.

Organize Your Thoughts

Do not overlook this important step. Your memo should have an opening, a middle, and a closing. Organizing the information into this structure does not have to be a formal process—you won't have time to create a full-blown outline, nor will one be necessary. Jot down the points you need to make in a sequence that makes sense. Keep it simple. In some cases, you will organize by classifying and dividing your subject matter, presenting the information on one subject before going on to another subject. Sometimes a problem-and-solution order makes sense. At other times, a chronological, sequential, or general-to-specific order will be appropriate.

◆ See pages 35–55 in Chapter 2, Organizing Your Information, for typical organizing strategies.

Write the Draft

With the right information and a structure for organizing it, the writing will not be difficult. Stick to your plan—your rough outline—and begin. Make the structure easy for you and your reader to follow. Cover only one subject in each paragraph. After a topic sentence, provide essential supporting information—facts, examples, policy, procedures, guidelines.

Write a quick draft first; you can polish it later. Put your ideas down as quickly as you can. Write without worrying about grammar, sentence structure, or spelling. Given the limited time available, your main focus should be on getting your ideas down.

Polish the Draft

You will not have much time left, but discipline yourself to read the draft several times, concentrating on different elements each time.

First, concentrate on larger issues. Is the information accurate? Is it complete? Have you made all your points? Are they organized in the right sequence? Have you provided too much information? Revise accordingly.

Next, focus on polishing at the sentence and word level. Aim for simple sentences in the active voice. Include some longer sentences to avoid the monotony of too many simple sentences strung together. Structure longer sentences so that subjects and verbs agree and primary ideas are distinct from subordinate ideas. Use parallel structure to convey matching ideas. Use lists where possible. Don't forget to review punctuation. A misplaced comma or semicolon can change the meaning of a sentence. In this situation, you do not have time for a cooling period, so watch for any emotionally charged language.

◆ For guidance on using e-mail for collaborative writing, see Chapter 5, Collaborative Writing.

As a final review, use your spell checker, but don't rely on it to catch all of your spelling errors. Make sure you read through a paper version of the memo at least once to catch any remaining errors. If you have time, ask a second reader to help.

Take a Well-Deserved Break

After your draft is written, you may e-mail it to a superior for review before you prepare the final form for signature and distribution. Now sit back and enjoy the sense of professional pride you have earned from a job well done under pressure!

CONSIDERING AUDIENCE AND PURPOSE
Writing Business Communications

- Determine the most-appropriate medium for your message based on your audience and your purpose. What would be most appropriate and best achieve your purpose? A letter? A memo? An e-mail message? A fax?

- Keep your readers' needs in mind as you write.

- Bring your reader more directly into the communication by appropriately using the "you" viewpoint.

- Consider whether a formal (somewhat restrained) or an informal writing style would be more appropriate for your purpose and your audience. Remember that an attempt to sound casual or friendly can instead seem insincere.

- Even when writing to a close associate, be considerate of your reader and use appropriate grammar, spelling, and punctuation.

- For international correspondence, be aware of how cultural differences may affect the reader's interpretation of your message.

■ Sending E-Mail and Instant Messages: Protocol and Strategies

E-mail (or *email*) and instant messages can function in the workplace to send information quickly, elicit discussions, collect opinions, and transmit documents and files of all types. Correspondence, reports, meeting notices, questionnaires, and digital files of all kinds are routinely sent to colleagues throughout an organization and to others worldwide through these media.

E-mail messages are particularly useful for facilitating discussions and collecting opinions. E-mail enables a collaborative writing team, for example, to exchange multiple drafts to produce a final document. When used for exchanging ideas rapidly, e-mail messages are often conversational in tone and can become something between a telephone conversation and a memo. Even in these informal exchanges, you need to think carefully about your reader and the accuracy and appropriate level of detail of the information you send.

Review and Confidentiality Implications

As with other workplace correspondence, maintain a high level of professionalism when you send e-mail and instant messages: A message should be grammatically and factually correct, with no ambiguities or unintended implications. When you send an informal message to a colleague, you can correct misunderstandings relatively easily—but at the expense of wasted time. Take even more care when sending messages to superiors in your organization or to people outside the organization.

Time spent reviewing your messages before sending them can save a great deal of time and embarrassment sorting out misunderstandings resulting from sending a careless message. One helpful strategy is to write the draft and revise your message before filling in the "To" line with the address of your recipient. Be careful as well to follow the rules of netiquette, discussed in the section that follows.

ETHICS NOTE

Confidentiality is another issue to keep in mind when you are sending e-mail and instant messages. All messages sent electronically, no matter how personal, sensitive, or proprietary, can be intercepted by someone other than the intended recipient. Remember, e-mail and instant messages are never truly deleted, even when you think you've removed them from your computer. Not only can the information be printed, circulated, and forwarded, but most companies back up and save all company e-mail messages. Employers can legally monitor e-mail and instant message communications. Some companies make this policy known, but others do not. Companies can also be legally compelled to provide these messages to a third party, such as a court of law. Consider the content of all your messages given these possibilities. The potential for the unintended release of inappropriate information makes the need for a careful review of your text before you click Send all the more important.

Observing Netiquette

ON THE WEB

For more advice on sending e-mail attachments, go to Chapter 8, bedfordstmartins.com/ writingthatworks

To maintain a high level of professionalism in workplace e-mail and instant messages, observe the rules of netiquette (*Internet + etiquette*).

- Use company e-mail and instant messages only for appropriate business.
  - Do not send or forward jokes or humorous stories, use biased language, or discuss office gossip.
  - Do not send *flames* (e-mail messages that contain abusive, obscene, or derogatory language) to attack someone.
  - Do not send *spams* (mass-distributed e-mail messages that often promote personal projects and interests).
- Respond to incoming messages promptly. If you receive an assignment by e-mail that will take a few days or longer to complete, send a response saying so.
- Be scrupulous about typing addresses and user names; ensure that the intended recipient (and nobody else) receives the message.
- Send mass mailings with care (including those to all members of your class). If you seek assistance with a project, make recipients feel special by sending each one a targeted message because mass e-mail messages are impersonal and easily ignored.
- Send an attachment only after verifying that your recipient wants or needs the file and that your recipient's software will accept it. Be aware that attachments can consume download time and disk space.

Dilbert

- Consider posting a large file at an Internet or intranet server and supplying the file's address so that your recipient may download the file at his or her convenience.

- Do not write in all-uppercase letters; such a message is difficult to read and is considered the equivalent of shouting. Likewise, do not write in all-lowercase letters; it is considered lazy and too informal for professional work.

- Avoid abbreviations used in personal e-mail messages, and chat rooms (*BTW* for *by the way*, for example).

- Do not use emoticons (keyboard characters used to create sideways faces conveying emotions) for business and professional messages. For advice on providing typographic emphasis, review the next section on design considerations.

- Observe memo protocol for courtesy copies and blind copies.

 DIGITAL TIPS: Sending an Attachment

Sending attachments with an e-mail or instant message is a quick, convenient alternative to sending paper copies or disks through the regular mail. However, large files, like graphics, slow transmission speed. In addition, the recipient's software or Internet provider may not be able to accept large files. Most people receive numerous attachments every day, so be sure that your attachment file names are meaningful to your recipients.

   A word of caution: Viruses can be embedded in e-mail attachments, so make sure you regularly update your virus-scanning software.

   For more on this topic, see <bedfordstmartins.com/writingthatworks> and select *Digital Tips,* "Sending an Attachment."

Composing Professional E-mail Messages

E-mail is a quick and easy way to communicate, but avoid the temptation to dash off a first draft and send it as is. The writing advice given earlier in this chapter also applies to e-mail messages, especially when they replace memos inside an organization or when they replace business letters for communications to those outside an organization. Be aware, however, that recipients outside an organization may consider e-mail messages to be less appropriate than business letters on printed organizational stationery. Moreover, some customers, clients, and others may have limited access to e-mail or may check their e-mail infrequently.

Design Considerations

The dynamics of a computer screen and the limitations of some Internet service providers require that you keep in mind some special design considerations when you are sending e-mail messages. The following are especially important:

- Break the text into brief paragraphs. No one wants to read long, dense blocks of text on a computer screen.

- Do not overwhelm your reader with lengthy passages. If your message runs much longer than a screen of text, consider sending it as an attached file along with a brief e-mail message that functions as a cover memo for the longer attachment.

- If you must send a document with tables and bulleted lists, do so in an attachment, making sure that the recipient has compatible software to view and save the attachment, as tables and lists do not always transmit well.

- Be considerate of the technical capabilities of your recipient. Check before sending memory-hungry attachments that may not be accepted by your recipient's software or Internet service provider or that may download very slowly.

- Put your response to someone else's e-mail message at the beginning (or top) of the e-mail window. Don't make the recipient scroll down to the end of the original message to find your response.

- In quoting the message you're replying to, include only those parts relevant to your reply. Clearly indicate the difference between your response and the text quoted in the incoming e-mail message by marking the beginning of the quoted text with a greater-than symbol (>).

- Always fill in the subject line with a concise phrase that describes the topic of your message. The recipient can then decide at a glance when he or she needs to read it. Subject lines also help your reader organize and file incoming messages.

Some e-mail systems allow you to use sophisticated typographical features, such as various fonts and bullets. These options increase your e-mail file size and may display unpredictably in other e-mail systems. Unless you are sure your recipient's software will display your formatted message correctly, set your e-mail software to send messages in "plain text" and use alternative highlighting devices. For example, capital letters or asterisks, used sparingly, can substitute for boldface, italics, and underlines as emphasis.

▶   Dr. Wilhoit's suggestions benefit doctors AND patients.

▶   Although the proposal is sound in *theory,* it will never work in *practice.*

Intermittent underlining can replace solid underlining or italics when referring to published works in an e-mail message:

▶   My report follows the format outlined in _The Business Writer's Handbook_.

Salutations, Closings, and Signature Blocks

E-mail can function as a letter, memo, or personal note; therefore, adapt your salutation to your audience and context. If your employer follows a certain form, adopt that practice. Otherwise, use the following guidelines:

- When e-mail functions as a memo, you may omit the salutation and closing because both your name and the name(s) of the recipient(s) appear in the "To" and "From" sections of the message. However, some e-mail users adopt a slightly more personal greeting, especially if the distribution list is relatively small or a single individual (*Project colleagues* or *Andreas* [recipient's first name]).

- When e-mail goes outside an organization to someone with whom you have not yet corresponded, you can use the standard letter salutation (*Dear Professor Tucker:* or *Dear Docuform Customer:*) and a slightly informal closing (*Best wishes,* or *Sincerely,*).

- When e-mail functions as a personal note to a friend, you can vary informal salutations (*Hi Mike,* or *Hello Jenny,*) and closings (*Take care,* or *Cheers,*).

Of course, you may wish to use some combination of these approaches, depending on your relationship with the recipients and the practice among those with whom you exchange e-mail. Be aware that in some cultures, business correspondents do not use first names as quickly as in U.S. correspondence. See examples of inappropriate and appropriate e-mail messages in Figures 8–9 and 8–10, respectively.

◆ *For guidelines applicable to writing e-mail messages for an international audience, see pages 300–305.*

Because e-mail does not provide letterhead with standard addresses and contact information, many companies and individual writers include *signature blocks* (called *signatures* for short) at the bottom of their messages. Signatures, usually preprogrammed to appear on every e-mail message sent, supply information that company letterhead usually provides in other correspondence. If your organization

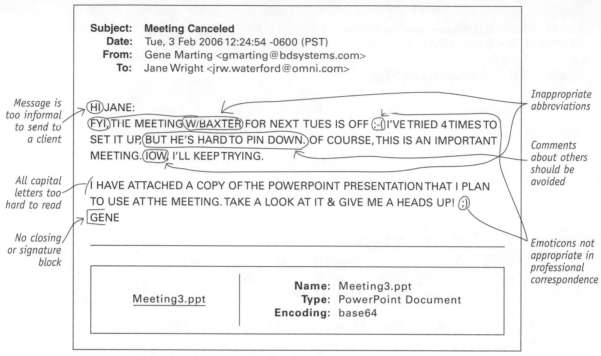

Figure 8–9   Inappropriate E-mail Message (with Attachment)

recommends a certain format or restricts the content of signatures, adhere to that standard. Otherwise, choose a signature that lets your reader know your full name, official title, department or division, and the organization for which you work. Other items often included in a signature are telephone and fax numbers, and mailing and Internet addresses. Some e-mail signature blocks can include auto-mated links that connect to a Web site. Many e-mail programs allow you to create multiple signature blocks, so you can have one for professional and one for per-sonal use.

When you use a signature block at the bottom of an e-mail message, separate the signature from the message by two or three spaces. Other cues can highlight the signature: A line of hyphens (-), underlines (_), equals signs (=), tildes (~), or asterisks (*) can effectively separate a signature from the e-mail message. Usually, typographical highlights begin at the left margin and continue until the end of the signature's longest line, as shown in Figure 8–10.

Avoid using quotations, aphorisms, and other messages ("May the Force be with you") in professional signatures. As with all design features, use signature blocks appropriate for the tone of your correspondence and the professional image of you and your organization.

Subject: **Baxter Meeting Canceled**
Date: Tue, 3 Feb 2006 12:24:54 -0600 (PST)
From: Gene Marting <gmarting@secsystems.com>
To: Jane Wright <jrw.waterford@omni.com>

Jane:

I need to cancel the meeting with Thomas Baxter for next Friday (Feb 17).
I will work to schedule another meeting because we need to meet with him.

I have attached a copy of the PowerPoint presentation that I'd like to use at the meeting. Let me know if you see possible improvements.

Thanks,

Gene

===================================
Gene Marting, Manager
Sales Division, Building Systems, Inc.
3555 South 47th Street, Boise, ID 83703
Off: 208-719-6620 Fax: 208-719-5500
http://www.building/sys/com
e-mail: gmarting@secsystems.com
===================================

Signature block separated from message

Meeting3.ppt	**Name:** Meeting3.ppt
	Type: PowerPoint Document
	Encoding: base64

Figure 8–10   Revised, Appropriate E-mail Message (with Attachment)

DIGITAL TIPS: Managing Your E-mail

■ Check your e-mail several times each day; try to clear your in-box by the end of the day.

■ Set priorities for reading e-mail by skimming sender names and subject lines.

■ Review all messages on a subject in date and time order before you respond, so you don't waste time responding to an issue that is no longer relevant.

(*continued*)

> ### DIGITAL TIPS: Managing Your E-mail (*continued*)
>
> - Learn the advanced features of your system so that you can use filters that organize messages (including junk mail) as they arrive. Test these filters carefully, as they may discard important messages because of faulty filtering rules.
> - Create electronic folders for e-mail, using personal names and key topics.
> - Send yourself a copy or save copies of important e-mails in your electronic folders.
> - Use the Search command to find topics and individual names.
> - Print and file hard copies of crucial e-mail messages that are complex or that you will need for meetings.
> - Keep an up-to-date address book.
> - If you will not check your in-box for an extended period, create an away-from-desk automatic response that informs senders when you are expected back and, if necessary, whom they can contact in your absence. (To learn how to set up an automated response, see <bedfordstmartins.com/writingthatworks> and select *Digital Tips,* "Leaving an Away-from-Desk Message.")

Instant Messaging in the Workplace

Instant messaging is a growing text-based communications medium because it fills a niche between telephone calls and e-mail messages. It permits both real-time communications, like a phone, while allowing the transfer of files, like e-mail. It is especially useful to people with cell phones who are working at sites without access to regular e-mail.

To set up routine IM exchanges, add the user names of the people you exchange messages with to your list of contacts (or "buddy list"). Choose a screen name that your colleagues will recognize. If you use IM routinely as part of your job, create an "away" message that signals when you are not available for IM interactions.

When writing instant messages, keep your messages simple and to the point, covering only one subject in each message to prevent confusion and inappropriate responses. Because screen space is often limited and speed is essential, many who send instant messages use abbreviations and shortened spellings ("u" for "you" and "L8R" for "later"). Be sure that your reader will understand such abbreviations; when in doubt, avoid them.

In Figure 8–11, the manager of a software development company in Maine ("Diana") is exchanging instant messages with a business partner in the Netherlands ("Andre"). Notice that the correspondents use an informal style that includes personal and professional abbreviations with which both are familiar ("NP" for "no problem"; "FYI" for "for your information"; and "QSG" for Quick Start Guide). These messages demonstrate how instant messaging can not only help exchange information quickly but also build rapport among distant colleagues and team members. The exchange also demonstrates why IM is not generally appropriate for highly complex messages or for more formal circumstances, such as when establishing new professional relationships.

ON THE WEB

For a detailed list of abbreviations used in IM exchanges and their definitions, go to Chapter 8, bedfordstmartins.com/ writingthatworks

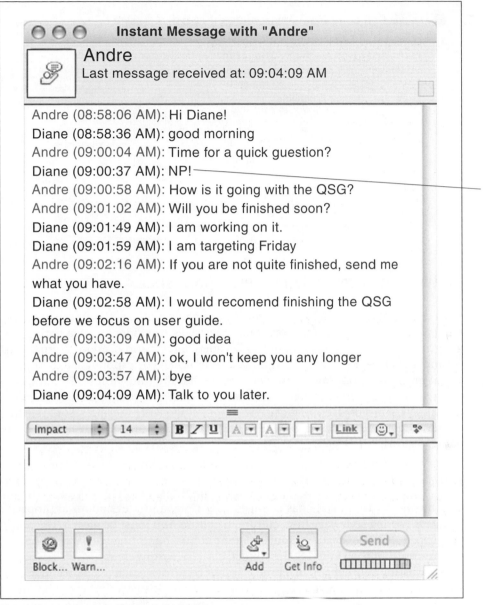

Each line of dialog preceded by the speaker's name

Informal language and terse statements

Use of abbreviations

Figure 8–11   Instant-Message Exchange

ETHICS NOTE

Be sure to follow your employer's IM policies, such as any limitations on sending personal messages during work hours or requirements concerning confidentiality. If no specific policy exists, assume that personal use of IM is not appropriate in your workplace.

DIGITAL TIPS: IM Privacy and Security

■ Organize your contact or "buddy lists" to separate workplace contacts from family and friends so that you do not inadvertently send personal messages to professional associates and vice versa. Consider restricting buddy lists on professional IM accounts to business associates.

■ Learn the options, capabilities, and security limitations of your IM system and set the preferences that best suit your use of the system.

■ Be especially alert to the possibilities of virus infections and security risks with messages, attachments, access to buddy lists, and other privacy issues.

■ Save significant IM logs for your future reference.

■ Be aware that instant messages can be saved by your recipients and may be archived by your employer.

■ Do not use professional IM for gossip or inappropriate exchanges.

■ Writing International Correspondence

With organizations participating in the increasingly global marketplace, you may need to write letters, memos, or e-mail messages to readers whose native language is not English. Because English is widely taught and used in international business, you will be able to send most international correspondence in English. If you must use a translator, however, be sure that the translator understands the purpose of your correspondence. It is also prudent to let your reader know (in the letter itself or in a postscript) that a translator helped write the letter. For first-time contacts, consider sending both the English version and a translation in the reader's native language.

Culture and Business Writing Style

U.S. business writing style has changed over time, and ideas about appropriate business writing style vary from culture to culture. You must be alert to the needs and expectations of readers from different cultural and linguistic backgrounds. For example, in the United States, direct, concise writing demonstrates courtesy by not wasting another person's time; in other countries (such as Spain and India), such directness and brevity suggests that the writer dislikes the reader so much that he or she wishes to make the communication as brief as possible. Whereas a U.S. business writer might consider one brief letter sufficient to communicate a request, a writer in another culture may expect an exchange of three or four longer letters to pave the way for action.

Japanese business writers, as another example, often use traditional openings that reflect on the season, compliment the reader's success, and offer hopes for the reader's continued prosperity. These traditional openings may strike some U.S. readers as being overly elaborate, literary, or even insincere. Likewise, Japanese business writers express negative messages and refusal letters indirectly to avoid embarrassing the recipient or causing a loss of face.

In U.S. business correspondence, traditional salutations such as *Dear* and complimentary closings such as *Yours truly* have, through custom and long use, acquired meanings quite distinct from their dictionary definitions. Understanding the unspoken meanings of these forms and using them naturally is routine for those who are a part of U.S. business culture. Likewise, people in many cultures are slower to use an individual's first name in communications than are most Americans. In fact, in some cultures, first names are never used in business settings—even if the individuals have worked together for years. Such customs vary from culture to culture and even within cultures. Therefore, when you read correspondence from businesspeople in other cultures or countries, be alert to these differences and consider how you should address them and your own colleagues in correspondence.

The first step in avoiding misunderstandings is to be aware that differences exist and to learn how they affect communication. To learn more about this subject, use the term *intercultural communication* to search library and reliable Internet sources.

ON THE WEB

Google's International Business and Trade Directory provides an excellent starting point for searching the Web for information related to customs, communications, and international standards. Go to Chapter 8, **bedfordstmartins.com/ writingthatworks,** and select *Web Links.*

Language and Usage

Take special care in international correspondence to avoid American idioms ("it's a slam dunk," "give a heads up," and the like), unusual figures of speech, and allusions to events or attitudes particular to American life. Such expressions could easily confuse your reader. Avoid humor, irony, and sarcasm because they are easily misunderstood outside their cultural context.

Pretentious or overly ornate writing will also impede the reader's understanding. Moreover, if you plan to use jargon or technical terminology, ask yourself whether the words you choose might be found in the abbreviated English-language dictionary that your reader would likely be using.

Write clear and complete sentences. Unusual word order or rambling sentences will frustrate and confuse a nonnative reader of English. Read your writing aloud to identify overly long sentences and to eliminate any misplaced modifiers or awkwardness. Long sentences that contain more information than the reader can comfortably absorb should be divided into two or more sentences. Also avoid using an overly simplified storybook style. A reader who has studied English as a second language might be insulted by a condescending tone and childish language.

Finally, proofread your correspondence carefully; a misspelled word such as *there* for *their* or *discreet* for *discrete* will be particularly troublesome for a nonnative reader of English—especially if that reader turns to a dictionary for help and cannot find the word because it is misspelled.

◆ *For advice on using appropriate language in business writing, see pages 108–114 in Chapter 4. Revising the Draft.*

Dates, Time, and Measurement

Countries differ in their use of formats to represent dates, time, and other kinds of measurement. To represent dates, most countries typically write the day before the month and year. For example, 1/11/06 means 1 November 2006 in most parts of the world; in the United States, it means January 11, 2006. To avoid uncertainty, write out the name of the month to make the entire date immediately clear to all international readers.

Clock time poses similar problems, so you may need to specify time zones or refer to international standards, such as Greenwich Mean Time (GMT) or Universal Coordinated Time (UCT), for clarity. In Europe and the U.S. Military, the 24-hour system is used for clock time. The hours between midnight and noon are numbered 1 to 12 and the hours between noon and midnight are numbered 13 to 24. In this system, four o'clock in the afternoon (4:00 p.m.) is 1600, and 30 minutes later (4:30 p.m.) is 1630. Do not separate the hour and minute with a period or colon. Using this system in letters and e-mail messages will avoid confusion for European correspondents.

◆ *For a list of subject-specific guides and manuals, see page 199.*

Using other international standards, such as commas for decimal points and the metric system (standard in most countries except the United States and the United Kingdom), will also help your reader. For up-to-date information about accepted conventions for numbers and symbols in chemical, electrical, data-processing, pharmaceutical, and other fields, consult guides and manuals specific to the subject matter.

Cross-Cultural Examples

When you write for international readers, rethink the ingrained habits that define how you express yourself, learn as much as you can about the cultural expectations of others, and focus on politeness strategies that demonstrate your respect for your readers. Doing so will help you achieve clarity and mutual understanding.

Consider the two versions of a letter written by a U.S. businessman to a Japanese businessman in Figures 8–12 and 8–13. The letter in Figure 8–12 does not respect the politeness norms important to Japanese readers. It contains jargon, idioms, and figures of speech that may confuse a nonnative speaker of English. The writer has used inappropriately informal language and an overly simplified style, which are likely to offend his reader.

Compare that letter to the one in Figure 8–13, which is written in language that is literal and specific. The letter opens by expressing concern about the recipient's family and prosperity because that type of expression honors Japanese traditional patterns in business correspondence. The letter is also free of American slang, idioms, and jargon. Bulleted lists are used to break up the paragraphs, contractions are not used, and months are spelled out.

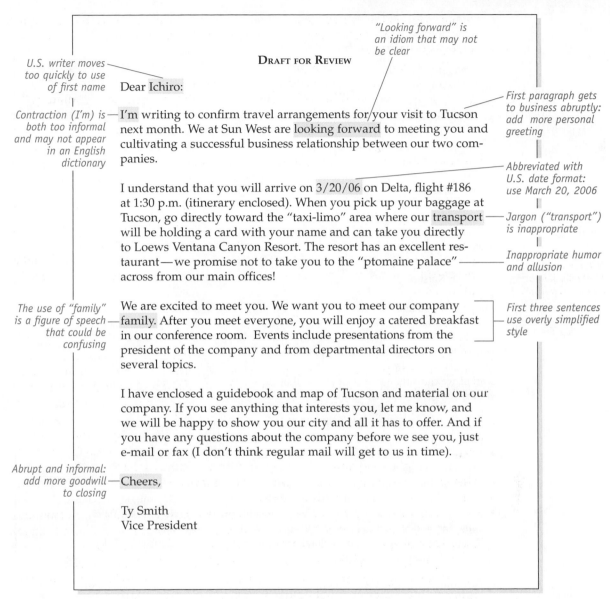

"Looking forward" is an idiom that may not be clear

DRAFT FOR REVIEW

U.S. writer moves too quickly to use of first name

Dear Ichiro:

Contraction (I'm) is both too informal and may not appear in an English dictionary

I'm writing to confirm travel arrangements for your visit to Tucson next month. We at Sun West are looking forward to meeting you and cultivating a successful business relationship between our two companies.

First paragraph gets to business abruptly: add more personal greeting

I understand that you will arrive on 3/20/06 on Delta, flight #186 at 1:30 p.m. (itinerary enclosed). When you pick up your baggage at Tucson, go directly toward the "taxi-limo" area where our transport will be holding a card with your name and can take you directly to Loews Ventana Canyon Resort. The resort has an excellent restaurant—we promise not to take you to the "ptomaine palace" across from our main offices!

Abbreviated with U.S. date format: use March 20, 2006

Jargon ("transport") is inappropriate

Inappropriate humor and allusion

The use of "family" is a figure of speech that could be confusing

We are excited to meet you. We want you to meet our company family. After you meet everyone, you will enjoy a catered breakfast in our conference room. Events include presentations from the president of the company and from departmental directors on several topics.

First three sentences use overly simplified style

I have enclosed a guidebook and map of Tucson and material on our company. If you see anything that interests you, let me know, and we will be happy to show you our city and all it has to offer. And if you have any questions about the company before we see you, just e-mail or fax (I don't think regular mail will get to us in time).

Abrupt and informal: add more goodwill to closing

Cheers,

Ty Smith
Vice President

Figure 8–12 Inappropriate International Correspondence (Marked for Revision)

Sun West Corporation, Inc.

2565 North Armadillo
Tucson, AZ 85719
Phone: (602) 555-6677
Fax: (602) 555-6678   <sunwest@aol.com>

February 27, 2006

Ichiro Katsumi
Investment Director
Toshiba Investment Company
1-29-10 Ichiban-cho
Tokyo 105, Japan

Formal salutation   Dear Mr. Katsumi:

*Polite opening
acknowledges
recipient and
his family*
I hope that you and your family are well and prospering in the new year. We at Sun West Corporation are very pleased that you will be coming to visit us in Tucson next month. It will be a pleasure to meet you, and we are very gratified and honored that you are interested in investing in our company.

So that we can ensure that your stay will be pleasurable, we have taken care of all of your travel arrangements. You will

- Leave Narita–New Tokyo International Airport on Delta Airlines flight #75 at 5:00 p.m. on March 20, 2006.
- Arrive at Los Angeles International Airport at 10:50 a.m. local time and depart for Tucson on Delta flight #186 at 12:05 p.m.

*Checklist-style
schedule with
times and dates
spelled out*
- Arrive at Tucson International Airport at 1:30 p.m. local time on March 20.
- Depart Tucson International Airport on Delta flight #123 at 6:45 a.m. on March 27.
- Arrive in Salt Lake City, Utah, at 10:40 a.m. and depart at 11:15 a.m. on Delta flight #34 and arrive in Portland, Oregon, at 12:10 p.m. local time.
- Depart Portland, Oregon, on Delta flight #254 at 1:05 p.m. and arrive in Tokyo at 3:05 p.m. local time on March 28.

*Courteous and
helpful contact
information*
If this information is not accurate or if you need additional information about your travel plans or information on Sun West Corporation, please call, fax, or e-mail me directly. That way, we will receive your message in time to make the appropriate changes or additions.

Figure 8–13   Appropriate International Correspondence (continued)

Mr. Ichiro Katsumi   2   February 27, 2006

After you arrive in Tucson, a chauffeur from Skyline Limousines will be waiting for you at Gate 12. He or she will be carrying a card with your name, will help you collect your luggage from the baggage claim area, and will then drive you to the Loews Ventana Canyon Resort. This resort is one of the most prestigious in Tucson, with spectacular desert views, high-quality amenities, and one of the best golf courses in the city. The next day, the chauffeur will be back at the Ventana at 9:00 a.m. to drive you to Sun West Corporation.

Specific arrival plans

We at Sun West Corporation are very excited to meet you and introduce you to all the members of our hardworking and growing company family. After you meet every-one, you will enjoy a catered breakfast in our conference room. At that time, you will receive a schedule of events planned for the remainder of your trip. Events include presentations from the president of the company and from departmental directors on

- The history of Sun West Corporation.
- The uniqueness of our products and current success in the marketplace.
- Demographic information and benefits of being located in Tucson.
- The potential for considerable profits for both our companies with your company's investment.

Specific trip event plans

We encourage you to read through the enclosed guidebook and map of Tucson. In ad-dition to events planned at Sun West Corporation, you will find many natural wonders and historical sites to see in Tucson and in Arizona in general. If you see any particular event or place that you would like to visit, please let us know. We will be happy to show you our city and all it has to offer.

Again, we are very honored that you will be visiting us, and we look forward to a suc-cessful business relationship between our two companies.

Polite closing

Sincerely,

Ty Smith

Ty Smith
Vice President
ts-sunwest@aol.com

Enclosures (2)

Figure 8–13 Appropriate International Correspondence (continued)

CHAPTER 8 SUMMARY: UNDERSTANDING THE PRINCIPLES OF BUSINESS COMMUNICATION

Selecting the Appropriate Medium

- Letters on your organization's stationery
  - To represent a commitment to the recipient
  - To formalize a business relationship
- Memos: printed and electronic
  - To communicate and circulate information within your organization
- E-mail and instant messages
  - To communicate quickly within your organization and with customers and others outside your organization
  - To transmit text and graphics files electronically
- Faxes
  - To transmit a document that is not available in electronic format
  - To transmit a document that must be viewed in its original form (for instance, a letter with a signature or an official seal)
- Telephone and conference calls
  - To provide an alternative to a face-to-face meeting
  - To enable participants to hear one another's voices
- Voice-mail messages
  - To record brief messages for later retrieval
- Face-to-face meetings
  - To make initial or early contacts with associates and customers
  - To plan a project or make group decisions about specific objectives
- Videoconferencing
  - To save money on the travel costs of face-to-face meetings
  - To enable participants to hear and see one another

Writing and Formatting Letters

- Follow the writing process.
- Use goodwill and the "you" viewpoint.
- Use the direct pattern for good news:
  1. Main point or good news
  2. Explanation of facts
  3. Goodwill close
- Use the indirect pattern for some negative messages:
  1. Context (or "buffer")
  2. Explanation
  3. Bad news
  4. Goodwill close

- Follow letter formatting conventions:
  - Prepare a heading or use printed letterhead.
  - Provide an inside address.
  - Create an appropriate salutation, body, and complimentary close.
  - Design a second page correctly, if needed.
  - Add end notations as required.

Writing and Formatting Memos

- Follow company routing and signature protocol.
- Organize your ideas into an opening, body, and closing.
- Adjust the style and tone to the recipient.
- Use lists and headings strategically.
- Use appropriate format.
- Make the subject line accurate.

Meeting the Deadline: The Time-Sensitive Memo

- Make sure that you understand the assignment.
- Gather pertinent background information.
- Organize your major points into a sequence that makes sense.
- Write the draft quickly, covering only one subject in each paragraph.
- Polish the draft, focusing on content and organization before revising at the sentence level.

Sending E-mail and Instant Messages

- Recognize that all electronic messages are subject to interception by someone other than the person or persons for whom the message is intended; write them accordingly.
- Observe the rules of netiquette.
- Review all e-mail messages for accuracy, readability, and tact before sending them.
- Consider the design needs of e-mail messages.
- Create an appropriate salutation, closing, and signature block.
- Keep IM communications brief.
- Cover only one topic in each IM.
- Use only IM abbreviations your recipients understand.
- Maintain accurate and current contacts (buddy lists).

Writing International Correspondence

- Use words likely to appear in your reader's English-language dictionary.
- Adjust for cultural preferences in pacing and organizing ideas.
- Consider the decision-making style of your recipient's culture.
- Avoid using humor and slang.
- Read the letter aloud for ambiguity and confusing sentence structure.
- Check for appropriate forms of dates, times, and measurements.

◆ *For an online quiz on communication principles, go to Chapter 8,* bedfordstmartins.com/ writingthatworks

ON THE WEB

For additional exercises, go to Chapter 8, bedfordstmartins.com/ writingthatworks

■ Exercises

1. You are the manager of accounting for a company that sells computer-software packages. You have just received word from the comptroller that there has been a change in the expense allowances for employees using their own cars on business. Previously, one rate was applied to all employees, but now there will be different allowance rates for regular and nonregular drivers. Effective immediately, regular drivers will receive 40¢ per mile for the first 650 miles driven per month, and 10¢ for each additional mile; nonregular drivers will receive 30¢ per mile for the first 150 miles per month, and 10¢ for each additional mile. Regular drivers are those who use their own cars frequently on the job to drive to their sales territories. Nonregular drivers are those employees—such as home-office personnel—who only occasionally use their cars on business. To ensure that these categories are used properly, you have requested that the manager of each department notify Accounts Payable, in writing, which employees in his or her department should be classified as regular drivers. Accounts Payable will reimburse those employees not identified by the letter according to the nonregular-driver formula. Prepare a memo or an e-mail message to communicate this information to all employees.

2. Complete this assignment either on your own or as part of a collaborative team.

   a. You are director of corporate communications for a nationwide insurance company called The Provider Group. Management has asked you to design a letterhead that reflects a "modern, yet responsible image." For this project, collect as many samples of letterhead stationery as you can. Then, using word-processing software with graphics capability, design a letterhead for The Provider Group (using a local address, phone number, and any other appropriate details). As you design, consider the image and personality your design will project, as well as the amount of information you should provide.

   b. Survey three or four organizations in your area (including your college) to determine the standard letter formats they use (full block, modified block, and so on). Evaluate the formats using the guidelines provided in this chapter and in Chapter 7, Designing Effective Documents and Visuals.

   c. Using the results in parts a and b, determine the best format for letters sent to clients by The Provider Group.

3. Briefly describe a work- or school-related e-mail message that you have received that was inappropriate or that communicated information so poorly that you had to ask for a clarification.

4. Prepare an e-mail message to inform a group of international customers of the following: Your company's newsletter will now be delivered electronically, by e-mail, and will be updated monthly instead of bimonthly. Customers who wish to receive the print version of the newsletter will be charged an annual handling fee of $30. New items listed in the newsletter can be ordered at your company's Web site at a 10 percent discount. Customers need to inform the company if they wish to cancel their subscriptions to the newsletter. Be sure to present these changes positively—with your customers' point of view in mind. Refer to the following sections of this chapter: Sending E-mail and Instant Messages: Protocol and Strategies (page 291) and Writing International Correspondence (page 300).

5. Rewrite the following statements, improving them as indicated.

   a. Rewrite the following statement to make it more positive and less blunt:

   ▶ I will not pay you because you have not sent the final software upgrade. If you do not send the right one immediately, I will not pay you at all.

   b. Rewrite the following passage to make it more friendly:

   ▶ I wrote for the Music Collection you advertised on TV, and, not only did it take six weeks to get here, but it was the wrong set of CDs. Can't you get anything right? I'm canceling payment on my check and sending this set of CDs back!

   c. Rewrite the following passage to make it clear and unpretentious:

   ▶ With reference to your recent automobile accident, I have been unable to contact you due to the fact that I have been in Chicago working day and night on a proposal—a biggie. I should be back in the office in the neighborhood of the 15th or so. In the unforeseen and unlikely event that I should be delayed, you can utilize Mr. Strawman, of my office, who will also endeavor in your behalf.

6. Imagine that you work for a company where many of the new hires have been using text messaging to pass on confidential material to each other or relay emergency information. This greatly concerns the chief executive officer (CEO), who especially has a problem with employees using business IM names like "Sexyguy2007" and "Squirrelgirl42". Draft a company memo, to be sent by the CEO, detailing the proper use of IM etiquette.

7. Draft an inquiry letter to Mr. José Espinosa of the Spanish Tourist Bureau in Madrid, Spain, asking for information about work opportunities in Spain. Explain that you are interested in relocating to Spain after you graduate. To draft the letter, first gather information about both the proper protocol and the format of the letter. With the approval of your instructor, ask an instructor at your college who teaches Spanish (and would understand the form and protocol of such a letter) to comment on the appropriateness of the letter you have drafted.

8. Based on your own experience as a student, write a memo to your instructor on one of the following topics in no more than 30 minutes:

   a. Should student tickets to athletic events on campus be included with the price of tuition?
   b. Should the library add a coffee kiosk in the reserve room?
   c. Should the college offer more Internet-access courses?

   Be sure to cover the points you feel must be included to support your conclusion.

9. You work for Smith Consultants, and your manager has asked you to draft a complaint letter to the software-supply company that developed your new customer-service database—the level of service and technical support to date has not met your manager's expectations. Include the following points:

   a. Telephone calls from your employees to the software help department are often not returned in a timely fashion. Sometimes they are not returned at all.
   b. Software-assistance personnel often blame your hardware for the problem; however, when consulted, the hardware representative reports that the problem is with the software.
   c. Promised monthly four-hour in-service training sessions have not been scheduled for the past three months.

You must also mention that your company is considering not paying the software provider the remaining 30 percent of the purchase amount. However, this is a very delicate matter because Smith Consultants has already invested thousands of dollars in the software system and would like to resolve the problem without losing the investment. Following the principles of business correspondence offered in this chapter, submit your draft in correct business-letter format to your instructor.

10. Explore the templates offered by your word-processing software. Most word-processing packages offer several styles of business-document templates, both contemporary and traditional. (Check your software's "help" menu for "templates.") Use a template for letters offered by your software to format a letter you have composed. Print out the letter and submit it to your instructor with a memo that addresses the following questions:

    a. Why did you choose this particular template?
    b. Did the template make writing your letter easier? Why or why not?
    c. Why might businesses request that their employees use a template when formatting business letters?
    d. What are the drawbacks, if any, of using templates?

ON THE WEB

For more collaborative classroom projects, go to Chapter 8, bedfordstmartins.com/ writingthatworks

■ Collaborative Classroom Projects

1. Divide into small groups (three or four students) and elect a group leader. As a writing team, draft a letter explaining the changes in shipping charges to customers of your wholesale office-supply company.

   For more than five years, your company has been able to offer online customers a flat shipping rate of $5.95 for any order under $300. This has been a strong advertising point for the company. However, profits have fallen steadily in the past two years, so the president of your company has announced that shipping charges will increase in two months. Shipping will be $5.95 for orders under $100 and will increase by $3 for each additional $1 to $100 worth of product.

   Your writing team must inform your existing customers of the change—a difficult task because the customers have been conditioned by your marketing representatives to expect "the industry's most reasonable" shipping charges. The letter should provide the context and explanation of the charges, the bad news, and a goodwill close. Follow the guidelines in this chapter for reference.

2. Imagine that members of your group work as interns for a new local nonprofit organization that works with parents to teach expressive skills to autistic toddlers. The organization has received several financial and automobile donations in response to a recent fund-raising drive, and it needs to send a form letter to donors that thanks them for their generosity and subtly encourages them to give again in the future. Because some donors have asked how they can write off their car donations, the organization has decided to supplement the letter with an information sheet that explains how to deduct noncash contributions from their income taxes. Create a thank-you letter and an information sheet as follows:

    a. For the letter,
       • Create a name and letterhead for the charity.
       • Begin with the donor's inside address and a salutation with the donor's name.
       • Write the letter using a "we" or "I" viewpoint.

- Thank the donor for the contribution to your charity and detail the amount donated.
- Describe the good works of the charity (who is helped by the charity and how).
- Let donors know that because no goods or services were exchanged, the donation is tax-deductible and they should keep this letter for their tax records.
- Provide a contact name and number.
- The director of the charity should sign the letter.

b. For the information sheet, use the following information paraphrased from the IRS Web site. Be sure to organize it logically and attractively (see Chapter 7, Designing Effective Documents and Visuals) and use the "you" viewpoint.

- If a donor claims a deduction on his or her return of over $500 for all contributed property, the donor must attach a Form 8283 (PDF), *Noncash Charitable Contributions*, to the return.
- If a donor claims a total deduction of $5,000 or less for all contributed property, the donor need complete only Section A of Form 8283.
- If a donor claims a deduction of more than $5,000 for an item or a group of similar items, the donor generally needs to complete Section B of Form 8283, which usually requires a qualified appraiser to appraise the vehicle and its value.
- The donor will need to keep records of the donation and substantiate the car's current fair market value. The charity will need to provide written acknowledgment (a description of the car and whether the charity provided any goods or services in exchange, including their value) if the donor is claiming a deduction of $250 or more for the car.

3. Divide into two groups of equal numbers. One group represents the local electric company's consumers, and the other group represents the company's marketing representatives. If you are in the consumer group, write a letter as a team to the utility commissioner asking that the rate increase requested by the electric company not be granted. If you are in the marketing group, write a letter as a team asking the utility commissioner to grant your rate-increase request. Each group has 30 minutes to write the letter, which should address the following issues:

a. Dependability of service of the utility
b. Need for a rate increase
c. Ability of customers to pay for the increase

Trade letters and, during the next 30 minutes, work as a group to write bad-news response letters from the utility commissioner's office. If you are writing to the consumers, break the bad news that the rate increase will be necessary. If you are writing to the electric company's marketing representatives, break the bad news that a rate increase will not be granted. Remember to provide a context, an explanation, the bad news, and a goodwill close when drafting your replies.

Research Projects

1. Imagine that several administrative assistants in your company have been sending sales letters to female customers randomly using *Ms.* and *Mrs.* as titles. Research the history of the title *Ms.* and write a memo to the assistants detailing

ON THE WEB

For extra research projects, go to Chapter 8, bedfordstmartins.com/writingthatworks

when the term was coined and for what reasons, and explaining the conventions they should use when addressing women in their written correspondence.

2. Assume you work for a company that is expanding to include several international branches. Research and write an informal investigative report on cultural differences in workplace communication: slang expressions and technical jargon, methods of addressing people, punctuation marks, colors, references to body parts, physical gestures, technology symbols, cultural symbols, or other aspects of written communication. You may choose one culture to compare to the United States in great detail or more than one culture to compare on different points. Before beginning your research and writing, determine your audience, your purpose, and the scope of your report.

ON THE WEB

For additional Web projects, go to Chapter 8, bedfordstmartins.com/ writingthatworks

▇ Web Projects

1. Search newspaper Web sites for three recent articles about e-mail etiquette. Write a brief analysis in which you compare and contrast the content of the articles. E-mail your analysis to your instructor and include links to the articles analyzed.

2. Imagine that your company is eager to sell its new nonlinear video editing system internationally, starting in Canada, then moving on to Switzerland. Your marketing director, who is very industrious, has already created business cards, brochures, and other marketing materials and planned a public relations campaign that will launch in six weeks. Unfortunately, she did not do enough research into Canadian business practices to know that the country is officially bilingual and the province of Quebec requires that there be a French translation for all promotional materials. You suspect there may be similar issues with the Swiss campaign. Address the situation by doing the following:

   a. Research official language requirements and business etiquette in Canada and Switzerland. A good starting point is Executive Planet at <www.executiveplanet .com/>.
   b. Search the Web for professional translation services and find a rough estimate for the cost of translating an eight-page brochure into French on a rush basis. Find out also what additional translations for the Swiss campaign might cost.
   c. Write a memo that commends the marketing director for working hard on the project but also describes the current translation issue. Being aware of your tone, advise the director of the need to thoroughly research any countries the system will be marketed in before creating final material, and give two or three examples of other issues she may find with regard to doing business in Canada and Switzerland. Advise the director to quickly have the materials translated into French by a professional translating service and describe how much money will be allocated from the marketing department's budget for this service and why (again, be aware of your tone). Conclude your memo with a form of goodwill that encourages the director to be as industrious as she has been, but to also be aware of cultural differences and the impact they can have on companies trying to do business internationally.

9 Writing Business Correspondence

This chapter applies the principles described in Chapter 8 to widely used types of workplace correspondence. Much of this correspondence involves routine information exchanges, but even straightforward communications provide opportunities to benefit you and your recipient. Equally important is correspondence that promotes a positive image of your organization's product or service. Finally, and most challenging, is correspondence that communicates sensitive or negative information.

Voices from the Workplace

Robert Repetto, Novia Associates, Inc.

Robert Repetto is the mechanical engineer for a small New Hampshire company that specializes in creating seismic-restraint and vibration-isolation materials for municipal construction projects. When he designs customized products for Novia's clients, Robert is careful to inform them of any potential problems, usually by e-mail or fax. "Project managers don't want to hear that their cost-saving modifications violate building codes or that an order will be delayed because somebody submitted the wrong specifications. When I have to tell customers something unpleasant, I always try to look at the situation from their point of view. It can be tempting to lay blame or say, 'I told you so,' but it's much more effective to explain what the problem is and focus on how it can be solved. Delivering the bad news in writing keeps the relationship professional and helps to prevent miscommunication, which is important when you're trying to stay on schedule."

Victoria Ravin, Translations.com

Project manager Victoria Ravin oversees the development of translated materials, ranging from textbooks and children's books to Web sites and training videos. Corresponding clearly and concisely is a priority for Victoria, who is responsible for ensuring that her client's material is market-appropriate and culturally sensitive. "Each project is different and there are often multiple parts, so I need to make sure that no step is missed. I do this by being as specific as possible in my e-mail transmittal memos and other correspondence. Most of the linguists are not native English speakers, so it is particularly important for me to make sure that they understand what needs to be done. Whenever the linguists have questions about the projects they're working on, they send me query sheets. I respond by indicating clearly what directions I'd like them to take."

◆ *For advice on selecting the form (or medium) most appropriate for your purpose and audience, see pages 263–267.*

◆ *For information on formatting letters and memos, see pages 267–289 in Chapter 8, Understanding the Principles of Business Communication.*

◆ *For advice on proposal cover letters and a sample, see pages 454 and 456 in Chapter 13, Writing Proposals.*

■ Routine and Positive Messages

The types of correspondence discussed in this section provide the opportunity to build goodwill with readers and create a positive image of your organization.

Covers (or Transmittals)

When you send a formal report, proposal, brochure, or similar material, you should include a short message, often called a cover (or transmittal) letter, that identifies what you are sending. An e-mail message used to send an electronic attachment also serves this purpose, as does a memo sent within an organization. The cover message also provides you with a record of when and to whom you sent the material.

Keep your remarks brief. Your opening should explain what is being sent and why. A cover letter that accompanies a report, for example, may identify its title, briefly describe its contents, state its purpose, and note who requested the report. In an optional second paragraph, you might summarize the information or point out any sections of particular interest to the reader. This paragraph could mention the conditions under which the material was prepared, such as limitations of time or budget. Your closing paragraph should contain acknowledgments, offer more assistance, or express the hope that the material will fulfill its purpose. If your letter accompanies a proposal, you could mention a key point or two as to why your firm is the best one to do the job.

Figure 9–1 is an example of a cover letter that is brief and to the point. Figure 9–2 shows a cover letter that is a bit more detailed, touching on the manner in which the information was gathered.

ECOLOGY SYSTEMS AND SERVICES

39 Beacon Street, Boston, Massachusetts 02106
(617) 351-1223 • Fax: (617) 351-2121
ecologysystems.com

May 24, 2006

Mario Espinoza, Chief Engineer
Louisiana Chemical Products
3452 River View Road
Baton Rouge, LA 70893

Dear Mr. Espinoza:

Enclosed is the final report on our installation of pollution-control equipment at Eastern Chemical Company, which we send with Eastern's permission. Please call me (ext. 1206) or e-mail me at the address below if I can answer any questions.

*Identification
of enclosure*

Offer of assistance

Sincerely,

Susan Wong

Susan Wong, Ph.D.
Technical Services Manager
swong@ecologysystems.com

SW/ls
Enclosure: Report

Figure 9–1 Brief Cover Letter (for a Report)

WATERFORD PAPER PRODUCTS
P.O. Box 413
WATERFORD, WI 53474

Phone: (414) 738-2191 • Fax: (414) 738-9122
waterfordpaper.com

January 16, 2007

Mr. Roger Hammersmith
Ecology Systems, Inc.
1015 Clarke Street
Chicago, IL 60615

Dear Mr. Hammersmith:

Identification of enclosure

Enclosed is the report estimating our power consumption for the year, as requested by John Brenan, Vice President, on September 5.

Background and purpose of report

The report is a result of several meetings with the manager of plant operations and her staff and an extensive survey of all our employees, delayed by the transfer of key staff in Building A. We believe, however, that the report will provide the information you need to furnish us with a cost estimate for the installation of your Mark II Energy Saving System.

Acknowledgment of help

We would like to thank Diana Biel of ESI for her assistance in preparing the survey. If you need any more information, please let me know.

Sincerely,

James G. Evans
New Projects Office
jge@waterfordpaper.com

Enclosure

Figure 9–2   Cover Letter (with Background Information)

Acknowledgments

One way to build goodwill with colleagues and clients is to let them know that you have received something they sent and to express thanks. A letter, an e-mail message, or a memo that serves these functions is usually a short, polite note. The example shown in Figure 9–3 is typical and could be sent as a letter or an e-mail message.

From: Wilbur Kohn <kohn@kohns.com>
To: Marsha Stein <stein39@macrofoods.com>
Sent: Friday, February 23, 2007 5:52 PM
Subject: Checkout Lane Reporting System

Dear Ms. Stein:

I received your comprehensive report today. When I finish studying it in detail, I'll send you our cost estimate for the installation of the Checkout Lane Reporting System.

    Acknowledgment

Thank you for preparing such a thorough analysis.

    Thanks to writer

Regards,

Wilbur Kohn

Figure 9–3   Acknowledgment Letter (Sent as an E-mail Message)

Inquiries

An inquiry letter or e-mail message can be as simple as a request for a free brochure or as complex as asking a consultant to define specific requirements for a usability testing lab.

◆ *For job applications, another type of inquiry letter, see Chapter 16, Finding the Right Job.*

    The two broad categories of inquiries include those that benefit the recipient and those that benefit the writer. Inquiries of obvious benefit to the recipient include requests for information about a recently advertised product. Inquiries that primarily benefit the writer include, for example, a request to a professional association to send demographic information about its members. If your inquiry is of the second kind, be particularly considerate of your reader's needs. Your objective will probably be to obtain, within a reasonable time, answers to specific questions. You will be more likely to receive a prompt, helpful reply if you follow the guidelines listed in Considering Audience and Purpose: Writing Inquiries on page 318 and illustrated in Figure 9–4.

Reason for request

> **From:** Kathryn J. Parsons <kjparsons@udayton.edu>
> **To:** Jane E. Metcalf <metcalf@mvpc.org>
> **Sent:** 16 March 2007 09:23:45 -0500 (EST)
> **Subject:** Inquiry on Heating Systems
>
> Dear Ms. Metcalf:
>
> Could you please send me some information on heating systems for a computer-Ized, energy-efficient house that a team of engineering students at the University of Dayton is designing?
>
> The house, which contains 2,000 square feet of living space (17,600 cubic feet), meets all the requirements in your brochure "Insulating for Efficiency." We need the following information, based on the southern Ohio climate:
>
> 1. The proper-size heat pump for such a home
> 2. The wattage of the supplemental electrical heating units required
> 3. The estimated power consumption and rates for those units for one year
>
> We will be happy to send you our preliminary design report. If you have questions or suggestions, please contact me at kjparsons@udayton.edu or call 513-229-4598.
>
> Thank you for your help.
>
> Kathryn Parsons

List of questions

Offer to share results and contact information

Figure 9–4   Inquiry (Sent as an E-mail Message)

➤ CONSIDERING AUDIENCE AND PURPOSE
Writing Inquiries

- Make your questions specific, clear, and concise.
- Phrase your questions so that the reader will know immediately the type of information you are seeking, why you need it, and how you will use it.
- If possible, present your questions in a numbered list to make it easy for your reader to address them.
- Keep the number of questions to a minimum.
- Offer some inducement for the reader to respond, such as promising to share the results of what you are doing.
- Promise to keep responses confidential, if appropriate.
- Close by thanking the reader for taking the time to respond. Provide contact information, such as a phone number or an e-mail address, to simplify a reply.

Responses to Inquiries

When you receive an inquiry, read it quickly to determine whether you have both the information and the authority to respond. If you do, reply as promptly as you can, answering every question asked. Adjust the length of your response to the questions and the information provided by the writer. Even if the writer has asked a question that seems silly or has what you feel is an obvious answer, respond courteously and as completely as you can. You may tactfully point out that the writer has omitted or misunderstood something.

If you feel you cannot answer an inquiry, find out who can and forward the inquiry to that person. Notify the writer that you have forwarded the inquiry, as shown in Figure 9–5. If you reply to a forwarded inquiry, state in the first paragraph why someone else is answering, as shown in Figure 9–6.

Sales and Promotions

A sales letter or promotional message requires a thorough understanding of the product, service, or business and the potential customer's needs. For this reason, many businesses (such as major retailers) employ specialists to compose their sales letters and other promotional material. However, if you work in a small business or are self-employed, you may need to write sales letters yourself. An effective

---

Subject: **Report Received**
Date: Fri, 21 March 2007 11:42:25 -0500 (EST)
From: Jane E. Metcalf <metcalf@mvpc.org>
To: Kathryn J. Parsons <kjparsons@udayton.edu>

Dear Kathryn Parsons:

Thank you for inquiring about the heating system we recommend for homes designed according to the specifications in our brochure "Insulating for Efficiency." *(Acknowledgment of inquiry)*

Because I cannot answer your specific questions, I have forwarded your inquiry to Michael Wang, Engineering Assistant in our Development Group. He should be able to answer your questions, and you should hear from him shortly. *(Notification of forwarding)*

Best wishes,

Jane E. Metcalf

==================================
Jane E. Metcalf, Director of Public Information
Miami Valley Power Company
P.O. Box 1444 ~ Miamitown, OH 45733
Office 513-264-4800 ~ Fax 513-264-4889
Web ~ mvpc.org
==================================

Figure 9–5   Acknowledgment of an Inquiry (Indicating That the Request Has Been Forwarded)

From: Michael Wang <mwang@mvpc.org>
To: Kathryn J. Parsons <kjparsons@udayton.edu>
Sent: 28 March 2007 16:09:22 -0500 (EST)
Subject: RE: Inquiry on Heating Systems

Dear Ms. Parsons:

Acknowledgment of inquiry

Jane Metcalf forwarded to me your inquiry of March 16 about the house that your engineering team is designing. I can estimate the heating requirements of a typical home of 17,600 cubic feet as follows:

Responses to list of questions

1. For such a home, we would generally recommend a heat pump capable of delivering 40,000 BTUs, such as our model AL-42 (17 kilowatts).
2. With the AL-42's efficiency, you don't need supplemental heating units.
3. Depending on usage, the AL-42 unit averages between 1,000 and 1,500 kilowatt-hours from December through March. To determine the current rate for such usage, check with Dayton Power and Light Company.

Offer of further help

I can give you an answer that would apply specifically to your house based on its particular design (such as number of stories, windows, and entrances). If you send me more details, I will be happy to provide more precise figures for your interesting project.

Sincerely,

Michael Wang

Engineering Assistant
mwang@mvpc.org

Figure 9–6 **Response to an Inquiry (Sent as an E-mail Message)**

sales message accomplishes the goals described in the Writing Effective Sales Messages checklist on page 321.

Your first task is to identify your audience: those who should receive your letter or other material. If you do not select your recipients carefully, your message will likely be dismissed as junk mail or spam (if sent by e-mail). Appropriate recipients may include existing customers, people who have purchased a product or service from you and may do so again. You also might want to seek new customers who may be interested in certain products or services. Companies that specialize in marketing techniques compile and sell such lists of members of professional, fraternal, and religious organizations, trade-show attendees, and the like. Because these lists tend to be expensive, select them with care.

Once you decide who should receive your sales letter, learn as much as you can about their age, sex, vocation, geographical location, educational level, financial status, and interests. You must be aware of your readers' needs so that you can effectively tell them how your product or service will satisfy those needs.

Analyze your product or service carefully to determine your strongest psychological sales points—the product's intangible benefits rather than its physical features—and build your sales letter around those points. Begin by identifying how your product or service will make your reader's job easier, status higher, personal life more pleasant, and so on. Then in the body of the letter, show how your product or service can satisfy the need or desire identified in your opening. Describe the physical features of your product in terms of their benefit to your reader. Help your reader imagine using your product or service—and enjoying its benefits.

If the price of your product or service is especially competitive, you may decide to emphasize the cost. However, if your product or service is relatively costly (even if priced competitively), you may be able to emphasize its high quality, reliability, or special benefits. If you feel a need to minimize the negative effect of price, you might state the cost in terms of a unit rather than a set ($20 per item instead of $600 per set); identify the daily, the monthly, or even the yearly cost based on the estimated life of the product; suggest a series of payments rather than the total; or compare the cost with that of something the reader accepts readily ("costs the same as a movie and a dinner out").

ETHICS NOTE

Be certain that any claim you make in a sales message is valid. Mail fraud carries heavy legal penalties. If you say that a product is safe, for example, you could be guaranteeing its absolute safety; therefore, say the product is safe "provided that normal safety precautions are taken." Further, do not exaggerate or speak negatively about a competitor. For further ethical and legal guidelines, visit the Direct Marketing Association at <www.the-dma.org>. See also the ethics note on page 104 in Chapter 4, Revising the Draft.

Figure 9–7 shows a typical sales letter. Notice its light, friendly tone—an approach frequently used by small, local businesses to make the reader feel comfortable about coming to them. The signature line of sales letters often shows the name of the company rather than the name of an individual, as is the case in this example. The e-mailed sales message in Figure 9–8 also uses an informal but professional tone, appealing to the readers' interests while instilling confidence in the company's ability to provide timely information.

WRITER'S CHECKLIST
Writing Effective Sales Messages

- ☑ Develop your letter to accomplish three basic goals.
  - – Open by attracting your reader's attention and arousing his or her interest.
  - – Describe features of the product or service that would appeal strongly to your reader's wants or needs.
  - – Suggest ways that the reader can immediately use the product or service.
- ☑ If sending an e-mail message, create a subject line that encourages recipients to read the message ("Special Offer When You Respond to This Message").

(continued)

WRITER'S CHECKLIST (continued)

☑ Be certain that any claim you make in a sales letter is truthful, not an overstatement.

☑ Present evidence to convince your reader that your product or service is everything you claim it to be. Don't exaggerate, make unreasonable claims, speak negatively of a competitor, or use other unfair tactics. You can build confidence with a money-back guarantee, a free trial offer, testimonials, or case histories.

☑ Make the customer's response easy and worthwhile. You might include a map to your store, a discount coupon, instructions for phone-in orders and free delivery, or a Web address for more information, special discounts, and online orders.

Janice's Cycle Shop
775 First Avenue, Ottumwa, IA 52501
(515) 273-5111 • fax (515) 273-5511

April 5, 2007

janicecycle.com

Mr. Raymond Sommers
350 College Place
Sharpsville, IA 52156

Dear Mr. Sommers:

Needs of reader   Are you ready to go bike riding this spring — but your bike isn't?

Benefits of service   Janice's Cycle Shop will get your bike in shape for the beautiful days ahead. We will lubricate all moving parts; check the tires, brakes, chain, lights, horn, and other accessories; and make any minor repairs — all for only $29.95 with the coupon enclosed with this letter.

Convenience of service   Just stop in any day, Monday through Saturday, between 8:00 a.m. and 9:00 p.m. We are conveniently located at the corner of First and Walker. If you bring your bike in before 10:00 a.m., you can enjoy a spring bike ride that evening.

Happy riding!

Janice's Cycle Shop

Figure 9–7   Sales Letter

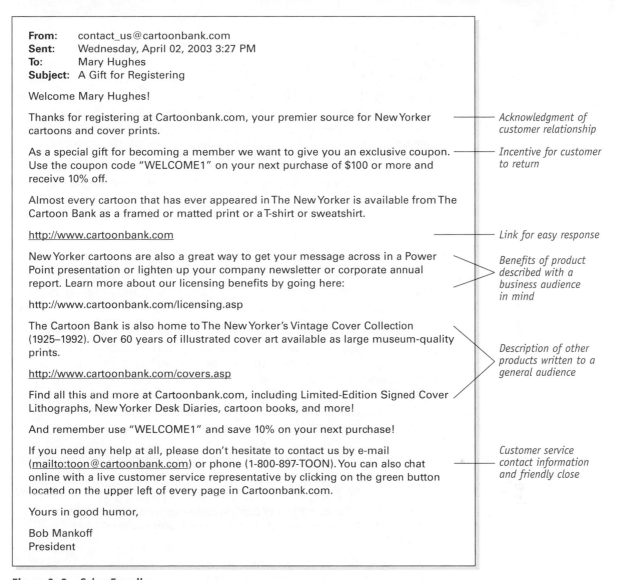

From: contact_us@cartoonbank.com
Sent: Wednesday, April 02, 2003 3:27 PM
To: Mary Hughes
Subject: A Gift for Registering

Welcome Mary Hughes!

Thanks for registering at Cartoonbank.com, your premier source for New Yorker cartoons and cover prints. — *Acknowledgment of customer relationship*

As a special gift for becoming a member we want to give you an exclusive coupon. Use the coupon code "WELCOME1" on your next purchase of $100 or more and receive 10% off. — *Incentive for customer to return*

Almost every cartoon that has ever appeared in The New Yorker is available from The Cartoon Bank as a framed or matted print or a T-shirt or sweatshirt.

http://www.cartoonbank.com — *Link for easy response*

New Yorker cartoons are also a great way to get your message across in a Power Point presentation or lighten up your company newsletter or corporate annual report. Learn more about our licensing benefits by going here: — *Benefits of product described with a business audience in mind*

http://www.cartoonbank.com/licensing.asp

The Cartoon Bank is also home to The New Yorker's Vintage Cover Collection (1925–1992). Over 60 years of illustrated cover art available as large museum-quality prints. — *Description of other products written to a general audience*

http://www.cartoonbank.com/covers.asp

Find all this and more at Cartoonbank.com, including Limited-Edition Signed Cover Lithographs, New Yorker Desk Diaries, cartoon books, and more!

And remember use "WELCOME1" and save 10% on your next purchase!

If you need any help at all, please don't hesitate to contact us by e-mail (mailto:toon@cartoonbank.com) or phone (1-800-897-TOON). You can also chat online with a live customer service representative by clicking on the green button located on the upper left of every page in Cartoonbank.com. — *Customer service contact information and friendly close*

Yours in good humor,

Bob Mankoff
President

Figure 9–8   Sales E-mail

■ Sensitive and Negative Messages

Writing sensitive or negative messages requires careful thought. You must decide, for example, how direct or indirect your message should be and then choose words that maintain a professional relationship with a correspondent despite any difficult circumstances.

◆ *See also Negative Messages and the Indirect Pattern on pages 271–272, Goodwill and the "You" Viewpoint on pages 267–269, and Sending a Resignation Letter on pages 580–582.*

Refusals

When you receive a request to which you must give a negative reply, you may need to write a refusal message containing bad news—something that a reader does not want to receive. Unless the stakes are very low, opening with the bad news can affect your reader negatively. The ideal refusal says *no* in such a way that you avoid antagonizing your reader while managing to maintain goodwill. To do so, you must convince your reader that the reasons for refusing are logical or understandable before you present the bad news. The following pattern effectively deals with this problem:

1. *Context.* In the opening (often called a "buffer"), introduce the subject and establish a professional tone.
2. *Explanation.* Review the facts that lead logically to the bad news, but try to see things from your reader's point of view.
3. *Bad news.* State your refusal, based on the facts, concisely and without apology.
4. *Goodwill.* In the closing, establish or reestablish a positive relationship by providing an option, assure the reader of your high opinion of his or her product or service, offer a friendly remark, or merely wish the reader success.

In the case of a rejected proposal, such as that in Figure 9–9, express appropriate and genuine appreciation for the reader's time, effort, and interest. Thoroughly detail the reasons for the refusal with the goal of convincing the reader that the conclusion is reasonable. State the negative message concisely, clearly, and as positively as possible. Close by working to reestablish goodwill and avoid rehashing the bad news (not writing "Again, we're sorry we can't use your idea").

Refusals often vary with what is at stake for the writer or the reader. The refusal in Figure 9–10 declines an invitation to speak, and the stakes for the writer are relatively low; however, the writer wishes to acknowledge the honor of being asked. Figure 9–11 shows a letter rejecting a job applicant in which the stakes are higher. Finally, Figure 9–12 shows a refusal sent to a supplier whose product was not selected, yet the writer wishes to maintain a harmonious relationship.

◆ *For advice about writing resignation and job refusal letters, see Chapter 16, Finding the Right Job.*

Complaints

By the time you need to write a complaint letter (sometimes called a "claim letter"), you may be irritated and angry. If you write a letter that reflects only your annoyance and anger, you may simply seem petty and irrational. As a result, the best complaint letters—the ones taken seriously—do not sound complaining. Remember, too, that the person who receives your complaint may not be the one who was directly responsible for the situation. An effective letter should assume that the recipient will conscientiously correct the problem. Although the circumstances and severity of the problem may vary, effective complaint letters (or e-mails) should generally follow this pattern:

1. Identify the problem or faulty item(s) and include relevant information such as invoice numbers, part names, and dates, as well as a copy of the receipt, bill, or contract.

2. Explain logically, clearly, and specifically what went wrong—especially for a problem with a service. (Avoid speculating about why you think a problem occurred.)

3. State what you expect the reader to do to solve the problem to your satisfaction.

Memo

To: Darrell Munro
From: Amelia Jackson, Screening Procedures Committee   *AJ*
Date: May 17, 2006
Subject: Response to Proposed Security-Clearance Procedures

The Screening Procedures Committee appreciates the time and effort you spent on your proposal for a new security-clearance procedure.

Context and thanks

We reviewed the potential effects of implementing your proposed security-clearance procedure on a company-wide basis. We asked the Systems and Procedures Department to review the data, survey industry practices, seek the views of senior management and department heads, and submit the idea to our legal staff. As a result of this process, we have reached the following conclusions:

Explanation with logical reasons

- The cost savings you project are correct only if the procedure could be universally required.
- The components of your procedure are legal, but most are not widely accepted by our industry.
- Based on our survey, some components could alienate employees who would perceive them as violating an individual's rights.
- Enforcing company-wide use would prove costly and impractical.

For these reasons, the committee recommends that divisions continue their current security screening procedures.

Refusal

However, some components of your procedure may apply in certain circumstances. As a result, the editor of *The Guardian* would like to feature your ideas in the next issue. She will contact you to discuss your ideas next week. On behalf of the committee, thank you for the thoughtful proposal.

Goodwill closing with option

Figure 9–9   Memo Rejecting an Internal Proposal

Positive context

Review of facts and refusal

Goodwill closing with option

From: Ralph Morgan <rpmorgan@wec.com>
To: Javier Lopez <jlopez@tnco.com>
Date: Wednesday, March 29, 2007
Subject: Speaking Invitation

Dear Mr. Lopez:

I am honored to have been invited to address your regional meeting in St. Louis on May 17. That you would consider me as a potential contributor to such a gathering of experts is indeed flattering.

On checking my schedule, I find that I will be attending the annual meeting of our parent corporation's Board of Directors on that date. Therefore, as much as I would enjoy addressing your members, I must decline.

I have been very favorably impressed over the years with your organization's contributions to the engineering profession, and I would welcome the opportunity to participate in a future meeting.

Sincerely,

Ralph P. Morgan

================================
Ralph P. Morgan
Research Director
Watashaw Engineering Company
301 Industrial Lane
Decatur, IL 62525
Phone: (708) 222-3700
Fax: (708) 222-3707
wec.com
================================

Figure 9–10   E-mail Refusing a Speaking Invitation

To reach someone who can help you in a large organization, first check its Web site or call its main office so that you can address your letter to the appropriate department (often Customer Service, Consumer Affairs, or Adjustments). In smaller organizations, you might write to a vice president in charge of sales or service. For very small businesses, write directly to the owner. As a last resort, you may find that sending copies of a complaint letter to more than one person in the company will get fast results. Each employee who receives the letter will know (because of the notation at the bottom of the page) that others, possibly higher in the organization, have received the letter and will take note of whether the problem is solved. Figure 9–13 shows a typical complaint letter.

Liberty Associates
3553 West Marshall Road
San Diego, California 92101

Phone (619) 555-1001
Fax (619) 555-0110
libertyassociates.com

January 19, 2007

Ms. Sonja Yadgar
2289 South 63rd Street
Hartford, CT 06101

Dear Ms. Yadgar:

Thank you for your interest in financial counseling at Liberty Associates. I respect your investment experience and professionalism, and I enjoyed our conversation.

Positive context

Shortly after our meeting, an especially appropriate, well-qualified internal candidate applied for the position, and we have decided to offer the job to that individual. I say in all honesty that the decision was very difficult. Both Nancy Linh and I were impressed with your qualifications and believe that you have a great deal to offer our profession.

Review of facts and refusal

Please do stay in touch. Best wishes for the future.

Goodwill closing

Sincerely,

Meike Künkel
Vice President
Director of Development

Figure 9–11 Letter Rejecting a Job Applicant

MARTINI BANKING AND DATA SYSTEMS

251 West 57th Street
New York, New York 10019
Phone (212) 555-1221   Fax (212) 555-2112
martinisystems.com

February 11, 2007

Mr. Henry Coleman
Abbott Office Products, Inc.
P.O. Box 544
Detroit, MI 48206

Dear Mr. Coleman:

Positive context

Thank you for your cooperation and your patience with us as we struggled to reach a decision. We believe our long involvement with your company indicates our confidence in your products.

Review of facts and refusal

Based on our research, we found that the Winton Check Sorter has all the features that your sorter offers and, in fact, has two additional features that your sorter does not. The more important one is a backup feature that retains totals in its memory, even if the power fails. The second additional feature is stacked pockets, which are less space-consuming than the linear pockets on your sorter. After much deliberation, therefore, we have decided to purchase the Winton Check Sorter.

Goodwill closing

Although we did not select your sorter, we were very favorably impressed with your system and your people. Perhaps we will be able to use other Abbott products in the future.

Sincerely,

Muriel Johnson

Muriel Johansen
Business Manager

Figure 9–12   Letter Rejecting a Sales Proposal

BAKER HEALTHCARE SYSTEMS

Purchasing Department
501 Main Street
Springfield, OH 45321
(513) 683-8100
Fax (513) 683-8000

September 22, 2007

Manager, Customer Relations
Medical Solutions, Inc.
521 West 23rd Street
New York, NY 10011

Subject: ST3 Diagnostic Scanners

On July 10, I ordered nine ST3 Diagnostic Scanners (order # ST3-1179R). The scanners were ordered from your customer Web site.

On August 2, I received from your Newark, New Jersey, parts warehouse seven HL monitors. I immediately returned these monitors with a note indicating the mistake that had been made. However, not only have I failed to receive the ST3 scanners I ordered, but I have also been billed repeatedly.

Explanation of error

I have enclosed a copy of my confirmation e-mail, the shipping form, and the most recent bill. If you cannot send me the scanners I ordered by November 1, please cancel my order.

Enclosures substantiating complaint

Request for solution

Sincerely,

Paul Denlinger
Manager
pld@baker.org

Enclosures

www.baker.org

Figure 9–13   Complaint Letter

Adjustments

An adjustment letter responds to a complaint and tells the customer what your company intends to do about the problem. You should settle such matters quickly and courteously, always trying to satisfy the customer at a reasonable cost to your company. An effective adjustment letter actually builds goodwill as it both repairs any damage that has been done and restores the customer's confidence in your company.

Open your letter with what the reader will consider good news.

- Grant the adjustment, if appropriate, for uncomplicated situations ("Enclosed is a replacement for the damaged part").

- Reveal that you intend to grant the adjustment by admitting that the customer was right ("Yes, you were incorrectly billed for the delivery"). Then explain the specific details of the adjustment. This method is good for adjustments that require detailed explanations.

- Apologize for the error ("Please accept our apologies for not acting sooner to correct your account"). This method is effective when the customer's inconvenience is as much an issue as money.

- Use a combination of these techniques. Often, situations that require an adjustment also require flexibility.

The tone of your correspondence is critical. Grant adjustments graciously; a settlement made grudgingly will do more harm than good. No matter how unreasonable the complaint, your response should be positive and respectful, focusing not on the unfortunate situation but on what you are doing to correct it. Not only must you be gracious, you must also acknowledge the error in such a way that the customer or client will not lose confidence in your organization. Before granting an adjustment to a claim for which your company is at fault, as illustrated in Figure 9–14, you must determine what happened and what you can do to satisfy the customer. Be certain that you are familiar with your company's adjustment policy. In addition, be careful about your wording; for example, "we have just received your letter of May 7 about our defective product" could be ruled in a court of law as an admission that the product is, in fact, defective. Treat every claim individually, and lean toward giving the customer the benefit of the doubt.

Sometimes you may decide to grant a partial adjustment to regain the customer's lost goodwill, even though the claim is not really justified, as in Figure 9–15.

You also might need to educate your reader about the use of your product or service. Customers sometimes submit unjustified claims honestly believing them to be fair (for example, a problem resulting from a customer not following maintenance instructions properly). You would grant such a claim only to build goodwill. When you write a letter of adjustment in such a situation, give the explanation before granting the claim—otherwise, your reader may never get to the explanation. If your explanation establishes customer responsibility, do so tactfully, as Figure 9–16 illustrates.

ON THE WEB

For additional examples of adjustment letters, go to bedfordstmartins.com/writingthatworks and select *Model Documents Gallery*.

International Hotels

EXECUTIVE OFFICE

September 26, 2007

Ms. Elizabeth Shapiro
2374 N. Kenwood Ave.
Fresno, CA 93650

Dear Ms. Shapiro:

We are sorry that you and your husband's stay with us did not go smoothly. *Gracious tone*
Providing dependable service is what's expected of us—and when our staff
doesn't provide high-quality service, it's easy to understand our guests' disap-
pointment. I truly wish we had performed better and that your vacation plans
had not been disrupted.

We are eager to restore your confidence in our ability to provide dependable, *Adjustment*
high-quality service. Please accept the enclosed certificate for one weekend's
stay at any of our 500 hotels worldwide. I hope we will have the pleasure of
welcoming you and your husband again soon.

Ms. Shapiro, in addition, we appreciate your taking the time to write. It helps *Positive closing*
to receive comments such as yours, and we conscientiously follow through
to be sure proper procedures are met. I assure you your letter is being put to
good use.

Yours truly,

M. J. Matthews

Ms. M. J. Matthews
Executive Office

Enclosure: Certificate

10113 Executive Drive/Chicago, Illinois 60601
800-964-9400   interhotel.com

Figure 9–14   Adjustment Letter (Company Takes Responsibility)

Computer Solutions, Inc.
521 West 23rd Street
New York, NY 10011

Customer Relations
Phone (212) 574-3894
Fax (212) 574-3899
ssiegel@compsol.com

September 28, 2006

Mr. Fred J. Swesky
7811 Ranchero Drive
Tucson, AZ 85761

Dear Mr. Swesky:

Thank you for your letter regarding the replacement of your CS5 Notebook Computer.

Explanation of customer responsibility

You said in your letter that you used the unit on an open deck. As our service representative pointed out, this model is not designed to operate in extreme heat. As the instruction manual accompanying your new CS5 states, such exposure can produce irreparable damage. Because your unit was used in such extreme heat conditions, we cannot honor the warranty.

Partial adjustment

However, we are enclosing a certificate entitling you to a trade-in allowance equal to your local CSI dealer's markup for the unit. This means you can purchase a new unit at wholesale, provided you return your original unit to your local dealer.

Sincerely yours,

Susan Siegel

Susan Siegel
Assistant Director

SS/mr
Enclosure

Figure 9–15   Partial Adjustment Letter (Customer Is Responsible)

9025 North Main Street
Butte, MT 59702

Phone (800) 233-5656
Fax (800) 233-3010

August 26, 2007

Mr. Carlos Ortiz
638 McSwaney Drive
Butte, MT 59702

Dear Mr. Ortiz:

Enclosed is your SWELCO Coffeemaker, which you sent to us on August 17.

In various parts of the country, tap water may have a high mineral content. If you fill your SWELCO Coffeemaker with water for breakfast coffee before going to bed, a mineral scale will build up on the inner wall of the water tube—as explained on page 2 of your SWELCO Instruction Booklet.

Education of customer

We have removed the mineral scale from the water tube of your coffeemaker and thoroughly cleaned the entire unit. To ensure the best service from your coffeemaker in the future, clean it once a month by operating it with four ounces of white vinegar and eight cups of water. To rinse out the vinegar taste, operate the unit twice with clear water.

Adjustment and instruction

With proper care, your SWELCO Coffeemaker will serve you faithfully and well for many years to come.

Positive closing

Sincerely,

Helen Upham

Helen Upham
Customer Services

HU/mo
Enclosure

swelco.com

Figure 9–16   Educational Adjustment Letter

WRITER'S CHECKLIST
Writing Tactful Adjustment Letters

☑ Address your reader respectfully, whether you apologize, explain, educate, or offer an adjustment.

☑ Explain what caused the problem if such an explanation will help restore your reader's confidence or goodwill.

☑ Explain specifically how you intend to make the adjustment if it is not obvious in your opening.

☑ Express appreciation to the customer for calling your attention to the situation, explaining that this helps your firm keep the quality of its product or service high.

☑ Point out any steps you may be taking to prevent a recurrence of whatever went wrong, giving the customer as much credit as the facts allow.

☑ Avoid recalling the problem in your closing ("Again, we apologize . . ."). Close positively, looking forward, not back.

Collections

Collection letters serve two purposes: (1) to collect the overdue bill and (2) to preserve the customer relationship. In some states, collection letters should be prepared by attorneys because certain language and requirements must be followed to demand payment. However, even if you never need to write a collection letter, understanding the principles behind such letters offers important insights into the strategies of sensitive correspondence.

Most companies use a series of collection letters in which the letters become increasingly demanding and urgent. The series usually proceeds in three stages, each of which may include several letters as well as follow-up phone calls. All letters should be courteous and show a genuine interest in the customer and whatever problems may be preventing prompt payment. The first stage consists of reminders stamped on the invoice ("overdue"), form letters, or brief personal notes. These early reminders should maintain a friendly tone that emphasizes the customer's good credit record. They should remind the customer of the debt and may even solicit more business by including promotional material for new items. As in the example in Figure 9–17, you might suggest that nonpayment may be a result of a simple error or oversight.

In the second stage, the collection letters are more than just reminders. You now assume that some circumstances are preventing payment. Ask directly for payment, and inquire about possible problems, perhaps inviting the customer to discuss the matter with you. You might suggest an optional installment payment plan if you are able to offer one. Mention the importance of good credit, appealing to the customer's pride, self-esteem, and sense of fairness. Remind the customer that he or she has always received good value from you. Make it easy to respond with a return envelope, a toll-free telephone or fax number, or a Web address where the payment can be made. At this stage, your tone should be firmer and more direct than in the early stage, but it should never be rude, sarcastic, or threatening. Notice how the second-stage letter shown in Figure 9–18 is more direct than the first-stage letter but no less polite.

ABBOTT OFFICE PRODUCTS, INC.

P.O. Box 544
Detroit, MI 48206
Phone (313) 567-1221
Fax (313) 567-2112
abbott.com

August 28, 2006

Mr. Thomas Holland
Walk Softly Shoes
1661 East Madison Boulevard
Garfield, AL 36613

Dear Mr. Holland:

With the new school year about to begin, your shoe store must be busier
than ever as students purchase their back-to-school footwear. Perhaps in
the rush of business you've overlooked paying your account of $1,200,
which is now 60 days overdue.

Enclosed is our fall sales list. When you send in your check for your outstanding account, why not send in your next order and take advantage
of these special prices.

Sincerely,

Henry Bliss

Henry Bliss
Sales Manager
hb@abbott.com

Tactful reminder

*Enclosure seeks
future business*

Figure 9–17   First-Stage Collection Letter

Third-stage collection letters reflect a sense of urgency, for the customer has
not responded to your previous letters. Although your tone should remain courteous, make your demand for payment explicit. Point out how reasonable you have
been, and urge the customer to pay at once to avoid legal action. Again, make it
easy to respond by providing a return envelope, a toll-free telephone or fax number, or a Web address, as shown in Figure 9–19.

ABBOTT OFFICE PRODUCTS, INC.

P.O. Box 544
Detroit, MI 48206
Phone (313) 567-1221
Fax (313) 567-2112
abbott.com

November 6, 2006

Mr. Thomas Holland
Walk Softly Shoes
1661 East Madison Boulevard
Garfield, AL 36613

Dear Mr. Holland:

Inquiry about problems   We are concerned that we have not heard from you about your overdue account of $1,200 even though we have written three times in the past 90 days. Because you have always been one of our best customers, we have to wonder if some special circumstances have caused the delay. If so, please feel free to discuss the matter with us.

Direct request   By sending us a check today, you can preserve your excellent credit record. Because you have always paid your account promptly, we are sure that you will want to settle this balance now. If your balance is more than you can pay at present, we will be happy to work out mutually satisfactory payment arrangements.

Options for response   Please use the enclosed envelope to send in your check, or call (800) 526-1945, toll-free, to discuss your account.

Sincerely,

Henry Bliss

Henry Bliss
Sales Manager
hb@abbott.com

Figure 9–18   Second-Stage Collection Letter

ABBOTT OFFICE PRODUCTS, INC.

P.O. Box 544
Detroit, MI 48206
Phone (313) 567-1221
Fax (313) 567-2112
abbott.com

December 28, 2006

Mr. Thomas Holland
Walk Softly Shoes
1661 East Madison Boulevard
Garfield, AL 36613

Dear Mr. Holland:

Your account in the amount of $1,200 is now 180 days overdue. You have already received a generous extension of time and, in fairness to our other customers, we cannot permit a further delay in payment.   *Urgent request*

Because you have not responded to any of our letters, we will be forced to turn your account over to our attorney for collection if we do not receive payment immediately. Such action, of course, will damage your previously fine credit rating.   *Explicit demand*

Why not avoid this unpleasant situation by sending your check in the enclosed return envelope within 10 days or by calling (800) 526–1945 to discuss payment.   *Options for response*

Sincerely,

Henry Bliss

Henry Bliss
Sales Manager
hb@abbott.com

Figure 9–19   Third-Stage Collection Letter

CHAPTER 9 SUMMARY: WRITING BUSINESS CORRESPONDENCE

Routine and Positive Messages

- *Cover* (or *transmittal*) messages accompany material sent to a recipient, identify what is being sent, and explain why it is being sent.

- *Acknowledgments* build goodwill with colleagues and clients by confirming the arrival of something they sent and expressing thanks.

- *Inquiries and responses* state clearly the information wanted, who wants it, and why. Answer inquiries by responding to all the questions or forwarding the inquiry to someone who can.

- *Sales and promotions* attract the reader's attention to a product, service, or business by arousing interest, emphasizing benefits, and inviting a response.

Sensitive and Negative Messages

- *Refusals* deny requests or give negative replies while working to maintain goodwill.

- *Complaints* use a professional tone to describe a problem and how you expect it to be corrected to your satisfaction.

- *Adjustments* tell customers how your company intends to redress a complaint and apologize if the company is at fault.

- *Collections* work to preserve the customer relationship while collecting payment on an overdue account.

ON THE WEB

For an online quiz on writing business correspondence, go to Chapter 9, bedfordstmartins.com/ writingthatworks

---

ON THE WEB

For additional exercises, go to Chapter 9, bedfordstmartins.com/ writingthatworks

■ Exercises

1. Write a cover letter for a report or a term paper that you are preparing for another course. Address your letter to the appropriate instructor.

2. The following situations require different types of correspondence. Read *a* through *e*, and then write the letters, memos, or e-mail messages assigned by your instructor, using the proper format for each.

   a. You are writing a letter requesting a free booklet that explains how college students can apply for scholarships to study abroad. Address the letter to Nancy Reibold, the executive director of the Global Initiative Center at 1012 Third Avenue, New York, NY 10021. You learned about this booklet when you were surfing the Web and came upon the Global Initiative Center Web site.

   b. Assume that you are Nancy Reibold and you received the request for the booklet. You are out of copies at the moment, however, because you have received more requests than anticipated. You expect to receive more copies within two weeks. Write a response to the inquiry explaining these circumstances. Tell the reader that you will send the booklet, titled "Study Abroad," as soon as you can—and offer the alternative of downloading a document that you will make available at your Web site.

   c. You are Nancy Reibold's assistant at the Global Initiative Center, and you are both angry. You have just received 10,000 copies of the booklet from the Jones Printing Company, 105 East Summit Street, New Brunswick, NJ 08910. When you opened the carton, you discovered each booklet is missing several pages.

This is the second printing mistake made by Jones Printing, and the shipment is late as well, even though Robert Mason, the sales representative, had promised that you would have no problems this time. Nancy Reibold wants to "get this problem corrected immediately." Write a complaint letter to Robert Mason for Ms. Reibold to sign.

    d. Assume that you are Robert Mason. You have received the complaint letter about the printing mistake. After checking, you discover that the booklets sent to the Global Initiative Center had been subcontracted to another printing firm (ILM Printing Company) because of the backlog at Jones. You know that Jones Printing will not be billed for the booklets if you return them to ILM Printing within five working days. You decide that you must write an adjustment letter to Ms. Reibold quickly, asking her to return the booklets.

    e. Assume that you are Robert Mason. Send a convincing, detailed memo to J. R. Jones, your boss and president of Jones Printing, recommending that ILM Printing Company not be used for future subcontracting work.

3. You manage Sunny River Resort. Charles James, director of the Sunny River Business League, has requested the free use of your lodge for a two-day staff meeting. You'd like the business league to use your meeting room, but you have a problem: You charge any group $500 per day to use the room. You can't afford to give it away. The room has a number of fixed and variable costs required to clean, pay for lighting and air-conditioning, and supply and repair equipment. Also, what might happen if others knew you had provided the room at no cost? Write a letter to Mr. James selling him on the idea of using your lodge while holding to the $500 fee. Use tact, a positive tone, and persuasive details.

4. You are the manager of Hamon's Fine Clothing. Dr. Klaus Müller, a busy cardiac surgeon, has purchased two suits (total $1,578) from you and is six months overdue in paying for them despite several standard form notices. You'll now need to start a series of collection letters, but you want to make the pace slow. Dr. Müller is highly respected in the community. Write a series of collection letters, spacing them appropriately (date the first letter January 2).

5. You are the membership director of a fitness center that caters to professional women. You decide to bring in additional revenue by offering personal training sessions at $60 per hour and hire three fitness instructors who have been certified as personal trainers by the Aerobics and Fitness Association of America. Unfortunately, clients have been slow to sign up. Write a sales letter to existing members, announcing your fitness center's personal training program. In addition to convincing your readers of the benefits of personal training, the letter should introduce the trainers, describe their backgrounds and interests, and emphasize the extensive training they received in their certification workshops. Their training includes

- Anatomy and kinesiology
- Fitness assessment testing procedures (including skin-fold caliper measuring and sit-up, reach, and abdominal strength tests)
- Weight management and nutrition for the average person as well as those with special medical needs
- Motivation

6. Imagine that the sales letter in the previous exercise worked well and many people signed up with the three trainers, especially C. J., who really knows how to

motivate people. However, a rumor spreads through the fitness center that she isn't certified, and members begin to complain about paying $60 an hour for an uncertified trainer. You check with a source at the Aerobics and Fitness Association of America who confirms that C. J. never completed the certification workshop. Write an adjustment letter to the members who scheduled personal training sessions with C. J. You'll want to consider that C. J. has a loyal following, but your fitness center's credibility is at risk. What solution can you offer that might appease C. J.'s clients and keep your fitness center's credibility intact?

7. You are Mr. Henry Coleman of Abbott Office Products, who received the letter in Figure 9–12. Write a memo to R. P. McMurphy, Vice President of Engineering (with a copy to Pat Smith, Director of Marketing), recommending improvements in the check sorter (or another office system of your choice). Collect facts by visiting a local office-systems store or examining its catalog.

8. You have recently purchased a local high-end camera store and wish to build your business. You have a mailing list of former customers, but many of them were unhappy with the previous owner's products and service. You would like to win them back. You specialize in the highest-quality digital and single-lens reflex (SLR) cameras as well as accessories. The shop is also an authorized repair service for Nikon and Sony cameras and lenses. Your partner is highly qualified as both a photographer and an expert in digital imaging for commercial and Web applications. The community you serve is relatively affluent, but the former owner's reputation included overcharging customers and refusing to service what he sold. Your store is located on East Capitol Drive near a variety of appliance stores and restaurants, and a chain electronics store that sells cameras but is not known for quality service. You believe that satisfied customers will improve your business. Write a sales letter, addressed to former customers, effectively promoting your services. Plan this letter as the basis for other promotional materials.

9. Eight years ago, you opened Tiny Tots Day Care with six children, and it has grown to a capacity of 65 children. Its reputation is so high that there is a waiting list of 78 children. As the director and owner of the center, you now face a problem that you have never before encountered. You must expel a child from the center. You need to write a letter to Mr. and Mrs. Brady, telling them that their four-year-old son, Brett, is being expelled from Tiny Tots. Since Brett entered your center, things haven't been the same. This child is not able to get along with other children. In his two months at Tiny Tots, he has bitten six children (causing one child to require stitches); kicked a teacher; and regularly scratched, hit, and pulled hair. Several parents have threatened to pull their children out of your center if Brett does not leave. Despite several conferences with Brett's parents, who seem reasonable and concerned about their son, you have observed no changes in his behavior. Write the letter to the Bradys, following the pointers for a refusal letter. Remember that this is the Bradys' only child, and choose your words carefully.

10. In a brief essay, discuss why you think e-mail may not replace the traditional paper business letter in all circumstances. Relate your essay to your field of study or occupational interest, and give examples of situations in the workplace that may call for formal letters that use professionally printed letterhead stationery. Consider all areas relevant to your field, such as customers, clients, international correspondence, job applications, suppliers, competitors, technology, and so forth.

■ Collaborative Classroom Projects

ON THE WEB

For more collaborative classroom projects, including a follow-up to Collaborative Classroom Project 3, go to Chapter 9, bedfordstmartins.com/writingthatworks

1. Form groups of five or fewer members. Your company, an office-supply business, has just mistakenly sent a letter to all your customers offering a 20 percent discount off the total of their next order. The letter was supposed to have offered a 20 percent discount off the most-expensive item in their next order. After receiving input from all appropriate departments, the company president has decided the business cannot afford to grant the overall 20 percent discount. You have been instructed to draft a letter to your customers explaining the mistake and clarifying that they will be allowed to take 20 percent off only the most expensive item, not the entire order. Your company president asks that you appeal to your customers' vested interest in your company's ability to keep prices competitive and advises you to ask for their understanding of the error. Appoint a team leader and, as a group, take no more than 20 minutes to brainstorm the points you want to include in the letter. During the next 20 minutes, draft your letters individually. As a group, select one letter that best represents your group's ideas.

2. Your class has been asked to organize a three-hour workshop on business writing for your university's continuing education department. As a class, you have discussed this workshop with your instructor and decided that because of your course loads, your jobs, and other outside responsibilities you are unable to volunteer to conduct a successful workshop at this time. Appoint a class leader or facilitator and a class recorder. As a group, draft a letter to the Department of Continuing Education explaining why your class cannot help. Brainstorm to develop a list of points to include in your letter. Open the letter with an explanation of the context, introducing the subject and establishing the tone. Then explain the facts, lead logically to your refusal, and conclude with goodwill to retain a positive relationship with the department. (Keep in mind that your class's refusal creates a sensitive situation for your instructor, who will be working again with the Department of Continuing Education.) After you have completed your letter, your instructor may want to give the class feedback.

3. Choose a partner in class and invent two companies that provide one of the products or services listed below. Imagine that your company is interested in one of the products or services that your partner's company offers. For example, your national telecommunications company, Teleservice, is opening a branch in another state and needs to relocate several senior managers. Your partner's company, Relocators, Inc., provides employee relocation services.

   - computer networking
   - small business tax preparation
   - ergonomic office furniture
   - organic cleaning products
   - telecommunications
   - employee relocation real estate services
   - office breakfast or lunch catering
   - promotional banners
   - fitness center memberships
   - leadership training

   a. Write an inquiry letter asking your partner's company for more information about the product or service offered.

   b. Switch drafts and write a response to your partner's inquiry. Remember to answer every question as completely as you can, and be sure to respond courteously. If appropriate, you may also tactfully point out that the writer has omitted or misunderstood something. Share your drafts with the person to whom you are responding.

ON THE WEB

For extra research projects, go to Chapter 9, bedfordstmartins.com/ writingthatworks

■ Research Projects

1. Imagine that you work in the public relations office of a national bank and you have to notify over 500,000 customers that their account information may have been stolen by hackers. You have received hundreds of phone calls from customers who are concerned about identity theft and who are threatening to take their business to another financial institution.

   a. Research previous instances of data theft at other banks or financial institutions. Be sure to look at what has happened and what, if anything, the banks offered their customers as compensation.
   b. Research identity theft and make a list of helpful tips for your customers. Be sure to use reputable sources as a means of keeping your readers' confidence.
   c. Write a letter to be sent to all of the bank's customers. Explaining the situation, offer reassurance, and (if appropriate) offer some form of compensation to keep them from pulling their money out of the bank.

   When you are finished writing your letter, present it to the class.

2. Choose one of the following topics:

   • How to write effective sales letters (or, generally, how to write persuasively)
   • How to write effective refusal letters ("bad news" or "negative messages")
   • How to write effective complaint letters
   • How to respond to complaint letters

   Find at least three recent articles on your topic in an academic journal or periodical, such as the *Journal of Business Communication* or *Business Communication Quarterly.* (Your reference librarian can suggest indexes or abstracting services that will help you find articles.) Write a brief critical analysis of what you find. Compare and contrast the articles and, in conclusion, give your opinion on the article with the most helpful advice. Support your analysis with examples from the articles.

ON THE WEB

For additional Web projects, go to Chapter 9, bedfordstmartins.com/ writingthatworks

■ Web Projects

1. You work for a small, budget-conscious company of fewer than 50 employees. Your supervisor has asked you to investigate one of the items listed below for possible purchase by your company. Your supervisor's primary consideration is cost. Using the Web, review information provided by at least three online vendors about the product or service you are interested in. E-mail the vendors to obtain any further information you may need. Which vendor offers the best value? Write a persuasive memo to your supervisor that explains your recommendation for the product or service. Include key points from your research, and support your recommendation with specific details. Possible products and services to investigate include the following:

   • A wireless communication system
   • A company vehicle (for purchase or lease)

- A computer software package
- A security system
- An accounting or other business-related service

2. Review at least three online companies that specialize in e-mail marketing. Begin by entering the key search term "e-mail marketing," "online marketing," "Internet marketing," or "Internet e-mail marketing," using at least three different search engines, such as go.com, Lycos, Yahoo!, AltaVista, or other browsing tools. In your review, explore what these companies promise to provide the customer, what the differences or similarities among these companies are in terms of their goals and business styles, and why these companies hire professional writers to develop their sales-oriented e-mail correspondence. Then consider how the sales e-mail is different from or similar to the traditional sales letter.

10 Writing Informal Reports

AT A GLANCE: Informal Reports

The successful operation of many organizations depends on reports that are either circulated within the organization or submitted to customers, clients, and others. This chapter discusses report-writing strategies (see pages 344–347) and the most-common types of informal reports:

What is a report? Although the term is used to refer to hundreds of different types of written communications, it can be defined as an organized presentation of factual information prepared for a specific audience.

Reports fall into two broad categories: formal and informal. Formal reports, explained in detail in Chapter 11, generally grow out of projects that require many months of work, large sums of money, and the collaboration of many people. They may run several hundred pages and usually include a table of contents and other devices to aid the reader because of their length and scope of coverage. Informal reports, however, generally run from a few paragraphs to a few pages and provide information on projects that typically take a few hours or days to complete. They include only the essential elements of a report: an introduction, a body, conclusions, and, when appropriate, recommendations. Because of their brevity and limited scope, informal reports are customarily written as letters (for recipients outside a company) or as memos (for recipients within an organization).

■ Planning and Writing Informal Reports

Informal reports often describe specific incidents, note the progress of ongoing activities or projects, or summarize the results of a completed project. They may also recommend follow-up work that should be performed based on the conditions described. These reports may be completed for distribution within an organization or submitted to an outside client or customer in a number of formats—typically as memos, letters, or e-mail messages.

Voices from the Workplace

Johan De Beer, Mitsubishi Engine North America

As a service and warranty manager for Mitsubishi Heavy Industries, Johan De Beer travels extensively to evaluate industrial engines and analyze problems for customers all over the world. His trip and trouble reports are read not only by his supervisors in Illinois and managers in New York and Japan but also by customers, suppliers, and third-party manufacturers as well. "It's very important that my reports are clear, concise, and comprehensive," says Johan. He explains, "My first language is Flemish, the manufacturer's first language is Japanese, and the end-user's first language might be anything from Spanish to Afrikaans, so I try to keep my writing simple and I include pictures and diagrams to illustrate details. The more thorough a report is, the fewer questions I will have to answer later." Johan offers: "Be prepared to have your report analyzed by other experts. Your writing must be able to stand up to the scrutiny of your peers." (For a sample of a trip report prepared by Johan De Beer, see Figure 10–5.)

David Noyes, HLM Design–Heery International

For David Noyes, a project manager at the full-service architecture firm HLM Design–Heery International, writing informal reports is a frequent and esssential part of his job. The most-common reports that he writes are project memos, office memos, and contact reports. When writing reports, David keeps the following strategies in mind. "First, I include the title of the project; the date; and the names, titles, and contact information of the participants. Next, I summarize the information as clearly and concisely as possible — if my reports were to be misunderstood, they could lead to potentially expensive and dangerous mistakes. I also make sure that my technical points are absolutely accurate. Finally, I edit my reports so that they are never longer than two or three pages — otherwise, people won't take the time to read them!"

Considering Audience

◆ For additional guidance on audience analysis, see Assessing Your Audience's Needs on pages 6–7.

As with all workplace writing, first consider the makeup of your audience. An informal report is almost always written for a specific small group of readers (or a single reader) — usually at their request. As a result, readers will likely be familiar with the subject of the report, making it easier for you to determine how much background information to provide and how much specialized or technical language to use. Note, for example, that the writer of the trouble report in Figure 10–1 assumes that the reader is familiar with "circle of safety" checks. Without such knowledge, the reader would be unable to interpret the writer's recommendations.

Collecting Information

For a report to be effective, you need to include all the information that will meet your objective (such as describing an accident or explaining the need to upgrade a staff training program) and address your reader's needs (such as keeping a project on schedule or having enough data to make a decision). To achieve these goals,

ON THE WEB

For more help with writing informal reports, see Chapter 10, bedfordstmartins.com/writingthatworks

◆ *For more on note-taking, see pages 172–174 in Chapter 6, Researching Your Subject.*

◆ *For more on organizing information, see Chapter 2, Organizing Your Information.*

keep notes through every stage of the activity on which you will be reporting. Otherwise, you may have trouble obtaining or trying to remember information when the time comes to write the report.

The purpose of taking notes is to record, in an abbreviated form, the background information that will go into your report. Be careful, however, not to make your notes so brief that you forget what you intended when you wrote them. Once you have prepared and gathered your notes, organize them into a sequence that makes sense from the perspective of your objective and audience. If you are working with an outline, add your notes to the appropriate places to flesh it out.

CONSIDERING AUDIENCE AND PURPOSE
Planning and Evaluating Informal Reports

- Who is the audience for your report?
- What specifically have your readers requested?
- How knowledgeable are your readers about the topic?
- Have you selected the right format—e-mail, memo, or letter—for your readers?
- Have you framed the topic for your audience and provided any necessary background information in your introduction?
- Do your graphics depict the findings accurately and clearly for your intended audience?
- Does the body of the report present an organized account of the topic? Is it sufficient in scope so that your audience can understand and interpret your findings, conclusions, and recommendations?

Parts of the Informal Report

Most informal reports that you will be called on to write will have three or four main parts: the introduction, the body, conclusions, and recommendations.

Introduction

The introduction announces the subject of the report, explains its purpose, and, when appropriate, names anybody who assisted with or provided information for the report. It may describe the scope of information covered, any limitations of the topic, or reason for the amount of detail presented. It may also provide any essential background information about the subject of the report. The introduction should also concisely preview any conclusions, findings, or recommendations made in the report. A concise overview is useful to your readers because it saves them time by providing essential information at a glance and helps them focus their thinking.

Body

The body presents a clearly organized account of the report's subject—the results of a market survey, the findings of a test carried out, the status of a construction project, and so on. The amount of detail you include in the body depends on your objective, the complexity of your subject, and your readers' familiarity with the subject. This information is frequently supported by tables, graphs, drawings, and other visuals to clarify ideas and concepts in ways that words alone cannot, as well as to save space.

◆ *For detailed advice on creating and using visuals, see Chapter 7, Designing Effective Documents and Visuals.*

Conclusions and Recommendations

The conclusion summarizes your findings and tells readers what you think the significance of those findings may be. Using only the topics discussed in the report, the conclusion may make a judgment or prediction, issue a call for action, or suggest ideas for further action.

Recommendations are sometimes combined with conclusions in one section at the end of the report. In this section, you recommend a course of action that you believe is warranted by your findings. Recommendations can range from suggestions for instituting new procedures, or for developing new products or marketing campaigns, to setting up new departmental responsibilities, or to hiring new employees.

■ Types of Informal Reports

Because there are so many different types of informal reports and because the categories sometimes overlap (a trip report, for example, might also be a progress report), it would be unrealistic to attempt to study or try to itemize every type. However, it is possible to become familiar with report writing in general and to examine some of the most frequently written kinds of informal reports in the workplace: trouble reports, investigative reports, progress reports, periodic reports, trip reports, and test reports.

Trouble Reports

Incidents involving personal injuries, accidents, and work stoppages (those caused by equipment failures, worker illnesses, and so on) occur in many industrial and construction settings. Problematic episodes may also occur in health care, social work, and criminal-justice settings. Every such incident must be reported so that management can determine its cause and take any necessary steps to prevent a recurrence. A trouble report—also called an accident report or an incident report, depending on the situation—is the record of an accident, mechanical breakdown, medical emergency, or conflict among residents of mental-health or other institutions that may even be used by the police or by a court of law in establishing guilt or liability.

The trouble report is usually a memo written by the person in charge of the site where the incident occurred, addressed to his or her superior. (Although some companies have printed forms for specific types of trouble reports, they include a section in which the writer must describe in detail what happened.)

Figure 10–1 shows a trouble report written by a safety officer after interviewing all the people involved in an accident.

ON THE WEB

To access guidelines and forms for incident reports prepared by the Occupational Safety and Health Administration (OSHA), go to Chapter 10, bedfordstmartins.com/ writingthatworks

Consolidated Energy, Inc.

To: Marvin Lundquist, Vice President
         Administrative Services
From: Kalo Katarlan, Safety Officer   KK
         Field Service Operations
Date: August 21, 2006
Subject: Field Service Employee Accident on August 9, 2006

An Accident Review was conducted on Friday, August 18, 2006, at the Reed Service Center. The attendees were as follows:

How accident was evaluated—employee interviews

Injured Representative:	John Markley
Union Representative:	Harry Hartsock
Employee's Supervisor:	Carl Timmerinski
Safety Officer:	Kalo Katarlan
Safety Officer, Field Service Operations:	Marie Sonora
Date of Accident:	August 9, 2006
Days of Lost Time:	2

Accident Summary

What happened, who was involved, what injury resulted

While John Markley loaded branches into the bed of the truck at the site of a rewiring job on German Road, a piece broke off in his right hand and struck his right eye. Following is a description of the accident.

Accident Details

Events listed in order of occurrence

1. Prior to the accident, Chico Ruiz was stringing new wire at the site and John checked with Chico about the materials he wanted for framing a pole. Some trees had been trimmed in the area, and John offered to help remove some of the debris by loading it into his pickup truck.
2. John's right eye was struck by a piece of tree branch. John had just undergone laser surgery on his right eye on Monday, August 7, to reattach his cornea. At the time of the accident, he was not wearing protective eyeware.
3. John immediately covered his right eye with his hand, and Chico Ruiz gave him a paper towel with ice to cover his eye and help ease the pain.
4. After the initial pain subsided, John got into his truck and began to back up to return to the Service Center. Chico reminded John about the pole trailer parked behind his truck and then returned to the crews he was supervising. John continued backing up, but did not see the tree behind him because his visibility was blocked by the tree debris in his truck bed.

Figure 10–1   Trouble Report (Memo with Recommendations) (continued)

Katarlan   2   August 21, 2006

5. When John struck the tree, his head struck the back window of the truck, shattering the glass. He was not wearing a safety helmet.
6. John returned to the Service Center to report the accident to his supervisor. However, because he had pieces of glass inside his clothes and on his neck, he decided to go home to shower and change clothes. He also used eyedrops prescribed to him after his surgery to thoroughly wash his injured right eye.
7. The next day, August 10, John went to Downtown Worker's Care because he was experiencing headaches. He was diagnosed with a bruised eyeball and eyelid. The headaches were caused by the impact to his head when it hit the rear window of his truck.
8. On Monday, August 14, John returned to his eye surgeon. Although bruised, his eye was not damaged, and the surgically implanted lens was still in place.

Preventive Measures

To prevent a recurrence of such an accident, the Safety Department will require the following actions in the future:

List of corrective actions

*   When working around and moving debris such as tree limbs or branches, all service-crew employees must wear helmets and safety eyewear with side shields.
*   Service-crew employees must always consider the possibility of shock for an injured employee. If crew members cannot leave the job site to care for the injured employee, someone on the crew must call for assistance from the Service Center. An injured employee should never be allowed to drive immediately after an accident. The Service Center phone number is printed in each service-crew member's handbook.
*   All service-crew employees must conduct a "circle of safety" check around any vehicle before moving it.

Figure 10–1   Trouble Report (Memo with Recommendations) (continued)

ETHICS NOTE

Because insurance claims, workers' compensation awards, and even lawsuits may hinge on the information contained in a trouble report, be sure to include precise times, dates, locations, treatment of injuries, names of any witnesses, and any other crucial information. Be thorough and accurate in your analysis of the problem and support any judgments or conclusions with facts. Be objective: Always use a neutral tone and avoid assigning blame. If you speculate about the cause of the problem, make clear to your reader that you are speculating.

WRITER'S CHECKLIST
Writing a Trouble Report

☑ On the *subject line* of your memo, state what you are reporting:

▶ SUBJECT: Personal-Injury Accident in Section A-40.

☑ Write a brief *introductory summary* of the incident.

☑ In the *body* of your memo:

– State exactly when and where the accident, breakdown, emergency, or conflict took place.

– Describe any physical injury or any property damage that occurred.

– Itemize any expenses that resulted from the incident (for example, an injured employee may have missed a number of workdays, or an equipment failure may have caused a disruption in service to the company's customers).

– Include precise data on times, dates, location, treatment of injuries, names of any witnesses, and any other crucial information.

☑ In your *conclusion*, provide a detailed analysis of what you believe caused the trouble.

– Avoid condemnation or blame; be thorough, exact, and objective, and support any opinion you offer with facts.

– Mention what was or will be done to correct the conditions that may have led to the incident.

☑ Include your *recommendations* for preventing further incidents (such as increased safety precautions, improved equipment, or the establishment of training programs). If you are speculating on the cause of the accident, make sure that this is clear to the reader.

Evaluating and Revising a Trouble Report

☑ Who is the audience for the report?

☑ Do you need to interview workers or others about the accident or incident?

☑ Are your notes thorough enough to accurately summarize the accident or incident?

☑ Have you organized your thoughts into a concise outline to guide your writing?

☑ Does the introduction state the subject and purpose of the report?

☑ Does the body include sufficient detail to lead the reader to the same findings and conclusions that you present?

☑ Do the findings and conclusions logically follow from the details described in the body?

☑ Do the recommendations make sense based on your conclusions?

Investigative Reports

Investigative reports are most often written in response to a request for information. You might be asked, for instance, to check the range of prices that companies charge for a particular item or service, to conduct an opinion survey among customers, to study alternative procedures for performing a specific operation, to review business trends in your line of work, and so on. You would then present your findings in an investigative report.

Investigative reports are usually prepared as *memos* if written within an organization and as *letters* if written by an outside consultant. The results of long, complex investigations are usually written as formal reports. For memo and letter reports, open with a brief introductory summary that includes a statement of the information you were seeking and any relevant background as to why the investigation was necessary and who requested it. Then, in the body of the memo or letter, describe the extent of or method used for your investigation. Finally, state your findings and any recommendations based on the findings.

◆ *For guidance on writing and formatting letters and memos, see Chapter 8, Understanding the Principles of Business Communication.*

In the example shown in Figure 10–2, a store manager has investigated three alternative ways of reducing shoplifting in his store and recommended the one most suitable for the store's size and budget.

◆ *For formal reports, see Chapter 11, Writing Formal Reports.*

Progress and Periodic Reports

Both progress reports and periodic reports are written to inform decision-makers about the status of work performed over the course of an ongoing project. The chief difference between them is when they are written. The progress report is issued at certain milestones during a project. Construction and manufacturing projects, for example, must be done in stages: Whether the project involves adding a sunroom to a private residence or building a deep-sea oil-drilling rig, it follows a coordinated sequence. Progress reports describe in detail the status of activities at each stage in the sequence: work in progress, work completed, special problems or delays, costs, worker availability, and anything else that affects the schedule for completing the project. The periodic report, sometimes called a status report, details the status of an ongoing project at regular intervals—weekly, monthly, quarterly. Both types of reports may be required for work being performed within an organization or by an outside consultant.

Progress Reports

The purpose of a progress report is to keep others—usually management or a client—informed of the status of a project. In answering various questions (Is the project on schedule? Running smoothly? Within its budget?), the report lets

Green Department Stores
Memo

To: William Bernardi, Regional Manager
From: Julius Chernoff, Department Manager *JC*
Date: September 24, 2007
Subject: Shoplifting at Store E-5150

Introduction and background

As we have discussed over the last several months, shoplifting at Store E-5150 has increased since the store opened one year ago this month. Although we have budgeted $30,000 a year for shoplifting losses, our monthly inventory check shows that we have lost $47,800 in merchandise this year. The loss was especially evident during the summer months. It is time to take action to reverse this trend.

Section heading and overview of options

Proposed Solutions

My staff and I have researched several different options for minimizing shoplifting in our store. They include hiring security guards, using strategically placed security cameras in the store, and using undercover employees. In investigating options available to us, we considered effectiveness, convenience, and cost.

Security Guards

First option investigated, with findings

We first considered hiring security guards. I met with the president of Hall Security on July 25. Hall Security is a local company that has been in business ten years. I also talked to other store managers in the area who have contracts with Hall Security—all are very pleased with the service and its effectiveness. They believe that the presence of uniformed security guards in their stores discourages theft. The managers surveyed report shoplifting reduction rates of from 50 to 70 percent. I can provide you with detailed data from these interviews at your request.

Recommendation

If we decide to have one security guard on duty during all store hours, we would pay a flat monthly rate of $4,300. One guard on duty from 4 p.m. until 10 p.m. daily, our busiest hours, would cost $2,100 a month. We are not considering the option of a night guard because we have not had any problems with break-in burglaries after hours.

Security Cameras

Second option investigated, with findings

We next considered the use of security cameras. The cameras provide a record of thefts in progress and make prosecuting shoplifters much easier once they're caught. The technicians from TSC, Inc., a camera service company, visited our store on August 6. They studied the floor plan to determine the most-effective placement of cameras throughout the store. They recommend six cameras placed so that we have a view of the whole store at all times. We would need to purchase a single

Figure 10–2   Investigative Report (Memo with Recommendations) (continued)

William Bernardi   2   September 24, 2007

monitor that would display each camera's view on a rotational basis every ten seconds. The monitor would be located in the store manager's office where I or, in my absence, someone I designate, can observe activity throughout the store's retail space. The videotapes can be kept for a week and then recorded over.

TSC, Inc., would install the system and train our employees to operate it. TSC, Inc., also provides a five-year on-site service warranty for the cameras and monitor. They make service calls to the store during business hours within four hours of being called. Total cost, including installation, will be $7,500. We were impressed with the knowledge, experience, and professionalism of the TSC representatives. They provided data for stores comparable to ours that showed an average 60 to 75 percent drop in the incidence of shoplifting after cameras were installed. I called several store managers where the cameras are in use, and they verified these results.

Impressions of service

Undercover Employees

The third option examined is the use of undercover employees. This option involves having store employees who pose as customers as they stroll through the store monitoring customers for shoplifting. We estimate that this option would require two employees each shift. They would alternate between their regular duties, such as stocking shelves, and performing inventory-control tasks. If we also employ security guards, these two units could work in conjunction to help discourage theft.

Third option investigated, with findings

However, the option has some risks associated with it. It would require that our employees receive training in the legal rights of customers and could potentially put our employees at risk in encounters with criminals. Hall Security can provide training over a one-week period at a cost of $1,500 per employee.

Risks associated with option

Recommendations

After completing our research on these possibilities for theft prevention, my staff and I believe that the best option is the installation of security cameras. After comparing the cost of the system with the amount of merchandise we are losing, we believe that the expense is worth the investment. Once the system is installed, there will be negligible expense in its use and maintenance. Our research shows that theft has declined in more than 90 percent of the stores that have had security cameras installed. Pending our approval, TSC, Inc., can install the system in four days. Once it is installed, we would evaluate the effectiveness of the system on a monthly basis and I would provide you with a monthly status report. I look forward to your assessment of this recommendation.

Section heading and recommendations based on findings

Figure 10–2   Investigative Report (Memo with Recommendations) (continued)

readers know precisely what work has been completed, what work remains to be done, and the reasons for any possible delays. Often the report will include recommendations for changes in procedure or will propose new courses of action. Progress reports are generally prepared when a particular stage of a project is reached. For a company-wide computer-system upgrade, for example, the significant steps could include electrical power enhancements to a building, hardware and software installation and testing, and employee training.

The projects most likely to generate progress reports are long-term and fairly complex. The construction of a building, the development of a new product, the opening of a branch office in another part of town, and a major reorganization of a company's Web site are examples of such projects. Progress reports are frequently required in the contract for a project that will take weeks, months, or longer to complete.

Progress reports allow managers and clients to keep track of the project and to make any necessary adjustments in assignments, schedules, and budget allocations while the project is under way. Progress reports can make it easier for management to schedule the arrival of equipment and supplies so that they will be available when needed. Such reports can, on occasion, avert crises. If a hospital had planned to open a new wing in February, for instance, but a shortage of wallboard caused a two-month lag in construction, a progress report would alert hospital managers to the delay in time for them to make alternative plans.

Many projects, of course, require more than one progress report. In general, the more complicated the project, the more frequently management will want to review it. All reports issued during the life of a project should be submitted in the same format to make it easier for readers to recognize at a glance where they need to focus their attention. Progress reports sent outside the company are normally prepared as letters (Figure 10–3); those circulated within a company can be written as memos.

The first in a series of reports should identify the project in detail and specify what materials will be used and what procedures will be followed throughout the project. Later reports in the series contain only a transitional introduction that briefly reviews the work discussed in the previous report. The body of the reports should describe in detail the current status of the project. Every report should end with any conclusions or recommendations—for instance, alterations in schedule, materials, or procedures.

In the example shown in Figure 10–3, a contractor reports to the county administrator on progress in renovating the county courthouse. Notice that the emphasis is on meeting specified costs and schedules.

 DIGITAL TIPS: Creating Styles and Templates

In most word-processing programs, you can create styles — sets of formatting characteristics for text elements such as headings, paragraphs, and lists — that allow you to automate much of the work of formatting your report. Once you have specified your styles, save them as a template and use it each time you create a report.

For step-by-step instructions, see <bedfordstmartins.com/writingthatworks> and select *Digital Tips*, "Creating Styles and Templates."

Hobard Construction Company
9032 Salem Avenue
Lubbock, TX 79406

www.hobardcc.com
Phone (808) 769-0832
Fax (808) 769-5327

August 15, 2007

Walter M. Wazuski
County Administrator
109 Grand Avenue
Manchester, NH 03103

Subject: Progress Report for July 31, 2007

Subject line identifies topic

Dear Mr. Wazuski:

The renovation of the County Courthouse is progressing on schedule and within budget. Although the cost of certain materials is higher than our original bid indicated, we expect to complete the project without exceeding the estimated costs because the speed with which the project is being completed will reduce overall labor expenses.

Project status summary

Costs

Materials used to date have cost $178,600, and labor costs have been $258,000 (including some subcontracted plumbing). Our estimate for the remainder of the materials is $59,000; remaining labor costs should not exceed $400,000.

Work Completed

Detailed status of project

As of July 31, we finished installation of the circuit-breaker panels and meters, level-one service outlets, and all subfloor wiring. The upgrading of the courtroom, the upgrading of the records-storage room, and the replacement of the air-conditioning units are in the preliminary stages.

Work Schedule

We have scheduled the upgrading of the courtroom to take place from August 27 to October 5, the upgrading of the records-storage room from October 6 to November 13, and the replacement of the air-conditioning units from November 15 to December 18. We see no difficulty in having the job finished by the scheduled date of December 21.

Sincerely yours,

Tran Nuguélen, Project Engineer
<ntran@hobardcc.com>

Figure 10–3   Progress Report (Letter to Client)

Periodic Reports

Periodic reports are issued at regular intervals—daily, weekly, monthly, quarterly, annually—rather than at the stages of a project where significant milestones were reached. Employees routinely submit status reports (also called "activity" reports) to their supervisors about their ongoing projects.

◆ *For a discussion of the scope and format of formal reports, see Chapter 11, Writing Formal Reports.*

Quarterly and annual reports, because of their scope, are usually presented as formal reports. Most other kinds of periodic reports seldom run longer than a page or two. Like progress reports, these shorter reports are most often written as memos or e-mail messages within an organization and as letters when sent to clients and customers outside an organization.

Many kinds of routine information that must be reported periodically—and that do not require a narrative explanation—can be recorded on forms, entered into networked computer databases or spreadsheets, or printed as graphs or tables in the body of a written report. Examples include human resources, accounting, and inventory records; production and distribution figures; sales numbers; and travel and task logs.

One- and two-page periodic reports can be organized in a variety of ways. The standard sequence of introduction, body, and conclusions and recommendations may serve your needs. Otherwise, modify the organizational pattern to suit your reader's reporting requirements. Once you have established a format and an organization, create a template and use it consistently for each consecutive report.

DESIGNING YOUR DOCUMENT
Formatting Progress and Periodic Reports

- For internal distribution, format the report as a memo or an e-mail message.
- If the report will be sent to clients or others outside your organization, format it as a letter.
- Use headings to organize the contents of your report.
- Keep narrative information brief and easy to skim.
- Present routine and numerical data in tables or graphs.
- Create a template and use the same format — headings, tables, organization, and so on — for each consecutive report in a series.

The sample periodic report shown in Figure 10–4 is sent monthly from a company's district sales manager to the regional sales manager. This periodic report would be sent to the regional sales manager either with a brief cover memo or as an attachment to a brief e-mail message. Notice that there is no traditional opening and closing, which are superfluous because the report is routine; that is, it goes to the same person every month and covers the same topics. It also goes to a high-level manager who receives many such reports each month, so he or she does not have time to read unnecessary narrative. Because this report is written to someone completely familiar with the background details of the projects discussed, the district sales manager can

Rockport
Customer Services
Monthly Report
June 2006

*Frequency
of report*

Mid-Atlantic District

*Standardized
heading*

Current personnel:	13
Changes this month:	None
Awards/relocations/promotions:	• Alonzo Berg attended the Field Business Conference.
	• Dawon Washington was honored by his peers for superior customer satisfaction at Southwest Utility.
Human resources issues:	None

*Routine categories
of information—
narrative introduc-
tion unnecessary*

Product Revenue

*Project status
grouped into
standard categories*

Customer	Equipment	Maint. $	Notes
Southwest Utility	6650–200	$ 6,200/mo	None
Demeter, Inc.	SVR	$ 800/mo	Installing a new SVR in February
Barg Aerospace	6650–900	$10,000	Installation charge
Barg Aerospace	6650–900	$ 9,000/mo	New monthly maintenance (2 years)

*Numerical infor-
mation formatted
as a table*

Top Prospects

Customer	Service	Revenue	Odds	Comments
Herndon Bank	PPR	$ 5,600	100%	LAR Services
Southwest Utility	PPR	$10,000	100%	Configuration
MacDonalds	PPR	$10,000	100%	Maintenance
MacDonalds	PPR	$ 6,900	100%	Conversion
Reece Corp.	PPR	$13,000	100%	Upgrades
Reece Corp.	PPR	$ 2,300	100%	Maintenance
Gabbard Mfg.	PPR	$25,000	80%	Cynergy Installation
Gabbard Mfg.	ERCAR	$95,000	50%	ERCAR Upgrades

Competitive Customer or Marketplace News

• Cynergy, Inc.'s new maintenance offering is not going over well with some customers. We should be able to take advantage of this.

• Watsorg's decision will be announced July 24–28. This is for $18 to $20 million, going either to us or to Cynergy. The problem is that we finished our "best and final" presentation in the first week of February, and Watsorg gave Cynergy an

Figure 10–4   Periodic Report (continued)

extension to the end of the month. Dragging this out increases Cynergy's odds of winning. However, the last word is that the negotiations are not going well with Cynergy, so we are keeping our fingers crossed.

- AREDOT is installing the largest Saki tape library system in the world. The sales rep said that Saki had been working with a company to develop a "virtual tape system" when Embry was sold to Jordan. This resulted in Jordan not getting the contract.

- Charlestown Customer Services met with a CARL team director from Columbus, Ohio, to discuss future services with CARL. He is considering Rockport as the prime contractor for all necessary services in Charlestown. He will base his decision on the cost analysis.

Significant Wins and Accomplishments

- Hector Martinez convinced Barg Aerospace to acquire two additional 6650A-900s from us on a rental basis with a two-year maintenance contract worth $9,000 per month per machine. The installation team has installed the second 900 and will install the third in the coming weeks.

- Charlestown Customer Services completed installation of a Cynergy 2063 and a Rockport 1006 at Ft. Lee, Virginia. We partnered with Rathbone Corporation to win the business.

Product Issues

Secard performance issues have continued from last month. We applied new code with high hopes, but no improvement was noted by the customer. Currently, ERT traces are running to gather more information. The customer is getting very concerned with this issue, and they are our only Secard customer in Charlestown.

2

Figure 10–4   Periodic Report (continued)

write a spare narrative with many shorthand references to equipment, customers, and project status. For example, the writer mentions a "best and final" presentation to Watsorg rather than writing that Rockport, his company, has presented its final sales proposal to Watsorg, Inc., for equipment and services. The writer need not spell out the details of the project because the regional sales manager is already familiar with them. Such an abbreviated narrative is appropriate for the intended reader.

Trip Reports

Many companies require or encourage employees to prepare reports on their business trips. A trip report not only provides a permanent record of a business trip and its accomplishments but also enables many employees to benefit from the information that one employee has gained.

A trip report is normally written as a memo or an e-mail message and addressed to an immediate supervisor, as shown in Figure 10–5. On the subject line, give the destination (or purpose) and dates of the trip. Explain the purpose of the trip in a brief introductory summary and note whom or where you visited and what you accomplished. The report should devote a brief section to each major event and may include a heading for each section (you needn't give equal space to each event; instead, elaborate on the more-important events). End the report with any appropriate conclusions and recommendations. Finally, if required, attach a record of expenses to the trip report.

ON THE WEB

For an example of an extended trip report, go to **bedfordstmartins** **.com/writingthatworks** and select *Model Documents Gallery*.

Test Reports

Test reports, also called laboratory reports when tests are performed in laboratories, record the results of tests and experiments. Normally, those who write test reports do so as a routine part of their work. Tests that form the basis of reports are not limited to any particular occupation; they commonly occur in many fields, from chemistry to fire science, from metallurgy to medical technology, and include studies on cars, blood, mercury thermometers, pudding mixes, smoke detectors—the list is endless. Information collected in testing may be used to upgrade or abandon products or to streamline testing or manufacturing procedures.

Because accuracy is the essential goal of a test report, be sure to take careful notes while you are performing the test. Then state your findings in clear, straightforward language. Use tables, graphs, or illustrations if they will help your readers interpret the findings. Because a test report should be objective, it is one of the few writing formats in which the passive voice is usually more suitable than the active voice. The format in which test reports are prepared depends on the intended audience: letters for customers outside your organization and memos for employees within your organization.

◆ *For guidance in preparing visuals, see Chapter 7, Designing Effective Documents and Visuals.*

◆ *For a discussion of active versus passive voice, see Chapter 4, Revising the Draft.*

On the subject line, identify the test you are reporting. If the purpose of the test is not obvious to your reader, explain it in the body of the report. Then, if it is helpful to your reader, outline the testing procedures. You need not give a detailed explanation of how the test was performed; rather, provide just enough information

Watson Engines

Memorandum

June 14, 2006

To: Jacob Stein, International Service Manager
From: Wilhelm Kurtz, Engine Specialist
Subject: Trouble-Shooting Trip to Garcia Tractor Company, Caracas, Venezuela,
         June 8–11, 2006

The Problem

I visited the Garcia Tractor Company's dealership in Caracas to determine the cause of severe overheating and the loss of power in one of their tractors.

Action Taken

I inspected the tractor's engine to find the cause of the problem and determined that the cooling water in the tractor's Watson engine (serial number L94847U) contained minerals that solidified when the engine temperature exceeded 65°C (149°F), thereby creating a layer of mineral deposits on the walls of the cooling spaces and rendering the engine incapable of rejecting heat. The ultimate result of this problem was the engine's loss of power because of overheating.

I further inspected the engine to determine whether other parts may have been harmed and discovered that the following lubricated moving parts were damaged.

- The crankshaft and all bearing contact surfaces showed signs of extensive wear, which could have been caused either by breakdown of the lubricating oil's viscosity or by contaminated lubricating oil.

- The engine block was damaged on the seating surface of the number three bearing, which could have been caused by either oil acidification or water condensation.

- The number five main bearing cap was also damaged because of either oil acidification or water condensation.

- On the rear half of the left camshaft, the lobe that operated the number eight fuel injection pump showed signs of aggravated wear.

- Twenty-one of the twenty-four pushrods were damaged on the surface where they make contact with the cam followers. This damage could have been caused by the breakdown in viscosity of the lubricating oil or by lack of scheduled maintenance.

Marginal annotations:

Subject line with destination and trip dates

Headings separate sections of the report

Purpose of the trip

Summary of actions

Findings based on actions

Figure 10–5   Trip Report (Memo)   Adapted with permission from a report prepared by Johan De Beer of Mitsubishi Engines, N.A. (continued)

Page Two   Wilhelm Kurtz   June 14, 2006

- Three of the twenty-four cam followers were damaged on the inside cup where they support the pushrods.

Recommendations

Recommendations based on findings

I recommend that the following actions be taken:

- The crankshaft should be machined down 0.25 millimeters for the connecting rods and the mains.
- The block and the main bearings should be machined and line bored.
- The damaged camshaft lobe should be sleeved and the damaged part of the camshaft replaced.
- The damaged pushrods and cam followers should be replaced.
- The vibration damper should be remanufactured to prevent heat developed by the engine from solidifying the viscous oil and nullifying the damping action.

I requested a sample of used oil from the engine, but the oil had been drained and discarded before my arrival. I recommend that the oil viscosity be tested after the engine has been operated for several hours.

Suggested Follow-Up

Because Garcia Motors uses many additional Watson engines that potentially could also be damaged, I strongly recommend sending a detailed report of these problems to the client and commissioning a set of Spanish-language maintenance guides for current and future customers in Venezuela.

Figure 10–5   Trip Report (Memo) (continued)

for your reader to have a general idea of the testing methods. Next, present the data—the results of the test. If an interpretation of the results would be useful to your reader, furnish such an analysis in your conclusion. Close the report with any recommendations you are making as a result of the test.

Figure 10–6 shows a test report that notes briefly how the test was conducted. Figure 10–7 shows a test report that explains in detail how the tests were performed and describes the federal standards on which the testing was based.

BIOSPHERICS
Inc.

4928 Wyaconda Road
Rockville, MD 20852
Phone (301) 492-3331
Fax (301) 492-1832
biosphericsinc.com

*Report in
letter format
for a customer*

March 14, 2007

Mr. Luigi Sebastiani, General Manager
Midtown Development Corporation
114 West Jefferson Street
Milwaukee, WI 53201

*Test identified
in subject line*

SUBJECT: Results of Analysis of Soil Samples for Arsenic

Dear Mr. Sebastiani:

The results of our analysis of your soil samples for arsenic showed considerable variation; a high iron content in some of the samples may account for these differences.

*Testing
methodology*

Following are the results of the analysis of eight soil samples. The arsenic values listed are based on a wet-weight determination. The moisture content of the soil is also given to allow conversion of the results to a dry-weight basis if desired.

*Table of areas
tested and findings*

Hole	Depth	Moisture (%)	Arsenic Total (ppm)
1	12"	19.0	312.0
2	Surface	11.2	737.0
3	12"	12.7	9.5
4	12"	10.8	865.0
5	12"	17.1	4.1
6	12"	14.2	6.1
7	12"	24.2	2,540.0
8	Surface	13.6	460.0

*Interpretation
of test findings*

I noticed that some of the samples contained large amounts of metallic iron coated with rust. Arsenic tends to be absorbed into soils high in iron, aluminum, and calcium oxides. The large amount of iron present in some of these soil samples is probably responsible for retaining high levels of arsenic. The soils highest in iron, aluminum, and calcium oxides should also show the highest levels of arsenic, provided the soils have had approximately equal levels of arsenic exposure.

If I can be of further assistance, please do not hesitate to contact me.

Yours truly,

Gunther Gottfried

Gunther Gottfried, Chemist
<ggottfried@biosphericsinc.com>

Figure 10–6 Test Report (Letter to Customer)

BIOSPHERICS Inc.

4928 Wyaconda Road
Rockville, MD 20852
Phone (301) 492-3331
Fax (301) 492-1832
biosphericsinc.com

April 4, 2007

Mr. Leon Hite, Administrator
The Angle Company, Inc.
1869 Slauson Boulevard
Waynesville, VA 23927

Dear Mr. Hite:

On March 21, Biospherics Inc. performed asbestos-in-air monitoring at your
Route 66 construction site, near Front Royal, Virginia. Six persons and three
construction areas were monitored.

All monitoring and analyses were performed in accordance with "Occupational
Exposure to Asbestos," U.S. Department of Health and Human Services, Public
Health Service, National Institute for Occupational Safety and Health, 1995.
Each worker or area was fitted with a battery-powered personal sampler pump,
operating at a flow rate of approximately two liters per minute. The airborne
asbestos was collected on a 37-mm Millipore-type AA filter mounted in an
open-face filter holder. Samples were collected over an eight-hour period.

In all cases, the workers and areas monitored were exposed to levels of asbestos
fibers well below the standard set by the Occupational Safety and Health
Administration. The highest exposure found was that of a driller exposed to
0.21 fibers per cubic centimeter. The driller's samples were analyzed by scanning electron microscopy followed by energy-dispersive X-ray techniques that
identify the chemical nature of each fiber, to identify the fibers as asbestos or
other fiber types. Results from these analyses show that the fibers present are
tremolite asbestos. No nonasbestos fibers were found.

Yours truly,

Allison Jones

Allison Jones, Chemist
AJ/jrm

*Report in letter
format for a
customer*

Scope of test

*Testing
methodology*

Test findings

Figure 10–7   Test Report with Methodology Explained (Letter to Customer)

CHAPTER 10 SUMMARY: WRITING INFORMAL REPORTS

Check informal reports to make sure that:

- The introduction states the subject and purpose and summarizes conclusions and recommendations.
- The body presents a detailed account of the work reported on.
- The conclusion summarizes findings and indicates their significance.
- The recommendations of actions you believe should be taken are based on the conclusions.

The following types of informal reports are typical:

- Trouble reports
  - Identify the precise details, such as time and place of an accident or other incident
  - Indicate any injuries or property damage
  - State a likely cause of the accident or incident
  - Specify what is being done to prevent a recurrence, if that's possible
- Investigative reports
  - Open with a statement of the information the writer has sought
  - Define the extent of the investigation
  - Present the findings, interpretations, conclusions, and, when appropriate, recommendations
- Progress and periodic reports
  - Inform the reader of the status of an ongoing project either at certain stages (progress) or at regular intervals (periodic)
  - Alert readers to any necessary adjustments in scheduling, budgeting, and work assignments
- Trip reports
  - Include the destination and dates of the trip
  - Explain why the trip was made, who was visited, and what was accomplished
  - State any findings or recommendations based on the purpose of the trip
- Test reports
  - State the purpose of the test and indicate the procedures used to conduct the test
  - Indicate the results of the test or experiment and any interpretations helpful to the reader

ON THE WEB

For an online quiz on informal reports, go to Chapter 10, bedfordstmartins.com/ writingthatworks

ON THE WEB

For additional exercises, go to Chapter 10, bedfordstmartins.com/ writingthatworks.

■ Exercises

1. Imagine that you are the traffic manager of a trucking company that has had four highway accidents within a one-week period. Using the following facts, write a trouble report to your company president, Michael Spangler.
   - Your company operates in your state.
   - The four accidents occurred in different parts of the state and on different dates (specify the date and location of each).

- Each accident resulted in damage not only to the truck (specify the dollar amount of the damage) but to the cargo (specify the type of cargo and the dollar amount of the damage).
- Only one of the accidents involved another vehicle (a company truck swerved into a parked car when a tire blew out). Give the make and year of the damaged car and its owner's name.
- Only one of the accidents involved injury to a company driver (give the name).
- Your maintenance division traced all four of the accidents to faulty tires, all the same brand (identify the brand), and all purchased at the same time and place (identify the place and date).
- The tires have now been replaced, and your insurance company, Acme Underwriters, has brought suit against the tire manufacturer to recover damages, including lost business while the four trucks were being repaired (specify the dollar amount of the lost business).

2. Worker's compensation allows employees who are injured on the job to receive benefits like medical expenses and lost wages, depending on when the injury happened, how the injury happened, and the severity of the injury. Imagine that you work for a human resources manager of a large online retailer. Most of your company's workers spend their days packing books, DVDs, and other products into mailing boxes, then lifting the boxes and putting them onto carts and pulling the carts to the mailing rooms. Your manager asks you to draft an investigative end-of-the-year report in the form of a memo that details the most common type of employee injury and other yearly information. Your research uncovers the following:

- Back injuries are the most common, occurring mostly in the warehouse.
- In 2005–2006, 956 injuries occurred.
- The total cost of the injuries was $3.5 million.
- There is still a cost of $8.2 million for all open claims.
- This information reflects a significant loss in productivity.

Be sure to open your memo with a brief introductory summary that details the information you were seeking, why the investigation was necessary, and who requested it. In the body of the memo or letter, describe the extent of or method used for your investigation. Then state your findings and any recommendations based on the findings.

3. In Exercise 2, you wrote an investigative report about back injuries and worker's compensation at a large online retailer. Your manager reported your findings to the company's board of directors, who were concerned about the impact of the worker's compensation expenses on the company's overall budget. You have been asked to head a task force of warehouse workers and managers to explore ways to prevent warehouse injuries, especially back injuries, and reduce the injuries by at least 35 percent by the end of the next fiscal year.

Write a three-month progress report on what your task force has investigated and its findings. Comment on such issues as the design of warehouse equipment, the weight of boxes being packed, the various postures and movements employees engage in throughout the day and how often, the level of training employees receive, and the amount of stress employees experience with mailing deadlines. Also discuss the early results of new back-injury-prevention programs you have implemented.

4. As the medical staff administrative assistant at a hospital, write a progress report to the director of the hospital outlining the current status of the annual reappointment of committees. Use the following facts to write the report:

   • A total of ten committees must be staffed.
   • The chief of staff has telephoned each person selected to chair a committee, and you have sent each of them a follow-up letter of thanks from the chief.
   • You have written letters to all physicians who are currently on committees but are not being reappointed, informing them of the fact.
   • You have written letters to all physicians being asked to serve on committees.
   • You expect to receive replies from those physicians declining the appointment by the 15th of the following month.
   • Once committee assignments have been completed, you will type the membership lists of all committees and distribute them to the complete medical staff.

5. You are a field-service engineer for a company that markets diesel-powered emergency generators. Based on the following information, write a trip report.

   You have just visited five cities to inspect the installation of your company's auxiliary power units in hospitals, and you need to report to your manager about your findings. You visited the following hospitals and cities:

   • May 22: Our Lady of Mercy Hospital in San Antonio
   • May 23: Dallas Presbyterian Hospital in Dallas
   • May 24: St. Elizabeth Hospital in Oklahoma City
   • May 25: New Orleans General Hospital in New Orleans
   • May 26: Jefferson Davis Memorial Hospital in Atlanta

   You found that each installation was properly done. With the cooperation of the administrators, you switched each hospital to auxiliary power for a one-hour trial run. All went well. You held a brief training session for the maintenance staff at each hospital, teaching them how to start the engine and how to regulate its speed to produce 220 volts of electricity from the generator at 60 hertz. You want to commend your company's sales staff and field personnel for creating a positive image of your company in the minds of all five customers you visited.

6. Locate a test report that you wrote for a laboratory class that you are taking or have taken. Rewrite the report according to the guidelines in this chapter, and submit it in memo form to your instructor.

7. Each of the following topics presents a situation in which a company plans a significant change that could threaten its existing customer base. Select one of the following topics (or create your own topic based on your area of study and professional interest) and write a memo in which you offer your recommendations for ensuring that the change that your company proposes will not jeopardize its existing customer base. With your customers in mind, make specific suggestions for facilitating as smooth and positive a transition as possible.

   a. Assume that you are part of the management team of a fast-food restaurant with a "burgers only" identity—and a loyal customer base—that wants to add distinctive and healthful menu items.
   b. Assume that you are part of the management team for an apparel manufacturing firm known for its conservative fashions. Your firm is about to introduce a new line of clothing with a distinctly contemporary appeal.

c. Assume that you work for a small medical insurance company concerned with the rising number of medical claims being submitted by your customers. To combat this, your company has initiated a campaign designed to entice your customers to adopt healthier lifestyles, and has begun sending brochures and personalized letters to customers. Some customers have expressed concern that this is an indication that the company will become more reluctant to pay their claims.

8. Try a new or better method to accomplish a task and document the steps and results. For example, try balancing your checkbook using the computer or try a different system for doing the week's laundry or grocery shopping. Then write a test report in the form of a memo to your instructor. Include each step of the process or the procedures you used and the results of your test. If appropriate, compare the test process to your old way of accomplishing the task. Include in your memo any observations that would be helpful in interpreting your test report.

9. Write a trip report to your boss, Monica Jenkins, CEO of Jenkins Marketing Specialists, Inc. Your goal in writing a trip report is to inform management about new procedures, equipment, or laws, or to supply information affecting products, operations, and services. Ms. Jenkins supported your request to attend the Business Etiquette Conference, sponsored by the Business Management Association and held at Delta State University in Cleveland, Mississippi, at Broom Hall, College of Business. The six-day conference was held April 18–23, 2006.

   Your goal is to let Ms. Jenkins know that you gathered valuable information that will benefit the company.

   a. Write an introductory paragraph in which you identify the event (exact date, sponsor name, conference theme and name, and location) and preview the topics to be discussed in your report.
   b. In the body, summarize three to five main points from one presentation you attended each day at the conference. State how you benefited from the conference and how what you learned will also benefit the reader and Jenkins Marketing Specialists, Inc.
   c. Express appreciation, suggest action to be taken, or synthesize the value of the trip or conference.

   In your report, highlight interesting and important facts using typographical tools such as boldface, headings, and bullets. Itemize your expenses on a separate page as an attachment to your report.

10. Imagine that you are a security consultant and have been hired by a company that creates security systems for the average homeowner. The company has hired you to test its new wireless camera—one that promises to work in low light and transmit pictures up to 100 meters—in a real-world environment. You decide to take several of the cameras home and place them within reception range under the eaves of the garage, in the baby's room, overlooking your front door, and in the yard near the pool. Although you appreciate the ease with which you could set up the system, it becomes apparent over the course of your week of testing that the picture and sound quality were negatively impacted by the interference of other electrical equipment in the house, such as the baby monitor, the microwave oven, and the cordless phone. Static noises and jumping lines made it nearly impossible to understand the sound and picture. Write a test report to the security systems corporation detailing your findings.

ON THE WEB

For more collaborative classroom projects, go to Chapter 10, bedfordstmartins.com/ writingthatworks

■ Collaborative Classroom Projects

1. In Collaborative Classroom Project 3 in Chapter 8, Understanding the Principles of Business Communication, your class broke into two groups, the local electric company's consumers and the company's marketing representatives. Both sides wrote letters asking that a rate increase be rejected or accepted, respectively. Now assume that before the marketing representatives wrote their letter, they had investigated the company's need for a rate increase to build a fourth natural gas–fired generating unit. The investigation uncovered the following information[1]:

   • The electric company supplies electricity to three cities and over 1.65 million customers.
   • Population growth is beginning to add strain to an already overloaded system (the company currently generates power using nuclear, coal, natural gas, and oil plants at 12 different sites).
   • Customers set two peak records for summer usage in 2006: They used approximately 8,992 megawatt-hours (MWh) of electricity on July 16 between 4:00 and 5:00 p.m., and approximately 9,027 MWh on July 18 in the same time period.
   • Despite the summer heat, peak energy use occurs during the winter: the highest demand (10,142 MWh) was recorded on January 15, 2006.
   • Company engineers report that a new natural gas–fired generating unit would add approximately 500 megawatts of capacity, which could generate electricity for about 320,000 additional consumers.

   Rewrite your group's marketing representatives' letter to include the research. When you are finished, exchange letters for peer reviews. Comment on the level of persuasion that these letters now contain with the added details and facts.

2. As a class, plan to visit a lab or learning center on campus, preferably one outside your department. Determine as a group which lab you would like to visit and the specific purposes of your visit. The lab may be a science lab, a computer lab, an engineering lab, or a writing center. After an explanation of the lab's procedures and a tour of the lab or center, your class will reconvene in your own classroom and write a trip report about the visit. Include the date of the visit, your destination, the purpose of your trip, and an explanation of what you learned during the visit.

3. In small groups, collaborate to write a trouble report about a problem on campus. Choose a topic that has a simple solution, like a busy campus intersection that needs a traffic signal or a parking problem that could be relieved by providing students with incentives to use the bus system. Other topics might address overly complicated procedures for dropping or adding a class or using online resources at the library. Submit your report to your instructor in memo form.

---

[1] Adapted from Florida Power's Web site <www.progress-energy.com/aboutus/news/article .asp?id=12022>

Research Projects

ON THE WEB

For extra research projects, including a continuation of Collaborative Classroom Project 1, go to Chapter 10, **bedfordstmartins.com/ writingthatworks**

1. The use of cell phones, laptop computers, and digital cameras has created a growing need for the recycling of portable rechargeable batteries. Many retail stores are helping to preserve the environment by shipping spent battery packs to recycling centers. In Chapter 6, Researching Your Subject, Exercise 8, you created a questionnaire designed to determine if people are aware of the need to recycle portable rechargeable batteries and how people feel about companies that provide recycling programs. Expand your investigation and write an investigative report on the recycling of portable rechargeable batteries. In this report, be sure you do the following:

   a. Define the many different types of rechargeable batteries being used today (like nickel cadmium and lithium ion).
   b. Explain how the recycling is accomplished.
   c. List the local businesses in your city that participate in recycling programs.
   d. Include the findings from your questionnaire.

2. You have been asked to determine for your campus organization where members can volunteer 10 to 12 hours a week for a local community service.

   a. Begin by investigating at least three organizations that accept volunteers, such as nursing homes, hospitals, political and civic groups, or schools. Detail the type of volunteer help needed, the hours and days when the help is needed, whether any training is required, and to whom you'll report. Also be sure to find out if volunteers do hands-on work with people—such as playing games with children or adults or bathing, lifting, or turning those who aren't mobile—or if volunteers work behind the scenes, making solicitation calls, addressing envelopes, stocking supplies, and so on.
   b. Then write an eight- to ten-page investigative report in which you evaluate each of the three organizations given the criteria above, as well as from the point of view of your own background, experience, and future vocational goals that are similar to those members of your organization.
   c. Finish by selecting the one that is most suitable for members of your organization and explain the reasons for your selection.

Web Projects

ON THE WEB

For more Web project options, go to Chapter 10, **bedfordstmartins.com/ writingthatworks**.

1. Assume that you work for a small business and the company president has asked you to gather information from the Small Business Administration (SBA) that will benefit your company, such as opportunities for government contracts, or special programs or training available through the SBA. Visit the SBA Web site at (<www.sba.gov>) and prepare an investigative report of 300 to 500 words to be submitted to your instructor.

2. Many large international companies target sections of their Web sites to the different world markets where their products are sold. For example, McDonald's (<www.McDonalds.com>) includes customized pages for each of the 50 plus countries where its restaurants are established. Assume that you work for a company that is considering expanding its Web site for international markets. You

have been assigned to investigate and report your findings on the differences and similarities between the regional sections of other companies' sites. To research your report, examine the Web sites of at least three international corporations. You might visit, for example, McDonald's American and European sites, or Sony's Asian and Eastern European sites. Note the translations of the company's slogan, the colors and graphics used on the sites, the presentation of products, and so on. (You may want to revisit the sections on international correspondence in Chapter 8, Understanding the Principles of Business Correspondence; on using graphics to communicate to global audiences in Chapter 7, Designing Effective Documents and Visuals; and on considering international Web users in Chapter 15, Writing for the Web: Rhetorical Principles.

11 Writing Formal Reports

At a Glance: Formal Reports

This chapter discusses the parts of formal reports, the information they should include, and how best to organize them into an effective final product. Depending on the subject, objective, and scope, a formal report is typically divided into three major parts—front matter, body, and back matter—and contains the following elements:

Formal reports are written accounts of major projects. Such projects include research into new developments in a field, explorations of the feasibility of a new product or a new service, or an end-of-year review of developments within an organization. Because of the variety of purposes they serve, formal reports can be called by many different names: feasibility study, annual report, investigative report, research report, analytical report, and the like. Regardless of their purpose, formal reports contain various components that make up the parts of the report. The purpose, scope, and complexity of the project will determine which components will be included and how they are organized. Most formal reports—certainly those that are long and complex—require a carefully planned structure and signposts that provide readers with an easy-to-recognize guide to the material in the report. Such aids as a table of contents, a list of figures, and an abstract (a brief summary of the report) make the information in the report more easily accessible. Making a formal topic outline, which lists the report's major facts and ideas and indicates their relationship to one another, should help you to write a well-organized report.

Formal reports are organized to address the needs of more than one audience. These audiences will occupy a variety of positions in the organization receiving the report, have different levels of knowledge about your topic, and be responsible for reading and responding to different parts of the report. Although everybody will skim the table of contents, managers and other decision-makers will focus on the executive summary because it concisely summarizes the report in full. These readers need to know the "bottom line" quickly for its potential impact on their staffing, organizational, and budget decisions. They may also need to refer to the glossary for definitions of special terms. Technical experts, however, will be responsible for implementing the report's recommendations, so they need to understand in detail how the conclusions and recommendations were reached. General readers whose needs are less immediate may read only the abstract to decide whether to read the whole report. Few in your audience will read the entire report, so an executive summary and abstract must be written to make sense independently of the rest of the report. Likewise, overlapping content is appropriate in the introduction, executive summary, abstract, and conclusions and recommendations.

As you read this chapter, keep in mind all that you've learned about the process of drafting and revising on-the-job writing tasks because careful planning, drafting, and revising, as much as using the organizational frameworks covered in this chapter, form the basis for a successful formal report. Formal-report

ON THE WEB

For more help with writing formal reports, go to Chapter 11, bedfordstmartins.com/ writingthatworks

Voices from the Workplace

Judy Prono, Los Alamos National Laboratory

At Los Alamos National Laboratory, Judy Prono leads a team of writers and editors who help lab scientists explain their research in print and on the Web. Considering a report's audience and purpose is critical for her team because readers can range from experts to the general public. Judy explains, "To reach such diverse audiences, we begin by explaining the 'what' and 'so what' of the research to nonexpert readers and add technical details as the report progresses. If it is a high-visibility brochure, we may also tell two stories, one in the text and one in the accompanying graphics, captions, and sidebars. The two become complementary explanations of the research that tell the full story together but capture its highlights if readers have time only for the 'pictures.'"

Ted Kalo, Congressional Staff Member

Ted Kalo is minority general counsel for the House Judiciary Committee for the office of Representative John Conyers Jr. Following the 2000 presidential election, he researched and wrote a report detailing voting irregularities across the country. Ted describes his approach to researching and organizing the report: "Based on the little knowledge I began with on the subject, I came up with a few categories that the research might fall under. After I did some more research, I came up with new categories and made an outline for each state. Then I began to fill in the outlines with data." As he drafted and revised his report, Ted was careful to provide his readers with clear conclusions. "Once the report was finished, I took a few days to think about what the larger lessons were. I knew my introduction had to be compelling."

---

preparation involves *researching* and generating a substantial amount of information, which you will need to evaluate, select, and organize before you begin the drafting process. The *research* required for a formal report can be extensive, so *brainstorming* and refining the scope of the topic are essential.

In addition, plan to write several *outlines* for your report: one as an overview of the whole project and smaller, more-specific outlines for individual sections. Breaking the work into parts can make the daunting task of pulling together a long report more manageable.

You will need to revise the report several times, evaluating each draft for coherence, clarity, and correctness. You will also need to review the drafts to see whether the individual sections of the report connect smoothly and logically, whether sources are used correctly and consistently, and whether *visuals*—drawings, tables, graphs, charts, photographs, and maps—are well designed and correctly positioned. Because of the extensive revisions required for a long report, collaborative reviews of your work will help you immensely; colleagues, fellow students, or instructors can offer revision suggestions to supplement your own evaluations of the report.

In the workplace, formal reports are often written by a team of specialists assembled for that purpose. Each member of the team is selected to contribute

◆ *For guidance on conducting research, see Chapter 6, Researching Your Subject.*

◆ *For brainstorming strategies, see Chapter 1, Assessing Audience and Purpose.*

◆ *For outlining, see Chapter 2, Organizing Your Information.*

◆ *For advice on planning, creating, and integrating visuals, see Chapter 7, Designing Effective Documents and Visuals.*

◆ *For a description of the collaborative review process, see Chapter 5, Collaborative Writing.*

◆ *For a review of revising strategies, see Chapter 4, Revising the Draft.*

material based on his or her specialty or background and collaborates on every facet of the writing process:

- Planning the report
- Researching the subject and writing a chapter or section of the report
- Reviewing the drafts of other team members
- Revising their drafts on the basis of comments from all other team members

A team leader usually coordinates the team's work by setting a schedule for the work, leading the effort to plan the report, assigning responsibilities, coordinating all content reviews, editing the final draft, and overseeing production and distribution of the final report. The team leader also performs the essential task of controlling the master draft to ensure that it is current and accurate, and that no parts are confused with earlier drafts that have been revised and superseded.

 DIGITAL TIPS: Automating Report Formatting

In most word-processing programs, you can create styles — sets of formatting characteristics for text elements such as headings, paragraphs, and lists — that allow you to automate much of the work of formatting your report. Once you have specified your styles, save them as a template and use it each time you create a formal report. Creating a template allows you to automate:

- Fonts and font sizes for text, headings, titles, footnotes, headers, and footers
- Paragraph formats, including indentation and margins
- Lists, including indentation from the margin and spacing
- Number of columns
- The table of contents based on a report's headings and subheadings

For step-by-step instructions, see <bedfordstmartins.com/writingthatworks> and select *Digital Tips*, Automating Report Formatting.

■ Transmittal Letter or Memo

When you submit a formal report, include with it a brief transmittal (or cover) letter or memo that identifies the topic the formal report addresses and explains why the report was prepared. Written in the form of a standard business letter or memo, the transmittal most often opens with a brief paragraph (one or two sentences) explaining what is being sent and why. The next paragraph contains a brief summary of the report's contents or stresses some feature that would be important to the audience. This section may also mention any special conditions under which the material was prepared (limitations of time or money, for instance). The closing paragraph may acknowledge any help received in preparing the report, or express the hope that the information fulfills its purpose.

Typically, most transmittal letters and memos are composed of these elements. In any case, they should be brief—usually one page. Figure 11–1 shows a sample transmittal memo.

◆ *Examples of transmittal letters are also shown in Figures 9–1 and 9–2.*

CGF Aircraft Corporation
Memo

To: Members of the Ethics and Business Conduct Committee
From: Susan Litzinger, Director of Ethics and Business Conduct 𝒮𝓛
Date: March 3, 2006
Subject: Reported Ethics Cases 2005

Enclosed is "Reported Ethics Cases: 2005 Annual Report." This report, required by CGF Policy CGF-EP-01, contains a review of the ethics cases handled by CGF ethics officers and managers during 2005, the first year of our Ethics Program.

The ethics cases reported are analyzed according to two categories: (1) major ethics cases, or those potentially involving serious violations of company policy or illegal conduct, and (2) minor ethics cases, or those that do not involve serious policy violations or illegal conduct. The report also examines the mode of contact in all of the reported cases and the disposition of the substantiated major ethics cases.

It is my hope that this report will provide the committee with the information needed to assess the effectiveness of the first year of CGF's Ethics Program and to plan for the coming year. Please let me know if you have any questions about this report or if you need further information. I may be reached at (555) 211-2121 and by e-mail at sl@cgf.com.

Enc.

Addressed to recipients designated by the program

Brief opening describes the enclosure

Brief summary of report contents

Closing with offer of additional support

Enclosure notation

Figure 11–1   Transmittal Memo for a Formal Report   *Source:* Reprinted and adapted by permission of Susan Litzinger, a student at Pennsylvania State University, Altoona.

■ Front Matter

The front matter, which includes all the elements that precede the body of the report, serves several purposes: (1) It gives the audience a general idea of the author's purpose in writing the report; (2) it indicates whether the report contains the kind of information that the audience is looking for; and (3) it lists where in the report the audience can find specific chapters, headings, illustrations, and tables. Not all formal reports require every one of these elements. A title page and table of contents are usually mandatory, but whether an abstract, a list of figures, a list of tables, a foreword, a preface, and a list of abbreviations and symbols are

ON THE WEB

For additional formal reports, go to bedfords/martins.com/ writingthatworks and select Model Documents Gallery.

included will depend on the scope of the report and its intended audience. Scientific and technical reports, for example, often include a separate listing of abbreviations and symbols, while in most business reports, such lists are unnecessary. The front-matter pages are numbered with lowercase Roman numerals. Throughout the report, page numbers are often centered either near the bottom or near the top of each page.

Title Page

Although the formats of title pages vary, the page could include the following information: (1) the full title of the report; (2) the name(s) of the writers, principal investigators, or compilers that prepared it; (3) the date the report was issued; (4) the name of the organization for which the writer(s) works; and (5) the name of the organization or person to which the report is submitted.

1. *Full title of the report.* The title should reflect the topic as well as the scope and objective of the report. Titles often provide the only basis on which audiences can decide whether to read a report. Aim for accuracy and conciseness: Titles too vague or too long not only hinder the audience but can prevent efficient filing and later retrieval. Follow these guidelines when creating the title:
   • Focus on the subject matter of the report. Avoid titles that begin "Notes on," "Studies on," "A Report on," or "Observations on." These phrases are often redundant and state the obvious. However, phrases such as "Annual Report" or "Feasibility Study" should be used in a title or subtitle because they help define the purpose and scope of the document.
   • Avoid using abbreviations in the title. Use them only when the report is intended for an audience familiar enough with the topic that the abbreviation will be understood.
   • Do not include the period covered by a report in the title; include that information in a subtitle:

   ▶ EFFECTS OF PROPOSED HIGHWAY CONSTRUCTION ON PROPERTY VALUES
   Tri-State Regional District
   Annual Report, 2006

2. *Names of the writers, principal investigators, or compilers, as appropriate.* Frequently, contributors simply list their names. Sometimes they identify themselves by their job title in the organization (Jane R. Lihn, Cost Analyst; Rodrigo Sánchez, Head, Research and Development). They also identify themselves by their tasks in contributing to the report (Antoine Baume, Compiler; Wanda Landowska, Principal Investigator).

3. *Date or dates of the report.* For one-time reports, list the date when the report is to be distributed. For periodic reports, which may be issued monthly or quarterly, list the period that the present report covers in a subtitle, as well as the date when the report is to be distributed.

4. *Name of the organization for which the writer works.*
5. *Name of the organization or individual to which the report is being submit-ted,* if the work is being done for an organization other than your own.

These categories are standard on most title pages. Some organizations may require additional information. A sample title page appears in Figure 11–2.

REPORTED ETHICS CASES
2005 Annual Report

*Report title
and subtitle*

Prepared by Susan Litzinger
Director of Ethics and Business Conduct

Report author

Report Distributed March 3, 2006

Date report issued

Prepared for
The Ethics and Business Conduct Committee
CGF Aircraft Corporation

Report recipient

Figure 11–2 Title Page of a Formal Report

The title page, although unnumbered, is considered page i (small Roman numeral one). The back of the title page, which is blank and unnumbered, is considered page ii, and the abstract then falls on page iii so that it appears on a right-hand (that is, an odd-numbered) page. For reports with printing on both sides of each sheet of paper, it is a long-standing printer's convention that right-hand pages are always odd-numbered and left-hand pages are always even-numbered. (Note the pagination in this book.) New sections and chapters of reports typically begin on a new right-hand page. Reports with printing on only one side of each sheet can be numbered consecutively regardless of where new sections begin.

Abstracts

An abstract is a condensed version of a longer work that summarizes and highlights the major points. One of its main purposes is to enable your prospective reader to decide whether to read the whole work. Usually 200 to 250 words long, an abstract must make sense independently of the work it summarizes. Depending on the kind of information they contain, abstracts are usually classified as either descriptive or informative.

A descriptive abstract includes information about the purpose, scope, and methods used to arrive at the findings contained in the report. It is thus a slightly expanded table of contents in paragraph form. Provided that it adequately summarizes the information, a descriptive abstract need not be longer than several sentences (Figure 11–3).

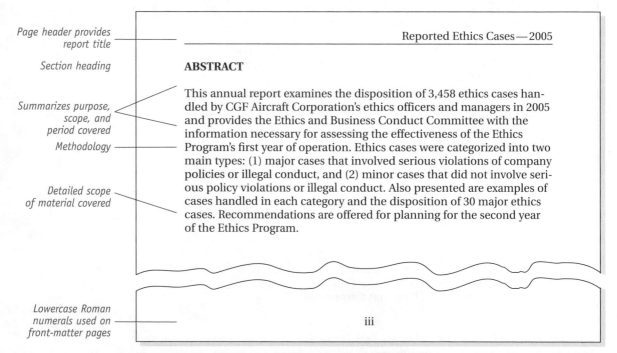

Page header provides report title

Reported Ethics Cases—2005

Section heading

ABSTRACT

Summarizes purpose, scope, and period covered

Methodology

This annual report examines the disposition of 3,458 ethics cases handled by CGF Aircraft Corporation's ethics officers and managers in 2005 and provides the Ethics and Business Conduct Committee with the information necessary for assessing the effectiveness of the Ethics Program's first year of operation. Ethics cases were categorized into two main types: (1) major cases that involved serious violations of company policies or illegal conduct, and (2) minor cases that did not involve serious policy violations or illegal conduct. Also presented are examples of cases handled in each category and the disposition of 30 major ethics cases. Recommendations are offered for planning for the second year of the Ethics Program.

Detailed scope of material covered

Lowercase Roman numerals used on front-matter pages

iii

Figure 11–3 **Descriptive Abstract of a Formal Report**

An informative abstract is an expanded version of the descriptive abstract. In addition to information about the purpose, scope, and methods of the original report, the informative abstract includes the results, conclusions, and recommendations, if any. The informative abstract thus retains the tone and essential scope of the report while omitting its details (Figure 11–4).

Which of the two types of abstract should you write? The answer depends on your employer. If it has a policy, comply with it. Otherwise, aim to satisfy the needs of the principal readers of your report. Informative abstracts satisfy the needs of the widest possible audience, but descriptive abstracts are preferable for information surveys, progress reports that combine information from more than one project, and any report that compiles a variety of information. For these types of reports,

---

Reported Ethics Cases—2005 · · · · · · · · · · · *Page header provides report title*

ABSTRACT · · · · · · · · · · · *Section heading*

This annual report examines the disposition of 3,458 ethics cases handled by CGF Aircraft Corporation's ethics officers and managers in 2005 and provides the Ethics and Business Conduct Committee with the information necessary for assessing the effectiveness of the Ethics Program's first year of operation. · · · · · · · · · · · *Purpose and scope*

Ethics cases were categorized into two main types: (1) major cases, that involved serious violations of company policies or illegal conduct, and (2) minor cases that did not involve serious policy violations or illegal conduct. Also presented are examples of cases handled in each category and the disposition of 30 major ethics cases. · · · · · · · · · · · *Methodology*

The effectiveness of CGF's Ethics Program during the first year of implementation is most evidenced by (1) the active participation of employees regarding ethics concerns, and (2) the action taken in the cases they reported. Disseminating information about the disposition of ethics cases sends a message to employees that unethical or illegal conduct will not be tolerated. · · · · · · · · · · · *Conclusions*

Recommendations for planning for the second year of the Ethics Program are (1) continuing the channels of communication now available in the Ethics Program, (2) increasing financial and technical support for the Ethics Hotline, (3) disseminating the annual ethics report to employees to ensure their awareness of CGF's commitment to uphold its Ethics Policy and Procedures, and (4) implementing measures to promote ethical behavior and reward ethical conduct. · · · · · · · · · · · *Recommendations*

Page footer provides page number

iii

Figure 11–4   Informative Abstract of a Formal Report

conclusions and recommendations either do not exist in the original or are too numerous to include in an abstract. Typically, an abstract follows the title page and is numbered page iii.

Write the abstract after finishing your report. Otherwise, your abstract may not accurately reflect the final product. Begin with a topic sentence that announces the subject and scope of the report. Then, using the major and minor heads of your table of contents to distinguish primary from secondary ideas, decide what material is relevant to your abstract. Write clearly and concisely, eliminating unnecessary words and ideas, but do not omit articles (*a, an, the*) and important transitional words and phrases (*however, therefore, but, in summary*). Write complete sentences, but avoid stringing a group of short sentences end to end; instead, combine ideas by using subordination and parallel structure. As a rule, spell out most acronyms and all but the most common abbreviations (°C, °F, mph). Finally, as you summarize, keep the tone and emphasis consistent with the original report.

◆ *For additional advice, review Summarizing on page 177 in Chapter 6, Researching Your Subject.*

WRITER'S CHECKLIST
Writing Abstracts

Include the following information:

- ☑ Subject
- ☑ Scope
- ☑ Purpose
- ☑ Methods used
- ☑ Results obtained (informative abstract only)
- ☑ Recommendations made, if any (informative abstract only)

Do not include the following kinds of information:

- ☑ Detailed discussion or explanation of the methods used
- ☑ Administrative details about how the research was undertaken, who funded it, who worked on it, and the like, unless such details have a bearing on the document's purpose
- ☑ Illustrations, tables, charts, maps, and bibliographic references
- ☑ Any information that does not appear in the original document

Table of Contents

A table of contents lists all the headings of the report in their order of appearance, along with their page numbers. It includes a listing of all front matter and back matter except the title page and the table of contents itself. The table of contents begins on a new right-hand page. Note that in Figure 11–5 the table of contents is numbered page v because it follows the abstract (page iii), and because page iv is blank.

Along with the abstract, a table of contents enables your audience to preview the information covered in a report and decide whether to read further. It also aids a reader who may want to look only at certain sections of the report. For this reason, the wording of chapter and section titles in the table of contents should always be identical to those in the text.

TABLE OF CONTENTS

v

Header provides report title

Major and subordinate headings differentiated by typeface and indentations

Page number for each section

Footer provides page number

Figure 11–6   Table of Contents of a Formal Report

    Sometimes, the table of contents is followed by lists of figures and tables contained in the report. These lists should always be presented separately, and a page number should be given for each item listed.

List of Figures

When a report contains more than five figures, list them by title, along with their page numbers, in a separate section beginning on a new page and immediately following the table of contents. Number figures consecutively with Arabic numbers.

Figures include all illustrations—drawings, photographs, maps, charts, and graphs—contained in the report.

List of Tables

When a report contains more than five tables, list them, along with their titles and page numbers, in a separate section immediately following the list of figures (if there is one). Number tables consecutively with Arabic numbers.

Foreword

A foreword is an optional introductory statement written by someone other than the author. It generally provides background information about the publication's significance and places it in the context of other works in the field. The author of the foreword is usually an authority in the field or an executive of the company. The author's name and affiliation and the date the foreword was written appear on a separate line below the foreword.

Preface

A preface is an optional introductory statement used to announce the purpose, background, or scope of the report. Sometimes a preface specifies the audience for whom the report is intended, and it may also highlight the relationship of the report to a given project or program. A preface may contain acknowledgments of help received during the course of the project or in the preparation of the report, and, finally, it may cite permission obtained for the use of copyrighted works. If a preface is not included, place this type of information, if it is essential, in the introduction (discussed later in this chapter). Figure 11–6 shows a sample preface.

The preface follows the table of contents (and the lists of figures and tables and the foreword, if these are present). It begins on a separate page, is numbered with Roman numerals, and is titled "Preface."

List of Abbreviations and Symbols

When the abbreviations and symbols used in a report are numerous, and when there is a chance that the audience will not be able to interpret them, the front matter should include a list of all abbreviations and symbols and what they stand for in the report. Such a list, which follows the preface, is particularly appropriate for technical reports whose audience is not restricted to technical specialists.

Figure 11–7 shows an example of a list of symbols that appear in a report as part of equations that calculate the transfer of heat and water vapor from the surface of cooling ponds at industrial sites. The list is made up of special symbols used in this report. The author assumes that the report readers have a technical education, however, because BTU (British thermal unit), Hg (chemical symbol for mercury), and similar terms are not identified.

Reported Ethics Cases — 2005

PREFACE

The CGF Aircraft Corporation takes its commitment to an ethical work environment seriously. Throughout its 64-year history, CGF has fostered high ethical standards in its relations with its customers, suppliers, and employees. The size, diversity, and decentralized locations of our workforce make it imperative that CGF's ethical commitment — both in principle and in practice — be formalized. To this end, the CGF Aircraft Corporation established a corporation-wide ethics program in August 2004. The goal of the program is to "promote a positive work environment that encourages open communication regarding ethics and compliance issues and concerns."

The Office of Ethics and Business Conduct (OEBC) was created to implement and administer the program. The director of the OEBC and seven ethics officers from throughout the corporation are responsible for the following program objectives:

- Communicate the values and standards for CGF's Ethics Program to employees.

- Inform employees about company policies regarding ethical business conduct.

- Establish company-wide channels for employees to obtain information and guidance in resolving ethics concerns.

- Implement company-wide ethics-awareness and education programs.

This report examines the nature and disposition of the ethics cases handled by the OEBC in 2005, the first year of operation. The report was compiled to provide the corporation's Ethics and Business Committee of the OEBC with the information necessary to assess the effectiveness of the first year of CGF's ethics program.

This report represents the efforts of the dedicated staff of the OEBC, the ethics officers, and the many managers and employees throughout CGF. We wish to acknowledge their active support and contributions to this report and to the program.

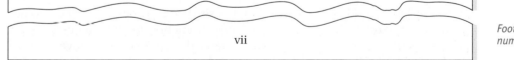

vii

Header provides report title

Section heading

Background and purpose of program

Program background

Bulleted list makes objectives easy to read

Purpose and scope of report

Audience for report

Acknowledgment of help in preparation of report

Footer provides page number

Figure 11–6   Preface of a Formal Report

SYMBOLS

A	Pond surface area, ft^2 or acres
A_0	One-half the daily insulation, BTU/ft^2
A_n	Surface area of nth segment of the plugflow model, ft^2
C	Cloud cover in tenths of the total sky obscured
C_1	Bowen's ratio, 0.26 mmHg/°F
C_P	Heat capacity of water, $BTU/lb/°F$
E_1, E_2	Estimation of equilibrium temperatures using data from off-site and on-site records, respectively, °F
$E(x)$	Estimation of equilibrium temperature using monthly average meteorologic data, °F
e_a	Saturation pressure of air above pond surface, mmHg
e_s	Saturation pressure of air at surface temperature, T_s, mmHg
g	Skew coefficient
H	Heat content, BTU

Figure 11–7   List of Symbols

■ Body

The body is the section of the report that describes in detail the methods and procedures used to generate the report, demonstrates how results were obtained, describes the results, draws conclusions, and, if appropriate, makes recommendations. It includes the following:

◆ *For guidance about page-level layout and design elements — typography, margins, columns, headers and footers, and the like — see pages 206–216 in Chapter 7, Designing Effective Documents and Visuals.*

- An executive summary
- An introduction
- The text (including headings, tables, illustrations, and references)
- Conclusions and recommendations

Number the first page of the body page 1 in Arabic rather than Roman numerals.

Executive Summary

The body begins with an executive summary that provides a more-complete overview of the report than the abstract does. It enables readers to quickly scan the report's primary points. The summary states the purpose of the investigation and gives major findings; provides background; states the scope; provides conclusions; and, if any are made, gives recommendations. It also describes the procedures used to conduct the study. Although more complete than an abstract, the executive summary should not contain a detailed description of the work on which the findings, conclusions, and recommendations were based. The length of the summary is proportional to the length of the report; typically, the summary should be approximately 10 percent of the length of the report.

Some executive summaries follow the organization of the report. Others high-light the findings, conclusions, and recommendations by summarizing them first, before going on to discuss procedures or methodology.

Like the abstract, the executive summary should be written so that it can be read independently of the report. It must not refer by number to figures, tables, or references contained elsewhere in the report. Because executive summaries are frequently read in place of the full report, all uncommon symbols, abbreviations, and acronyms must be spelled out.

Figure 11–8 shows an executive summary of the report on the Ethics Program at CGF Aircraft Corporation.

WRITER'S CHECKLIST
Writing Executive Summaries

- ☑ Write the executive summary after you have completed the original document.
- ☑ Avoid using terminology that may not be familiar to your readers.
- ☑ Spell out all uncommon symbols, abbreviations, and acronyms.
- ☑ Do not refer by number to figures, tables, or references contained elsewhere in the report.
- ☑ Make the summary concise, but do not omit transitional words and phrases (such as *however*, *moreover*, *therefore*, *for example*, and *in summary*).
- ☑ Include only information discussed in the original document.

Introduction

The introduction provides your audience with any general information — such as why the report has been written — required to understand the details of the rest of the report. State the subject, the purpose, the scope, and the way you plan to develop the topic. You may also describe how the report will be organized, but, as with the descriptive abstract, exclude specific findings, conclusions, and recommendations. Figure 11–9 shows the introduction to the report on the CGF Ethics Program. Note that the contents of the introduction and the contents of the preface may overlap in some cases.

Introducing the Subject

The introduction should state the subject of the report. However, it should also include any necessary background information on the definition, history, or theory of the subject that provides context for the audience.

Stating the Purpose

The statement of the purpose in your introduction should function as a topic sentence does in a paragraph. It should make your audience aware of your goal as they read your supporting statements and examples and tell them whether your material provides a new perspective or clarifies an existing perspective.

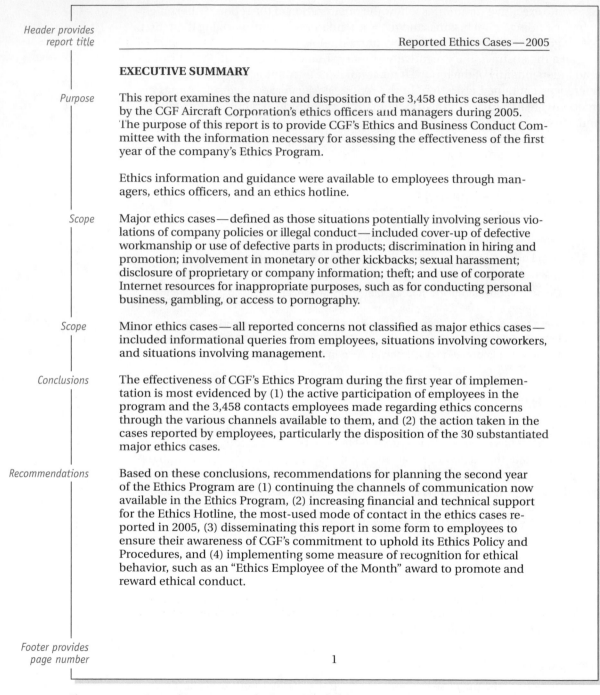

Header provides report title

Reported Ethics Cases—2005

EXECUTIVE SUMMARY

Purpose

This report examines the nature and disposition of the 3,458 ethics cases handled by the CGF Aircraft Corporation's ethics officers and managers during 2005. The purpose of this report is to provide CGF's Ethics and Business Conduct Committee with the information necessary for assessing the effectiveness of the first year of the company's Ethics Program.

Ethics information and guidance were available to employees through managers, ethics officers, and an ethics hotline.

Scope

Major ethics cases—defined as those situations potentially involving serious violations of company policies or illegal conduct—included cover-up of defective workmanship or use of defective parts in products; discrimination in hiring and promotion; involvement in monetary or other kickbacks; sexual harassment; disclosure of proprietary or company information; theft; and use of corporate Internet resources for inappropriate purposes, such as for conducting personal business, gambling, or access to pornography.

Scope

Minor ethics cases—all reported concerns not classified as major ethics cases—included informational queries from employees, situations involving coworkers, and situations involving management.

Conclusions

The effectiveness of CGF's Ethics Program during the first year of implementation is most evidenced by (1) the active participation of employees in the program and the 3,458 contacts employees made regarding ethics concerns through the various channels available to them, and (2) the action taken in the cases reported by employees, particularly the disposition of the 30 substantiated major ethics cases.

Recommendations

Based on these conclusions, recommendations for planning the second year of the Ethics Program are (1) continuing the channels of communication now available in the Ethics Program, (2) increasing financial and technical support for the Ethics Hotline, the most-used mode of contact in the ethics cases reported in 2005, (3) disseminating this report in some form to employees to ensure their awareness of CGF's commitment to uphold its Ethics Policy and Procedures, and (4) implementing some measure of recognition for ethical behavior, such as an "Ethics Employee of the Month" award to promote and reward ethical conduct.

Footer provides page number

1

Figure 11–8   Executive Summary of a Formal Report

Header provides report title

INTRODUCTION

This annual report examines the disposition of the 3,458 reported ethics cases in 2005 and provides the Ethics and Business Conduct Committee with the information necessary for assessing the effectiveness of the first year of CGF's Ethics Program. Recommendations are given for planning the second year of the Ethics Program.

Purpose

Ethics and Business Conduct Policy and Procedures

Subheading signals shift in topic

Effective January 1, 2005, the Ethics and Business Conduct Committee implemented Policy CGF-EP-01 and Procedure CGF-EP-02 for the administration of CGF's new Ethics Program. The purpose of the Ethics Program is to "promote ethical business conduct through open communication and compliance with company ethics standards" (CGF "Ethical Business Conduct").

Background

The Office of Ethics and Business Conduct (OEBC) administers the Ethics Program. The director of OEBC, along with seven ethics officers throughout CGF, is responsibile for the following objectives:

- Communicate the values, standards, and goals of CGF's Ethics Program to employees.
- Inform employees about company ethics policies.
- Provide channels for employee education and guidance in resolving ethics concerns.
- Implement company-wide programs in ethics awareness, education, and recognition.

Bulleted list makes information easy to read

Employee accessibility to ethics information and guidance became the immediate goal of the OEBC in its first year of operation. The following channels were set up in 2005:

Background

- Managers throughout CGF received intensive ethics training and employees were encouraged to go to their managers as the first point of contact.
- Ethics officers were available to employees through face-to-face or telephone contact, to managers, to callers using the Ethics Hotline, and by e-mail.
- The Ethics Hotline was available to all employees, 24 hours a day, 7 days a week, to report ethics concerns anonymously.

Confidentiality Issues

Subheading signals shift in topic

CGF's Ethics Policy ensures confidentiality and anonymity for employees who raise genuine ethics concerns. Procedure CGF-EP-02 guarantees appropriate discipline, including dismissal, for retaliation or retribution against any employee who reports any genuine ethics concern.

Footer provides page number

Figure 11–9   Introduction to a Formal Report (continued)

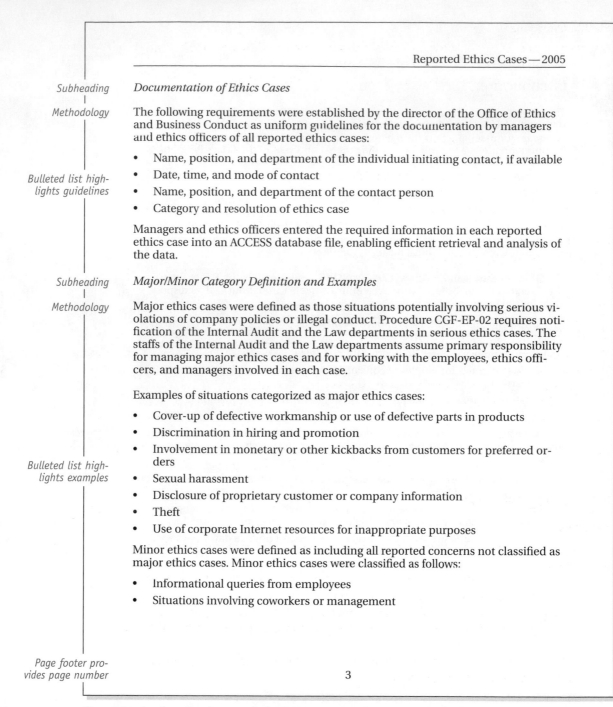

Reported Ethics Cases — 2005

Subheading

Documentation of Ethics Cases

Methodology

The following requirements were established by the director of the Office of Ethics and Business Conduct as uniform guidelines for the documentation by managers and ethics officers of all reported ethics cases:

- Name, position, and department of the individual initiating contact, if available
- Date, time, and mode of contact

Bulleted list high-lights guidelines

- Name, position, and department of the contact person
- Category and resolution of ethics case

Managers and ethics officers entered the required information in each reported ethics case into an ACCESS database file, enabling efficient retrieval and analysis of the data.

Subheading

Major/Minor Category Definition and Examples

Methodology

Major ethics cases were defined as those situations potentially involving serious violations of company policies or illegal conduct. Procedure CGF-EP-02 requires notification of the Internal Audit and the Law departments in serious ethics cases. The staffs of the Internal Audit and the Law departments assume primary responsibility for managing major ethics cases and for working with the employees, ethics officers, and managers involved in each case.

Examples of situations categorized as major ethics cases:

- Cover-up of defective workmanship or use of defective parts in products
- Discrimination in hiring and promotion
- Involvement in monetary or other kickbacks from customers for preferred orders

Bulleted list high-lights examples

- Sexual harassment
- Disclosure of proprietary customer or company information
- Theft
- Use of corporate Internet resources for inappropriate purposes

Minor ethics cases were defined as including all reported concerns not classified as major ethics cases. Minor ethics cases were classified as follows:

- Informational queries from employees
- Situations involving coworkers or management

Page footer provides page number

3

Figure 11–9 Introduction to a Formal Report (continued)

Stating the Scope

The statement of scope tells the audience how much or how little detail to expect. Does your report present a broad survey of the topic, or does it concentrate on one part of the topic? Once you state your scope broadly, stop. Save the details for the main body of the report.

Previewing How the Topic Will Be Developed

In a long report, state how you plan to develop or organize your topic. Is the report an analysis of the component parts of some whole? Is it an analysis of selected parts (or samples) of a whole? Is the material presented in chronological order? Does it move from details to general conclusions, or from a general statement to the details that verify the statement? Does it set out to show whether a hypothesis is correct or incorrect? Stating your topic allows your audience to anticipate how the subject will be presented and gives them a basis for evaluating how you arrived at your conclusions or recommendations.

Text (Body)

Generally the longest section of the report, the text (or body) presents the details of how the topic was investigated, how the problem was solved, how the best choice from among alternatives was selected, or whatever else the report covers. This information is often clarified and further developed by the use of illustrations and tables and may be supported by references to other studies.

Most formal reports have no single best organization—it will depend on the topic and on how you have investigated it. The text is ordinarily divided into several major sections, comparable to the chapters in a book. These sections are then subdivided to reflect logical divisions in your main sections. See the sample table of contents (Figure 11–5) for an example of how the text for the report on the Ethics Program at the CGF Aircraft Corporation was organized. Figure 11–10 shows the body of the same report.

Headings

The use of headings (or heads) in the body of formal reports is important. Headings make the report more accessible to the audience by (1) dividing the body into manageable segments, (2) calling attention to the main topics, and (3) signaling changes of topics. Especially for long and complicated reports, you may need several levels of headings to indicate major divisions and subdivisions of the topic. Make headings most effective by following these guidelines on pages 389 and 394:

- Use headings to signal a new topic or, if it is a lower-level heading, a new subtopic within the larger topic.
- Avoid too many or too few headings or levels of headings; too many clutter a document and too few fail to provide a recognizable structure.

Header provides report title

Heading

Figure labeled and cross-referenced in text (cross-reference precedes figure)

Figure boxed and set off by white space above and below

Heading signals shift in topic

Cross-reference precedes figure

Page footer provides page number

ANALYSIS OF REPORTED ETHICS CASES

Reported Ethics Cases by Major/Minor Category

CGF ethics officers and managers company-wide handled a total of 3,458 ethics situations during 2005. Of these cases, only 172, or 5 percent, involved reported concerns of a serious enough nature to be classified as major ethics cases (see Figure 1). Major ethics cases were defined as those situations potentially involving serious violations of company policy or illegal conduct.

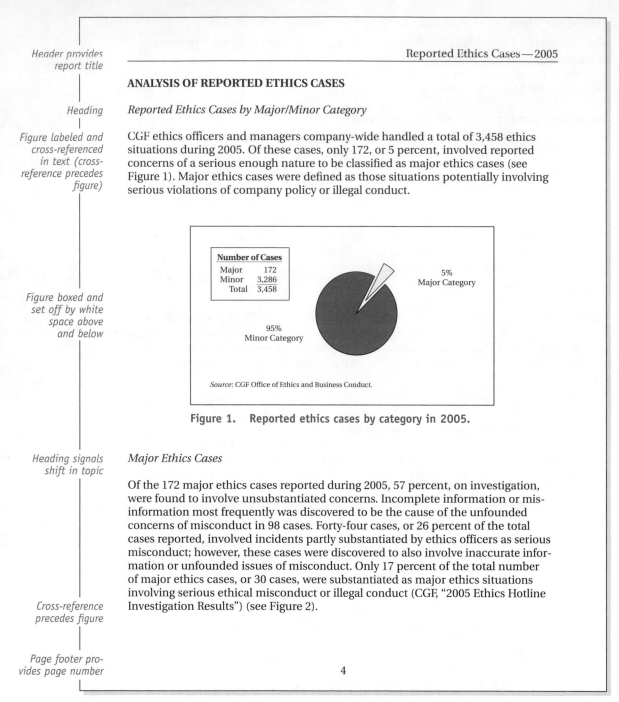

Number of Cases	
Major	172
Minor	3,286
Total	3,458

5%
Major Category

95%
Minor Category

Source: CGF Office of Ethics and Business Conduct.

Figure 1.   Reported ethics cases by category in 2005.

Major Ethics Cases

Of the 172 major ethics cases reported during 2005, 57 percent, on investigation, were found to involve unsubstantiated concerns. Incomplete information or misinformation most frequently was discovered to be the cause of the unfounded concerns of misconduct in 98 cases. Forty-four cases, or 26 percent of the total cases reported, involved incidents partly substantiated by ethics officers as serious misconduct; however, these cases were discovered to also involve inaccurate information or unfounded issues of misconduct. Only 17 percent of the total number of major ethics cases, or 30 cases, were substantiated as major ethics situations involving serious ethical misconduct or illegal conduct (CGF, "2005 Ethics Hotline Investigation Results") (see Figure 2).

Figure 11–10   Body of a Formal Report (continued)

Header provides report title

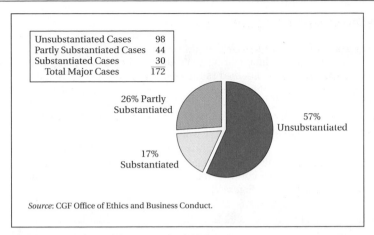

Unsubstantiated Cases	98
Partly Substantiated Cases	44
Substantiated Cases	30
Total Major Cases	172

Source: CGF Office of Ethics and Business Conduct.

Pie chart showing percentages and augmented with specific values

Figure 2.   Major ethics cases in 2005.

White space above and below figure boxes

Of the 30 substantiated major ethics cases, seven remain under investigation and two cases are currently in litigation. Of the remaining substantiated cases, five resulted in severe disciplinary action: two employees were dismissed and three were demoted. Seven employees were given written warnings, and nine employees received verbal warnings (see Figure 3).

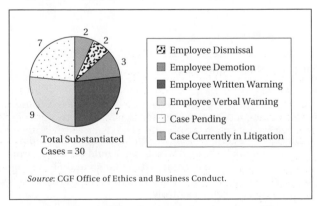

Total Substantiated Cases = 30

- Employee Dismissal
- Employee Demotion
- Employee Written Warning
- Employee Verbal Warning
- Case Pending
- Case Currently in Litigation

Source: CGF Office of Ethics and Business Conduct.

Figure with key to shading of values on pie chart

Figure 3.   Disposition of substantiated major ethics cases in 2005.

Footer provides page number

Figure 11–10   Body of a Formal Report (continued)

Header provides report title

Subheading

Bulleted list highlights information

Cross-reference precedes figure

White space above and below figure box

Footer provides page number

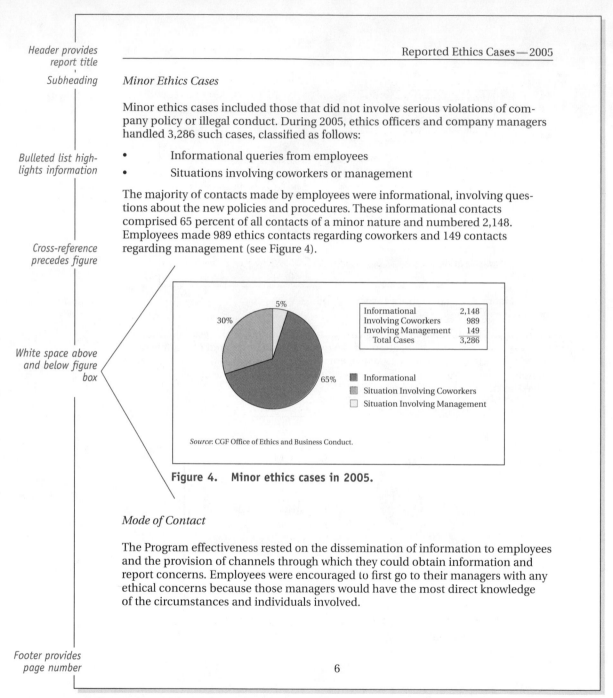

Reported Ethics Cases—2005

Minor Ethics Cases

Minor ethics cases included those that did not involve serious violations of company policy or illegal conduct. During 2005, ethics officers and company managers handled 3,286 such cases, classified as follows:

• Informational queries from employees

• Situations involving coworkers or management

The majority of contacts made by employees were informational, involving questions about the new policies and procedures. These informational contacts comprised 65 percent of all contacts of a minor nature and numbered 2,148. Employees made 989 ethics contacts regarding coworkers and 149 contacts regarding management (see Figure 4).

Informational	2,148
Involving Coworkers	989
Involving Management	149
Total Cases	3,286

■ Informational
▨ Situation Involving Coworkers
☐ Situation Involving Management

Source: CGF Office of Ethics and Business Conduct.

Figure 4.   Minor ethics cases in 2005.

Mode of Contact

The Program effectiveness rested on the dissemination of information to employees and the provision of channels through which they could obtain information and report concerns. Employees were encouraged to first go to their managers with any ethical concerns because those managers would have the most direct knowledge of the circumstances and individuals involved.

Figure 11–10   Body of a Formal Report (continued)

Header provides report title

Other options were available, however, for employees who did not feel able to go to their manager. The ethics officers were available to employees through telephone conversations, face-to-face meetings, and e-mail messages. Ethics officers also served as contact points for managers in need of support and assistance in handling the ethics concerns reported to them by their subordinates.

The Ethics Hotline, operational in mid-January 2005, offered employees anonymity and confidentiality. It was accessible to all employees on a 24-hour, 7-day basis. Ethics officers handled calls reported through the hotline on a rotational basis.

In summary, ethics information and guidance was available to all employees during 2005 through the following channels:

- Employee to manager
- Employee telephone, face-to-face, and e-mail contact with ethics officers
- Manager to ethics officer
- Ethics Hotline

Bulleted lists summarize parallel information in parallel form

The mode of contact in the 3,458 reported ethics cases was as follows (see Figure 5):

Cross-reference precedes figure

- In 19 percent or 657 of the reported cases, employees went to managers with concerns.
- In 9 percent or 311 of the reported cases, employees contacted an ethics officer.
- In 5 percent or 173 of the reported cases, managers sought assistance from ethics officers.
- In 67 percent or 2,317 of the reported cases, employees used the Ethics Hotline.

Source: CGF Office of Ethics and Business Conduct.

White space above and below figure

Figure 5.   Mode of contact in reported ethics cases in 2005.

Footer provides page number

Figure 11–10   Body of a Formal Report   (continued)

- Use varying type styles and formatting conventions to distinguish among levels of headings (see Figure 11–11 and Designing Your Document on page 395).
- Ensure that headings at the same level are of relatively equal importance and follow parallel structure.
- Subdivide sections only as needed; not every section requires lower-level headings.
- When subdividing a section, always use two or more headings (a topic cannot logically be divided into fewer than two parts).
- Do not allow a heading to substitute for discussion; the text should read as if the heading were not there.
- Do not leave a heading as the final line of a page. If two lines of text cannot fit below a heading, start the section at the top of the next page.

FIRST-LEVEL HEADING

The text of the document begins here.

SECOND-LEVEL HEADING

The text of the document begins here.

Third-Level Heading

The text of the document begins here.

Fourth-Level Heading

The text of the document begins here.

Fifth-level heading. The text of the document begins here and continues normally to the next line of the page.

Figure 11–11   Common Type Style for Headings

The decimal numbering system uses a combination of numbers and decimal points to subordinate levels of headings in a report. The system is used primarily for scientific and technical reports. The outline in Figure 11–12 shows the correspondence between different levels of headings and the decimal numbers used. (Note that although the second-, third-, and fourth-level headings are indented in an outline or table of contents, as headings they are flush with the left margin in the body of the report.)

DESIGNING YOUR DOCUMENT
Heading Styles

Although various systems exist, the following guidelines for formatting up to five levels of headings are common:

First-Level Head

- All capital letters underlined or in 18-point boldface type
- Centered or flush left on the line by itself
- Two spaces above and one below

Second-Level Head

- All capital letters or in 14-point boldface type
- Flush left on a line by itself
- One space above and one space below

Third-Level Head

- Capital and lowercase letters underlined or in boldface type
- Flush left on a line by itself
- One space above and one space below

Fourth-Level Head

- Capital and lowercase letters *not* underlined or in boldface type
- One space above and one space below

Fifth-Level Head

- Indented as a paragraph on the same line as the first line of material it introduces
- Underlined or in italic typeface
- First letter capitalized; all others lowercase except proper nouns
- Ends with a period
- One space above the heading

Figure 11–11 illustrates this system.

```
1.       MAJOR IDEA
1.1      Supporting idea for 1
1.2      Supporting idea for 1
1.2.1    Example or illustration of 1.2
1.2.2    Example or illustration of 1.2
1.2.2.1 Detail for 1.2.1
1.2.2.2 Detail for 1.2.1
1.3      Supporting idea for 1
2.       MAJOR IDEA
```

Figure 11–12   Decimal Numbering System for Headings

Explanatory Notes

Occasionally, reports contain notes that amplify terms or points for some readers that would be a distraction for others. This type of explanation is generally placed at the foot of the page on which the idea appears.

▶   A description of the 76 variables identified for inclusion in the regression equations, together with their method of construction, data, source, means, and ranges, is given in Appendix A. The following discussion elaborates on those variables that proved most important in explaining housing-price variations.[1]

       [1]The number in parentheses in the following discussion refers to the variable number as used in regression equations.

For additional guidance on the purpose of these notes, see Chapter 6, Researching Your Subject.

If such comments are very long, or if offering them as footnotes would crowd the pages of the report body, they may appear in a final "Notes" section instead.

Graphic and Tabular Matter

Formal reports often contain illustrations and tables that clarify and support the text. These materials may be numbered and sequenced in varying ways. If your organization has a preferred system, use it. If not, the following guidelines offer a typical system for numbering and smoothly integrating such materials into the text.

Identify each figure with a title and a number, in Arabic numerals, above or below the figure. For fairly short reports, number figures sequentially throughout the report (Figure 1, Figure 2, and so forth). For long reports, number figures by chapter or by section. According to this system, the first figure in Chapter 1 would be Figure 1.1 (or Figure 1–1), and the second figure would be Figure 1.2 (or Figure 1–2). In Chapter 2, the first figure would be Figure 2.1 (or Figure 2–1), and so on.

For a full discussion of creating and using illustrations, see Chapter 7, Designing Effective Documents and Visuals.

In the text, refer to figures by number rather than by location ("Figure 2.1" [or Figure 2–1] rather than "the figure below"). When the report is laid out and printed, the figures may not fall exactly where you originally expected. The figure or table should always be placed *after* its first mention in the text.

Identify each table with a title and a number, centering both of these lines above the table. For fairly short reports, number the tables sequentially throughout the report (Table 1, Table 2, and so on). For long reports, number tables by chapter or by section, according to the system described for figure numbering. As with figures, refer to tables in the text by number rather than by location ("Table 4.1" [or "Table 4–1"] rather than "the above table").

Conclusions

The conclusions section of a report pulls together the results or findings presented in the report and interprets them in the light of its purpose and methods. Consequently, this section is the focal point of the work, the reason for the report in the first place. The conclusions must grow out of the findings discussed in the body of the report; moreover, they must be consistent with what the introduction states as the purpose of the report and the report's methodology. For instance, if the introduction states that the report's objective is to assess the market for a new product, then the conclusion should focus on the requirements of the market examined and on how appropriate the new product is for that market.

Recommendations

Recommendations, which are sometimes combined with the conclusions, suggest a course of action that should be taken based on the results of the study. (Whether the report should make recommendations is determined when the report is being planned.) What consulting group should the firm hire for a special project? Which Web-page designer should the company sign a contract with? What new and emerging markets should the firm target? Which make of delivery van should the company purchase to replace the existing fleet? The recommendations section says, in effect, "I think we should purchase this, or do that, or hire them."

The emphasis here is on the verb *should*. Recommendations advise the audience on the best course of action based on the researcher's findings. Generally, a decision-maker in the organization, or a customer or client, makes the final decision about whether to accept the recommendations.

Figure 11–13 shows the conclusions and recommendations from the report on the CGF Ethics Program.

Works Cited (or References)

If you refer to material in, or quote directly from, a published work or other research source, you must cite those sources in the body of the text and provide a list of references in a separate section. Citing sources and listing references allows readers to locate and consult your sources and to find further information about the subject; the practice also enables you to avoid plagiarism while supporting your assertions and arguments with expert opinion and valid data. If your instructor or employer has a preferred reference style, follow it; otherwise, use the MLA or APA documentation guidelines shown in Chapter 6, Researching Your Subject. (*Note:* If you use the MLA style, the list is titled "Works Cited"; in APA style, it is titled "References.") For a relatively short report, place the references at the end of the body of the report, as shown in Figure 11–14. For a report with a number of sections or chapters, place the references at the end of each major section or chapter. In either case, title the reference or works-cited section as such and begin it on a new page. If a particular reference appears in more than one section or chapter, repeat it in full in each appropriate reference section.

◆ *For detailed guidance for documenting sources and avoiding plagiarism, see pages 179–199 in Chapter 6, Researching Your Subject.*

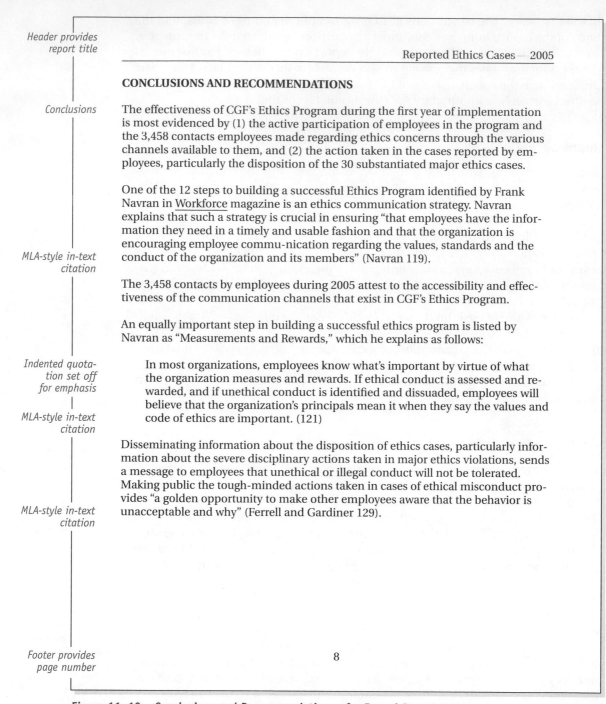

Header provides report title

CONCLUSIONS AND RECOMMENDATIONS

Conclusions

The effectiveness of CGF's Ethics Program during the first year of implementation is most evidenced by (1) the active participation of employees in the program and the 3,458 contacts employees made regarding ethics concerns through the various channels available to them, and (2) the action taken in the cases reported by employees, particularly the disposition of the 30 substantiated major ethics cases.

One of the 12 steps to building a successful Ethics Program identified by Frank Navran in <u>Workforce</u> magazine is an ethics communication strategy. Navran explains that such a strategy is crucial in ensuring "that employees have the information they need in a timely and usable fashion and that the organization is encouraging employee commu-nication regarding the values, standards and the conduct of the organization and its members" (Navran 119).

MLA-style in-text citation

The 3,458 contacts by employees during 2005 attest to the accessibility and effectiveness of the communication channels that exist in CGF's Ethics Program.

An equally important step in building a successful ethics program is listed by Navran as "Measurements and Rewards," which he explains as follows:

Indented quotation set off for emphasis

> In most organizations, employees know what's important by virtue of what the organization measures and rewards. If ethical conduct is assessed and rewarded, and if unethical conduct is identified and dissuaded, employees will believe that the organization's principals mean it when they say the values and code of ethics are important. (121)

MLA-style in-text citation

Disseminating information about the disposition of ethics cases, particularly information about the severe disciplinary actions taken in major ethics violations, sends a message to employees that unethical or illegal conduct will not be tolerated. Making public the tough-minded actions taken in cases of ethical misconduct provides "a golden opportunity to make other employees aware that the behavior is unacceptable and why" (Ferrell and Gardiner 129).

MLA-style in-text citation

Footer provides page number

8

Figure 11–13 Conclusions and Recommendations of a Formal Report (continued)

Header provides report title

With these two points in mind, I offer the following recommendations for planning the Ethics Program's second year:

Recommendations

- Continue the channels of communication now available in the Ethics Program.
- Increase financial and technical support for the Ethics Hotline, the most highly used mode of contact in the reported ethics cases in 2005.
- Disseminate this report in some form to employees to ensure employees' awareness of CGF's commitment to uphold its Ethics Policy and Procedures.
- Implement some measure of recognition for ethical behavior, such as an "Ethics Employee of the Month," to promote and reward ethical conduct.

Bulleted list highlights information

To ensure that employees see the value of their continued participation in the Ethics Program, feedback is essential. The information in this annual review, in some form, should be provided to employees. Knowing that the concerns they reported were taken seriously and resulted in appropriate action by Ethics Program administrators would reinforce employee involvement in the program. While the negative consequences of ethical misconduct contained in this report send a powerful message, a means of communicating the *positive* rewards of ethical conduct at CGF should be implemented. Various options for recognizing employees who exemplify ethical conduct should be considered and approved.

Recommendations

Continuation of the Ethics Program's successful 2005 operations, with the implementation of the above recommendations, should ensure the continued pursuit of the Ethics Program's purpose: "to promote a positive work environment that encourages open communication regarding ethics and compliance issues and concerns."

Footer provides page number

Figure 11–13   Conclusions and Recommendations of a Formal Report (continued)

Header provides report title

Works-cited listing follows MLA format

Footer provides page number

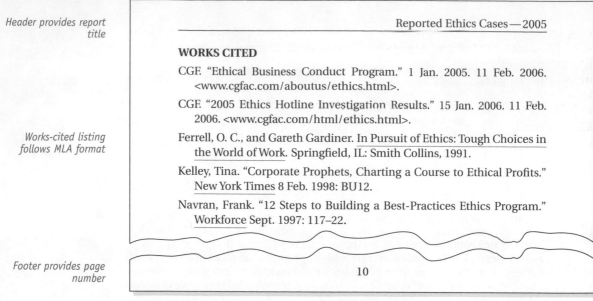

Figure 11–14   **Works-Cited Section of a Formal Report**

ETHICS NOTE

Always identify the sources of any facts, ideas, quotations, and paraphrases you in-clude in a report. Plagiarism — even if unintentional — is unethical and in some cases il-legal. Plagiarism in a college course may result in formal academic misconduct charges; on the job, it can get you fired. Avoid trouble by giving proper credit to others.

■ Back Matter

The back matter of a formal report contains supplementary material, such as where to find additional information about the topic (bibliography), and expands on certain subjects (appendixes). Other back-matter elements define the terms used (glossary) and provide information on how to easily locate information in the report (index). For very long formal reports, back-matter sections may be in-dividually numbered.

Bibliography

The bibliography is an alphabetical listing of all the sources you consulted to prepare the report—not just the ones you cite specifically—and suggests additional re-sources readers might want to consult. Accordingly, the bibliography may be longer than the works-cited section. A bibliography is not necessary if the Works Cited (or References) page contains a complete list of sources. Like other elements in the front and back matter, the bibliography starts on a new page and is labeled by name.

Appendixes

An appendix clarifies or supplements the body with information that is too detailed or lengthy for the primary audience but that is relevant to secondary audiences. Appendixes might provide long charts and supplementary graphs or tables, copies of questionnaires and other material used in gathering information, texts of interviews, pertinent correspondence, and explanations too long for explanatory footnotes. Generally, each appendix contains one type of material. For example, a report may have one appendix presenting a questionnaire and a second appendix presenting a detailed computer printout tabulating questionnaire results.

Place the first appendix on a new page directly after the bibliography; each additional appendix also begins on a new page. Identify each appendix with a title and a heading. Appendixes are ordinarily labeled Appendix A, Appendix B, and so on. If your report has only one appendix, label it "Appendix," followed by the title. To call it Appendix A implies that an Appendix B will follow.

If a report has only one appendix, the pages are generally numbered 1, 2, 3, and so forth. If it has more than one appendix, the pages are double-numbered according to the letter of each appendix (for example, the first page of Appendix B would be numbered B–1).

Glossary

A glossary is an alphabetical list of definitions of terms used in a formal report. If you are writing a report that will go to readers unfamiliar with many of the terms you use, include a glossary. If you do, keep the entries concise and be sure they are written in plain language to improve reader understanding.

▶   *Capital gain:* The difference between an assets purchase price and selling price, when the difference is positive.

Arrange the terms alphabetically, with each entry beginning on a new line. The definitions then follow the terms, dictionary style. In a formal report, the glossary appears as a separate section after the appendix(es) and bibliography, and it begins on a new page.

Regardless of whether you include a glossary, you must also define any specialized terms when they are first mentioned in the text.

Index

An index is an alphabetical list of all the major topics and subtopics found in the report. It cites the pages where each topic can be found and allows readers to find information on particular topics quickly and easily, as shown in Figure 11–15. Indexes are especially useful for reports that will serve as reference documents in a subject area for at least several years. The index always comes at the very end of the report.

Do not attempt to compile an index until the final manuscript is completed because terminology and page numbers will not be accurate before then. The key to a useful index is selectivity. Instead of listing every possible reference to a topic, select references to passages where the topic is discussed fully or where a significant point is made about it. Use the words or phrases that best represent a topic—those that a reader would most likely look for in an index. For example, the key terms in a reference to the development of legislation about environmental impact statements would probably be *legislation* and *environmental impact statement.*

An index entry can consist solely of a main entry and its page number; it can also include a main entry, subentries, and even sub-subentries, as shown in Figure 11–15. The first word of an entry should be the principal word because the reader will look for topics alphabetically by their main words. An index entry should be written as a noun or a noun phrase rather than as an adjective alone.

When you have compiled a list of key terms and cross-references for the entire work, sort the main entries alphabetically, then sort all subentries and sub-subentries alphabetically beneath their main entries.

ON THE WEB

The American Society of Indexers lists software available for indexing at its Web site, <www.asindexing.org>

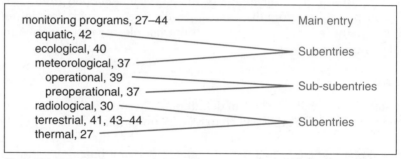

Figure 11–15   Index Entry (with Main Entry, Subentries, and Sub-subentries)

🖱 DIGITAL TIPS: Creating an Index

Word-processing software can help you save time when creating an index for your report.

■ Review the document to identify entries (the words, phrases, figure captions, or symbols that you wish to index).

■ Following your software's instructions, highlight and code these entries. (In Microsoft Word, for example, you can mark a keyword, and the software can automatically mark all other instances of the word.)

■ The software sorts the coded entries, eliminates duplications, and arranges the entries alphabetically with their page numbers in a separate section at the end of the document.

■ If you wish, create headings for each alphabetical grouping of the index (A, B, C, and so on).

■ Your draft index will still need careful review and revisions, but using the software to create the first draft can certainly save time. Review for what might be missing as well as for what is there.

For further instructions, see <bedfordstmartins.com/writingthatworks> and select *Digital Tips,* Creating an Index.

CHAPTER 11 SUMMARY: WRITING FORMAL REPORTS

Formal reports require thoughtful planning because of their varied audiences, purposes, scope, and complexity. To ensure that your formal reports are adequately planned and written, review the following summary checklist.

- Who is the principal audience for the report? Who is the secondary audience?
- Is the transmittal letter or memo necessary and addressed to the principal audience?
- Are the elements that make up the front matter, body, and back matter of the report organized correctly?
- Does the title page include the report title, preparer, and recipient?
- Does the abstract highlight the report's major points?
- Does the table of contents list section titles exactly as they appear throughout the report?
- Does the executive summary describe the purpose, major findings, conclusions, recommendations, and methodology used to reach the findings? Can it be read independently of the report?
- Does the body of the report enable the principal audience to interpret your findings, conclusions, and recommendations?
- Does the introduction state the purpose of the report, the scope of material it covers, how you plan to develop the topic, and how the report will be organized?
- Is the body of the report organized into logically divided sections that best represent how the topic was developed to reach its findings, conclusions, and recommendations?
- Do the conclusions grow logically from the report's findings?
- Do the recommendations advise the audience on the appropriate course of action to take based on the findings?
- Do the works cited or references provide enough information to permit a reader to locate a source of interest?
- Is the material in the appendixes of sufficient importance to be included but so voluminous or ancillary that its presence in the body of the report would impede the reader?
- Does the report include a large number of technical terms that should be defined for your audience in an alphabetically arranged glossary?
- Are the index terms sufficiently selective that they allow the audience to locate key topics throughout the report quickly and accurately?

ON THE WEB

For an online quiz on formal reports, go to Chapter 11, bedfordstmartins.com/ writingthatworks

Exercises

1. Write a brief analysis identifying different types of formal reports and list different situations in which each might be used.

2. Prepare a statement that defines the scope of a formal report, covering the benefits, risks, and costs of establishing an on-site fitness center at a local business with more than 200 employees.

3. Complete the following audience-profile questionnaire for the fitness-center report in Exercise 2 or for a hypothetical research, investigative, or annual report that you have been asked to prepare. Briefly explain the topic of your formal report and then answer the following questions:

ON THE WEB

For additional exercises on writing formal reports, go to Chapter 11, bedfordstmartins.com/ writingthatworks

    a. Who is your audience? (Write a 75- to 100-word description.)

    b. What does your audience already know about the subject?

    c. What do you want your audience to know?

    d. What might be your readers' attitude toward the topic? (Explore several alternatives.)

    e. Why will your audience be reading the report?

    f. How will your readers' perception of the report affect the project?

4. Keeping in mind that design is an important part of a formal report, prepare a title page for the fitness-center report in Exercises 2 and 3 or for a hypothetical research, investigative, or annual report that you have been asked to prepare and bring it to class. Refer to pages 376–378 for guidelines as you design your title page.

5. Considering your audience and purpose, determine what elements you would need to include in the fitness-center or hypothetical report from Exercises 2, 3, and 4. Then prepare a table of contents that details the materials the final report would include.

6. Make a list of the many kinds of reports that the professionals with whom you or your family interact on a yearly basis might need to write. Consider, for example, your medical doctor, dentist, accountant, or contractor. With permission of the writer, obtain a copy of an actual report. (If you cannot obtain a sample from your personal contacts, you may use the annual report of a large company with which you interact regularly, such as Proctor and Gamble or Staples.) Outline the body of this report and present it to the class.

7. Write a brief explanation of why you think either the executive summary or the abstract is the most important single piece of a formal report. Refer to the report included in this chapter or to another sample report to support your conclusions.

8. Assume you are starting a business of your own. First, determine what type of business you would start, depending on your knowledge or experience. Based on what you know about such a business, write an introduction for a formal report, explaining what your business will be and identifying what city would be the best location for your business and why. Assume that you are preparing this report to attach to a request for funding from the Small Business Administration. Submit an outline to your instructor before you begin your draft.

9. Assume that you work in the corporate office of a high-end automotive manufacturer and that you are coordinating a report that analyzes the effectiveness of new management initiatives that have gone into effect in the last year. Two of the people on your team, who have been lax in meeting periodic deadlines, submit hastily written drafts on the day before the entire report must be printed. To your dismay, you realize that each of them has peppered his section with abbreviations for trendy managerial phrases, such as "JIT" for "Just-in-Time" delivery and "CSR" for "Corporate Social Responsibility." There is no time left to revise these sections, but you know that several of the report's readers will not understand the abbreviations. Using the following terms, create a List of Abbreviations for the report to explain what phrases they stand for and what those phrases mean. (You may have to do a little research to learn what the abbreviations stand for and what business concepts they refer to.)

ALF	BID	KAS
ALO	CSR	KISS
ASK	FMCG	MOP
ATNA	JIT	SONTTAP

10. Using the guidelines on pages 401–402, create an index for the sample formal re-port reprinted in Figures 11–9, 11–10, 11–13, and 11–14. As your instructor directs, exchange your index with another student and make a list of terms that differ in the indexes. Write a brief note for each distinctive index entry, evaluating whether you think it would be good to add to your index.

Collaborative Classroom Projects

ON THE WEB

For more collaborative classroom projects, go to Chapter 11, bedfordstmartins.com/ writingthatworks

1. Bring to class a sample abstract for a journal article related to your major field of study. Divide into teams with classmates who share a similar major area of study. Appoint a group leader and a recorder. As a group, review the abstracts and answer the following questions about each:
    a. How many words are in the abstract?
    b. Is the abstract descriptive or informative? How do you know?
    c. What is the abstract's purpose? What is its scope?
    d. Is the abstract clear and concise?
    e. Does the abstract encourage you to read the rest of the report?
    f. How would you improve the abstract?

2. Everyone at one time or another has to take his or her automobile in for repair. In groups of three or four, create an outline of a report that will examine the number and names of automobile repair shops in your city; the number and names of the local repair shops with technicians who have been certified by the nonprofit National Institute for Automotive Service Excellence (ASE); whether any complaints have been lodged against these shops with the local Better Business Bureau; and any correlation you find (or don't find) between repair shops with certified workers or noncertified workers and numbers of complaints. Each person in the group should be assigned one of the parts to research. All members should bring in their findings, then, as a group, determine the type, scope, and organization of the report. After the outline is created, present it and the findings to the class.

3. As a class, discuss the executive summary shown in Figure 11–8. Assume that the audience is, for example, the board of directors of CGF Aircraft Corporation. Consider the following questions:
    a. How does the executive summary introduce the report? Does it include the appropriate information?
    b. Is the background information sufficient?
    c. What is the purpose of the report?
    d. What is the scope of the report?
    e. Are costs an important concern of this report?
    f. Are the conclusions effective?
    g. How long would you expect the report to be?

Research Projects

ON THE WEB

For extra research proj-ects, go to Chapter 11, bedfordstmartins.com/ writingthatworks

1. Imagine that you work for a consulting firm that specializes in attractions, like theme parks, aquariums, and zoos. Your firm has been hired by TRC, Inc., a company that owns several theme parks in the United States and is now inter-ested in opening a new park in your state.

   a. Write an investigative report for TRC, Inc., that includes the following:

- An introduction
- A short history of theme parks
- The current state of the theme-park industry across the country and in your state
- An analysis of what makes theme parks successful (like popular themes that appeal to families, cutting-edge rides, quality service and cleanliness, and acceptable admissions prices)
- The local audience for theme parks (demographics) and what appeals to them
- A description of the competition in the area and their strong and weak points
- Developing trends in theme parks (what the theme park of the future will look like and offer to the public)
- Conclusions
- Recommendations
- Works Cited

   b. Include the following types of graphics and visuals in your report (be sure to cite them and label them as described in Chapter 7, Designing Effective Documents and Visuals):

- A line graph of attendance at theme parks across the country during the last five years
- A chart of services and offerings that make theme parks successful and the national theme parks that offer all or some of those services and offerings
- A pie graph of tourism in your state, broken down by the popularity of each kind of tourist activity (for example, theme parks, nature activities, museums, and so on)
- Photographs of local theme parks

2. Conduct research to prepare an analytical formal report that compares two possible courses of action. Imagine you work for a small company that has revenues of about $100 million in sales (and profits of about $4 million a year). Your company's sales force numbers 20 members who collectively travel approximately 1,000 miles a week. Your company now needs a new fleet of cars, all the same make and model, for the sales force. The cars should be economical but large enough to accommodate the samples (of equipment, books, and so on). You have been asked to determine whether the fleet should be purchased or leased.

    Begin by developing a profile of your company so that you understand its needs and resources. Next, select three or four makes and models of cars. Choose specific features of the cars that you can compare. Analyze these features to determine (1) which car is the most cost-effective and the most suitable choice for your company and (2) whether to purchase or lease a fleet of these cars. In your report, clearly define, justify, and explain your findings:

- State the purpose of your report and your findings.
- Inform readers of how and where you gathered information.
- Define the criteria on which you based your research, given your company and its needs.
- Compare and contrast available options.
- Explain your conclusions and recommendations.

Web Projects

ON THE WEB

For additional Web projects, go to Chapter 11, bedfordstmartins.com/ writingthatworks

1. Using the *Occupational Outlook Handbook* at the Bureau of Labor Statistics Web site at <www.bls.gov/oco/home.htm>, write a formal report in which you analyze two different job positions in your major area of study. Include in your report the required background, working conditions, pay scale, geographic expectations, and job outlook. Prepare your report as if you are trying to decide objectively between two occupations, and include a conclusion and recommendations section.

2. The Federal Highway Administration (FHWA) of the U.S. Department of Transportation (DOT) works with states to conduct studies that explore the funding and feasibility of highway projects. According to the FHWA's Procedural Guidelines for Highway Feasibility Studies, six to nine tasks must occur within studies. See <www.fhwa.dot.gov/hep10/corbor/feastudy.html>. Only the last two steps of each case involve drafting the report; the first steps involve gathering and analyzing data.

   a. Write an abstract of the FHWA's Procedural Guidelines. Include a breakdown of the tasks required for (1) "improving an existing facility" or (2) "making major improvements to . . . a multi-State transportation corridor."

   b. Visit your state's DOT Web site and find a link to current construction projects. You can also research a project that local citizens and government officials are exploring, like monorail service.

   c. Imagine that you work for your state's DOT and you've been asked to draft an outline of a feasibility study for one or two current or future construction projects to get funding from the FHWA. Consider how you would address each task leading to the final report. Describe what kind of information you would try to put in each task and from where you would get these data. Sources could include the public affairs office of the local DOT, local newspapers, and the U.S. DOT's Web site links to transportation information regarding each state. Create a transmittal memo directed to the secretary of transportation for your state.

12 Writing Instructions

AT A GLANCE: Instructions

When you tell someone how to perform a procedure or task, you are giving instructions. Instructions may describe how to carry out a particular task in the workplace (send a file to a digital copier); perform a procedure (process a Medicare form); operate equipment (use a spray-paint gun); or assemble, repair, or maintain equipment (replace a seal on a high-pressure pump). This chapter provides guidance for the following:

- Planning Instructions / 408
- Writing Instructions / 418
- Illustrating Instructions / 422
- Testing the Effectiveness of Instructions / 428

How many times have you heard people complain about instructions being unclear, inaccurate, or poorly illustrated? Poor instructions can cause miscommunication and delays in an important project or, worse, be directly responsible for an injury, which could result in damage claims and lawsuits. If your instructions are based on clear thinking and careful planning, they should enable your audience to carry out the procedure or task successfully. Clear, easy-to-follow instructions can also build goodwill for your company. Keep in mind that the most-effective instructions often combine written elements and visual elements that reinforce each other. Finally, consider testing your instructions with someone unfamiliar with them and record and evaluate their behavior as they do so.

Planning Instructions

To write effective instructions, you must first learn how the operation is performed, assess the needs of your audience, and organize the instructions in the proper sequence. If possible, perform the operation yourself and record the details for each step in the process. Then assess your audience. Are they fellow employees within your firm, North American customers for your company's products, or non-English readers? Adapt your language and the design features of your instructions—their layout and packaging—for your target audience. After writing an introduc-

Voices from the Workplace

James Bates, U.S. Department of Housing and Urban Development

As a senior community planning and development representative with the U.S. Department of Housing and Urban Development (HUD), James Bates leads projects designed to help communities reduce homelessness, increase homeownership, finance shopping centers in low-income neighborhoods, and respond to natural disasters. Whether he's reporting on a project or providing instructions, James keeps in mind some basic principles. "Tell people only what is most relevant for them to know given their position and level of interest. Technical staff want to know about resources, timetables, and the processes they need to follow. Clients want to know what they are going to get and when they will get it. Managers want to know the bottom line: solutions, recommendations, and actions. I make sure that our mission and message are always conveyed in an audience-sensitive manner."

Beth Blazon, St. Joseph's Hospital

Beth Blazon is an occupational therapist at St. Joseph's Hospital in Nashua, New Hampshire, where she develops rehabilitation plans and works one-on-one with her patients to help them perform occupational exercises. Before her patients are discharged, Beth equips each with written instructions for exercises to be completed at home. She explains, "I make my instructions simple, taking into account any language or cognitive barriers the patient may have. I also tailor the instructions to each person." Beth's strategy for writing instructions is to keep them focused, brief, and visual. "I don't want my readers to have to sift through paragraphs of information they will not need. I keep my instructions as basic as possible, using as few words as possible. I've found that the use of pictures helps a lot, especially when demonstrating exercises."

---

tion, listing or describing any essential tools or materials, as necessary, organize the instructions in the sequence and exact number of steps necessary to perform the task.

ON THE WEB

For more help with writing instructions, go to Chapter 12, bedfordstmartins.com/ writingthatworks

Learn to Perform the Operation Yourself

To write accurate and easily understood instructions, you must thoroughly understand the task you are describing. Otherwise, your instructions could be inaccurate or even dangerous. For example, the container of a brand-name drain cleaner directs the user to do the following:

▶   Fill sink with 1 to 2 inches of water, then close off drain opening.

Users would find it difficult to raise the water level in the sink *before* closing the drain! The writer of these instructions did not carefully observe the actual sequence of steps required to use the product, or he or she would have written the instructions accurately. In this case, users simply ignored the instructions and performed the task according to common sense, so no harm was done. Suppose such confusing instructions were given for administering an intravenous fluid or for assembling high-voltage electrical equipment. The results of such inaccurate advice could be both dangerous and costly.

The writer of the drain-cleaning instructions undoubtedly knew better and was just careless. Sometimes, though, a writer may be asked to write instructions for a procedure that he or she does not understand adequately. Don't let that happen to you. If you cannot perform a task yourself, request permission to watch someone else do it. As you watch, take careful notes and ask questions about any step that is not clear to you. Direct observation should enable you to write instructions that are exact, complete, and clear. Also make certain that you know the reason for the procedure, the materials and tools required, and the end result of the task.

Once you understand the procedure, you must determine the most effective way to present it to your audience.

Assess Your Audience and Purpose

In the workplace, you may need to prepare instructions for coworkers, domestic and international customers, or other users of your company's products or services. Start by determining who will use your instructions. Remember that you and your readers share a common purpose: the successful completion of a task or procedure after reading your instructions. To write instructions that best meet readers' requirements, learn as much as you can about your audience. You and your coworkers, for example, share a large amount of knowledge already. For customers and others outside the company, begin by learning their level of knowledge and experience, and try to put yourself in their position as they follow your instructions. Is the audience skilled in the kind of task for which you are writing instructions? If they are knowledgeable about the subject, use the specialized vocabulary and abbreviations appropriate to the subject. If they have little or no knowledge of the subject, use plain language or include a glossary, defining specialized terms in plain language. For international readers, learn about their proficiency in English.

◆ For advice on creating a glossary, see Chapter 11, Writing Formal Reports, page 401.

Coworkers

Employees write many kinds of informal, nontechnical instructions to coworkers every day. The advantage of communicating with coworkers is that you share with them a large body of information about the organization for which you work. You can assume their familiarity with the company's organization and hierarchy, job titles, products, customers, and numerous other details that need not be spelled out. In the e-mail instructions in Figure 12–1, for example, a budget analyst requests data about an office's copier program from the manager of that program to plan for the upcoming fiscal year's budget. Note that this guidance is sent annu-

From: Carol Quenten <cquenten@techquest.com>
To: Gene Carruthers <gcarruthers@techquest.com>
Sent: March 1, 2007 09:27:42
Subject: Planning Call for FY 2009 Budget

Gene,

We are planning the 2009 budget cycle, and I'll need the following information about the copier program in your organization.

Please gather and enter the following data on the budget form located on the shared S:\ drive at S:\OCIOO\IMD\copiers:

- Current and projected monthly maintenance charges for each copier and the totals
- Any indication of projected maintenance increases from our vendors
- The number of copiers we lease and the number we own
- The number of copiers we need to replace based on a seven-year life cycle per machine
- The projected costs for replacing our current copiers with networked copiers

Do not project toner and paper costs at this time.

The information is due for my review on 4/3/2007. Thanks.

```
===============================
Carol Quenten, Budget Analyst
Office of the Chief Financial Officer
TechQuest Inc.
119 Trowbridge Rd., Minneapolis, MN 55401
(507) 333-3333 Fax: (507) 333-3334
cquenten@techquest.com
techquest.com
===============================
```

Bulleted list for ease of reading and response

Qualifying guidance

Details on submitting answers

Figure 12–1   Informal Employee-to-Employee Instructions

ally to the head of the copier program, so both the sender and the recipient are familiar with the process. The scope of the request, its language ("seven-year life cycle"), and their shared access to an online form require no special explanations.

More-detailed instructions to coworkers may describe how to perform routine workplace activities. The instructions in Figure 12–2 address the crucial corporate responsibility of responding to consumer correspondence in a timely and responsible manner. They lay out the steps from the point when the correspondence is received until the company's response is sent. Note the use of headings, the step-by-step organization of the required tasks, and the uncomplicated language of the memo. These instructions assume that all recipients are familiar with the company's departments and job titles.

XYZ Corporation

Consumer Response Department
Procedures for Handling Correspondence

Instructions arranged in sequential order

1. Intake

When the Customer Response Department receives a written consumer query or comment, the department assistant

Bullets identify tasks within each major step

- Logs in the correspondence in the electronic tracking system.
- Makes a paper copy.
- Gives the copy to the section analyst for review.
- Retains the original in the section tracking folder.

Boldface headings identify major steps

2. Content Review

The department analyst

- Reviews the content.
- Meets with the department chief to discuss response strategy, staff assigned to respond, and date due to the department supervisor.

The due date is two working days before the response is due to the vice president for consumer affairs.

3. Staff Assignment

The department analyst

- Informs the department assistant of who will respond and the due date.
- Meets with the assistant and provides any necessary background for the reply.

4. Staff Response

- The respondent e-mails the draft reply to the department assistant on or before the due date.
- The department assistant logs the draft into the database and forwards it to the department analyst for review.

5. Response Review

The department chief and department analyst meet to

- Make any necessary revisions to the draft.
- Forward the draft to the department assistant for incorporation into the final draft.

The department assistant

- Enters the final draft into the company electronic document database.
- Maintains a record of concurrences on the final draft.
- Prepares a paper correspondence package for signature.

6. Approval

- The department supervisor approves the correspondence package.
- The department assistant forwards the correspondence package to the vice president for consumer affairs for review and signature.

Figure 12–2   Coworker Instructions for Processing Correspondence

DIGITAL TIPS: Organizing and Highlighting Instructions

When writing instructions, use the following features of your word-processing software to organize and highlight information:

- Font size and boldface
- Outlining feature
- Numbered-list feature
- Bulleted-list feature
- Clip-art icons and symbols

Consumers

Some instructions are intended to help customers assemble and maintain products. The instructions can range in scope from directions for assembling a model ship to guidance for installing and testing software on the computer network of a multibranch commercial bank. These instructions tend to be formally written and carefully reviewed for accuracy and for their adherence to policy and legal requirements before they are used. The requirements common to all consumer instructions are that they be accurate, written in language appropriate to the audience, illustrated in sufficient detail (if necessary), and packaged in the medium most useful to the customer—brochure, print manual, compact disk.

You must assess your customers carefully to meet these requirements. Consider their familiarity with your product based on their previous knowledge or experience, how broad your audience is (Is it a narrow group of specialists or a large cross-section of the population?), and the medium most useful to them. Also consider your audience's motivation for reading your instructions. Although instructions are essential to the successful use of consumer products, many readers ignore them. Methods for increasing the likelihood that such readers will look at your instructions are discussed in this chapter under Design for Ease of Use. (The instructional needs of international readers are addressed in the following section.) Figure 12–3 shows a set of instructions in a customer booklet for maintaining a propane gas outdoor grill.

International Readers

Language differences create the biggest obstacle to writing instructions for readers whose primary language is not English. When you must write instructions for such an audience, find out as much as possible about their English-language proficiency and adjust your writing accordingly. If your text will be translated into another language, write to the extent possible in plain language and define specialized terms or abbreviations in a glossary. Help your audience by becoming familiar with their terminology for important concepts or even the names of commonly

Instructions written in imperative mood

Instructions organized into numbered steps

Cleaning the Inside of the Grill

1. Disconnect the igniter wire from the igniter before cleaning the grill. Do not mistake the brown and black accumulation of grease and smoke for paint. The interiors of gas grills are not painted at the factory (and should never be painted).
2. Remove the grill lid, cooking grate, grease cup, and Drip VapoRISER Bar. Discard old lava rocks or briquettes. Attach the grease cup to the grease hanger and empty it after each use.
3. Using a scrub brush, apply a strong solution of detergent and water or grill cleaner to the insides of the grill lid and the bottom. Rinse and allow the equipment to air dry completely.

Figure 12–3   Product-Maintenance Instructions

◆ *For a fuller discussion of writing for international readers, see* Writing for an International Audience, *pages 69–71, in Chapter 3,* Writing the Draft; Using Graphics to Communicate Internationally, *pages 246–252, in Chapter 7,* Designing Effective Documents and Visuals; *and* Writing International Correspondence, *pages 300–305, in Chapter 8,* Understanding the Principles of Business Communication.

used objects. Consider, for example, the following passage from a computer printer service manual that was translated from Japanese to English for American field engineers.

▶ Remove cover panel with great care, using plus driver to remove screws. Inside control box, wires are held in place with different screws. Take minus driver and loosen screws to remove wire from red and green terminals.

The terms "plus driver" and "minus driver" refer to a Philips-head screwdriver and a flat-head screwdriver. The Japanese translator apparently did not know the appropriate American terminology for the tools, so he used what seemed logical descriptions of them. The result was a lot of confusion by English-speaking readers over what these terms could mean.

Well-illustrated instructions are effective in clarifying directions for international readers. In fact, instructions for many kinds of devices that require assembly are completely visual, such as the laminated cards aboard airplanes that illustrate how to buckle and unbuckle passenger seatbelts. Using visual instructions is especially effective for international audiences because they avoid the pitfalls common when information is translated from one language to another. If visual-only instructions are not possible, consult with someone from your intended audience's country or culture as you plan and draft your instructions. The instructions in Figure 12–4 illustrate how to install a box shelf on drywall. The product, manufactured in China, is sold internationally.

The need for cross-cultural understanding of commonly used concepts led to the development by the International Organization for Standardization (ISO) of agreed-on symbols like those shown in Figure 7–37 (page 251) for use in public signs, guidebooks, and manuals.

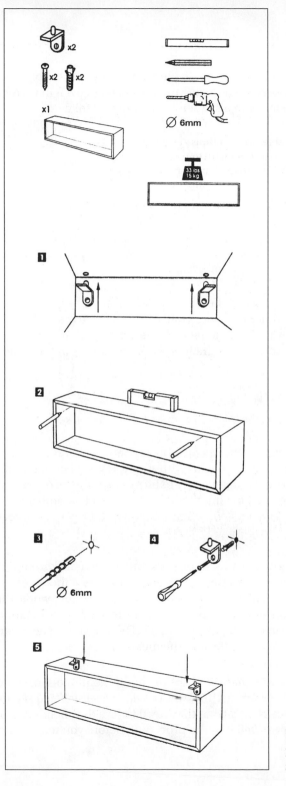

Product parts, tools needed, and width of holes

Icon of weight capacity for shelf

Placement of brackets in predrilled holes

How to mark wall for bracket holes

Sequence for installing drywall anchor and screw to wall

How to position shelf on brackets against wall

Figure 12–4   Visual Instructions Created for International Customers   *Source:* Rubbermaid Frame Shelf Kit Product Packaging.

Organize the Instructions

To make your instructions easy to follow, divide them into short, simple steps, and arrange the steps in the correct sequence. The steps can be given in either of two ways. You can label each step with a sequential number, as follows:

▶ 1. Connect each black cable wire to a brass terminal.
2. Attach one 4-inch green jumper wire to the back.
3. Connect both jumper wires to the bare cable wires.

Or, you can use words that indicate time or sequence, as follows:

▶ *First*, assess the problem that the customer reports to you. *Next*, observe and test the system in operation. *At that time*, question the customer until you understand the problem completely. *Then*, test the following. . . .

Think ahead for your reader. If the instructions in step 2 will affect a process in step 9, say so in step 2. Sometimes your instructions have to make clear that two operations must be performed simultaneously. Either state that fact in an introduction to the specific instructions or include both operations in the same step.

◆ *Review the information on sequential organization on pages 36–38, in Chapter 2, Organizing Your Information.*

CONFUSING 1. Hold the Control key down.
2. Press the Bell key before releasing the Control key.

CLEAR 1. While holding the Control key down, press the Bell key.

If your instructions involve many steps, break them into stages, each with a separate heading so that each stage begins with step 1. Using headings as dividers is especially important if your reader is likely to be performing the operation as he or she reads the instructions. Many instructions for product assembly are organized into four parts: Introduction, Required Equipment and Materials, Procedure, and Conclusion.

1. *Introduction.* Use an introduction to provide any needed background information, to state the purpose of the procedure, or to offer a theory of operation to help your audience understand why the product works the way it does. Figure 12–5 shows an excerpt from the introduction to a manual for the setup and operation of a digital video disk (DVD) system. The excerpt describes the scope of the manual and the meaning of symbols used throughout.

2. *Required Equipment and Materials.* If special equipment, tools, or materials are needed to complete your instructions, provide a well-labeled section that tells your audience clearly what they need before they begin the procedure—don't let them get well into the procedure before you tell them about such requirements.

About this Manual

- The instructions in this manual describe the controls on the remote. You can also use the controls on the system if they have the same or similar names as those on the remote.
- The symbols used in this manual are explained below:

Symbol	Meaning	Symbol	Meaning
DVD	Functions available in DVD video mode	**MP3**	Functions available for MP3* audio tracks
VIDEO CD	Functions available in VIDEO CD mode	**JPEG**	Functions available for JPEG files
CD	Functions available in CD mode	☼	More convenient features

* MP3 (MPEG1 Audio Layer 3) is a standard format
defined by ISO/MPEG, which compress audio data.

Purpose and scope of manual

Table of symbols

Footnote to define standard audio format

Figure 12–5   Introduction for Instructions   *Source:* "Home Theater System," Courtesy of Sony Corporation, 2003.

3. *Procedural Steps.* The procedural steps are the sequential steps required to complete the task. Review the section on sequential organization on pages 36–38 in Chapter 2, Organizing Your Information, for a full discussion of this method of development.

4. *Conclusion.* Brief instructions can simply end with the last step in the procedure. For longer and more-complex instructions, add a conclusion section that satisfies your audience's sense of confidence about completing the job successfully.

> ▶ Congratulations on successfully assembling your gas grill. With proper care, it will serve you well for many years to come.

Many instructions are organized into sections similar to this structure but are titled to more specifically describe the process. The instructions for installing a ceramic countertop in a kitchen or bathroom, for example, are organized into the following sections:

1. Introduction
2. Tools Needed
3. Surface Preparation
   - Choosing the Edge Trim
   - Selecting the Sink
4. Planning the Layout
5. Setting the Tile
6. Applying Grout
7. Caulking and Sealing the Grout

CONSIDERING AUDIENCE AND PURPOSE
Planning to Write Instructions

■ Can you perform or carefully observe others perform the task you are describing?

■ Will someone unfamiliar with the task you are describing be able to follow your instructions?

■ What vocabulary is appropriate to your audience?

■ Are your instructions to coworkers sufficiently specific to ensure that the task can be completed accurately and within the allotted schedule?

■ Did you take into account your customers' level of knowledge about your product before you began writing?

■ Are your instructions written and illustrated appropriately for international readers?

■ Have you organized the instructions in the proper sequence for the task?

■ Writing Instructions

Effective instructional writing follows a precise pattern dictated by the instruction-writer's goal: telling someone how to perform a task. The most direct way of doing so is to word the instructions as commands, using the imperative mood: (1) Perform step 1. (2) Wait 5 minutes and perform step 2, and so on.

Assume that the reader will not be familiar with the task or procedure described. For that reason, use the plainest language possible to communicate with the broadest audience.

Finally, you are obligated to warn the audience explicitly of any potential risks or hazards associated with the task being explained. These warnings must be clearly spelled out, stand out from the surrounding text, and, if possible, illustrated.

Write Directly to Your Reader

The clearest and simplest instructions are written as commands. Addressing each sentence directly to your audience in the imperative mood and the active voice makes your instructions easier to follow and less wordy than if you were to write them in the passive voice.

PASSIVE	The access lid should be closed by the operator.
ACTIVE/IMPERATIVE	Close the access lid.

◆ *See also Active and Passive Voice on pages 102–105 in Chapter 4, Revising the Draft.*

Although instructions should be concise, do not try to achieve conciseness by leaving out needed words such as articles (*a, an, the*), pronouns (*you, this, these*), and verbs. Doing so will certainly shorten sentences, but sentences shortened this way usually have to be read more than once to be understood—actually defeating the purpose of brevity. The following instruction for cleaning a power punch press assembly (a machine that punches holes and other patterns into materials), for example, is not easily understood at first reading.

UNCLEAR	Pass brush through punch area for debris.

The meaning of the phrase *for debris* needs to be made clearer. Revised, the instruction is readily understandable.

CLEAR	Pass a brush through the punch area to clear away any debris.

In any operation, certain steps must be performed with more exactness than others. Anyone who has boiled a three-minute egg for four minutes understands this all too well. Alert your audience to the steps that require exact timing or measurement.

VAGUE	Let the liquid cool.
PRECISE	Let the liquid cool for 30 minutes at room temperature.

WRITER'S CHECKLIST
Writing Instructions in Plain Language

- ☑ Identify and write to your average reader.
- ☑ Keep in mind your average reader's level of technical knowledge.
- ☑ Avoid unnecessary jargon.
- ☑ Avoid confusing terms and constructions; for example,
  - – Do not include undefined abbreviations and acronyms.
  - – Do not use two different words for the same thing.
  - – Do not give an obscure meaning to a word.
- ☑ Write in the imperative mood.
- ☑ Use the active voice.
  - – It makes clear who is supposed to do what.
  - – It uses fewer words.
- ☑ Use *you* and other pronouns.
  - – They allow you to write directly to the reader rather than to a group.
  - – They pull the reader into the writing and make the writing relevant to the reader.

(continued)

WRITER'S CHECKLIST (continued)

☑ Write short sentences.
- Aim for one message in each sentence.
- Break up information into smaller, easier-to-understand units.

☑ Use simple tenses; use the present tense as much as possible.

☑ Select word placement carefully.
- Keep subjects and objects close to their verbs.
- Put *only*, *always*, and other conditional words next to the words they modify.
- Put *if* phrases after the main clauses to which they apply, not before.

Include Warnings and Cautions

Warnings and cautions are essential to instructions involving potentially hazardous equipment or materials. Many processes in industrial, medical, law enforcement, and other settings involve the use of potentially dangerous equipment, chemicals, and explosives. Instruction writers have legal and ethical reasons for ensuring that warnings and cautions are included with such instructions. Even instructions for tasks not overtly hazardous may require cautionary statements. In either case, you may need legal guidance on the appropriate language to use.

ETHICS NOTE

Product liability laws require a manufacturer to warn potential users of (1) dangers in the *normal use* of the product and (2) dangers in the *foreseeable misuse* of the product. A manufacturer, however, need not warn of *open and obvious* dangers. Hence, instructions for an electric knife need not warn the user not to use the knife for shaving a beard — an obvious danger that is also neither "normal use" nor "foreseeable" by the manufacturer. Instructions for an electric knife would need to warn users to take care when holding food to be sliced, because a slip of the hand could result in injury — a danger in normal use. Even if the danger is open and obvious, the manufacturer may have a duty to warn users who may not be aware of the extent or degree of danger. If the likelihood of injury is serious, the manufacturer is also required to display a warning on the product itself.

Language of Warnings

In general, all instructions for the proper use of a product should be *clear*, *readable*, and *understandable*. However, readers must also be warned specifically of dangers that they might expect and dangers that they might not. Remember, a danger that is obvious to you as the writer of the instructions may not be obvious to the user. Instructions not only must warn of all risks and hazards but also must warn *adequately*. An adequate warning must do three things:

- Identify the hazard and the potential seriousness of the risk.
- Give the likely results of ignoring the warning.
- Describe how to avoid the hazard and thus the injury.

To ensure that a warning is adequate, the language in it must be clear and explicit.

VAGUE   Failure to disengage the blades may result in bodily harm.

EXPLICIT   If you do not disengage the blades, they can amputate your fingers.

Avoid words that are open to interpretation or need further defining: *proper, excessive, frequently, often, seldom, may, might, could, recommended, occasionally.* If potential users comprise a diverse group, consider their familiarity (if any) with the product, level of literacy, and nationality.

Visual Symbols and Signal Words

Alert your readers to any potentially hazardous materials or actions before they reach the step for which the material is needed or the action will be performed. Caution readers handling hazardous materials about any requirements for special clothing, tools, equipment, and other safety measures. Highlight warnings, cautions, and precautions to make them stand out visually from the surrounding text—use an open, uncrowded format so that they do not blend in with the instructions. A clear border of heavy lines or white space adds visual emphasis to warnings. You can also place warning notices in all uppercase letters, in large and distinctive fonts, or in color.

   Use symbols and icons in the text to reinforce warnings, as illustrated in Figure 12–6. Use line drawings of products that depict the physical sources of

ON THE WEB

For more guidelines on the use of terminology, colors, and symbols in instructions and labeling, visit the American National Standards Institute at <www.ansi.org/> and the International Organization for Standardization at <www.iso.org/>.

READ SAFETY SIGNS CAREFULLY AND FOLLOW THEIR INSTRUCTIONS

Danger signs identify the most-serious hazards and are attached to machines near specific hazard areas.

Keep safety signs in good condition. Replace any missing or damaged safety signs.

Turn off power before removing service cover.

Do not operate machine without guards in place.

Icons depict types of hazards

Figure 12–6 Typical Warning Icons with Text

hazards and, if possible, the nature of the hazard. Don't show a picture of what *not* to do unless you put a slash (/) through the image, as shown in Figure 12–7. And don't use cartoons for safety warnings because they dilute warnings, trivialize the hazard, may imply that you are "talking down" to readers, and are difficult to design simply.

Figure 12–7   Icon Depicting a Prohibited Activity

Warning words, symbols, icons, and labels are increasingly becoming standardized, although industry practices do vary. Certain signal words in boldface and their corresponding colors are becoming standards in North America:

DANGER (red): hazard or unsafe practice that *will* result in severe injury or death

WARNING (orange): *could* result in severe injury or death

CAUTION (yellow): could result in *minor* injury or property damage

NOTICE (blue): information unrelated to safety

The hazard-alert symbol—an international standard—should appear with the signal word.

Use cautions and warnings only when necessary, however. Too many may cause your audience to ignore those that are essential.

■ Using Illustrations and Design Principles

Well-thought-out illustrations can make even the most complex instructions easier to understand. In addition to demonstrating the steps of your instructions, drawings, photographs, and diagrams can help your audience identify parts and the relationships between them. In fact, some instructions, including those for international audiences, use only illustrations. (See Figure 12–4.)

Consider the layout and design of your instructions to most effectively integrate text and visuals. Highlight important visuals, like warnings, by making them stand out from the surrounding text. Consider using boxes and boldface or distinctive headings. Experiment with font style, size, and color to determine which devices are most effective. If you use color, be aware that certain colors (red, green, yellow, for example) have well-established meanings in North America but may be interpreted differently in other countries.

Illustrate for Clarity

The value of illustrations will depend on your audience's needs and on the nature of the project. Generally, instructions for inexperienced readers should be more thoroughly illustrated than those for experienced readers. Enhance the value of the illustration by referring to it in the instructions to explain what it shows, and use labels on the illustration to further clarify its purpose.

Ensure that step-by-step instructions are placed next to the steps illustrated so that the audience immediately recognizes the connection between the two. Figure 12–8 shows instructions that guide a medical lab technician through the steps of

---

STREAKING AN AGAR PLATE

Distribute the inoculum over the surface of the agar in the following manner:

Step 1. After sterilizing the loop in an open flame, beginning at one edge of the saucer, thin the inoculum by streaking back and forth over the same area several times, sweeping across the agar surface until approximately one quarter of the surface has been covered. *Sterilize the loop.*

Step 2. Streak at right angles to the originally inoculated area, carrying the inoculum out from the streaked areas onto the sterile surface with only the first stroke of the wire. Cover half of the remaining sterile agar surface. *Sterilize the loop.*

Step 3. Repeat as described in step 2, covering the remaining sterile agar surface.

Single illustration shows a three-step process

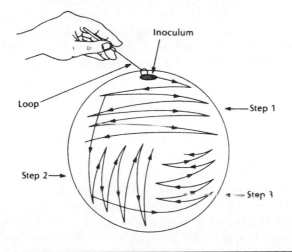

Labels on the illustration link it to the steps in the instructions

Plate enlarged to emphasize the pattern and sequence of strokes

Figure 12–8   Step-by-Step Instructions with Illustration

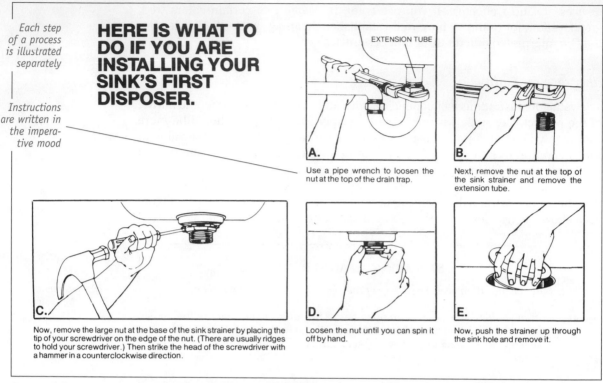

Each step of a process is illustrated separately

Instructions are written in the imperative mood

HERE IS WHAT TO DO IF YOU ARE INSTALLING YOUR SINK'S FIRST DISPOSER.

EXTENSION TUBE

A. Use a pipe wrench to loosen the nut at the top of the drain trap.

B. Next, remove the nut at the top of the sink strainer and remove the extension tube.

C. Now, remove the large nut at the base of the sink strainer by placing the tip of your screwdriver on the edge of the nut. (There are usually ridges to hold your screwdriver.) Then strike the head of the screwdriver with a hammer in a counterclockwise direction.

D. Loosen the nut until you can spin it off by hand.

E. Now, push the strainer up through the sink hole and remove it.

Figure 12–9   Illustrating Each Step in a Set of Instructions   *Source:* "Installation of Kenmore Waste Disposers," Courtesy of Sears, Roebuck and Company, 1997, Hoffman Estates, Illinois.

streaking a saucer-sized disk of material (called *agar*) used to grow bacterial colonies for laboratory examination. The purpose is to thin out the original specimen (the *inoculum*) so that bacteria will grow in small, isolated colonies. When necessary or advisable, illustrate each step in your instructions (Figure 12–9), making certain that the illustration represents the current model of the equipment.

A technique especially useful for inexperienced readers is to show a close-up of a portion of a larger image, as in Figure 12–10, which illustrates installation of a shower floor drain. The "magnified" image can show essential details impossible to see in a larger picture. Linking the two images visually puts the close-up in context for the reader.

◆ *For a complete discussion of how to create and use effective illustrations, see Chapter 7, Designing Effective Documents and Visuals.*

Design for Ease of Use

Even clear, well-illustrated instructions are of no value if no one reads them. Customers want to use a new device as soon as they receive it. However, if the product comes with a thick user's manual of dense, legalistic text, they will avoid it. This attitude can lead to accidents, increased calls to customer help lines, dissatisfied customers, and lost time and productivity.

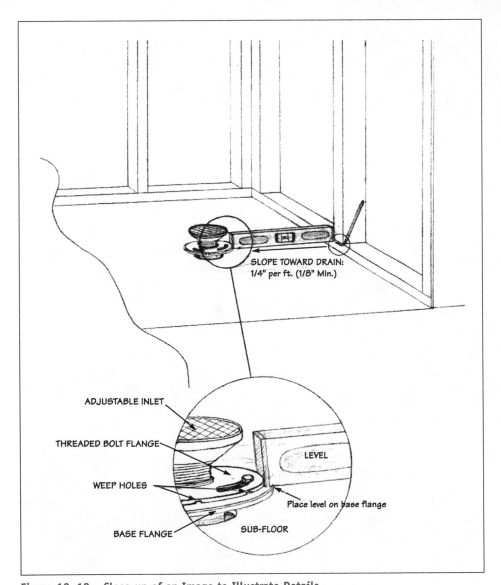

Overview illustration linked to an enlarged detail

Figure 12–10   Close-up of an Image to Illustrate Details

To address this problem, many firms have adopted a two-tier approach in their instructions. In addition to a full-scale user's manual, essential for products such as automobiles, cell phones, washers, dryers, or ovens, they produce a quick-start guide with pictures, easy-to-follow diagrams, and minimal text. When users are given a choice between a 200-page owner's manual and an eight-page glossy color booklet, they opt for the booklet. In another approach, many companies now provide quick-setup posters with few words and large photographs that are often color coded to parts on the equipment, as shown in Figure 12–11. Other

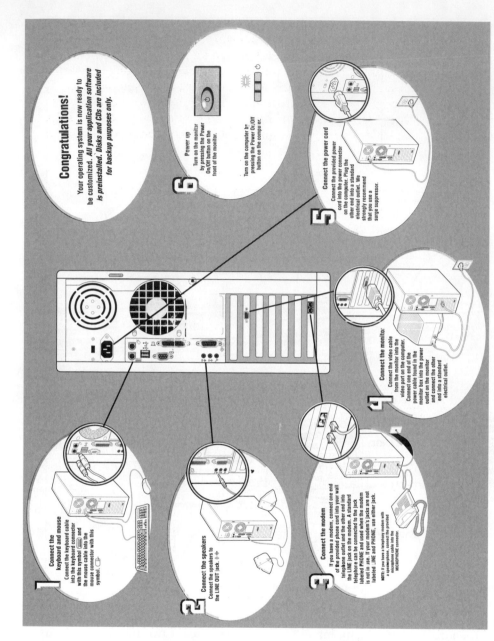

Figure 12–11   Poster of Illustrated Instructions

426

firms produce laminated cards and booklets with indexed tabs that permit readers to find at a glance what they're looking for—the correct air pressure for tires, how to set an oven timer, and the like, as shown in Figure 12–12. Other options include 3 × 5-inch laminated cards (for phone use), stickers (warning of poisons and providing information about emergency treatment), and even magnets. To create instructions for complex procedures, consider using the two-tier approach. (Although many other options exist for providing customers with product help, such as CD-ROMs, Web sites, help lines, and instructor-led classes, a description of these options is outside the scope of this text.)

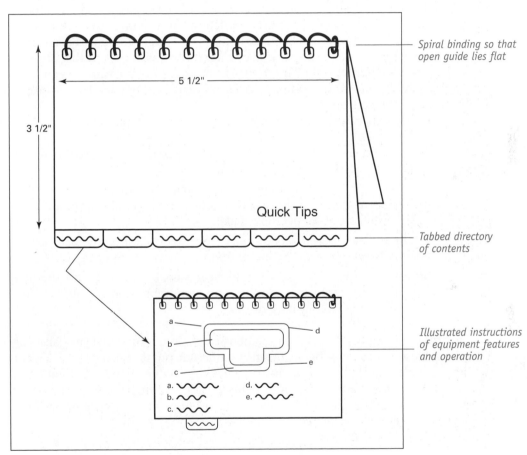

Figure 12–12   Laminated Pocket-Size Owner's Guide

■ Testing for Usability

To test the accuracy and clarity of your instructions, ask someone who is not familiar with the operation to use the instructions you have written to perform the task or procedure. A first-time user of your instructions can spot missing steps or point out passages that should be worded more clearly. As you watch your tester follow your instructions, note any steps that seem especially puzzling or confusing and revise them for clarity.

Usability testing is a common method for diagnosing potential problems by having a test subject follow the draft instructions to perform a task. It involves bringing users into the development process—for example, by testing periodic drafts on users and then revising the instructions in response to the test results. Test participants typically are members of the actual target audience for the product or procedure. If the participants encounter problems, it is likely that other actual users will experience similar problems. For example, if instructions for filling out a section of a tax form are unclear to test participants, they are likely to be confusing to most taxpayers.

Usability tests can rely on one or more of the following methods:

- *User testing.* Testers observe and record the actions of test participants who perform real tasks using the instructions.

- *Protocols.* Test participants comment aloud as they follow the instructions and perform the tasks described to reveal their thought processes, attitudes, and reasons for decision-making.

- *Comprehension tests.* Users complete tests to determine whether they understand and can recall the information, such as visuals or tables.

- *Surveys and interviews.* Testers interview users both before and after they read the instructions to determine their comprehension and attitudes and the clarity of what they have read.

ON THE WEB

For more help planning and conducting usability tests, go to **bedfordstmartins.com/ writingthatworks** and select *Links Library*, Usability Testing.

Analyzing the results of those test methods can help instructional specialists detect and resolve problems before the instructions are put to use. If test participants have trouble understanding the instructions, the language and organization, as well as layout and design, may need to be revised. Although usability testing can be time-consuming, the extra time can pay off in greater safety, improved efficiency, and fewer customer complaints.

CHAPTER 12 SUMMARY: WRITING INSTRUCTIONS
Planning Instructions

■ Make sure that you understand the task thoroughly. (For technical instructions to accompany products, learn to perform the operation yourself or carefully observe others performing the operation.)

■ Learn the needs and experience level of your audience.

- Organize the task into short, simple steps.
- Present each step in the correct sequence.

Writing Instructions

- Write directly to your readers, using the active, imperative voice.
- Write clearly and concisely — short sentences are best.
- In an introduction at the beginning of your instructions,
  - Mention any necessary details, background information, and preparation.
  - List all required equipment and materials.
- Use plain language (avoid technical jargon).
- Within procedural steps, include necessary warnings and cautions.

Using Illustrations and Design Principles

- Use visuals to illustrate steps and procedures where needed.
- Create visuals at the level of detail appropriate to your audience.
- If you are creating instructions for users averse to reading manuals, consider creating a quick-start guide with images, easy-to-follow diagrams, and minimal text.

Testing for Usability

- Test the readability and effectiveness of your instructions by having someone unfamiliar with the task test them while you observe.
- Analyze the results of your observations to improve the instructions.
- Revise the instructions as necessary.

ON THE WEB

For an online quiz on writing instructions, go to Chapter 12, bedfordstmartins.com/writingthatworks

■ Exercises

ON THE WEB

For additional exercises, go to Chapter 12, bedfordstmartins.com/writingthatworks

1. Write a set of instructions for either of the following topics. Assume that your audience has no knowledge of the subject. Use illustrations where they would be helpful to your audience.
   a. How to program your VCR/DVR to record a television show that will be broadcast in several hours from the time you programmed your machine
   b. How to use a particular type of software to create a document

2. Create a set of interview questions that you could rely on as a means of checking the usability of the instructions you created in Exercise 1. Remember that you would interview users both before and after they read the instructions to determine their comprehension and attitudes and the clarity of what they have read.

3. Collect examples of instructions written in the passive voice and rewrite them using the active voice.

4. As this chapter describes, most firms have developed a two-tier approach for instructions because consumers will gravitate toward illustrated quick-start guides, easy-to-follow diagrams, and booklets instead of 200-plus-page instruction manuals. Locate a large instructional book or manual (for example, for new software or a new automobile), or go to a Web site that features lengthy instructions for consumer goods, and create a set of 3 × 5-inch laminated cards or a four- to

eight-page booklet that will be easy to follow and thus encourage consumers to follow instructions.

5. Locate two sets of assembly, how-to-use, or cleaning instructions from products that you have recently purchased. Key the instructions on your word processor (or scan them with OCR software). Using the insert-comment technique explained in Chapter 5 (Digital Tips: Reviewing Collaborative Documents, page 134), critique the instructions you have copied, then, using the Writing Instructions in Plain Language checklist on pages 419–420, compare their use of plain language. Discuss ways that the instructions could have been improved and comment on what is well written.

6. Write two sets of instructions on how to get from the closest airport to your school's student center. Assume your audience is made up of two groups of potential students: native speakers of English and non-native speakers of English. (See Chapter 8, Understanding the Principles of Business Communication, for helpful information on international communication strategies.)

7. Imagine that you are the Web master for a large online chat group that is visited by thousands of people each day. You have been concerned about visitors conducting themselves unprofessionally by doing things like attacking others, linking your site with other sites, and trying to sell products and services to other visitors. Define your site's topic and purpose, then create a list of at least ten instructions regarding conduct for your site and explain the penalties for ignoring the instructions.

8. Collect examples of instructions that are written using ambiguous words like "might" or "may" and revise them using explicit words.

9. Many grocers and large retailers now offer self-checkout systems that encourage customers to scan, pay for, and bag their merchandise themselves. These systems allow the store to place employees in other areas where one-on-one attention is needed, and they reduce the need to hire more cashiers. Imagine that you work for a company that manufactures these checkout systems. Write a set of instructions for store managers that will help them prevent the following problems that could discourage customers from using the equipment (*hint:* Many of these problems could be prevented before the customer has to face them):

   - The customer is unfamiliar or uncomfortable with the self-checkout system.
   - The customer scans the bar code, but the product does not appear in the register's inventory database.
   - The customer has difficulty following the steps needed to work the self-checkout system (for example, he or she can't figure out how to use the scales to weigh produce).

10. People who are not fluent in the language of a country in which they are visiting or residing often need visual instructions to help them read or fill out an official government document. In response, agencies may place numbers on a picture of the document that explains where different personal information is located or required. For example, to help English-speakers traveling to China understand their Chinese visa, officials might enlarge an image of a Chinese visa, place a *1* where the visitor's name would appear and a *2* where the visa expiration date would appear, and so on, then place a list of the numbers and what they correspond to below the sample visa. Using an image of a driver's license or another official doc-

ument, create a visual using numbers that would explain to a non-native reader of English the information on each line or the information required for each line.

Collaborative Classroom Projects

ON THE WEB

For more collaborative classroom projects, go to Chapter 12, bedfordstmartins.com/ writingthatworks

1. Many companies offer sweepstakes competitions as a means of increasing interest in their products and services. In addition to requiring entrants' names and contact information, these companies often create very specific rules to reduce the number of successful entries. The rules may, for example, require that answers to an essay question fall within a set word count or that a certain word be printed in capital letters. In groups of two, create a sweepstakes for an imaginary company and include a list of instructions for completing the entry. When you are finished, hand your instructions to other students in your class to complete. By the end of class, analyze how many applications were completed successfully and how many would have been immediately rejected.

2. In groups of four to six, write assembly instructions for a product in the classroom. For example, assume that the instructor's desk needs to be assembled. Write an introduction, a required equipment and materials section, a procedural-steps section, and a conclusion. Share your instructions with the class.

3. For any of the exercises or projects in this chapter that ask you to create instructions, conduct a usability test with protocols as a means of checking the usability of those instructions. Sit next to your usability test participants as they comment aloud while they follow the instructions and perform the tasks. This should reveal their thought processes, attitudes, and reasons for decision-making, which should help you determine areas of helpfulness or confusion in your instructions. Form groups of three or four, as directed by your instructor.

Research Projects

ON THE WEB

For extra research projects, go to Chapter 12, bedfordstmartins.com/ writingthatworks.

1. Numerous chemicals are used in the cleaning of educational institutions' bathrooms, offices' carpeting, and so on. For this assignment, research and write a formal report on the cleaning products used by your institution's cleaning or maintenance crews.
   a. Begin by interviewing the director of maintenance (or someone in a similar position) at your institution about the kinds of cleansers and chemicals used for specific types of cleaning. Ask about the precautions needed and specific instructions given to those who work with these chemicals. Ask about the amount and cost of these products on a monthly or yearly basis.
   b. Next, inquire about training given to employees in the use of these chemicals (your Human Resources Department may conduct this training). Ask how much training and instruction is offered and what subjects are covered. Ask if there are any special sessions offered to non-native speakers or readers of English.
   c. Research "green," or environmentally friendly, products that can be used in place of more toxic cleansers. Be sure to address the ability of such cleansers to

clean heavily populated environments, the potential cost of such products, and the training or instruction needed for their use.

Write a formal report to the head of maintenance that summarizes your findings, makes recommendations on product safety and worker training and instruction, and recommends a course of action regarding the use of traditional cleansers, environmentally friendly cleansers, or a combination of both. Include a graph or chart with your report.

2. As explained in this chapter, warning words, symbols, icons, and labels are increasingly standardized, although industry practices do vary. Certain signal words in boldface and their corresponding colors are becoming standards in North America, like **DANGER** in red, **WARNING** in orange, and **CAUTION** in yellow. And certain icons, like the no-smoking symbol depicted in Figure 12–7, are universally understood. Research appropriate icons that you could place in the formal report described in Research Project 1. For example, what icons and signal words with corresponding colors would you use, or would you create, that might represent a dangerous bathroom-cleaning product used by your university? How would you differentiate it for a product that might be less toxic but is still dangerous if ingested? Report your findings to your instructor in a memo.

ON THE WEB

For additional Web projects, go to Chapter 12, bedfordstmartins.com/ writingthatworks

■ Web Projects

1. Explore the following two Web sites to discover how they use illustrations to help convey their messages to the consumer: SafetyStore at <www.safetystore.com/>, an online catalog of safety and preparedness products, and the U.S. Coast Guard at <www.uscg.mil/USCG.shtm>, Office of Boating Safety. Make a list of the variety of illustrations used and their individual purposes. Analyze the style of text that accompanies the illustrations. Determine the goals of these sites and whether these sites accomplish their goals. Support your conclusions with examples, as directed by your instructor.

2. Imagine that you give how-to-travel seminars for people in different occupational fields who will be flying on airlines throughout the United States. In your earlier seminars, some people were confused about what is allowed in carry-on luggage and what has to be checked into the cargo bay. You decide to create lists for your seminar attendees that break down acceptable and prohibited items by the following categories: male and female models traveling to fashion shoots, semiprofessional athletes traveling to their sporting events, construction vendors heading for conventions, and martial artists heading to competitions. Using the list of permitted and prohibited carry-on items from the Transportation Security Administration at <www.tsa.gov/public/display?theme=177>, create two handouts for one or two of the groups above, complete with the appropriate symbols or icons, to accommodate members of these groups that include the following:

a. English-speaking American travelers
b. American immigrants and international travelers who are not familiar with symbols and icons used in this country and for whom English is a second language

13 Writing Proposals

AT A GLANCE: Proposals

This chapter discusses the audience for, the management and organization of, and the writing strategies used to develop the following kinds of proposals:

A proposal is a document written to persuade readers—colleagues or potential customers, for example—to adopt a plan or course of action that you believe will solve a problem or fulfill a need. If your objective is to persuade your organization's management to make a change or an improvement or perhaps to fund a project you would like to launch, you would write an *internal proposal*. If your objective is to persuade someone outside your company to agree to a plan or take a course of action, you would write an *external proposal*, such as a sales proposal. A *sales proposal*, which may be either solicited or unsolicited, seeks to convince a potential customer to purchase your products or services. Often, you will collaborate with others in preparing a proposal.

■ Planning and Writing Proposals

Regardless of the type of proposal you write, begin by considering its target audience and purpose, the project management, and the proposal structure. The company or agency soliciting a proposal will often specify its purpose, organization, and due date. When you prepare an unsolicited proposal, you must determine what approach will be most effective and specify a schedule for completing the project that is realistic for your company.

Voices from the Workplace

Brian Manning, Molecular, Inc.

User experience consultant Brian Manning designs Web sites for companies based on their business goals and the demands of their customers. Brian writes proposals to communicate key project information — objective, delivery, and cost — to prospective clients. He also uses proposals as an opportunity to outline the responsibilities of the people involved. "A good proposal will include any assumptions you've made about the solution or the work you will be providing," Brian asserts. "It is impossible to forecast everything that will impact how and when you will deliver a solution, so it is critical to ensure that the client knows the dependencies on which you base your proposal. Providing this information up front allows the client to validate or correct assumptions and mitigates the risk of a potential conflict at a critical stage of the project."

Sarah Schwerdel, Bay State Community Services

Sarah Schwerdel a licensed mental health counselor who works with a community-based social services agency, writes documentation of client treatment daily. Because her agency's budget relies on grants, she also often works with a collaborative group to write formal proposals. "The purpose of a proposal in our agency is to apply for contracts with government agencies to provide services for mutual clients," Sarah explains. "Proposals are an essential part of this process; they give us the opportunity to develop new and exciting programs and the potential to share those programs with our clients. My advice when writing a proposal is to have a very clear idea of key concepts, as well as the strategies and goals you are hoping to achieve. The proposal needs to be thorough and supported by relevant research."

ON THE WEB

For more help with writing proposals, go to Chapter 13, bedfordstmartins.com/ writingthatworks

Audience and Purpose

Because a proposal offers a plan to fill a need, readers will evaluate your plan based on how well you answer the following questions: What is the existing problem that the proposal addresses? What do you propose to do? What are the benefits of what you propose? How do you plan to do it? When do you plan to do it? How much will it cost?

To answer these questions effectively, make certain that your proposal is organized and written to address the needs of your entire audience. You will likely have more than one reader because proposals often require more than one level of review and approval. As you assess your readers, take into account their role in the organization.

- *Executives* and other high-level decision-makers, for example, will want to know the long-term benefits of what you propose, as well as the amount of money and the number of personnel that your plan requires.
- *Managers* will need to evaluate your credibility and consider how your plan addresses their problem. They will also need to know how they would put

your plan into action. They would be responsible for site preparation, staff training and motivation, and the schedule.

- *Technical staff* will need even more information on how to put your plan to work and will focus on the sections in your proposal that cover your previous experience and the proposed detailed solution, including the work plan, schedule, blueprints, and diagrams.

For example, if your primary reader is an expert on your subject, but his or her supervisor is not, you would provide an executive summary for the supervisor, summarizing the goal of the project and its budget, schedule, and personnel estimates in nontechnical language. To further address the needs of nontechnical readers, consider including a glossary of specialized terms used throughout the proposal, or an appendix that explains highly detailed information in nontechnical language. Also consider adding a list of acronyms and other abbreviations as appropriate, especially for nontechnical readers.

Writing a persuasive and even complex proposal can be simplified by composing a concise statement of exactly the problem or opportunity that your

◆ *For advice on writing executive summaries, preparing a glossary, and creating a list of abbreviations, see Chapter 11, Writing Formal Reports, pages 384–385, 401, and 382–384, respectively.*

◆ *Review Determining Your Purpose on page 6 and Assessing Your Audience's Needs on pages 6–7 in Chapter 1, Assessing Audience and Purpose.*

CONSIDERING AUDIENCE AND PURPOSE
Writing Proposals

- ■ Is your audience a manager within your organization or a potential customer outside your organization?
- ■ Does your proposal answer clearly the following questions?
  - What problem does your proposal address?
  - What do you propose to do?
  - What benefits does your proposed plan offer?
  - How do you plan to do it?
  - When do you plan to undertake and complete it?
  - How much do you estimate it will cost?
- ■ Does your proposal address the functional needs of those who must evaluate it by including:
  - An executive summary in nontechnical language for decision-makers?
  - A summary of the proposed solution, budget, schedule, and training requirements for managers?
  - Technical details and visuals of the proposed solution for the specialists who must assess your degree of expertise to perform the work?
- ■ Is the language professional and respectful?
- ■ Is the proposal written, organized, and submitted exactly as specified in the request for proposal?
- ■ Have you carefully revised material used from your workplace to fit seamlessly into the proposal?

proposal is designed to address. Stating the problem or opportunity concisely helps you and your readers understand the value, scope, and limitations of your proposed solution.

Project Management

Because organizations are frequently faced with the need to prepare high-quality, persuasive proposals under tight deadlines, proposals are often written by teams. When you are working with a collaborative team, designate a project leader to guide the process, organize the content, and ensure that the deadline is met.

Start by creating a broad outline of the proposal, dividing it into sections, and assigning each section to team members on the basis of their expertise. Check your organization's files for boilerplate material—such as standard language for a product description or a company profile—that can be adapted for your purposes. The project manager should establish a schedule that includes due dates for drafts, reviews of the drafts, revisions, and the final proposal.

Give each member of the team responsibility for researching and drafting his or her assigned segment of the document. Keeping the client's needs and the proposal's purpose in mind, each member should review the other team members' work and offer advice to help improve it.

Individual writers then evaluate their colleagues' reviews and accept, reject, or build on their suggestions. When each segment is finalized, the project manager consolidates all of the completed drafts into a final master copy.

For additional guidance on preparing a proposal on a tight schedule, see Meeting the Deadline: The Time-Sensitive Proposal on pages 468–469.

◆ *For a detailed overview of the collaborative writing process, see Chapter 5, Collaborative Writing.*

WRITER'S CHECKLIST
Writing Proposals with a Team

☑ Hold a planning meeting with the proposal team to assign work and establish due dates for all tasks.

☑ Assign project coordinators to ensure that all sections and elements are complete and consistent and comply with the requirements of the request for proposal.

☑ Set priorities so that the most-important sections of the proposal receive adequate attention.

☑ Delegate work to ensure that subject-area experts are available within the schedule established.

☑ Schedule the project so that work begins on the sections that will take the longest, doing as many sections as possible simultaneously.

☑ Use boilerplate as extensively as possible, being careful to adapt it to the prospective customer.

☑ Select the best medium to communicate among proposal team members.

☑ Track the status of each part of the proposal carefully, sending periodic reminders about upcoming deadlines.

Organization

Any proposal—whether it is internal or external, or whether it is short and un-complicated or long and complex—should be planned and organized carefully. A short or medium-length proposal consists at least of an introduction, a body, and a conclusion. A long proposal, as will be discussed, generally contains more parts to accommodate the increased variety of information it represents.

Writing the Introduction

In the introduction of your proposal, state your purpose and scope; state the problem you propose to solve and your solution to it. Indicate in your introduc-tion the dates on which you propose to begin and complete work on the project, any special benefits of your proposed approach, and the total cost of the project. If you are writing a sales proposal, you could also refer to any previous positive as-sociation your company may have had with the potential customer.

Writing the Body

In the body of your proposal, explain in detail (1) what products and services you are offering (for a sales proposal), (2) how the job will be done, (3) the procedures you will use to perform the work and the materials you will use (if applicable), (4) a schedule indicating when each stage of the project will be completed, and (5) a breakdown of the costs of the project.

Writing the Conclusion

In the conclusion of your proposal, emphasize the benefits of your solution, prod-ucts, or services, and persuade the reader to take action. Use an encouraging and confident tone. If you are concluding a sales proposal, express your appreciation for the opportunity to submit the proposal and your confidence in your com-pany's ability to do the job. You might add that you look forward to establishing good working relations with the client and that you would be glad to provide any additional information that might be needed. Your conclusion could also review any advantages your company may have over its competitors. It should specify the time period during which your proposal can be considered a valid offer. If any supplemental material (such as blueprints or price sheets) accompany the pro-posal, include a list of them at the end of the proposal.

Persuasive Writing

A proposal, by definition, is persuasive writing because you are attempting either to convince your readers to do something or to believe that you are the right per-son or firm to provide a product or service. Your goal is to prove to your readers that they need what you are proposing to do, and that it is practical and appropri-ate. For an unsolicited proposal, you may even need to convince your readers that they have a problem serious enough to require a solution. You would then offer your solution by first building a convincing case, demonstrating the validity of your approach.

In persuasive writing, how you present your ideas is as important as the ideas themselves. Avoid ambiguity, do not wander from your main point, and, above all, never make false claims. Support your appeal with relevant facts, statistics, and examples. Your supporting evidence must lead logically, even inevitably, to your conclusions and your proposed solution—that is, begin with the most-important evidence and end with valid but secondary evidence. Finally, cite the relevant sources of information used to support your position. Doing so gives your arguments strong credibility.

◆ *For a detailed overview of researching and citing evidence and supporting information, see Chapter 6, Researching Your Subject.*

ETHICS NOTE

As you develop the points in your proposal, be careful to acknowledge any contradictory evidence or potentially conflicting opinions; doing so allows you to anticipate and overcome objections to your proposal and even helps support your argument. By acknowledging negative details or opposing views, you not only gain credibility but also demonstrate good ethics.

The tone of your proposal should be positive, confident, and tactful. The following example, addressed to the Qualtron Corporation, is inappropriate because of its arrogant and condescending tone:

▶ The Qualtron Corporation has obviously not considered the potential problem of not having backup equipment available when a commercial power failure occurs. The corporation would also be wise indeed to give a great deal more consideration to the volume of output expected per machine.

The following version of the same passage is positive, confident, and tactful:

▶ The system would be redesigned so that it can provide backup equipment in the event of a commercial power failure. The system would also be based on realistic expectations of the output of each machine. For example, . . .

WRITER'S CHECKLIST
Writing Persuasive Proposals

☑ Analyze your audience carefully to determine how to best meet your readers' needs or requirements.

☑ Write a concise purpose statement to clarify your proposal's goals.

☑ Emphasize the proposal's benefits to readers and anticipate their questions or objections.

☑ Incorporate evidence to support the claims of your proposal, being careful to cite your sources.

☑ Divide the writing task into manageable segments and develop a work schedule.

☑ Review the descriptions of proposal sections and their uses in this chapter.

☑ Select an appropriate, visually appealing format (see Chapter 7, Designing Effective Documents and Visuals).

☑ Use a confident, upbeat tone throughout the proposal.

Internal Proposals

The purpose of an internal proposal is to suggest a change or an improvement within an organization. An internal proposal, often in memo format, is sent to a superior within the organization who has the authority to accept or reject the proposal. Two common types of internal proposals—routine and formal—are often distinguished from each other by the frequency with which they are written and by the degree of change proposed.

◆ *The telecommuting proposal by Christine Thomas (see Figure 1–6, pages 17–20) is an example of an internal proposal.*

Routine Internal Proposals

Routine internal proposals are the most frequent type of proposal and typically include small spending requests, requests for permission to hire new employees or increase salaries, and requests to attend conferences or purchase new equipment. In writing routine proposals, highlight any key benefits to be realized.

Figure 13–1 shows a typical internal proposal. It was written as a memo by a plant safety officer to the plant superintendent and recommends changes in specific safety practices at the company.

Formal Internal Proposals

Formal internal proposals usually involve requests to commit relatively large sums of money. They are usually organized into the introduction, body, and conclusion pattern described on page 437. The body, in turn, is further divided to reflect the subject matter. It may begin with a section describing the background or history of an issue and go on to discuss options for addressing the issue in separate sections.

The introduction of your internal proposal should establish that a problem exists and needs a solution. This section is sometimes called a "problem statement." (Internal proposals are sometimes referred to as *problem-solution memos*.) If the audience is not convinced that there is a problem, your proposal will not succeed. After you identify the problem, summarize your proposed solution and indicate its benefits and estimated total cost. Notice how the introduction in Figure 13–2 states the problem directly and then summarizes the writer's proposed solution.

The body of your internal proposal should offer a practical solution to the problem and provide the details necessary to inform and persuade your readers. Put yourself in your readers' position—ask what information would convince you to make the decision you are asking them to make. Then, being as specific as possible, provide the following information:

1. Sufficient background information to describe the extent of the problem (if the information is based on research, cite your sources)
2. The methods or optional approaches to be used in achieving the proposed solution
3. Information about equipment, materials, and staff requirements
4. A breakdown of costs
5. A schedule for completing the project, possibly broken down into separate tasks

◆ *For guidance on researching and citing background information, see Chapter 6, Researching Your Subject.*

Figure 13–3 shows the body of the internal proposal introduced in Figure 13–2.

Memo

To: Harold Clurman, Plant Superintendent
CC: Carla Hernandez, Supervisor, Group 333
From: Fred Nelson, Safety Officer   *Fn*
Date: August 4, 2006
Subject: Safety Practices for Group 333

Introduction that states a problem

Many accidents and near-accidents have occurred in Group 333 because of the hazardous working conditions in this area. This memo identifies those hazardous conditions and makes recommendations for their elimination.

Hazardous Conditions

Employees inside the factory must operate the walk-along crane through aisles that are frequently congested with scrap metal, discarded lumber, and other refuse from the shearing area. Many surfaces in the area are coated in oil.

Detailed explanation of the problem

The containers for holding raw stock and scrap metal are also unsafe. On many of the racks, the hooks are bent inward so far that the crane cannot fit into them properly unless it is banged and jiggled in a dangerous manner. To add to the hazard, employees in the press group do not always balance the load in the racks. As a result, the danger of falling metal is great as the unbalanced racks swing practically out of control overhead. These hazards endanger employees in Group 333 and also employees in the raw-stock and shearing areas because the crane passes over these areas.

Additional details

Hazards also exist in the yard and in the chemical building. Dumping strip metal into the scrap bins is the most-dangerous practice of all. To dump this metal, the tow-motor operator raises the rack over the edge of the scrap-metal bin and rotates the forks to permit the scrap-metal to fall from one end of the rack. As the weight shifts, the rack slams into one of the tow-motor forks (raised 12 feet above the ground). This method has resulted in two tow-motor tip-overs in the past month. In neither incident was the driver injured, but injuries are very likely. Group 333 employees must also dump tubs full of scrap metal from the tow motor into the 10-foot-high scrap bins. Because of the unpredictable way the metal falls from the tubs, employees have received many facial cuts and body bruises. In winter weather, all employees have been cut and bruised in falls that occurred as they were climbing up on scrap bins covered with snow and ice to dump scrap from pallets that had not been banded.

Finally, nearly all Group 333 employees who handle the caustic chemicals report damaged clothing and ruined shoes. Poor lighting in the chemical building (lights 20 feet above the floor), storage racks positioned less than two feet apart, and container caps incorrectly fastened have made these accidents impossible to prevent.

1

Figure 13–1   **Routine Internal Proposal**   (continued)

Recommendations

To eliminate these hazards as quickly as possible, I recommend that the following actions be taken:

Recommended solution

1. Group 333 supervisors must rigorously initiate and enforce a policy to free aisles of obstructions.
2. All dangerous racks must be repaired and replaced.
3. The Engineering Group must develop a safe rack dumper.
4. Heavy wire-mesh screens must be mounted on the front of all tow motors.
5. Group 333 employees must not accept scrap in containers that have not been properly banded.
6. Illumination must be increased in the chemical building and a compulsory training program for the safe handling of caustic chemicals must be scheduled.

I would like to meet with you and the supervisor of Group 333 before the end of the month, as your schedule permits. You will have my complete cooperation in working out all of the details of the proposed recommendations.

Conclusion

2

Figure 13–1   Routine Internal Proposal   (continued)

ABO, Inc.
Memo

To: Joan Marlow, Director, Human Resources Division
From: Leslie Galusha, Chief, Employee Benefits Department   *LG*
Date: June 12, 2007
Subject: Employee Fitness and Health-Care Costs Proposal

Health-care and worker's compensation insurance costs at ABO, Inc., have risen 100 percent over the last four years. In 2002, costs were $5,675 per employee per year; in 2006, they reached $11,560 per employee per year. This doubling of costs mirrors a national trend in which health-care costs are anticipated to rise at the same rate for the next ten years. Controlling these escalating expenses will be essential. They are eating into ABO's profit margin because the company currently pays 70 percent of the costs for employee coverage.

Introduction clearly states problem

Healthy employees bring direct financial benefits to companies in the form of lower employee insurance costs, lower absenteeism rates, and reduced turnover. Regular physical exercise promotes fit, healthy people by reducing the risk of coronary heart disease, diabetes, osteoporosis, hypertension, and stress-related problems. I propose that to promote regular, vigorous physical exercise for our employees, ABO implement a health-care program that focuses on employee fitness. . . .

Introduction summarizes proposal solution

Figure 13–2   Introduction of an Internal Proposal (Transmittal Memo Excerpt)

Problem of Health-Care Costs

Information explaining extent of problem

The U.S. Department of Health and Human Services recently estimated that health-care costs in the United States will triple by the year 2014. Corporate expenses for health care are rising at such a fast rate that, if unchecked, in eight years they will significantly erode corporate profits.

According to Health and Human Services, people who do not participate in a regular and vigorous exercise program incur double the health-care costs and are hospitalized 30 percent more days than people who exercise regularly. Nonexercisers are also 41 percent more likely to submit medical claims over $10,000 at some point during their careers than are those who exercise regularly.

My study of Tenneco, Inc., found that the average health-care claim for unfit men was $2,006 per illness compared with an average claim of $862 for those who exercised regularly. For women, the average claim for those who were unfit was $2,535, more than double the average claim of $1,039 for women who exercised. In addition, Control Data Corporation found that each nonexerciser cost the company an extra $515 a year in health-care expenses (Kozar).

Information explaining extent of problem

Citations identify sources of information

These figures are further supported by data from independent studies. A model created by the National Institutes of Health (NIH) estimates that the average white-collar company could save $596,000 annually in medical costs (per 1,000 employees) just by promoting wellness. NIH researchers estimated that for every $1 a firm invests in a health-care program, it saves up to $3.75 in health-care costs (Goetzel 342). In an overview of studies that evaluated the benefits of company wellness programs, the Public Health & Health Policy Institute of Wisconsin reported that "an unhealthy lifestyle or modifiable risk factors . . . account for at least 25 percent of employee health-care expenditures" (Zank and Friedsam 1).

Proposed Solutions for ABO

The benefits of regular, vigorous physical activity for employees and companies are compelling. To achieve these benefits at ABO, I propose that we choose from one of two possible options: build in-house fitness centers at our warehouse facilities, or offer employees several options for membership at a national fitness club.

In-House Fitness Center

Explanation of proposed solution

Building in-house fitness centers would require that ABO modify existing space in its five warehouses and designate an area outside for walking and running. To accommodate the weight-lifting and cardiovascular equipment and an aerobics area would require a minimum of 4,000 square feet. Lockers and shower stalls would also have to be built adjacent to the men's and women's bathrooms.

Figure 13–3   Body of an Internal Proposal   (continued)

Joan Marlow   3   Employee Fitness Proposal

The costs to equip each facility are as follows:

1	Challenger 3.0 Treadmill	$4,395	*Required*
3	Ross Futura exercise bicycles @ $750 each	$2,250	*equipment*
1	CalGym S-370 inner thigh machine	$2,250	*and materials*
1	CalGym S-325 outer thigh machine	$2,250	
1	CalGym S-260 lat pull-down machine	$2,290	
1	CalGym S-360 leg-extension, combo-curl	$1,900	
1	CalGym S-390 arm-curl machine	$2,235	
1	CalGym S-410 side-lat machine	$1,950	
1	CalGym S-430 pullover machine	$2,110	
1	CalGym S-440 abdominal machine	$2,250	*Breakdown of costs*
1	CalGym S-460 back machine	$2,250	
1	CalGym S-290 chest press	$2,000	
1	CalGym S-310 pectoral developer	$1,950	
10	5710321 3-wide lockers @ $81 each	$810	
4	5713000 benches and pedestals @ $81 each	$324	
	Carpeting for workout area	$3,000	
3	showers each, men's/women's locker room	$15,000	
	Men's and women's locker-room expansion	$15,000	
	Remodeling expenses	$450,000	
	Total per ABO site	$514,214	
	Grand Total	**$2,571,070**	

At headquarters and at the regional offices, our current Employee Assistance Program staff would need to be available several hours each workday to provide instructions for the use of exercise equipment. Aerobics instructors can be hired locally on a monthly basis for classes. The Buildings and Maintenance Department staff would clean and maintain the facilities.

Required staff

Fitness-Club Membership

Offering a complimentary membership to a national fitness club for all employees can also help reduce company health-care costs. AeroFitness Clubs, Inc., offers the best option for ABO's needs. They operate in over 45 major markets, with over 300 clubs nationwide. Most important, AeroFitness Clubs are located here in Bartlesville and in all four cities where our regional warehouses are located.

Explanation of proposed solution

AeroFitness staff are trained and certified in exercise physiology and will design individualized fitness programs for our employees. They offer aerobics classes for all levels, taught by certified instructors. Each club also features the latest in resistance exercise equipment from Nautilus, Universal, Paramount, and Life Fitness. Most AeroFitness facilities provide competition-size swimming pools, cushioned indoor running tracks, saunas, whirlpools, steam rooms, and racquetball courts.

Figure 13–3   Body of an Internal Proposal   (continued)

Joan Marlow   4   Employee Fitness Proposal

AeroFitness offers a full range of membership programs that include corporate discounts. The basic membership of $600 per year includes the following:

- Unlimited use of exercise equipment
- Unlimited aerobics classes
- Unlimited use of racquetball, sauna, and whirlpool facilities
- Free initial consultation with an exercise physiologist for exercise and nutrition programs
- Free child care during daytime working hours

The club offers a full range of membership programs for companies. ABO may choose to pay all or part of employee membership costs. Three membership program options are available with AeroFitness:

- *Corporate purchase.* ABO buys and owns the memberships. With 10 or more memberships, ABO receives a 35-percent discount.

   ABO costs: $600 per employee × 1,200 employees – 35% discount
   = $468,000 per year.*

- *Corporate subsidy.* Employees purchase memberships at a discount and own them. With 10 or more memberships, employees and the company each pay one-half of annual membership dues and receive a 30-percent discount off annual dues. The corporation also pays a one-time $50 enrollment fee per employee.

   ABO costs: $300 per employee × 1,200 employees – 30% discount
   = $252,000 per year. The one-time enrollment fee of $50 per employee
   adds $60,000 to first-year costs.*

- *Employee purchase.* Employees purchase memberships on their own. With five or more memberships, employees receive 25 percent off regular rates. Club sales representatives conduct an on-site open-enrollment meeting. Employees own memberships.

   ABO costs: None.

Breakdown of costs

*Assumes that all employees will enroll.

Figure 13–3   Body of an Internal Proposal   (continued)

Joan Marlow   5   Employee Fitness Proposal

Conclusion and Recommendation

I recommend that ABO, Inc., participate in the corporate membership program at AeroFitness Clubs, Inc., by subsidizing employee memberships. By subsidizing memberships, ABO shows its commitment to the importance of a fit workforce. Club membership allows employees at all five ABO warehouses to participate in the program. The more employees who participate, the greater the long-term savings in ABO's health-care costs. Building and equipping fitness centers at all five warehouse sites would require an initial investment of over $2.5 million. These facilities would also occupy valuable floor space—on average, 4,000 square feet at each warehouse. Therefore, this option would be very costly.

Enrolling employees in the corporate program at AeroFitness would allow them to attend on a trial basis. Those interested in continuing could then join the club and pay half of the membership cost, less a 30-percent discount on the $600 yearly fee. The other half of the membership fee ($300) would be paid for by ABO. If an employee leaves the company, he or she would have the option of purchasing ABO's share of the membership to continue at AeroFitness or selling their half of the membership to another ABO employee wishing to join AeroFitness.

Implementing this program will help ABO, Inc., reduce its health-care costs while building stronger employee relations by offering employees a desirable benefit. If this proposal is adopted, I have some additional thoughts about publicizing the program to encourage employee participation. I look forward to discussing the details of this proposal (including the implementation schedule for each option) with you and answering any questions you may have.

Conclusion restates recommendation

Conclusion closes with spirit of cooperation

Figure 13–4   Conclusion of an Internal Proposal

The conclusion of your internal proposal should tie everything together, restate your recommendation, and close with a spirit of cooperation (offering to set up a meeting, supply additional information, or provide any other assistance that might be needed). Keep your conclusion brief, as in Figure 13–4.

If your proposal cites information that you obtained through research, such as published reports, government statistics, or interviews, follow the conclusion with a Works Cited list that provides complete publication information for each source, as in Figure 13–5.

Joan Marlow   6   Employee Fitness Proposal

Works Cited

Works-cited section lists research sources

Centers for Medicare & Medicaid Services. "Projected." National Health Expenditure
    Data, 2006. 20 Sept. 2007 <http://www.cms.hhs.gov/
    NationalHealthExpendData>.

Goetzel, R. Z., et al. "Health Care Costs of Worksite Health Promotion Participants
    and Nonparticipants." Journal of Occupational and Environmental
    Medicine, Apr. 1998. PubMed. 18 Sept. 2007 <http://ncbi.nih.gov/entrez>.

Kozar, Marcie. "Re: Company Costs for Nonexercisers." E-mail to the author. 15 May
    2007. Office of the Comptroller, Tenneco, Inc.

U.S. Department of Health and Human Services, Office of the Assistant Secretary
    for Planning and Evaluation. "Physical Activity Fundamental to Preventing
    Disease." 2002. 12 Sept. 2007. <http://aspe.hhs.gov/health/reports/
    physicalactivity.index.shtml>.

Zank, D., and D. Friedsam. "Employee Health Promotion Programs: What Is the
    Return on Investment?" Issue Brief. Aug. 2005. Wisconsin Public Health
    & Health Policy Institute. Sept. 2007 <http://www.pophealth.wisc.edu/
    uwphi>.

Figure 13–5   Works Cited Page of an Internal Proposal

WRITER'S CHECKLIST
Creating Internal Proposals

☑ Prepare your proposal for someone in your organization with the power to act on it.

☑ Describe the problem clearly, providing any essential technical or historical background to clarify why the problem exists.

☑ Offer your solution in sufficient detail so that a decision-maker can evaluate your approach.

  – Note any resource requirements necessary for a solution (personnel, equipment, materials).

  – Provide a schedule for implementing the solution.

☑ Specify the benefits expected to result from your solution.

External Proposals

External proposals are prepared for clients and customers outside your company. They are either submitted in response to a request for goods and services from another organization (a solicited proposal) or sent to them without a prior request (an unsolicited proposal). Research and grant proposals, a type of external proposal, are usually submitted to medical and research institutions, as well as to local, state, and federal government agencies to request funding to support research that could benefit the funding organization.

Solicited and Unsolicited Proposals

Solicited proposals are written in response to a request for bids on goods or services by another company or by a local, state, or federal government agency. To find the best method of doing a job and the most-qualified company to do it, procuring organizations commonly issue a request for proposal (RFP) or an invitation for bids (IFB) that asks competing companies such as yours to bid for a job. An RFP may be rigid in specifying how the proposal should be organized and what it should contain, but it is normally quite flexible about the approaches that bidding firms may propose. Ordinarily, the RFP simply defines the basic work that the procuring organization needs and leaves it up to the proposers to put forth their method of performing the work economically and within their stated schedule. An IFB, however, is restrictive, binding the bidder to produce an item or service that meets the exact requirements of the agency or company.

When you respond to an RFP or IFB, pay close attention to any specifications in the request governing the preparation of the proposal and follow them carefully. Such specifications usually state how the proposal should be organized, the kind of technical expertise required, the basis for calculating cost estimates, the location of the work site, and the like. Figure 13–6 shows a short solicited sales

ON THE WEB

To see sample RFPs, and to locate RFPs for government agencies, go to Chapter 13, **bedfordstmartins.com/writingthatworks**

Jerwalted Nurseries

Ronald Malcomson, President

12 Rogers Highway West
St. Louis, MO 63101
Ph. 1-800-212-1212
Fax 314-999-1111

February 1, 2007

Ms. Tricia Olivera, Vice President
Watford Valve Corporation
1600 Swanson Avenue
St. Louis, MO 63121

Dear Ms. Olivera:

Introduction states purpose and scope of proposal, and indicates when project can be started and completed

Jerwalted Nurseries, Inc., proposes to landscape the new corporate headquarters of the Watford Valve Corporation, on 1600 Swanson Avenue, at a total cost of $14,871. The lot to be landscaped is approximately 600 feet wide and 700 feet deep. Landscaping will begin no later than April 30, 2007, and will be completed by May 31.

The following trees and plants will be planted, in the quantities given and at the prices specified.

Body lists products to be provided and cost per item

4	maple trees	@ $110 each	$440
41	birch trees	@ $135 each	$5,535
2	spruce trees	@ $175 each	$350
20	juniper plants	@ $15 each	$300
60	hedges	@ $12 each	$720
200	potted plants	@ $12 each	$2,400
		Total Cost of Plants =	$9,745
		Labor =	$5,126
		Total Cost =	$14,871

Conclusion specifies time limit of proposal, expresses confidence, and looks forward to working with prospective customer

All trees and plants will be guaranteed against defect or disease for a period of 90 days, the warranty period to begin June 1, 2007.

The prices quoted in this proposal will be valid until June 30, 2007.

Thank you for the opportunity to submit this proposal. Jerwalted Nurseries has been in the landscaping and nursery business in the St. Louis area for 30 years, and our landscaping has won several awards and commendations, including a citation from the National Association of Architects. We are eager to put our skills and knowledge to work for you, and we are confident that you will be pleased with our work. If we can provide any additional information or assistance, please call us at the number listed above.

Sincerely,

Ronald Malcomson

Ronald Malcomson

Figure 13–6   Short Solicited Sales Proposal

proposal that responds to a property-management company's invitation for bids on a landscaping project.

Unsolicited proposals are those submitted to a company without a prior request and are not as unusual as they may sound: Companies often operate for years with a problem they have never recognized (unnecessarily high maintenance costs, for example, or poor inventory-control methods). You might prepare an unsolicited proposal for such a company if you were convinced that the potential customer could realize substantial benefits by adopting your solution to a problem. Of course, you would need to convince the customer of the need for what you are proposing and that your solution would be the best one (Figure 13–7). Many unsolicited proposals are preceded by a letter of inquiry that specifies the problem or unmet need to determine whether there is any potential interest. If you receive a positive response, you would conduct a detailed study of the prospective client's needs to determine whether you can be of help and, if so, exactly how. You would then prepare your proposal on the basis of your study.

ETHICS NOTE

Always keep in mind that, once submitted, a sales proposal is a legally binding document that promises to offer goods or services within a specified time and for a specified price. Many sales proposals also note that the offer is valid for a limited period (usually 90 days).

Grant and Research Proposals

Grant and research proposals are written to request the approval of, and usually funding for, particular projects. For example, a professor of education might submit a research proposal to the state or federal Department of Education to request funding for research on the relationship of class size to educational performance; similarly, a community center might submit a grant proposal to obtain funding from a local government agency for an after-school job-training program.

Many government and private foundations solicit research and grant proposals. Granting agencies typically post opportunities, along with detailed application guidelines, at their Web sites, and usually specify their own requirements for the format and content of proposals, as shown in Figures 13–8 and 13–9. Tailor your grant or research proposal to your audience by carefully following the guidelines provided by the granting agency. In addition, remember that proposals must always be persuasive: Explain your project's goals, your plan for achieving those goals, and your qualifications to perform the project.

ON THE WEB

For samples of research and grant proposals, go to **bedfordstmartins.com/ writingthatworks,** and select *Model Documents Gallery.*

Aerolite Bicycle Supply

1536 Bicycle Road
Bedford, Pennsylvania 16802

aerolitecycle.com
Phone 1-800-331-1221

November 20, 2006

Mr. Eric Shoop
Shoop Bicycle Shop
Squall Valley, Utah 19542

Dear Mr. Shoop:

Introduction states the purpose and range of products offered

Aerolite would like to congratulate you on the grand opening of your bicycle shop in Squall Valley, Utah. As you know, Aerolite makes quality equipment for bicycling. We carry bicycles, shorts, jerseys, helmets, and a variety of bicycle parts. We are eager to introduce you to our line of high-quality equipment offered at an affordable price. Please read on!

Bicycles

Our high-end bicycle frames are made of titanium, which makes them the strongest and the lightest frames on the market today. All of our other bicycle frames are made of butted aluminum, a very strong, anticorrosive, patented material that is very durable for all kinds of riding.

Body details the product line and specific features

Our dual-suspended mountain bikes are unique because we developed the only Y frame used in such bikes. This frame eliminates the "pogo-ing" that compresses the rear shock in normal dual-suspended bikes instead of putting the power to the ground and to forward momentum. Our design puts the power the rider puts into the pedals straight to the ground, which pushes the rider forward instead of up and down.

All of our bikes have Natsuya components, ranging from the ALUMA at the low end to the XRT at the high end. Each component has a groupo, which includes derailleurs (front and back), shifters, gears, brakes, brake levers, crank, pedals, headset, handlebars, and wheel hubs. Every bike has a groupo for its specific level. As the level of bike increases, the prices increase—but the quality goes right along with the price.

Figure 13–7   Short Unsolicited Sales Proposal   (continued)

Mr. Eric Shoop   2   November 20, 2006

Shorts and Jerseys

Aerolite shorts are made of spandex with comfortable fleece padding in the seat.
Our jerseys are made of an acrylic material that keeps the rider warm in the winter
and cool in the summer. They pull the sweat away from the rider's body in summer
and block the wind in winter.

Helmets

Our helmets—able to withstand a 300-foot vertical drop onto a hard surface without getting scratched—are the strongest on the market. With soft interior padding
and generous vents, they're also the most comfortable.

Please Consider Our Line of Merchandise

Bikers of the rough terrain of Squall Valley know they can count on the durability of
Aerolite bicycles and merchandise. If you choose to carry our line, you will be the
exclusive Aerolite dealer in Utah, offering equipment known around the world for
its quality and performance.

Persuasive conclu-
sion describes
advantages over
competitors, and
follow-up with
a salesperson

I have enclosed a brochure that contains our entire line of merchandise. An Aerolite
representative will visit your store in three weeks to see if you are interested in carrying the Aerolite line of merchandise and to answer any questions you may have.

Sincerely,

James Eugene

James Eugene
Sales Manager

Enclosure

Figure 13–7   Short Unsolicited Sales Proposal   (continued)

Sponsoring agency
Participating agencies

Title of grant topic

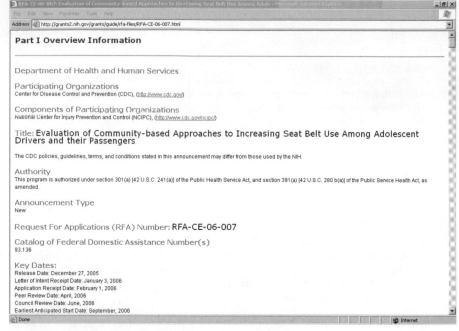

Figure 13–8   Web Page Listing a Grant-Proposal Topic   *Source:* Department of Health and Human Services.

Topics and methods required for a research-grant proposal

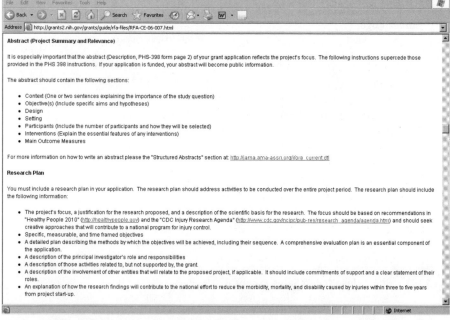

Figure 13–9   Web Page Describing Content Requirements for the Grant Proposal shown in Figure 13–8   *Source:* Department of Health and Human Services.

Sales Proposals

The sales proposal, a major marketing tool for business and industry, is a company's offer to provide specific goods or services to a potential buyer within a specified period of time and for a specified price. The primary purpose of a sales proposal is to demonstrate that the prospective customer's purchase of the seller's products or services will solve a problem, improve operations, or offer other benefits.

Sales proposals vary greatly in length and sophistication. Some are a page or two written by one person; others are many pages written collaboratively by several people; still others are hundreds of pages written by a proposal-writing team. A short sales proposal might bid for painting the outside of a single-family home, a sales proposal of moderate length might bid for the installation of a network operating system for a small company, and a very long sales proposal might bid for the construction of a multimillion-dollar shopping center or sports complex. Short sales proposals are often written on standardized forms that are available from office-supply and stationery stores.

Your first task in writing a sales proposal is to find out exactly what your prospective customer needs. Then determine whether your organization can satisfy that customer's needs. If appropriate, compare your company's strengths with those of competing firms, determine your advantages over them, and emphasize those advantages in your proposal. For example, say a small biotechnology company is bidding for the contract to supply several types of medical test kits to a regional hospital. The proposal writer who believes that the company has a better-qualified staff than its competitors might include the résumés of the key people who would be involved in the project as a way of emphasizing that advantage.

While the simple sales proposal typically follows the introduction-body-conclusion pattern outlined on page 437, the long sales proposal contains more parts to accommodate the increased variety of information that it must present. The long sales proposal may include some or all of the following sections:

- Cover, or transmittal, letter (Figure 13–10)
- Title page
- Executive or project summary (Figure 13–11)
- General description of products (Figure 13–12)
- Detailed solution or rationale (Figure 13–13)
- Cost analysis (Figure 13–14)
- Delivery schedule or work plan (Figure 13–14)
- Site-preparation description (Figure 13–15)
- Training requirements (Figure 13–16)
- Statement of responsibilities (Figure 13–17)
- Description of vendor (Figure 13–18)
- Organizational sales pitch (optional) (Figure 13–18)
- Conclusion (optional) (Figure 13–19)
- Appendixes (optional)

Optional sections may be included at the discretion of the proposal-writing team. A conclusion, for example, may be added to a very long proposal as a convenience to the reader, but it is not mandatory. A site-preparation section, however, is essential if the work proposed requires construction, remodeling, or such preparatory work as facility rewiring before equipment can be installed.

◆ For additional guidance on writing cover letters and transmittals, see pages 314, 316, and 317 in Chapter 9, Writing Business Correspondence, and pages 374–375 in Chapter 11, Writing Formal Reports.

A long sales proposal begins with a cover letter—sometimes called a *transmittal letter*—which expresses your appreciation for the opportunity to submit your proposal and for any assistance you may have received in studying the customer's requirements. The letter should acknowledge any previous positive association with the customer. Then it should summarize the recommendations offered in the proposal and express your confidence that they will satisfy the customer's needs. Figure 13–10 shows the cover letter for the proposal illustrated in Figures 13–11 through 13–19—a proposal that the Waters Corporation of Tampa provide a computer system for the Cookson's chain of retail stores.

◆ For more advice on preparing a title page, see pages 376–378 in Chapter 11, Writing Formal Reports.

◆ For a discussion of executive summaries, see pages 384–385 in Chapter 11, Writing Formal Reports.

A title page and an executive summary—sometimes called a *project summary*—follow the cover letter. The title page contains the title of the proposal, the date of submission, the company to which it is being submitted, your company's name, and any symbol or logo that identifies your company. The executive summary is addressed to the executive who will ultimately accept or reject the proposal and should summarize in nontechnical language how you plan to approach the work. Figure 13–11 shows the executive summary of the Waters Corporation proposal.

If your proposal offers products as well as services, it should include a general description of the products, as in Figure 13–12. In many cases, product descriptions will already exist as company boilerplate; be sure to check your company's files or server before drafting a description from scratch.

Following the executive summary and the general description, explain exactly

---

 DIGITAL TIPS: Sharing Existing Company Material (Boilerplate)

■ In the workplace, if written material (company profiles, instructions, procedures, product descriptions, or reports created by colleagues) that meets your needs exists in other company documents, copy and paste the information into your document. Don't redo work that has already been done.

■ Discuss sources of existing material in team planning meetings and store them in electronic folders, on network drives, or on internal Web sites for sharing with other team members. Be sure to edit the material to make it an exact fit.

■ Sources of boilerplate need not be acknowledged. Borrowing these passages is neither plagiarism nor a violation of copyright because the information is simply being used in a different setting by the organization to which it already belongs.

■ In the classroom, borrowing published and Web-based information is necessary and acceptable, whether quoted or paraphrased, but you must document its source. Not citing the source of such information is plagiarism, unless the information is common knowledge. (See Avoiding Plagiarism and Copyright Violations on pages 178–179 in Chapter 6, Researching Your Subject.)

how you plan to do what you are proposing. This section, called the detailed solution or rationale, will be read by specialists who can understand and evaluate your plan, so you can feel free to use technical language and discuss complicated concepts. Figure 13–13 shows one part of the detailed solution appearing in the Waters Corporation proposal, which included several other applications in addition to the payroll application. Notice that the detailed solution, like the discussion in an unsolicited sales proposal, begins with a statement of the customer's problem, follows with a statement of the solution, and concludes with a statement of the benefits to the customer. In some proposals, the headings "Problem" and "Solution" are used for this section.

A cost analysis and delivery schedule are essential to any sales proposal. The cost analysis — also called a budget — itemizes the estimated cost of all the products and services that you are offering; the delivery schedule — also called a *work plan* — commits you to a specific timetable for providing those products and services. Figure 13–14 shows the cost analysis and delivery schedule of the Waters Corporation proposal.

If your recommendations include modifying your customer's physical facilities, you would include a site-preparation description that details the modifications required. In some proposals, the headings "Facilities" and "Equipment" are used for this section.

If the products and services you are proposing require training the customer's employees, your proposals should specify the required training and its cost. Figure 13–15 shows the site-preparation section and Figure 13–16 the training-requirements section of the Waters proposal.

To prevent misunderstandings about what you and your customer's responsibilities will be, you should draw up a statement of responsibilities (Figure 13–17), which usually appears toward the end of the proposal. Also toward the end of the proposal is a description of the vendor, which gives a profile of your company, its history, and its present position in the industry. The description-of-the-vendor section typically includes a list of people or subcontractors and the duties they will perform. The résumés of key personnel may also be placed here or in an appendix. Following this description, many proposals add what is known as an organizational sales pitch. To this point, the proposal has attempted to sell specific goods and services. The sales pitch, striking a somewhat different chord, is designed to sell the company and its general capability in the field. The sales pitch promotes the company and concludes the proposal on an upbeat note. Figure 13–18 shows the vendor-description and sales-pitch sections of the Waters proposal.

Some long sales proposals include a conclusion section that summarizes the proposal's salient points, stresses your company's strong points, and includes information about whom the potential client can contact for further information. It may also end with a request for the date the work will begin should the proposal be accepted. Figure 13–19 shows the conclusion of the Waters proposal.

Depending on length and technical complexity, some proposals include appendixes made up of statistical analyses, maps, charts, tables, and résumés of the principal staff assigned to the project. Appendixes to proposals should contain only supplemental information; the primary information should appear in the body of the proposal.

ON THE WEB

For a complete, annotated version of the proposal shown in Figures 13–11 to 13–19, as well as the RFP to which the proposal responded, go to **bedfordstmartins.com/ writingthatworks** and select *Model Documents Gallery*.

The Waters Corporation

17 North Waterloo Blvd., Tampa, Florida 33607
Phone: (813) 919-1213 Fax: (813) 919-4411
waterscorp.com

September 1, 2006

Mr. John Yeung, General Manager
Cookson's Retail Stores, Inc.
101 Longuer Street
Savannah, Georgia 31399

Dear Mr. Yeung:

Opening expresses appreciation for chance to bid on the project and stresses success of past working relationship

The Waters Corporation appreciates the opportunity to respond to Cookson's Request for Proposal dated July 26, 2006. We would like to thank Mr. Becklight, Director of your Management Information Systems Department, for his invaluable contributions to the study of your operations before preparing our proposal. Waters's close working relationship with Cookson's has resulted in a clear understanding of your philosophy and needs.

Body describes purpose of work proposed and belief in its success in meeting the customer's need

Our proposal describes a Waters Interactive Terminal/Retail Processor System designed to meet Cookson's network and processing needs. It will provide all of your required capabilities, from the point-of-sale operational requirements at the store terminals to the host processor. The system is easily installed without extensive customer reprogramming and is compatible with much of Cookson's present equipment. It will provide the flexibility to add new features and products in the future. The system's unique hardware modularity, microprocessor design, and flexible programming capability greatly reduce the risk of obsolescence.

Ending assures customer of company's commitment to success

Thank you for the opportunity to present this proposal. We will use all the resources available to the Waters Corporation to ensure the successful implementation of the new system.

Sincerely yours,

Janet A. Curtain

Janet A. Curtain
Executive Account Manager
General Merchandise Systems
jcurtain@netcom.tf.com

Enclosure: Cookson Proposal

Figure 13–10   Cover Letter for a Sales Proposal

The Waters Proposal September 1, 2006

EXECUTIVE SUMMARY

The Waters 319 Interactive Terminal/615 Retail Processor System will provide your management with the tools necessary to manage people and equipment more profitably with procedures that will yield more cost-effective business controls for Cookson's.

Opens with overview of the proposed system

The equipment and applications proposed for Cookson's were selected through the combined effort of Waters and Cookson's Management Information Systems Director, Mr. Becklight. The architecture of the system will respond to your current requirements and allow for future expansion.

The features and hardware in the system were determined from data acquired through the comprehensive survey we conducted at your stores in February of this year. The total of 71 Interactive Terminals proposed to service your four store locations is based on the number of terminals currently in use and on the average number of transactions processed during normal and peak periods. The planned remodeling of all four stores was also considered, and the suggested terminal placement has been incorporated into the working floor plan. The proposed equipment configuration and software applications have been simulated to determine system performance based on the volumes and anticipated growth rates of the Cookson's stores.

Summarizes scope of system proposed

The information from the survey was also used in the cost justification, which was checked and verified by your controller, Mr. Deitering. The cost effectiveness of the Waters Interactive Terminal/615 Retail Proces-sor System is apparent. Expected savings, such as the projected 46 percent reduction in sales audit expenses, are realistic projections based on Waters's experience with other installations of this type.

Ends with projected cost savings of interest to the executive reader

-1-

Figure 13–11 **Executive Summary of a Sales Proposal**

The Waters Proposal   September 1, 2006

GENERAL SYSTEM DESCRIPTION

The point-of-sale system that Waters is proposing for Cookson's includes two primary Waters products. These are the 319 Interactive Terminal and the 615 Retail
Processor.

Waters 319 Interactive Terminal

Detailed breakdown of system components and functions essential for technical readers

The primary component in the proposed retail system is the 319 Interactive
Terminal. It contains a full microprocessor, which gives it the flexibility that
Cookson's has been looking for.

The 319 Interactive Terminal provides you with freedom in sequencing a transaction to suit your needs rather than limiting you to a preset list of available steps
or transactions. The terminal program can be adapted to provide unique transaction sets, each designed with a logical sequence of entry and processing to accomplish required tasks. In addition to sales transactions recorded on the selling floor,
specialized transactions such as theater-ticket sales and payments can be designed
for your customer-service area.

The 319 Interactive Terminal also functions as a credit-authorization device, either
by using its own floor limits or by transmitting a credit inquiry to the 615 Retail
Processor for authorization.

Data-collection formats have been simplified so that transaction editing and formatting are much more easily accomplished. The information systems manager has
already been provided with documentation on these formats and has outlined all
data-processing efforts that will be necessary to transmit the data to your current
systems. These projections have been considered in the cost justification.

Waters 615 Retail Processor

The Waters 615 Retail Processor is a minicomputer system designed to support the
Waters family of retail terminals. The processor will reside in your data center in
Buffalo. Operators already on your staff will be trained to initiate and monitor its
activities.

-2-

Figure 13–12   General-Description-of-Products Section of a Sales Proposal   (continued)

The Waters Proposal   September 1, 2006

The 615 will collect data transmitted from the retail terminals, process credit- and check-authorization inquiries, maintain files to be accessed by the retail terminals, accumulate totals, maintain a message-routing network, and control the printing of various reports. The functions and level of control performed at the processor depend on the peripherals and software selected.

Software

The Retail III software used with the system has been thoroughly tested and is operational in many Waters customer installations.

Additional system details for technical specialists

The software provides the complete processing of the transaction, from the interaction with the operator on the sales floor through the data capture on cassette or disk in stores and in your data center.

Retail III provides a menu of modular applications for your selection. Parameters condition each of them to your hardware environment and operating requirements. The selection of hardware will be closely related to the selection of the software applications.

Figure 13–12 General-Description-of-Products Section of a Sales Proposal (continued)

The Waters Proposal   September 1, 2006

PAYROLL APPLICATION

Current Procedure

A primary system feature described in problem-solution form with supporting cost analysis

Your current system of reporting time requires each hourly employee to sign a time sheet; the time sheet is reviewed by the department manager and sent to the Payroll Department on Friday evening. Because the week ends on Saturday, the employee must show the scheduled hours for Saturday and not the actual hours; therefore, the department manager must adjust the reported hours on the time sheet for employees who do not report on the scheduled Saturday or who do not work the number of hours scheduled.

The Payroll Department employs a supervisor and three full-time clerks. To meet deadlines caused by an unbalanced work flow, an additional part-time clerk is used for 20 to 30 hours per week. The average wage for this clerk is $9.00 per hour.

Advantage of the Waters System

The 319 Interactive Terminal can be programmed for entry of payroll data for each employee on Monday mornings by department managers, with the data reflecting actual hours worked. This system would eliminate the need for manual batching, controlling, and data input. The Payroll Department estimates conservatively that this work consumes 30 hours per week.

Hours per week	30
Average wage (part-time clerk)	×9.00
Weekly payroll cost	$270.00
Annual Savings	$14,040

Elimination of the manual tasks of tabulating, batching, and controlling can save 0.25 hourly units. Improved work flow resulting from timely data in the system without data-input processing will allow more efficient use of clerical hours. This would reduce payroll by the 0.50 hourly units currently required to meet weekly check disbursement.

Eliminate manual tasks	0.25
Improve work flow	0.50
40-hour unit reduction	1.00
Hours per week	40
Average wage (full-time clerk)	11.00
Savings per week	$440.00
Annual Savings	$22,880

TOTAL ANNUAL SAVINGS: $36,920

-4-

Figure 13–13   Detailed Solution of a Sales Proposal

The Waters Proposal   September 1, 2006

COST ANALYSIS

This section of our proposal provides detailed cost information for the Waters 319 Interactive Terminal and the Waters 615 Retail Processor. It then multiplies these major elements by the quantities required at each of your four locations.

319 Interactive Terminal

	Price	Maintenance (1 year)
Terminal	$2,895	$167
Journal Printer	425	38
Receipt Printer	425	38
Forms Printer	525	38
Software	220	—
Totals	**$4,490**	**$281**

615 Retail Processor

	Price	Maintenance (1 year)
Processor	$57,115	$5,787
CRT I/O Writer	2,000	324
Laser Printer	4,245	568
Software	12,480	—
Totals	**$75,840**	**$6,679**

Breakdown of hardware, software, and maintenance costs

The following breakdown itemizes the cost per store:

Store No. 1

Description	Quantity	Price	Maintenance (1 year)
Terminals	16	$68,400	$4,496
Digital Cassette	1	1,300	147
Laser Printer	1	2,490	332
Software	16	3,520	—
Totals		**$75,710**	**$4,975**

Store No. 2

Description	Quantity	Price	Maintenance (1 year)
Terminals	20	$85,400	$5,620
Digital Cassette	1	1,300	137
Laser Printer	1	2,490	332
Software	20	4,400	—
Totals		**$93,590**	**$6,089**

-5-

Figure 13–14   **Cost Analysis and Delivery Schedule of a Sales Proposal**   (continued)

The Waters Proposal   September 1, 2006

Store No. 3

Description	Quantity	Price	Maintenance (1 year)
Terminals	17	$72,590	$4,777
Digital Cassette	1	1,300	147
Laser Printer	1	2,490	332
Software	17	3,740	—
Totals		**$80,120**	**$5,256**

Store No. 4

Description	Quantity	Price	Maintenance (1 year)
Terminals	18	$76,860	$5,058
Digital Cassette	1	1,300	147
Laser Printer	1	2,490	332
Software	18	3,960	—
Totals		**$84,610**	**$5,537**

Data Center at Buffalo

Description	Quantity	Price	Maintenance (1 year)
Processor	1	$57,115	$5,787
CRT I/O Writer	1	2,000	324
Laser Printer	1	4,245	568
Software	1	12,480	—
Totals		**$75,840**	**$6,679**

The following summarizes all costs:

Location	Hardware	Maintenance (1 year)	Software
Store No. 1	$72,190	$4,975	$3,520
Store No. 2	89,190	6,099	4,400
Store No. 3	76,380	5,256	3,740
Store No. 4	80,650	5,537	3,960
Data Center	63,360	6,679	12,480
Subtotals	$381,770	$28,546	$28,100

Total $438,416

Further cost breakdown and delivery schedule

DELIVERY SCHEDULE

Waters is normally able to deliver 319 Interactive Terminals and 615 Retail Processors within 90 days of the date of the contract. This can vary depending on the rate and size of incoming orders.

All the software recommended in this proposal is available for immediate delivery. We do not anticipate any difficulty in meeting your tentative delivery schedule.

-6-

Figure 13–14   Cost Analysis and Delivery Schedule of a Sales Proposal   (continued)

The Waters Proposal   September 1, 2006

SITE PREPARATION

Waters will work closely with Cookson's to ensure that each site is properly prepared prior to system installation. You will receive a copy of Waters's installation and wiring-procedures manual, which lists the physical dimensions, service clearance, and weight of the system components in addition to the power, logic, and environmental requirements. Cookson's is responsible for all building alterations and electrical facility changes, including the purchase and installation of communication cables, connecting blocks, and receptacles.

Details of system requirements and division of responsibilities for the work

Wiring

For the purpose of future site considerations, Waters's in-house wiring specifications for the system call for two twisted-pair wires and 22 shielded gauges. The length of communications wires must not exceed 2,500 feet.

As a guide for the power supply, we suggest that Cookson's consider the following:

1. The branch circuit (limited to 20 amps) should service no equipment other than 319 Interactive Terminals.
2. Each 20-amp branch circuit should support a maximum of three 319 Interactive Terminals.
3. Each branch circuit must have three equal-size conductors—one hot leg, one neutral, and one insulated isolated ground.
4. Hubbell IG 5362 duplex outlets or the equivalent should be used to supply power to each terminal.
5. Computer-room wiring will have to be upgraded to support the 615 Retail Processor.

-7-

Figure 13–15   Site-Preparation Section of a Sales Proposal

The Waters Proposal   September 1, 2006

TRAINING

To ensure a successful installation, Waters offers the following training course for your operators.

Interactive Terminal/Retail Processor Operations

Employee training costs and length

Course number: 8256
Length: three days
Tuition: $500.00

This course provides the student with the skills, knowledge, and practice required to operate an Interactive Terminal/Retail Processor System. Online, clustered, and stand-alone environments are covered.

We recommend that students have a department-store background and that they have some knowledge of the system configuration with which they will be working.

-8-

Figure 13–16   Training-Requirements Section of a Sales Proposal

The Waters Proposal   September 1, 2006

RESPONSIBILITIES

Based on its years of experience in installing information-processing systems, Waters believes that a successful installation requires a clear understanding of certain responsibilities.

Waters's Responsibilities

Generally, it is Waters's responsibility to provide its users with needed assistance during the installation so that live processing can begin as soon thereafter as is practical.

- Provide operations documentation for each application that you acquire from Waters.
- Provide forms and other supplies as ordered.
- Provide specifications and technical guidance for proper site planning and installation.
- Provide adviser assistance in the conversion from your present system to the new system.

Customer's Responsibilities

Cookson's will be responsible for the suggested improvements described earlier, as well as the following:

- Identify an installation coordinator and system operator.
- Provide supervisors and clerical personnel to perform conversion to the system.
- Establish reasonable time schedules for implementation.
- Ensure that the physical site requirements are met.
- Provide personnel to be trained as operators and ensure that other employees are trained as necessary.
- Assume the responsibility for implementing and operating the system.

Division of tasks between customer and vendor

-9-

Figure 13–17   Statement-of-Responsibilities Section of a Sales Proposal

The Waters Proposal   September 1, 2006

DESCRIPTION OF VENDOR

Statements of the vendor's history and commitment to its core business to highlight its experience and reputation

The Waters Corporation develops, manufactures, markets, installs, and services total business information-processing systems for selected markets. These markets are primarily in the retail, financial, commercial, industrial, health-care, education, and government sectors.

The Waters total-system concept encompasses one of the broadest hardware and software product lines in the industry. Waters computers range from small business systems to powerful general-purpose processors. Waters computers are supported by a complete spectrum of terminals, peripherals, and data-communication networks, as well as an extensive library of software products. Supplemental services and products include data centers, field service, systems engineering, and educational centers.

The Waters Corporation was founded in 1934 and presently has approximately 26,500 employees. The Waters headquarters is located at 17 North Waterloo Boulevard, Tampa, Florida, with district offices throughout the United States and Canada. For a comprehensive listing of Waters products and services, visit our Web site at waterscorp.com.

WHY WATERS?

Corporate Commitment to the Retail Industry

Waters's commitment to the retail industry is stronger than ever. We are continually striving to provide leadership in the design and implementation of new retail systems and applications that will ensure our users of a logical growth pattern.

Research and Development

Over the years, Waters has spent increasingly large sums on research-and-development efforts to ensure the availability of products and systems for the future. In 2005, our research-and-development expenditures for advanced-systems design and technological innovations reached the $70 million level.

Leading Point-of-Sale Vendor

Waters is a leading point-of-sale vendor, having installed over 150,000 units. The knowledge and experience that Waters has gained over the years from these installations ensure well-coordinated and effective systems implementations.

-10-

Figure 13–18   Description-of-Vendor and Sales-Pitch Sections of a Sales Proposal

The Waters Proposal   September 1, 2006

CONCLUSION

Waters welcomes the opportunity to submit this proposal to Cookson's. The Waters Corporation is confident that we have offered the right solution at a competitive price. Based on the hands-on analysis we conducted, our proposal takes into account your current and projected workloads and your plans to expand your facilities and operations. Our proposal will also, we believe, afford Cookson's future cost-avoidance measures in employee time and in enhanced accounting features.

Final summary of system advantages

Waters has a proven track record of success in the manufacture, installation, and servicing of retail business information systems, stretching over many decades. We also have a demonstrated record of success in our past business associations with Cookson's. We believe that the system we propose will extend and strengthen this partnership.

Restatement of vendor's experience and reputation

Should you require additional information about any facet of this proposal, please contact Janet A. Curtain, who will personally arrange to meet with you or arrange for Waters's technical staff to meet with you or send you the information you need.

Contact information

We look forward to your decision and to continued success in our working relationship with Cookson's.

-11-

Figure 13–19   Conclusion of a Sales Proposal

■ MEETING THE DEADLINE: The Time-Sensitive Proposal

Proposal writers must give top priority to meeting the procuring organization's deadline, while also producing a high-quality, persuasive proposal likely to receive favorable evaluations. The following time-management strategies can help toward meeting these goals.

1. *Hold an initial planning session.* The project manager should hold a planning meeting with the coordinator, the compiler, the budget specialist, and the key subject-matter specialists to introduce the project team members, set priorities, determine and delegate tasks, and set milestone deadlines for each task.

2. *Assign coordinators.* During the planning meeting, the project manager should choose a writing coordinator to organize the creation and production of text and graphics, and a compiler (often an administrative assistant) to integrate all sections and elements of the final proposal and to make sure that those sections and elements adhere to the potential customer's requirements in the request for proposal.

3. *Set priorities.* The proposal sections or features likely to weigh most heavily during the prospective customer's evaluation of the proposal should receive the most attention from the writers and the most space in the final product. Make this determination at the beginning of the project. These sections tend to be longer than sections of lesser importance. For example, for a ten-page proposal that includes four sections, the two most important sections might be four pages each, while the two least important sections might be one page each.

4. *Delegate tasks.* To expedite research and writing, assign more than one person to work on each section, and allow them to work out a way to collaborate efficiently to meet the deadline for submitting their section. This strategy works best when the contributors have diverse schedules and areas of specialization. Often, two or three subject experts coauthor parts of a single section and the writing coordinator edits the resulting draft for clarity and coherence.

5. *Work out a schedule.* During the initial planning session, determine how much time each task is likely to require. Start work immediately on tasks likely to take longer to complete, but also begin to collect other important pieces, such as résumés, biographies, and project descriptions. Decide which tasks can be done simultaneously and which tasks must precede others. When establishing a schedule, work backward from the proposal deadline, leaving at least a day for the proposal to reach its destination by express delivery, half a day before that for collecting company signatures and making multiple copies of the proposal, and half a day before that for last-minute edits and proofreading.

6. *Use boilerplate material.* When possible, import into the proposal standard pieces of information from previous proposals, such as résumés, descriptions of past projects, and company goals and accomplishments. This is known as boilerplate material. For additional information about the use of boilerplate, see Digital Tips: Sharing Existing Company Material (Boilerplate) on page 454.

7. *Select the best media.* Choose the most efficient means for collecting information and draft sections for the proposal. For example, if you need written material immediately, use e-mail attachments, internal servers, wikis (collaborative Web sites), or faxes; if you need written material within a day or two, interoffice mail, Express Mail, or a delivery service might suffice. If you need information immediately that is not yet drafted, rely on phone calls or in-person meetings.

8. *Track progress and deadlines.* Use e-mail or phone messages periodically to send out reminders about deadlines or prompt someone to deliver material that you need right away. Hold interim meetings if doing so will speed up your work. If interim task deadlines are missed and you need information, materials, or finished products immediately, ask everyone on the project team to abandon other projects to devote full-time and extra hours to the proposal effort so that you can meet the final deadline.

9. *Hold a lessons-learned meeting, if necessary.* Even when these strategies are used, problems can arise that jeopardize the quality of your proposal or your ability to meet the final deadline. After sending out the proposal, hold a debriefing session in which you identify those problems and plan strategies for avoiding them when planning and writing future proposals.

CHAPTER 13 SUMMARY: WRITING PROPOSALS

A proposal

- Is written to persuade a reader to follow a plan or course of action.
- Is written from the perspective and needs of the audience.
- Is organized to address specific readers in specific sections.
  - Overviews for executives
  - Implementation plans and schedules for managers
  - Details for the technical staff
- Is produced by a collaborative team of specialists when the proposal is complex.
- Consists of the following parts (and may include additional parts, based on the needs of your topic).
  - An *introduction* that states
    - The problem you propose to solve and your solution to it
    - The dates on which you propose to begin and complete work
    - Any special benefits of your proposed approach
    - The total cost of the project
    - Any previous positive association between your company and the potential customer (if a sales proposal)

- A *body* that explains
  - What products and services you are offering (if a sales proposal)
  - How the job will be done
  - The procedures you propose to use to perform the work
  - The materials you will use (if applicable)
  - The schedule for each stage of the project
  - Detailed costs
- A *conclusion* that emphasizes
  - The benefits of your solution, products, or services that persuade the reader to take action
  - Your appreciation for the opportunity to submit the proposal
  - Your confidence in your ability — or, if a sales proposal, of your company's ability — to carry out the project
  - Your willingness to provide further information
  - The advantages of your company over its competitors

  And includes:
  - The time period during which the proposal is valid
  - A list or description of any supplemental materials

■ Bolsters your case with credible facts, arguments, and examples.

An internal proposal

■ Is written to a manager within your organization.

■ Is usually written to persuade management to make a change or an improvement, or to fund a project that you would like to launch.

An external proposal

■ Is written to a potential client outside your organization.

■ May be solicited or unsolicited.

■ Might be written to persuade a potential customer to purchase your company's products or services.

■ Might be written to persuade a government agency or private foundation to fund a project.

■ May be short or long, depending on the complexity of the topic.

■ Is often time sensitive and must be produced by a collaborative writing team under the pressure of a tight deadline.

ON THE WEB

For an online quiz on proposals, go to Chapter 13, bedfordstmartins.com/ writingthatworks

---

■ Exercises

1. Address an internal proposal to your supervisor, recommending that your company begin a tuition-refund plan or specific technology-training program. Propose at least three major advantages to having either of these educational programs, and present them in decreasing order of importance.

2. You are a landscaping contractor and would like to respond to the following RFP, which appears in your local newspaper:

   ▶ Lawn-mowing agreement for the Town of Augusta, Oregon. Weekly mowing of 5 miles of Route 24 median and sidings, 10 acres in Willoughby Park, and 23 acres at Augusta Memorial Golf Course, May 30 through September 30. Proposals are due April 30.

   Write a proposal in which you estimate the number of labor-hours the contract would require, what you would charge, the ability of your staff and equipment to do the job, your firm's experience and qualifications, and the weekly schedule that you propose to follow.

3. Write a proposal letter in which you recommend a change in a government process—for example, in the way Americans pay taxes, the way the census is completed, the way voter registration is handled, or the way immigrants become citizens. Be specific when listing the advantages of your idea. Address your short, informal proposal to a local, state, or federal legislator, as appropriate.

4. Write a proposal letter to change a specific rule or regulation of an organization to which you belong, such as your school, religious organization, professional association, or fitness club. List the current rule or regulation, then present your proposed changes and explain the advantages of your new rule. Address your short proposal to the president or head of the organization.

5. Prepare a short, internal proposal to persuade your instructor to accept one of the following ideas. Present as many logical and persuasive reasons as possible to support your proposal.

   • Students should automatically be excused from class on Mondays immediately following school vacations.
   • There should be no penalty for missing class.
   • Students should be allowed up to three days to submit papers late without penalty.
   • If students have more than three tests in one week, they should be allowed to make up one exam the following week.
   • If students are within three percentage points of reaching the next highest grade, extra-credit opportunities should be granted for the purpose of raising the grade.

6. Imagine that you work as a proposal writer for an electronics company that makes specialized equipment for the U.S. Navy. You have been informed that should your company win a contract next year, a record will be kept of your performance assessments and evaluations. Both positive and negative information will be recorded, such as quality reviews, over-budget cost reports, user comments, and technical successes and failures (see <www.cpars.navy.mil> for detailed information on the Navy's Contractor Performance Assessment Reporting System). Draft an internal proposal to your boss detailing this new information and suggesting procedures and processes that could be put into place so that your company's performance assessments and evaluations will be positive.

7. As a human resources coordinator of a large company, you've noticed an increase in the number of employee medical emergencies, some serious, over the past two years. Write an internal proposal memo to your supervisor, offering plans that would (1) contribute to employees' good health and (2) help employees respond to medical emergencies. Plans for improving employees' health could include a more-comprehensive medical-benefits package, on-site health screening, stress-management and nutrition counseling, and corporate memberships to fitness centers. Plans for helping employees handle medical emergencies could include on-site cardiopulmonary resuscitation (CPR) and first-aid training. Explain the benefits of each solution you propose.

8. Imagine that you run your own business and want to expand your client base. First, choose a small business concept that interests you and identify a service or product that such a business might provide. Prepare a one-page cost analysis for

a sales proposal that you would submit to a prospective client. Your cost analysis should be clearly written and well formatted, and should include the following breakdown for the project:

- Cost of personnel or labor
- Cost of overhead
- Cost of new equipment
- Total cost of project

Submit any amounts you wish in these categories and change the category titles as needed. Each category except total cost must contain at least four different line items. For example, cost of personnel or labor might include the hourly rate for the time the company president will spend on this project and the cost of other staff specialists required on the project. Overhead might include the cost of support staff, supplies, company vehicles, and so forth. The cost of new equipment would include the cost of items purchased solely for the client. Although you may use any numbers you wish in the line items, all subtotals should equal the total cost when added together.

9. In Exercise 10 in Chapter 10, you were asked to imagine that you were a consultant hired by a company that creates security systems for the average homeowner. While its new wireless surveillance camera was supposed to work in low light and transmit pictures up to 100 meters, your tests revealed that the camera's picture and sound quality were negatively impacted by the interference of other electrical equipment in the house, such as baby monitors, microwave ovens, and cordless phones. Static noises and jumping lines made it nearly impossible to understand the sound and picture.

   Now, imagine that you are the head of the security systems company's development team. Based on the test report you wrote for Exercise 10 in Chapter 10, write an internal proposal to the head of the company detailing the test results and requesting funds to hire an electronics consultant who specializes in solving such problems.

10. Identify a problem that you feel needs to be solved either at work or at school. For example, the increasing number of students and limited number of parking spaces is causing a major parking problem. Or sealed windows in your office building are creating sick-building syndrome, and many employees are getting ill more frequently and for longer periods of time. Your assignment is to write a proposal offering a solution to the problem. (Your instructor may want to approve your topic selection.) Assume that your proposal is internal, and include the following in your proposal:

   a. Transmittal letter
   b. Executive summary
   c. Introduction, body, and conclusion
   d. Cost analysis (you may invent the numbers)
   e. Timeline or schedule of delivery
   f. Description of vendor

Your completed proposal will be seven to ten pages long, with the executive summary less than one page, single-spaced. Your introduction, body, and conclusion will be approximately three pages of text, 1.5-spaced. Insert at least two visuals within the text.

Collaborative Classroom Projects

ON THE WEB

For more collaborative classroom projects, go to Chapter 13, bedfordstmartins.com/writingthatworks

1. In teams of three to five members, review the description of the vendor included in Figure 13–18, and develop and design an organizational sales pitch. Referring back to this chapter, develop a rough draft, including an original layout and design created by your team. Set priorities for the information to be included and be creative in the manner you choose to present the information. Take 45 minutes to one hour to complete this assignment.

2. Divide into teams with classmates who share a similar major area of study. If you have more than seven students in your group, divide into two smaller groups. During the next hour, your team assignment is to write a short proposal in the form of a persuasive letter directed to your instructor. In your letter, propose an educational field trip to a place of interest. Include the following in your proposal:
   - Why this place is of educational value to your team
   - What you expect to learn from the trip
   - Suggested mode of travel, accommodations, and arrangements for meals
   - A breakdown of costs
   - Suggested sources for funding
   - Any other relevant points

3. In teams of five to seven members, develop an internal proposal asking the dean's office to upgrade or expand a facility, technology, or course offering (or another topic approved by your instructor). Your proposal is due in three weeks. Spend 45 minutes developing a plan for completing your group's proposal. Refer to Meeting the Deadline: The Time-Sensitive Proposal on pages 468–469.
   a. Your team will need to assign a project manager, a writing coordinator, a compiler, and a budget specialist.
   b. Once chosen, the project manager will begin the session by introducing team members, setting priorities, and determining and delegating tasks.
   c. In a collective effort, make a list of the tasks that will need to be completed.
   d. Decide what sections will be included in the proposal.
   e. Develop a timeline, including scheduling and sequencing of the tasks. Include any other details you feel are relevant as you develop your plan.

   As directed by your instructor, present your plan for how your team will meet the deadline orally to the class or submit the plan in writing to your instructor. Submit the finished proposal to your instructor.

Research Projects

ON THE WEB

For extra research projects, go to Chapter 13, bedfordstmartins.com/writingthatworks

1. Many government and research proposals have very specific instructions on the format and content of each proposal. For example, a proposal's instructions may specify the number of characters per inch allowed in the text, and the size of the margins and number of lines allowed per page. Assume that you and three other classmates are interested in pursuing a career as professional grant writers for medical and educational institutions. Research at least six specific grants dealing with medical or educational products or research. Create a report of your findings

(review Chapter 10, Writing Informal Reports) that gives many examples of the instructions you found and also explains why agencies that fund research projects would be so specific about such seemingly inconsequential details.

2. For Exercises 2 and 3 in Chapter 10, you wrote an investigative report detailing back injuries and worker's compensation claims at a large online retailer. You were asked to head a task force of warehouse workers and managers to explore ways to prevent warehouse injuries, especially back injuries, and write a three-month progress report that explains what your task force has investigated and summarizes its findings. Research warehouse equipment companies and manufacturers of safety equipment and use your findings to create an internal proposal that comments on such issues as the design of warehouse equipment, especially the kind that transports heavy boxes, and makes suggestions for the purchase of new equipment that would help the warehouse workers prevent injuries.

ON THE WEB

For more Web projects, go to Chapter 13, bedfordstmartins.com/writingthatworks

■ Web Projects

1. Your high-tech company is interested in changing its security procedures to include biometric verification technology. Employees' fingerprints or retina patterns (or both) would now be scanned before they could enter top-secret areas. You have been asked to investigate at least three Web sites of companies that provide this kind of technology. Write a proposal letter to your boss that details how the technology works, the cost, and the advantages over traditional security methods.

2. Assume that you run the Adult Basic Education (ABE) program at your local county jail. Your job is to offer instructional and support services that will help incarcerated adult students improve their literacy and English-speaking skills through the high school levels, to the point that they are ready, upon their release, to continue and succeed in postsecondary education. Search the Web for educational grants that might help you meet your goals. You may apply for funds to address potential courses in ABE, literacy, pre-adult secondary education, English for speakers of other languages (ESOL), preliteracy ESOL, and adult diploma classes, among others.

   a. Begin by searching the Web site of your state's Department of Education, then move to the federal agencies. Create a report of at least three sources of funding available, what they give money for, and the requirements for applying for the funding. (These may include required forms, like letters of intent and budget details.) Also note all of the deadlines.

   b. Draft a proposal to your state's Department of Education that answers the questions in Considering Audience and Purpose: Writing Proposals on page 435.

   c. Now rework your proposal draft according to the Writing Persuasive Proposals checklist on page 438. Remember that you are arguing that your program has the greatest need and offers the most for its students, so persuasive writing is essential. (You won't be rewriting the proposal in a specific format for a specific funding source unless you wish to, but rather reworking the existing draft.)

14 Giving Presentations and Conducting Meetings

AT A GLANCE: Presentations and Meetings

Although most of this book covers the principles of writing that work in business and industry, much workplace information is communicated orally as well, and the components of such communications—listening and responding effectively—are both critically important. This chapter offers practical guidelines for the following:

Writing and presentations have much in common. Both must be logically organized and are most effective when clear and succinct. The principles of writing discussed throughout this text are also applicable to preparing presentations in the workplace: Know your purpose and audience, organize your information, and determine the amount of information necessary to convey your message. However, much is different between writing and presentations, and this chapter explores those elements unique to this form of communication. Oral communication is most widely used in the workplace for giving presentations and in conducting meetings. Central to the success of both is effective listening.

ON THE WEB

For more help with giving presentations and conducting meetings, go to Chapter 14, bedfordstmartins.com/ writingthatworks

■ Preparing and Delivering Presentations

The steps required to prepare an effective presentation parallel the steps you follow to write a document: (1) determine your purpose and analyze your audience, (2) find and gather the facts to support your point of view and proposal, and (3) logically organize your information. However, presentations are intended for listeners, not readers. Because you are giving a talk rather than writing a memo or report, your manner of delivery, the way you organize the material, and your supporting visual aids require as much attention as your content.

Determining Your Purpose

Every presentation is given for a purpose—even if only to share information. To determine the purpose of your presentation, use the following question as a guide: What do I want the audience to know, to believe, or to do when I have finished the presentation? Based on the answer to that question, write a purpose statement that answers the questions *what* and *why.*

▶   The purpose of my presentation is to explain to my classmates the various tasks I performed last semester as a part-time volunteer at the Maplewood Adult Day Care Center [*what*] so that other members of the class will want to become volunteers at Maplewood [*why*].

▶   The purpose of my presentation is to convince my company's chief information officer of the need to improve the appearance, content, and customer use of our company's Web site [*what*] so that she will be persuaded to include additional funds in the budget for site-development work next fiscal year [*why*].

◆ For a fuller discussion of determining purpose, analyzing an audience, considering your context, and gathering information, see pages 6–10 in Chapter 1, Assessing Audience and Purpose.

Keep in mind that your purpose and your audience's receptiveness will be affected by the context of the presentation. Will your audience be expecting you to address an existing company or industry-wide issue important to them? Will your organization's goals, expectations, even jargon be relevant or appropriate when you address outside groups? Will your gestures and use of eye contact affect how your presentation is received because of your audience's background or cultural frame of reference? These and other matters all make up the context affecting the success of your presentations.

Analyzing Your Audience

Once you determine the desired end result of the presentation, you need to analyze your audience so that you can tailor your presentation to your audience's needs. Answer the following five questions about your audience:

1.   What is your audience's level of experience or knowledge about your topic?
2.   What is the general educational level and age of your audience?

Voices from the Workplace

Stephen Lin, Smarter Living, Inc.

Product manager Stephen Lin provides leadership, direction, and planning for his company's travel search tool, <www.BookingBuddy.com>. Meetings and presentations are an integral part of how Stephen communicates with his team. Who he invites to a meeting is paramount. He says, "Covering your bases is a good thing to do; however, overkill is a bad thing. You run the risk of bringing operational efficiency to a halt if there are too many people who don't really need to be there." When giving a presentation, Stephen tries to keep his participants engaged. He suggests, "While going off topic is typically a bad idea, sometimes it's the curveball needed to bring people's attention back to the main issue at hand. I find that entertaining anecdotes are the best way to do this as they still keep you relatively on target."

Paul B. Greenspan, EMC Corporation

As senior director of business development for EMC, a company that specializes in information management and storage, Paul Greenspan spends much of his time meeting with prospective and established customers. "A good presenter," he advises, "uses techniques to minimize the amount of work the audience has to do. For example, I learned to use arresting visuals and to avoid long, bulleted lists that basically duplicate my notes. Body language is also important—how you use your arms, how you gesture. The 'big' gesture that may seem exaggerated to the presenter looks natural to the audience. Finally, you have to demand interactivity from your audience. The day of the 'droning, talking head' with an inch-thick stack of transparencies is gone forever. Insist on your audience engaging and interacting with you."

3. What is your audience's attitude toward the topic you are speaking about, and—based on that attitude—what concerns, fears, or objections might your audience have?

4. Are there subgroups in your audience that might have different concerns or needs?

5. What questions could your audience ask about this topic?

Gathering Information

Once you have focused the presentation, you need to find the information that will support your point of view or the action you propose. Give the audience only the information necessary to accomplish your goals; too much information will overwhelm the audience, and too little information will leave the audience either with a sketchy understanding of your topic or with the feeling that you have not provided enough information to support the course of action you wish them to take.

Structuring Your Presentation

When structuring your presentation, keep the focus on your audience as listeners. As such, they remember openings and closings best because your listeners are freshest at the outset and refocus their attention as you complete your remarks. Take advantage of this pattern. Give your audience a brief overview of your presentation at the beginning, use the body to develop your ideas, and end with a summary of what you covered and, if appropriate, a call to action.

Introduction

The introduction to your presentation may include an opening—something designed to catch and focus the audience's attention. The following opening defines a problem:

▶ You have to write an important report, but you'd like to incorporate the bulk of an old report into your new one. The problem is that you don't have an electronic version of the old report. You'll have to re-key many pages. You groan because that seems an incredible waste of time. Have I got a solution for you!

You could also use any of the following types of openings:

- *An attention-getting statement:* As many as 50 million Americans have high blood pressure.
- *A rhetorical question:* Would you be interested in a full-sized computer keyboard that is waterproof, is noiseless, and can be rolled up like a rubber mat?
- *A personal experience:* As I sat at my computer one day last month deleting my eighth junk e-mail of the day, I decided to find a way to eliminate this time-waster.
- *An appropriate quotation:* According to researchers at the Massachusetts Institute of Technology, "Garlic and its cousin the onion confer major health benefits—including fighting cancer, infections, and heart disease."

◆ *For additional examples of openings, see Writing an Opening on pages 84–86 in Chapter 3, Writing the Draft.*

Following your opening, set the stage for your audience by giving an overview of the presentation. The overview may include general or background information that your audience will need to understand the more-detailed information in the body of your presentation. It may also be an overview of how you've organized the material.

▶ This presentation explains the options available to you, the employees of Acme Corporation, for making payroll contributions to a long-term retirement plan that will enhance the income you will receive from Social Security and pension benefits.

▶ This presentation will answer your questions about:
  - How much can I save?
  - How much does Acme contribute to the plan?
  - What are my investment options?

Body

In the body of your presentation, persuade your audience of the validity of your conclusion. If you are addressing a problem, demonstrate that the problem exists and offer a solution or range of possible solutions. If your introduction stated that the problem was low profits, high costs, outdated technology, or high employee absenteeism, for example, you might use the following approach:

- Offer a solution.
  - Increase profits by lowering production costs.
  - Cut overhead to reduce costs.
  - Upgrade existing technology to improve productivity.
  - Offer employees more flexibility in their work schedules or other incentives.
- Prove your point.
  - Gather the facts and data you need.
  - Present the facts and data using easy-to-understand visual aids.
- Call for action.
  - Convince your audience to agree, to change their minds, or to do something.
- Anticipate questions ("How much will it cost?") and objections ("We're too busy now. When will we have time to learn the new software?") and be ready for them.

Closing

Your closing should achieve the goals of your presentation. If your purpose is to motivate your audience to take action, ask them to do what you want them to do; if your purpose is to get your audience to think about something, summarize what you want them to think about. Many presenters make the mistake of not actually closing—they simply quit talking, shuffle papers around, and then walk away.

Because your closing is what your audience is most likely to remember, it is the time to be strong and persuasive. Returning to the retirement savings plan example, consider the following possible closing:

▷   This is the first step toward your future security.
- Decide how much you can save each month.
- Remember Acme's contribution.
- Choose the investment options that best fit your needs.
- ENROLL NEXT WEEK!

This closing brings the presentation full circle and asks the audience to act on the information provided in the presentation—exactly what a closing should do.

Transitions

Transitions should appear between the introduction and the body, between the points in the body, and between the body and the closing. Transitions, simply a sentence or two, let the audience know that you're moving from one topic to the next. They also prevent a choppy presentation and provide you, the speaker, with assurance that you know where you're going and how to get there.

▶   Before getting into the specifics of the fund families available to you, I'd like to describe the investment goals and strategies of each. That information will provide you with the background you'll need to compare the differences among them to make an informed decision about what works best for you.

It is also a good idea to pause for a moment after you've delivered a transitional line between topics to let the audience shift gears with you. Remember, they don't know where you're headed.

The typical presentation follows a pattern made up of the components shown in Figure 14–1, although the number of slides and their content will vary, depending on the speaker's topic. The complete presentation for the savings and investment program is shown in Figure 14–2. Note the conciseness and layout of the language and visuals.

Model presentation pattern: introduce key content, support key content with data, summarize content, end with a call to action

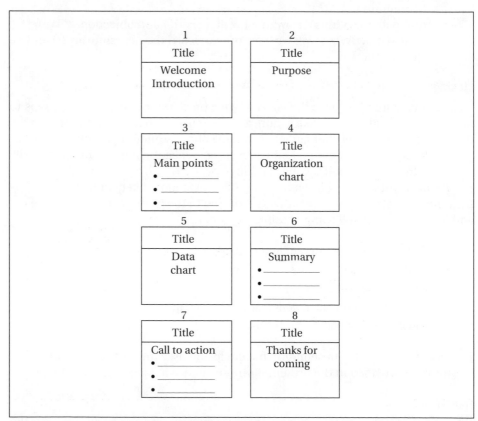

Figure 14–1   Pattern for a Typical Presentation

EMPLOYEE BENEFITS

Acme Corporation

Presented by Laura Phelps

Office of Human Resources

June 2007

Cover slide for presentation information — who, what, when

Savings and Investment Program

Saving for Your Future

This presentation will explain our options for contributing to the employee savings plan through payroll deductions.

Acme Corporation considers this program a long-term retirement-oriented plan to enhance your retirement security above the level of your pension and Social Security benefits.

-1-

Introductory slide with overview of topic and attention-getting statement

**Acme Corporation
Savings and Investment Program**

Questions to Ask Yourself

- How much can I save?
- How much does Acme Corporation contribute?
- What are my investment options?

-2-

Rhetorical questions to pique audience interest and announce organization of information

Figure 14–2   Sample Presentation (continued)

Response to first question

Acme Corporation
Savings and Investment Program

How Much Can I Save?

- Save from 2% to 20% of your gross earnings
- Elect to save on the following basis:
  - Pre-tax basis
  - After-tax basis
  - Combination of both

-3-

Response to second question

Acme Corporation
Savings and Investment Program

How Much Does Acme Corporation Contribute?

- Acme Corporation matches 25¢ of every dollar you save each month!
- Example based on earning $2,000 per month.

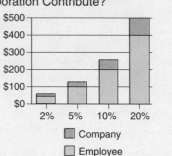

-4-

Response to third question

Acme Corporation
Savings and Investment Program

What Are My Investment Options?

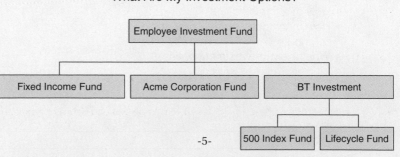

-5-

Figure 14–2   Sample Presentation   (continued)

Acme Corporation
Savings and Investment Program

The Next Step to Your Future Security

- Decide how much you can save each month.
- Remember Acme's contribution.
- Choose the investment options that best fit your needs.
- ENROLL NEXT WEEK!

-6-

Call to action

Acme Corporation
Thank You for Coming

Your Future Is Important to Us

- Consider your options.
- Enroll next week.
- Questions? Call or e-mail the Benefits Office:
  - (301) 990-1200, extension 03
  - E-mail: benefits@acme.com

-7-

Instructions for response to call to action

Figure 14–2   Sample Presentation (continued)

WRITER'S CHECKLIST
Organizing a Presentation

☑ When preparing a presentation, follow the same guidelines that you follow for writing.

☑ Use a logical structure based on that of the written essay: Include an introduction, a body, and a conclusion.

☑ Be clear, direct, and precise.

☑ Support your presentation with specific examples.

☑ Between subtopics, use transitions to help your listeners understand how the parts are related.

Using Visual Aids

Well-planned visual aids can clarify and simplify your message because they communicate clearly, quickly, and vividly. They are also attention-getters that help retain audience interest. Charts, graphs, and illustrations greatly increase audience understanding and retention of the information, especially for complex issues and technical information that could otherwise be misunderstood or glossed over by your audience. A bar graph, pie chart, diagram, or concise summary of key points can eliminate misunderstanding and save many words. Note that visuals in presentations require titles; however, they generally do not need figure or table numbers because the presenter refers to them in the proper sequence during the presentation.

◆ Use the guidelines for preparing visuals discussed in Chapter 7, Designing Effective Documents and Visuals.

You can create and present your visual aids in a variety of media, including computer-presentation software; flip charts, whiteboards, and chalkboards; overhead transparencies; 35mm slides; and handouts.

Using Presentation Software

Visual information in workplace presentations is frequently displayed on computer monitors, for a small audience, or by projectors connected to a laptop computer, for larger audiences (Figure 14–3).

Laptop computer, projector, and pull-down screen

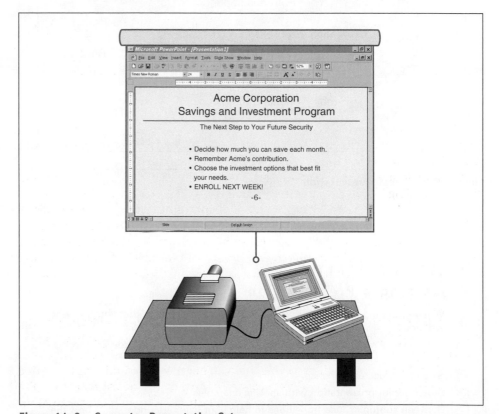

Figure 14–3   Computer-Presentation Setup

Presentation software, such as PowerPoint, Corel Presentations, Freelance Graphics, and other packages, permits you simultaneously to create your slides as you write your presentation. You can import content, charts, and graphs from other files, and use standard templates and other aids that help you design effective visuals. Possible enhancements include a selection of layouts, typefaces, background textures and colors, as well as clip-art images, sound (including music), and video (such as animation) from outside sources, such as the Internet. Avoid using too many enhancements, however, because they could distract viewers from your message. (Figure 14–4 shows a slide that uses a bulleted list and clip art.)

ON THE WEB

For a helpful tutorial on creating effective slides, see **bedfordstmartins.com/ writingthatworks** and select *Tutorials,* Preparing Presentation Slides. For links to additional information and tutorials for using presentation software, select *Web Links*.

Plain-Language Award of the Month

What Are the Criteria for the Award?

Use "Plain-Language Principles," such as

- Common, everyday words
- Short sentences
- Active voice
- "You" and other pronouns (as appropriate)
- Logical organization
- Easy-to-read design features (lists and tables)

Figure 14–4   Presentation Slide with Bulleted List and Clip Art

Presentation software also makes it possible to convert a presentation to Web format and post it to your company's intranet site, a feature that makes your slides accessible to your colleagues during or after your presentation.

Be sure to integrate your visuals with your presentation when you rehearse. Practice loading the presentation and anticipate any technical difficulties that might arise. Should you encounter a technical snag during the presentation, stay calm and give yourself time to solve the problem. If you can't, say so and move on. As a backup, carry a copy of your electronic presentation printed onto transparencies in case there's a problem with the computer projection system. Also carry an extra copy of your presentation on a disk for backup.

ON THE WEB

For another example of presentation slides, go to **bedfordstmartlns .com/writingthatworks** and select *Model Documents Gallery*.

Using Flip Charts, Whiteboards, and Chalkboards

Flip charts are large sheets of white paper bound like a tablet and fastened to the top of an easel (Figure 14–5). The charts are ideal for smaller groups in a conference room or a classroom. The presenter writes on the sheets with colored felt-tip pens, often during the presentation. To avoid distracting your audience by writing as you speak, prepare text and sketches ahead of time on a series of sheets and flip through them during your presentation. Flip charts are also an ideal medium for brainstorming with your audience. You can fill sheet after sheet with ideas, tape

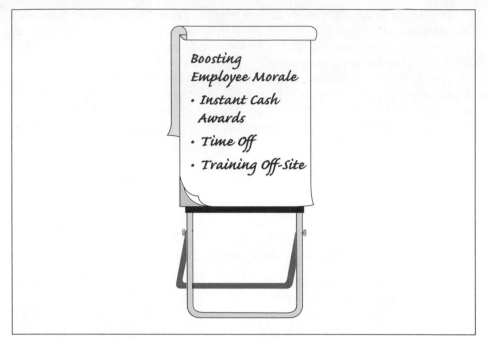

Figure 14–5 Flip Chart

them around the walls for everyone to see, and use a clean sheet or sheets to organize the ideas into an outline for follow-up work.

Whiteboards and chalkboards, common to classrooms, are convenient for creating impromptu sketches and for jotting notes during your presentation. If your presentation requires extensive notes or complex drawings, create them before the presentation to minimize audience restlessness. Ensure before the presentation that you have ample chalk or marking pens and an eraser. If you need to keep ideas that will be erased because you're running out of space, assign someone in the audience to record them for future reference.

Using Overhead Transparencies and Slides

Transparencies are page-sized sheets of clear plastic on which the text and graphics for your presentation are copied, using a computer printer or copy machine. During the presentation, you place the transparencies on an overhead projector (Figure 14–6), and the images are projected onto a screen or blank wall. The images can range from black text on clear film to multicolored computer images.

You could, depending on the complexity of the topic, create a series of overlays to cover selected areas and then remove them to reveal the next key point or illustration in the presentation. You can also lay a sheet of paper over a list of bulleted items on a transparency, uncovering one at a time as you discuss it, to focus audience attention on each point in the sequence.

Slides are 2-by-2-inch 35mm film color transparencies inserted into a carousel and projected onto a screen or a blank wall. Color transparencies are especially

Figure 14–6   Overhead Projector and Transparency Sheet

useful if you need to include photographs in your presentation. (The individual screens produced using presentation software are also called slides.)

Overhead transparencies and slides are best seen in a darkened room, unlike flip charts and chalkboards or whiteboards, which are best seen in a fully lighted room.

DESIGNING YOUR DOCUMENT
Creating Slides for Presentations

- Use text sparingly. Instead of blocks of text, use bulleted or numbered lists and keep them parallel in content and grammatical form. Use numbers if sequence is important and bullets if not.

- Limit the number of bulleted or numbered items to five or six per slide. The slide should contain no more than 40 to 45 words. (See Figure 14–4.) Any more will clutter the slide and force you to use a smaller type size that could impair your audience's ability to read.

- Make your slides consistent in type style, type size, and spacing.

- Use a type size visible to members of the audience in the back of the room. Type should be no smaller than 30 point bold. For headings, 45 or 50 point is even better.

- Use graphs and charts rather than tables to show data trends. Use only one or two graphs or charts per slide; otherwise, the data will look cluttered and may be hard to see.

- Ensure that the contrast between your text and background is sharp. (See Figure 14–3.) Use light backgrounds with dark lettering and avoid textured or fancy "wallpaper" backgrounds.

- Aim for 12 or fewer slides per presentation. More than that will tax any audience's concentration.

- Don't read the text on your slides word for word. Instead, summarize the content of the slide and cover salient points in detail.

Using Handouts

Handouts typically are paper copies of your presentation slides, although they may be a summary of key points; supporting data in tables, charts, and graphs; or other supplementary information. They benefit you and your audience by reinforcing what is said and by permitting your listeners to take notes and retain the material for future reference. They are usually distributed before the presentation, although some presenters distribute them afterward to avoid having the handouts distract their audience during the presentation.

Delivering Your Presentation

Once you've outlined and drafted your presentation and prepared your visuals, you are ready to think about practice and delivery techniques.

Practicing Your Presentation

Begin by familiarizing yourself with the sequence of the material—major topics, notes, and visuals—in your outline. Once you feel comfortable with the content, you're ready to practice the presentation itself.

Practice on your feet and out loud. Try to practice in the room where you'll give the presentation. Practicing here will help you learn the idiosyncrasies of the room: acoustics, lighting, how the chairs will most likely be arranged, where the electrical outlets and switches are located, and so forth. Practicing out loud is more effective than just rehearsing mentally because you process the information in your mind many times faster than you can possibly speak it. Rehearsing out loud will make clear exactly how long your presentation will take and will highlight any problems, such as awkward transitions. Rehearsing also helps you to eliminate or reduce verbal tics, such as "um," "you know," and "like."

Practice with your visuals. Be sure to integrate your slides, transparencies, or other visuals into your practice sessions. This will help your presentation go more smoothly. Operate the equipment (computer, slide projector, or overhead projector) until you're comfortable with it. Even if things go wrong, being prepared and having practiced will give you the confidence and poise to go on. You can also use your visuals as cues to the next point you wish to make.

Videotape your practice session. Videotape is a very effective and sometimes painful way to catch what you are doing wrong. The tape will reveal how you present your material from the audience's perspective. If you do not have access to a videotape recorder, at the very least use an audiotape recorder to evaluate your vocal presentation. Another effective technique is to ask a friend or colleague watch you rehearse and comment on your delivery.

> ## WRITER'S CHECKLIST
> ## Practicing Your Presentation
>
> ☑ Practice out loud and, if possible, in the room where you'll deliver the presentation.
>
> ☑ Incorporate your visuals as you practice, using the computer, slide projector, or overhead transparencies.

☑ Videotape or audiotape your practice session and evaluate it critically, or have a colleague or classmate observe and comment.

☑ Because the meaning of gestures differs greatly from culture to culture, carefully choose and rehearse those that you will use during presentations.

☑ Practice your presentation in front of colleagues or friends and have them watch for any gestures that could be misinterpreted by your audience.

Using Delivery Techniques That Work

In addition to your words and message, nonverbal communication can engage and inspire your audience. If you want your audience to share your point of view, show them your enthusiasm for your topic. Your words will have more staying power when you deliver them with physical and vocal animation. Be sure to make eye contact; use movement and gestures; and vary your vocal inflection, pace, and projection.

Make eye contact.   The best way to establish rapport with your audience is with eye contact. For smaller audiences, make eye contact with as many people as possible. In a large audience, directly address those people who seem most responsive to you in different parts of the audience. Address each person separately, and focus your attention on him or her for several seconds before moving on. Doing so helps you establish rapport with your audience by holding their attention. It also gives you important visual cues as to how you're doing. Are people engaged and actively listening? Are they looking around or staring at the floor? These cues may tell you that you need to speed up or slow down the pace of your presentation.

Use movement and gestures.   Animate your presentation with physical movement. The easiest way to integrate movement into your presentation is to step to the screen and point to a visual as you discuss it. Touch the screen with the pointer and turn back to the audience before beginning to speak (touch, turn, and talk). If you are using an overhead projector, you can place the pointer directly on the overhead so that it casts a shadow that points to the appropriate item on the screen. Otherwise, simply take a step or two to one side or to the other after you have been talking for a minute or so. This type of movement is most effective at transitional points in your presentation, between major topics, or after pauses for emphasis. Too much movement, however, can be distracting—so try not to pace or wave your arms. Hand gestures will come more naturally during your presentation if you include them in your practice sessions.

Adjust your vocal inflection, pace, and volume.   Your voice can be an effective tool in communicating your sincerity, enthusiasm, and command of your topic. Use it to your advantage to project your credibility. *Vocal inflection* is the rise and fall of your voice at different times, such as the way your voice naturally rises at the end of a question ("You want it *when?*"). Keep your audience's attention by using this pattern as you would in a conversation. Do not fall into a monotone speech pattern that can hypnotize your audience and make them drowsy. Vocal variety also allows you to highlight differences between key and subordinate points in your presentation. Using a conversational delivery and making eye contact also promote the feeling among members of the audience that you're addressing each one directly.

Pace is the speed at which you deliver your presentation. If you speak too fast, your words will run together, making it difficult for your audience to follow you. If you speak too slowly, the audience will get impatient and their minds may wander.

Speak up to be heard. If anyone in the audience cannot hear you, your presentation has been ineffective for that person. If the audience has to strain to hear you, they may give up trying to listen. You can correct for these problems by practicing out loud with someone listening from the back of the room.

> ## CONSIDERING AUDIENCE AND PURPOSE
> ### Engaging Your Audience When Speaking
>
> ■ Establish rapport and trust by looking into the eyes of as many audience members as possible.
>
> ■ Use your voice to communicate sincerity and enthusiasm, and, above all, do not speak in a monotone. Project your voice so that you're heard by everyone, and pace your delivery so that your words don't run together.
>
> ■ Be animated, moving to the screen to emphasize points and gesturing naturally.
>
> ■ Hold the interest of your audience by looking at your notes as little as possible. (Never read directly from your notes.)
>
> ■ Deliver your talk from a prepared outline on slides rather than memorizing it word for word. This way, it
>
> - Sounds more natural and less monotonous
>
> - Helps audience attention and comprehension
>
> - Enables more eye contact with your audience, which helps convey your interest in and enthusiasm for the topic

Dealing with Presentation Anxiety

Everyone experiences nervousness before a presentation. Survey after survey reveals that dread of speaking in front of others ranks among the top five fears for most people. Typical reactions to this stress include shortness of breath, a racing heartbeat, trembling, perspiration, and even nausea. Some people react by clearing their throats repeatedly, tugging at their clothing or earlobes, or moving continuously during the presentation. Instead of letting this stress inhibit you, focus on channeling your nervous energy into a helpful stimulant. That is, if you can't eliminate your stress entirely, manage it. The best way to master this feeling is to know your topic thoroughly. If you know what you are going to say and how you are going to say it, you will gain confidence and reduce anxiety as you become immersed in your subject.

Rehearsing your presentation will help. Do so alone or, if possible, in front of one or more listeners. If you're anxious because you may forget something or get lost during your delivery, you may find it helpful to write out the presentation in full, put it aside, and rehearse using only brief notes. If you falter, refer to your written version. After a practice session, imagine yourself in front of your audience delivering your material point by point. Begin by saying to yourself, "My subject is important. I am ready. My listeners are here to listen to what I have to say." If you cannot remember every point you wish to make during the practice presentation, review your notes or visuals. These will trigger your memory both as you imagine the presentation and when you're actually giving it.

You can use several techniques to quell the butterflies immediately before a presentation. Fill your lungs with a deep breath and hold it for a count of ten. Then exhale and repeat, doing so several times or until you feel your body begin to relax. Tensing and relaxing muscles is another effective stress reducer. Clench both fists tightly and count to ten while inhaling and then exhale. Repeat several times until your stress begins to diminish.

During the presentation, do not be upset if you say the wrong word, refer to the wrong visual, or otherwise do something unplanned. Simply take a deep breath, correct your mistake, and move forward. Do not refer to your mistake unless you must—chances are that the audience will think you are moving according to plan.

Reaching Global Audiences

The prevalence of multinational corporations and multinational trade agreements, the increasing diversity of the U.S. workforce, and even increases in immigration have made the ability to reach audiences with varied cultural backgrounds an essential skill. The multicultural audiences for your presentations may include clients, business partners, colleagues, and current and potential employees and customers of varied backgrounds.

Presentations to global audiences involve special challenges. As with all materials intended for global readers and listeners, keep your language simple and consistent. Don't call something a "ratio" in one place and a "rate" in another. Puns and wordplay may entertain a U.S. audience but will likely confuse foreign listeners. State the main points of your presentation often and in the identical language each time. Follow this guidance whether you are addressing an audience for whom English is a second language or speaking through an interpreter. As you deliver your presentation, speak slowly and deliberately, enunciating clearly and pausing often. Keep in mind the following additional points about delivering presentations:

- Bland is better than colorful. Avoid idioms ("dog and pony show," "barking up the wrong tree"), jargon ("emoticons," "debugging"), and acronyms. They will put an unnecessary impediment between you and your audience. Avoid U.S.-centered examples of business, political, or sports figures unless they are essential to your discussion. They will not be understood and, worse, they will suggest to your audience that your perspective about the world is narrowly focused on the United States.

◆ For additional information and tips on communicating with multicultural audiences, see
- *Writing for an International Audience on pages 69 and 71 in Chapter 3, Writing the Draft*
- *Writing International Correspondence on pages 300–305 in Chapter 8, Understanding the Principles of Business Correspondence*
- *Using Graphics to Communicate Internationally on pages 246–252 in Chapter 7, Designing Effective Documents and Visuals*

- Do not use the trite sports metaphors that are all too common in American speech ("slam dunk," "touchdown," "home run"). They will puzzle your international audience and suggest to them that you are insensitive about their culture and customs.

- Jokes can backfire even with U.S. audiences, so they are especially tricky with international listeners. If you think that humor is important to your message, try it out on someone familiar with the languages and cultures of your audience beforehand and revise accordingly.

- With U.S. audiences, maintaining eye contact enhances the speaker's credibility and connectedness with the audience. In some Asian cultures, however, making direct eye contact is seen as an invasion of privacy. For these listeners, try instead to sweep your gaze across them rather than looking at anyone too long.

CONSIDERING AUDIENCE AND PURPOSE
Evaluating Your Presentation

■ Have you analyzed the purpose of your presentation so that it focuses on what you want your audience to know, to believe, or to do when they leave?

■ Do you know the makeup of your audience so that your presentation accommodates their level of knowledge of, experience with, and attitude toward your topic?

■ Is your presentation structured in the best sequence for an audience of listeners?

■ Are your presentation's visual aids concise, informative, and visible to everyone in the room?

■ Have you practiced your presentation so that your delivery is animated, shows mastery of the topic, can be heard by everyone, and is not rushed?

■ For international audiences, is your presentation free of U.S.-centered idioms, references, and jargon?

■ Listening

Active listening enables the listener to understand the directions of an instructor, the message in a speaker's presentation, the goals of a manager, and the needs and wants of customers. Above all, it lays the foundation for cooperation. Productive communication occurs when both the speaker and the listener focus clearly on the content of the message and attempt to eliminate as much interference as possible.

Fallacies about Listening

Most people assume that because they can hear, they know how to listen. In fact, *hearing* is passive and *listening* is active. Hearing voices in a crowd or a ringing telephone requires no analysis and no active involvement. We hear such sounds without choosing to listen to them—we have no choice but to hear them. Listening, however, requires taking action, interpreting the message, and assessing its worth. Listening also requires that you consider the context of messages and the differences in meaning that may be the result of differences in the speaker's and the listener's occupation, education, culture, language, sex, race, or other factors.

Steps to More-Effective Listening

To listen more effectively, you should (1) make a conscious decision to listen actively, (2) define your purpose for listening, (3) take specific actions to listen more efficiently, and (4) adapt to the situation.

Make a Conscious Decision

The first step to effective listening is simply making up your mind to do so. Effective listening requires conscious effort, something that does not come naturally. To listen actively, the well-known precept is true: "Seek first to understand and then to be understood."[1] If you follow this rule, you may find it easier to take the steps or the time required to ensure that you are indeed exerting a conscious effort to listen effectively.

Define Your Purpose

To listen effectively, you must know *why* you're listening. Focusing on your purpose will help manage the most-common problems people have with listening: drifting attention, formulating a response while the speaker is still talking, and interrupting the speaker. When you know a situation will require active listening, take the time to focus on the following questions:

- What kind of information do I hope to get from this conversation or meeting?
- How will this information benefit me?
- What kind of message do I want to send while I'm listening (understanding, determination, flexibility, competence, patience)?
- Do I foresee any problems—boredom, wandering attention, anger, impatience? How can I keep these problems from preventing me from listening effectively?

Take Specific Actions

Becoming an active listener requires a willingness to become a responder rather than a reactor. A *responder* is a listener who slows down the communication to be certain that he or she is accurately receiving the message being sent by the speaker. A *reactor* simply says the first thing that comes to mind, without checking to make sure that he or she accurately understands the message. Take the following actions to help you become a responder and not a reactor.

---

[1]Steven R. Covey, *The 7 Habits of Highly Effective People: Powerful Lessons in Personal Change,* 15th ed. (New York: Free Press, 2004).

- Make a conscious decision to be impartial when evaluating a message. For example, do not dismiss a message because you dislike the speaker or are distracted by the speaker's appearance, mannerisms, or accent.

- Slow down the communication by asking for more information or by paraphrasing the message received before you offer your thoughts. Paraphrasing lets the speaker know that you are listening, gives the speaker an opportunity to clear up any misunderstanding, keeps you focused, and helps you remember the discussion.

- Listen with empathy by putting yourself in the speaker's position or looking at things from the speaker's perspective. Try to understand the speaker's feelings, wants, and needs—appreciate his or her point of view. When people feel they are being listened to, they tend to respond with appreciation and cooperation.

- Take notes while you are listening. Note-taking provides several benefits. It helps you stay focused on what the speaker is saying, especially during a presentation or lecture. It helps you remember what you've heard because you reinforce the message by writing it. (You can also check the notes at a later date, when you need to recall what was said.) Finally, it communicates to the speaker that you are listening and that you are interested in what he or she is saying.

Adapt to the Situation

Listening at peak efficiency at all times is not necessary. When someone stops you in the hall for an idle conversation, you may legitimately listen without giving the conversation your full attention. Even during a lecture, you may be listening for specific information only. However, if you are on a team project where the success of the project depends on everyone's contribution, listening efficiently will enable you to gather information important to the project as well as other nuances, such as the ongoing relationships among team members.

 CONSIDERING AUDIENCE AND PURPOSE
Listening Effectively

- Make a conscious decision to become a better listener.
- Define your purpose for listening in a given situation:
  - What kind of information do I want from this exchange?
  - How can I use this information?
- Block out background distractions to focus on the message.
- Screen out personal biases or preconceptions that may hinder an impartial evaluation of the message.
- Slow down the speaker by asking for more information or by paraphrasing the message before responding to the speaker.
- Take notes to help stay focused on what the speaker is saying.
- Adapt to the situation.

MEETING THE DEADLINE: The Time-Sensitive Presentation

When you need to prepare a presentation under a tight deadline, it helps to follow a structured approach—one that will help you work efficiently, reduce anxiety, and feel confident in what you have to say. As you begin this process, remember that your goal is to create and deliver a logically organized and visually appealing presentation that is appropriate for your audience, fulfills your purpose, and is appropriate in scope.

Use the following guidelines to help you plan, create, practice, and deliver a presentation that will satisfy you and your audience while meeting your deadline.

Part I: Planning Your Presentation (45 Minutes)

Focus on each of the following points as you prepare your presentation.

1. *Analyze your audience.* While considering the needs of all of your listeners, concentrate on the key decision-makers in your audience and gear your presentation toward them. Based on your audience, decide how technical your presentation will be, use language suitable to your listeners' level of expertise, and avoid jargon.

2. *Know the purpose of your presentation.* Think of what you want your audience to know, to believe, or to do as a result of your presentation. Write a purpose statement that defines the scope of your presentation and indicates what you plan to cover. After writing your purpose statement, think about how to introduce your topic, decide what key points will explain your topic, and choose a closing point that will make a clear statement to your audience.

3. *Gather your information.* Your presentation probably covers a topic you have already written about in a proposal or report. Organize all relevant information on your topic into one electronic file. If this is not possible, collect hard copies of the materials into a folder.

4. *Plan your delivery time frame.* As you plan and develop your presentation, remember that you will need to get your points across within a set time period. Whether your presentation is scheduled for five minutes or an hour, think of your main points in relation to your time frame.

5. *Structure the content of your presentation.* Outline what you want to say in a logical manner that will achieve your goals and meet the needs of your listeners. As you do this, think of how many slides you will need to convey your message. For a five-minute PowerPoint presentation, you will need no more than five to ten slides. If you decide to work with five slides, plan to discuss these for about a minute each. For ten slides, plan to discuss each for about 30 seconds. Some slides—those covering key points and benefits—will require more time than, say, an introductory slide. Consider the following structure:

Slide 1	Introduce yourself.
Slide 2	Introduce your topic.
Slide 3	State your purpose.
Slides 4–6	State and explain your key points—points that will inform or persuade your audience.
Slides 7 and 8	Explain how what you propose will benefit your listeners.
Slide 9	Close by reviewing the most important parts of your presentation. Choose carefully what you want your listeners to remember most.
Slide 10	Thank your listeners for their attention. Credit outside sources, if necessary, and include your contact information.

Part II: Creating Your Presentation (90 Minutes)

Given your time frame, use your energy wisely when preparing your slides.

- Work within one of PowerPoint's basic templates to create your slides.

- To write your notes simultaneously, work in the Notes Page option, available under View in the menu.

- For each slide, cover no more than five to seven ideas or "bullet points."

- Keep your slides uncluttered and easy to read, even from the back of the room.

- Import existing charts and graphs to your presentation, but don't spend time creating and designing new ones. If time permits, add inoffensive clip art where appropriate or a tasteful color background (use light background colors to ensure a contrast between the type and background). If not, focus on the clear presentation of your content. (*Note:* For visuals you are unable to import but that are important, bring printouts to hand out to your audience.) See Figure 14–7.

- Once your slides are complete, work within the Notes Page to write the text of your presentation. You can later print out your notes for practice or for reference if you need them when delivering your presentation.

- Preview and evaluate your slides by selecting Slide Sorter (under View in your menu bar). Edit, rearrange, delete, or add to slides and visuals as needed. See Figure 14–8.

Part III: Practicing Your Presentation (45 Minutes)

Keep the following points in mind while practicing your presentation.

- Speak energetically. Your enthusiasm will energize your listeners and help persuade them to consider what you propose.

- Avoid memorizing your presentation. A spontaneous delivery will be more credible and engaging to your audience.

What Are the Benefits to Employees?

- Access The Sports Center for $20/month— includes all athletic facilities, whirlpool, and sauna.

- Support of personal trainers or massage therapists, for an additional $15/month.

- Free cholesterol and blood-pressure screening.

- Free nutrition and weight-management counseling.

- Employee incentive "wellness points" that earn discounts on fitness gear and clothing at The Sports Center Shop.

-2-

The Healthy Life Program offers your employees one of the best and most-affordable wellness packages available nationwide. For modest monthly fees, your employees can become members of The Sports Center and Day Spa, a facility that won the "Best of Chicago" award in 2002, and that was recently rated #1 by *In-Shape Magazine*. Here they can enjoy numerous benefits that include not only a generous offering of classes such as aerobics, spinning, kickboxing, Pilates, and yoga, all taught by top-notch instructors—but they will also enjoy the support of the highly qualified personal trainers, nutrition counselors, and health-care professionals on staff. We do all we can to make sure our members approach exercise, diet, and lifestyle change safely and sensibly.

The Notes pages of your presentation give you a space in which to expand the ideas of your slide with concrete details

Figure 14–7   Notes Page of a PowerPoint Presentation

- Refer to your slides during your presentation, but don't read them word for word—what you say should provide detail and depth to what appears on the screen.

- Know what you want to say about each slide. If necessary, refer to the notes you created when you developed your slides. Tape notes for each slide onto index cards for a less-intrusive way to check them during the presentation.

- Use vocal inflection to emphasize key points; a monotone voice will put your audience to sleep.

- Breathe deeply. Bringing oxygen to the brain keeps you composed and mentally sharp and helps you to speak slowly and more clearly.

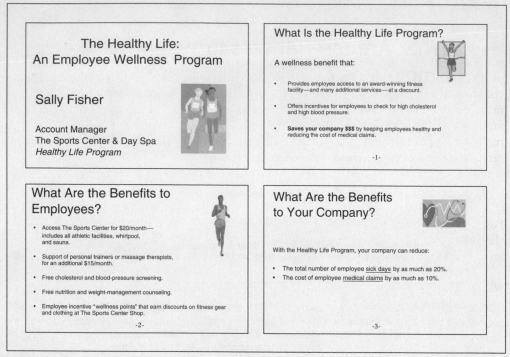

The Slide-Sorter view allows you to evaluate the structure of your presentation

Figure 14–8   Slide-Sorter View of a PowerPoint Presentation

Before you give your presentation:

1. Practice your delivery at least three times.

2. Time yourself and make any necessary adjustments. If you edit your presentation at this point, practice it again at least twice.

3. Use your time constructively. If you find yourself worrying, practice again or mentally run through your slides and key points.

4. The night before your presentation, choose and prepare attire that is appropriate and professional.

5. Try to visit the room where you will be presenting beforehand, preferably a day ahead of time. If this is not possible, arrive at least 45 minutes before your presentation. Check out the presentation equipment—making sure it is in good working order and that you know how to operate it. Evaluate the setup of the room, the lighting, and the temperature, and make any necessary adjustments.

Conducting Productive Meetings

Meetings are a fact of workplace life. Though essential, they are seldom looked forward to. They can be time-consuming and even stressful if the topic is contentious or if there are personality conflicts among participants. None of these potential concerns is avoidable entirely, but the suggestions in this section will help you minimize or avoid them. In basic terms, a meeting is a face-to-face exchange among a group of people who have come together for a common purpose — to make a contribution to a collective effort. A meeting requires planning and preparation, just as writing and oral presentations do.

Planning a Meeting

For a meeting to be successful, determine the focus of the meeting, decide who should attend, and choose the best time and place to hold the meeting. Prepare an agenda for the meeting and determine who should take the minutes.

What Is the Purpose of the Meeting?

The first step in planning a meeting is to focus on your desired outcome. Ask yourself what those attending want to know, to believe, or to do as a result of attending the meeting.

Suppose you called a meeting of your sales staff to design a sales campaign for a new scanner that will result in a successful launch of the product. In response to the questions above, you could jot down the following answers:

▶ As a result of this meeting:
  - I want the salespeople *to know* that this is an outstanding scanner that can increase their sales considerably.
  - I want the salespeople *to believe* that this is the best scanner on the market and that their customers want it.
  - I want the salespeople *to offer* their ideas for the sales campaign.

Once you focus on your desired outcome, use the information to write a purpose statement for the meeting that answers the questions *what* and *why*.

▶ The purpose of this meeting is to gather ideas from the sales force [*what*] that will create an effective sales campaign for our new scanner [*why*].

Who Should Attend?

Invite to the meeting only those who can contribute to fulfilling your planned outcome. If a meeting must be held without some key participants, send or e-mail the agenda to them prior to the meeting and ask for any contributions they would like to make. If employees from regional offices or other geographic locations need to participate, they can do so by speakerphone or a video link. Circulate the meeting minutes to everyone, including those who could not attend, following the meeting.

When Should the Meeting Be Held?

Schedule a meeting when all or most of the key people can be present. The time of day and the length of the meeting can affect its outcome. Consider the following when planning your meeting:

- People need Monday morning to focus on work after being off for two days.
- People need Friday afternoon to wrap up the week and take care of anything that must be finished before the week ends.
- Avoid scheduling meetings the hour following lunch because most people feel sleepy then.
- Avoid scheduling early morning meetings because attendees may be delayed by traffic and everyone likes a few minutes in the morning to check messages, get a cup of coffee, and so on.
- Include adequate breaks in meetings scheduled to last longer than two hours so that attendees can check their messages, make important phone calls, or use the restroom.
- Avoid scheduling a meeting during the last 15 minutes of the day. You can be assured of a quick meeting, but it is likely that no one will remember what went on.
- Schedule the meeting at a time convenient to those participating remotely by speakerphone who are in different time zones.

Where Should the Meeting Be Held?

Having a meeting in your office or conference room can give you an advantage. You feel more comfortable, and your guests' newness to the surroundings may give you an edge. Agreeing to hold the meeting at their location, however, signals your cooperation. For balance, especially for first-time gatherings, meet at a neutral site, such as at an off-site conference center. That way, no one has a distinct advantage and attendees often feel freer to participate.

What's on the Agenda?

A tool for focusing the participants, the agenda is an outline of the issues the meeting will address. Never begin a meeting without an agenda, even if it is only a handwritten list of topics you want to cover. Distribute the agenda a day or two before the meeting so that those attending have time to prepare or gather the necessary materials. For a longer meeting in which participants will make a presentation or need to be prepared to discuss an issue in detail, try to distribute the agenda a week or more in advance. If you have no time to distribute the agenda early, however, be sure to distribute it at the beginning of the meeting.

The agenda should cover only a few major items: the names of attendees, the time and place of the meeting, and the topics to be discussed. If people are presenting material, the agenda should indicate the amount of time allotted for each speaker. Finally, the agenda should give the start and stop times for the meeting so that participants can plan the rest of their day. Figure 14–9 shows a sample agenda.

Sales-Meeting Agenda

Purpose: To Get Input for a Sales Campaign for the New Scanner

Date: May 10, 2007

Place: Conference Room 14-C

Time: 9:30 a.m.–11 a.m.

Attendees: Advertising Manager, Sales Manager and Reps, Customer
Service Manager

What, where, when, who details

Topic	Presenter	Time
The Scanner	Bob Arbuckle	Presentation, 9:30–9:45
The Sales Strategy	Mary Winifred	Presentation, 9:45–10:00
The Campaign	Maria Lopez	Presentation, 10:00–10:15
Discussion	Led by Dave Grimes	Presentation, 10:15–11:00

Topics of meeting, presenters, and periods scheduled

Figure 14–9   Meeting Agenda

If distributed in advance of the meeting, the agenda should be accompanied by a memo or an e-mail message that invites people to the meeting. The message should include the following:

- The purpose of the meeting. Everyone should know not only exactly why this meeting is being held but also what you hope to accomplish.
- The meeting start and stop times. People need to know how to budget their time. A word of warning: When you advertise an ending time for the meeting, be sure to end it on time unless everyone agrees to extend the meeting beyond the promised stop time.
- The date and place.
- The names of the people invited. Knowing the names of everyone who will be attending often affects how people prepare for the meeting.
- Instructions on how to prepare for the meeting. Different participants may need to prepare differently, so tell them collectively and individually how to get ready for the meeting.

Figure 14–10 shows an e-mail message transmitting a meeting agenda.

E-mail message announcing what, when, who, where; transmitting agenda (attached) and preparation instructions

Subject:	Planning Meeting
Date:	Thurs, 03 May 2007 13:30:12 EST
From:	qSusan Chaney <schaney@millenniumscanners.com>
To:	Advertising Manager; Sales Manager, Sales Representatives, Customer Service Manager
Attachments:	▯ Sales Meeting Agenda.doc (29 KB)

Purpose of the Meeting

The purpose of this meeting is to get your ideas for the upcoming introduction and sales campaign for our new scanner.

Date, Time, and Location

Date: May 10, 2007
Time: 9:30 a.m.–11:00 a.m.
Place: Conference Room E (go to the ground floor, take a right off the elevator, third door on the left)

Attendees

The groups addressed above.

Meeting Preparation

Everyone should be prepared to offer suggestions on the following items:

- Sales features of the new scanner
- Techniques for selling the scanner
- Customer profile of potential buyers
- FAQs — questions customers may ask
- Anticipated support services

Agenda

Please see the attached document.

Figure 14–10   E-mail Message Transmitting an Agenda

Who Should Take Minutes?

Delegate the minute-taking to someone other than the meeting leader. The minute-taker records major decisions made and tasks assigned. To avoid misunderstandings, the minute-taker must record each assignment, the person responsible for it, and the date on which it is due. For a standing committee, either rotate responsibility for taking minutes or assign someone permanently to the task.

Running a Meeting

To lead a successful meeting, follow your agenda—the topics that must be covered and the outcomes that you wish—and ensure that you have invited the right people with the necessary information. Equally important, keep in mind how the personalities of those attending a meeting may affect its success. Members of any

CONSIDERING AUDIENCE AND PURPOSE
Attending Meetings

- Be punctual. When attending a meeting, always arrive several minutes early. Being aware of time shows that you acknowledge the value of another person's time.

- Be attentive. If you are new to the organization, spend time listening and observing, but do speak.

- Meetings are considered an opportunity for everyone to share ideas; share yours even if they differ from those expressed by other attendees.

- Feel comfortable responding as your ideas come to you. Also, because meetings are considered a place for brainstorming, don't be too concerned about expressing your thoughts in complete sentences or in perfect grammatical form.

group are likely to vary greatly in their personalities and attitudes. Most of the time you need only be tactful and diplomatic in your dealings with everyone in attendance, and the meeting will go well. Begin by setting an example for the group by listening carefully and by encouraging participants to listen to each other. (Review the section about listening earlier in this chapter.) To create an environment in which people listen to each other, adopt a "you" attitude by being considerate of other people's points of view.

1. Seek first to understand and then to be understood. Consider the feelings, thoughts, ideas, and needs of others; don't ignore other points of view.

2. Make others feel valued and respected by listening to them and commenting on their statements.

3. Respond positively to the comments of others as best you can.

4. Widen your acceptance level of new thoughts, different ways of doing things, and the differences between you and other people (particularly people from other cultures).

Be aware, however, that members of any group vary greatly in their personalities and attitudes. Despite your best efforts, it's not uncommon to encounter people whose personalities hinder effective communication during the meeting. The following guidelines should help you to deal with these potential impediments and keep the group's focus on successfully working through the agenda.

- *The Interruptive Person.* An interruptive person rarely lets anyone finish a sentence and can intimidate the group's quieter members. When such a person begins to be detrimental to the group, tell him or her in a firm but nonhostile tone to let the others finish what they are saying in the interest of getting everyone's best thinking. By addressing the issue directly, you signal to the group the importance of putting its common goals first.

- *The Negative Person.* A negative person generally has difficulty accepting change and will often oppose a new idea or project. If left unchecked, this attitude can demoralize the group as a whole. Of course, not all negative views are invalid. As long as the negative person is making valid points, ask the group for its suggestions as to how to remedy the issues being raised. When these issues are outside the agenda of the meeting in progress, announce that you will schedule a separate meeting to see that the issues are addressed. Then move the meeting to the next item on the agenda. If the person's points are not valid, you may need to schedule a separate meeting with this person to sort out any misunderstandings.

- *The Rambling Person.* The rambling person cannot collect his or her thoughts quickly enough to state them succinctly. It's easy for the group to become impatient with such people and try to finish their sentences for them. Although a rambling person has trouble saying what he or she means, this doesn't mean that the thoughts are of no value. You can actively help by restating or clarifying the ideas. Quite often, the person will nod in agreement, and you can move on. Try to strike a balance between providing your own interpretation and drawing out the person's intended meaning.

- *The Quiet Person.* A quiet person may be reluctant to speak in a group setting or may be deep in thought. Your job, however, is to get everyone's best thinking, regardless of how disinclined a person is to share it. Instead of putting the person on the spot by asking directly what he or she thinks, try indirect prompting instead. You could go around the table asking everyone by name if they have any thoughts on an issue, being careful to not begin the questioning with the quiet person. This gives such a person time to collect his or her thoughts. If this approach fails, ask such a person *before the meeting* to jot down his or her thoughts for use during the meeting.

- *The Territorial Person.* The territorial person fiercely defends his or her group against all threats—real and perceived. This narrow focus can polarize a meeting by driving others to protect their own territories at the cost of pursuing the organization's goals. To deal with this situation, point out that although the individual's territorial concerns may be valid, everyone is working for the same organization and its overall goals take precedence.

Dealing with Conflict

Despite your best efforts, conflict is inevitable. However, conflict is potentially valuable; when managed positively, it can stimulate creative thinking by challenging complacency and showing ways to achieve goals more efficiently or economically.

Try to deal with conflict so that its benefits are retained and its negative effects are minimized. First, be sure that those involved in the conflict are aware of any areas of agreement, and emphasize these areas to establish common ground. Then identify any differences and ask why they exist. If facts seem to be at issue, determine which are correct. If goals differ, encourage each party to try to look at the problem from the other person's point of view. You can take any of a number of approaches to resolve a conflict, including the following:

- *Noncombative tactics.* Avoid accusations, threats, or disparaging comments, and emphasize common interests and mutual goals. Reward conciliatory acts by praising them and reciprocating, and express a desire for harmonious relations. This can have a very disarming effect on an aggressive person.

- *Persuasion.* Try to convince the other party to accept your point of view. How successful this is likely to be will depend on your credibility with the other person and his or her willingness to consider your views. Provide facts or previous practices to support your position. Point out how your position benefits the other person (if true). Show how your position is consistent with precedent, prevailing norms, or accepted standards. Tactfully point out any overlooked costs, any disadvantages, or any errors in logic in the other party's point of view.

- *Bargaining.* Exchange concessions until a compromise is reached. Compromising means settling for half a victory rather than risking an all-out win-or-lose struggle. A compromise must provide each side with enough benefits to satisfy minimal needs.

- *Collaborating.* Each side accepts the other's goal as well as its own, and works to achieve the best outcome for both. For such a win-win approach to succeed, each side must understand the other's point of view and discover the needs that must be satisfied. A flexible, exploratory attitude is a prerequisite for collaboration. Trust must be high, but collaborating to resolve conflict often leads to very creative results. Define the problem, then define alternative solutions, and then select the one that provides both sides with the most benefits.

Making a Record of Decisions and Assignments

Not all meetings require formal notes (called *minutes*), but if they are necessary, be sure that the person taking notes records each assignment, the person responsible for it, and the date on which it is due.

The preferable way to record decisions and assignments is to allow everyone present to see what's written. Flip charts are commonly used for this purpose (see Figure 14–5). Information on the charts can be revised for clarity later and distributed to those who attended. Another option is to use a laptop computer to record decisions and assignments and to have these notes projected on a screen so that participants can see what is being recorded. The electronic document can be revised for clarity and distributed to all attendees by e-mail or on paper. It can also serve as the basis for official meeting minutes.

Closing the Meeting

Just before closing the meeting, review all decisions and assignments by having the minute-taker read them aloud. Doing so helps the group focus on what they have collectively agreed to do. This process also allows for any questions to be raised or misunderstandings to be clarified and promotes everyone's agreement about the group's decisions. Set a date by which everyone at the meeting can expect to receive the minutes. Finally, thank everyone for their participation and close the meeting on a positive note.

CONSIDERING AUDIENCE AND PURPOSE
Planning and Conducting Meetings

■ Call a meeting to address a specific need; develop a purpose statement to focus your thoughts.

■ Determine who should attend; invite only those essential to fulfilling the purpose of the meeting.

■ Select a meeting time and place convenient to all attendees.

■ Create an agenda and distribute it a day or two before the meeting.

■ Assign someone to take notes and make clear what the notes should include.

■ Follow the agenda to keep everyone focused on the purpose of the meeting and the time available.

■ Be respectful of the views of others and their ways of expressing those views.

■ Review the strategies in this chapter for dealing with attendees whose style of expression in some way prevents your getting everyone's best thinking.

■ Deal with conflict positively to maximize its benefits.

■ Ensure that meeting minutes record major decisions; assignments; other due dates; and, if necessary, the date, time, and location of a follow-up meeting.

■ Close the meeting by reviewing all decisions and assignments so that attendees collectively agree to them.

Taking Minutes

Many organizations and committees keep official records of their meetings; such records are known as minutes and are taken by someone designated before the meeting to do so. The person designated writes and distributes the minutes before the next meeting. At the beginning of each meeting, those attending vote to accept the minutes from the previous meeting as prepared or to revise or clarify specific items.

ETHICS NOTE

Because minutes are often used to settle disputes, they must be accurate, complete, and clear. When approved, minutes become the official record of decisions made at the meeting and can be used as evidence in legal proceedings.

If you are assigned to write minutes, keep them brief and to the point. Give complete information on each topic, but do not ramble—conclude the topic and go on to the next one. Following a set format, such as that shown in Figure 14–11, will help you to keep the minutes concise.

Keep abstractions and generalities to a minimum and, most important, be specific. If you are referring to a nursing station on the second floor of a hospital, say "the nursing station on the second floor," not simply "the second floor."

WARETON MEDICAL CENTER
DEPARTMENT OF MEDICINE

Minutes of the Monthly Meeting of the Credentials Committee

DATE: April 18, 2006

PRESENT: M. Valden (Chairperson), R. Baron, M. Frank, J. Guern, L. Kingston,
L. Kinslow (Secretary), S. Perry, B. Roman, J. Sorder, F. Sugihana

Dr. Mary Valden called the meeting to order at 8:40 p.m. The minutes of the previous meeting were unanimously approved, with the following correction: the
secretary of the Department of Medicine is to be changed from Dr. Juanita Alvarez
to Dr. Barbara Golden.

Old Business

None.

New Business

The request by Dr. Henry Russell for staff privileges in the Department of Medicine
was discussed. Dr. James Guern made a motion that Dr. Russell be granted staff
privileges. Dr. Martin Frank seconded the motion, which passed unanimously.

Similar requests by Dr. Ernest Hiram and Dr. Helen Redlands were discussed. Dr.
Fred Sugihana made a motion that both physicians be granted all staff privileges
except respiratory-care privileges because the two physicians had not had a sufficient number of respiratory cases. Dr. Steven Perry seconded the motion, which
passed unanimously.

Dr. John Sorder and Dr. Barry Roman asked for a clarification of general duties for
active staff members with respiratory-care privileges. Dr. Richard Baron stated that
he would present a clarification at the next scheduled staff meeting, on May 15.

Dr. Baron asked for a volunteer to fill the existing vacancy for Emergency Room
duty. Dr. Guern volunteered. He and Dr. Baron will arrange a duty schedule.

There being no further business, the meeting was adjourned at 9:15 p.m. The next
regular meeting is scheduled for May 15, at 8:40 p.m.

Respectfully submitted,

Lester Kinslow   *Mary Valden*

Leslie Kinslow   Mary Valden, M.D.
Medical Staff Secretary Chairperson

Meeting attendees

*Meeting opening
time, a correction,
and acceptance of
previous minutes*

*Terse coverage
of topics and
decisions*

*Meeting adjourn-
ment time*

*Signatures of
minute-taker
and committee
chairperson*

Figure 14–11   Minutes of a Monthly Meeting

Remember that meeting minutes may be used, at some time in the future, by a lawyer, a judge, or a jury who probably won't be familiar with the situation you are describing—and that you may not be available to explain what you wrote or you may not remember any of the details of the situation. After all, the reason for taking minutes is to create a permanent record that will be available should it be needed.

The minutes must list all meeting attendees, so, unless you know everyone there, circulate a lined sheet of paper at the beginning of the meeting so that people can write their names and titles or organizations for you to incorporate into the minutes. Be specific when you refer to people. Instead of using titles ("the chief of the Marketing Division") use names and titles ("Florence Johnson, chief of the Marketing Division"). If a member of the committee is to report to the committee at its next meeting, state the member's name and the topic so that there is no uncertainty about the assignment and who is responsible for it. Be consistent in the way you refer to people. Do not call one person Mr. Jarrell and another Janet Wilson. It may be unintentional, but a lack of consistency in titles or names may imply a deference to one person at the expense of another. Minutes should always be objective and impartial.

When you have been assigned to take the minutes at a meeting, go adequately prepared. A laptop computer is an ideal tool for this task. If you handwrite the minutes, bring more than one pen and plenty of paper. If it is convenient, you may bring a tape recorder as backup to your notes. Bring the minutes of the previous meeting and any other material that you may need. Take memory-jogging notes during the meeting and then expand them with the appropriate details immediately after the meeting. Remember that minutes are primarily a record of specific actions taken, although you may sometimes need to summarize what was said or state the essential ideas in your own words.

WRITER'S CHECKLIST
Writing Minutes of Meetings

Include the following information in meeting minutes:

- ☑ The name of the group or committee holding the meeting
- ☑ The topic of the meeting
- ☑ The kind of meeting (a regular meeting or a special meeting called to discuss a specific subject or problem)
- ☑ Names of attendees and their titles or organizations
- ☑ The place, time, and date of the meeting
- ☑ A statement that the chair and the secretary were present or the names of any substitutes
- ☑ A statement that the minutes of the previous meeting were approved or revised
- ☑ A list of any reports that were read and approved
- ☑ All the main motions that were made, with statements as to whether they were carried, defeated, or tabled (vote postponed), and the names of those who made and seconded the motions (motions that were withdrawn are not mentioned)
- ☑ A full description of resolutions that were adopted and a simple statement of any that were rejected

WRITER'S CHECKLIST (continued)

☑ A record of all ballots with the number of votes cast for and against resolutions

☑ The time the meeting was adjourned (officially ended) and the place, time, and date of the next meeting, if any

☑ The recording secretary's signature and typed name, and, if desired, the signature of the chairperson

CHAPTER 14 SUMMARY: GIVING PRESENTATIONS AND CONDUCTING MEETINGS

In planning a presentation, ask the following questions:

■ What is my purpose?

■ Who is my audience?

■ What amount of information should I prepare to adequately cover the topic for my audience in the time available?

In preparing the presentation:

■ Gather the needed information.

■ Decide how to organize the information.

■ Structure the presentation around this organization.

■ Decide on the types of visuals you will need.

In rehearsing your presentation:

■ Become familiar with your presentation.

■ Practice on your feet, out loud, and with your visuals.

■ Videotape your practice sessions, if possible, and review the video for posture, gestures, and voice, as well as for content.

■ Try to rehearse in the room where the presentation will take place to familiarize yourself with its layout.

When delivering the presentation:

■ Remember that nervousness before a presentation is normal.

■ Show enthusiasm for your topic through the effective use of movement, eye contact, gestures, and your voice.

To maximize your effectiveness as a listener:

■ Adapt your level of concentration to the situation.

■ Take the time to understand what the speaker is saying before speaking yourself.

■ Acknowledge the speaker through questions and gestures.

■ Define what you need or hope to take away from listening to someone else.

■ Consciously work to control yourself from letting boredom, distractions, anger, or other impediments affect you.

In conducting effective meetings:

■ Determine the purpose of the meeting.

■ Decide who should be invited.

■ Determine the best time and place for the meeting.

■ Create and distribute an agenda before the meeting.

■ Select someone to take minutes.

■ Manage different types of people effectively to achieve the best outcome for the group.

■ Deal with conflict positively by adopting noncombative tactics, persuasion, bargaining, or collaborating.

■ Review all decisions made and assignments to participants at the close of the meeting.

To record the minutes of a meeting:

■ Be prepared. Bring the necessary tools for recording the proceedings — a laptop computer is ideal. Also bring minutes from the previous meeting and any other necessary materials.

■ Be accurate, complete, and clear because minutes of a meeting may be used to settle disputes or as evidence in legal proceedings. Follow a set format for taking notes.

■ Be concise and avoid generalities.

■ Be specific and consistent when referring to people, places, and events.

■ Be objective and impartial, avoiding adjectives and adverbs that suggest either good or bad qualities.

■ Record tasks and the names of attendees who will perform these tasks.

■ Expand your notes immediately after the meeting, adding appropriate details, if necessary.

ON THE WEB

For an online quiz on presentations and meetings, go to Chapter 14, bedfordstmartins.com/ writingthatworks

ON THE WEB

For additional exercises, go to Chapter 14, bedfordstmartins.com/ writingthatworks

■ Exercises

1. Select a topic for a presentation and write a purpose statement that is based on your answers to the three questions discussed on page 476: (1) What do I want my audience to know? (2) What do I want my audience to believe? and (3) What do I want my audience to do? Possible topics include the following:

   • Should Congress censor the Internet?
   • Are many heads always better than one? Is collaboration essential in the workplace?
   • Are printed books a thing of the past?
   • What responsibility do the media have toward the public? Are the media objective?
   • Should local, state, and federal governments tax Internet purchases?
   • Should high school cafeterias ban hamburgers, hot dogs, pizza, and carbonated soft drinks?
   • Would you and one or more partners stand a better chance of business success if you opened a coffee kiosk (in a hospital lobby, in a shopping mall, or on a busy street corner, for example) or if you invested in and ran a coffee shop for a coffee-chain franchise (Seattle's Best, Starbucks, Cosi, and so on)?

2. Complete the following statements about the audience for the presentation topic you selected for Exercise 1:

   a. The experience or level of knowledge that my audience currently has about my subject is _____. Based on their existing knowledge, I should _____.

   b. The general educational level of my audience is _____.
      Based on their general educational level, I'll need to _____.
   c. The type of information I should provide this audience to achieve my objective is _____.
   d. Some of the questions that the audience may have throughout the presentation include the following:

        • _____
        • _____
        • _____

3. Continuing with the presentation topic you used in Exercises 1 and 2, prepare an introduction for your presentation that includes the following:

    • An interesting opening
    • A statement of purpose
    • An explanation of how you are going to present the topic (method of development)

4. Using the same presentation topic and materials from Exercises 1, 2, and 3, create a closing for your presentation that asks your audience to take a specific action or that summarizes the main points and restates the purpose of your presentation.

5. Prepare an outline for the presentation you've been working on in the previous four exercises. Use at least four headings and three subheadings under each heading. Include an opening, introduction, body, and closing. Next, prepare at least six transparencies using bullet statements and keywords that will help keep the audience focused during your presentation. For this assignment, concentrate on using effective text and clip art, if desired, when preparing each transparency. You will discover that your finished product serves not only as an aid to your presentation but as an outline for you to follow during the presentation, possibly eliminating the need for notes.

6. Add two of the following to the set of visuals you prepared for Exercise 5.

    • Table
    • Chart
    • Graph
    • Map
    • Pictorial other than clip art

7. Write a brief explanation of the impact that the audience has on any presentation you might prepare. Consider the following:

    • How does the education or reading level of the audience guide your choices in what information to include and how you will convey it?
    • If the audience shares your field or major, how will that affect your choices in what information to include and how you will convey it?
    • How might your understanding of your audience affect the purpose of your presentation? How do your purpose and understanding of your audience affect the way that you organize your presentation? (It may be helpful to review How Audience and Purpose Shape Organization on pages 32–35 in Chapter 2, Organizing Your Information.)

8. A popular expression used to describe ineffective presentations is "death by PowerPoint." Whether the problem lies with the presentation or the presenter, examples include pointlessly long presentations, presenters who read each slide word for word, cluttered slides in a tiny font, or presentations that are either too

plain and boring or too filled with distracting text animations. Using at least three of the presentation exercises or projects that are offered in this chapter, write a memo to the class cautioning your classmates against "death by PowerPoint" and suggesting how to avoid it. Give specific examples of where the PowerPoint creator could go wrong in each instance.

9. Choose an educational, work-related, or motivational presentation topic. Using an 8 1/2-by-11 spiral notebook, draft a flip chart of sketches to accompany your presentation. Submit an outline of your presentation with your flip-chart sketches to your instructor.

10. Attend a lecture on campus given by a speaker with whom you are likely to disagree (you may also choose to attend a lecture on a topic about which you have a strong opinion). Take to the presentation the list of the points about listening in Take Specific Actions on pages 497–498. As you listen to the presentation, make brief notes of your reactions; for example, note when you are tempted to be distracted by the speaker's appearance, mannerisms, or accent. Immediately after the presentation, expand your notes and review this chapter for advice on listening. Turn your observations of your own use of listening techniques into a report on how using them can help others listen better based on your experience.

ON THE WEB

For more collaborative classroom projects, go to Chapter 14, **bedfordstmartins.com/ writingthatworks**

■ Collaborative Classroom Projects

1. During a presentation, verbal, visual, and nonverbal communications affect your audience. To make a positive impression on your audience and to keep their attention, you must convey your genuine enthusiasm for your topic. With this principle in mind, take turns in front of the class introducing yourselves and explaining what you plan to accomplish in your career. Speak for no more than three minutes, and pay attention to the nonverbal communication signals that you and your classmates use. Do some students seem more excited about their future careers than others? Do some seem bored? Think about which gestures and expressions work well and which should be avoided while speaking.

2. Imagine that you work for an ophthalmologist who specializes in laser surgery. The doctor often gives free PowerPoint presentations on cataract surgery to the community to attract more patients. During the last presentation, people complained that the slides were very hard to read. One common complaint was that there was poor contrast between background and the text. In teams of three or four students, discuss what other readability problems an audience that is visually impaired could experience with PowerPoint presentations. As a group, propose solutions to these problems and present them to the class.

3. Plan a meeting, to take place outside of class, to organize a particular class activity or trip; to decide on a specific policy; or to vote on a specific campus, national, or international issue. The meeting will require the participation of everyone in your class. As a group, determine what you expect to achieve at the meeting and prepare a short agenda. Appoint a meeting facilitator to keep the meeting focused and a meeting secretary to record the minutes. At the meeting, maintain an atmosphere in which students listen to each other and practice adopting the "you" attitude as discussed in Running a Meeting on pages 502–506. When the meeting is concluded and decisions are made or actions decided, write a brief analysis of

the interaction that occurred during the session. What, if anything, could have been improved? Did the environment encourage participation?

Research Projects

ON THE WEB

For extra research projects, go to Chapter 14, **bedfordstmartins.com/ writingthatworks**

1. PowerPoint has been heralded and criticized by many scholars and experts. Prepare a five-minute presentation in which you give the history of PowerPoint and describe the reasons people support and denigrate the tool. Be sure to both paraphrase and directly cite each of the experts you use as a source. Structure your presentation so that the introduction has an attention-getting opening, a body that presents your research, and a closing that summarizes major points and asks your audience to ponder some of the major issues with PowerPoint.

2. In Collaborative Classroom Project 2, you were asked to consider problems someone with visual disabilities might encounter when watching a presentation. Research cataracts, the most-popular surgeries used to correct them, and the costs and benefits associated with each surgery. Create a visual presentation that could be used by an ophthalmologist to inform new cataract patients about their surgical options. Assume these patients have vision problems already and adjust the slides accordingly.

Web Projects

ON THE WEB

For additional Web projects, go to Chapter 14, **bedfordstmartins.com/ writingthatworks**

1. Imagine that you are the CEO for a national property group interested in building a shopping mall in your state. You have several national and international chain stores interested in establishing stores in your mall, so you want to establish your mall in a county where customers of various economic and racial demographics reside. Begin by going to the U.S. Census Bureau Web site at <www.census.gov>, selecting the regional office closest to you, and clicking the "Regional Fun Facts" link for your state. Look at the demographics for your state and explore the data from several local counties. Narrow your choice to two counties that offer the best customer base for the type of mall you are considering. Prepare a table, graph, or chart on a transparency or in PowerPoint, comparing relevant information regarding the two counties and listing the U.S. Census Bureau as your source. The transparency should be simple, with a font large enough for an audience to read it from a distance. Be ready to share the visuals and your recommendation with the class.

2. Imagine that you work with several other college students at a carpet cleaning company that puts coupons in local flyers and newspapers to solicit business. Potential customers often call to discuss their carpets and schedule a free consultation. Employees take turns answering the phones when the receptionist is on break, but Lee and Janice let the phone ring four or five times before picking it up because they like to finish what they're doing before beginning what could be a long discussion. If another employee accidentally transfers a call to Lee, he bounces it back to the front desk or transfers it to Janice so that he can focus on something else. Because Janice is on the phone all day, she often has to eat at her desk, and occasionally answers the phone mid-chew. Sometimes Janice stops by Lee's desk to ask him about orders; Lee usually puts his hand over the receiver

before answering her. Because Lee, Janice, and others like them will soon be fired unless they improve their telephone skills, you have decided to hold a meeting to address the problem.

a. Determine what the purpose of your meeting is and who should attend it.

b. Search the Web for at least three sites that describe proper phone etiquette, then create a list of what employees should be doing to create a good impression to potential customers.

c. Use your list to prepare an agenda for the meeting.

d. Keeping in mind that employees are sensitive to criticism and that you want to maintain a positive attitude among the staff—but that you also want to solve the phone etiquette problem—write a transmittal memo that will be distributed with the meeting agenda.

15 Writing for the Web: Rhetorical Principles

AT A GLANCE: Web Content

This chapter offers guidance in the following areas to help you write and organize Web content, and it emphasizes the importance of collaborating closely with a site's Web master to optimize content for speed and accessibility:[1]

The prevalence and availability of Web technology in the workplace for news, marketing, research, and shopping may make it necessary for you to write a report, an article, or an introduction to a content area for a Web site. In several important ways, writing for the Web is very much like writing for print: You need to understand your purpose and your audience, carefully research your subject, organize your thoughts, use plain language, and make your text free of typographical or grammatical errors. However, writing for the Web is different from writing for other media—and more challenging—because your audience is scanning a computer screen and expects to get information quickly and efficiently. Ease of access to your content will be affected both by how it's written and organized and by the speed at which it loads to your readers' screens.

---

[1] In the workplace, the Web master or site designer maintains site-wide technical and design standards. On campus, your instructor or the campus computer support staff can guide you on standards for posting content.

Voices from the Workplace

Rebecca Schlei, Harry W. Schwartz Bookshops

Writer and marketing media coordinator Rebecca Schlei helps to handle all of her company's marketing publications, from signage to author events to promotional material to print and e-mail newsletters. Over 19,000 people subscribe to Rebecca's biweekly e-newsletter, an HTML-rich document with graphics, links, and purchasing options. "While the e-newsletter is popular for its marketing ideas," Rebecca explains, "we have found that accuracy and sensitivity to content matter tremendously in our online communications — perhaps even more so than in printed materials. When a document containing typos or broken links goes out to the subscribers, we often receive immediate criticism and requests to be taken off the list. In a time when spam floods their in-boxes, it's especially important to be sensitive to readers' tastes and preferences."

Annika Tamura, Boston.com

Annika Tamura is the design director at Boston.com, a regional Web site that provides the entire contents of the *Boston Globe* along with breaking news and entertainment features. When developing the site's current design, Annika and her colleagues conducted several usability tests, inviting groups of users to navigate and evaluate the site. "We learned that we needed to scale back on the amount of content and streamline the presentation." Based on usability tests, they revised the design three times. "People read differently online," explains Annika. "They jump around and read short amounts." She notes that "we needed to label and organize information into logical groupings that made it clear if a section was about news or travel." Annika's advice to anyone who writes or designs for the Web is, "Always keep your user in mind. Use multimedia to enhance content, not to create a barrier between the information and the user. Respect that information is what people come to your site for."

ON THE WEB

For Web-design resources, go to Chapter 15, bedfordstmartins.com/ writingthatworks

■ Writing for Rapid Consumption

People read text on Web sites differently than they read paper text. Reading rates on the Web slow by 25 percent and more compared with rates for reading paper text, in part because of eyestrain caused by the flickering monitor. Few people read Web content word for word. Most — up to 80 percent — scan the screen for what interests them or for what they need. They don't linger — they usually scan a page for about ten seconds before moving on, unless they find what they want.[2]

Given the reader's brief attention span and other features unique to Web sites, you must plan and organize your information to promote ease of use and comprehension.

In the workplace, content you create will likely appear on one or more pages of your organization's or company's Web site. Familiarize yourself with the site's existing overall design and content areas. Before submitting your content, review recently published material at the site to get a sense of the site's purpose and audience and how your content works in relationship to both.

---

[2] Data pertaining to reader practices at Web sites appears in Jakob Nielson's *Designing Web Usability* (Indianapolis, IN: New Riders, 2000), p. 106.

■ Crafting Content for the Web

Whether you plan to write original content for a Web site or adapt content from an existing document, use the following guidelines to plan and organize your text and graphics.

Using the Inverted Pyramid

As you organize and draft your information, begin with the bottom line—your conclusions—by using the inverted-pyramid method traditionally used by journalists to organize your writing. State your conclusions or most-important points before providing the detailed background information—facts, data, and logic—to support them. Because most Web readers do not read word for word, the inverted-pyramid presentation of information promotes speed of access to your content. By placing the most-important information at the beginning, you allow readers to grasp what is significant without their having to read to the end. Of course, you still need to provide the background details, explanations, documentation, and other information essential to your content for readers wishing the additional level of detail. Figure 15–1 depicts this method in principle, and Figure 15–2 shows how it works in practice.

◆ *The inverted-pyramid method is also described as Decreasing Order of Importance on page 46 in Chapter 2, Organizing Your Information.*

Using a Simple Style and an Appropriate Tone

If you want your ideas to make an impact on the Web, your writing style must be plain, honest, and to the point. Web users are looking for information, not unsupported claims—whether you are describing a product (such as a digital camera) or a public-policy idea (such as charter schools). To this end, avoid promotional

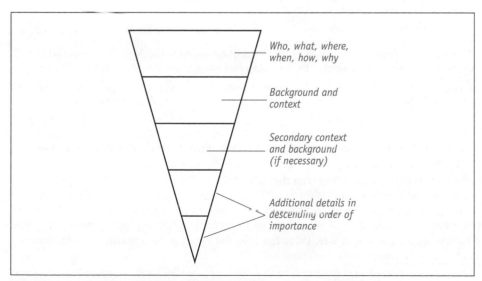

Figure 15–1   The Inverted-Pyramid Method of Organizing Information

close window

Press Release

Contact: Les Dorr, Jr.
Phone: 202-267-3883
APA 08-05
Date Posted: February 24, 2005

FAA Moves to Upgrade Black Boxes

Answers who, what, when — WASHINGTON, DC—The U.S. Department of Transportation's Federal Aviation Administration (FAA) today proposed a series of significant upgrades to aircraft "black boxes" that will increase the quality, quantity, and survivability of recorded data.

Answers why — Stronger cockpit voice recorder and flight data recorder standards that require newer recording technology and greater recording frequency will ensure that more valuable data is retrieved from aircraft incidents and accidents, FAA Administrator Marion C. Blakey said.

Provides background and context — Under the proposed rules, all voice recorders must record the last two hours of cockpit audio instead of the currently required 15 to 30 minutes. Also, a 10-minute independent backup power source for the voice recorders would be required to allow recording even if all aircraft power sources were lost or interrupted. Voice recorders also would have to use technology other than magnetic tape, which is vulnerable to damage and decreased reliability, Blakey said.

Expands context by describing scope of activity — Airplanes (but not helicopters) currently in service would have to retrofit some of the equipment within four years of the rule's effective date. The rule also mandates these enhancements on all newly built aircraft and helicopters two years from the effective date.

"Good data is often the key to deciphering what went wrong in an aircraft incident or accident," Blakey said. "Increasing the likelihood that recorders yield crucial data improves overall safety by giving us the chance to analyze these events."

Expands context by describing additional scope of activity — The proposed rule also clarifies operating requirements for voice recorders, which would have to operate continuously from when pilots begin their checklist before starting the engines until completion of the final checklist when the flight ends.

The FAA is proposing that data recorders measure the aircraft's primary flight control movements, and how hard the pilots move the controls, more frequently than is now required. The data recorders also would be required to retain the last 25 hours of recorded information. These provisions would affect newly manufactured aircraft starting two years from the rule's effective date.

The proposed rule formalizes current FAA policy that both types of recorder be housed in separate units (excluding helicopters) and that no single electrical failure disable the recorders.

Concludes with secondary details — The proposed rule, published in today's Federal Register, affects manufacturers and operators of airplanes and helicopters holding certificates for aircraft with 10 or more seats. The FAA estimates that the total cost to operators and manufacturers would be approximately $256 million in today's dollars.

Details of the proposed rule can be found on the Web at
http://www.faa.gov/avr/arm/nprm.cfm?nav=nprm.

Figure 15–2 **Press Release at a Web Site, Using the Inverted-Pyramid Presentation of Information**
Source: Federal Aviation Administration (<www.faa.gov>).

language that inflates the claims of the product or idea but provides no corroborating information to support those claims.

UNSUPPORTED CLAIM	Amco's All-in-One Mini Sound System is the best product in its class on the Internet! Buy one today!
SUPPORTED CLAIM	Amco's All-in-One Mini Sound System is a proven leader in compact systems based on <u>industry tests</u> and was voted the #1 mini sound system for 2005 by <u>*Audio Magazine*</u>.

Note that the improved version links directly to the source of the evidence (*industry tests* and *Audio Magazine*) that supports the company's claims about the product.

Like e-mail, the Web often invites informality. Remember that regardless of the technology used to reach your reader, your words and tone represent your company or project. Eliminate any biased or sexist language and resist the temptation to insert unnecessary and inappropriate humor in any writing—Web or otherwise—intended for the public. Also avoid puns, which suggest too much informality and can confuse your international readers. This guidance applies equally to the language of the captions and call-outs for graphics.

◆ *For comprehensive guidance on style, tone, and the avoidance of biased language, see Chapter 4, Revising the Draft.*

Writing Concisely

Revise your text for conciseness. Your readers will appreciate your effort because they are looking for useful content in a hurry. Concise content also reduces reader eyestrain caused by prolonged reading on a computer screen. Use the following guidelines to achieve conciseness:

- Cover one idea in each paragraph.
- Begin each paragraph with a topic sentence.
- Try to limit each paragraph to three or four sentences.
- Aim for short sentences with simple sentence structure; use concrete nouns and active verbs.
- Use plain language.

Figure 15–3 depicts a page at the Web site of the Argonne National Laboratory, a research facility, that describes its work in developing hydrogen-powered fuel cells. The page is effective because each paragraph is introduced by a pertinent heading, opens with a topic sentence, and covers one facet of the project in plain language. The page integrates an informative visual as well.

◆ *For additional guidelines on using topic sentences, achieving conciseness, and using plain language, see Chapter 4, Revising the Draft.*

Chunking Content

Another way to focus reader attention is to break up dense blocks of text by dividing them into short paragraphs so that they stand out and can be quickly scanned and absorbed. Each chunked passage should coherently focus on one facet of

Heading signals topic coverage

Short paragraphs each describe one facet of the project

Concise definition of the concept with illustration

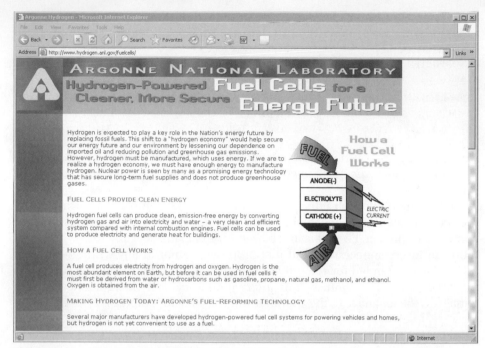

Figure 15–3   Web Page Featuring Chunked Content   *Source:* Argonne National Laboratory (<www.anl.gov>).

your topic. Identify such passages with captions or headings that announce the topic and help the reader decide at a glance whether to read the material. Include links for more-detailed secondary or background information to avoid slowing readers not interested in that level of information. Use the inverted-pyramid principle to organize these passages.

The content shown in Figures 15–2 and 15–3 both effectively divide their content into short paragraphs. Each paragraph in Figure 15–2 focuses on one point and for ease of access is set off from the others by white space. The use of headings for the short paragraphs in Figure 15–3 makes the information even easier to scan. The passages in both figures are grouped in a logical sequence for the information covered.

Linking to Internal Content

Use *hyperlinks*—words or images that act as gateways to other content areas—to expand access to your information. To provide facts, data, charts, glossaries, or documentation to support or expand coverage of information on the screen, create hyperlinks from your page to additional content. Hyperlinks give readers quick access to material and save them the trouble of having to scroll through screen after screen to locate content. Hyperlinks can take viewers to another page at your site or to an external Web site.

If your coverage on a single page stretches beyond two or three screens, as for a short report, booklet, or pamphlet, create a table of contents for it at the top of the Web page. Hyperlink each element in the table of contents to content further down the page. Make sure these links are visible on the first screen so that readers need not scroll down to see them. Use hyperlinks to connect the headings in the table of contents to their locations in the document so that the reader can access a specific section quickly and easily. A good example of a hyperlinked table of contents is shown in Figure 15–4. Each topic is linked to paragraphs further down the page under boldface subheadings. The reader can either scroll down to read the whole document or use the hyperlinks in the table of contents to access a piece of the information quickly and easily. Depending on the overall site design,

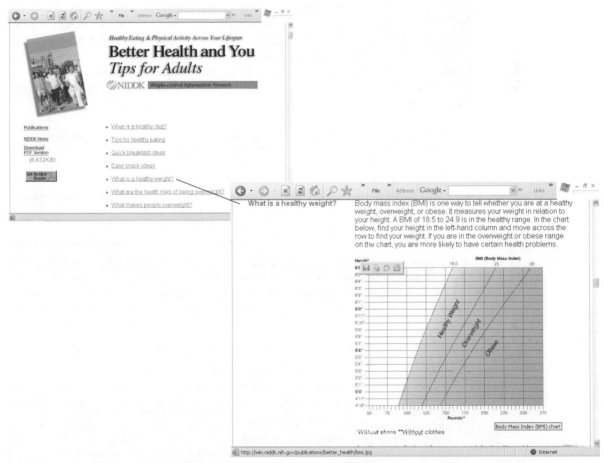

Figure 15–4   Table of Contents Linking to Content on the Same Web Page   *Source:*
National Institutes of Health (<www.nih.gov>).

the complete document may even be located at a different part of the site, such as in a collection of similar documents, thus eliminating the need for the reader to scroll down a single screen to review it.

For lengthy content on a single page, include helpful directional cues, such as links at convenient breaks so that users can get to the top of the page without having to scroll.

Back to Top

These links are placed between text passages where they do not interrupt readers.

Use links to focus user attention, not distract it. Keep to a minimum hyperlinks *within* text paragraphs. Otherwise, they are visually distracting (underlined or colored) and make scanning the text difficult. Embedded links also allow readers to leave the page before reaching the end of your content. Figure 15–5 shows a page from a site that contains too many distracting links embedded in the text. Rather than embedding hyperlinks throughout the body of your text, combine them into short, well-organized lists that are introduced with explanatory text. Be sure to inform readers where the link will take them. In some cases, the title of the link is self-explanatory: Glossary or For Additional Information. At other times, you need to add a brief explanatory passage:

▶ Refer to the section on Plug-ins, Viewers, and Other Tools for information on icons associated with document formats (e.g., PDF) used at this site.

You can place lists of hyperlinks periodically throughout your document to break up large blocks of text, or place a list of links at the end of your document, as you would with footnotes. In Figure 15–6, the hyperlinks at the end of the document

Numerous embedded links distract and slow readers

> The W3C, the standards-setting body for the World Wide Web, has addressed these issues through its Web Accessibility Initiative (WAI), which issued a set of Web Content Accessibility Guidelines (version 1.0) in May, 1999. They were followed in 2000 by WAI guidelines for user agents and authoring tools. The WAI Content Guidelines include a list of checkpoints for evaluating Web pages for their degree of accessibility to people with physical, visual, hearing and cognitive/neurological disabilities. Each checkpoint is assigned one of three priority levels. Priority One are checkpoints which must be met to prevent lack of access for some groups of users. Compliance to Priority One checkpoints is known as "Single-A" conformance. Priority Two ("Double-A" conformance) are checkpoints which should be met to prevent difficulties in access for some users, and Priority Three ("Triple-A" conformance) are checkpoints which authors may satisfy to ensure good access for all users. The fact that there are three ordered levels of conformance allows Web site developers to focus first on eliminating the most serious barriers to accessibility. The WAI Guidelines correspond closely to those for conformance with Section 508.

Figure 15–5 **Overuse of Embedded Links (Links Underlined for Emphasis)** *Source:* Language Learning and Technology (<http://llt.msu.edu/vol5no1/emerging/default.html>).

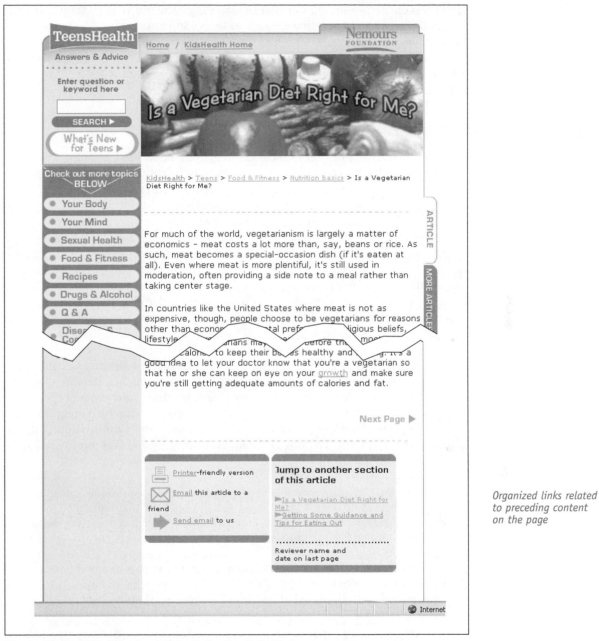

Organized links related to preceding content on the page

Figure 15-6   Well-Organized Links Following Main Text   *Source:* The Nemours Foundation © 1995–2006.

are still available without being distracting. Finally, avoid cuing readers with the phrase "Click Here." The phrase offers no useful information and is considered a Web cliché.

AVOID   To learn more about our company, <u>Click Here</u>.

BETTER   Learn more about the <u>XYZ Corporation</u>.

Linking to External Content

◆ *For detailed guid-
ance on reviewing
outside sites and other
Internet sources of
information, see the
Evaluating Online
Resources checklist
on page 171.*

Links to external (or outside) sites can be an invaluable way of expanding your content. However, be sure to review such sites and their content carefully before acti-
vating your link to them. Is the site's author or sponsoring organization reputable?
Is the content accurate and current? Does the site date-stamp its content (such as
"This page was last updated on January 12, 2007")? Is the information unbiased?

Some Web sites request that you ask their permission before linking to them.
To determine a site's policy in this regard, review its <u>About Us</u> page, usually accessible from the homepage. Although linking to another site can be done electronically without the other site being aware of the link, your organization may have a
policy of asking permission of outside sites before linking to them. In either case,
you would e-mail a request to the site's Web master asking for permission. Check
with your site's Web master to find out if standardized language exists for making
such requests.

You should link directly to the page or specific area of an external site that is
relevant to your users. When you hyperlink to an external site, be sure that your
writing provides a clear context for why you're sending your readers there, and
what they will find. The following passage appears at a Tips for Doing Business
with Us section of the Web site for the Nuclear Regulatory Commission (NRC). It
directs users to a non-NRC site to obtain automatic updates about business opportunities with the agency.

▶   **FedBizOpps.** NRC usually publicizes proposed business opportunities valued at
       greater than $25,000 on the <u>FedBizOpps</u> Web site EXIT. You may register on this site
       for automatic notification of business opportunities by product or service classifica-
       tion code the day they are posted.

Note the *Exit* label in this passage. Many sites place an icon or a text label next to
links to outside sites to inform users that they are leaving the host site. A site's Help
page may explain the purpose of the practice, such as the following passage:

▶   The EXIT label is placed directly after an external link to let you know that the link is
       going to take you away from the XYZ Corporation site. These links are provided as a
       service and do not imply any official endorsement of or responsibility for the opin-
       ions, ideas, data, or products presented at these locations, or guarantee the validity
       of the information provided.

Check with your Web master or site administrator about site policy for these notices if your content includes links to external sites.

Once you link to another site, you are responsible for checking frequently to ensure that the content remains accurate and current—or that it hasn't disappeared. It may be corporate or organizational legal policy at your site to post a disclaimer, such as the following, to inform users that information at outside sites is not under your control and may at times be erroneous.

▶ *Disclaimer:* The XYZ Corporation cannot guarantee the accuracy, completeness, or reliability of all information on non-XYZ servers and Web sites to which the XYZ site links.

WRITER'S CHECKLIST
Crafting Content for the Web

☑ Organize content from the top down — begin with your most important point, adding supporting details and background information in descending order of importance.

☑ Present ideas as concisely as possible and express them in plain language.

☑ Support all claims with facts.

☑ Chunk dense blocks of text into shorter passages that stand out for ease of reading, and introduce them with informative headings.

☑ Create hyperlinks to additional information to reduce content on your page and to enrich coverage of your topic.

☑ Review hyperlinks periodically to ensure that their content continues to be relevant to your purposes.

■ Highlighting Information

Writing and organizing text for rapid consumption are essential first steps to promoting ease of access to your content. You can further augment access through a variety of highlighting techniques, some of which are common to printed text and some of which are unique to Web content.

Using Headings and Subheadings

Headings reduce the complexity of text by highlighting structure and showing organization. They also signal breaks in coverage from one topic to the next. Readers use them to scan rapidly for meaningful information on-screen as well as in printed documents. Set off headings in boldface on a separate line either directly above or in the left margin directly across from the text they describe. Figure 15–3 uses headings effectively to introduce and divide content.

◆ *For additional guidance about the use of headings to highlight content, see page 211 in Chapter 7, Designing Effective Documents and Visuals, and pages 389 and 394–395 in Chapter 11, Writing Formal Reports.*

Using Bulleted and Numbered Lists

Like headings, bulleted and numbered lists break up dense paragraphs. They also reduce text length and highlight relevant content instead of embedding it within paragraphs. Bulleted lists show readers that the items displayed are parallel in importance. Numbered lists inform readers immediately that the sequence of your

◆ *For more information about creating numbered and bulleted lists, see lists on page 105 in Chapter 4, Revising the Draft.*

information is crucial. Regardless of the form the list takes, make all items in it grammatically parallel.

Note that not all text passages should be broken into bulleted lists. Doing so would make your pages look like a PowerPoint presentation but without a speaker to fill in the context for the bulleted points. Lists without supporting explanatory text lack coherence. The bulleted items in Figure 15–7 are effective because they highlight the questions—each on a separate line—meant to be considered. They also link to additional background information about each question.

Bulleted items encourage evaluation of each issue

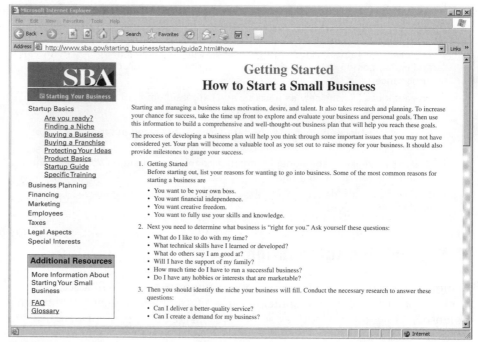

Figure 15–7   Effective Use of a Numbered List with Bullets   *Source:* Small Business Administration (<www.sba.gov>).

Giving Directional Cues

Avoid directional cues that make sense on the printed page but not on a Web screen, such as "as shown in the example below" or "in the graph at the top of this page." Directional phrases like these can be confusing when there is no real reference for "above" and "below," and no "top" or "bottom" of the document. Instead, position links so that they are tied directly to the content to which they pertain. For example, when the terms "above" and "below" refer to content on a single page, insert links on the page that take readers to the top or bottom of your page. (See the sample <u>Back to Top</u> link on page 522.)

The terms *next* and *previous* can also cause confusion. Use these terms only when you know users accessed your page from an immediately preceding page.

These terms are, however, used appropriately to navigate through PDF (portable document format) files.

Providing Keywords for Content Retrieval

One challenge of writing for the Web is making sure that your desired audience can find your page. To increase the odds that Web search engines will locate your site, be specific in describing your important points. Using keywords and concepts throughout your text will help the search engine find your page.

NO KEYWORDS	We are proud to introduce a new commemorative coin honoring our company's founder and president. The item will be available on this Web site after December 1, 2008, which is the 100th anniversary of our first sale.
WITH KEYWORDS *(IN ITALICS)*	The new *Reynolds* commemorative coin features a portrait of *George G. Reynolds*, the founder and president of *Reynolds Corporation*. The *coin* can be purchased on our Web site (<<u>www.reynoldswidgetcorp .com/coin.htm</u>>) after December 1, 2008, in honor of the 100th anniversary of the sale of the first *Reynolds widget*.

By using words such as "Reynolds," "George G. Reynolds," and the "coin" instead of "our company's," "our founder," and "the item," you will give the search engines much more specific information that they, in turn, can give to users. The revised paragraph also includes a link to the company's Web site for ease of access to those wishing to purchase the coin.

Using Graphics and Typography

The way your content looks on the screen when published will be affected by the site's existing design. The page on which your content appears will likely display a banner at the top featuring the organization or company name; navigational tool bars at the top, bottom, or left side of the screen; links to other content areas; and other elements. The site's design standards may affect the line length of your text, the default type sizes and styles in use at the site, the preferred format for graphics files, and a variety of other features. Meet with the site's Web master to ensure that your content fits smoothly into the existing design and that it is consistent with site technical and design standards.

As with print publications, your audience and purpose should determine *why* graphics are important to your content. At times, graphic elements provide visual relief from dense text and make the site attractive and appealing, as in Figure 15–4. For the most part, however, use only images that illustrate essential information, as in Figure 15–3. If users depend on the site for accessible and visually clear information, use graphics that load as quickly as possible. Large or high-resolution graphics, like color photographs or animated images, can cause long delays as they download to the user's system. If these images are gratuitous, they will frustrate your readers because they offer no relevant content to justify the slow load times. For high-resolution graphics that are essential, consider using thumbnails on your page that link to the original-size image. (Thumbnails are images reduced to 10 to 15 percent of the original file size for quick access.) Work with the Web master to optimize all graphics for speed of access. Ask about the preferred file compression format—JPEGs, GIFs, or other?—for visuals you submit. Also consider giving visitors a graphics-free option for quicker access to your content.

Font sizes and styles affect screen legibility. Computer screens display fonts at lower resolutions than in most printed text. Thus, sans serif fonts work better for text passages on-screen because serifs "fuzz out" on low-resolution monitors, adversely affecting legibility and causing eyestrain. Consult with your Web master about the site's font preferences and review the text of your content on an internal browser for legibility before posting it for public access. Be aware, however, that even with your best efforts to ensure legibility, the user's browser, operating system, and font preferences can affect how your text looks on the user's screen.

◆ *For more information about type sizes and styles, see* Typography *on pages 208–209 in Chapter 7,* Designing Effective Documents and Visuals.

Line length also affects legibility. Short line lengths reduce the amount of eye movement and eyestrain necessary to scan text. Optimal length is approximately half the width of the screen.[3] To achieve this length, draft text that's between 50 and 70 characters, or 10 to 12 words to a line. Longer lines make it difficult for readers to

---

DESIGNING YOUR DOCUMENT
Highlighting Information

- Use headings and subheadings to introduce text passages, to signal changes in topics, and to provide visual breaks on the page.
- Use bulleted lists to display text in easy-to-scan format when the ideas are parallel in meaning.
- Use numbered lists to display content when the sequence of the information matters.
- Make all bulleted and numbered lists grammatically parallel.
- Provide hyperlinks to additional content rather than written directions for finding it elsewhere on the site.
- Use keywords to describe important content so that Web search engines will find your page.
- Select graphics that are essential to your audience and purpose.
- Optimize graphics files so that they download quickly.
- If you cannot avoid large file sizes, use thumbnails of your graphics on your page that link to the original-size image.
- Use appropriate font styles, sizes, and line lengths to enhance the legibility of your content.

---

[3] Patrick L. Lynch and Sara Horton, *Web Style Guide: Basic Design Principles for Creating Web Sites,* Second Edition (New Haven, CT: Yale University Press, 2002), page 123. See also <www.webstyleguide.com/type/lines.html>.

locate the next line of text at the left margin, particularly for single-spaced para-graphs. Finally, as with printed material, do not use all capital letters or boldface type for blocks of text. They slow reader speed and comprehension.

For content that contains special or international characters, consult with the Web master about the best way to submit the files for HTML coding. These characters include, among others, bullets, dashes, and asterisks; symbols for chemical and mathematical equations; or fonts and accent marks for non-English languages. In general, aim for consistency to establish a visual sense of unity and to provide visual cues that help visitors find information.

Enhancing Access to Content

The techniques discussed in the previous sections will help you organize and present text and graphics for the Web that are easy for your audience to understand. This section describes your responsibility as a content provider to ensure that your information is accessible to people with disabilities and that it meets the needs of international users.

Ensuring Access for People with Disabilities

Many of the advantages of Web sites include colorful graphics, animation, and streaming video and audio. However, these design elements can be barriers to people with impaired vision or hearing or those who are color-blind. To overcome these barriers to your content, discuss the following strategies with the site Web master or site-accessibility specialist.

ON THE WEB

For guidelines for improving Web-site accessibility, go to Chapter 15, **bedfordstmartins.com/ writingthatworks**

- Avoid frames, complex tables, animation, JavaScript, and other design elements that are incompatible with text-only browsers and adaptive technologies, such as voice or large-print software.[4]
- Provide HTML versions of pages and documents whenever possible because this format is most compatible with the current generation of screen readers.
- Include text-equivalent captions that describe the graphic or audio elements of your content (for example, "Photograph of Harriet V. Sullivan, President HVS Accounting Services").
- Design for the color-blind reader using captions and other text to make meaning independent of color (Green, labeled **G**, means **All Safe**).

Implementing these measures requires the expertise of a Web-technology specialist. However, as the content provider, you will be expected to write text

---

[4] Adaptive technologies, such as screen readers, use software to activate a voice synthesizer that reads aloud the text and captions for nontext elements (e.g., graphics) on a computer screen.

captions for all graphics and sound features—as described in the third item of the preceding list. You may also want to offer different options for site visitors, such as full-graphics, light-graphics, and text-only versions of your content. Discuss these options with the Web master.

Finally, test your pages using "Bobby" at <www.cast.org/bobby>, a site that will provide an on-screen analysis of a Web page to ensure its accessibility.

Considering International Users

◆ *For more on international audiences, see the following:*
• *Writing for an International Audience, pages 69 and 71*
• *Writing International Correspondence, pages 300–305*
• *Using Graphics to Communicate Internationally, pages 246–252*
• *Reaching Global Audiences, pages 495–496*

Consider the needs of international readers if they are part of your target audience. You need not write simplistic prose to do so, nor do you need to write separate versions of your content for domestic and international readers. As with other writing aimed at readers of English as a second language, you should, however, review your text to eliminate expressions and references that make sense only to someone very familiar with American English. Avoid expressions such as "throw in the towel" and "a no-brainer." Likewise, express dates, clock times, and measurements in accordance with international practices. If your content includes visuals, choose symbols and icons, colors, representations of human beings, and captions that can be easily understood.

 CONSIDERING AUDIENCE AND PURPOSE

Enhancing Access to Content

■ Work with your site's Web master or accessibility specialist to provide content— text, graphics, audio—that is compatible with adaptive technologies used by people with disabilities.

■ Create captions that accurately describe the graphics and audio features of your content.

■ Describe color-coded content so that its meaning can be understood independent of color.

■ Test your content for accessibility using the "Bobby" site at <www.cast.org/bobby>.

■ Create text, graphics, and units of measurement to accommodate international readers.

■ Posting an Existing Document

This chapter has focused on how to organize and write original content or adapt existing content for Web sites. However, you may be asked to submit an existing paper document to a Web site. The document may be a report, user manual, or policy and procedure handbook, for example. In its original form, it will be organized to be read in the sequence written for paper publication. If the document is lengthy, it makes sense to retain the document's original sequence and page layout. If you shorten or revise your original document for posting on the Web, footnote or otherwise mark the Web content accordingly, as follows, so that readers will know that it differs from the original.

▶ *The data in Appendix A of this report are updated monthly and vary from the data in the printed report, which is published each February.

Documents posted on the Web are frequently converted to PDF files, which display the pages on-screen exactly as they appear on paper. The PDF files are viewable with free, downloadable Adobe Acrobat software, which allows the pages to be enlarged for ease of online reading. Readers can read the document online, download it to a hard drive, or print it in whole or in part. Regardless of format or version used, before you prepare existing paper documents for public availability at a Web site, do the following:

- Review the document for compliance with your organization's publishing guidelines:
  - Is it appropriate for public access?
  - Is it consistent with current policies and practices for the organization's products and services?
  - Does it contain proprietary and privacy information that must be protected or deleted?
- Obtain permission for Web publication if the document contains copyrighted text, tables, or images. (Some copyright holders require separate permissions for paper and Web publication of their content.)
- Contact the site Web master about the preferred electronic file format in which to submit the document for coding and posting: MS Word, PageMaker, PDF, FrameMaker, or other format.
- Ask the Web master to optimize any slow-loading graphics files for quicker access.
- Review the coded document on an internal Web site *before* it is posted to the public site to ensure that it is the correct version, that no information is missing, and that all links work and go to the right places.

If your document is long, assume that users will print it to read offline. Consult your site's Web master about creating a single-file version of the document to optimize printing.

 DIGITAL TIP: Using PDF Files

Converting documents such as reports, articles, and brochures to PDF files allows you to retain the identical look of the printed documents. The PDF pages will display on-screen exactly as they appear on the printed page. Readers can read the document online, download and save it, or print it in whole or in part. For more on this topic, see <bedfortstmartins.com/writingthatworks> and select *Digital Tip*, Using PDF Files.

■ Protecting the Privacy of Your Users

You may find it necessary to collect information on your page submitted by site users. You may ask them, for example, to respond to a questionnaire that you've posted, to subscribe to a service, to comment on a document, or to give you general feedback about your page. Many users also submit unsolicited e-mail questions to Web sites about some aspect of the site. Be aware that most Internet users wish to have information about themselves—name, residential and e-mail addresses, phone number, credit-card number, personal opinions, and the like—kept confidential. In response to this concern, all reputable Web sites post a privacy notice—usually on the homepage—informing users about how it intends to handle the solicited and unsolicited information from individuals received at the site.

If you plan to collect such information on your page or if your page has an e-mail link, contact the site Web master about putting a link on your page to the site-wide privacy statement. As an example, the privacy policy in Figure 15–8, excerpted

---

Privacy Policy

Thank you for visiting the Nuclear Regulatory Commission's Web site and reviewing our privacy policy. . . . When you visit our site, we automatically collect and store the following information about you:

- The IP address . . .
- The pages you visit
- The date and time you access our site

For site management, NRC maintains an operational log of site user addresses. This log is used to generate site usage statistics, track operational problems, and investigate suspected unauthorized activities. Information in this log about individual users is shared only with appropriate law enforcement entities, if necessary, to investigate or prosecute unlawful activities conducted on or against this site. . . .

Public Disclosure of Submitted Information

Your submissions **may** be made public unless, at the point of collection, we have stated the information will be maintained in an NRC Privacy Act system of records or unless you seek protection of the information. . . .

If you send us an e-mail message or online form that includes personally identifiable information . . . your information will be used for the purposes described at the point of collection. . . .

Use of Cookies

"Cookies" are small bits of text that are used either for the length of a visit ("session cookies") or saved on a user's hard drive to identify that user, or information about that user, the next time the user logs on to a Web site ("persistent cookies"). We use "session cookies" as place-keepers to retain context during an individual user session. They assist with movement throughout the site during that visit without any capacity to track users over time and across different Web sites. Session cookies are deleted at the end of a visit or they expire in a short time. They are not used to track personal information.

Figure 15–8   Privacy Statement (Excerpt)   *Source:* U.S. Nuclear Regulatory Commission (<www.nrc.gov>).

from the U.S. Nuclear Regulatory Commission's Web site, appears on its homepage (<www.nrc.gov>) and other locations throughout the site where the public can contact or submit information to the agency.

Some corporate privacy statements describe their policy for sharing user information, such as subscriber lists, to third parties for marketing purposes. Informing users of this practice is both candid and ethical. These sites often give users the opportunity to refuse permission to use their addresses for marketing, as in the following example:

▶ **Opt Out Choice**
Our users are given the opportunity to "opt out" of having their information used for purposes not directly related to our site at the point where we ask for the information. For example, our order form has an "opt out" mechanism so that users who buy a product from us but don't want any marketing material can keep their e-mail address off our lists.

CONSIDERING AUDIENCE AND PURPOSE
Protecting the Privacy of Your Users

■ Provide users with a link to the site's privacy statement, particularly if you solicit comments or provide an e-mail link for unsolicited comments.

■ Inform users if you intend to use their information for marketing or if you intend to share their information with third parties.

■ Give visitors the option of refusing permission to have their information used for marketing.

■ Documenting Sources of Information

As with print publications, you must document and acknowledge outside sources of information or of help received—text, images, streaming video, and other multimedia material. If any of this source material is copyrighted, you must seek prior approval before using it. Documenting sources at your site has at least two major advantages: (1) It discloses where you obtained your information, thereby bolstering the site's credibility, and (2) it allows users to locate it, if necessary. The site should also document information in the public domain, such as publications and Web sites of the federal government.

Site credibility is further enhanced by acknowledging help received in the creation or review of content at the site. Note the passage in the third paragraph of the Weight Control Information Network of the National Institutes of Health's Web site, shown in Figure 15–9. These acknowledgments attest to the accuracy, quality, and objectivity of the information provided.

◆ *For guidance on the use and documentation of source material, including electronic information, see Chapter 6, Researching Your Subject.*

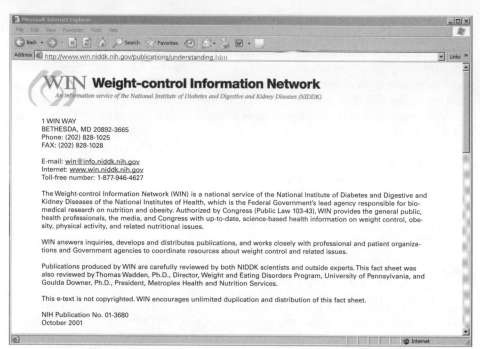

Detailed listings of content reviewers

Figure 15–9 **Page Acknowledging Expert Review of Content** *Source:* National Institutes of Health (<www.nih.gov>).

CHAPTER 15 SUMMARY: WRITING FOR THE WEB

Use the following revision checklist to make sure that content you develop or adapt for the Web is crafted for ease of reading by site visitors and is accessible to people with disabilities as well as to international users.

■ Plan, organize, and write Web content that can be grasped quickly and efficiently using the following techniques:

  ● Use the inverted-pyramid method to organize content "top down" so that key points and conclusions appear first.

  ● Develop content that is accurate, backed up by supporting evidence, and expressed in a tone appropriate for your audience.

  ● Write concisely and use plain-language principles consistent with your content.

  ● Break up dense blocks of text into coherent paragraph-length passages that are sequenced by the inverted-pyramid method.

  ● Expand access to your information by hyperlinking it to content at your or other Web sites.

■ Augment access to your content using the following highlighting techniques:

  ● Introduce topics with headings and subheadings to signal the shift from one topic to another.

  ● Use bulleted and numbered lists to further break up dense blocks of text and focus reader attention on relevant points.

- Use directional cues appropriate to a Web page and avoid those that make sense only in printed material.
- Describe important passages using key terms and concepts that allow search engines to locate your content.
- Select graphics pertinent to your audience and purpose, and optimize them for quick access.
- Choose type sizes and fonts to enhance legibility.
- Limit line length to promote ease of scanning.

■ Provide for the special needs of people with disabilities and international site visitors by adhering to the following guidelines:

- Create content compatible with adaptive technologies.
- Use language, units of measurement, and graphics that are consistent with the practices of international and U.S. site visitors.

■ Submit a previously published document to a Web site according to the following guidelines:

- Submit the document in the most-suitable file format for the site.
- Inform site users if the Web version is abridged or otherwise differs from the printed version.
- Obtain prior permission to publish works that contain copyrighted text or graphics.
- Examine the document on an internal Web server for accuracy and effectiveness before it is posted for public access.
- For a long document, post a single-file version for users wishing to print the document.

■ Inform site users of how or whether their privacy is protected if they submit solicited or unsolicited information to you.

■ Give credit to outside sources of content at your site, including approval to use copyrighted material.

ON THE WEB

For an online quiz on writing for the Web, go to Chapter 15, bedfordstmartins.com/writingthatworks

■ Exercises

1. Bring in a report, a research paper, or an essay written for another course and rework it so that it is appropriately chunked for online reading. Use appropriate captions and headings.

2. As your instructor directs, post a report, a research paper, an essay, or another text you have already written, to your personal or class Web site. (Review Posting an Existing Document on pages 530–531 in this chapter before you begin.) You can also use your text from Exercise 1.

3. Using this textbook (or a textbook from another class that you are taking) as a model, analyze the use of headings, subheadings, white space, models and examples, visuals, and so on. Note the consistency in the use of these and other textual elements. Do they invite the reader to continue to read from section to section and chapter to chapter? Present your findings to the class.

4. Imagine that you are a writer who wants to publish an online book because it is much less expensive to present your book in a PDF file and let readers print the pages than it is to print a hard-copy book yourself. Create an idea for your book,

then create the specifications for the design of the pages, including font sizes, heading styles, line width, and so on. Use your findings from Exercise 3 to help in your design choices.

5. Create a ten-item online sample questionnaire that you could use to gather information about the television and music preferences of today's college students. Create your questions, then decide how you would design the layout of this questionnaire. Consider chunking, concise text, headings and subheadings, bulleted and numbered lists, and so on. Present your document to the class.

6. For Collaborative Classroom Project 2 in Chapter 8, you created an information sheet that explains to donors how to deduct a car donation to a local nonprofit organization on their taxes. Revise this information sheet into content to be posted on the nonprofit organization's Web site. Remember that tax information is often very wordy and difficult to follow, so you will need to be very strategic about presenting it online. Review the Highlighting Information checklist on page 528 before you begin.

7. Many companies have intranets that they use to share information with employees as well as selected vendors and clients. For Exercise 9 in Chapter 12, you were asked to write a set of instructions to help grocery-store managers assist customers who use self-checkout systems. Rework those instructions for uploading to the system manufacturer's intranet site. Consider adding links as well as highlighting techniques, like directional cues.

8. For Web Project 2 in Chapter 13, you were asked to research and apply for a grant to fund an Adult Basic Education program at your local county jail. Assume that your organization received the grant. Using the example of the press release in this chapter as a model (Figure 15–2), write a press release that announces your organization's success in obtaining the grant and telling readers how the funds will be used to further the organization's mission. Use the inverted pyramid structure explained on pages 516–517.

9. For Research Project 2 in Chapter 14, you created a visual presentation that informs an ophthalmologist's new cataract patients of their surgical options. Write a memo to the doctor that describes how you would adapt this presentation for inclusion on the practice's Web site. Remember that many of the people who will visit this Web page have vision problems, so you will have to make adjustments accordingly.

10. Review the reworked research paper or essay that you prepared for Exercise 1 and note places where you could link elements in your text to existing Web sites. Find Web sites to link to and list them on a separate page.

ON THE WEB

For more collaborative classroom projects, go to Chapter 15, bedfordstmartins.com/ writingthatworks

Collaborative Classroom Projects

1. Using several printed issues of a local community newspaper, find three to five stories on a general topic. Read these stories, then write an online article on this topic that uses the inverted-pyramid style.

2. In groups of three or four students who share your major, bring to class information from three Web sites that you might use to research a career of your choice.

Print out relevant pages from each site and together review the guidelines in this chapter for documenting sources of information. Draft a list of questions to consider when evaluating online text as a research resource specific to your field. Evaluate and compare each of the sites that your group members have found and decide which sites would be the most reliable for career research. Write a brief group summary of your findings to share with the class.

3. Assume that you and two other students are consultants who work with various groups who represent disabled people. One of your tasks is to write letters to companies whose Web sites do not adhere to "Bobby" standards, explaining that because disabled customers cannot use their sites, the companies are losing potential business.

Before the next class, decide on a type of company to investigate (for example, insurance companies, movie theaters, grocery stores, and so on), then run several of the companies' Web sites through "Bobby" at <www.cast.org/bobby> (you will need to know their URLs). Print the results and bring them to class. As a group, analyze your findings, looking closely at quality and accessibility. Which of these companies would you write to in order to explain Web-site accessibility? What changes would you suggest be made to the site and why?

■ Research Projects

ON THE WEB

For extra research projects, go to Chapter 15, **bedfordstmartins.com/ writingthatworks**

1. For your major department's Web site, write an online article that describes five databases to which your college library has access that are pertinent to your field of study.

2. For Exercises 2 and 3 in Chapter 10 and Research Project 2 in Chapter 13, you prepared reports about back injuries and worker's compensation at the warehouse of a large online retailer and proposed ways to improve employee safety. Now assume that you work for the Human Resources Department of this company and you want to create a page for the company intranet to explain safe lifting procedures.

   a. Begin by researching ways to safely lift heavy objects. Remember that you will need to cite your sources. (You may use any research you've already completed as a starting point.) You also want to consider what sources (if any) you might link to from your page.

   b. Consider your audience for this page: You may have workers who speak English as a second language or have low literacy skills, for example. It may be prudent to use more graphics than text. (Review Chapter 7, Designing Effective Documents and Visuals.) Remember that many graphics on the Web are copyrighted: Be sure to determine if you need permission before cutting and pasting any images into your document.

   c. Draft your page either in hard copy (through thumbnail sketches) or in a Web-site design program if you have access to one. Then, with a classmate, conduct a usability test (see Chapter 12, Writing Instructions) of your instructions. Take any comments regarding the page layout into consideration as well.

   d. Finish your page.

ON THE WEB

For additional Web projects, go to Chapter 15, bedfordstmartins.com/ writingthatworks

■ Web Projects

1. On the Web you can find several sites that explain how things work. (One excellent resource is <www.howstuffworks.com>.) Review the guidelines in this chapter for creating documents and integrating visuals, then

   a. Choose an electronic object, such as a cell phone or digital camera, and explore how it works. Print the explanation of how the object works and evaluate both the explanation and the Web page according to the criteria described in this chapter.

   b. Mark up the Web-page layout and the explanation, indicating any changes you would make to improve its design. You may focus on one aspect of the explanation, such as its use of chunking, or many aspects. Feel free to sketch out your ideas.

   c. Write a memo to your instructor in which you explain what does and does not work for the original design of the Web page and the explanation, supporting your ideas with information in this chapter. Specify how your changes would improve the document's design. Attach to your memo the marked-up print-out of the explanation and any sketches you've created.

2. Many local convention and visitors-bureau sites describe local attractions, provide listings of educational institutions in the area, recommend shopping and art areas, and so on. Go to such a Web site and analyze the material already on the site. Then get the name and e-mail address of the site's Web master and write a letter to that person with ideas for stories on colorful characters or events or places in the city that would be relevant for that site.

At a Glance: The Job Hunt

The search for a job can be logically divided into five steps, each of which is covered in this chapter:

- Determining the best job for you / 540
- Preparing an effective résumé / 545
- Writing an effective letter of application / 567
- Doing well in the interview / 574
- Sending follow-up correspondence / 578
- Sending a resignation letter or memo / 580

You have enviable advantages as you look for a job. You've prepared for the world of work with an education, training, and experience. You have desirable skills to offer — some directly applicable to a specific job, others more general that are applicable regardless of the job. (The writing skills acquired in this and other classes are also applicable across a broad range of occupations.) Your awards, honors, extracurricular activities, and life experiences all demonstrate these broadly applicable abilities and your willingness to take on challenging work, whether in an office, a laboratory, a hospital, a community clinic, an industrial site, or a wilderness area.

Whether you are applying for your first professional job, changing jobs, or returning to the job market after an absence, you'll need to be systematic and persistent in your job search. Occasionally a desirable job comes your way without much effort, but the odds are against that happening. As well prepared as you may be, you need to plan your job search carefully. The detailed guidance in this chapter will increase your chances of translating your skills into a successful job search.

Before you begin your search for a job, do some serious thinking about your future. Decide first what you would most like to be doing now. Then think about the kind of work you'd like to be doing two years from now and five years from now. Once you have established your goals, you can begin your job hunt with greater confidence because you'll have a better idea of what kind of position you are looking for and in what companies or other organizations you are most likely to find that position.

ON THE WEB

For more advice on finding the right job, go to Chapter 16, bedfordstmartins.com/ writingthatworks

◆ *Brainstorming is discussed on pages 9–10 in Chapter 1, Assessing Audience and Purpose.*

■ Determining the Best Job for You

Begin by assessing your skills, interests, and abilities, perhaps through brainstorming. Next, consider your career goals and values. Ask yourself questions like the following: What courses have I most enjoyed? Does helping others interest me? How important are career stability and a certain standard of living? Where do I want to live? Do I prefer working independently or collaboratively?[1]

Once you've reflected and brainstormed about the job that's right for you, a number of sources can help you locate the job you want:

- Networking
- Campus career services
- Web resources
- Advertisements
- Trade and professional journal listings
- Private and temporary employment services
- Government employment agencies
- Letters of inquiry and informational interviews

Finding the job that's right for you may take many months. If you face unemployment during this period, consider working for a temporary employment agency, as described on page 544.

Networking

Networking is communicating with people who might provide useful advice or connect you with potential employers. They may be people already working in your chosen field, contacts in professional organizations and volunteer groups, professors and former employers, family members, friends, or neighbors; any of them might direct you to exactly the job lead you need. Use your contacts to expand your network of contacts. Consider that of all open positions, an estimated 80 percent are filled through networking.[2]

Campus Career Services

Visiting your school's career center—and working with a counselor who understands your strengths and interests—is a great way to begin your job search. Recruiters from business, industry, and government often visit college job-

---

[1] A good source for stimulating your thinking is the most recent edition of *What Color Is Your Parachute? A Practical Manual for Job-Hunters & Career Changers* by Richard Nelson Bolles, published by Ten Speed Press and updated annually.

[2] From JobStar Central, an online job-search guide hosted by the *Wall Street Journal* at <http://jobstar.org>.

Voices from the Workplace

Sherri Pfennig, University of Wisconsin–Milwaukee

Sherri Pfennig is senior career counselor at the University of Wisconsin–Milwaukee's Career Development Center. Sherri stresses the importance of considering audience and purpose for effective résumé writing: "Your résumé is a commercial, just like the commercials you see on TV or anywhere else. For a commercial to be successful, the creator has to know both the product and the audience inside out. Advertisers adapt product language and packaging to successfully attract the interest of different audiences. Likewise, you need to know what you are trying to sell with your résumé, what your audience is buying, and how to adapt the language of your résumé regarding your skills and qualities to attract the interest of different employer groups you approach."

Anne Basanese, Toxics Use Reduction Institute

Manager of Toxics Use Reduction Institute (TURI), Anne Basanese is involved in hiring all new employees for the institute. When choosing candidates to interview, Anne looks for a concise cover letter that highlights how the applicant's skills will relate to specific job requirements. During the interview, she tries to determine whether a candidate is a good fit for the institute: "While the cover letter and résumé list skills and experience, the interview is a way of viewing applicants' presence and assessing their professional and interpersonal skills," Anne says. A candidate who "does research about the position and the company before the interview, and who demonstrates an appropriate office demeanor in person, really stands out." Anne believes that candidates who can articulate what they want from the position, as well as what they can contribute to the institute, have an advantage. She also recommends that job seekers always promptly send a follow-up letter after the interview. A letter that "indicates interest in the position, acknowledges the time and attention received in the interview, and reinforces how a candidate's skills will meet the job requirements leaves a lasting and positive impression."

placement offices to interview prospective employees. Recruiters will also keep your school's career counselors aware of current employment needs and current job openings. Career counselors can not only help you in the brainstorming phase of your career selection but also put you in touch with the best, most current resources—identifying where to begin your search and saving you time. Career centers often hold job fairs and workshops on such topics as preparing your résumé for your particular field and doing well in an interview; they also offer other job-finding resources on their Web sites.

Web Resources

Using the Internet can enhance your job search in a number of ways. In addition to providing access to job listings in newspapers and professional journals, the Web provides a wealth of sites that give advice about careers, job seeking, and résumé preparation; several databases make it possible to search job listings, post

ON THE WEB

For job-hunting tips, sample documents, and links to these and several other job-search sites, see bedfordstmartins.com/writingthatworks and select *Finding an Internship or Job* and *Web Links.*

your résumé, and apply for positions confidentially. The following general-interest sites include job-search guidance as well as job listings.

- America's Job Bank at
  Sponsored by the U.S. Department of Labor, America's Job Bank is a comprehensive listing of job postings categorized by state. It also contains such information as salary and demographic employment profiles for job seekers interested in relocating to a region.

- Monster at <www.monster.com>
  One of the best-known sites, Monster.com contains such information as career advice and job postings (including international listings). Specialized sites cater to the interests of occupational groups.

- CollegeGrad.com at <www.collegegrad.com>
  CollegeGrad.com is a site for the entry-level job seeker. It has user-friendly design links to sections on résumés and cover letters, interviews and negotiations, what to do when you get an offer, and an E-Zine for job hunters.

- Riley Guide: Employment Opportunities and Job Resources on the Internet at <www.rileyguide.com>
  The Riley Guide contains introductions and annotated links to resources by career field, employer type, and location. It also has sections on résumé preparation and online recruiting.

- What Color Is Your Parachute? JobHuntersBible.com at <www.jobhuntersbible.com>
  What Color Is Your Parachute? is a site for job seekers and career changers based on the best-selling book of the same name by Richard N. Bolles. It provides such resources as an interactive test for career counseling, tips for using the Internet, tips for preparing an effective résumé, and links to job postings and other useful sites.

◆ *See also Internet Research on pages 165–169 in Chapter 6, Researching Your Subject.*

Always visit the Web sites of companies you are interested in. In addition to helping you learn about the company's background and current activities, most corporate Web sites list job openings, provide instructions for applicants, and offer other information, such as employee benefits. Many include an option that allows you to e-mail your cover letter and résumé directly to the appropriate department or person.

You might also consider exploring Internet discussion groups that relate to your career interests. Discussion groups can provide a useful way to keep up with the trends in your profession and general employment conditions over time — and some also post job openings that may be appropriate for you. One resource for finding professional discussion groups is Google Groups, organized by subject and available at <http://groups.google.com>.

Finally, consider posting your résumé at your personal Web site. Although posting your résumé at an employment database will undoubtedly attract more potential employers, including your résumé at your own site has benefits. For example, you might provide a link to your site in e-mail correspondence or provide your Web site's URL in an inquiry letter to a prospective employer. If you use a personal Web site, however, it should contain only material that would be of interest to prospective employers, such as examples of your work, awards, and other professional items. If you decide to post your résumé on the Web, keep in mind the advice regarding electronic résumés on pages 554–557.

◆ *Before you create your own Web site, see the introductory material on pages 516–525 in Chapter 15, Writing for the Web.*

Employment specialists suggest that you spend time on the Web later in the evening or very early in the morning so that you can focus on in-person contacts during working hours.

ETHICS NOTE

Many employers now routinely check the Web (including personal sites, blogs, and networking portals such as Facebook and Friendster) for materials posted by and about job candidates and current employees. Remember that your Web presence is available for anybody to see and that you must maintain a professional demeanor when searching for a job. Be very careful that you do not post any comments, photographs, or links that a potential employer may find objectionable or inappropriate. Even seemingly harmless materials, such as pictures from a party or expressions of support for a particular sports team, could compromise your chances of being considered for employment.

Advertisements

Many employers advertise in the classified sections of print and online newspapers. Occasionally, newspapers print special supplements that provide valuable information on résumé preparation, job fairs, and other facets of the job market. Check the Sunday editions or help-wanted Web pages of major newspapers for the widest selection of employment listings. Keep in mind that a position may be listed under various classifications. A clinical medical technologist seeking a job, for example, might find the specialty listed under "Medical Technologist," "Clinical Medical Technologist," or "Laboratory Technologist." Depending on a hospital's or a pathologist's needs, the listing could be even more specific, such as "Blood Bank Technologist" or "Hematology Technologist." So try to read or search all areas that may be pertinent to your interests.

As you read the ads, take notes on such things as salary ranges, job locations, job duties and responsibilities, and even the terminology used in the ads to describe the work. A knowledge of the words and expressions that are generally used to describe a particular type of work can be helpful when you prepare your résumé and letters of application. Using the appropriate terminology is especially important for résumés that you submit electronically. (See Electronic Résumés on pages 554–557.)

Trade and Professional Journal Listings

In many industries, associations publish periodicals of interest to people working in the industry. Such periodicals (print and online) often contain job listings. If you were seeking a job in forestry, for example, you could check the job listings in the *Journal of Forestry*, published by the Society of American Foresters. To learn

◆ *See also Library Research on pages 158–165 in Chapter 6, Researching Your Subject.*

ON THE WEB

For access to professional organizations and publications, go to Chapter 16, bedfordstmartins.com/writingthatworks

about the trade or professional associations for your occupation, consult resources on the Web, such as Google's *Directory of Professional Organizations*, or online resources offered by your library or campus career office. You may also consult the following references at a library: *Encyclopedia of Associations, Encyclopedia of Business Information Sources*, and *National Directory of Employment Services*.

Private and Temporary Employment Agencies

Private employment agencies are organizations that are in business to help people find jobs—for a fee. Reputable agencies provide you with job leads, help you to organize your job search, and supply information on companies during the hiring.

Choose a private employment agency carefully, preferably through a personal recommendation. Some are very well established and reputable; others are not. Check with your local Better Business Bureau and with friends, acquaintances, or your school's career office before you sign an agreement with a private employment agency. Before signing a contract, be sure you understand who is paying the agency's fee. Often the employer pays the agency's fee; however, if you have to pay, make sure you know exactly how much. As with any written agreement, read the fine print carefully.

ON THE WEB

For access to employment agencies approved by the Better Business Bureau, go to Chapter 16, bedfordstmartins.com/writingthatworks

Temporary employment agencies and services offer a chance to determine what jobs or fields may be a good fit for you while giving you experience. For example, if you are interested in—but not certain about—a professional area, consider working in that area as a temporary or part-time employee. Even as a short-term member of a support staff, you can gain valuable experience that can help you decide whether a particular profession is right for you. Temporary work in a professional area will also build your network while you continue your job search.

Government Employment Services

Local, state, and federal government agencies offer many employment services. Local government agencies are listed in telephone and Web directories under the name of your city, county, or state. For detailed information on the trends of over 250 occupations, see the most recent edition of the *Occupational Outlook Handbook* published by the U.S. Department of Labor at <http://bls.gov/OCO>. For information about jobs with the federal government, contact the U.S. Office of Personnel Management at <http://usajobs.opm.gov/>.

ON THE WEB

For access to government employment resources, go to Chapter 16, bedfordstmartins.com/writingthatworks

Keep records of job ads, the dates they were published, the period during which applications will be accepted, copies of letters of application and résumés, notes requesting interviews, and the names of important contacts. Use your records as a future resource and reminder.

Letters of Inquiry and Informational Interviews

If you would like to work for a particular firm, write and ask whether it has any openings for people with your qualifications. Normally, you should send the letter either to the director of human resources or to the department head; for a small firm, however, you may write to the head of the firm. Your letter should present a general summary of your employment background or training. (See Writing an Effective Letter of Application on pages 567–573.)

In your letter of inquiry, ask if you can meet with someone for an informational interview, and whether you may bring your résumé with you. Some organizations welcome the opportunity to talk with prospective employees, even when they have no immediate job openings. It's a way for them to assess fresh talent, promote their firm, and expand their file of eligible prospects. Although the interview is informal, dress appropriately and do some homework beforehand: What's the firm's core business or mission and its size? Does the firm plan to expand? (Review the list of topics discussed in Doing Well in the Interview on pages 574–577.) Use the interview as an opportunity to practice your interview skills, to learn about accepted workplace standards, and to gain insight into the organization's expectations for prospective employees.

■ Preparing an Effective Résumé

A résumé is a summary of your qualifications and your main tool for finding a job.[3] Generally limited to one page (or two if you have a great deal of experience), your résumé itemizes the qualifications that you can mention only briefly in your application letter. The information in your résumé is key to helping employers decide whether to contact you for a personal interview. It can also serve as the source for specific questions asked during an interview.

Because résumés form the basis for a potential employer's first impression, make sure that yours is well organized, carefully designed, consistently formatted, easy to read, and free of errors. Keep the following guidelines in mind.

- Consider first an organization that needs your strengths and fits your goals, as suggested by the examples shown in this chapter.

- Experiment to determine a layout and design that is attractive and uncluttered.

- Be consistent. Be sure to use, for example, the same date formats (5/2007 or May 2007), punctuation, and spacing throughout.

- Proofread carefully, verify the accuracy of the information, and have at least one other person—preferably your instructor or someone in your professional field—review it.

- Use a high-quality printer and high-grade paper.

◆ *See also Designing Documents on pages 206–216 in Chapter 7, Designing Effective Documents and Visuals, and Proofreading on pages 115–116 in Chapter 4, Revising the Draft.*

---

[3] A detailed résumé for someone in academic and scientific areas is often called a *curriculum vitae* (also *vita* or *c.v.*). It may include education, publications, projects, grants, and awards as well as a full work history. Outside the United States, the term *curriculum vitae* is often used as a synonym for the word *résumé*.

Analyzing Your Background

In preparing to write your résumé, determine what kind of job you are seeking. Then ask yourself what information about you and your background would be most important to a prospective employer in the field you have chosen. On the basis of your answers, decide what details to include in your résumé and how you can most effectively present your qualifications. Brainstorm about yourself and your background, answering the following questions:

- What college or colleges did you attend? What degree(s) do you hold? What was your major field of study? What was your grade point average? What academic honors have you been awarded? What particular academic projects reflect your best work?

- What internships or jobs have you held? What were your principal and secondary duties in each of them? When and for how long did you hold each job? Have you been promoted?

- What skills have you developed that potential employers value and seek in ideal job candidates? What projects or accomplishments reflect your important contributions?

- What other experiences and activities would be of value in the kind of job you are seeking? Consider extracurricular activities that have contributed to your learning experience; leadership, interpersonal, and communication skills you have developed; any collaborative work you have performed; and language and computer skills that you have acquired.

Use your answers as a starting point and let one question lead to another.

If you are returning to the workplace after an absence, most career experts say that it is important to acknowledge the gap in your career rather than try to hide it. That is particularly true if, for example, you are reentering the workforce because you have devoted a full-time period to care for children or dependent adults. Do not undervalue such work. Although unpaid, it often provides experience that develops important time-management, problem-solving, organizational, and interpersonal skills. Figure 16–1 illustrates how you might reflect such experiences in a résumé.

Unpaid home-care tasks feature organizational and time-management responsibilities

Primary Child-Care Provider, 2004 to 2007
   Furnished full-time care to three preschool children at home. Instructed in beginning scholastic skills, time management, basics of nutrition, arts, and swimming. Organized activities, managed household, and served as neighborhood-watch captain.

Home Caregiver, 2005 to 2006
   Provided 60 hours per week in-home care to Alzheimer's patient. Coordinated medical care, developed exercise programs, completed and processed complex medical forms, administered medications, organized budget, and managed home environment.

Figure 16–1 Unpaid Experience Included in a Résumé

If you have done volunteer work during such a period, list that experience. Volunteer work often results in the same experience as full-time, paid work, a fact that your résumé should reflect, as in Figure 16–2.

School Association Coordinator, 2005 to 2006
　　Managed special activities of the Briarwood Elementary School Parent-Teacher Association. Planned and coordinated meetings, scheduled events, and supervised fund-drive operations. Raised $70,000 toward refurbishing the school auditorium.

Volunteer tasks feature coordination, organizational, and funds-management skills

Figure 16–2　Volunteer Experience Included in a Résumé

Organizing Your Résumé

A number of different organizational patterns can be used effectively. The following categories are typical—which you choose should depend on your experience and goals, the employer's needs, and any standard practices in your profession.

　　Heading (name and contact information)

　　Job objective (optional)

　　Qualifications summary

　　Education

　　Employment experience

　　Related skills and abilities

　　Honors and activities

　　References

　　Portfolios (optional)

Whether you place education or employment experience first depends on the job you are seeking and which credentials would strengthen your résumé more. If you are a recent graduate without much work experience, you would list education first. If you have years of job experience, including jobs directly related to the kind of position you are seeking, you would list employment experience first. In your education and employment sections, use a reverse chronological sequence: List the most recent experience first, the next most recent experience second, and so on.

The Heading

At the top of your résumé, include your name, address, telephone number (home or cell), and e-mail address. Make sure that your name stands out on the page. A centered heading usually works best (Figure 16–3). If you have both a school address and a permanent home address, place your school address on the left side of the page and your permanent home address on the right side of the page. Place both underneath your name, as shown in Figure 16–4.

CONSUELA B. SANDOVAL
6819 Elm Street
Somerville, Massachusetts 02144
(617) 635-1552
cbsand@cpu.fairview.edu

Figure 16–3   Centered Résumé Heading

VIKRAM L. MATHUR

SCHOOL
148 University Drive
Bloomington, Indiana 47405
(812) 652-4781
mathur2@iu.edu

HOME (AFTER JUNE 2007)
1482 Marengo Lane
Nashville, Tennessee 37204
(615) 343-0406
vlmathur@yahoo.com

Figure 16–4   Résumé Heading for a Student with Two Addresses

Job Objective

The job objective introduces the material in a résumé and helps the reader quickly understand your goal. If you decide to include an objective, use a heading such as "Objective," "Employment Objective," "Career Objective," or "Job Objective." State your immediate goal and, if you know that it will give you an advantage, the direction that you hope your career will take. Try to write your objective in no more than three lines, and tailor it to the specific job for which you are applying, as illustrated in the following examples.

- A full-time computer-science position aimed at solving engineering problems and contributing to a management team.
- A position involving meeting the concerns of women, such as family planning, career counseling, or crisis management.
- Full-time management of a high-quality local restaurant.
- A summer research or programming position providing opportunities to use problem-solving skills.

Keep in mind that the objective section is optional. Although some potential employers prefer to see a clear employment objective in résumés, many employment specialists counsel against them because they can have the unintended consequence of limiting your options.

Qualifications Summary

You may wish to include a brief summary of your qualifications to persuade hiring managers to select you for an interview. Sometimes called a *summary statement* or *career summary*, a qualifications summary can include skills, achievements, experience, or personal qualities that make you especially well suited to the position. You may wish to give this section a heading such as "Profile," "Career Highlights," or simply "Qualifications." Or, you may use a headline, such as "Award-Winning Senior Financial Analyst," to capture a prospective employer's attention, as shown in Figure 16–13 (page 563).

Education

List the college(s) you have attended, the degrees you received and the dates you received them, your major field(s) of study, and any academic honors you have earned (Figure 16–5). Include your grade point average only if it is 3.0 or higher — or include your average in your major if that is more impressive. List courses only if they are unusually impressive or if your résumé is otherwise sparse. Mention your high school only if you want to call attention to special high school achievements, awards, projects, programs, internships, or study abroad.

EDUCATION
Georgia Institute of Technology, Atlanta, GA
Bachelor of Science in Engineering (expected June 2008)
Cumulative Grade Point Average: 3.46 out of possible 4.0

College, degree, and field of study

> *Related Courses*
> Methods of Digital Computations
> Differential Equations
> Graphic Display
> Software Design

Related courses pertinent to job

> *Activities and Honors*
> Phi Chi Epsilon — Honor Society for Women in Business and Engineering
> Society of Women Engineers — Secretary-Treasurer (2006–2007)
> American Institute of Industrial Engineers — Secretary (2006–2007)
> Engineering Science Club
> Doris Harlow Scholarship recipient (2005, 2006)
> Dean's List six of eight semesters

Activities and honors to highlight accomplishments

Figure 16–5   Education Section of a Résumé

Employment Experience

Organize your employment experience in reverse chronological order, starting with your most-recent job and working backward under a single major heading called "Experience," "Employment," "Professional Experience," or the like (Figure 16–6). You could also organize your experience functionally by clustering similar types of jobs or experience into one or several sections with specific headings such as

Chronological listing of job experience

EMPLOYMENT EXPERIENCE

Computer Systems International, Atlanta, Georgia
ASSISTANT TRAINING DIRECTOR
September 2006 to Present
    Prepared professional training program for the Design, Data Entry, and
    Engineering departments.

Vacationland Amusement Park, Toccoa, Georgia
CHIEF LIFEGUARD
April 2005 to August 2006
    Supervised three other lifeguards and trained them in emergency first-aid
    techniques.

Figure 16–6 **Employment Experience Organized Chronologically**

"Management Experience," "Major Accomplishments," or "Summary of Qualifications" (Figure 16–7).

One type of arrangement might be more persuasive than the other, depending on the situation. For example, if you are applying for an accounting job but have no specific background in accounting, you would probably do best to list past and present jobs in chronological order, from most to least recent. If you are applying for a supervisory position and have had three supervisory jobs in addition to two nonsupervisory positions, you might choose to create a single section called "Supervisory Experience" and list only your three supervisory jobs. Or, you could create two sections—"Supervisory Experience" and "Other Experience"—and include the three supervisory jobs in the first section and your nonsupervisory jobs in the second section.

The functional résumé groups work experience by types of workplace activities or skills rather than by jobs in chronological order. Organization by function is useful for applicants who want to stress certain skills important to the prospective employer or industry or who have been employed at only one job and want to demonstrate the diversity of their experience in that position. Functional arrangement is also useful if you are changing careers and want to highlight transferable skills. However, many employers are suspicious of functional résumés because they can be used to hide a poor work history, such as excessive job hopping

SUMMARY OF QUALIFICATIONS

SPANISH-LANGUAGE SKILLS
- Fluent speaking, reading, and writing in Spanish (native language is English)
- Judged highly proficient in medical vocabulary and interpreting by Harvard Pilgrim Health Care
- Write and report in Spanish for *Siglo 21*, a newspaper based in Lawrence, Massachusetts
- Translate newspaper articles from English to Spanish

INTERPERSONAL SKILLS
- Conduct culturally appropriate bilingual interviews under stressful conditions
- Trained to remain calm and focused when talking to people at the scene of fires, crimes, and in the wake of family tragedies
- Bicultural as well as bilingual

COMMUNICATION SKILLS
- Relay speakers' words and ideas to others with accuracy and speed
- Write press releases for the largest immigrant advocacy group in Massachusetts

EMPLOYMENT HISTORY

Freelance reporter and copy editor, Boston, Massachusetts	2005-present
Reporter, *News & Record*, Greensboro, North Carolina	2003-2005
Reporter, *Gaston Gazette*, Gastonia, North Carolina	2001-2003
Reporter, *Press & Standard*, Walterboro, South Carolina	2000-2001

VOLUNTEER WORK

Writer, Mass. Immigrant and Refugee Advocacy Coalition, Boston, Massachusetts	2005-present
Interpreter, blood drives and United Way campaigns, Greensboro, North Carolina	2003-2005
Intake worker, El Vínculo Hispano, Siler City, North Carolina	2003-2004
English as a Second Language teacher, Walterboro, South Carolina	2000-2001

Opens with qualifications and career accomplishments

Uses active verbs to describe experiences

Lists job history and volunteer work following qualifications and accomplishments

Figure 16-7 Employment Experience Organized Functionally

or extended unemployment gaps. Functional elements can be combined with a chronological arrangement by using a qualifications summary or skills category, as shown in Figure 16–7.

ETHICS NOTE

Be truthful in your résumé. If you give false information and are found out, the consequences could be serious. The truthfulness of your résumé reflects not only your personal ethics but also the integrity with which you would represent the organization.

In general, follow these conventions when working on the "Experience" section of your résumé.

- Include jobs or internships when they relate directly to the position you are seeking. Although some applicants choose to omit internships and temporary or part-time jobs, including such experiences can make a résumé more persuasive if they have helped you develop specific related skills.
- Include volunteer experiences, such as taking on a leadership position in a college organization or directing a community-service project, if they demonstrate that you have developed skills valued by potential employers.
- List military service as a job; give the dates served, the duty specialty, and the rank at discharge. Discuss military duties if they relate to the job you are seeking.
- For each job or experience, list both the job and company titles. Throughout each section, consistently begin with either the job or the company title, depending on which will likely be more impressive to potential employers.
- Under each job or experience, provide a concise description of your primary and secondary duties. If a job is not directly relevant, provide only a job title and a brief description of duties that helped you develop skills valued in the position you are seeking. For example, if you were a lifeguard and now seek a management position, focus on supervisory experience or even experience in averting disaster to highlight your management, decision-making, and crisis-control skills.
- Use action verbs (for example, "managed" rather than "as the manager") and state ideas succinctly, as shown in Figure 16–7. Even though the résumé is about you, do not use "I" (for example, instead of "I was promoted to Section Leader," use "Promoted to Section Leader").
- Focus as much as possible on your achievements in your work history ("Increased employee retention rate by 16 percent by developing a training program"). Employers want to hire doers and achievers.

Related Skills and Abilities

Employers are interested in hiring applicants with a variety of skills or the ability to learn new ones fairly quickly. Depending on the position, you might list in a skills section items such as fluency in a foreign language; writing and editing abilities; specialized technical knowledge; equipment or mechanical training; or computer skills, including knowledge of specific languages, software, hardware, and Web sites created.

Honors and Activities

If you have room on your résumé, list any honors and unique activities near the end. Include items such as student or community activities, professional or club mem-

DIGITAL TIPS: Creating a Résumé Using a Template

Microsoft Word and Corel WordPerfect offer templates for a variety of résumé styles.

- Click on File/New/Templates in your toolbar and follow the guidance provided. Note that the templates may be stored on your computer or accessed through a Web site.

- Select from a variety of ways to organize and present the content:
  - Entry level
  - Chronological
  - Functional
  - Elegant
  - Contemporary
  - Professional

- Adapt the template to your needs or preferences by applying an array of design features:
  - Add lines across the page.
  - Change fonts.
  - Standardize headings.

- Spell check before printing. Proofread carefully.

berships, awards received, or works published. Be selective; do not duplicate information given in other categories, and include only information that supports your employment objective. Provide a heading for this category that fits its contents, depending on which skills or activities you want to emphasize, such as "Activities," "Honors," "Professional Affiliations," or "Publications and Memberships."

References

Avoid listing references unless that is standard practice in your profession or your résumé is sparse. You might include a phrase such as "References available upon request" to signal the end of a long résumé, or write "Available on request" after the heading "References" as a design element to balance a page. In any case, you should have a separate list of references to give to prospective employers after interviews; your list should include the main heading "References for [your name]" and the names, affiliations, titles, and contact information for each of your references. Do not give anyone as a reference without first obtaining his or her permission.

Portfolios

The résumé may also state that a "Portfolio is available on request." Portfolios have traditionally been used by artists and writers to illustrate their work. However, a portfolio also may provide samples of your most-impressive written work (reports, proposals, presentations), copies of letters of praise, certificates that attest to special abilities, newspaper clippings, and other items that visually display your accomplishments and potential contributions to a prospective employer. Present your portfolio professionally and attractively in a folder or binder; if you create a Web résumé, you can post your portfolio with it (see Electronic

ON THE WEB

For further advice on portfolios, go to Chapter 16, bedfordstmartins.com/ writingthatworks and select *Web Links,* Kimeldorf Library.

Résumés on pages 554–557). For an interview, it is best to bring a portfolio containing ten items or fewer.

Salary

Avoid listing the salary you desire in your résumé. On the one hand, you may price yourself out of a job you want if the salary you list is higher than a potential employer is willing to pay. On the other hand, if you list a low salary, you may not get the best possible offer. (See Salary Negotiations on page 577.)

Electronic Résumés

In addition to the traditional paper résumé, you can post a Web-based résumé. You may also need to submit a résumé on disk or through e-mail to a potential employer to be included in an organization's database. As Internet and database technologies converge, remain current with the forms and protocols that employers prefer by reviewing popular job-search sites, such as HotJobs at <http://hotjobs.yahoo.com> and Monster.com at <www.monster.com>.

Scannable and Plain-Text Résumés

Large companies often electronically scan résumés into a database, which allows them a time-saving way to screen a large pool of applicants for job openings. With this practice in mind, be prepared to submit your résumé in more than one format. In addition to the traditional paper résumé, prepare and submit a no-frills or plain-text version for ease of scanning.

A plain-text version is easier to scan than the traditional résumé because OCR (optical character recognition) scanning software does poorly in recognizing unusual typefaces, graphics, boxes, and other typographic and design features common in traditional paper résumés. The easiest way around these limitations is to format a version of your résumé as a plain-text file (.txt) or to use ASCII-compatible[4] characters so that it can be read accurately across most applications and systems.

A scannable résumé is normally mailed to an employer in paper form, scanned, and downloaded into a company's searchable database. Avoid decorative, uncommon, or otherwise fancy typefaces; use simple font styles (a sans serif font such as Ariel) and sizes between 10 and 14 points. Use white space generously because scanners use it to recognize where one topic has ended and another has begun. Although a paper résumé is best kept to one page, you need not limit an electronic résumé to a single page. However, keep the résumé as simple, clear, and concise as possible. Use white or beige paper and do not fold it for mailing because a scanner can misread a folded line. Scan such a résumé yourself to make sure there are no problems.

---

[4]ASCII (pronounced ăs'-kēy) is an acronym for American Standard Code for Information Interchange and is the most basic format for transferring files between different programs. In word-processing terms, it can be thought of as unformatted text.

Some employers request ASCII or plain-text résumés via e-mail, which can be added directly into the résumé database without scanning. ASCII résumés also allow employers to read the file regardless of the type of software they are using. You can copy and paste such a résumé directly into the body of the e-mail message.

For résumés that will be downloaded into databases, use nouns rather than verbs to describe experience and skills (*designer* and *management* rather than *designed* and *managed*). You may also include a section in such a résumé titled "Keywords" (or perhaps give a descriptive name, such as "Areas of Expertise"). Keywords, also called *descriptors,* allow potential employers to search the database for qualified candidates. So, be sure to use keywords that are the same as those used in the employer's descriptions of the jobs that best match your interests and qualifications. This section can follow the main heading of your résumé or appear near the end of your résumé. Figure 16–8 is an example of a plain-text résumé that demonstrates the use of keywords for electronic searches.

E-mail–Attached Résumés

An employer may request or you may prefer to submit a résumé as an e-mail attachment to be printed out by the employer. If so, consider using a relatively plain design and sending the résumé as a rich text format (.rtf) document. Or, if precise design is important, send the résumé as a PDF file that will preserve the fonts, images, graphics, and layout. You can attach this file to an e-mail message that will then serve as your application letter.

◆ *See also Digital Tip: Using PDF Files on page 531 in Chapter 15, Writing for the Web.*

 DIGITAL TIPS: Preparing an ASCII Résumé

When preparing an ASCII document, proper formatting is critical. Keep the following points in mind.

■ Do not use word-processing elements, such as graphic lines or boxes, bullets, underlining, italics, or boldface.

■ Avoid uncommon typefaces; use simple font styles and sizes between 10 and 14 points.

■ Create horizontal lines by using a series of hyphens or asterisks (up to 60 characters).

■ Replace bullets with hyphens or asterisks, and use white space between sections rather than indenting.

■ Set the margins so that you do not exceed 65 characters per line, including spaces.

   – Use the space bar instead of tabs and column formats.

   – Align everything to the left margin.

   – Use hard returns, not the word-wrap feature, to insert line breaks.

■ Save your document as an ASCII or MS-DOS text using the .txt extension (for example, "resume.txt").

For more on preparing an ASCII résumé, go to <bedfordstmartins.com/writingthatworks> and select *Digital Tips,* "Preparing an ASCII Résumé."

DAVID B. GROENING
6819 Locustview Drive
Topeka, Kansas 66614
(913) 233-1552
dbgroening@cpu.fairview.edu

JOB OBJECTIVE
Work as a programmer with writing, editing, and training responsibilities,
leading to a career in information design management.

Keywords listed in
a separate section

KEYWORDS
Programmer, Operating Systems, Unipro, Newsletter, Graphics,
Cybernetics, Listserv, Professional Writer, Editor, Trainer, Instructor,
Technical Writer, Tutor, Designer, Manager, Information Design.

Asterisks replace
bullets

EDUCATION
** Fairview Community College, Topeka, Kansas
** Associate's Degree, Computer Science, June 2006
** Dean's Honor List Award (six quarters)

RELEVANT COURSE WORK
** Operating Systems Design
** Database Management
** Introduction to Cybernetics
** Technical Writing

EMPLOYMENT EXPERIENCE
** Computer Consultant: September 2003 to Present

Line width limited
to 65 characters

Fairview Community College Computer Center: Advised and trained
novice users; wrote and maintained Unipro operating system
documentation.
** Tutor: January 2002 to June 2003
Fairview Community College: Assisted students in mathematics and
computer programming.

SKILLS AND ACTIVITIES

All lines begin at
left margin

** Unipro Operating System: Thorough knowledge of word-processing,
text-editing, and file-formatting programs.
** Writing and Editing Skills: Experience in documenting computer
programs for beginning programmers and users.
** Fairview Community Microcomputer Users Group: Co-founder and
editor of monthly newsletter ("Compuclub"); listserv manager.

FURTHER INFORMATION
** References, college transcripts, a portfolio of computer programs,
and writing samples available upon request.

Figure 16–8   Résumé in ASCII Format

Web Résumés

Another option is to post your résumé on your own Web site. Doing so makes it available to potential employers at their convenience—you need only send them your Web address. A Web résumé can also be updated as often as necessary without the need to mail updates to everyone. Perhaps the chief advantage of a Web résumé is that it allows you to create an electronic portfolio linked to samples of your work—reports, articles, graphics projects, presentations, and the like. An interactive résumé with links to the portfolio will work only if you create an HTML (hypertext markup language) version of your work. If you wish to post a résumé and portfolio without hyperlinks, you could use a plain-text version or PDF image file instead. If you plan to post your résumé on your own Web site, keep the following points in mind:

- Follow the general advice for writing for the Web, outlined in Chapter 15.
- View your résumé on several browsers to see how it looks.
- Just below your name, you may wish to provide a series of internal links to such important categories as "Experience" and "Education."
- Consider building a multipage site for displaying a work portfolio, publications, reference letters, and the like.
- Use a counter to keep track of the number of times your résumé Web page has been visited.
- If privacy is an issue, include an e-mail link ("mailto") at the top of the résumé rather than your home address and phone number.

Make the most of posting your résumé on your own Web site by e-mailing links to potential employers. Keep in mind that personal Web sites are by their nature less effective than commercial services that attract recruiters with their large databases of candidates.

Sample Résumés

The sample résumés in this section are provided to stimulate your thinking about how to tailor your résumé to your own job search. Before you design and write your résumé, look at as many samples as possible, and then organize and format your own to best suit your previous experience and your professional goals and to make the most persuasive case to your target employers.

- Figure 16–9 presents a conventional résumé in which a recent college graduate is seeking an entry-level position.
- Figure 16–10 shows a résumé with a variation of the conventional headings to highlight professional credentials.

- Figure 16–11 shows a résumé that focuses on the applicant's management experience.

- Figure 16–12 focuses on how the applicant advanced and was promoted within a single company.

- Figure 16–13 illustrates how an applicant can organize a résumé by combining functional and chronological elements.

During your job search, apply for as many positions as possible that are acceptable to you and for which you qualify. However, be careful to adapt your core résumé to the specific requirements of each job listing before you submit it. Note how the applicant, Joshua Goodman, tailors the two résumés in Figures 16–14 and 16–15 in response to two different job listings for a graphics designer. Both résumés are formatted in an unconventional style to highlight his graphics-design skills. The ABC Services listing (Figure 16–16) describes a candidate who can use graphics and desktop-publishing software to produce printed products ("ads, brochures, signs, flyers, etc."). Joshua's résumé (Figure 16–15) focuses on his experience with this work under Graphics-Design Experience. For the listing in Figure 16–17, his résumé (Figure 16–15) gives equal coverage to his graphics- and Web-design capabilities in response to the XYZ Group's listing for someone with both skills. He specifically inserts a new section (Web-Design Experience) for this purpose. If he's interviewed by ABC Services and asked about Web design, he can discuss his background then.

ON THE WEB

For more examples of résumés with helpful annotations, go to bedfordstmartins.com/writingthatworks and select *Model Documents Gallery.*

PEGGY EDWARDS
144 Elm Street, Apt. 4
West Orange, New Jersey 07052
(973) 741-0134
peggy-edwards@hotmail.com

Heading with name and contact information

OBJECTIVE To work at a local health department as a Registered Environmental Health Specialist.

EDUCATION Montclair State University, Upper Montclair, New Jersey
B.S., Health Education (concentration in Community Health), 2006
Magna Cum Laude (GPA: 3.75/4.0)

Education and listing of course work appropriate for a recent graduate

Essex County Community College, West Caldwell, New Jersey
A.S., Social Sciences, 2003

RELATED COURSES:
- Public Health
- Health Promotion
- Environmental Health
- The Teaching of Health
- School Health and Community Service
- Environment and Public Health

HONORS:
Dean's List, Phi Theta Kappa, Golden Key National Honor Society

RELATED EXPERIENCE *Intern, Bergen County Health Department, 1/2004–4/2004*
(North Bergen, New Jersey)
Conducted Chapter 12 food inspections, reviewed septic plans, and responded to community complaints under the supervision of trained health inspectors.

Internship and part-time job experience relevant to a recent graduate

Substitute Health Teacher, West Orange High School, 9/2001–1/2002
(West Orange, New Jersey)

Dental Assistant, Daniel R. Korb, D.D.S., P.A., 8/2000–3/2001
(Cedar Grove, New Jersey)
Took dental radiographs of all patients, sterilized instruments, and sanitized rooms.

LICENSES New Jersey Registered Environmental Health Specialist
New Jersey Dental Radiologist
New Jersey Commercial Drivers license with air brake endorsement

Licenses related to job objective

REFERENCES Furnished upon request

Figure 16–9   Résumé for an Entry-Level Position

CHRIS RENAULT, RN

3785 Raleigh Court, #46 • Phoenix, AZ 67903 •
(555) 467-1115 • chris@resumepower.com

Opens with listing of professional qualifications

Qualifications

➤ *Recent Honors Graduate of Approved Nursing Program*
➤ *Current Arizona Nursing Licensure and BLS Certification*
➤ *Presently Completing Clinical Nurse Internship Program*

Highlights education and license credential

Education & Licensure

ARIZONA STATE UNIVERSITY Tempe, AZ
Bachelor of Science in Nursing (BSN), 2007
Graduated summa cum laude (GPA: 4.0)

MOHAVE COMMUNITY COLLEGE Kingman, AZ
Associate's Degree in Nursing (AN), 2005
Graduated cum laude (GPA: 3.5)

Course-work Highlights: Family and Community Nursing, Health-Care Delivery Models, Health Assessment, Pathology, Microbiology, Nursing Research, Nursing of Older Adults, Health-Care Ethics

Arizona RN License, 2007
BLS Certification, 2007

Lists responsibilities in ongoing internship program

Clinical Internship

CAMELBACK MEDICAL CENTER — Phoenix, AZ
Nurse Intern, 2006 to Present

• Accepted into new-graduate RN training program and completing in-depth, eight-month rotation working under a trained preceptor.

• Gaining valuable clinical experience to assume the role of a professional nurse within an acute-care setting. Rotating through all medical-center areas, including Post Surgical, Orthopedics, Pediatrics, Oncology, Emergency Department, Psychiatric Nursing, Cardiac Telemetry, and Critical Care.

• Developing speed and skill in the day-to-day functions of a staff nurse. Participating in patient assessment, treatment, medication disbursement, and surgical preparation as a member of the health-care team.

• Earned written commendations from preceptor for *". . . excellent ability to interact with patients and their families, showing a high degree of empathy, medical knowledge, and concern for quality and continuity of patient care."*

Establishes professional involvement in outside activities

Community Involvement

Active Volunteer and Fund-raising Coordinator, The American Cancer Society — Scottsdale, AZ, Chapter (2005 to Present)
Participant, Annual AIDS Walkathon (2002 to 2005) and "Find the Cure" Breast Cancer Awareness Marathon (2004, 2005)

Figure 16–10   Résumé, Highlighting Professional Credentials. Prepared by Kim Isaacs, Advanced Career Systems, Inc.

ROBERT MANDILLO
7761 Shalamar Drive
Dayton, Ohio 45424
(513) 255-4137
mand@juno.com

OBJECTIVE

A management position in the aerospace industry with responsibility for developing new designs and products.

MANAGEMENT EXPERIENCE

MANAGER, ENGINEERING DRAFTING DEPARTMENT — May 1998–Present
Wright-Patterson Air Force Base, Dayton, Ohio

Supervise 17 drafting mechanics in support of the engineering design staff. Develop, evaluate, and improve materials and equipment for the design and construction of exhibits. Write specifications, negotiate with vendors, and initiate procurement activities for exhibit design support.

SUPERVISOR, GRAPHICS ILLUSTRATORS — June 1985–April 1998
Henderson Advertising Agency, Cincinnati, Ohio

Supervised five illustrators and four drafting mechanics after promotion from Graphics Technician. Analyzed and approved work-order requirements. Selected appropriate media and techniques for orders. Rendered illustrations in pencil and ink. Converted department to CAD system.

EDUCATION

BACHELOR OF SCIENCE IN MECHANICAL ENGINEERING TECHNOLOGY, 1985
Edison State College, Wooster, Ohio

ASSOCIATE'S DEGREE IN MECHANICAL DRAFTING, 1983
Wooster Community College, Wooster, Ohio

PROFESSIONAL AFFILIATION

National Association of Mechanical Engineers and Drafting Mechanics

REFERENCES

References, letters of recommendation, and a portfolio of original designs and drawings available online at <www.juno.com/mand>.

Begins with job experience relevant to prospective employers

Education and affiliations emphasize rigorous preparation in field and continuing professional interests

Figure 16–11   Résumé for an Applicant with Management Experience

CAROL ANN WALKER
1436 West Schantz Avenue
Laurel, Pennsylvania 17322
(717) 399-2712
caw@yahoo.com

FINANCIAL EXPERIENCE

KERFHEIMER CORPORATION, Philadelphia, Pennsylvania

Job-experience opening highlights promotion

Senior Financial Analyst, June 2002–Present
Report to Senior Vice President for Corporate Financial Planning. Develop manufacturing cost estimates totaling $30 million annually for mining and construction equipment with Department of Defense.

Financial Analyst, November 1999–June 2002
Developed $50-million funding estimates for major Department of Defense contracts for troop carriers and digging and earth-moving machines. Researched funding options, resulting in savings of $1.2 million.

FIRST BANK, INC., Bloomington, Indiana

Planning Analyst, September 1994–November 1999
Developed successful computer models for short- and long-range planning.

EDUCATION

Ph.D. in Finance: expected, June 2007
The Wharton School of the University of Pennsylvania

M.S. in Business Administration, 1998
University of Wisconsin–Milwaukee
"Executive Curriculum" for employees identified as promising by their employers.

B.S. in Business Administration (*magna cum laude*), 1994
Indiana University
Emphasis: Finance   Minor: Professional Writing

PUBLISHING AND MEMBERSHIP

Published "Developing Computer Models for Financial Planning," *Midwest Finance Journal* 34.2 (2004): 126–36.

Association for Corporate Financial Planning, Senior Member.

REFERENCES

References and a portfolio of financial plans are available upon request.

Figure 16–12   Advanced Résumé, Showing Promotion within a Single Company

———— CAROL ANN WALKER ————

1436 West Schantz Avenue • Laurel, PA 17322
(717) 399-2712 • caw@yahoo.com

Award-Winning Senior Financial Analyst

Astute senior analyst and corporate financial planner with 11 years of experience and proven success enhancing P&L scenarios by millions of dollars. Demonstrated ability to apply critical thinking and sound strategic/economic analysis to multi-dimensional business issues. Advanced computer skills include Hyperion, SQL, MS Office, and Crystal Reports.

Opens by highlighting career accomplishments and functional areas of expertise

---

Financial Analyst of the Year, 2005

Recipient of prestigious national award from the Association for Investment Management and Research (AIMR)

Areas of Expertise

- Financial Analysis & Planning
- Forecasting & Trend Projection
- Trend/Variance Analysis
- Comparative Analysis

- Expense Analysis
- Strategic Planning
- SEC & Financial Reporting
- Risk Assessment

Career Progression

KERFHEIMER CORPORATION–Philadelphia, PA   1999 to Present

Senior Financial Analyst, June 2002 to Present
Financial Analyst, November 1999 to June 2002

Rapidly promoted to lead team of 15 analysts in the management of financial/SEC reporting and analysis for publicly traded, $2.3-billion company. Develop financial/statistical models used to project and maximize corporate financial performance. Support nationwide sales team by providing financial metrics, trends, and forecasts.

Continues with chronological history that features accomplishments

Key Accomplishments:

- **Developed long-range funding requirements crucial to firm's subsequent capture of $1 billion** in government and military contracts.
- **Facilitated a 45% decrease in company's long-term debt** during several major building expansions through personally developed computer models for capital acquisition.
- **Jointly led large-scale systems conversion to Hyperion**, including personal upload of database in Essbase. Completed conversion without interrupting business operations.

Figure 16–13 Advanced Résumé, Combining Functional and Chronological Elements. (continued)
Prepared by Kim Isaacs, Advanced Career Systems, Inc.

—————————— CAROL ANN WALKER ——————————

Résumé • Page Two

Career Progression (*continued*)

FIRST BANK, INC.–Bloomington, IN   1994 to 1999

Planning Analyst, September 1994 to November 1999
Compiled and distributed weekly, monthly, quarterly, and annual closings/financial reports, analyzing information for presentation to senior management. Prepared depreciation forecasts, actual-vs.-projected financial statements, key-matrix reports, tax-reporting packages, auditor packages, and balance-sheet reviews.

Key Accomplishments:

- **Devised strategies to acquire over $1 billion at 3% below market rate.**
- **Analyzed financial performance for consistency to plans and forecasts**, investigated trends and variances, and alerted senior management to areas requiring action.
- **Achieved an average 23% return on all personally recommended investments**. Applied critical thinking and sound financial and strategic analysis in all funding options research.

Education

THE WHARTON SCHOOL OF THE UNIVERSITY OF PENNSYLVANIA–Philadelphia, PA
Ph.D. in Finance Candidate, Expected June 2007

UNIVERSITY OF WISCONSIN–Milwaukee, WI
M.S. in Business Administration, May 1998

INDIANA UNIVERSITY–Bloomington, IN
B.S. in Business Administration, Emphasis in Finance
(*magna cum laude*), May 1994

Affiliations

- Association for Investment Management and Research (AIMR), Member, 2001 to Present
- Association for Corporate Financial Planning (ACFP), Senior Member, 1999 to Present

Portfolio of Financial Plans Available on Request
(717) 399-2712 • caw@yahoo.com

Figure 16–13　Advanced Résumé, Combining Functional and Chronological Elements. (continued)
Prepared by Kim Isaacs, Advanced Career Systems, Inc.

Joshua S. Goodman
222 Morewood Avenue
Pittsburgh, PA 15212
(878) 111-1234
Jgoodman@aol.com

OBJECTIVE

A position as a graphics designer with responsibilities in information design, packaging, and media presentations.

EMPLOYMENT EXPERIENCE

Job experience highlights qualifications for position described in Figure 16–16

Assistant Designer • Dyer/Khan
Los Angeles, California
Summer 2006, Summer 2007
Assistant Designer in a versatile design studio. Responsible for design, layout, comps, mechanicals, pre-press production for four-color posters, booklets, brochures, etc.
Clients: Paramount Pictures, Mattel Electronics, and Motown Records.

Highlights publications experience from design through the print-production cycle

Graphics Designer • Barton & Barton
Los Angeles, California
Summer 2005
Graphics Designer for advertising firm. Designed Web sites and created templates for two corporate clients. Created interactive banners and screen interfaces to facilitate online advertising for three corporate clients.

Features graphics design background

Production Assistant • Grafis
Los Angeles, California
Summer 2004
Production assistant at fast-paced design firm. Assisted with comps, mechanicals, and miscellaneous studio work.
Clients: ABC Television, A&M Records, and Ortho Products Division.

EDUCATION

Carnegie Mellon University, Pittsburgh, Pennsylvania BFA in Graphics Design — May 2006.

Graphics Design
Corporate Identity
Industrial Design
Graphics Imaging Processes
Color Theory
Computer Graphics
Typography
Serigraphy
Photography
Video Production

Relevant course work

COMPUTER SKILLS

XML, HTML, JavaScript, Forms, Macromedia Dreamweaver 3, Macromedia Flash 4, Photoshop 5.5, Image Ready (Animated GIFs), CorelDRAW, DeepPaint, iGrafx Designer, MapEdit (Image Mapping), Scanning, Microsoft Access/Excel, QuarkXPress.

ACTIVITIES

Member, Pittsburgh Graphics Design Society; Member, The Design Group

Figure 16–14   Résumé Tailored to a Job Listing for a Traditional Graphics Designer (for ABC Services, see Figure 16–16)

Joshua S. Goodman
222 Morewood Avenue
Pittsburgh, PA 15212
(878) 111-1234
Jgoodman@aol.com

OBJECTIVE

A position as a graphics designer with responsibilities in Web and document design, packaging, and media presentations.

WEB-DESIGN EXPERIENCE

Revised version of résumé in Figure 16–14 targets job listing requiring Web-design skills and experience

Separate Web section calls atention to mandatory skills for the position

**Graphics Designer • Barton & Barton
Los Angeles, California
Summer 2005**
Graphics Designer for advertising firm. Planned major revision of Barton & Barton's corporate Web site. Designed Web sites and created templates for two corporate clients. Created interactive banners and screen interfaces to facilitate online advertising.

GRAPHICS-DESIGN EXPERIENCE

**Assistant Designer • Dyer/Khan
Los Angeles, California
Summer 2006, Summer 2007**
Assistant designer in a versatile design studio. Responsible for design, layout, comps, mechanicals, and project management.
Clients: Paramount Pictures, Mattel Electronics, and Motown Records.

**Production Assistant • Grafis
Los Angeles, California
Summer 2004**
Production assistant at fast-paced design firm. Assisted with comps, mechanicals, and miscellaneous studio work.
Clients: ABC Television, A&M Records, and Ortho Products Division.

EDUCATION

Carnegie Mellon University, Pittsburgh, Pennsylvania BFA in Graphics Design — May 2006.

*Web Design
Computer Graphics
Graphics Design
Corporate Identity
Industrial Design
Graphics Imaging Processes
Color Theory
Typography
Serigraphy
Photography
Video Production*

Relevant course work as recent graduate

COMPUTER SKILLS

CorelDRAW, DeepPaint, iGrafx Designer, MapEdit (Image Mapping), Scanning, Microsoft Access/Excel, QuarkXPress, PageMaker, Illustrator, Adobe Acrobat Writer, MS Word.

Highlights Web-software capabilities

ACTIVITIES

Member, Pittsburgh Graphics Design Society; Member, The Design Group.

Figure 16–15   Résumé Tailored to a Job Listing for a Graphics Designer with Web-Development Experience (for XYZ Group, see Figure 16–17)

GRAPHICS DESIGNER

ABC Services, Inc., a hospitality management company located in Anywhere, USA, is in search of a full-time graphics designer able to multitask and proficient in Adobe PageMaker, Illustrator, Photoshop, Acrobat, and Word to create ads, brochures, signs, flyers, etc. Must be familiar with print process and IBM platforms. ABC offers great benefits, competitive salary, and flexible work environment. Please send résumé and salary requirements to ABC Group, etc.

Figure 16–16 Job Listing for a Traditional Graphics Designer (ABC Services)

GRAPHICS DESIGNER

The XYZ Group, a prestigious scientific organization located in Anyplace, USA, seeks a graphics designer. Position requires an experienced and creative graphics designer with strong concept and design skills to work on a wide range of projects, including logos, brochures, posters, annual reports, and Web-site design. Candidate must be able to manage many projects simultaneously and work with minimal supervision on all aspects of projects from start to finish. Must have good interpersonal skills for interaction with a wide variety of staff and volunteers to ensure timely production of all projects.

Candidates must have expert-level knowledge of PageMaker, Photoshop, and Illustrator/FreeHand in the Windows environment and Macromedia Dreamweaver (current release). Must have previous print-buying experience. Web-page development experience, good proofreading skills, and scanner experience are essential. Bachelor's degree in graphics design, fine arts, communications, or related field with a minimum 3–5 years recent experience using all required skills. Send cover letter and résumé, including salary history, to: XYZ Group, etc.

Figure 16–17 Job Listing for a Graphics Designer with Web-Development Experience (XYZ Group)

■ Writing an Effective Letter of Application

When applying for a job, you almost always need to submit an application letter with your résumé. The letter of application is essentially a sales letter in which you market your skills, abilities, and knowledge. Therefore, your application letter must be persuasive. The successful application letter accomplishes four tasks: (1) it catches the reader's attention favorably by describing how your skills will contribute to the organization, (2) it explains which particular job interests you

◆ *For a discussion of sales letters, see pages 319–323 in Chapter 9, Writing Business Correspondence.*

and why, (3) it convinces the reader that you are qualified for the job by drawing your reader's attention to particular elements in your résumé or portfolio, and (4) it requests an interview.

Opening Paragraph

In the opening paragraph, provide context and show your enthusiasm.

1. Indicate how you heard about the opening. If you have been referred to a company by an employee, a career counselor, a professor, or someone else, be sure to mention this even before you state your job objective ("I recently learned from Jodi Hammel of an opening in your firm").

2. State your job objective and mention the specific job title ("Karen Jarrett informed me of a possible opening for a district manager"). Those who make hiring decisions review many application letters. To save them time while also calling attention to your strengths as a candidate, state your job objective directly in your first paragraph.

3. Explain why you are interested in the job and demonstrate your initiative as well as knowledge of the organization by relating your interest to some facet of the organization. ("Your position interests me greatly not only because your firm is number one in the region but also because I am impressed with Advertising Media's Employee Development Program.")

Note how the following opening paragraph cites where the position was advertised, states the position title, and expresses interest in line with a career objective.

▶ Dear Mr. Lupert:

In the February 24, 2007, issue of the *Butler Gazette,* I learned that you have summer technical training internships available. This opportunity interests me because I have the professional and educational background necessary to make positive contributions to your firm.

Body Paragraphs

In the second paragraph (and third, if necessary), show through examples that you are highly qualified for the job. Limit each of these paragraphs to just one basic point that is clearly stated in the topic sentence. For example, your second paragraph might focus on work experience and your third paragraph on educational achievements. Don't just *tell* readers that you're qualified—*show* them by including examples and details. Come across as proud of your achievements and refer to your enclosed résumé, but do not simply summarize your résumé. Indicate how (with your talents) you can make valuable contributions to the company you are interested in, such as "I was the national winner of TI's 'Outstanding Customer Service Award' for 2003, 2004, and 2005. I have strong contacts with key buyers at all the major firms in our industry."

Note how the following two paragraphs from the application letter for the internship position give specific examples of project experience, provide information on course work and degree goals, reference the enclosed résumé, and emphasize how these experiences can contribute to the company.

▶ My professional experiences are representative of my abilities. My current project, a computer tutoring system that teaches LISP (an artificial intelligence programming language), is the first of its kind and is now being sold across the country to corporations and universities. I work with a team to test and revise our work until we have solved each problem. I have also developed leadership and collaborative skills that I could contribute to a summer position at Applied Sciences. As a co-founder of a project to target and tutor high school students with learning disabilities, I organized and implemented many of the training and tutoring sessions. My ability to take the initiative on challenging projects would be a valuable asset to your company.

   Pursuing degrees in industrial management and computer science has prepared me well to make valuable contributions to your goal of successfully implementing new software. Through varied courses, described in my résumé, I have the ability to learn new skills and to interact effectively in a technical environment. I would look forward to applying all these abilities at Applied Sciences, Inc.

Closing Paragraph

In the final paragraph, request an interview. Let the reader know how to reach you by including your phone number or e-mail address. End with a statement of goodwill, even if it is only "thank you."

▶ I would appreciate the chance to interview with you at your earliest convenience. If you have questions or would like additional information, contact me at (435) 228-3490 any Tuesday or Thursday after 10 a.m. or e-mail me at <sennett@excepr.com>. Thank you for your time.

Sincerely,

Molly Sennett

Molly Sennett

Enclosure: Résumé

Proofread your letter very carefully. Research indicates that if employers notice even one spelling, grammatical, or mechanical error, they often eliminate the candidate from consideration immediately. Such errors will give employers the impression that you lack writing skills or that you are generally sloppy and careless in the way you present yourself professionally.

◆ *See also Proofreading on pages 115–116 in Chapter 4, Revising the Draft.*

WRITER'S CHECKLIST
Writing a Letter of Application

☑ In the opening paragraph:
  – Indicate how you heard about the opening.
  – State your job objective and interest in the job.
  – Mention the job title.

☑ In the body of the letter:
  – Cite project and previous employment experiences that demonstrate your quali-fications for the job.
  – Indicate how college course work, your degree, and pertinent training add to your qualifications for the job.
  – Refer to your enclosed résumé.
  – Explain how your qualifications and achievements can contribute to the prospective employer.

☑ In the closing paragraph:
  – Request an interview.
  – Provide your phone number and e-mail address so that you can be contacted.
  – End with a goodwill statement.

Sample Letters

The three sample application letters shown in Figures 16–18 through 16–20 follow the application-letter structure described in this section. Each is adapted according to the emphasis, tone, and style to fit its particular audience.

ON THE WEB

For more sample cover letters, go to **bedfordstmartins.com/ writingthatworks** and select *Model Documents Gallery*.

- In Figure 16–18, a college student seeks an internship in a retailing business.
- In Figure 16–19, a recent college graduate applies for a job in an advertising company. Note that she refers the addressee to her Web site to view her résumé and design portfolio.
- In Figure 16–20, a person with many years of work experience applies for a job as a district manager.

From: Marsha S. Parker <msparker@ubi.edu>
To: Patrice C. Crandall <pcrandall@abels.com>
Sent: Monday, February 27, 2007 10:47AM
Subject: Application for Summer Internship
Attachment: 📄 Parker_Resume.doc

Dear Ms. Crandall:

I have learned from your Web site that you are hiring undergraduates for summer internships. The internship is appealing to me because I have discovered through personal research that Abel's buyer-training program is one of the most effective in the industry.

Opens by demonstrating initiative in researching the company, locating the program, and noting its value to the applicant's career

The professional and analytical qualities that my attached résumé describe match the job description on your Web site. My experiences with the Alumni Relations Program and the University Center Committee have enhanced my communication and persuasive abilities and my understanding of compromise and negotiation. For example, in the alumni program, I persuaded both uninvolved and active alumni to become more engaged with the direction of the university. On the University Center Committee, I balanced the students' demands with the financial and structural constraints of the administration. With these skills, I can ably assist the members of your department with their summer projects and successfully juggle multiple responsibilities.

Continues by linking the applicant's personal characteristics to tangible accomplishments

I would appreciate the opportunity to meet with you to discuss your summer internship further. If you have questions or would like to speak with me, please contact me at (412) 863-2289 any weekday after 3 p.m or you can e-mail me at <msparker@ubi.edu>. Thank you for your consideration.

Sincerely,

Marsha S. Parker

Figure 16–18   Application Letter Sent as an E-mail Message from a College Student Applying for an Internship

449 Samson Street, Apt. 19
Providence, RI 02906
September 19, 2007

Alice Tobowski
Employee Relations Department
Advertising Media, Inc.
1007 Market Street
Providence, RI 02912

Dear Ms. Tobowski:

Opens by referencing a personal contact at the firm

I recently learned from Jodi Hammel, a graphics designer at Advertising Media, Inc., and a former colleague, that you are recruiting advertising assistants. Your position interests me greatly not only because your firm is number one in the region but also because I am impressed with Advertising Media's Employee Development Program.

Continues with a strong emphasis on her bilingual and other skills to stand out from many other applicants

Ms. Tobowski, I am aware that hundreds of applicants are applying for this position, but I have a combination of qualities probably few can match. As noted in my résumé, I not only possess multilingual skills (Spanish, French, and English) but also hold a degree in advertising.

Closes by referring to a personal Web site for her résumé and portfolio of design work

Through several internships in advertising companies, I have developed outstanding verbal and written communication skills as well as an ability to work well with colleagues. Most recently, I developed a successful advertising campaign for Quilted Bear in Providence, which resulted in a 25 percent increase in customer inquiries from the French Canadian and South American markets. My résumé and a portfolio of my graphics design work are available at my Web site at <SarahsGraphics.com>.

Could we schedule a meeting at your convenience to discuss this career opportunity further? Feel free to call me any weekday morning at (401) 578-1241 or e-mail me at <singh@SarahsGraphics.com> if you have questions or need further information. Thank you for your consideration.

Sincerely,

Sarah Singh

Sarah Singh

Encloses a résumé

Enclosure: Résumé

Figure 16–19   Application Letter from a Recent College Graduate Applying for a Job

522 Beethoven Drive
Roanoke, VA 24016
November 15, 2007

Ms. Cecilia Smathers
Vice President, Dealer Sales
Hamilton Office Machines, Inc.
6194 Main Street
Hampton, VA 23661

Dear Ms. Smathers:

During the recent NOMAD convention in Washington, one of your sales representatives, Karen Jarrett, informed me of a possible opening for a district manager in your Dealer Sales Division. My extensive background in the office-systems industry makes me an ideal candidate for the position.

Opens by referencing a personal contact at the firm

I was with Technology, Inc., Dealer Division from its formation in 1994 until TI's merger and reorganization last year. During that period, I was involved in all areas of dealer sales, both within Technology, Inc., and through personal contact with a number of independent dealers. From 2000–2006, I served as Dealer Sales Manager and Special Representative. As described in the enclosed résumé, I was the national winner of TI's "Outstanding Customer Service Award" for 2003, 2004, and 2005. I have strong contacts with key buyers at all the major firms in our industry.

Continues with a concise career summary

I would be happy to discuss my qualifications in an interview at your convenience. Please telephone me at (804) 449-6743 or e-mail me at <gm302.476@sys.com>.

Closes with contact information

Sincerely,

Gregory
Mindukakis

Gregory Mindukakis

Enclosure: Résumé

Encloses a résumé

Figure 16–20   Application Letter from an Applicant with Many Years of Experience

■ Doing Well in the Interview

Preparing a professional résumé and writing an effective letter of application are essential to obtaining a job interview; that preparation helps you understand your strengths as a potential employee and articulate your career objectives. Nevertheless, the interview is often the most difficult part of the job search because it is so pivotal in the hiring process. A job interview may last for 30 minutes, or it may take several hours; it may be conducted by one person or by several, either at one time or in a series of interviews, in person, by phone, or by teleconference. Because it is impossible to know exactly what to expect, it is important that you be as prepared as possible. If you are interviewed by phone, set aside a time and place where you won't be interrupted and have your résumé and note-taking tools (notepad, computer) available.

Before the Interview

ON THE WEB

For online access to major national newspapers and other business references, go to Chapter 16, **bedfordstmartins.com/ writingthatworks**, and select *Web Links*.

The interview is not a one-way communication. It presents you with an opportunity to ask questions of your potential employer and to demonstrate your knowledge of the position and the organization itself. In preparation, learn everything you can about the company before the interview by answering the questions listed in the Learning about Employers checklist on page 576. You can obtain information from the company's Web site, current employees, company literature, and the business section of local and national newspapers, such as the *New York Times*, the *Los Angeles Times*, the *Wall Street Journal*, and the *Washington Post* (available online and in the library). You may be able to learn about the company's size, sales volume, product line, credit rating, branch locations, subsidiary companies, new products and services, building programs, and other such information from its annual reports; publications such as *Moody's Industrials* at <www.moodys.com>, *Dun and Bradstreet* at <www.dnb.com>, *Standard & Poor's* at <www2.standardandpoors.com>, and *Thomas' Register* at <www.5.thomasnet.com>; and other business reference sources a librarian might suggest. What you cannot find through your own research, ask your interviewer. Now is your chance to make certain that you are considering a healthy and growing company. It is also your chance to show your interest in the company and find out as much as possible about company-employee relations, including opportunities for career growth. To that end, you may want to ask your interviewer some or all of the following questions:

- How often are employees formally evaluated on their performance?
- Does the company require training or certification?
- Does the company fund career-related training and outside education?
- Does the position I'm applying for have promotion potential?
- Is there a probationary period for new employees?

Finally, as a way of gaining insight into how the company operates, you could ask your interviewer how he or she started at the company—if time permits.

Try to anticipate the questions your interviewer might ask, and prepare your answers in advance. Be sure you understand a question before answering it, and avoid responding too quickly with a rehearsed answer — be prepared to answer in a natural and relaxed manner. Interviewers typically ask the following questions:

- What are your short-term and long-term occupational goals?
- Where do you see yourself five years from now?
- What are your major strengths and weaknesses?
- Do you work better with others or alone?
- How do you spend your free time?
- What accomplishments are you particularly proud of and why?
- Why are you leaving your current job?
- Why do you want to work for this company?
- Why should I hire you?
- What salary and benefits do you expect?

Some of these questions are difficult. Give them careful thought, try to be as concrete as possible by offering examples when appropriate, and remember that there is no one correct answer.

Many employers use behavioral interviews. Rather than traditional, straightforward questions, the behavioral interview focuses on asking the candidate to provide examples or respond to hypothetical situations. Interviewers who use behavior-based questions are looking for specific examples from your experience. Prepare for the behavioral interview by recollecting challenging situations or problems that were successfully resolved. Examples of behavior-based questions include the following:

- Can you tell me about a time when you experienced conflict on a team?
- If I were your boss and you disagreed with a decision I made, what would you do?
- How have you used your leadership skills to bring about change?
- Can you tell me about a time when you failed?

Be sure that you arrive for your interview at the appointed time. In fact, it is usually a good idea to arrive early because you may be asked to fill out an application before you meet your interviewer. Read the application form before filling it out, and proofread it when you are finished. Not only does the application form provide the company with a record for its files, but it also gives the company an opportunity to see how closely you follow directions, how thoroughly you complete a task, and how well you express your ideas in writing. Always bring extra copies of your résumé and samples of your work (if applicable). Some of the people you meet may not have a copy of your résumé, and it contains much of the same information the application asks for: personal data, work experience, and education.

Finally, bring a tablet and pen or personal digital assistant (PDA) to record pertinent information. Do not, however, bring a laptop computer—doing so creates a distraction and a barrier between you and your interviewer.

WRITER'S CHECKLIST
Learning about Employers

As you search for information about potential employers, use these questions as a guide.

- ☑ What kind of organization is it?
- ☑ How diversified is it?
- ☑ Is it a nonprofit organization?
- ☑ If it is government employment, at what level or sector is it?
- ☑ Does it provide a service or product? If so, what kind?
- ☑ How large is the business? How large are its assets?
- ☑ Is it locally owned? Is it a subsidiary of a larger organization? Is it expanding?
- ☑ How long has it been in business?
- ☑ Where will you fit in?

During the Interview

The interview actually begins before you are seated: What you wear and how you act make a first impression. In general, dress simply and conservatively, avoid extremes in fragrance and cosmetics, and be well-groomed.

Behavior

◆ *See also the discussion of listening on pages 496–498 in Chapter 14, Giving Presentations and Conducting Meetings.*

First, thank the interviewer for his or her time, express your pleasure at meeting him or her, and remain standing until you are offered a seat. Then sit up straight (good posture suggests self-assurance), look directly at the interviewer, and try to appear relaxed and confident. Never chew gum. During the interview, you may find yourself feeling a little nervous. Use that nervous energy to your advantage by channeling it into alertness. Listen carefully and record important information in your memory. Jot down a few facts and figures as needed, but do not attempt to take extensive notes during the interview.

Responses

When answering questions, don't ramble or stray from the subject. Say only what you must to answer each question properly and then stop, but avoid giving just yes or no answers—they usually don't permit the interviewer to learn enough about you. Some interviewers allow a silence to fall just to see how you will react. The burden of conducting the interview is the interviewer's, not yours—and he or she may interpret your rush to fill a void in the conversation as a sign of insecurity. If such a silence makes you uncomfortable, be ready to ask pertinent questions about the company from your prepared list. If the interviewer overlooks important points, bring them up.

Interviewers look for a degree of self-confidence and understanding of the field in which the applicant is applying for a job, as well as genuine interest in the field, the company, and the job. Less is expected of a beginner, but even a newcomer must show some self-confidence and command of the subject. One way to communicate your interest in the job and company is to ask questions. Interviewers respond favorably to applicants who can communicate and present themselves well.

Salary Negotiations

Although it is better to negotiate salary after you have a job offer or certainly late in the interview, you may be asked, "What are your salary requirements?" You cannot answer such a question without solid preparation. Make sure that you are aware of prevailing salaries in your field so that you will be better prepared to discuss salary. If you are a recent graduate, it is usually unwise to attempt to bargain. Many companies have inflexible starting salaries for beginners.

First, your goal should be to work toward a win-win situation for you and your prospective employer. Avoid overemphasizing money because it tends to make your potential loyalty to an organization suspect. The issue is not simply one of dollar amounts but of your own job satisfaction and what value you can bring to your employer. Consider the following guidelines:

- Seek advice ahead of time from a professional with relevant experience.
- Determine the lowest salary you would accept, perhaps based on your most-recent employment.
- Determine the typical salary ranges for positions in your area.
- Determine possible fringe benefits that would be valuable to you.
- Determine the firm's opportunities for promotion.

ON THE WEB

For links to Web sites offering useful resources for salary negotiations, see Chapter 16, bedfordstmartins.com/writingthatworks, and select *Web Links*.

If questioned directly about salary, you can give an answer such as, "I was considering a range of $— to $—, but that would also depend on the benefits available and the potential or timetable for promotions or salary increases." Remember, it's always acceptable to say to a prospective employer that you would like to think about an offer.

Conclusion

At the conclusion of the interview, thank your interviewer for his or her time. Indicate that you are interested in the job (if true), and try to get an idea of when you can expect to hear from the company (do not press too hard). Reaffirm friendly contact with a firm handshake.

◼ Sending Follow-up Correspondence

After you leave the interview, review your notes for accuracy and fill in any gaps while the information is fresh — it may be helpful in comparing job offers. As soon as possible after the interview (no later than two days), send the interviewer a note of thanks in a brief letter or e-mail message. Such notes often include the following:

- Your thanks for the interview and to individuals or groups that gave you special help or attention during the interview
- The name of the specific job for which you interviewed
- Your impression that the job is attractive
- Your confidence that you can perform the job well
- An offer to provide further information or answer further questions

Figure 16–21 shows a typical example of follow-up correspondence. If you have not heard back from the company about the status of your application in two weeks, send another brief and courteous letter or e-mail message. Beyond that period, it is the responsibility of the company to contact you.

From: pming@juno.com (Philip Ming)
To: vallone@infosystems.com
Subject: Re: Employment Interview
Sent: 16 May 06 3:59:56 PM Eastern Daylight Time

Dear Mr. Vallone:

Opens with an expression of appreciation

Thank you for the informative and pleasant interview we had yesterday. Please extend my thanks to Mr. Wilson of the Media Group as well.

Continues with a strong statement of interest in the job

I came away from our meeting most favorably impressed with Information Systems. I find the position of ACR Designer in the Medical Division to be an attractive one and feel confident that my qualifications would enable me to perform the duties to everyone's advantage.

If I can answer any further questions, please let me know.

Sincerely yours,

Philip Ming

=====================
Ends with relevant contact information

Philip Ming
9672 Patton Drive
Kearney, NE 68849
(308) 841-9782
=====================

Figure 16–21   Follow-up E-mail Thanking the Interviewer

If you are offered a job you want, accept the offer verbally and write a brief letter of acceptance as soon as possible—certainly within a week. The organization of such a message is simple. Begin by accepting the job you have been offered. Identify the job by title and state the exact salary so that there will be no confusion on these two important points. The second paragraph might go into detail about moving dates and the time for reporting to work. The details will vary, depending on the nature of the job offer. Conclude with a statement that you are looking forward to working for your new employer, as in the acceptance letter written by a college student in Figure 16–22.

9672 Patton Drive
Kearney, NE 68849
(308) 841-9782

June 9, 2006

Mr. F. E. Vallone
Manager of Human Resources
Information Systems, Inc.
3275 Commercial Park Drive
Raleigh, NE 68501

Dear Mr. Vallone:

Opens by accepting job and verifying the salary, title, and organizational unit

I am pleased to accept your offer of $36,500 per year as a junior ACR designer in the Medical Group.

Continues with near-term schedule and start date

After graduation, I plan to leave Kearney on Tuesday, June 20. I should be able to find suitable living accommodations within a few days and be ready to report for work on the following Monday, June 26. Please let me know if this date is satisfactory to you.

Ends with goodwill statement

I look forward to working with the design team at Information Systems.

Very truly yours,

Philip Ming

Philip Ming

Figure 16–22   Acceptance Letter Written by a College Student

◆ *For additional advice on writing refusal letters, see Negative Messages and the Indirect Pattern on pages 271–272 in Chapter 8, Understanding the Principals of Business Communication, and Refusals on page 324 in Chapter 9, Writing Business Correspondence.*

Because you will probably have applied to more than one organization, you will need to write a letter of refusal if you receive more than one job offer. Be especially tactful and courteous because the employer you are refusing has spent time and effort interviewing you and may have counted on your accepting the job. It is also possible that you may apply for another job at this company in the future. Figure 16–23 is an example of a job-refusal letter. It acknowledges the consideration given the applicant, offers a logical reason for refusal of the offer, and then concludes on a pleasant note.

Opens with a tactful reason for refusing the job offer

Closes by acknowledging the effort of the prospective employer

Dear Mr. Vallone:

I enjoyed talking with you about your opening for a technical writer, and I was gratified to receive your offer. Although I have given the offer serious thought, I have decided to accept a position as a copywriter with an advertising agency. I feel that the job I have chosen is better suited to my skills and long-term goals.

I appreciate your consideration and the time you spent with me. I wish you the best of luck in filling the position.

Figure 16–23   Letter of Refusal

■ Sending a Resignation Letter or Memo

When you are planning to leave a job, for any reason, you usually write a resignation letter to your supervisor or to an appropriate person in the Human Resources Department.

- Start on a positive note, regardless of the circumstances under which you are leaving.
- Consider pointing out how you have benefited from working for the company or say something complimentary about the company.
- Comment on something positive about the people with whom you have been associated.
- Explain why you are leaving in an objective, factual tone.
- Avoid angry recriminations because your resignation will remain on file with the company and could haunt you in the future when you need references.

◆ *For strategies concerning negative messages, see pages 271–272 in Chapter 8, Understanding the Principles of Business Communication.*

Your letter or memo should give enough notice to allow your employer time to find a replacement. It might be no more than two weeks, or it might be enough time to put your files in order and train your replacement. Some organizations may ask for a notice equivalent to the number of weeks of vacation you receive. Check the policy of your employer before you begin your letter.

The sample resignation memo in Figure 16–24 is from an employee who is leaving to take a job offering greater opportunities. The resignation memo in Figure 16–25 is written by an employee who is leaving under unhappy circumstances; notice that it opens and closes positively and that the reason for the resignation is stated without apparent anger or bitterness.

ON THE WEB

For another sample resignation letter, go to bedfordstmartins.com/ writingthatworks and select *Model Documents Gallery*.

MEMO

To: W. R. Johnson, Director of Purchasing
From: J. L. Washburn, Purchasing Agent   *JLW*
Date: January 9, 2007
Subject: Resignation from Barnside Appliances,
           effective January 23, 2007

My three years at Barnside Appliances have been an invaluable period of learning and professional development. I arrived as a novice, and I believe that today I am a professional—primarily as a result of the personal attention and mentoring I have received from my superiors and the fine example set by both my superiors and my peers.

Positive opening

I believe, however, that the time has come for me to move on to a larger company that can give me an opportunity to continue my professional development. Therefore, I have accepted a position with General Electric, where I am scheduled to begin on January 30. Thus, my last day at Barnside will be January 23. I will be happy to train my replacement during the next two weeks.

Reason for leaving

Many thanks for the experiences I have gained and best wishes for the future.

Positive closing

Figure 16–24   Resignation Memo to Accept a Better Position

MEMO

To: T. W. Haney, Vice President, Administration
From: L. R. Rupp, Executive Assistant
Date: February 9, 2007
Subject: Resignation from Winterhaven, effective March 2, 2007

Positive opening

My five-year stay with the Winterhaven Company has been a very pleasant experience, and I believe that it has been mutually beneficial.

Reason for leaving

Because the recent restructuring of my job leaves no career path open to me, I have accepted a position with another company that I feel will offer me greater advancement opportunities. I am, therefore, submitting my resignation, to be effective on March 2, 2007.

Positive closing

I have enjoyed working with my coworkers at Winterhaven and wish the company success in the future.

Figure 16–25   Resignation Memo under Negative Conditions

CHAPTER 16 SUMMARY: FINDING THE RIGHT JOB

Follow these five steps for finding a job:

- Determine the best job for you.
- Prepare an effective résumé.
- Write an effective letter of application.
- Conduct yourself professionally during the interview.
- Send a follow-up message after the interview.

Research the following sources of information for locating jobs:

- Campus career center
- Web resources
- Tips from family, friends, and acquaintances
- Letters of inquiry
- Informational interviews
- Advertisements in newspapers
- Advertisements in trade and professional journals
- Private and temporary employment agencies
- Local, state, and federal agencies

Plan your résumé carefully.

- Determine the type of job you seek and compile a list of prospective employers.
- Consider the type of information about you and your background of most importance to potential employers.

■ Determine, based on this information, the details that should be included and the most-effective way to present them.

Write an effective letter of application.

■ Catch the reader's attention.

■ Create the desire for your services.

■ Include a brief summary of your qualifications for the specific job for which you are applying.

■ State when and where you can be reached.

Follow these steps to prepare for a job interview:

■ Learn everything you can about your prospective employer.

■ Arrive on time.

■ Highlight those strengths most useful to the job you are applying for.

■ Demonstrate your knowledge of your field.

■ Send the interviewer a brief note of thanks after the interview.

When you receive a job offer, write one of the following letters:

■ If you plan to accept the offer, send a letter of acceptance as soon as possible after you receive the offer.

■ If you plan to refuse, send a letter as soon as possible refusing the offer but expressing your appreciation for the organization's time and effort in considering you.

Follow these guidelines in preparing a letter or memo of resignation:

■ Begin and end the message on a positive note.

■ Explain the reason for your departure factually and objectively.

■ Give at least two weeks' notice (and preferably longer) to allow your employer to prepare for your departure.

ON THE WEB

For an online quiz on finding the right job, go to Chapter 16, bedfordstmartins.com/ writingthatworks

■ Exercises

1. Write a letter to a past or present teacher, an employer, or another appropriate person, asking permission to use him or her as a job reference. Be prepared to explain in class why you think this person is especially well qualified to comment on your job qualifications.

2. Obtain a sample résumé at your school's career-development center or local copy center. Annotate and write a brief critical analysis of the résumé for your instructor, pointing out its strong points and how it might be improved in content, organization, or design.

3. List five specific features a company or other employer would need to have to make you interested in working for them. Next, list what you would want to gain from your work experience, such as learning more about a specific technology that interests you.

4. Prepare a list of at least six job-related assets that you have and explain why and how these qualities would be useful to a potential employer. Consider things like your educational experiences and course work, and work and volunteer

ON THE WEB

For additional exercises go to Chapter 16, bedfordstmartins.com/ writingthatworks

experiences. Include any honors you have received, high grade point averages, specific skills such as advanced computer knowledge or creative design talent, and unique work experience. List good work habits such as accuracy, dependability, and the ability to manage large projects, and back them up with supporting examples from your work or educational experience. Be ready to read your list aloud to others so that they can provide feedback.

5. Following the guidelines on pages 554–557, create a résumé to send in response to an electronic posting advertising a summer position in your field of study. Submit your résumé either on a disk or as an e-mail attachment, or both, as required by your instructor.

6. Using the guidelines in this chapter, write a letter of application and a résumé in response to an advertisement for a job you will be qualified for when you graduate. Use high-quality white bond paper and make sure the letter and résumé are error- and blemish-free.

7. Assume that you have been interviewed for the job in Exercise 6. Write a follow-up letter expressing thanks for the interview.

8. If your current résumé is prepared by job chronology, prepare a second résumé— a functional résumé—that not only organizes work experience by type but also helps you identify important skills, abilities, or experiences. Follow the guidelines on pages 548–550. Your instructor may ask you to submit your chronological résumé with your functional résumé.

9. Review your existing résumé to make sure that your use of verbs and nouns in your job descriptions are consistent and parallel in structure. (See Parallel Structure on pages 104–105 in Chapter 4, Revising the Draft.)

10. Create an ASCII or a plain-text résumé that you could send via e-mail or upload to your Web site. (Use the guidelines provided in Digital Tips: Preparing an ASCII Résumé on page 555.)

ON THE WEB

For more collaborative classroom projects, go to Chapter 16, bedfordstmartins.com/ writingthatworks

■ Collaborative Classroom Projects

1. Divide into groups of four to six classmates who share your major area (or a similar area) of study. Appoint a group leader and a recorder. For the first 30 minutes, brainstorm a list of action words that could be used to describe your collective skills, abilities, and experiences, and which could work well in a résumé to be used to apply for a job in your field. During the next 15 minutes, brainstorm a list of positions that you could apply for when you graduate. Be ready to share your information with your classmates.

2. Assume you are a liberal arts major and that you plan to apply for one of the jobs in the following list.

Technical Writer/Editor
Public Relations Coordinator
Content Developer for Corporate Training Department
Web Editor
Recruiting Coordinator
Field Investigator for personnel security company
Grant Writer

After individually examining job listings on the Web and scanning your college catalog, divide into groups of three or four and make a list of skills that might be required for the position. Then, for each required job skill, brainstorm a list of related skills and experiences that might be gained from courses and extracurricular activities in a liberal arts degree program, such as internships or service learning, as well as from any volunteer or paid work. For example, for a position as a membership sales director for a fitness center, required skills include listening, speaking, writing, researching, and being physically fit; related experiences might include membership in a debate team, writing for a social club's newsletter, a summer job as a camp counselor, library research, proficiency in a second language acquired during a semester abroad, membership in an athletic team, and so on.

3. Working in pairs, spend 20 minutes during which you play the role of the job interviewer, while your partner plays the role of the interviewee. Then switch roles for the next 20 minutes. Begin by referring to the interview section of this chapter, and decide the name and type of company where you are interviewing, the position, and other details about the job. Include the following questions in the interview:

- What are your short-term and long-term professional goals?
- What are your major strengths and weaknesses?
- Why do you want to work for our company?
- What are your personal goals?
- What accomplishment are you particularly proud of? Describe it.
- Why should I hire you?

In conclusion, consider what answers you would change in preparation for your next interview.

■ Research Projects

ON THE WEB

For extra research projects, go to Chapter 16, bedfordstmartins.com/ writingthatworks

1. Research three major employers in your field and, in an outline format, answer the following questions about each:

    a. What kind of an organization is it?
    b. Is it a profit or nonprofit organization?
    c. Does it provide a service or services? If so, what kind(s)?
    d. What does its mission statement reveal?
    e. How large is the business? How large are its assets?
    f. Is it locally owned? Is it a subsidiary of a larger operation? Is it expanding?
    g. How long has it been in business?
    h. If it is government employment, at what level or sector is it?
    i. Where would you fit in?

    You can obtain information from the Internet, current employees, company literature such as employee publications, and the business section of back issues of local and national newspapers (available in the library and on the Web).

2. Imagine that you work for a large consulting company that has been hired to give a presentation in several European countries on how to seek employment in the United States. You've received several samples of would-be applicants' résumés and have noticed many differences between the structure of their résumés and what is expected in the United States. Research job hunting and résumé writing

strategies used in two other countries of your choice, then create a presentation on American-style résumé writing for job seekers from those countries (review Chapter 14, Giving Presentations and Conducting Meetings). Be sure to address the following issues:

- The use of the title "motivation letter" instead of "cover letter"
- The inclusion of an applicant's date of birth, marital status, and children on résumés
- Personal photographs
- Chronological order versus reverse chronological order
- Spelling
- College-level education described as "tertiary" education
- Paper size

ON THE WEB

For more Web projects, go to Chapter 16, bedfordstmartins.com/ writingthatworks

■ Web Projects

1. Review the Web sites of at least three online college or university placement centers, including the one hosted by your school. These centers offer links and general job-search information and can be helpful as you plan your own specific job search. Begin with the Center for Career Opportunities at Purdue University at <www.purdue.edu>. Write a brief analysis of at least three career-planning sites you reviewed (including the URLs). Be ready to share your results with the class.

2. Find information about the future employment potential of graduates in your major field of study by using at least five Web sources. In a brief memo to your instructor, answer the following questions about your major field:

   a. Based on current indicators, what are the job projections in your field in this country?
   b. Is there a worldwide demand for people in your field?
   c. Do employees in your field have an opportunity to advance?
   d. In your field, is there a wide range in salary expectations based on geographic location?
   e. What other relevant information can you provide?

PART FOUR

Revision Guide: Sentences, Punctuation, and Mechanics

MARK/SYMBOL	MEANING	EXAMPLE	CORRECTED TYPE
ℯ	Delete	the ~~manager's~~ report	the report
∧	Insert	*manager's* the ∧ report	the manager's report
dots (stet)	Let stand	the manager's report	the manager's report
≡ (cap)	Capitalize	the monday meeting	the Monday meeting
/ (lc)	Lowercase	the Monday Meeting	the Monday meeting
∼ (tr)	Transpose	the cover lettre	the cover letter
⌒	Close space	a loud speaker	a loudspeaker
#	Insert space	a loudspeaker	a loud speaker
¶	Paragraph	...report. The meeting...	...report. The meeting...
⊃	Run in with previous line or paragraph	...report. The meeting...	...report. The meeting...
— (ital)	Italicize	the New York Times	the *New York Times*
∿ (bf)	Boldface	Use boldface sparingly.	Use **boldface** sparingly.
⊙	Insert period	I wrote the e-mail	I wrote the e-mail.
⌃	Insert comma	However we cannot...	However, we cannot...
=	Insert hyphen	clear cut decision	clear-cut decision
⊢M⊣	Insert em dash	Our goal productivity	Our goal—productivity
⌄ or :/	Insert colon	We need the following	We need the following:
⌄ or ;/	Insert semicolon	we finished we achieved	we finished; we achieved
⌄⌄	Insert quotation marks	He said, I agree.	He said, "I agree."
⌄	Insert apostrophe	the managers report	the manager's report

Proofreaders' Marks

Sentences

A sentence is the most fundamental and versatile tool available to writers, but sentence faults and issues with pronouns, adjectives, adverbs, and verbs can cause difficulties for your readers. To help you avoid these problems, this section describes common sentence errors and how to correct them.

■ Sentence Faults

Sentence-level errors, like inaccurate facts or incomplete information, can confuse, irritate, or even mislead your readers. These errors can make your meaning hard to determine or, even worse, alter the meaning entirely. The most serious sentence problems are run-on sentences, comma splices, sentence fragments, and dangling and misplaced modifiers.

Run-on Sentences and Comma Splices

An independent clause expresses a complete thought by itself. Although it might be part of a larger sentence, it always can stand alone as a separate sentence:

▶ The training division will offer three new courses.

▶ Interested employees should sign up by Wednesday.

When two independent clauses are joined without any punctuation, the result is a *run-on*, or *fused, sentence*. When two independent clauses are joined with only a comma, the result is called a *comma splice* or *comma fault*. Either problem can be corrected by (1) making two sentences, (2) joining the two clauses with a semicolon (if they are closely related and of equal weight), (3) joining the two clauses with a comma and a coordinating conjunction, or (4) subordinating one clause to the other.

◆ *For tips on subordinating clauses effectively, see pages 102–104 in Chapter 4, Revising the Draft.*

RUN-ON	The training division will offer three new courses interested employees should sign up by Wednesday.
COMMA SPLICE	The training division will offer three new courses, interested employees should sign up by Wednesday.
CORRECT	The training division will offer three new courses. Interested employees should sign up by Wednesday. [two sentences]
CORRECT	The training division will offer three new courses; interested employees should sign up by Wednesday. [semicolon]
CORRECT	The training division will offer three new courses, *so* interested employees should sign up by Wednesday. [comma plus coordinating conjunction]
CORRECT	*When* the training division offers the new courses, interested employees should sign up for them. [one clause subordinated to the other]

Sentence Fragments

A sentence fragment is an incomplete grammatical unit that is punctuated as a sentence.

FRAGMENT	And quit his job.
SENTENCE	He quit his job.

A sentence fragment either lacks a subject or a verb or is a subordinate clause or phrase. Sentence fragments are often introduced by relative pronouns (*who, whom, whose, which, that*) or subordinating conjunctions (such as *although, because, if,* and *while*). When you use these introductory words, you must combine the dependent clause that follows with a main clause to form a complete sentence.

▶ The new manager instituted several new procedures. ~~Although~~ , *although* she didn't obtain approval for them with Human Resources.

A sentence must contain a main, or finite, verb; verbals (gerunds, participles, and infinitives) cannot function as verbs. The following examples are sentence fragments because they lack main verbs.

FRAGMENT	*Providing* all employees with disability insurance.
SENTENCE	The company *provides* all employees with disability insurance.
FRAGMENT	*To work* a 40-hour week.
SENTENCE	Most of our employees *work* a 40-hour week.

Explanatory phrases beginning with *such as, for example, because,* and similar terms may lead to sentence fragments.

▶ The staff wants additional benefits. *, such as* ~~For example,~~ the use of company cars.

Dangling and Misplaced Modifiers

Phrases that do not clearly and logically refer to the correct noun or pronoun are called *dangling modifiers*. Correct this problem by adding the appropriate noun or pronoun for the phrase to modify or by rewriting the phrase as a clause.

▶ While *I was* eating lunch, the computer malfunctioned.

▶ After finishing the negotiations, *we relaxed at dinner.* ~~dinner was relaxing.~~

A *misplaced modifier* refers, or appears to refer, to the wrong word or phrase. Avoid this problem by placing modifiers as close as possible to the words they modify. Position each modifier carefully so that it says what you mean.

▶ We ~~just~~ bought the property *just* for expansion.

▶ Our copier was used to duplicate materials ~~for other departments~~ that needed to be *for other departments* reduced.

A *squinting modifier* is located between two sentence elements and might refer to either one. To eliminate the ambiguity, move the modifier or revise the sentence.

▶ *During the next week, the* ~~The~~ union agreed ~~during the next week~~ to return to work.

▶ The union agreed during the next week *to return to work* ~~to return to work~~.

■ Pronouns

A *pronoun* is used as a substitute for a noun (the noun for which a pronoun substitutes is called the *antecedent*). An unclear link between a pronoun and its antecedent can sometimes cause confusion.

Pronoun Case

Grammatical case indicates the functional relationship of a noun or a pronoun to the other words in a sentence. The case of a pronoun is always determined by its function in a phrase, clause, or sentence. If it functions as the subject, it is in the subjective case; if it functions as an object, it is in the objective case; if it reflects possession or ownership and modifies a noun, it is in the possessive case. The subjective case can indicate the person or thing acting (*He* sued the vendor), the person or thing acted on (*He* was sued by the vendor), or the topic of description (*He* is the vendor). The objective case can indicate the thing acted on (The vendor sued *him*) or the person or thing acting but in the objective position (The vendor was sued by *him*). The possessive case indicates the person or thing owning or possessing something (It was *his* company).

Singular	*Subjective*	*Objective*	*Possessive*
First person	I	me	my, mine
Second person	you	you	your, yours
Third person	he, she, it	him, her, it	his, her, hers, its

Plural	*Subjective*	*Objective*	*Possessive*
First person	we	us	our, ours
Second person	you	you	your, yours
Third person	they	them	their, theirs

Determining Case

One test to determine the proper case of a pronoun is to try using it with a transitive verb that requires a direct object—a person or thing to receive the action expressed by the verb. *Hit* is a useful verb for this test. If the pronoun would logically precede the verb, use the subjective case; if it would logically follow the verb, use the objective case.

▶ *She* hit the volleyball. [subjective case]
▶ The volleyball hit *her*. [objective case]

An *appositive* is a noun or noun phrase that follows and amplifies another noun or noun phrase. A pronoun appositive takes the case of its antecedent.

▶ Two systems analysts, *Joe and I*, were selected to represent the company.
[*Joe and I* is in apposition to the subject, *systems analysts*, and therefore must be in the subjective case.]
▶ The systems analysts selected two members of our department—*Joe and me*.
[*Joe and me* is in apposition to *two members*, the object of the verb *selected*, and therefore must be in the objective case.]

The reverse situation can also present problems. To test for the proper case when the pronouns *we* and *us* are followed by an appositive noun that defines them, try the sentence without the noun.

SENTENCE	(*We/us*) pilots fly our own airplanes.
INCORRECT	*Us* fly our own airplanes.
	[The incorrect usage sounds wrong.]
CORRECT	*We* fly our own airplanes.
	[This correct usage sounds right.]

To determine the case of a pronoun that follows *as* or *than*, mentally add the words that are omitted but understood.

▶ The other sales representative is not paid as well as *she* [is paid].
  [You would not write, "*her* is paid."]

▶ His partner was better informed than *he* [was informed].
  [You would not write, "*him* was informed."]

If pronouns in compound constructions cause problems, try using them singly to determine the proper case.

▶ In his report, Jamel thanked Sam and (*me/I*).

▶ In his report, Jamel thanked *Sam*.

▶ In his report, Jamel thanked *me*.

Using *Who* or *Whom*

Writers are often unsure whether to use *who* or *whom*. *Who* is the subjective case form, whereas *whom* is the objective case form. When in doubt about which form to use, substitute a personal pronoun to see which one fits. If *he, she*, or *they* fits, use *who*.

▶ *Who* is the training coordinator?
  [You would say, "*She* is the training coordinator."]

If *him, her*, or *them* fits, use *whom*.

▶ It depends on *whom*?
  [You would say, "It depends on *them*."]

Pronoun Reference

A pronoun should refer clearly to a specific antecedent. Avoid vague and uncertain references.

▶ *, which was a big one,*
    We got the account after we wrote the proposal. ~~It was a big one.~~

For coherence, place pronouns as close as possible to their antecedents.

▶ *, praised for its design, is   .*
    The office building next to City Hall ~~was praised for its design.~~

A general (or broad) reference or one that has no real antecedent is a problem that often occurs when the word *this* is used by itself.

▶ *experience*
    He deals with personnel problems in his work. This helps him in his personal life.

Another problem is a hidden reference, which has only an implied antecedent.

▶ *the   of ketone bodies*
    A high-lipid, low-carbohydrate diet is "ketogenic" because it favors ~~their~~ formation.

Do not repeat an antecedent in parentheses following the pronoun. If you feel you must identify the pronoun's antecedent in this way, rewrite the sentence.

AWKWARD   The senior partner first met Bob Evans when he (Evans) was a trainee.

IMPROVED   Bob Evans was a trainee when the senior partner first met him.

Pronoun-Antecedent Agreement

A pronoun must agree, or correspond in form, with its antecedent in person, gender, and number.

Person

A pronoun must agree with its antecedent in person. For example, use either the third person or the second person. Don't mix them.

INCORRECT   *Employees* must sign the logbook when *you* enter a restricted area.

CORRECT   *Employees* must sign the logbook when *they* enter a restricted area.

CORRECT   *You* must sign the logbook when *you* enter a restricted area.

Gender

A pronoun must agree with its antecedent in gender.

▶   *Isabel* was wearing *her* identification badge, but *Tom* had to clip *his* on before they could pass the security guard.

Traditionally, a masculine pronoun was used to agree with antecedents that include both sexes, such as *everybody, nobody, one, person, someone,* or *student.*

However, because most people are sensitive to the implied sexual bias in such usage, it is better to use the following alternatives:

GENDER BIAS   *Everybody* completed *his* report on time.

FREE OF BIAS   *Everybody* completed *his or her* report on time.

FREE OF BIAS   *Everybody* completed a report on time.

Often, the best solution is to rewrite the sentence in the plural. Do not, however, resort to a plural pronoun when the antecedent is singular.

INCORRECT   *Everybody* completed *their* reports on time.

                [The antecedent, *Everybody*, is singular, but the pronoun, *their*, is plural.]

CORRECT   The *employees* completed *their* reports on time.

                [The antecedent, *employees*, is plural; the pronoun, *their*, is also plural.]

◆ *See also Sexist Language on pages 110–111 in Chapter 4, Revising the Draft.*

ESL TIPS	**Using Possessive Pronouns**

In many languages, possessive pronouns agree in number and gender with the nouns they modify. In English, however, possessive pronouns agree in number and gender with their antecedents. Check your writing carefully for agreement between a possessive pronoun and the word, phrase, or clause to which it refers.

▶ The *woman* bought *her* brother lunch.

▶ *Robert* sent *his* mother flowers on Mother's Day.

Number

A pronoun must agree with its antecedent in number.

▶ Although the typical *engine* runs well in moderate temperatures, ~~they~~ *it* often stall*s* in extreme cold.

In formal English, indefinite pronouns (*anybody, anyone, anything, each, either, everybody, everyone, everything, neither, nobody, none, no one, somebody, someone,* and *something*) are considered singular and must be referred to by singular pronouns.

INCORRECT   When *someone* has conducted research, *they* are likely to write an effective report.

You can use the following options for revision: (1) replace the plural pronoun with *he or she* or *his or her*; (2) make the antecedent plural; or (3) rewrite the sentence so that no problem of agreement exists.

CORRECT   When *someone* has conducted research, *he or she* is likely to write an effective report.

CORRECT   When *writers* have conducted research, *they* are likely to write an effective report.

CORRECT   A writer who has conducted research is likely to write an effective report.

Collective nouns may be singular or plural, depending on meaning.

CORRECT   The *staff* prepared *its* annual report.

[*Staff* refers to the group as a single unit.]

CORRECT   The *staff* returned to *their* offices after the meeting.

[*Staff* refers to members of the group as individuals.]

A compound antecedent joined by *or* or *nor* is singular when both elements are singular and plural when both are plural. If one of the antecedents is singular and the other plural, the pronoun agrees with the nearer antecedent.

CORRECT   Either the *receptionist* or the *secretaries* should go on *their* lunch breaks.

CORRECT   Either the *secretaries* or the *receptionist* should go on *his or her* lunch break.

A compound antecedent with its elements joined by *and* requires a plural pronoun.

CORRECT   The *architect* and the *designer* prepared *their* plans.

■ Adjectives and Adverbs

An adjective modifies or describes a noun or pronoun. An adverb modifies the action or condition expressed by a verb. An adverb may also modify an adjective, another adverb, or a clause.

Comparatives and Superlatives

The three degrees of comparison are called the *positive* (the basic form of the adjective or adverb), the *comparative* (showing comparison with one other item), and the *superlative* (showing comparison with two or more other items).

Most adjectives and adverbs in the positive form show the comparative form with the suffix *-er* for two items and the superlative form with the suffix *-est* for three or more items.

▶ The first report is *long*. [adjective in positive form]

▶ The second report is *longer*. [adjective in comparative form]

▶ The third report is *longest*. [adjective in superlative form]

▶ This copier is *fast*. [adverb in positive form]

▶ This copier is *faster* than the old one. [adverb in comparative form]

▶ This copier is the *fastest* of the three tested. [adverb in superlative form]

Many two-syllable adjectives and most three-syllable adjectives are preceded by the word *more* or *most* to form the comparative or the superlative.

▶ The new library is *more* impressive than the old one. It is the *most* impressive in the country.

Most adverbs with two or more syllables end in *-ly*, and most adverbs ending in *-ly* are compared by inserting the comparative *more* or *less* or the superlative *most* or *least* in front of them.

▶ Her sales rose *more quickly* last quarter than those of any other company's sales representative.

▶ *Most surprisingly*, the engine failed during the final test phase.

A few adjectives have irregular forms of comparison (*much, more, most; little, less, least*). A few irregular adverbs require a change in form to indicate comparison (*well, better, best; worse, worst; far, farther, farthest*).

Absolute words (such as *unique, perfect, exact,* and *infinite*) are not logically subject to comparison, especially in workplace writing, where accuracy and precision are often crucial.

                          closely
▶ We modified our mission statement to more ~~exactly~~ reflect our long-term goals.

Placement

Within a sentence, adjectives may appear before the nouns they modify (the attributive position) or after the nouns they modify (the predicative position).

▶ We negotiated a *bigger* contract than our competitor did.
   [attributive position]

▶ We negotiated a contract *bigger* than our competitor's.
   [predicative position]

Using Adjectives

In English, unlike many other languages, adjectives have only one form. Do not add *-s* or *-es* to an adjective to make it plural.

▶ the *long* letter
▶ the *long* letters

Likewise, adjectives in English do not change to show gender.

▶ The *tall* man (masculine noun)
▶ The *tall* woman (feminine noun)
▶ The *tall* building (neuter noun)

Capitalize adjectives of origin (city, state, nation, continent).

▶ the *Venetian* canals
▶ the *Texas* legislature
▶ the *French* government
▶ the *African* continent

In English, verbs of feeling (for example, *bore, interest, surprise*) have two adjectival forms: the present participle (*-ing*) and the past participle (*-ed*). Use the present participle to describe what causes the feeling. Use the past participle to describe the person who experiences the feeling.

▶ We heard the *surprising* election results.

[The *election results* cause the feeling of surprise.]

▶ Only the losing candidate was *surprised* by the election results.

[The *candidate* experienced the feeling of surprise.]

Adjectives follow the noun in English in only two cases: when the adjective functions as a subjective complement, as in:

▶ That project is not *finished*.

and when an adjective phrase or clause modifies the noun, as in:

▶ The project *that was suspended temporarily* has a new deadline.

In all other cases, adjectives are placed before the noun.

When there are multiple adjectives, the order illustrated in the following example would apply in most circumstances, with some exceptions. (Normally, do not use a phrase with so many stacked modifiers.)

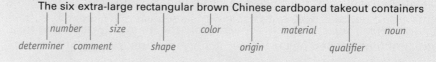

The six extra-large rectangular brown Chinese cardboard takeout containers

determiner | number | comment | size | shape | color | origin | material | qualifier | noun

An adjective is called a predicate adjective when it follows a linking verb, such as a form of the verb *to be*. By completing the meaning of a linking verb, a predicate adjective describes, or limits, the subject of the verb.

▶   The job is *easy*.

▶   The manager was very *demanding*.

An adjective also can follow a transitive verb and modify its direct object (the person or thing that receives the action of the verb).

▶   They painted the office *white*.

An adverb may appear almost anywhere in a sentence, but its position can affect meaning. Avoid placing an adverb between two verb forms where it will be ambiguous because it can be read as modifying either.

AMBIGUOUS   The man who was making calculations *hastily* rose from his desk and left the room.

[Did the man calculate hastily or did he rise hastily?]

IMPROVED   The man who was making calculations rose *hastily* from his desk and left the room.

IMPROVED   The man who was *hastily* making calculations rose from his desk and left the room.

■ Verbs

A verb is a word or group of words that describes an action (The copier *jammed* at the beginning of the job), states the way in which something or someone is affected by an action (He *was disappointed* that the proposal was rejected), or affirms a state of existence (She *is* a district manager now). This section focuses on those areas of verb usage that can cause inexperienced writers problems.

Subject-Verb Agreement

Agreement, grammatically, means the correspondence in form between different elements of a sentence. A verb must agree with its subject in person and number.

▶   *I am* going to approve his promotion.

[The first-person singular subject, *I*, requires the first-person singular form of the verb, *am*.]

▶   His *colleagues are* envious.

[The third-person plural subject, *colleagues*, requires the third-person plural form of the verb, *are*.]

Intervening Words

Subject-verb agreement is not affected by intervening phrases and clauses.

▶ *One* in twenty hard drives we receive from our suppliers *is* faulty.
   [The verb, *is*, must agree in number with the subject, *one*, not *hard drives* or *suppliers*.]

The same is true when nouns fall between a subject and its verb.

▶ Only *one* of the emergency lights *was* functioning.
   [The subject of the verb is *one*, not *lights*.]

▶ *Each* of the managers *supervises* a very large region.
   [The subject of the verb is *each*, not *managers*.]

Note that *one* and *each* are normally singular.
   Modifying phrases can obscure a single subject.

▶ The *advice* of two engineers, one lawyer, and three executives *was* obtained prior to making a commitment.
   [The subject of the sentence, *advice*, requires the single verb, *was*.]

Inverted Word Order

Inverted word order can confuse agreement between subject and verb.

▶ From this work *have come* several important *improvements*.
   [The subject of the verb is *improvements*, not *work*.]

Collective Subjects

Subjects expressing measurement, weight, mass, or total often take singular verbs even though the subject word is plural. Such subjects are treated as a unit.

▶ *Four years is* the normal duration of the apprenticeship program.

However, when such subjects refer to the individual items that make up the unit, a plural verb is required.

▶ If you're looking for oil, *three quarts are* on the shelf in the garage.

Similarly, collective subjects take singular verbs when the group is thought of as a unit. They take plural verbs when the individuals are thought of separately.

▶ The *committee is* holding its meeting on Thursday.

▶ The *majority are* opposed to delivering their reports at the meeting.

Compound Subjects

A compound subject is composed of two or more elements joined by a conjunction such as *and, or, nor, either . . . or,* or *neither . . . nor.* Usually, when the elements are connected by *and*, the subject is plural and requires a plural verb.

▶ *Chemistry and finance are* prerequisites for this position.

If the elements connected by *and* form a unit or refer to the same person, however, the subject is regarded as singular and takes a singular verb.

▶ Peaches and cream *is* his favorite dessert.
▶ His accountant and business partner *prepares* the tax forms.
  [His accountant is also his business partner.]

A compound subject joined by *or* or *nor* requires a singular verb with two singular elements and a plural verb with two plural elements.

▶ Neither the doctor nor the nurse *is* on duty.
▶ Neither the doctors nor the nurses *are* on duty.

A compound subject with a singular and a plural element joined by *or* or *nor* requires that the verb agree with the element closer to it.

▶ Neither the office manager nor the *accountants were* there.
▶ Neither the accountants nor the *office manager was* there.

Indefinite Pronouns

Indefinite pronouns such as *some, none, all, more,* and *most* may be singular or plural, depending on whether they are used with a mass noun (*Most* of the oil *has* been used) or with a count noun (*Most* of the drivers *know* why they are here). Mass nouns are singular, and count nouns are plural. Other words, such as *type, part, series,* and *portion*, take singular verbs even when they precede a phrase containing a plural noun.

◆ *See also Count and Mass Nouns on pages 636–637.*

▶ A *series* of meetings *was* held about the best way to market the new product.
▶ A large *portion* of most annual reports *is* devoted to promoting the corporate image.

Relative Pronouns

A relative pronoun (*who, which, that*) may take either a singular or a plural verb, depending on whether its antecedent is singular or plural.

▶ He is an *auditor* who *takes* work home at night.
▶ He is one of those *auditors* who *take* work home at night.

Singular Nouns Ending in *-s*

Some abstract nouns are singular in meaning though plural in form; examples include *mathematics*, *news*, *physics*, and *economics*.

▷ Textiles *is* an industry in need of import quotas.

▷ Statistics *is* a branch of mathematics that analyzes and interprets data based on samples and populations.

Some words, such as the plural *jeans* and *scissors*, cause special problems.

▷ The *scissors were* ordered last week.

[The subject is the plural *scissors*.]

▷ A *pair* of scissors *is* on order.

[The subject is the singular *pair*.]

Book Titles

A book with a plural title requires a singular verb.

▷ *Monetary Theories is* a useful source.

Subject Complements

A *subject complement* is a noun or an adjective in the predicate of a sentence following a linking verb. The number of a subject complement does not affect the number of the verb — the verb must always agree with the subject.

▷ The topic of his report *was* rivers.

[The subject of the sentence is *topic*, not *rivers*.]

Voice

In grammar, *voice* indicates the relation of the subject to the action of the verb. When the verb is in the *active voice*, the subject acts; when it is in the *passive voice*, the subject is acted on. Because the active voice is generally more direct, more concise, and easier for readers to understand, use the active voice in most cases.

The agency

▷ ~~It was~~ reported ~~by the agency~~ that the new model is defective.

Whether you use the active or the passive voice, be careful not to shift voices in a sentence.

identified it

▷ David Cohen corrected the inaccuracy as soon as ~~it was identified by~~ the editor.

◆ *For additional guidance on choosing between active and passive voice, see pages 102–103 in Chapter 4, Revising the Draft.*

he does not permit them
▶ The captain permits his crew to go ashore, but ~~they are not permitted~~ to go downtown.
                                                          ^

Mood

Mood in grammar indicates whether a verb is intended to make a statement or ask a question, give a command, or express a hypothetical possibility.

The *indicative mood* states a fact, gives an opinion, or asks a question.

▶ The setting *is* correct.
▶ *Is* the setting correct?

The *imperative mood* expresses a command, suggestion, request, or plea. In the imperative mood, the implied subject *you* is not expressed.

▶ *Install* the wiring today.
▶ Please *let* me know if I can help.

The *subjunctive mood* expresses something that is contrary to fact, conditional, hypothetical, or purely imaginative; it can also express a wish, a doubt, or a possibility. In the subjunctive mood, *were* is used instead of *was* in clauses that speculate about the present or future, and the base form (*be*) is used following certain verbs, such as *propose, request,* or *insist.*

▶ If we *were* to close the sale today, we would meet our monthly quota.
▶ The senior partner insisted that she *be* in charge of the project.

The most common use of the subjunctive mood is to express clearly that the writer considers a condition to be contrary to fact. If the condition is factual, use the indicative mood.

SUBJUNCTIVE   If I *were* president of the firm, I would change several hiring policies.

INDICATIVE   Although I *am* president of the firm, I don't control every aspect of its policies.

Do not shift haphazardly from one mood to another within a sentence; to do so makes the sentence unbalanced as well as ungrammatical.

INCORRECT   *Depress* the clutch first [imperative]; then you *should put* the truck in gear [indicative].

CORRECT   *Depress* the clutch first [imperative]; then *put* the truck in gear [imperative].

CORRECT   You *should depress* the clutch first [indicative]; then you *should put* the truck in gear [indicative].

ESL TIPS	Determining Mood

In written and especially in spoken English, there is an increasing tendency to use the indicative mood where the subjunctive traditionally has been used. Note the differences between traditional and contemporary usage in these examples:

Traditional (Formal) Use of the Subjunctive Mood

▷ I wish he *were* here now.

▷ If I *were* going to the conference, I would room with him.

▷ I requested that she *show* up on time.

Contemporary (Informal) Use of the Indicative Mood

▷ I wish he *was* here now.

▷ If I *was* going to the conference, I would room with him.

▷ I requested that she *shows* up on time.

As a nonnative speaker of English, you are faced with a choice: Do you use the subjunctive and, with some groups of people, sound sophisticated, intellectual, or even weird? Or, do you use the indicative and, with other groups, sound uneducated? The answer might be to master both uses and be able to move freely between the different groups. In business and technical writing, however, it is best to use the more traditional expressions.

Tense

Tense is the grammatical term for verb forms that indicate time distinctions. There are six simple tenses in English: past, past perfect, present, present perfect, future, and future perfect. Each tense also has a corresponding progressive form.

Tense	*Basic Form*	*Progressive Form*
Present	I start	I am starting
Present perfect	I have started	I have been starting
Past	I started	I was starting
Past perfect	I had started	I had been starting
Future	I will start	I will be starting
Future perfect	I will have started	I will have been starting

Use the *simple present tense* to represent action occurring in the present, without any indication of time duration (I *use* the calculator); to present actions or conditions that have no time restrictions (Water *boils* at 212°F); or to indicate habitual action (I *pass* the coffee shop every day). A general truth is always expressed in the present tense (Time *heals* all wounds). In addition, the present tense can be used as a "historical present" to make things that occurred in the past more vivid (Dow Jones *Reaches* a Record High).

Use the *present perfect tense* to describe something from the recent past that has a bearing on the present—a period of time before the present but after the simple past. The present perfect tense is formed by combining the present tense of the helping verb *have* with the past participle of the main verb (We *have finished* the draft and can now revise it).

To indicate an action that took place entirely in the past, use the *simple past tense*. The past tense is usually formed by adding *-d* or *-ed* to the root form of the verb (We *closed* the office early yesterday).

To indicate that one past event preceded another, use the *past perfect tense*, which is formed by combining the helping verb *had* with the past participle of the main verb (He *had finished* by the time I arrived).

ESL TIPS   ## Using the Progressive Form

English uses the progressive form, particularly the present progressive, more frequently than other languages do. The progressive form of the verb is composed of two features: a form of the helping verb *be* and the *-ing* form of the base verb.

PRESENT PROGRESSIVE   I *am updating* the Web site.

PAST PROGRESSIVE   I *was updating* the Web site last week.

FUTURE PROGRESSIVE   I *will be updating* the Web site regularly.

The present progressive is used in three ways:

1. To refer to an action that is in progress at the moment of speaking or writing
   ▶ My assistant *is taking* the meeting minutes.
2. To highlight that a state or action is not permanent
   ▶ The office temp *is helping* us for a few weeks.
3. To express future plans
   ▶ The summer intern *is leaving* to return to school this Friday.

The past progressive is used to refer to a continuing action or condition in the past, usually with specified limits.

▶ I *was failing* calculus until I got eyeglasses.

The future progressive is used to refer to a continuous action or condition in the future.

▶ We *will be monitoring* his condition all night.

Verbs that express mental activity or the senses of sight, smell, touch, sound, and taste are generally not used in the progressive.

▶ I *believe* the defendant's testimony.

Such verbs generally not used in the progressive include:

appear	forget	own	see
appreciate	have	prefer	seem
be	hear	recognize	sound
belong	know	remember	think
consist of	mean	represent	understand
contain	need	resemble	

Use the *simple future tense* to indicate a time that will occur after the present. The helping verb *will* (or *shall*) is used along with the main verb. (I *will finish* the job tomorrow.) Do not, however, use the future tense needlessly; doing so merely adds complexity.

▶ This system ~~will be~~ *is* explained on page 3.

▶ When you press this button, the feeder ~~will move~~ *moves* the paper into position.

Use the *future perfect tense* to indicate an action that will be completed at the time of or before another future action. It is formed by linking the helping verbs *will have* to the past participle of the main verb. (He *will have driven* 400 miles by the time he returns.)

Be consistent in your use of tense. The only legitimate shift in tense records a real change in time. Illogical shifts in tense will only confuse your readers.

▶ Before he visited the facility, the manager ~~meets~~ *met* with the staff.

Punctuation

Punctuation is a system of symbols that helps the reader to understand the intention of a sentence and the structural relationships within it. Misuse of punctuation can cause your reader to misunderstand your meaning. Marks of punctuation may link, separate, enclose, terminate, classify, and indicate omissions from sentences. Most of the 13 punctuation marks can perform more than one function. Their use is determined by grammatical conventions and by the writer's intention.

■ Commas

The *comma* (,) is used more than any other mark of punctuation because it has such a wide variety of uses: it can link, enclose, and separate. Used with care, the comma can clarify and emphasize how ideas fit together; used carelessly, it can cause confusion.

Linking Independent Clauses

Use a comma before a coordinating conjunction (*and, but, or, nor,* and sometimes *so, yet,* and *for*) that links independent clauses.

◆ *See also semicolons, page 612.*

▶ The new microwave disinfection system was delivered, *but* the installation will require an additional week.

However, if two independent clauses are short and closely related—and there is no danger of confusing the reader—the comma may be omitted. Both of the following examples are correct.

▶ The cable snapped and the power failed.
▶ The cable snapped, and the power failed.

Introducing Elements

Clauses and Phrases

Generally, place a comma after an introductory clause or phrase, especially if it is long, to identify where the introductory element ends and where the main part of the sentence begins.

▶ *Because we have not yet contained the new strain of influenza,* we recommend vaccination for high-risk patients.

A long modifying phrase that precedes the main clause should always be followed by a comma.

▶ *During the first series of field-performance tests at our Colorado proving ground,* the new engine failed to meet our expectations.

When an introductory phrase is short and closely related to the main clause, the comma may be omitted.

▶ *In two seconds* a 5°C temperature rise occurs in the test tube.

A comma should always follow an absolute phrase, which modifies the whole sentence.

▶ *The tests completed,* we organized the data for the final report.

Words

Certain types of introductory words are followed by a comma. One example is a transitional word or phrase (*however, in addition*) that connects the preceding clause or sentence with the thought that follows.

▶ *Furthermore,* steel can withstand a humidity of 99 percent, provided there is no chloride or sulfur dioxide in the atmosphere.

▶ *For example,* this change will make us more competitive in the marketplace.

When adverbs closely modify the verb or entire sentence, they should not be followed by a comma.

▶ *Perhaps* we can still solve the turnover problem. *Certainly* we should try.

A proper noun used in an introductory direct address is followed by a comma, as is an interjection (such as *oh, well, why, indeed, yes,* and *no*).

▶ *Nancy,* enclosed is the article you asked me to review. [direct address]

▶ *Indeed,* I will ensure that your request is forwarded. [interjection]

Quotations

Use a comma to separate a direct quotation from its introduction.

▶ Morton and Lucia White said, "People live in cities but dream of the countryside."

Do not use a comma when giving an indirect quotation.

▶ Morton and Lucia White said that people dream about country life, even though they live in cities.

◆ *See also Quotation Marks, pages 617–619, and Quoting from Your Sources, pages 174–176.*

Enclosing Elements

Use commas to enclose nonrestrictive and parenthetical sentence elements. Nonrestrictive elements add subordinate information about the things they modify; parenthetical elements also insert extra information into the sentence. Each is set off by commas to show its loose relationship with the rest of the sentence.

▶ Our new Detroit factory, *which began operations last month*, should add 25 percent to total output. [nonrestrictive clause]
▶ We can, *of course*, expect their lawyer to call us. [parenthetical element]

Similarly, enclose a nonrestrictive participial phrase (any form of a verb used as an adjective) within commas.

▶ The lathe operator, *working quickly and efficiently*, finished early.

In contrast, restrictive elements—as their name implies—restrict the meaning of the words to which they apply and cannot be set off with commas.

▶ The boy *in the front row* is six years old. [restrictive]
▶ The boy, *who is sitting in the front row*, is six years old. [nonrestrictive]

In the first sentence, *in the front row* is essential to the sentence: The phrase identifies the boy by his location. In the second sentence, the relative clause *who is sitting in the front row* is incidental: The main idea can be communicated without it.

An appositive phrase (which reidentifies another expression in the sentence) is enclosed in commas.

▶ Our company, *the Blaylok Precision Tool Company*, is doing well this year.

Separating Elements

Items in a Series

Although the comma before the last item in a series is sometimes omitted, it is generally clearer to include it.

▶ Random House, Bantam, Doubleday, and Dell were individual publishing companies before the industry's restructuring.

[Without the final comma, *Doubleday and Dell* might refer to one company or two.]

Phrases and clauses in coordinate series are also punctuated with commas.

▶ Plants absorb noxious gases, act as receptors of dirt particles, and cleanse the air of other impurities.

When phrases or clauses in a series contain commas, separate them with semi-colons.

▶ Our new products include amitriptyline, which has sold very well; dipyridamole, which has not sold well; and cholestyramine, which was just introduced.

Adjectives

When adjectives modifying the same noun can be reversed and make sense, or when they can be separated by *and* or *or*, they should be separated by commas.

▶ The drawing was of a *modern, sleek, swept-wing* airplane.

When an adjective modifies a phrase, no comma is required.

▶ She was investigating the *damaged inventory-control system.*

[The adjective *damaged* modifies the phrase *inventory-control system.*]

Never separate a final adjective from its noun.

▶ He is a conscientious, honest, reliable/worker. [omit comma]

Dates

A full date that is written in the month-day-year format uses a comma preceding and following the year.

▶ Note that November 30, 2015, is the payoff date for the bond.

◆ *See also Writing International Correspondence, pages 300–305.*

Do not use commas for dates in the day-month-year format, which is used in many parts of the world and by the U.S. military.

▶ Note that 30 November 2015 is the payoff date for the bond.

Do not use commas if only the day or the year is included.

▶ The target date of May 2009 is optimistic, so I would like to meet on March 4 to discuss our options.

Numbers

Use commas to separate the elements of Arabic numbers.

▶   1,528,200 bytes

However, because many countries use the comma as the decimal marker, use periods or spaces rather than commas in international documents.

▶   1.528.200 bytes *or* 1 528 200 bytes

Addresses

Commas are conventionally used to separate the elements of an address written on the same line (but they are not inserted between the state and the ZIP code).

▶   Kristen James, 4119 Mill Road, Dayton, Ohio 45401

Use commas to separate elements of geographic names.

▶   Toronto, Ontario, Canada

Names

Use a comma to separate names that are reversed or that are followed by an abbreviation of an earned title, such as Ph.D., M.D., and C.P.A.

▶   Smith, Alvin
▶   Jane Rogers, Ph.D.

In current usage, however, no comma is necessary before abbreviations of personal and corporate names (such as Jr., Sr., and Inc.).

▶   Ray Aragon Jr.
▶   Grace Inc.

Using Commas with Other Punctuation

When a comma should follow a phrase or clause that ends with words in parentheses, the comma always appears outside the closing parenthesis.

▶   Although we left late (at 7:30 p.m.), we arrived in time for the keynote address.

Commas always go inside quotation marks.

▶   The operator placed the discharge bypass switch at "normal," which triggered a second discharge.

A comma should not be used with a dash, an exclamation mark, a period, or a question mark.

▶ "Have you finished the project?/" I asked.

Avoiding Unnecessary Commas

Writers often add commas where they do not belong because they assume that a pause should be indicated by a comma. It is true that commas usually signal pauses, but it is not true that pauses *necessarily* call for commas.

Be careful not to place a comma between a subject and its verb or between a verb and its object.

▶ The wet weather across the region/makes spring planting difficult. [omit comma]
▶ The firm employs/four writers, two artists, and one photographer. [omit comma]

Do not use a comma between the elements of a compound subject or a compound predicate consisting of only two elements.

▶ The chairman of the board/and the president prepared the press release. [omit comma]
▶ The manager revised the schedules/and improved morale. [omit comma]

Placing a comma after a coordinating conjunction (*and, but, for, nor, or, so, yet*) is an especially common error.

▶ We doubled our sales, but/we still did not dominate the market. [omit comma]

Do not place a comma before the first item or after the last item of a series.

▶ We purchased new office furniture, including/desks, chairs, and tables. [omit comma]

Except with abbreviations, a comma should not be used with a period, a question mark, an exclamation mark, or a dash.

▶ "I have finished the project,/." he said. [omit period]
▶ "Have you finished the project?/," I asked. [omit comma]

◼ Semicolons

The *semicolon* (;) links independent clauses or other sentence elements that are of equal weight and grammatical rank. The semicolon indicates a longer pause than a comma would, but not so long a pause as a period would.

Two closely related independent clauses can be linked by a semicolon.

▶   No one applied for the position; the job was too difficult.

The relationship between the two statements should be so clear that a reader will understand why they are linked without further explanation. Often, such clauses balance or contrast with each other.

▶   Our last supervisor allowed only one long break; our new supervisor allows two short ones.

Use a semicolon between two main clauses connected by a coordinating conjunction (*and, but, for, or, nor, yet, so*) if the clauses are long and contain other punctuation.

▶   In most cases these individuals are corporate executives, bankers, or Wall Street lawyers; but they do not, as the economic determinists seem to believe, simply push the button of their economic power to affect fields remote from economics.

A semicolon should be used before conjunctive adverbs (such as *therefore, moreover, furthermore, indeed, in fact, however*) that connect independent clauses.

▶   I won't finish today; moreover, I doubt that I will finish this week.

Do not use a semicolon between a dependent clause and its main clause. Elements joined by semicolons must be of equal grammatical rank or weight.

▶   No one applied for the position; even though it was heavily advertised.

■ Colons

The *colon* (:) is a mark of anticipation and introduction that alerts the reader to the close connection between the first statement and the one following.

▶   We carry three brands of watches: Timex, Bulova, and Omega.

Do not, however, place a colon between a verb and its objects.

▶   The three fluids for cleaning pipettes are: water, alcohol, and acetone. [omit colon]

Do not use a colon between a preposition and its object.

▶   I would like to be transferred to: Tucson, Boston, or Miami. [omit colon]

A colon can link one statement to another that develops, explains, amplifies, or illustrates the first, including two independent clauses.

▶ Any large organization must confront two separate, though related, information problems: It must maintain an effective internal communication system, and it must maintain an effective external communication system.

Occasionally, a colon may be used to link an appositive phrase to its related statement if special emphasis is needed.

▶ Only one thing will satisfy Mr. Sturgess: our finished report.

Colons separate sections of works in citations and time designations.

▶ Genesis 10:16 [refers to chapter 10, verse 16]
▶ 9:30 a.m.

In a ratio, the colon indicates the proportion of one amount to another. (The colon replaces *to*.)

▶ The cement is mixed with the water and sand at a ratio of 7:5:14.

A colon follows the salutation in business correspondence, even when the salutation refers to a person by first name.

▶ Dear Ms. Jeffers:

The first word after a colon may be capitalized if it begins a complete sentence, a formal resolution or question, or a direct quotation.

▶ The conference attendance was low: We did not advertise widely enough.

Begin a subordinate element following a colon with a lowercase letter.

▶ We have only one way to stay within our present budget: to reduce expenditures for research and development.

▪ Apostrophes

An *apostrophe* (') is used to show possession; to mark the omission of letters; and sometimes to indicate the plural of numbers, letters, and acronyms.

Showing Possession

A noun or pronoun is in the possessive case when it represents a person, place, or thing that possesses something. Possession is generally expressed with *'s* (the *report's* title), with a prepositional phrase using *of* (the title *of the report*), or with the possessive form of a pronoun (*our* report). Practices vary for some possessive forms, but the following guidelines are widely used in business writing. Above all, be consistent.

◆ *See also Pronoun Case, pages 591–593.*

Singular Nouns

Most singular nouns indicate possession with *'s*.

▶ a *manager's* office
▶ an *employee's* job satisfaction
▶ the *company's* stock value
▶ the *witness's* testimony
▶ the *bus's* schedule

When pronunciation is difficult or when a multisyllable noun ends in a *z* sound, you may use only an apostrophe.

▶ *New Orleans'* levee reconstruction plans

Plural Nouns

Plural nouns that end in *-s* or *-es* show the possessive case with only an apostrophe.

▶ the *managers'* reports
▶ the *employees'* paychecks
▶ the *companies'* joint project
▶ the *witnesses'* reports
▶ the *buses'* schedules

Plural nouns that do not end in *-s* or *-es* show the possession with *'s*.

▶ *children's* clothing
▶ *women's* resources
▶ *men's* room

Compound Nouns

Compound nouns form the possessive with *'s* following the final letter.

▶ the *vice president's* proposal

▶ the *editor-in-chief's* desk

Plurals of some compound expressions are often best expressed with a prepositional phrase (presentations of the *editors-in-chief*).

Coordinate Nouns

Coordinate nouns show joint possession with *'s* following the last noun.

▶ *Fischer and Goulet's* partnership was the foundation of their business.

Coordinate nouns show individual possession with *'s* following each noun.

▶ The difference between *Barker's* and *Washburne's* test results was statistically insignificant.

Possessive Pronouns

The possessive pronouns (*yours, its, his, her, ours, whose, theirs*) do not require apostrophes. (Even good systems have *their* flaws.) *Its* is a possessive pronoun and does not use an apostrophe; *it's* is a contraction of *it is* and does not show possession.

▶ *It's* important that the sales department meet *its* quota.

ESL TIPS   **Indicating Possession**

English expresses possession in two ways: apostrophe *s* (*'s*) and *of*.

Use *'s* with personal names, personal nouns, collective nouns, and animals. (Use just an apostrophe for plural nouns that end with *s*.)

▶ *Joan's* class
▶ the *secretary's* lunch hour
▶ the *government's* pension plan
▶ the *dog's* tail
▶ the *employees'* stock portfolios

You can also use *'s* (or just an apostrophe) with some inanimate nouns: geographical and institutional names, nouns that refer to time, and nouns of special interest to human activity.

▶ the *company's* investors
▶ *today's* agenda
▶ a *week's* rest
▶ *business'* influence on politics

Use *of* with inanimate objects and measurements.

▶ the title *of* the monthly report
▶ a cup *of* coffee
▶ the length *of* the memo

Indicating Omission

An apostrophe is used to mark the omission of letters or numbers in a contraction or a date (*can't, I'm, I'll*; the class of *'06*, the crash of *'29*.) Although this usage is in no sense wrong, it is less formal than the longer forms and should be applied sparingly in business and professional writing.

Forming Plurals

An apostrophe can be used in forming the plurals of letters, words, or lowercase abbreviations if confusion might result from using *s* alone.

▶ The search program does not find *a*'s and *i*'s.

▶ *I*'s need to be distinguished from the number 1.

▶ Check for any *c.o.d.'s*.

Generally, however, add only *s* (in roman type) when referring to words as words or capital letters (which should be set in italics).

▶ Five *and*s appear in the first sentence.

▶ The applicants received *A*s and *B*s in their courses.

Do not use an apostrophe for plurals of abbreviations with all capital letters (DVDs) or a final capital letter (ten Ph.D.s) or for plurals of numbers (7s, the late 1990s).

■ Quotation Marks

Quotation marks (" ") are used to enclose direct repetition of spoken or written words. Quotation marks have other special uses, but they should not be used for emphasis.

◆ *For tips on achieving emphasis, see Chapter 4, pages 101–106.*

Identifying Quotations

Enclose in quotation marks anything that is quoted word for word (a direct quotation) from speech or written material.

▶ She said clearly, "I want the progress report before three o'clock."

Do not enclose indirect quotations—usually introduced by the word *that*—in quotation marks. Indirect quotations paraphrase a speaker's words or ideas.

◆ *See also Paraphrasing, pages 176–177.*

▶ She said that she wanted a copy of the progress report by three.

◆ *For further informa-tion on incorporating quoted material and inserting comments, see Avoiding Plagiarism and Copyright Viola-tions, pages 178–179; Quoting from Your Sources, pages 174–176; Brackets, pages 621–622; and Ellipses, pages 625–626.*

Material quoted directly and enclosed in quotation marks cannot be changed from the original unless you show the change in brackets.

Use single quotation marks (' ') to enclose a quotation that appears within another quotation.

▶   John said, "Jane told me that she would 'hang in there' until the deadline."

Setting Off Words, Phrases, and Titles

Words and Phrases

Use quotation marks to set off special words or terms only to point out that the term is used in context for a unique or special purpose (that is, in the sense of the term *so-called*).

▶   A remarkable chain of events caused the sinking of the "unsinkable" *Titanic* on its maiden voyage.

Slang, colloquial expressions, and attempts at humor, although infrequent in workplace writing, should not be set off by quotation marks unless they indicate a direct quote.

▶   Our first six months in the new office amounted to little more than a ⸢shakedown cruise⸣ for what lay ahead. [omit quotation marks]

Titles of Works

◆ *See also Italics, pages 633–635.*

Use quotation marks to enclose titles of short stories, articles, essays, chapters of books, radio and television programs, and songs. However, do not use quotation marks for titles of books and periodicals, which should appear in italics.

▶   Did you see the article "No-Fault Insurance and Your Motorcycle" in last Friday's *Wall Street Journal?*

Using Quotation Marks with Other Punctuation

Commas and periods always go inside closing quotation marks.

▶   "We hope," said Ms. Abrams, "that the merger will be announced this week."

Semicolons and colons always go outside closing quotation marks.

▶   He said, "I will pay the full amount"; this was a real surprise to us.

◆ *See also use of quotation marks with question marks, page 620.*

All other punctuation follows the logic of the context: If the punctuation is part of the material quoted, it goes inside the quotation marks; if the punctuation is not part of the material quoted, it goes outside the quotation marks.

ESL TIPS	**Using Quotation Marks with Other Punctuation**

The use of quotation marks and other punctuation in North American English differs from usage in some languages.

Style of quotation marks

▶ "exceptional" not „exceptional" or <<exceptional>>

Comma inside closing quotation mark

▶ "as a last resort," *not* "as a last resort",

Period inside closing quotation mark

▶ "to the bitter end." *not* "to the bitter end".

Semicolon or colon outside closing quotation mark

▶ "there is no doubt"; *not* "there is no doubt;"

■ Periods

A *period* (.) usually indicates the end of a declarative or an imperative sentence. Periods may also end questions that are actually polite requests and questions to which an affirmative response is assumed. (Will you please send me the financial statement.)

Use a comma, not a period, after a declarative sentence that is quoted in the context of another sentence.

▶ "The project has every chance of success," she stated.

A period is, by convention, placed inside quotation marks.

▶ He stated clearly, "My vote is yes."

◆ *See also Quotation Marks, pages 617–619 and Quoting from Your Sources, pages 174–176.*

If a sentence ends with an item in parentheses, the period should follow the end parenthesis.

▶ The institute was founded by Harry Denman (1902–1972).

When a complete sentence within parentheses stands independently, however, the end punctuation goes inside the final parenthesis.

▶ The project director listed the problems her staff faced. (This was the third time she had complained to the board.)

When a sentence ends with an abbreviation that ends with a period, do not add another period.

▶ Please meet me at 3:30 p.m.

■ Question Marks

The *question mark* (?) has several uses, but most often ends a sentence that is a direct question or request.

▶ Where did you put the tax report?

▶ Will you e-mail me if your shipment does not arrive by June 10?

Use a question mark to end a statement that has an interrogative meaning—a statement that is declarative in form but asks a question. (The tax report is finished?)

Question marks may follow a series of separate items within an interrogative sentence.

▶ Do you remember the date of the contract? Its terms? Whether you signed it?

Use a question mark to end an interrogative clause within a declarative sentence.

▶ It was not until July (or was it August?) that we submitted the report.

Retain the question mark in a title that is being cited, even if the sentence in which it appears has not ended.

▶ *Can Investments Be Protected?* is the title of her book.

Never use a question mark to end a sentence that is an indirect question.

◆ *See also Periods, pages 619–620.*

▶ He asked me where I put the tax report.

When used with quotations, the placement of the question mark is important. If the writer is asking a question, the question mark belongs outside the quotation marks.

▶ Did she say, "I don't think the project should continue"?

If the quotation itself is a question, the question mark goes inside the quotation marks.

◆ *See also Quoting from Your Sources, pages 174–176 in Chapter 6, Researching Your Subject.*

▶ She asked, "Do we have enough funding?"

If both cases apply—the writer is asking a question and the quotation itself is a question—use a single question mark inside the quotation marks.

▶ Did she ask, "Do we have enough funding?"

■ Exclamation Marks

The *exclamation mark* (!) indicates strong feeling, urgency, elation, or surprise (*Hurry! Great! Wow!*). However, it cannot make an argument more convincing, lend force to a weak statement, or call attention to an intended irony.

An exclamation mark can be used after a whole sentence or an element of a sentence.

▶   This meeting—please note it well!—concerns our budget deficit.

When used with quotation marks, the exclamation mark goes outside, unless what is quoted is an exclamation.

▶   The manager yelled, "Get in here!" Then Ben, according to Ray, "jumped like a kangaroo"!

In instructional writing, the exclamation mark is often used in cautions and warnings (*Danger! Stop!*).

■ Parentheses and Brackets

Parentheses (( )) and *brackets* ([ ]) are used to enclose explanatory or digressive words, phrases, or sentences.

Material in parentheses often clarifies or defines the preceding text without altering its meaning.

▶   She severely bruised her shin (or *tibia*) in the accident.

Parentheses are also used to enclose numerals or letters that indicate sequence.

▶   The following sections deal with (1) preparation, (2) research, (3) organization, (4) writing, and (5) revision.

The primary use of brackets is to enclose a word or words inserted by the writer or an editor into a quotation.

▶   The text stated, "Hypertext systems can be categorized as either modest [not modifiable] or robust [modifiable]."

Use brackets to set off a parenthetical item that is already within parentheses.

▶   We should be sure to give Emanuel Foose (and his brother Emilio [1812–1882]) credit for his part in founding the institute.

Parenthetical material does not affect the punctuation of a sentence. If a parenthesis or bracket appears at the end of a sentence, the ending punctuation should appear after the parenthesis or bracket. Likewise, a comma following a parenthetical word, phrase, or clause appears outside the closing parenthesis or bracket.

▶   She severely bruised her shin (or *tibia*), and he tore the cartilage (or *meniscus*) in his knee.

When a complete sentence within parentheses stands independently, however, the ending punctuation goes inside the final parenthesis.

▶   The project director listed the problems her staff faced. (This was the third time she had complained to the board.)

■ Hyphens

The *hyphen* (-) serves both to link and to separate words. The hyphen, for example, joins compound words (able-bodied, self-contained, self-esteem), forms compound numbers from twenty-one through ninety-nine, and divides fractions when they are written out (three-quarters).

Linking Modifiers

Two- and three-word modifiers that express a single thought are hyphenated when they precede a noun.

▶   It was a *well-written* report.

However, a modifying phrase is not hyphenated when it follows the noun it modifies.

▶   The report was *well written.*

If each of the words can modify the noun without the aid of the other modifying word or words, do not use a hyphen.

▶   a *new laser* printer

If the first word is an adverb ending in -*ly*, do not use a hyphen.

▶   a *privately* held company

A hyphen is always used as part of a letter or number modifier.

▶   9-inch, A-frame

In a series of unit modifiers that all have the same term following the hyphen, the term following the hyphen need not be repeated throughout the series; for greater smoothness and brevity, use the term only at the end of the series.

▶   The third-, fourth-, and fifth-floor rooms were recently painted.

Separating Prefixes and Suffixes

When a prefix precedes a proper noun, use a hyphen to connect the two.

▶   pre-Internet
▶   anti-Stalinist
▶   post-Newtonian

A hyphen may (but does not have to) be used when the prefix ends and the root word begins with the same vowel. When the repeated vowel is *i*, a hyphen is almost always used.

▶   re-elect
▶   re-enter
▶   anti-inflationary

A hyphen is used when *ex-* means "former."

▶   ex-partners
▶   ex-wife

The suffix -*elect* is connected to the word it follows with a hyphen.

▶   president-elect
▶   commissioner-elect

Hyphens identify prefixes, suffixes, or syllables written as such.

▶   *Re-*, -*ism*, and *ex-* are word parts that cause spelling problems.

Other Uses

Hyphens separate letters showing spelling (or misspelling).

▶ In his letter, he spelled "believed" b-e-l-e-i-v-e-d.

To avoid confusion, some words and modifiers should always be hyphenated. *Re-cover* does not mean the same thing as *recover*, for example; the same is true of *re-sent* and *resent*, *re-form* and *reform*, *re-sign* and *resign*.

A hyphen can stand for *to* or *through* between letters, numbers, and locations.

▶ pp. 44-46
▶ The Detroit-Toledo Expressway
▶ A-L and M-Z

Hyphens are also used to divide words at the end of a line. Avoid dividing words if possible; however, if you must divide them, consult a dictionary.

■ Dashes

The *dash* (—) is a versatile, yet limited, mark of punctuation. It is versatile because it can perform all the functions of punctuation (to link, to separate, to enclose, and to show omission). It is limited because it is especially emphatic and easily overused. Use the dash cautiously, therefore, to indicate more informality, emphasis, or abruptness than the conventional marks would show. In some situations, a dash is required; in others, a dash is a forceful substitute for other marks.

A dash can indicate a sharp turn in thought.

▶ That is the end of the project—unless the company provides additional funds.

A dash can indicate an emphatic pause.

▶ The project will begin—after we are under contract.

Sometimes, to emphasize contrast, a dash is also used with *but*.

▶ We completed the survey quickly—but the results were not accurate.

A dash can be used before a final summarizing statement or before repetition that has the effect of an afterthought.

▶ It was hot near the ovens—steaming hot.

A dash can be used to set off an explanatory or appositive series.

▶ Three of the applicants—John Evans, Mary Stevens, and Thomas Brown—seem well qualified for the job.

Dashes set off parenthetical elements more sharply and emphatically than commas or parentheses, which tend to reduce the importance of what they enclose. Contrast the following sentences.

▶ Only one person—the president—can authorize such activity.
▶ Only one person, the president, can authorize such activity.
▶ Only one person (the president) can authorize such activity.

Use dashes for clarity when commas appear within a parenthetical element.

▶ Retinal images are patterns in the eye—made up of light and dark shapes, in addition to areas of color—but we do not see patterns; we see objects.

The first word after a dash is never capitalized unless it is a proper noun. When keying in the dash, use two consecutive hyphens (--), with no spaces before or after the hyphens.

■ Ellipses

An *ellipsis* is the omission of words from quoted material; it is indicated by three spaced periods called *ellipsis points* (. . .). When you use ellipsis points, omit marks of internal punctuation at the point of omission, unless they are necessary for clarity or the omitted material comes at the end of a quoted sentence.

| ORIGINAL TEXT | Promotional material is sometimes charged for, particularly in high volume distribution to schools, although prices for these publications are much lower than the development costs when all factors are considered. |
| WITH OMISSION AND ELLIPSIS POINTS | Promotional material is sometimes charged for . . . although prices for these publications are much lower than the development costs. . . . |

Notice that the final period is retained and what remains of the quotation is grammatically complete.

When the omitted part of the quotation is preceded by a period, retain the period and add the three ellipsis points after it.

| ORIGINAL TEXT | Of the 172 major ethics cases reported, 57 percent were found to involve unsubstantiated concerns. Misinformation was the cause of unfounded concerns of misconduct in 72 cases. |
| WITH OMISSION AND ELLIPSIS POINTS | Of the 172 major ethics cases reported, 57 percent were found to involve unsubstantiated concerns. . . . |

◆ *See also Quoting from Your Sources, pages 174–176 in Chapter 6, Researching Your Subject.*

Do not use ellipsis points when the beginning of a quoted sentence is omitted.

▶ The ethics report states that "26 percent of the total cases reported involved incidents partly substantiated by ethics officers as serious misconduct."

▣ Slashes

The *slash* (/)—called a variety of names, including *slant line, diagonal, virgule, bar,* and *solidus*—both separates and shows omission.

The forward slash (/) is often used to separate items in the URL (uniform resource locator) addresses for sites on the Internet (<bedfordstmartins.com/writingthatworks>). The backward slash (\) is used to separate parts of file names (c:\myfiles\reports\annual07.doc).

The slash can indicate alternatives or combinations.

▶ David's telephone numbers are (333) 549-2278/2235.

▶ Check the on/off switch before you leave.

The slash often indicates omitted words and letters.

▶ miles/hour (miles per hour)

▶ w/o (without)

In fractions and mathematical expressions, the slash separates the numerator from the denominator (3/4 for three-fourths; x/y for x over y).

Although the slash is used informally with dates (5/11/08), do not use this form in international communications because many countries in Europe reverse the day/month order using this system. Thus, 5/11/08 would mean November 5, 2008, rather than May 11, 2008.

Mechanics

Certain mechanical questions tend to confound the writer on the job. Such questions as whether a number should be written as a word or figure, how acronyms should be used, whether a date should be stated day-month-year or month-day-year, and many others frequently arise when you are writing a letter or report. This section will help you answer these and other perplexing questions.

■ Capitalization

The use of capital, or uppercase, letters is determined by custom. Capital letters are used to call attention to certain words, such as proper nouns and the first word of a sentence. Use them carefully, especially when they affect a word's meaning (march/March, china/China, turkey/Turkey).

Proper Nouns

Proper nouns name specific persons, places, things, concepts, or qualities and are capitalized (Business Writing 205, Microsoft, Pat Wilde, Peru).

Common Nouns

Common nouns name general classes or categories of people, places, things, concepts, or qualities rather than specific ones and are not capitalized (business writing, company, person, country).

First Words

The first letter of the first word in a sentence is always capitalized. (Of the plans submitted, ours is best.) The first word after a colon is capitalized when the colon introduces an independent clause or a complete sentence.

▶ The meeting will address only one issue: What is the firm's role in environmental protection?

If the colon introduces a list or an appositive (a word or phrase that renames something else in the sentence, as in the following example), use a lowercase letter following the colon.

▸ We kept working for one reason: the approaching deadline.

The first word of a complete sentence in quotation marks is capitalized.

▸ Peter Drucker said, "The most important thing in communication is to hear what isn't being said."

The first word of a complete sentence enclosed in dashes, brackets, or parentheses is not capitalized when it appears as part of another sentence.

▸ We must make an extra effort in safety this year (accidents last year were up 10 percent).

Specific Groups

Capitalize the names of ethnic groups, religions, and nationalities (Native American, Christianity, Mongolian). Do not capitalize the names of social and economic groups (middle class, working class, unemployed).

Specific Places

Capitalize the names of all political divisions (Ward Six, Chicago, Cook County, Illinois). Capitalize the names of geographical divisions (Europe, Asia, North America, the Middle East). Do not capitalize geographic features unless they are part of a proper name.

▸ The mountains in some areas, such as the *Great Smoky Mountains*, make cell phone reception difficult.

The words *north*, *south*, *east*, and *west* are capitalized when they refer to sections of the United States. They are not capitalized when they refer to directions.

▸ I may travel *north* when I relocate, but my family will remain in the *South*.

Specific Institutions, Events, Concepts

Capitalize the names of institutions, organizations, and associations (U.S. Department of Health and Human Services). An organization usually capitalizes the names of its internal divisions and departments (Aeronautics Division, Human Resources). Types of organizations are not capitalized unless they are part of an official name (a business communication association; Association for Business Communication). Capitalize historic events (the Great Depression of the 1930s). Capitalize words that designate holidays, specific eras, months, or days of the week (Labor Day, the Renaissance, January, Monday). Do not capitalize seasons of the year (spring, autumn, winter, summer).

Titles of Works

Capitalize the initial letters of the first and last words of the title of a book, an article, a play, or a film, as well as all major words in the title. Do not capitalize articles (*a, an, the*), coordinating conjunctions (*and, but, for, or, nor, yet,* so), unless they begin or end the title (*The Lives of a Cell*). Capitalize prepositions within titles only when they contain more than four letters (*Between, Within, Until, After*), unless you are following a style that recommends otherwise. The same rules apply to the subject line of an e-mail message or a memo.

Professional and Personal Titles

Titles preceding proper names are capitalized (Ms. Berger, Senator McCain). Appositives following proper names normally are not capitalized (John McCain, *senator* from Arizona). However, the word *President* is capitalized when it refers to the chief executive of a national government.

Job titles used with personal names are capitalized (Ho-shik Kim, *Division Manager*). Job titles used without personal names are not capitalized (The *division manager* will meet us tomorrow).

Use capital letters to designate family relationships only when they occur before a name (my uncle; Uncle Fred).

Abbreviations, Letters, and Units

Capitalize abbreviations if the words they stand for would be capitalized, such as M.B.A. (Master of Business Administration). Also capitalize the following:

- Letters that serve as names or indicate shapes (vitamin B, T-square, U-turn, I-beam)
- Certain units, such as parts and chapters of books and rooms in buildings, when specifically identified by number (Chapter 5, Ch. 5; Room 72, Rm. 72)

Minor divisions within such units are not capitalized unless they begin a sentence (page 11, verse 14, seat 12).

■ Numbers

The standards for how to express numbers in workplace writing vary; however, unless you are following an organizational or a professional style manual, observe the following guidelines.

Words or Figures

Write numbers from zero to ten as words, and write numbers above ten as figures.

▷ I rehearsed my presentation *three* times.

▷ The meeting was attended by *150* people.

Do not follow a word representing a number with a numeral in parentheses that represents the same number. Doing so is redundant.

▷ Send five ~~(5)~~ copies of the report.

Spell out numbers that begin a sentence, even if they would otherwise be written as figures. If spelling out such a number seems awkward, rewrite the sentence so that the number does not appear at the beginning.

▷ *Last month, 273*
  ~~Two hundred seventy-three~~ defective products were returned ~~last month.~~

Spell out approximate and round numbers.

▷ We've had *over a thousand* requests this month.

In most writing, spell out ordinal numbers, which express degree or sequence (first, second; but 27th, 42nd) when they are single words (our *third* draft) or when they modify a century (the *twenty-first* century). However, avoid ordinal numbers in dates on correspondence (use March 30 or 30 March, not March 30th).

In general, use figures to express exact amounts of money. (We charge $28.95 per unit.) Use words to express indefinite amounts of money. (The printing system may cost several thousand dollars.) Use figures and words for rounded amounts of money over one million dollars; use figures alone for more complex or exact amounts.

▷ The contract is worth $6.8 million.

▷ The corporation paid $2,452,500 in taxes last year.

When several numbers appear in the same sentence or paragraph, write them the same way, regardless of other rules and guidelines.

▷ The company employs *271* people, leases *7* warehouses, and owns *150* trucks.

Plurals

Indicate the plurals of numerals by adding -*s* (7s, the late 1990s). Form the plural of a written number (like any noun) by adding -*s* or -*es* or by dropping -*y* and adding -*ies* (elevens, sixes, twenties).

Measurements

Express units of measurement as numerals (3 miles, 45 cubic feet, 9 meters). When numbers run together in the same phrase, write one as a numeral and the other as a word.

twelve

▷ The order was for ~~12~~ *twelve* 6-inch pipes.

Generally give percentages as numerals and write out the word *percent*, except when the number is in a visual, like a figure or table. (Approximately *85 percent* of the land has been sold.)

Express fractions as numerals when they are combined with whole numbers (27 1/2 inches, 4 1/4 miles). Spell out fractions when they are expressed without a whole number (one-fourth, seven-eighths). Always write decimal numbers as numerals (5.21 meters).

Time and Dates

Express hours and minutes as figures when a.m. or p.m. follows (11:30 a.m., 7:30 p.m.). Spell out time that is not followed by a.m. or p.m. (four o'clock, eleven o'clock).

In the United States, dates are usually written in a month-day-year sequence (August 11, 2007). Never use the strictly numerical form for dates (8/11/07) in business writing because the date is not always immediately clear, especially in international correspondence.

ESL TIPS **Punctuating Numbers**

Some rules for punctuating numbers in American English are summarized as follows.

Use a comma to separate numbers with four or more digits into groups of three, starting from the right.

▷ 2,500
▷ 57,890 cubic feet
▷ $187,291

Do not use a comma in years, house numbers, ZIP codes, and page numbers.

▷ June *2005*
▷ *92401* East Alameda Drive
▷ The ZIP code is *91601*
▷ Page *1204*

Use a period to represent the decimal point (*4.2* percent; *$3,742,097.43*).

Addresses

Spell out numbered streets from one to ten unless space is at a premium (East Tenth Street). Write building numbers as numerals. The only exception is the building number *one* (4862 East Monument Street; One East Monument Street). Write highway numbers as numerals (U.S. 40, Ohio 271, I-94).

Documents

In manuscripts, page numbers are written as numerals, but chapter and volume numbers may appear as numerals or as words (page 37, Chapter 2 or Chapter Two, Volume 1 or Volume One). Express figure and table numbers as numerals (Figure 4 and Table 3).

■ Abbreviations

Abbreviations are shortened versions of words or combinations of the first letters of words (Corp./Corporation, URL/*u*niform *r*esource *l*ocator). Abbreviations that combine the first letter or letters of several words—and can be pronounced as words—are called *acronyms* (PIN/*p*ersonal *i*dentification *n*umber, laser/*l*ight *a*mplification by *s*timulated *e*mission of *r*adiation). Abbreviations and acronyms, if used appropriately, can be convenient for both the writer and the reader. Like symbols, they can be important space savers in business writing.

The most important consideration in the use of abbreviations and acronyms is whether they will be understood by your readers. Even the same abbreviation, for example, can have several different meanings (NEA stands for both the National Education Association and the National Endowment for the Arts in the United States; British readers would associate it with the Nuclear Energy Association). In business, industry, and government, specialists and people working together on particular projects often use abbreviations. Shortened forms will be easily understood within a group of specialists; outside of the group, however, they might be incomprehensible. Remember that memos, e-mail messages, or reports addressed to specific people may be read by other people—you must consider those secondary readers as well. A good rule to follow: When in doubt, spell it out.

Names of Organizations

A company may include in its name a term such as *Brothers*, *Incorporated*, *Corporation*, or *Company*. If the term is abbreviated in the official company name that appears on letterhead stationery or on its Web site, use the abbreviated form: *Bros.*, *Inc.*, *Corp.*, or *Co.* If the term is not abbreviated in the official name, spell it out in writing, except with addresses, footnotes, bibliographies, and lists where abbreviations may be used. Likewise, use an ampersand (&) only if it appears in the official company name. For names of divisions within organizations, terms such as *Department* and *Division* should be abbreviated (*Dept., Div.*) only when space is limited.

Measurements

Except for abbreviations that may be confused with words (*in.* for *inch* and *gal.* for *gallon*), abbreviations of measurement do not require periods (*yd* for *yard* and *qt* for *quart*). Abbreviations of units of measure are identical in the singular and plural: 1 *cm* and 15 *cm* (*not* 15 *cms*). Some abbreviations can be used in combination with other symbols (°*F* for *degrees Fahrenheit* and *ft*² for *square feet*).

The following list includes abbreviations for the basic units of the International System of Units (SI), the metric system. This system not only is standard in science but also is used in international commerce and trade.

Measurement	Unit	Abbreviation
length	meter	m
mass	kilogram	kg
time	second	s
electric current	ampere	A
thermodynamic temperature	kelvin	K
amount of substance	mole	mol
luminous intensity	candela	cd

ON THE WEB

For additional definitions and background, see the National Institute of Standards and Technology Web site at <http://physics.nist.gov/cuu/Units/units.html▷.

Personal Names and Titles

Personal names generally should not be abbreviated: Thomas (*not* Thos.) and William (*not* Wm.). An academic, civil, religious, or military title should be spelled out and in lowercase when it does not precede a name. (The *captain* wanted to check the orders.) When they precede names, some titles are customarily abbreviated (*Dr.* Smith, *Mr.* Mills, *Ms.* Katz).

An abbreviation of a title may follow the name; however, be certain that it does not duplicate a title before the name (Angeline Martinez, Ph.D. *or* Dr. Angeline Martinez, *not* Dr. Angeline Martinez, Ph.D.). When addressing correspondence and including names in other documents, you normally should spell out titles (The Honorable Mary J. Holt; Professor Charles Martin). Traditionally, periods are used with academic degrees, although they are sometimes omitted (M.A./MA, M.B.A./MBA, Ph.D./PhD).

ON THE WEB

For links to Web sites specifying standard abbreviations and acronyms, including U.S. Postal Service abbreviations, see bedfordstmartins.com/writingthatworks and select *Web Links*.

■ Italics

Italics is a style of type used to denote emphasis and to distinguish foreign expressions, book titles, and certain other elements. *This sentence is printed in italics.* Italic type is signaled by underlining in a manuscript submitted for publication or

◆ *For more-effective ways to achieve emphasis, see pages 101–106 in Chapter 4, Revising the Draft.*

where italic font may not be available, such as in e-mail messages. Italicize words that require special emphasis in a sentence. (Contrary to projections, sales have *not* improved.) Do not overuse italics for emphasis, however. (*This* will hurt *you* more than *me*.)

Foreign Words and Phrases

Foreign words and phrases that have not been assimilated into the English language are italicized (*sine qua non, coup de grâce, in re, in camera*). Foreign words that have been fully assimilated into the language need not be italicized. A word may be considered assimilated if it appears in most standard dictionaries and is familiar to most readers (cliché, etiquette, vis-à-vis, de facto, siesta).

Titles

Italicize the titles of separately published documents, such as books, periodicals, newspapers, pamphlets, brochures, legal cases, movies, and television programs.

▶ *Turning Workplace Conflict into Collaboration* by Joyce Richards was reviewed in the *New York Times*.

Italicize the titles of compact disks, videotapes, plays, long poems, paintings, sculptures, and musical works.

CD-ROM	*Computer Security Tutorial on CD-ROM*
PLAY	Arthur Miller's *Death of a Salesman*
LONG POEM	T. S. Eliot's *The Waste Land*
MUSICAL WORK	Gershwin's *Porgy and Bess*

◆ *See also Quotation Marks, pages 617–619*

Do not italicize the titles of holy books and legislative documents (Old Testament, Magna Carta).

Proper Names

The names of ships, trains, and aircraft (but not the companies or governments that own them) are italicized (U.S. Aircraft Carrier *Independence*; U.S. Space Shuttle *Endeavor*). Craft that are known by model or serial designations are not italicized (DC-7; Boeing 747).

Words, Letters, and Figures

Words, letters, and figures discussed as such are italicized.

▶ The word *inflammable* is often misinterpreted.

▶ The *S* and *6* keys on my keyboard do not work.

Subheads

Subheads in a report are sometimes italicized.

▶ *Training managers.* We are leading the way in developing first-line managers who not only are professionally competent but . . .

◆ *For guidance on using italics as a design element, see page 211 in Chapter 7, Designing Effective Documents and Visuals.*

English as a Second Language (ESL)

Learning to write well in a second language takes a great deal of effort and practice. The most-effective way to improve your command of written English is to read widely beyond the reports and professional articles your job requires, such as magazines, newspapers, essays, novels, biographies, short stories, or any other writing that interests you. In addition, listen carefully to native speakers on television, on radio, and in person. Do not hesitate to consult a native speaker of English, especially for important writing tasks, such as e-mail messages, memos, and reports. Focus on those particular areas of English that give you trouble.

This section is a guide to some of the common problems nonnative speakers experience when writing English. For additional help, ask a native speaker or refer to the earlier sections of this guide.

ON THE WEB

For Web sites and electronic grammar exercises intended for speakers of English as a second language, see **bedfordstmartins.com/ writingthatworks** and select *Web Links* and *Exercise Central*.

ESL TIPS   **Finding Additional ESL Guidance in *Writing That Works***

Most of the information in this revision guide will be helpful to writers of English as a second language; however, the entries listed in the index under "ESL Tips" address specific issues that often cause problems.

■ Count and Mass Nouns

Count nouns refer to things that can be counted (tables, pencils, projects, reports). *Mass nouns* (also called *noncount nouns*) identify things that cannot be counted (electricity, water, air, loyalty, information). This distinction can be confusing with words like *electricity* and *water*. Although we can count kilowatt-hours of electricity and bottles of water, counting becomes inappropriate when we use the words in a general sense, as in "*Water* is an essential resource." Count nouns have plural forms; mass nouns do not. Following is a list of common mass nouns.

acid	coffee	information	precision
advice	education	knowledge	research
air	electricity	loyalty	technology
anger	equipment	machinery	transportation
biology	furniture	money	water
business	health	news	weather
clothing	honesty	oil	work

This distinction between whether something can or cannot be counted determines the form of the noun to use (singular or plural), the kind of article that precedes it (*a*, *an*, *the*, or no article), and the kind of comparative adjective it requires (*fewer* or *less*, *many* or *much*, and so on).

■ Articles

This discussion of articles applies only to common nouns (not to proper nouns, such as the names of people) because count and mass nouns are always common nouns.

The general rule is that every count noun must be preceded by an article (*a*, *an*, *the*), a demonstrative adjective (*this*, *that*, *these*, *those*), a possessive adjective (*my*, *your*, *her*, *his*, *its*, *their*), or some expression of quantity (such as *one*, *two*, *several*, *many*, *a few*, *a lot of*, *some*, *no*). The article, adjective, or expression of quantity appears either directly in front of the noun or in front of the whole noun phrase.

▶ Beth read *a* report last week. [article]

▶ *Those* reports Beth read were long. [demonstrative adjective]

▶ *Their* report was long. [possessive adjective]

▶ *Some* reports Beth read were long. [indefinite adjective]

The articles *a* and *an* are used with count nouns that refer to one item of the whole class of like items.

▶ Matthew has *a* pen. [Matthew could have *any* pen.]

The article *the* is used with nouns that refer to a specific item that both the reader and the writer can identify.

▶ Matthew has *the* pen. [Matthew has a *specific* pen that is known to both the reader and the writer.]

The article *the* is used with the superlative form of adjectives and adverbs.

▶ His report was *the* best the board ever read.

Do not use *the* with the comparative form.

▶   Which of these two restaurants is ~~the~~ better?

When making generalizations with count nouns, writers can either use *a* or *an* with a singular count noun or use no article with a plural count noun. Consider the following generalization using an article.

▶   *An* egg is a good source of protein. [any egg, all eggs, eggs in general]

However, the following generalization uses a plural count noun with no article.

▶   Eggs are good sources of protein. [any egg, all eggs, eggs in general]

When you are making a generalization with a mass noun, do not use an article in front of the noun.

▶   Sugar is bad for your teeth.

■ Prepositions

Prepositions are words that help connect nouns or pronouns to other parts of a sentence. They help to specify a relationship between items.
The word *on* is used with days of the week.

▶   We have staff meetings *on* Mondays.

At is used with hours of the day and with noon, night, and dawn.

▶   We leave work *at* 5:00.
▶   Lunch will be served *at* noon.

In is used with other parts of the day and with months, years, and seasons.

▶   I check my e-mail *in* the morning.
▶   I started to work for the firm *in* May.

The word *on* indicates a surface on which something rests.

▶   The files are *on* the desk.

At refers to an area or to a place.

▶   My assistant is *at* her desk.

In indicates a place that is inside an enclosure.

▶   The documents are *in* the file folder.

Gerunds and Infinitives

Nonnative writers are often puzzled by which form of a verbal (a verb used as another part of speech) to use when it functions as the direct object of a verb—or a complement. No structural rule exists for distinguishing between the use of an infinitive or a gerund as an object of a verb. Any specific verb may take an infinitive as its object, others may take a gerund, and yet others take either an infinitive or a gerund. At times, even the base form of the verb is used.

▶   He enjoys *working*. [gerund as a complement]

▶   She promised *to fulfill* her part of the contract. [infinitive as a complement]

▶   The president had the manager *assign* her staff to another project. [basic verb form as a complement]

To make such distinctions accurately, rely on what you hear native speakers use or what you read. Many ESL texts contain chapters on infinitive and gerund usage that lists verbs with their appropriate complements.

Adjective Clauses

Because of the variety of ways adjective clauses are constructed in different languages, they can be particularly troublesome for nonnative writers of English. The following guidelines will help you form adjective clauses correctly.

Place an adjective clause directly after the noun it modifies.

who is standing across the room
▶   The tall woman is a vice president of the company ~~who is standing across the room~~.

The adjective clause *who is standing across the room* modifies *woman*, not *company*, and thus comes directly after *woman*.

Avoid using a relative pronoun with another pronoun in an adjective clause.

▶   The man who ~~he~~ sits at that desk is my boss.

Verb Tenses

To determine which verb tense to use, consider the time in which the action you are describing occurs in relation to other actions.

◆ *For an overview of how to choose the appropriate tense, see pages 604–606.*

Present Perfect

Because it is so closely related to the past tense, the present perfect tense remains one of the most problematic of all tenses. In general, use the present perfect tense to refer to events completed in the past that have some implication for the present.

PRESENT PERFECT She *has revised* that report three times.

[She might revise it again.]

When a specific time is mentioned, however, use the simple past.

SIMPLE PAST I *wrote* the letter yesterday morning.

[The action, *wrote*, does not affect the present.]

Use the present perfect with a *since* or *for* phrase to describe actions that began in the past and will continue in the present.

▶ This company *has been* in business *for* seventeen years.

▶ This company *has been* in business *since* I was a child.

Present Progressive

◆ *See ESL Tips: Using the Progressive Form on page 605.*

The present progressive tense is especially difficult for those whose native language does not use this tense. The present progressive tense is used to describe some action or condition that is ongoing (or in progress) in the present and may continue into the future.

PRESENT PROGRESSIVE I *am searching* for an error in the document.

[The search is occurring now and may continue.]

In contrast, the simple present tense more often relates to habitual actions.

SIMPLE PRESENT I *search* for errors in my documents.

[I regularly search for errors, but I am not necessarily searching at this moment.]

■ Helping Verbs

In English, 23 helping verbs (forms of *have, be,* and *do*) may also function as main verbs. In addition, nine modal verbs (*can, could, may, might, must, shall, should, will, would*) function only as helping verbs. *Have, be,* and *do* change form to indicate tense; the nine modals do not.

The following guidelines will help you determine the proper use of modals. One-word modals do not change form to show a change in subject.

▶ I *could* quit. She *could* quit.

Most two- and three-word modals do change form, like other helping verbs.

▶ I *have to* finish the project. She *has to* finish the project.

Never use *to* between a one-word modal and the main verb.

▶ I can ~~to~~ type.
  [Most of the two- and three-word modals include *to*, as in *ought to drive*.]

Never use two one-word modals together.

▶ I might ~~could~~ work tomorrow.

Conditional Sentences

In *conditional sentences*, clauses that follow the words *if, when*, and *unless* show whether the result is possible or real, depending on other circumstances. Conditional sentences have two parts: a subordinate clause that begins with *if, when*, and *unless*, and a main clause that expresses a result.

A *prediction* foretells something based on conditional circumstances. Use a present-tense verb within the *if* clause. The clause that expresses the result is formed with a modal helping verb (usually *will*) and the base form of the verb.

▶ *If* you treat employees fairly, they *will be* better workers.

A *fact* explains a factual relationship between two or more occurrences. Use the same verb tense in both the conditional clause and the result clause.

▶ When it *snows*, I *leave* for work an hour earlier.
▶ When the chairperson *started* the meeting, he *welcomed* all new employees.

A *hypothetical sentence* explains that a result is impossible, did not happen, or is unlikely to happen. Use a past-tense verb within the *if* clause, and *would, could*, or *might* in the result clause.

▶ *If* I were CEO, I *would take* three months' vacation every year.

Index

List of Sample Documents